Sue Pemberton

Cambridge IGCSE® and O Level
Additional Mathematics
Coursebook

CAMBRIDGE UNIVERSITY PRESS

CAMBRIDGE
UNIVERSITY PRESS

University Printing House, Cambridge CB2 8BS, United Kingdom

One Liberty Plaza, 20th Floor, New York, NY 10006, USA

477 Williamstown Road, Port Melbourne, VIC 3207, Australia

4843/24, 2nd Floor, Ansari Road, Daryaganj, Delhi – 110002, India

79 Anson Road, #06–04/06, Singapore 079906

Cambridge University Press is part of the University of Cambridge.

It furthers the University's mission by disseminating knowledge in the pursuit of education, learning and research at the highest international levels of excellence.

Information on this title: education.cambridge.org

© Cambridge University Press 2016

This publication is in copyright. Subject to statutory exception and to the provisions of relevant collective licensing agreements, no reproduction of any part may take place without the written permission of Cambridge University Press.

First published 2016

20 19 18 17 16 15 14 13 12 11 10 9 8 7 6 5 4 3

Printed in Spain by GraphyCems

A catalogue record for this publication is available from the British Library

ISBN 978-1-316-60564-6 Paperback

Cambridge University Press has no responsibility for the persistence or accuracy of URLs for external or third-party internet websites referred to in this publication, and does not guarantee that any content on such websites is, or will remain, accurate or appropriate. Information regarding prices, travel timetables, and other factual information given in this work is correct at the time of first printing but Cambridge University Press does not guarantee the accuracy of such information thereafter.

®IGCSE is the registered trademark of Cambridge International Examinations.
Past exam paper questions throughout are reproduced by permission of Cambridge International Examinations.
Cambridge International Examinations bears no responsibility for the example answers to questions taken from its past question papers which are contained in this publication.
All exam-style questions and sample answers have been written by the authors.

....

NOTICE TO TEACHERS IN THE UK
It is illegal to reproduce any part of this work in material form (including photocopying and electronic storage) except under the following circumstances:
(i) where you are abiding by a licence granted to your school or institution by the Copyright Licensing Agency;
(ii) where no such licence exists, or where you wish to exceed the terms of a licence, and you have gained the written permission of Cambridge University Press;
(iii) where you are allowed to reproduce without permission under the provisions of Chapter 3 of the Copyright, Designs and Patents Act 1988, which covers, for example, the reproduction of short passages within certain types of educational anthology and reproduction for the purposes of setting examination questions.

Contents

Acknowledgements vi
Introduction vii
How to use this book viii

1 Sets **1**
  1.1 The language of sets 2
  1.2 Shading sets on Venn diagrams 6
  1.3 Describing sets on a Venn diagram 9
  1.4 Numbers of elements in regions on a Venn diagram 10
  Summary 15
  Examination questions 16

2 Functions **19**
  2.1 Mappings 20
  2.2 Definition of a function 21
  2.3 Composite functions 23
  2.4 Modulus functions 25
  2.5 Graphs of $y = |f(x)|$ where $f(x)$ is linear 28
  2.6 Inverse functions 30
  2.7 The graph of a function and its inverse 33
  Summary 36
  Examination questions 37

3 Simultaneous equations and quadratics **41**
  3.1 Simultaneous equations (one linear and one non-linear) 43
  3.2 Maximum and minimum values of a quadratic function 46
  3.3 Graphs of $y = |f(x)|$ where $f(x)$ is quadratic 52
  3.4 Quadratic inequalities 55
  3.5 Roots of quadratic equations 57
  3.6 Intersection of a line and a curve 60
  Summary 62
  Examination questions 64

4 Indices and surds **67**
  4.1 Simplifying expressions involving indices 68
  4.2 Solving equations involving indices 69
  4.3 Surds 73
  4.4 Multiplication, division and simplification of surds 75
  4.5 Rationalising the denominator of a fraction 78
  4.6 Solving equations involving surds 81
  Summary 85
  Examination questions 85

5 Factors and polynomials **88**
  5.1 Adding, subtracting and multiplying polynomials 89
  5.2 Division of polynomials 91
  5.3 The factor theorem 93
  5.4 Cubic expressions and equations 96
  5.5 The remainder theorem 100
  Summary 104
  Examination questions 105

6 Logarithmic and exponential functions **107**
  6.1 Logarithms to base 10 108
  6.2 Logarithms to base a 111
  6.3 The laws of logarithms 114
  6.4 Solving logarithmic equations 116

iii

6.5	Solving exponential equations		118
6.6	Change of base of logarithms		120
6.7	Natural logarithms		122
6.8	Practical applications of exponential equations		124
6.9	The graphs of simple logarithmic and exponential functions		125
6.10	The graphs of $y = ke^{nx} + a$ and $y = k \ln(ax + b)$ where n, k, a and b are integers		126
6.11	The inverse of logarithmic and exponential functions		129
	Summary		130
	Examination questions		131

7 Straight-line graphs — 134

7.1	Problems involving length of a line and mid-point	136
7.2	Parallel and perpendicular lines	139
7.3	Equations of straight lines	141
7.4	Areas of rectilinear figures	144
7.5	Converting from a non-linear equation to linear form	147
7.6	Converting from linear form to a non-linear equation	151
7.7	Finding relationships from data	155
	Summary	161
	Examination questions	161

8 Circular measure — 166

8.1	Circular measure	167
8.2	Length of an arc	170
8.3	Area of a sector	173
	Summary	176
	Examination questions	177

9 Trigonometry — 180

9.1	Angles between 0° and 90°	181
9.2	The general definition of an angle	184
9.3	Trigonometric ratios of general angles	186
9.4	Graphs of trigonometric functions	189
9.5	Graphs of $y = |f(x)|$, where $f(x)$ is a trigonometric function	199
9.6	Trigonometric equations	202
9.7	Trigonometric identities	208
9.8	Further trigonometric equations	210
9.9	Further trigonometric identities	212
	Summary	214
	Examination questions	215

10 Permutations and combinations — 218

10.1	Factorial notation	219
10.2	Arrangements	220
10.3	Permutations	223
10.4	Combinations	227
	Summary	231
	Examination questions	232

11 Binomial expansions — 236

11.1	Pascal's triangle	237
11.2	The binomial theorem	242
	Summary	245
	Examination questions	245

12 Differentiation 1 — 247

12.1	The gradient function	248
12.2	The chain rule	253
12.3	The product rule	255

12.4	The quotient rule	258
12.5	Tangents and normals	260
12.6	Small increments and approximations	264
12.7	Rates of change	267
12.8	Second derivatives	271
12.9	Stationary points	273
12.10	Practical maximum and minimum problems	278
Summary		283
Examination questions		284

13 Vectors — 288
13.1	Further vector notation	290
13.2	Position vectors	292
13.3	Vector geometry	296
13.4	Constant velocity problems	300
13.5	Interception problems	304
13.6	Relative velocity	307
13.7	Relative velocity using $\mathbf{i}, \mathbf{j}$ notation	314
Summary		315
Examination questions		316

14 Matrices — 319
14.1	Addition, subtraction and multiplication by a scalar	320
14.2	Matrix products	322
14.3	Practical applications of matrix products	325
14.4	The inverse of a 2×2 matrix	330
14.5	Simultaneous equations	334
Summary		336
Examination questions		340

15 Differentiation 2 — 341
15.1	Derivatives of exponential functions	342
15.2	Derivatives of logarithmic functions	346
15.3	Derivatives of trigonometric functions	350
15.4	Further applications of differentiation	355
Summary		361
Examination questions		362

16 Integration — 365
16.1	Differentiation reversed	366
16.2	Indefinite integrals	369
16.3	Integration of functions of the form $(ax+b)^n$	371
16.4	Integration of exponential functions	372
16.5	Integration of sine and cosine functions	374
16.6	Further indefinite integration	376
16.7	Definite integration	380
16.8	Further definite integration	383
16.9	Area under a curve	385
16.10	Area of regions bounded by a line and a curve	391
Summary		396
Examination questions		397

17 Kinematics — 400
17.1	Applications of differentiation in kinematics	402
17.2	Applications of integration in kinematics	410
Summary		416
Examination questions		417

Answers — 419

Index — 449

Acknowledgements

Past examination paper questions throughout are reproduced by permission of Cambridge International Examinations.

Thanks to the following for permission to reproduce images:

Cover artwork: Shestakovych/Shutterstock
Chapter 1 YuriyS/Getty Images; Chapter 2 Fan jianhua/Shutterstock; Chapter 3 zhu difeng/Shutterstock; Chapter 4 LAGUNA DESIGN/Getty Images; Fig. 4.1 Steve Bower/Shutterstock; Fig. 4.2 Laboko/Shutterstock; Fig. 4.3 irin-k/Shutterstock; Chapter 5 Michael Dechev/Shutterstock; Chapter 6 Peshkova/Shutterstock; Chapter 7 ittipon/Shutterstock; Chapter 8 Zhu Qiu/EyeEm/Getty Images; Chapter 9 paul downing/Getty Images; Fig. 9.1 aarrows/Shutterstock; Chapter 10 Gino Santa Maria/Shutterstock; Fig. 10.1snake3d/Shutterstock; Fig. 10.2 Keith Publicover/Shutterstock; Fig. 10.3 Aleksandr Kurganov/Shutterstock; Fig. 10.4 Africa Studio/Shutterstock; Chapter 11 Ezume Images/Shutterstock; Chapter 12 AlenKadr/Shutterstock; Chapter 13 muratart/Shutterstock; Fig. 13.1 Rawpixel.com/Shutterstock; Fig. 13.2 & 13.3 Michael Shake/Shutterstock; Chapter 14 nadla/Getty Images; Chapter 15 Neamov/Shutterstock; Chapter 16 Ahuli Labutin/Shutterstock; Chapter 17 AlexLMX/Getty

Introduction

This highly illustrated coursebook offers full coverage of the *Cambridge IGCSE®* and *O Level Additional Mathematics* syllabuses (0606 and 4037). It has been written by a highly experienced author, who is very familiar with the syllabus and the examinations. The course is aimed at students who are currently studying or have previously studied *Cambridge IGCSE® Mathematics* (0580) or *Cambridge O Level Mathematics* (4024).

The coursebook has been written with a clear progression from start to finish, with some later chapters requiring knowledge learned in earlier chapters. Where the content in one chapter includes topics that should have already been covered in previous studies, a recap section has been provided so that students can build on their prior knowledge.

At the start of each chapter, there is a list of objectives that are covered in the chapter. These objectives have been taken directly from the *Cambridge IGCSE® Additional Mathematics* (0606) syllabus.

'Class discussion' sections have been included. These provide students with the opportunity to discuss and learn new mathematical concepts with their classmates, with their class teacher acting as the facilitator. The aim of these class discussion sections is to improve the student's reasoning and oral communication skills.

Worked examples are used throughout to demonstrate each method using typical workings and thought processes. These present the methods to the students in a practical and easy-to-follow way that minimises the need for lengthy explanations.

The exercises are carefully graded. They offer plenty of practice via 'drill' questions at the start of each exercise, which allow the student to practise methods that have just been introduced. The exercises then progress to questions that typically reflect the kinds of questions that the student may encounter in the examinations. 'Challenge' questions have also been included at the end of most exercises to challenge and stretch high-ability students.

Towards the end of each chapter, there is a summary of the key concepts to help students consolidate what they have just learnt. This is followed by a 'Past paper' questions section, which contains *real* questions taken from past examination papers.

The answers to all questions are supplied at the back of the book, allowing self- and/or class-assessment. A student can assess their progress as they go along, choosing to do more or less practice as required. The answers given in this book are concise and it is important for students to appreciate that in the examination they should show as many steps in their working as possible.

A Practice Book is also available in the *Additional Mathematics* series, which offers students further targeted practice. This book closely follows the chapters and topics of the coursebook, offering additional exercises to help students to consolidate concepts learnt and to assess their learning after each chapter. 'Clues' and 'Tips' are included to help students with tricky topics. A Teacher's resource CD-ROM, to offer support and advice, is also available.

How to use this book

Chapter – each chapter begins with a set of learning objectives to explain what you will learn in this chapter.

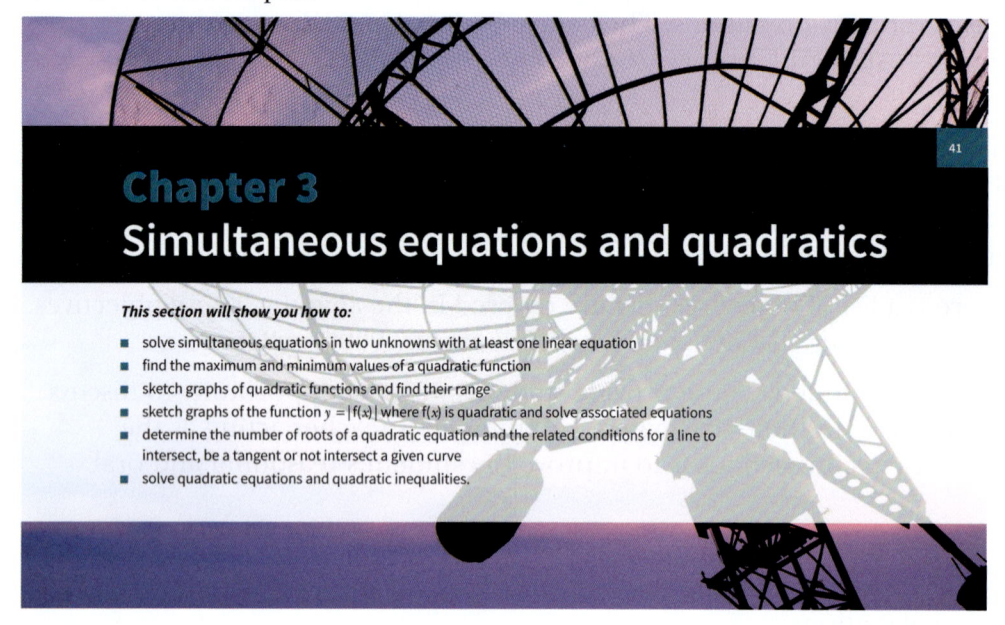

Chapter 3
Simultaneous equations and quadratics

This section will show you how to:
- solve simultaneous equations in two unknowns with at least one linear equation
- find the maximum and minimum values of a quadratic function
- sketch graphs of quadratic functions and find their range
- sketch graphs of the function $y = |f(x)|$ where $f(x)$ is quadratic and solve associated equations
- determine the number of roots of a quadratic equation and the related conditions for a line to intersect, be a tangent or not intersect a given curve
- solve quadratic equations and quadratic inequalities.

Recap – check that you are familiar with the introductory skills required for the chapter.

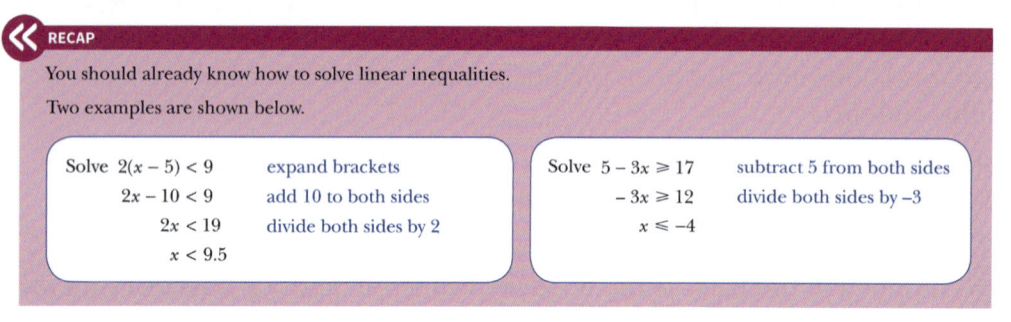

« RECAP

You should already know how to solve linear inequalities.
Two examples are shown below.

Solve $2(x - 5) < 9$	expand brackets	Solve $5 - 3x \geqslant 17$	subtract 5 from both sides
$2x - 10 < 9$	add 10 to both sides	$-3x \geqslant 12$	divide both sides by -3
$2x < 19$	divide both sides by 2	$x \leqslant -4$	
$x < 9.5$			

Class Discussion – additional activities to be done in the classroom for enrichment.

CLASS DISCUSSION

Solve each of these three pairs of simultaneous equations.

$8x + 3y = 7$ $\quad$ $3x + y = 10$ $\quad$ $2x + 5 = 3y$
$3x + 5y = -9$ $\quad$ $2y = 15 - 6x$ $\quad$ $10 - 6y = -4x$

Discuss your answers with your classmates.
Discuss what the graphs would be like for each pair of equations.

How to use this book

Worked Example – detailed step-by-step approaches to help students solve problems.

WORKED EXAMPLE 1

Find the value of:

a $\dfrac{8!}{5!}$ b $\dfrac{11!}{8!3!}$

Answers

a $\dfrac{8!}{5!} = \dfrac{8 \times 7 \times 6 \times \cancel{5} \times \cancel{4} \times \cancel{3} \times \cancel{2} \times \cancel{1}}{\cancel{5} \times \cancel{4} \times \cancel{3} \times \cancel{2} \times \cancel{1}}$

$= 8 \times 7 \times 6$

$= 336$

b $\dfrac{11!}{8!3!} = \dfrac{11 \times 10 \times 9 \times \cancel{8} \times \cancel{7} \times \cancel{6} \times \cancel{5} \times \cancel{4} \times \cancel{3} \times \cancel{2} \times \cancel{1}}{\cancel{8} \times \cancel{7} \times \cancel{6} \times \cancel{5} \times \cancel{4} \times \cancel{3} \times \cancel{2} \times \cancel{1} \times 3 \times 2 \times 1}$

$= \dfrac{990}{6}$

$= 165$

Note – quick suggestions to remind you about key facts and highlight important points.

> **Note:**
> $\log_{10} 30$ can also be written as $\lg 30$ or $\log 30$.

Challenge Q – challenge yourself with tougher questions that stretch your skills.

CHALLENGE Q

11 Copy the diagram and shade the region representing $(A \cap C) \cap B'$.

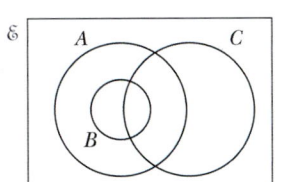

Summary – at the end of each chapter to review what you have learnt.

Summary

Position vectors

$\overrightarrow{AB}$ means the position vector of B relative to A.

$\overrightarrow{AB} = \overrightarrow{OB} - \overrightarrow{OA}$ or $\overrightarrow{AB} = \mathbf{b} - \mathbf{a}$

If an object has initial position $\mathbf{a}$ and moves with a constant velocity $\mathbf{v}$, the position vector $\mathbf{r}$, at time t, is given by the formula: $\mathbf{r} = \mathbf{a} + t\mathbf{v}$.

Velocity

$\text{Velocity} = \dfrac{\text{displacement}}{\text{time taken}}$

Relative velocity

The velocity of one body relative to another is called its relative velocity.

${}_A\mathbf{v}_B = \mathbf{v}_A - \mathbf{v}_B$ where ${}_A\mathbf{v}_B$ = the velocity of A relative to B

$\mathbf{v}_A$ = the velocity of A relative to the Earth

$\mathbf{v}_B$ = the velocity of B relative to the Earth

Cambridge IGCSE and O Level Additional Mathematics

Examination questions – exam-style questions for you to test your knowledge and understanding at the end of each chapter.

Examination questions

Worked past paper example

Matrices **A** and **B** are such that $\mathbf{A} = \begin{pmatrix} 3a & 2b \\ -a & b \end{pmatrix}$ and $\mathbf{B} = \begin{pmatrix} -a & b \\ 2a & 2b \end{pmatrix}$ where a and b are non-zero constants.

a Find $\mathbf{A}^{-1}$. [2]

b Using your answer to **part a**, find the matrix **X** such that $\mathbf{XA} = \mathbf{B}$. [4]

Cambridge IGCSE Additional Mathematics 0606 Paper 11 Q7i,ii Nov 2014

Answer

a $\mathbf{A} = \begin{pmatrix} 3a & 2b \\ -a & b \end{pmatrix}$

$|\mathbf{A}| = (3a \times b) - (-a \times 2b) = 3ab - (-2ab) = 5ab$

$\mathbf{A}^{-1} = \dfrac{1}{5ab}\begin{pmatrix} b & -2b \\ a & 3a \end{pmatrix}$

- swap the numbers on the leading diagonal
- change the signs of the numbers on the other diagonal

$\mathbf{A}^{-1} = \dfrac{1}{5ab}\begin{pmatrix} b & -2b \\ a & 3a \end{pmatrix}$

- divide by the determinant

b $\mathbf{XA} = \mathbf{B}$

$\mathbf{XAA}^{-1} = \mathbf{BA}^{-1}$ post-multiply both sides by $\mathbf{A}^{-1}$

$\mathbf{X} = \mathbf{BA}^{-1}$ $\mathbf{AA}^{-1} = \mathbf{I}$

$= \begin{pmatrix} -a & b \\ 2a & 2b \end{pmatrix} \dfrac{1}{5ab}\begin{pmatrix} b & -2b \\ a & 3a \end{pmatrix}$

$= \dfrac{1}{5ab}\begin{pmatrix} -a & b \\ 2a & 2b \end{pmatrix}\begin{pmatrix} b & -2b \\ a & 3a \end{pmatrix}$

$= \dfrac{1}{5ab}\begin{pmatrix} 0 & 5ab \\ 4ab & 2ab \end{pmatrix}$

So, $\mathbf{X} = \begin{pmatrix} 0 & 1 \\ \dfrac{4}{5} & \dfrac{2}{5} \end{pmatrix}$

Chapter 1
Sets

This section will show you how to:

- use set language and notation, and Venn diagrams to describe sets and represent relationships between sets.

Cambridge IGCSE and O Level Additional Mathematics

RECAP

You should already be familiar with the following set notation:

$A = \{x : x \text{ is a natural number}\}$
$B = \{(x, y) : y = mx + c\}$
$C = \{x : a \leqslant x \leqslant b\}$
$D = \{a, b, c, \ldots\}$

You should also be familiar with the following set symbols:

Union of A and B	$A \cup B$	The empty set	$\varnothing$
Intersection of A and B	$A \cap B$	Universal set	$\mathscr{E}$
Number of elements in set A	$n(A)$	A is a subset of B	$A \subseteq B$
'… is an element of …'	$\in$	A is a proper subset of B	$A \subset B$
'… is not an element of …'	$\notin$	A is not a subset of B	$A \nsubseteq B$
Complement of set A	A'	A is not a proper subset of B	$A \not\subset B$

You should also know how to represent the complement, union and intersections of sets on a Venn diagram:

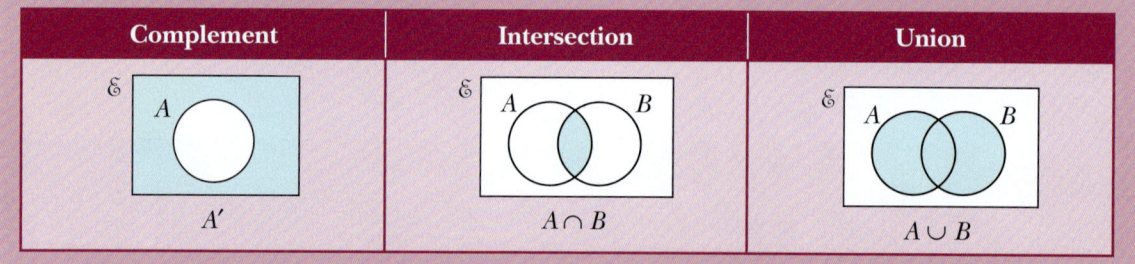

Complement	Intersection	Union
A'	$A \cap B$	$A \cup B$

The special conditions $A \cap B = \varnothing$ and $A \subset B$ can be represented on a Venn diagram as:

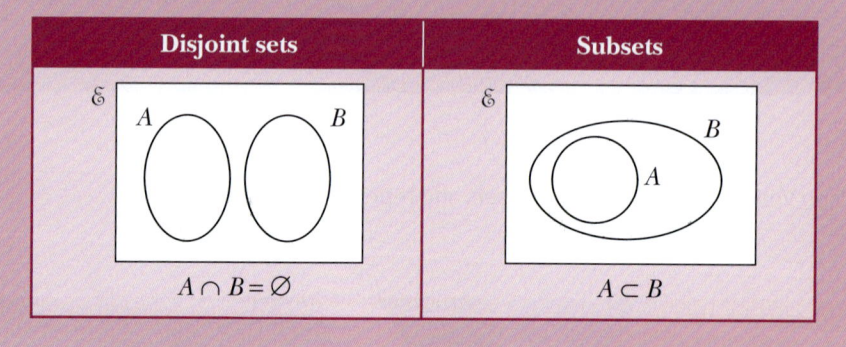

Disjoint sets	Subsets
$A \cap B = \varnothing$	$A \subset B$

1.1 The language of sets

You have already studied sets (for either IGCSE or O level).

The worked examples and exercises in this chapter consolidate your earlier work.

It is important that you re-familiarise yourself with the set notation that is covered in the recap.

There are some special number sets and symbols that represent these sets that you should also be familiar with:

the set of natural numbers {1, 2, 3, ...} $\mathbb{N}$
the set of integers {0, ±1, ±2, ±3, ...} $\mathbb{Z}$
the set of real numbers $\mathbb{R}$
the set of rational numbers $\mathbb{Q}$

You have already met the set notation $\{x : -1 < x < 3\}$.

This is read as: the set of numbers x such that x lies between −1 and 3.

The set notation can also be written as $\{x : -1 < x < 3,$ where $x \in \mathbb{R}\}$.

This is read as: the set of numbers x such that x lies between −1 and 3 where x is a real number.

> **WORKED EXAMPLE 1**
>
> $\mathscr{E} = \{x : 1 \leq x \leq 7,$ where $x \in \mathbb{R}\}$
> $A = \{x : 3 \leq x < 5\}$ $B = \{x : 2x - 1 > 7\}$
>
> Find the sets
> **a** A' **b** $A \cap B$.
>
> **Answers**
>
> **a** Draw a number line from 1 to 7.
> The set A is shown in blue.
> The set A' is shown in orange.
> $A' = \{x : 1 \leq x < 3 \cup 5 \leq x \leq 7\}$
>
> **b** The set A is shown in blue.
> $2x - 1 > 7$
> $2x > 8$
> $x > 4$
> $B = \{x : 4 < x \leq 7\}$ B is shown in green on the number line.
> The intersection of A and B are the numbers that are common to the two sets.
> $A \cap B = \{x : 4 < x < 5\}$

Exercise 1.1

1 $\mathscr{E} = \{x : 5 < x < 16, x$ is a integer$\}$
$A = \{x : 9 < x \leq 12\}$
List the elements of A'.

2 $\mathscr{E} = \{x : 1 \leq x \leq 12, x$ is a integer$\}$
$A = \{x : 5 \leq x \leq 8\}$
$B = \{x : x > 6\}$
$C = \{x : x$ is a factor of 8$\}$

List the elements of
a $A \cap B$
b $(A \cap B)'$
c $(A \cap B)' \cap C$.

3 $\mathscr{E} = \{x : 0 < x < 10, x \text{ is an integer}\}$

$P = \{x : x^2 - 6x + 5 = 0\}$

$Q = \{x : 2x - 3 < 7\}$

Find the values of x such that
a $x \in P$
b $x \in Q$
c $x \in P \cap Q$
d $x \in (P \cup Q)'$.

4 $\mathscr{E} = \{x : 1 \leqslant x \leqslant 10, x \in \mathbb{R}\}$

$A = \{x : 3 < x \leqslant 8\}$

$B = \{x : 5 < x < 9\}$

Find the sets
a A'
b B'
c $A \cap B$
d $A \cup B$.

5 $\mathscr{E} = \{\text{members of an outdoor pursuits club}\}$

$C = \{\text{members who go cycling}\}$

$R = \{\text{members who go running}\}$

$W = \{\text{members who go walking}\}$

Write the following statements using set notation.
a There are 52 members of the club.
b There are 35 members who go running.
c There are 21 members who go running and cycling.
d Every member who goes running also goes walking.

6 $\mathscr{E} = \{\text{members of a youth club}\}$

$M = \{\text{members who like music}\}$

$R = \{\text{members who like rock-climbing}\}$

$S = \{\text{members who like sailing}\}$

Describe the following in words
a $M \cup R$
b $M \cap S$
c R'
d $R \cap S = \varnothing$.

7 $\mathscr{E} = \{\text{students in a school}\}$

$A = \{\text{students studying art}\}$

$M = \{\text{students studying mathematics}\}$

$P = \{\text{students studying physics}\}$

a Express the following statements using set notation
   i all physics students also study mathematics
   ii no student studies both art and physics.
b Describe the following in words
   i $A \cap M \cap P'$
   ii $A' \cap (M \cup P)$.

8 $\mathscr{E} = \{x : 1 \leq x \leq 50, \text{ where } x \text{ is an integer}\}$
$C = \{\text{cube numbers}\}$
$P = \{\text{prime numbers}\}$
$S = \{\text{square numbers}\}$
Express the following statements using set notation

  a 17 is a prime number
  b 30 is not a cube number
  c there are 3 cube numbers between 1 and 50 inclusive
  d there are 35 integers between 1 and 50 inclusive, that are not prime
  e there are no square numbers that are prime.

9 $\mathscr{E} = \{\text{students in a school}\}$
$A = \{\text{students in the athletics team}\}$
$C = \{\text{students in the chess team}\}$
$F = \{\text{students in the football team}\}$
$G = \{\text{students who are girls}\}$
Express the following statements using set notation

  a all students in the chess team are girls
  b all students in the football team are boys
  c there are no students who are in both the athletics team and the chess team
  d there are 3 people who are in both the athletics team and the football team.

10 Illustrate each of the following sets on a graph.

  a $\{(x, y) : y = x + 2\}$
  b $\{(x, y) : x + y = 3\}$
  c $\{(x, y) : y = 2x - 1\}$
  d $\{(x, y) : x + y \geq 2\}$

11 $A = \{(x, y) : y = 2x + 3\}$
$B = \{(x, y) : y = 3\}$
$C = \{(x, y) : x + y = 6\}$
$D = \{(x, y) : y = 2x + 4\}$

  a List the elements of
   i $A \cap B$ **ii** $A \cap C$.
  b Find
   i $n(B \cap D)$ **ii** $n(A \cap D)$.

12 In each of the following sets, $x \in \mathbb{R}$.

$A = \{x : 7 - 2x = 3\}$
$B = \{x : x^2 - 3x - 10 = 0\}$
$C = \{x : x^2 + 6x + 9 = 0\}$
$D = \{x : x(x + 2)(x - 7) = 0\}$
$E = \{x : x^2 + 4x + 5 = 0\}$

a Find
  i $n(A)$ **ii** $n(B)$ **iii** $n(C)$ **iv** $n(E)$.

b List the elements of the sets
  i $B \cup D$ **ii** $B \cap D$.

c Use set notation to complete the statement: $C \cap D = \ldots$

1.2 Shading sets on Venn diagrams

When an expression is complicated, you may need to use some diagrams for your working out before deciding on your answer.

WORKED EXAMPLE 2

On a Venn diagram shade the regions:
a $A' \cap B$ **b** $A' \cup B$

Answers

First shade a Venn diagram for set A' and a Venn diagram for set B:

a $A' \cap B$ is the region that is in both A' and B.

b $A' \cup B$ is the region that is in A' or B or both so you need all the shaded regions.

Chapter 1: Sets

CLASS DISCUSSION

$(A \cap B)'$	$(A \cap B')'$	$A' \cap B$	$A' \cup B$
$(A \cup B)'$	$(A \cup B')'$	$A' \cup B'$	$A' \cap B'$
$(A' \cup B)'$	$(A' \cap B)'$	$A \cup B'$	$A \cap B'$

Each blue expression has an equivalent orange expression.

By considering the Venn diagrams for each expression, find the six pairs of equivalent expressions.

Discuss these matching pairs with your classmates.

Describe any rules that you have discovered.

Now copy and complete the following:

$(A \cap B)' = A' \ldots B'$

$(A \cup B)' = A' \ldots B'$

Exercise 1.2

1. On copies of this diagram shade the following regions. 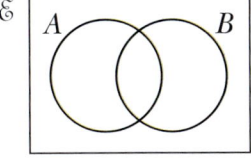
   a. $A \cap B'$
   b. $(A \cup B)'$
   c. $(A' \cap B)'$
   d. $(A \cap B)' \cap B$

2. $F \cap G = \emptyset$

   Show sets F and G on a Venn diagram.

3. $Q \subset P$

   Show sets P and Q on a Venn diagram.

4. 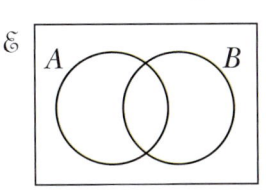
   a. Copy the Venn diagram and shade the region $A \cup B'$.
   b. Use set notation to express the set $A \cup B'$ in an alternative way.

5. Investigate whether the following statements are true or false:
   a. $A \cup B = A' \cap B'$
   b. $A \cap B = A' \cup B'$

6. On copies of this diagram, shade the following regions. 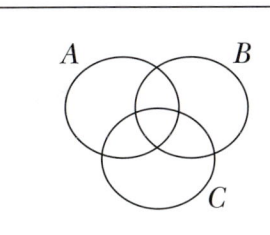
   a. $(A \cap B) \cup C$
   b. $(A \cup B) \cap C$
   c. $A \cup (B' \cap C)$
   d. $A \cup (B' \cap C')$
   e. $A \cap B \cap C'$
   f. $A' \cap (B \cup C)$
   g. $(A \cup B) \cap C'$
   h. $(A \cup B \cup C)'$

7 In the class discussion you discovered that
$(A \cap B)' = A' \cup B'$
$(A \cup B)' = A' \cap B'$.

Investigate whether the following statements are true or false:
a $(P \cap Q \cap R)' = P' \cup Q' \cup R'$
b $(P \cup Q \cup R)' = P' \cap Q' \cap R'$

8 $(A \cup B) \subset C$

Show sets A, B and C on a Venn diagram.

9 $A \cap B = \emptyset$ and $(A \cup B) \subset C$

Show sets A, B and C on a Venn diagram.

10 Investigate whether the following statement is true or false:
$(P \cap Q) \cup (P \cap R) = P \cap (Q \cup R)$

CHALLENGE Q

11 Copy the diagram and shade the region representing $(A \cap C) \cap B'$.

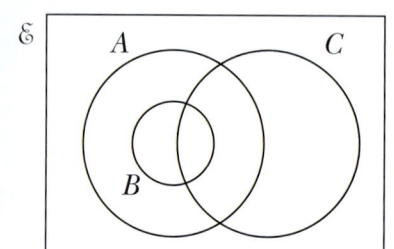

CHALLENGE Q

12 $\mathcal{E}$ = {students in a class}
C = {students who have a calculator}
P = {students who have a protractor}
R = {students who have a ruler}

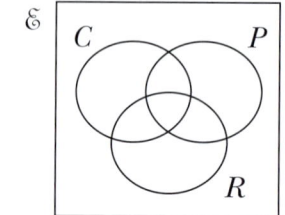

a Draw a copy of the Venn diagram. Shade the region which represents those students who have a calculator and a ruler, but no protractor.

b Draw a second copy of the Venn diagram. Shade the region which represents those students who have either a calculator or a ruler or both, but not a protractor.

1.3 Describing sets on a Venn diagram

You may be given a Venn diagram and then be asked to use set notation to describe the shaded region. This is illustrated in the following example.

WORKED EXAMPLE 3

Describe the shaded regions using set notation.

a, b, c (three Venn diagrams with sets A, B, 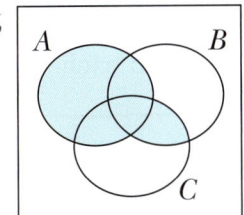 C)

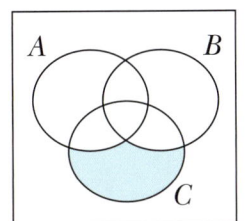

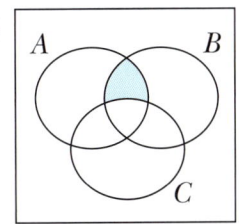

Answers

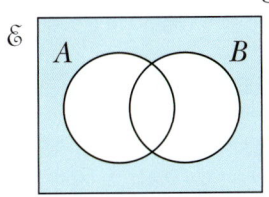

a The shaded region is outside $A \cup B$ and is inside C.
   The region is $(A \cup B)' \cap C$.

b The shaded region contains A and $B \cap C$
   The region is $A \cup (B \cap C)$.

c The shaded region is inside $A \cap B$ and outside C.
   The region is $(A \cap B) \cap C'$.

Exercise 1.3

1 Describe the shaded regions using set notation.

   a, b, 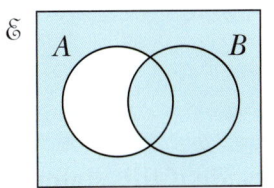 c (two-set Venn diagrams with A and B)

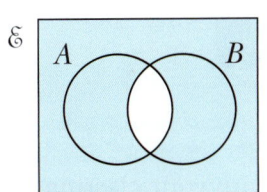

2 Describe the shaded regions using set notation.

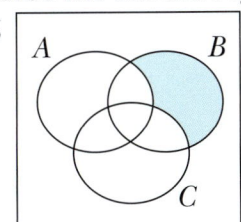

   a, b, 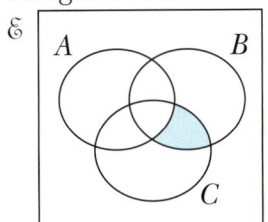 c, 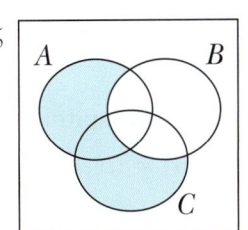 d, 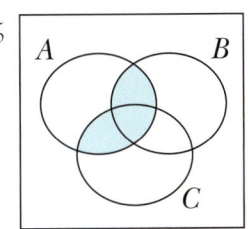 e, 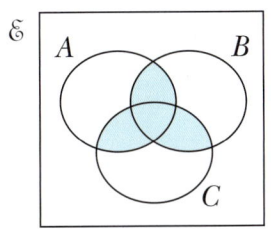 f (three-set Venn diagrams with A, B, C)

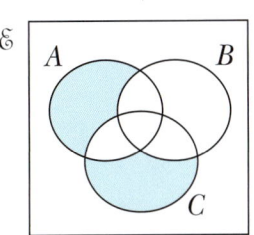

CHALLENGE Q

3 Describe the shaded region using set notation.

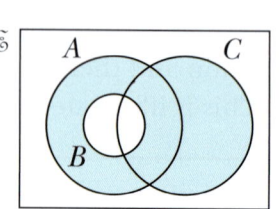

1.4 Numbers of elements in regions on a Venn diagram

You can use Venn diagrams to show the number of elements in each set.

WORKED EXAMPLE 4

$n(\mathcal{E}) = 35 \quad n(A) = 13 \quad n(B) = 20 \quad n(A \cap B) = 8$
Find $n(A \cup B)'$.

Answers

Draw a Venn diagram and put 8 in the intersection.

There are a total of 13 items in A, so 5 must go in the remaining part of A.

There are a total of 20 items in B, so 12 must go in the remaining part of B.

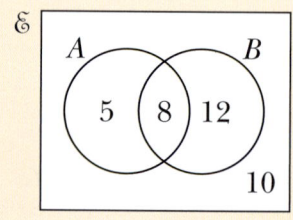

There are a total of 35 items in $\mathcal{E}$, so $\quad n(A \cap B)' = 35 - (5 + 8 + 12)$
$n(A \cup B)' = 10.$

CLASS DISCUSSION

Paul says that: $n(A \cup B) = n(A) + n(B)$

Discuss this statement with your classmates and decide if this statement is:

| Always true | Sometimes true | Never true |

You must justify your decision.
Discuss how you could adapt this statement so that it is always true.
Complete the rule: $n(A \cup B) = n(A) + n(B) - \ldots$

WORKED EXAMPLE 5

There are 75 tourists in a hotel.

  E = {tourists who speak English}

  F = {tourists who speak French}

  $n(E) = 18$ $n(F) = 21$ $n(E \cap F) = x$ $n(E' \cap F') = 51$

Write down an equation in x and hence find the number of tourists in the hotel who speak both English and French.

Answers

Method 1

$n(E' \cap F') = 51$ means that 51 tourists speak neither English nor French.

51 goes outside the sets E and F.

x goes in the intersection of the sets E and F.

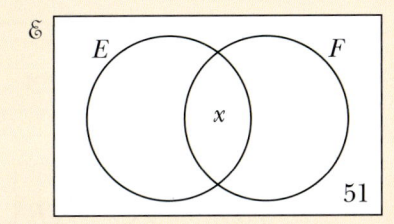

The number of tourists who speak English but not French = $18 - x$.
The number of tourists who speak French but not English = $21 - x$.
So the Venn diagram becomes:

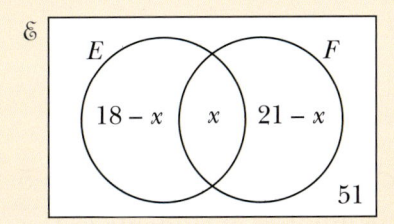

There is a total of 75 tourists.

So $(18 - x) + x + (21 - x) + 51 = 75$
            $100 - x = 75$
                 $x = 15$

The number of tourists who speak English and French = 15.

Method 2

$n(E \cup F) = 75 - 51 = 24$

Using the rule

$n(E \cup F) = n(E) + n(F) - n(E \cap F)$
      $24 = 18 + 21 - x$
       $x = 15$

The number of tourists who speak English and French = 15.

Exercise 1.4

1 The Venn diagram shows information about the number of elements in the sets.

For example $n(B) = 4 + 8 = 12$.

Find

- **a** $n(A)$
- **b** $n(B')$
- **c** $n(A \cap B)$
- **d** $n(A \cap B)'$
- **e** $n(A \cup B)$
- **f** $n(A' \cap B)$
- **g** $n(A' \cap B)'$
- **h** $n(A \cap B')$
- **i** $n(A \cap B')'$.

2 $n(A) = 13$ $n(B) = 20$ $n(A \cap B) = 10$

Find $n(A \cup B)$.

3 $n(A) = 12$ $n(B) = 14$ $n(A \cup B) = 20$

Find $n(A \cap B)$.

4 $n(A) = 11$ $n(A \cap B) = 8$ $n(A \cup B) = 25$

Find $n(B)$.

5 $n(\mathcal{E}) = 30$ $n(P) = 17$ $n(Q) = 15$ $n(P \cup Q)' = 3$

Find $n(P \cap Q)$.

6 $n(\mathcal{E}) = 40$ $n(A) = 26$
$n(B) = 21$ $n(A' \cap B) = 10$

In a copy of the Venn diagram insert the numbers of elements in the set represented by each of the four regions.

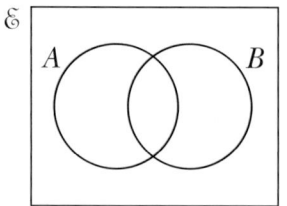

7 There are 36 students in a class.

$F = \{$students who speak French$\}$

$G = \{$students who speak German$\}$

$n(F) = 20$ $n(G) = 15$ $n(F \cap G) = x$ $n(F' \cap G') = 5$

Write down an equation in x and hence find the number of students in the group who speak French but not German.

8 There are 30 teachers in a school.

$F = \{$teachers who are female$\}$

$X = \{$teachers who are under 35 years old$\}$

$n(F) = 18$ $n(X) = 11$

State the maximum and minimum possible values of

- **a** $n(F \cap X)$
- **b** $n(F \cup X)$.

10 $n(A) = 10$ $n(B) = 14$ $n(C) = 9$
$n(A \cap B) = 4$ $n(A \cap C) = 3$ $n(B \cap C) = 6$ $n(A \cap B \cap C) = 1$

Draw a Venn diagram to find $n(A \cup B \cup C)$.

10 n(A) = 17   n(B) = 13   n(C) = 10
n(A ∪ B) = 23   n(A ∩ C) = 6   n(B ∩ C) = 4   n(A ∩ B ∩ C) = 3
Draw a Venn diagram to find n(A ∪ B ∪ C).

CHALLENGE Q
11 n(A) = 19   n(B) = 21   n(C) = 18
n(A ∩ B) = 12   n(A ∩ C) = 8   n(B ∩ C) = 9
n(A ∩ B ∩ C) = 5   n(A ∪ B ∪ C)' = 10
Draw a Venn diagram to find n(ℰ).

12 ℰ = {x : 5 ⩽ x ⩽ 40, x is an integer}
M = {multiples of 5}
O = {odd numbers}
P = {prime numbers}

a The circles are to be labelled with the letters M, O and P. Copy the Venn diagram and label each circle with the appropriate letter.

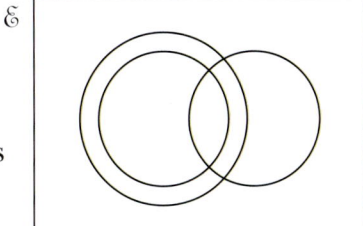

b Write each of the numbers 5, 7, 12 and 20 in the appropriate region on your diagram.

c Find   i n(M ∩ O)   ii n(O ∩ P').

The following exercise involves problem solving.

Start each question by displaying the given information on a Venn diagram.

Then use your Venn diagram to solve the problem.

Exercise 1.5

1 30 students go on an adventure holiday.

17 have canoed before, 10 have done horse riding before and 8 have done neither.

How many have done both before?

2 There are 52 members in an athletics club.

23 are sprinters and 16 are high jumpers and 20 do not do either of these.

How many members do both?

3 There are 30 students in a class.

21 like mango juice, 18 like pineapple juice and 4 students do not like either drink.

How many students like pineapple juice but not mango juice?

4 There are 28 students in a class.

15 study physics, 13 study biology and 7 are studying both of these subjects.

Find the number of students studying

   a neither of these subjects   **b** exactly one of these subjects.

CHALLENGE Q

5 There are 80 students in a small school.

26 study geography, 30 study history and 29 study economics.

22 study both history and economics, 8 study both geography and history and 7 study both geography and economics.

5 students study all three subjects.

Find the number of students studying

   a geography only   **b** none of these subjects

   c history but not economics   **d** exactly one of these subjects.

CHALLENGE Q

6 A group of 33 students are given three problems to solve, problems A, B and C.

20 solve problem A, 18 solve problem B and 12 solve problem C.

13 solve problem A and B, 7 solve problem B and C and 8 solve problem A and C.

7 solve all three problems.

Find the number of students who solve

   a problem B only   **b** none of the problems

   c exactly one problem   **d** exactly two problems.

Summary
The language of sets

Union of A and B	$A \cup B$	The empty set	$\varnothing$
Intersection of A and B	$A \cap B$	Universal set	$\mathscr{E}$
Number of elements in set A	$n(A)$	A is a subset of B	$A \subseteq B$
'... is an element of...'	$\in$	A is a proper subset of B	$A \subset B$
'... is not an element of...'	$\notin$	A is not a subset of B	$A \nsubseteq B$
Complement of set A	A'	A is not a proper subset of B	$A \not\subset B$

Some special number sets

The set of natural numbers $\{1, 2, 3, ...\}$ $\mathbb{N}$

The set of integers $\{0, \pm 1, \pm 2, \pm 3, ...\}$ $\mathbb{Z}$

The set of real numbers $\mathbb{R}$

The set of rational numbers $\mathbb{Q}$

Venn diagrams

You should also know how to represent the complement, union and intersections of sets on a Venn diagram:

Complement	Intersection	Union
A'	$A \cap B$	$A \cup B$

Disjoint sets	Subsets
$A \cap B = \varnothing$	$A \subset B$

Useful rules to remember

$(A \cap B)' = A' \cup B'$

$(A \cup B)' = A' \cap B'$

$n(A \cup B) = n(A) + n(B) - n(A \cap B)$

Cambridge IGCSE and O Level Additional Mathematics

Examination questions

Worked past paper example

a Sets A and B are such that $n(A) = 15$ and $n(B) = 7$.

Find the greatest and least possible values of

  i $n(A \cap B)$, [2]

  ii $n(A \cup B)$. [2]

b On a Venn diagram draw 3 sets P, Q and R such that

$P \cap Q = \emptyset$ and $P \cup R = P$. [2]

Cambridge IGCSE Additional Mathematics 0606 Paper 11 Q1ai,ii,b Nov 2011

Answers

a $n(A) = 15$ and $n(B) = 7$

The two critical cases are:

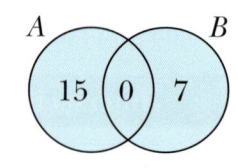

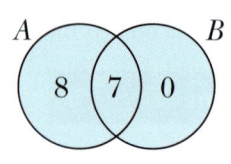

$n(A \cap B) = 7$ $n(A \cap B) = 0$
$n(A \cup B) = 15$ $n(A \cup B) = 22$

i greatest value of $n(A \cap B)$ is 7   least value of $n(A \cap B)$ is 0

ii greatest value of $n(A \cup B)$ is 22   least value of $n(A \cup B)$ is 15

b $P \cap Q = \emptyset$ and $P \cup R = P$

$P \cap Q = \emptyset$ means that P and Q do not intersect.

$P \cup R = P$ means that R must be contained in P.

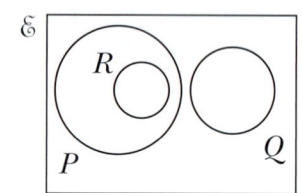

Exercise 1.6

Exam Exercise

1 a In a copy of the Venn diagrams below shade the region which represents the given set.

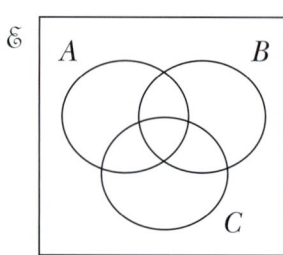

$(A \cap B) \cup C'$ 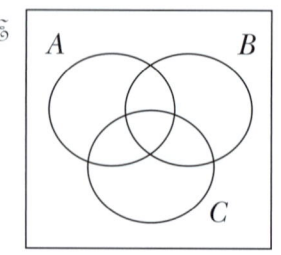 $A' \cap (B \cup C)$ [2]

b In a year group of 98 pupils, F is the set of pupils who play football and H is the set of pupils who play hockey. There are 60 pupils who play football and 50 pupils who play hockey. The number that play both sports is x and the number that play neither is $30 - 2x$. Find the value of x. [3]

Cambridge IGCSE Additional Mathematics 0606 Paper 21 Q1a,b Nov 2014

2 a In a copy of the Venn diagrams below, shade the regions indicated.

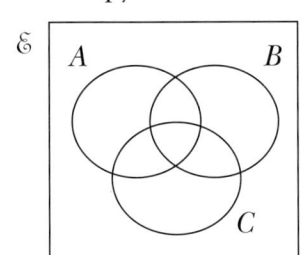

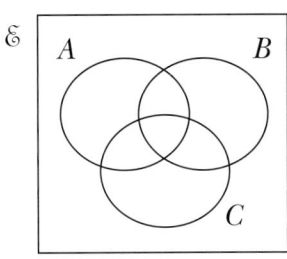

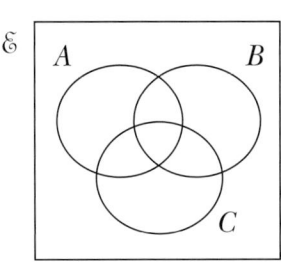

  i $A \cap B \cap C$ **ii** $(A \cup B) \cap C'$ **iii** $A \cup (B \cap C')$ [3]

b Sets P and Q are such that
$P = \{x : x^2 + 2x = 0\}$ **and** $Q = \{x : x^2 + 2x + 7 = 0\}$, **where** $x \in \mathbb{R}$.

  i Find n(P). [1]
  ii Find n(Q). [1]

Cambridge IGCSE Additional Mathematics 0606 Paper 11 Q3ai,ii,iii,bi,ii Jun 2014

3 a It is given that $\mathcal{E}$ is the set of integers, P is the set of prime numbers between 10 and 50, F is the set of multiples of 5 and T is the set of multiples of 10. Write the following statements using set notation.

  i There are 11 prime numbers between 10 and 50. [1]
  ii 18 is not a multiple of 5. [1]
  iii All multiples of 10 are multiples of 5. [1]

b i In a copy of the Venn diagram below shade the region that represents $(A' \cap B) \cup (A \cap B')$. [1]

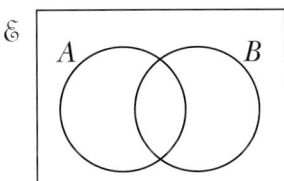

  ii In a copy of the Venn diagram below shade the region that represents $Q \cap (R \cup S')$. [1]

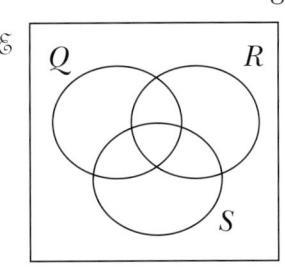

Cambridge IGCSE Additional Mathematics 0606 Paper 21 Q2ai,ii,iii,bi,ii Nov 2012

4 In a copy of the Venn diagram shade the region corresponding to the set given below.

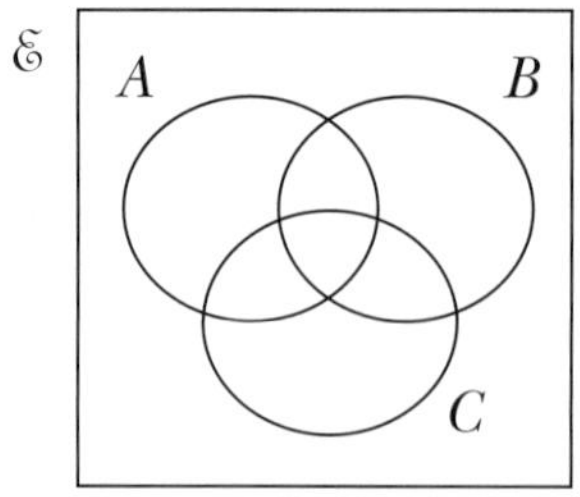

$(A \cup B) \cap C'$ 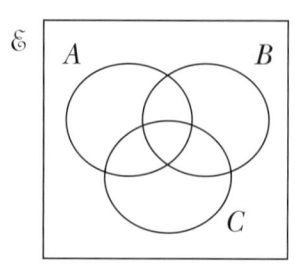 $(A \cup B \cup C)'$ 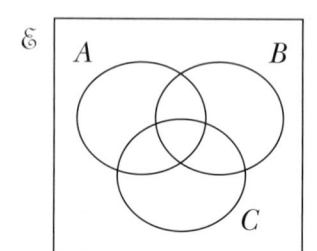 $(A \cap B) \cup (B \cap C) \cup (C \cap A)$ [3]

Cambridge IGCSE Additional Mathematics 0606 Paper 11 Q3a Jun 2011

Chapter 2
Functions

This section will show you how to:

- understand and use the terms: function, domain, range (image set), one-one function, inverse function and composition of functions
- use the notation $f(x) = 2x^3 + 5$, $f : x \mapsto 5x - 3$, $f^{-1}(x)$ and $f^2(x)$
- understand the relationship between $y = f(x)$ and $y = |f(x)|$
- explain in words why a given function is a function or why it does not have an inverse
- find the inverse of a one-one function and form composite functions
- use sketch graphs to show the relationship between a function and its inverse.

2.1 Mappings

Input → Output (1→2, 2→3, 3→4, 4→5) is called a **mapping diagram**.

The rule connecting the input and output values can be written algebraically as: $x \mapsto x + 1$.
This is read as 'x is mapped to $x + 1$'.

The mapping can be represented graphically by plotting values of $x + 1$ against values of x.

The diagram shows that for one input value there is just one output value.
It is called a **one-one** mapping.
The table below shows one-one, many-one and one-many mappings.

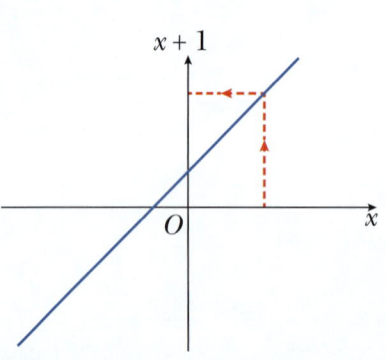

one-one	many-one	one-many
$x+1$	x^2	$\pm\sqrt{x}$
For one input value there is just one output value.	For two input values there is one output value.	For one input value there are two output values.

Exercise 2.1

Determine whether each of these mappings is one-one, many-one or one-many.

1. $x \mapsto x + 1$ $x \in \mathbb{R}$
2. $x \mapsto x^2 + 5$ $x \in \mathbb{R}$
3. $x \mapsto x^3$ $x \in \mathbb{R}$
4. $x \mapsto 2^x$ $x \in \mathbb{R}$
5. $x \mapsto \dfrac{1}{x}$ $x \in \mathbb{R}, x > 0$
6. $x \mapsto x^2 + 1$ $x \in \mathbb{R}, x \geq 0$
7. $x \mapsto \dfrac{12}{x}$ $x \in \mathbb{R}, x > 0$
8. $x \mapsto \pm x$ $x \in \mathbb{R}, x \geq 0$

Chapter 2: Functions

2.2 Definition of a function

A **function** is a rule that maps each x value to just one y value for a defined set of input values.

This means that mappings that are either $\begin{cases} \text{one-one} \\ \text{many-one} \end{cases}$ are called functions.

The mapping $x \mapsto x + 1$ where $x \in \mathbb{R}$, is a one-one function.

It can be written as $\begin{cases} f: x \mapsto x + 1 & x \in \mathbb{R} \\ f(x) = x + 1 & x \in \mathbb{R} \end{cases}$

($f : x \mapsto x + 1$ is read as 'the function f is such that x is mapped to $x + 1$')

$f(x)$ represents the output values for the function f.

So when $f(x) = x + 1$, $f(2) = 2 + 1 = 3$.

The set of input values for a function is called the **domain** of the function.

The set of output values for a function is called the **range** (or image set) of the function.

> **WORKED EXAMPLE 1**
>
> $f(x) = 2x - 1 \quad x \in \mathbb{R}, -1 \leqslant x \leqslant 3$
>
> **a** Write down the domain of the function f.
> **b** Sketch the graph of the function f.
> **c** Write down the range of the function f.
>
> **Answers**
>
> **a** The domain is $-1 \leqslant x \leqslant 3$.
> **b** The graph of $y = 2x - 1$ has gradient 2 and a y-intercept of -1.
> When $x = -1$, $y = 2(-1) - 1 = -3$
> When $x = 3$, $y = 2(3) - 1 = 5$
>
> [Graph showing line from $(-1, -3)$ to $(3, 5)$ with Domain on x-axis and Range on y-axis]
>
> **c** The range is $-3 \leqslant f(x) \leqslant 5$.

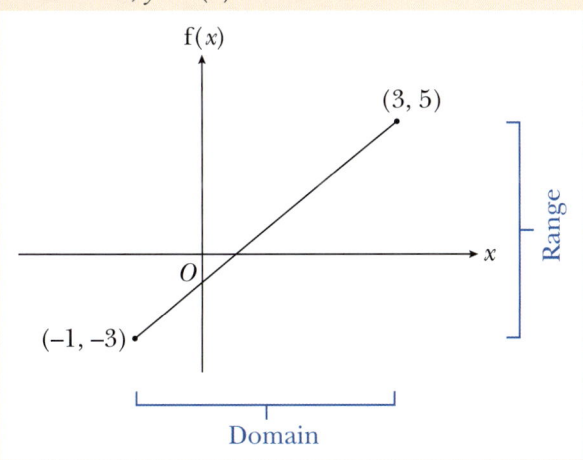

21

Cambridge IGCSE and O Level Additional Mathematics

WORKED EXAMPLE 2

The function f is defined by $f(x) = (x-2)^2 + 3$ for $0 \leq x \leq 6$.

Sketch the graph of the function.

Find the range of f.

Answers

$f(x) = (x-2)^2 + 3$ is a positive quadratic function so the graph will be of the form $\bigvee$

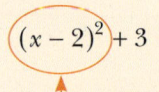

$\boxed{(x-2)^2} + 3$ This part of the expression is a square so it will always be ≥ 0. The smallest value it can be is 0. This occurs when $x = 2$.

The minimum value of the expression is $0 + 3 = 3$ and this minimum occurs when $x = 2$.

So the function $f(x) = (x-2)^2 + 3$ will have a minimum point at the point $(2, 3)$.

When $x = 0$, $y = (0-2)^2 + 3 = 7$.

When $x = 6$, $y = (6-2)^2 + 3 = 19$.

The range is $3 \leq f(x) \leq 19$.

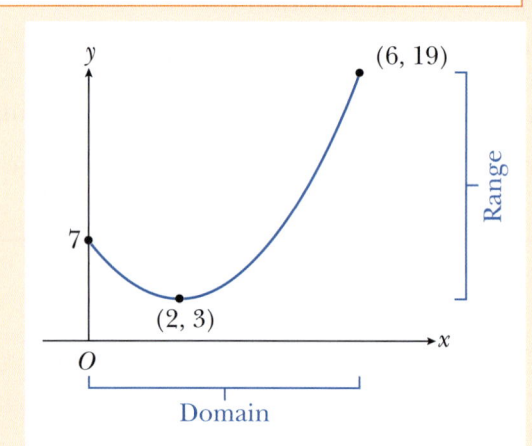

Exercise 2.2

1. Which of the mappings in **Exercise 2.1** are functions?

2. Find the range for each of these functions.

   a $f(x) = x - 5$, $-2 \leq x \leq 7$
   b $f(x) = 3x + 2$, $0 \leq x \leq 5$
   c $f(x) = 7 - 2x$, $-1 \leq x \leq 4$
   d $f(x) = x^2$, $-3 \leq x \leq 3$
   e $f(x) = 2^x$, $-3 \leq x \leq 3$
   f $f(x) = \dfrac{1}{x}$, $1 \leq x \leq 5$

3. The function g is defined as $g(x) = x^2 + 2$ for $x \geq 0$.
   Write down the range of g.

4. The function f is defined by $f(x) = x^2 - 4$ for $x \in \mathbb{R}$.
   Find the range of f.

5. The function f is defined by $f(x) = (x-1)^2 + 5$ for $x \geq 1$.
   Find the range of f.

6. The function f is defined by $f(x) = (2x+1)^2 - 5$ for $x \geq -\dfrac{1}{2}$.
   Find the range of f.

7. The function f is defined by $f : x \mapsto 10 - (x-3)^2$ for $2 \leq x \leq 7$.
   Find the range of f.

8 The function f is defined by $f(x) = 3 + \sqrt{x-2}$ for $x \geqslant 2$.

Find the range of f.

2.3 Composite functions

Most functions that you meet are combinations of two or more functions.

For example, the function $x \mapsto 2x + 5$ is the function 'multiply by 2 and then add 5'. It is a combination of the two functions g and f where:

$g : x \mapsto 2x$ (the function 'multiply by 2')

$f : x \mapsto x + 5$ (the function 'add 5')

So, $x \mapsto 2x + 5$ is the function 'first do g then do f'.

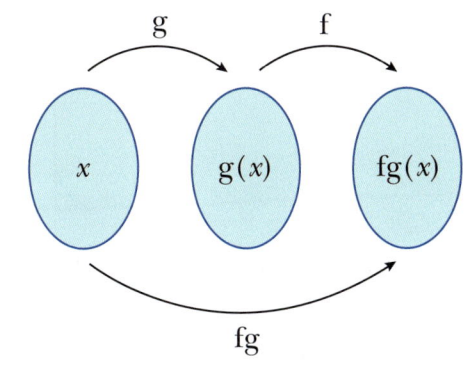

When one function is followed by another function, the resulting function is called a **composite function**.

> fg(x) means the function g acts on x first, then f acts on the result.

Note:
$f^2(x)$ means ff(x), so you apply the function f twice.

WORKED EXAMPLE 3

The function f is defined by $f(x) = (x-2)^2 - 3$ for $x > -2$.

The function g is defined by $g(x) = \dfrac{2x+6}{x-2}$ for $x > 2$.

Find fg(7).

Answers

fg(7)   g acts on 7 first and $g(7) = \dfrac{2(7)+6}{7-2} = 4$

$= f(4)$ f is the function 'take 2, square and then take 3'

$= (4-2)^2 - 3$

$= 1$

Cambridge IGCSE and O Level Additional Mathematics

> **WORKED EXAMPLE 4**
>
> $f(x) = 2x - 1$ for $x \in \mathbb{R}$ $g(x) = x^2 + 5$ for $x \in \mathbb{R}$
>
> Find   **a** $fg(x)$ **b** $gf(x)$ **c** $f^2(x)$.
>
> **Answers**
>
> **a** $fg(x)$ g acts on x first and $g(x) = x^2 + 5$
> $= f(x^2 + 5)$ f is the function 'double and take 1'
> $= 2(x^2 + 5) - 1$
> $= 2x^2 + 9$
>
> **b** $gf(x)$ f acts on x first and $f(x) = 2x - 1$
> $= g(2x - 1)$ g is the function 'square and add 5'
> $= (2x - 1)^2 + 5$ expand brackets
> $= 4x^2 - 4x + 1 + 5$
> $= 4x^2 - 4x + 6$
>
> **c** $f^2(x)$ $f^2(x)$ means $ff(x)$
> $= ff(x)$ f acts on x first and $f(x) = 2x - 1$
> $= f(2x - 1)$ f is the function 'double and take 1'
> $= 2(2x - 1) - 1$
> $= 4x - 3$

Exercise 2.3

1 $f : x \mapsto 2x + 3$ for $x \in \mathbb{R}$
    $g : x \mapsto x^2 - 1$ for $x \in \mathbb{R}$
    Find $fg(2)$.

2 $f(x) = x^2 - 1$ for $x \in \mathbb{R}$
    $g(x) = 2x + 3$ for $x \in \mathbb{R}$
    Find the value of $gf(5)$.

3 $f(x) = (x + 2)^2 - 1$ for $x \in \mathbb{R}$
    Find $f^2(3)$.

4 The function f is defined by $f(x) = 1 + \sqrt{x - 2}$ for $x \geq 2$.
    The function g is defined by $g(x) = \dfrac{10}{x} - 1$ for $x > 0$.
    Find $gf(18)$.

5 The function f is defined by $f(x) = (x - 1)^2 + 3$ for $x > -1$.
    The function g is defined by $g(x) = \dfrac{2x + 4}{x - 5}$ for $x > 5$.
    Find $fg(7)$.

6 h : $x \mapsto x + 2$ for $x > 0$
   k : $x \mapsto \sqrt{x}$ for $x > 0$
   Express each of the following in terms of h and k.
   a $x \mapsto \sqrt{x} + 2$ b $x \mapsto \sqrt{x+2}$

7 The function f is defined by f : $x \mapsto 3x + 1$ for $x \in \mathbb{R}$.
   The function g is defined by g : $x \mapsto \dfrac{10}{2-x}$ for $x \neq 2$.
   Solve the equation gf(x) = 5.

8 $g(x) = x^2 + 2$ for $x \in \mathbb{R}$
   $h(x) = 3x - 5$ for $x \in \mathbb{R}$
   Solve the equation gh(x) = 51.

9 $f(x) = x^2 - 3$ for $x > 0$
   $g(x) = \dfrac{3}{x}$ for $x > 0$
   Solve the equation fg(x) = 13.

10 The function f is defined, for $x \in \mathbb{R}$, by f : $x \mapsto \dfrac{3x+5}{x-2}$, $x \neq 2$.
   The function g is defined, for $x \in \mathbb{R}$, by g : $x \mapsto \dfrac{x-1}{2}$.
   Solve the equation gf(x) = 12.

11 $f(x) = (x+4)^2 + 3$ for $x > 0$
   $g(x) = \dfrac{10}{x}$ for $x > 0$
   Solve the equation fg(x) = 39.

12 The function g is defined by $g(x) = x^2 - 1$ for $x \geqslant 0$.
   The function h is defined by $h(x) = 2x - 7$ for $x \geqslant 0$.
   Solve the equation gh(x) = 0.

13 The function f is defined by f : $x \mapsto x^3$ for $x \in \mathbb{R}$.
   The function g is defined by g : $x \mapsto x - 1$ for $x \in \mathbb{R}$.
   Express each of the following as a composite function, using only f and/or g:
   a $x \mapsto (x-1)^3$ b $x \mapsto x^3 - 1$ c $x \mapsto x - 2$ d $x \mapsto x^9$

2.4 Modulus functions

The **modulus** of a number is the magnitude of the number without a sign attached.

The modulus of 4 is written $|4|$.

$|4| = 4$ and $|-4| = 4$

It is important to note that the modulus of any number (positive or negative) is always a positive number.

The modulus of a number is also called the **absolute value**.

The modulus of x, written as $|x|$, is defined as:

$$|x| = \begin{cases} x & \text{if } x > 0 \\ 0 & \text{if } x = 0 \\ -x & \text{if } x < 0 \end{cases}$$

CLASS DISCUSSION

Ali says that these are all rules for absolute values:

$$|x+y| = |x| + |y| \qquad\qquad |x-y| = |x| - |y|$$

$$|xy| = |x| \times |y| \qquad \left|\frac{x}{y}\right| = \frac{|x|}{|y|} \qquad (|x|)^2 = x^2$$

Discuss each of these statements with your classmates and decide if they are:

| Always true | Sometimes true | Never true |

You must justify your decisions.

The statement $|x| = k$, where $k \geqslant 0$, means that $x = k$ or $x = -k$.

This property is used to solve equations that involve modulus functions.

So, if you are solving equations of the form $|ax + b| = k$, you solve the equations

$ax + b = k$ and $ax + b = -k$

If you are solving harder equations of the form $|ax + b| = cx + d$, you solve the equations

$ax + b = cx + d$ and $ax + b = -(cx + d)$.

When solving these more complicated equations you must always check your answers to make sure that they satisfy the original equation.

Chapter 2: Functions

WORKED EXAMPLE 5

Solve.
a $|2x+1| = 5$ b $|4x-3| = x$ c $|x^2 - 10| = 6$ d $|x-3| = 2x$

Answers

a $|2x+1| = 5$
   $2x+1 = 5$ or $2x+1 = -5$
   $2x = 4$ $2x = -6$
   $x = 2$ $x = -3$
   CHECK: $|2 \times 2 + 1| = 5$ ✓ and
   $|2 \times -3 + 1| = 5$ ✓
   Solution is: $x = -3$ or 2.

b $|4x-3| = x$
   $4x-3 = x$ or $4x-3 = -x$
   $3x = 3$ $5x = 3$
   $x = 1$ $x = 0.6$
   CHECK: $|4 \times 0.6 - 3| = 0.6$ ✓ and
   $|4 \times 1 - 3| = 1$ ✓
   Solution is: $x = 0.6$ or 1.

c $|x^2 - 10| = 6$
   $x^2 - 10 = 6$ or $x^2 - 10 = -6$
   $x^2 = 16$ $x^2 = 4$
   $x = \pm 4$ $x = \pm 2$
   CHECK: $|(-4)^2 - 10| = 6$ ✓,
   $|(-2)^2 - 10| = 6$ ✓, $|(2)^2 - 10| = 6$ ✓
   and $|(4)^2 - 10| = 6$ ✓
   Solution is: $x = -4, -2, 2$ or 4.

d $|x-3| = 2x$
   $x-3 = 2x$ or $x-3 = -2x$
   $x = -3$ $3x = 3$
                    $x = 1$
   CHECK: $|-3-3| = 2 \times -3$ ✗
   and $|1-3| = 2 \times 1$ ✓
   Solution is: $x = 1$.

Exercise 2.4

1 Solve.

a $|3x-2| = 10$ b $|2x+9| = 5$ c $|6-5x| = 2$

d $\left|\dfrac{x-1}{4}\right| = 6$ e $\left|\dfrac{2x+7}{3}\right| = 1$ f $\left|\dfrac{7-2x}{2}\right| = 4$

g $\left|\dfrac{x}{4} - 5\right| = 1$ h $\left|\dfrac{x+1}{2} + \dfrac{2x}{5}\right| = 4$ i $|2x-5| = x$

2 Solve.

a $\left|\dfrac{2x-5}{x+3}\right| = 8$ b $\left|\dfrac{3x+2}{x+1}\right| = 2$ c $\left|1 + \dfrac{x+12}{x+4}\right| = 3$

d $|3x-5| = x+2$ e $x + |x-5| = 8$ f $9 - |1-x| = 2x$

3 Solve.

a $|x^2 - 1| = 3$ b $|x^2 + 1| = 10$ c $|4 - x^2| = 2 - x$

d $|x^2 - 5x| = x$ e $|x^2 - 4| = x + 2$ f $|x^2 - 3| = x + 3$

g $|2x^2 + 1| = 3x$ h $|2x^2 - 3x| = 4 - x$ i $|x^2 - 7x + 6| = 6 - x$

4 Solve each of the following pairs of simultaneous equations.

a $y = x + 4$ b $y = x$ c $y = 3x$
   $y = |x^2 - 16|$ $y = |3x - 2x^2|$ $y = |2x^2 - 5|$

2.5 Graphs of $y = |f(x)|$ where $f(x)$ is linear

Consider drawing the graph of $y = |x|$.

First draw the graph of $y = x$.

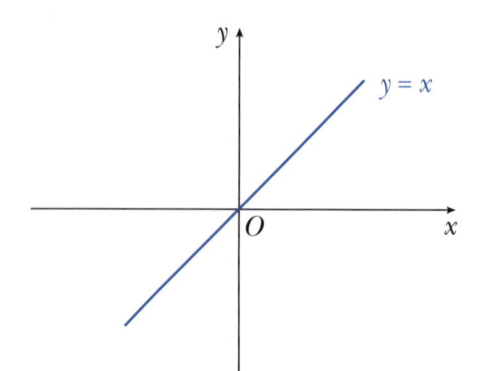

You then reflect in the x-axis the part of the line that is below the x-axis.

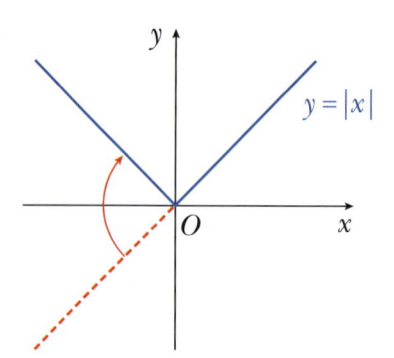

WORKED EXAMPLE 6

Sketch the graph of $y = \left|\dfrac{1}{2}x - 1\right|$, showing the coordinates of the points where the graph meets the axes.

Answers

First sketch the graph of $y = \dfrac{1}{2}x - 1$.

The line has gradient $\dfrac{1}{2}$ and a y-intercept of -1.

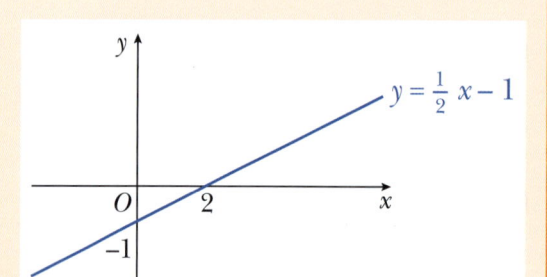

You then reflect in the x-axis the part of the line that is below the x-axis.

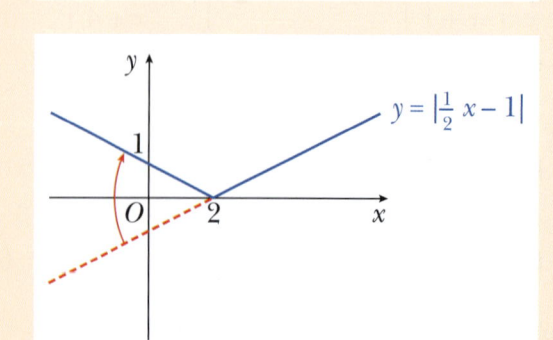

In **Worked example 5** you saw that there were two answers, $x = -3$ or $x = 2$, to the equation $|2x + 1| = 5$.

These can also be found graphically by finding the x-coordinates of the points of intersection of the graphs of $y = |2x + 1|$ and $y = 5$ as shown.

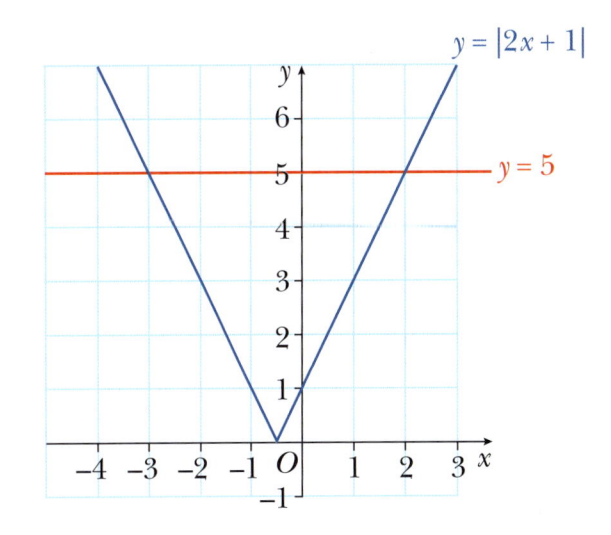

In the same worked example you also saw that there was only one answer, $x = 1$, to the equation $|x - 3| = 2x$.

This can also be found graphically by finding the x-coordinates of the points of intersection of the graphs of $y = |x - 3|$ and $y = 2x$ as shown.

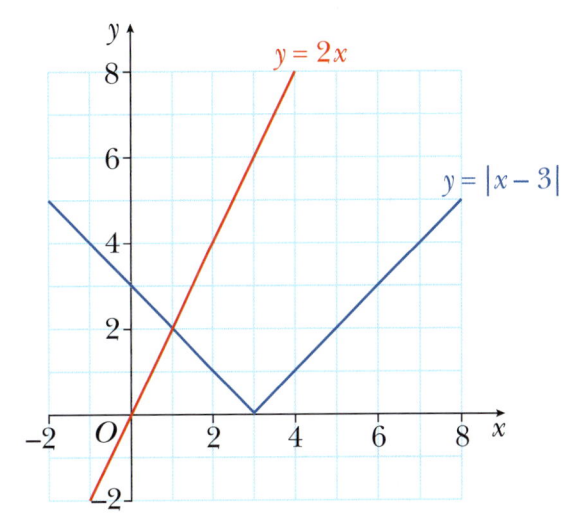

Exercise 2.5

1 Sketch the graphs of each of the following functions showing the coordinates of the points where the graph meets the axes.

   a $y = |x + 1|$ **b** $y = |2x - 3|$ **c** $y = |5 - x|$

   d $y = \left|\dfrac{1}{2}x + 3\right|$ **e** $y = |10 - 2x|$ **f** $y = \left|6 - \dfrac{1}{3}x\right|$

2 a Complete the table of values for $y = |x - 2| + 3$.

x	−2	−1	0	1	2	3	4
y		6		4			

  b Draw the graph of $y = |x - 2| + 3$ for $-2 \leq x \leq 4$.

3 Draw the graphs of each of the following functions.

   a $y = |x| + 1$ **b** $y = |x| - 3$ **c** $y = 2 - |x|$

   d $y = |x - 3| + 1$ **e** $y = |2x + 6| - 3$

4 Given that each of these functions is defined for the domain $-3 \leq x \leq 4$, find the range of

   a $f : x \mapsto 5 - 2x$ **b** $g : x \mapsto |5 - 2x|$ **c** $h : x \mapsto 5 - |2x|$.

5 $f : x \mapsto 3 - 2x$ for $-1 \leq x \leq 4$
   $g : x \mapsto |3 - 2x|$ for $-1 \leq x \leq 4$
   $h : x \mapsto 3 - |2x|$ for $-1 \leq x \leq 4$
   Find the range of each function.

6 **a** Sketch the graph of $y = |2x + 4|$ for $-6 < x < 2$, showing the coordinates of the points where the graph meets the axes.
   b On the same diagram, sketch the graph of $y = x + 5$.
   c Solve the equation $|2x + 4| = x + 5$.

7 A function f is defined by $f(x) = |2x - 6| - 3$, for $-1 \leq x \leq 8$.
   a Sketch the graph of $y = f(x)$.
   b State the range of f.
   c Solve the equation $f(x) = 2$.

8 **a** Sketch the graph of $y = |3x - 4|$ for $-2 < x < 5$, showing the coordinates of the points where the graph meets the axes.
   b On the same diagram, sketch the graph of $y = 2x$.
   c Solve the equation $2x = |3x - 4|$.

CHALLENGE Q

9 **a** Sketch the graph of $f(x) = |x + 2| + |x - 2|$.
   b Use your graph to solve the equation $|x + 2| + |x - 2| = 6$.

2.6 Inverse functions

The inverse of a function f(x) is the function that undoes what f(x) has done.

The inverse of the function f(x) is written as $f^{-1}(x)$.

The domain of $f^{-1}(x)$ is the range of f(x).

The range of $f^{-1}(x)$ is the domain of f(x).

It is important to remember that not every function has an inverse.

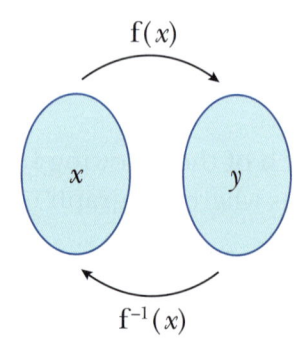

An inverse function $f^{-1}(x)$ can exist if, and only if, the function f(x) is a one-one mapping.

You should already know how to find the inverse function of some simple one-one mappings.

The steps to find the inverse of the function $f(x) = 5x - 2$ are:

Step 1: Write the function as $y =$ ⟶ $y = 5x - 2$

Step 2: Interchange the x and y variables. ⟶ $x = 5y - 2$

Step 3: Rearrange to make y the subject. ⟶ $y = \dfrac{x + 2}{5}$

$f^{-1}(x) = \dfrac{x + 2}{5}$

Chapter 2: Functions

CLASS DISCUSSION

Discuss the function $f(x) = x^2$ for $x \in \mathbb{R}$.
Does the function f have an inverse?
Explain your answer.
How could you change the domain of f so that $f(x) = x^2$ does have an inverse?

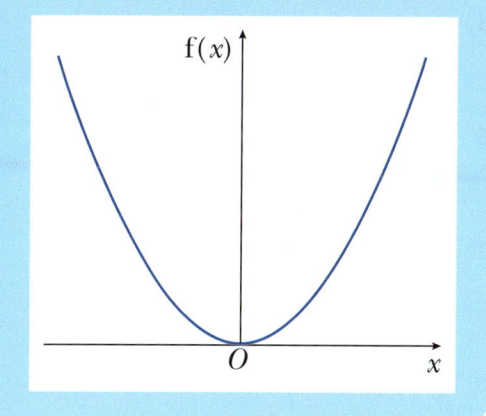

WORKED EXAMPLE 7

$f(x) = \sqrt{x+1} - 5$ for $x \geq -1$

a Find an expression for $f^{-1}(x)$.
b Solve the equation $f^{-1}(x) = f(35)$.

Answers

a $f(x) = \sqrt{x+1} - 5$ for $x \geq -1$

Step 1: Write the function as $y =$ ⟶ $y = \sqrt{x+1} - 5$
Step 2: Interchange the x and y variables. ⟶ $x = \sqrt{y+1} - 5$
Step 3: Rearrange to make y the subject. ⟶ $x + 5 = \sqrt{y+1}$
$(x+5)^2 = y + 1$
$y = (x+5)^2 - 1$

$f^{-1}(x) = (x+5)^2 - 1$

b $f(35) = \sqrt{35+1} - 5 = 1$
$(x+5)^2 - 1 = 1$
$(x+5)^2 = 2$
$x + 5 = \pm\sqrt{2}$
$x = -5 \pm \sqrt{2}$
$x = -5 + \sqrt{2}$ or $x = -5 - \sqrt{2}$
The range of f is $f(x) \geq -5$ so the domain of f^{-1} is $x \geq -5$.
Hence the only solution of $f^{-1}(x) = f(35)$ is $x = -5 + \sqrt{2}$.

Exercise 2.6

1 $f(x) = (x+5)^2 - 7$ for $x \geq -5$. Find an expression for $f^{-1}(x)$.

2 $f(x) = \dfrac{6}{x+2}$ for $x \geq 0$. Find an expression for $f^{-1}(x)$.

3 $f(x) = (2x-3)^2 + 1$ for $x \geq 1\dfrac{1}{2}$. Find an expression for $f^{-1}(x)$.

4 $f(x) = 8 - \sqrt{x-3}$ for $x \geq 3$. Find an expression for $f^{-1}(x)$.

5 $f : x \mapsto 5x - 3$ for $x > 0$ $g : x \mapsto \dfrac{7}{2 - x}$ for $x \neq 2$

   Express $f^{-1}(x)$ and $g^{-1}(x)$ in terms of x.

6 $f : x \rightarrow (x + 2)^2 - 5$ for $x > -2$

   a Find an expression for $f^{-1}(x)$.   b Solve the equation $f^{-1}(x) = 3$.

7 $f(x) = (x - 4)^2 + 5$ for $x > 4$

   a Find an expression for $f^{-1}(x)$.   b Solve the equation $f^{-1}(x) = f(0)$.

8 $g(x) = \dfrac{2x + 3}{x - 1}$ for $x > 1$

   a Find an expression for $g^{-1}(x)$.   b Solve the equation $g^{-1}(x) = 5$.

9 $f(x) = \dfrac{x}{2} + 2$ for $x \in \mathbb{R}$ $g(x) = x^2 - 2x$ for $x \in \mathbb{R}$

   a Find $f^{-1}(x)$.   b Solve $fg(x) = f^{-1}(x)$.

10 $f(x) = x^2 + 2$ for $x \in \mathbb{R}$ $g(x) = 2x + 3$ for $x \in \mathbb{R}$

   Solve the equation $gf(x) = g^{-1}(17)$.

11 $f : x \mapsto \dfrac{2x + 8}{x - 2}$ for $x \neq 2$ $g : x \mapsto \dfrac{x - 3}{2}$ for $x > -5$

   Solve the equation $f(x) = g^{-1}(x)$.

12 $f(x) = 3x - 24$ for $x \geqslant 0$. Write down the range of f^{-1}.

13 $f : x \mapsto x + 6$ for $x > 0$ $g : x \mapsto \sqrt{x}$ for $x > 0$

   Express $x \mapsto x^2 - 6$ in terms of f and g.

14 $f : x \mapsto 3 - 2x$ for $0 \leqslant x \leqslant 5$

   $g : x \mapsto |3 - 2x|$ for $0 \leqslant x \leqslant 5$

   $h : x \mapsto 3 - |2x|$ for $0 \leqslant x \leqslant 5$

   State which of the functions f, g and h has an inverse.

15 $f(x) = x^2 + 2$ for $x \geqslant 0$ $g(x) = 5x - 4$ for $x \geqslant 0$

   a Write down the domain of f^{-1}.   b Write down the range of g^{-1}.

16 The functions f and g are defined, for $x \in \mathbb{R}$, by

   $f : x \mapsto 3x - k$, where k is a positive constant

   $g : x \mapsto \dfrac{5x - 14}{x + 1}$, where $x \neq -1$.

   a Find expressions for f^{-1} and g^{-1}.

   b Find the value of k for which $f^{-1}(5) = 6$.

   c Simplify $g^{-1}g(x)$.

17 $f : x \mapsto x^3$ for $x \in \mathbb{R}$ $\quad\quad\quad$ $g : x \mapsto x - 8$ for $x \in \mathbb{R}$

Express each of the following as a composite function, using only f, g, f^{-1} and/or g^{-1}:

a $x \mapsto (x - 8)^{\frac{1}{3}}$ $\quad$ **b** $x \mapsto x^3 + 8$ $\quad$ **c** $x \mapsto x^{\frac{1}{3}} - 8$

d $x \mapsto (x + 8)^{\frac{1}{3}}$

2.7 The graph of a function and its inverse

In **Worked example 1** you considered the function $f(x) = 2x - 1$ $x \in \mathbb{R}$, $-1 \leqslant x \leqslant 3$.

The domain of f was $-1 \leqslant x \leqslant 3$ and the range of f was $-3 \leqslant f(x) \leqslant 5$.

The inverse function is $f^{-1}(x) = \dfrac{x + 1}{2}$.

The domain of f^{-1} is $-3 \leqslant x \leqslant 5$ and the range of f^{-1} is $-1 \leqslant f^{-1}(x) \leqslant 3$.

Drawing f and f^{-1} on the same graph gives:

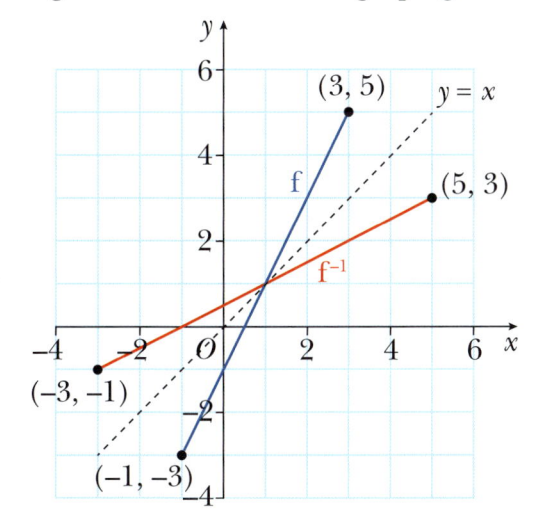

> **Note:**
> The graphs of f and f^{-1} are reflections of each other in the line $y = x$.
> This is true for all one-one functions and their inverse functions.
> This is because: $ff^{-1}(x) = x = f^{-1}f(x)$.

Some functions are called **self-inverse functions** because f and its inverse f^{-1} are the same.

If $f(x) = \dfrac{1}{x}$ for $x \neq 0$, then $f^{-1}(x) = \dfrac{1}{x}$ for $x \neq 0$.

So $f(x) = \dfrac{1}{x}$ for $x \neq 0$ is an example of a self-inverse function.

When a function f is self-inverse, the graph of f will be symmetrical about the line $y = x$.

Cambridge IGCSE and O Level Additional Mathematics

WORKED EXAMPLE 8

$f(x) = (x-2)^2$, $2 \leqslant x \leqslant 5$.

On the same axes, sketch the graphs of $y = f(x)$ and $y = f^{-1}(x)$, showing clearly the points where the curves meet the coordinate axes.

Answers

$y = (x-2)^2$ — This part of the expression is a square so it will always be $\geqslant 0$. The smallest value it can be is 0. This occurs when $x = 2$.

When $x = 5$, $y = 9$.

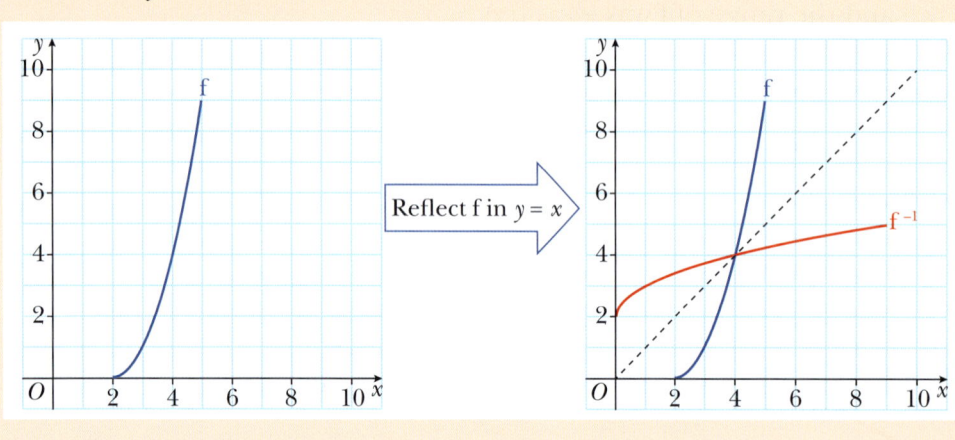

Reflect f in $y = x$

CLASS DISCUSSION

Sundeep says that the diagram shows the graph of the function $f(x) = x^x$ for $x > 0$, together with its inverse function $y = f^{-1}(x)$.

Is Sundeep correct?

Explain your answer.

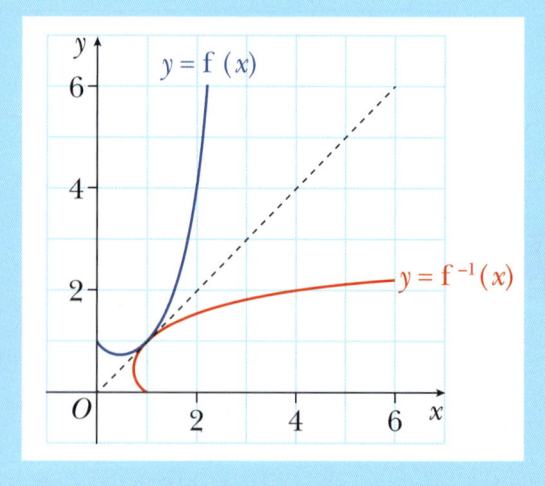

Chapter 2: Functions

Exercise 2.7

1. On a copy of the grid, draw the graph of the inverse of the function f.

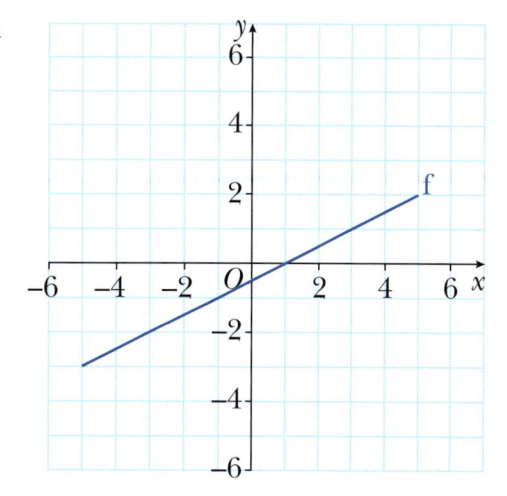

2. On a copy of the grid, draw the graph of the inverse of the function g.

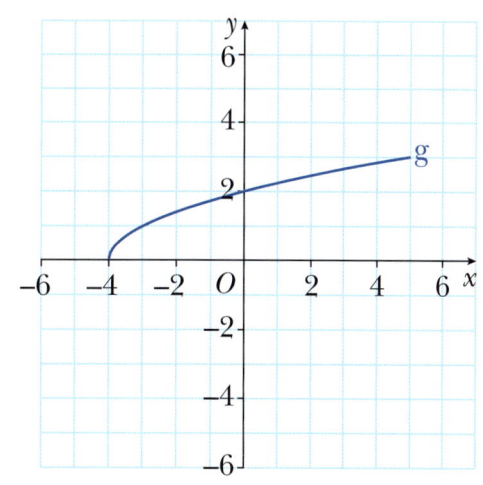

3. $f(x) = x^2 + 3$, $x \geqslant 0$.

   On the same axes, sketch the graphs of $y = f(x)$ and $y = f^{-1}(x)$, showing the coordinates of any points where the curves meet the coordinate axes.

4. $g(x) = 2^x$ for $x \in \mathbb{R}$

   On the same axes, sketch the graphs of $y = g(x)$ and $y = g^{-1}(x)$, showing the coordinates of any points where the curves meet the coordinate axes.

5. $g(x) = x^2 - 1$ for $x \geqslant 0$.

   Sketch, on a single diagram, the graphs of $y = g(x)$ and $y = g^{-1}(x)$, showing the coordinates of any points where the curves meet the coordinate axes.

6. $f(x) = 4x - 2$ for $-1 \leqslant x \leqslant 3$.

   Sketch, on a single diagram, the graphs of $y = f(x)$ and $y = f^{-1}(x)$, showing the coordinates of any points where the lines meet the coordinate axes.

7. The function f is defined by $f : x \mapsto 3 - (x+1)^2$ for $x \geqslant -1$.

   a Explain why f has an inverse.

   b Find an expression for f^{-1} in terms of x.

   c On the same axes, sketch the graphs of $y = f(x)$ and $y = f^{-1}(x)$, showing the coordinates of any points where the curves meet the coordinate axes.

CHALLENGE Q

8 $f : x \mapsto \dfrac{2x + 7}{x - 2}$ for $x \neq 2$

   a Find f^{-1} in terms of x.

   b Explain what this implies about the symmetry of the graph of $y = f(x)$.

Summary

Functions
A function is a rule that maps each x-value to just one y-value for a defined set of input values.

Mappings that are either $\begin{cases} \text{one-one} \\ \text{many-one} \end{cases}$ are called functions.

The set of input values for a function is called the **domain** of the function.

The set of output values for a function is called the **range** (or image set) of the function.

Modulus function
The modulus of x, written as $|x|$, is defined as:

$$|x| = \begin{cases} x & \text{if } x > 0 \\ 0 & \text{if } x = 0 \\ -x & \text{if } x < 0 \end{cases}$$

Composite functions
$fg(x)$ means the function g acts on x first, then f acts on the result.

$f^2(x)$ means $ff(x)$.

Inverse functions
The inverse of a function $f(x)$ is the function that undoes what $f(x)$ has done.

The inverse of the function $f(x)$ is written as $f^{-1}(x)$.

The domain of $f^{-1}(x)$ is the range of $f(x)$.

The range of $f^{-1}(x)$ is the domain of $f(x)$.

An inverse function $f^{-1}(x)$ can exist if, and only if, the function $f(x)$ is a one-one mapping.

The graphs of f and f^{-1} are reflections of each other in the line $y = x$.

Examination questions

Worked past paper example

The functions f and g are defined by

$$f(x) = \frac{2x}{x+1} \quad \text{for } x > 0,$$

$$g(x) = \sqrt{x+1} \quad \text{for } x > -1.$$

a Find fg(8). [2]

b Find an expression for $f^2(x)$, giving your answer in the form $\dfrac{ax}{bx+c}$ where a, b and c are integers to be found. [3]

c Find an expression for $g^{-1}(x)$, stating its domain and range. [4]

Cambridge IGCSE Additional Mathematics 0606 Paper 21 Q12i,ii,iii Jun 2014

Answers

a $g(8) = \sqrt{8+1} = 3$

$fg(8) = f(3)$ — substitute 3 for x in $\dfrac{2x}{x+1}$

$= \dfrac{2(3)}{3+1}$

$= 1.5$

b $f^2(x) = ff(x)$

$= f\left(\dfrac{2x}{x+1}\right)$ — substitute $\dfrac{2x}{x+1}$ for x in $\dfrac{2x}{x+1}$

$= \dfrac{2\left(\dfrac{2x}{x+1}\right)}{\left(\dfrac{2x}{x+1}\right)+1}$ — simplify

$= \dfrac{\dfrac{4x}{x+1}}{\dfrac{3x+1}{x+1}}$ — multiply numerator and denominator by $x+1$

$= \dfrac{4x}{3x+1}$

$a = 4$, $b = 3$ and $c = 1$

c $g(x) = \sqrt{x+1}$ for $x > -1$

Step 1: Write the function as $y = \quad\longrightarrow\quad y = \sqrt{x+1}$

Step 2: Interchange the x and y variables. $\longrightarrow\quad x = \sqrt{y+1}$

Step 3: Rearrange to make y the subject. $\longrightarrow\quad x^2 = y+1$

$$y = x^2 - 1$$

$f^{-1}(x) = x^2 - 1$

The range of f is $f(x) > 0$ so the domain of f^{-1} is $x > 0$.

The domain of f is $x > -1$ so the range of f^{-1} is $x > -1$.

Exercise 2.8

Exam Exercise

1 Solve the equation $|4x - 5| = 21$. [3]

Cambridge IGCSE Additional Mathematics 0606 Paper 21 Q1 Nov 2011

2 a Sketch the graph of $y = |3 + 5x|$, showing the coordinates of the points where your graph meets the coordinate axes. [2]

   b Solve the equation $|3 + 5x| = 2$. [2]

Cambridge IGCSE Additional Mathematics 0606 Paper 11 Q1i,ii Nov 2012

3 a Sketch the graph of $y = |2x - 5|$, showing the coordinates of the points where the graph meets the coordinate axes. [2]

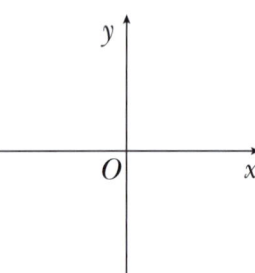

   b Solve $|2x - 5| = 3$. [2]

Cambridge IGCSE Additional Mathematics 0606 Paper 11 Q1i,ii Jun 2012

4 A function f is such that $f(x) = 3x^2 - 1$ for $-10 \leqslant x \leqslant 8$.

   a Find the range of f. [3]

   b Write down a suitable domain for f for which f^{-1} exists. [1]

Cambridge IGCSE Additional Mathematics 0606 Paper 11 Q12ai,ii Nov 2013

5 The functions f and g are defined for real values of x by

$$f(x) = \sqrt{x-1} - 3 \quad \text{for } x > 1,$$

$$g(x) = \frac{x-2}{2x-3} \quad \text{for } x > 2.$$

   a Find gf(37). [2]
   b Find an expression for $f^{-1}(x)$. [2]
   c Find an expression for $g^{-1}(x)$. [2]

Cambridge IGCSE Additional Mathematics 0606 Paper 21 Q4 Nov 2014

6 A function g is such that $g(x) = \dfrac{1}{2x-1}$ for $1 \leq x \leq 3$.
   a Find the range of g. [1]
   b Find $g^{-1}(x)$. [2]
   c Write down the domain of $g^{-1}(x)$. [1]
   d Solve $g^2(x) = 3$. [3]

Cambridge IGCSE Additional Mathematics 0606 Paper 11 Q9i-iv Nov 2012

7 a The functions f and g are defined, for $x \in \mathbb{R}$, by

$$f : x \mapsto 2x + 3$$
$$g : x \mapsto x^2 - 1.$$

   Find fg(4). [2]

  b The functions h and k are defined, for $x > 0$, by

$$h : x \mapsto x + 4$$
$$k : x \mapsto \sqrt{x}.$$

   Express each of the following in terms of h and k.
   i $x \mapsto \sqrt{x+4}$ [1]
   ii $x \mapsto x + 8$ [1]
   iii $x \mapsto x^2 - 4$ [2]

Cambridge IGCSE Additional Mathematics 0606 Paper 21 Q5a,bi,ii,iii Nov 2011

8 a The function f is such that $f(x) = 2x^2 - 8x + 5$.

   i Show that $f(x) = 2(x+a)^2 + b$, where a and b are to be found. [2]

   ii Hence, or otherwise, write down a suitable domain for f so that f^{-1} exists. [1]

 b The functions g and h are defined respectively by
   $$g(x) = x^2 + 4, \ x \geq 0, \quad h(x) = 4x - 25, \ x \geq 0,$$

   i Write down the range of g and of h^{-1}. [2]

   ii On a copy of the axes below sketch the graphs of $y = g(x)$ and of $y = g^{-1}(x)$, showing the coordinates of any points where the curves meet the coordinate axes. [3]

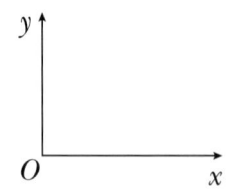

   iii Find the value of x for which $gh(x) = 85$. [4]

   Cambridge IGCSE Additional Mathematics 0606 Paper 11 Q11ai,ii,bi,ii,iii Jun 2011

Chapter 3
Simultaneous equations and quadratics

This section will show you how to:

- solve simultaneous equations in two unknowns with at least one linear equation
- find the maximum and minimum values of a quadratic function
- sketch graphs of quadratic functions and find their range
- sketch graphs of the function $y = |f(x)|$ where f(x) is quadratic and solve associated equations
- determine the number of roots of a quadratic equation and the related conditions for a line to intersect, be a tangent or not intersect a given curve
- solve quadratic equations and quadratic inequalities.

Cambridge IGCSE and O Level Additional Mathematics

> **RECAP** (simultaneous equations)
>
> You should already know how to use a graphical method or an algebraic method to solve simultaneous equations where both equations are linear.
>
> To solve simultaneous linear equations algebraically you should know both the elimination method and the substitution method.
>
> **Elimination method**
>
> Solve $5x + 2y = 25$ ---------------(1)
> $2x - y = 1$ ---------------(2)
>
> Multiply (2) by 2.
> $5x + 2y = 25$
> $4x - 2y = 2$
> Add the equations to eliminate y.
> $9x = 27$
> $x = 3$
> Substitute for x in equation (2).
> $6 - y = 1$
> $y = 5$
> Solution is $x = 3$, $y = 5$.
>
> **Substitution method**
>
> Solve $5x + 2y = 25$ ------------(1)
> $2x - y = 1$ ------------(2)
>
> Make y the subject of equation (2).
> $y = 2x - 1$
> Substitute for y in equation (1).
> $5x + 2(2x - 1) = 25$
> $9x - 2 = 25$
> $9x = 27$
> $x = 3$
> Substitute for x in equation (2).
> $6 - y = 1$
> $y = 5$
> Solution is $x = 3$, $y = 5$.

CLASS DISCUSSION

Solve each of these three pairs of simultaneous equations.

$8x + 3y = 7$	$3x + y = 10$	$2x + 5 = 3y$
$3x + 5y = -9$	$2y = 15 - 6x$	$10 - 6y = -4x$

Discuss your answers with your classmates.

Discuss what the graphs would be like for each pair of equations.

Chapter 3: Simultaneous equations and quadratics

RECAP (quadratic equations)

You should already know how to use a graphical method or an algebraic method to solve quadratic equations.

To solve quadratic equations algebraically you should know the factorisation method, the quadratic formula method and the completing the square method.

Factorisation method
Solve $x^2 - 4x - 12 = 0$.
Factorise:
$$(x - 6)(x + 2) = 0$$
$$x - 6 = 0 \text{ or } x + 2 = 0$$
Solution is $x = 6$ or $x = -2$.

Completing the square method
Solve $x^2 - 4x - 12 = 0$.
Complete the square.
$$(x - 2)^2 - 4 - 12 = 0$$
$$(x - 2)^2 = 16$$
Square root both sides.
$$x - 2 = \pm 4$$
$$x - 2 = 4 \text{ or } x - 2 = -4$$
Solution is $x = 6$ or $x = -2$.

Quadratic formula method
Solve $x^2 - 4x - 12 = 0$.
Identify a, b and c
$a = 1$, $b = -4$ and $c = -12$.
Use the formula:
$$x = \frac{-b \pm \sqrt{b^2 - 4ac}}{2a}$$
Substitute for a, b and c.
$$x = \frac{4 \pm \sqrt{(-4)^2 - 4 \times 1 \times (-12)}}{2 \times 1}$$
$$x = \frac{4 \pm \sqrt{64}}{2}$$
$$x = \frac{4 \pm 8}{2}$$
$$x = \frac{4 + 8}{2} \text{ or } x = \frac{4 - 8}{2}$$
Solution is $x = 6$ or $x = -2$.

CLASS DISCUSSION

Solve each of these quadratic equations.

$x^2 - 8x + 15 = 0$ $x^2 + 4x + 4 = 0$ $x^2 + 2x + 4 = 0$

Discuss your answers with your classmates. Discuss what the graphs would be like for each of the functions $y = x^2 - 8x + 15$, $y = x^2 + 4x + 4$ and $y = x^2 + 2x + 4$.

3.1 Simultaneous equations (one linear and one non-linear)

In this section you will learn how to solve simultaneous equations where one equation is linear and the second equation is not linear.

The diagram shows the graphs of $y = x + 1$ and $y = x^2 - 5$.

The coordinates of the points of intersection of the two graphs are $(-2, -1)$ and $(3, 4)$.

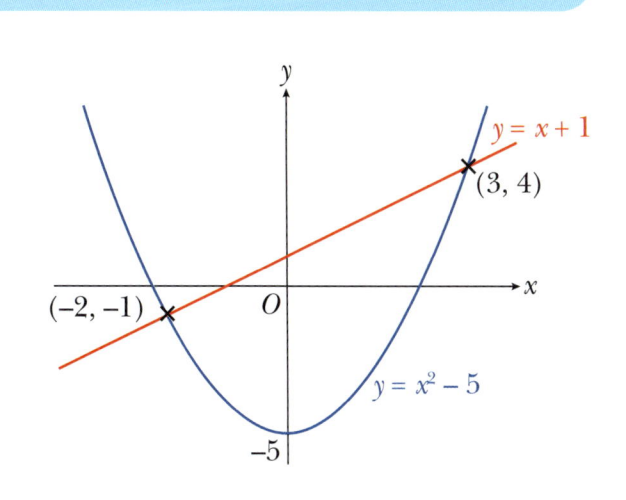

We say that $x = -2$, $y = -1$ and $x = 3$, $y = 4$ are the solutions of the simultaneous equations $y = x + 1$ and $y = x^2 - 5$.

The solutions can also be found algebraically:

$y = x + 1$ -------(1)
$y = x^2 - 5$ ------(2)

Substitute for y from (1) into (2):

$$x + 1 = x^2 - 5 \qquad \text{rearrange}$$
$$x^2 - x - 6 = 0 \qquad \text{factorise}$$
$$(x + 2)(x - 3) = 0$$
$$x = -2 \text{ or } x = 3$$

Substituting $x = -2$ into (1) gives $y = -2 + 1 = -1$.
Substituting $x = 3$ into (1) gives $y = 3 + 1 = 4$.
The solutions are: $x = -2$, $y = -1$ and $x = 3$, $y = 4$.

WORKED EXAMPLE 1

Solve the simultaneous equations.
$$2x + 2y = 7$$
$$x^2 - 4y^2 = 8$$

Answers

$2x + 2y = 7$ -------(1)
$x^2 - 4y^2 = 8$ ------(2)

From (1), $x = \dfrac{7 - 2y}{2}$.

Substitute for x in (2):

$$\left(\dfrac{7 - 2y}{2}\right)^2 - 4y^2 = 8 \qquad \text{expand brackets}$$

$$\dfrac{49 - 28y + 4y^2}{4} - 4y^2 = 8 \qquad \text{multiply both sides by 4}$$

$$49 - 28y + 4y^2 - 16y^2 = 32 \qquad \text{rearrange}$$

$$12y^2 + 28y - 17 = 0 \qquad \text{factorise}$$

$$(6y + 17)(2y - 1) = 0$$

$$y = -2\dfrac{5}{6} \text{ or } y = \dfrac{1}{2}$$

Substituting $y = -2\dfrac{5}{6}$ into (1) gives $x = 6\dfrac{1}{3}$.

Substituting $y = \dfrac{1}{2}$ into (1) gives $x = 3$.

The solutions are: $x = 6\dfrac{1}{3}$, $y = -2\dfrac{5}{6}$ and $x = 3$, $y = \dfrac{1}{2}$.

Exercise 3.1

Solve the following simultaneous equations.

1. $y = x^2$
   $y = x + 6$

2. $y = x - 6$
   $x^2 + xy = 8$

3. $y = x - 1$
   $x^2 + y^2 = 25$

4. $xy = 4$
   $y = 2x + 2$

5. $x^2 - xy = 0$
   $x + y = 1$

6. $3y = 4x - 5$
   $x^2 + 3xy = 10$

7. $2x + y = 7$
   $xy = 6$

8. $x - y = 2$
   $2x^2 - 3y^2 = 15$

9. $x + 2y = 7$
   $x^2 + y^2 = 10$

10. $y = 2x$
    $x^2 + xy = 3$

11. $xy = 2$
    $x + y = 3$

12. $y^2 = 4x$
    $2x + y = 4$

13. $x + 3y = 0$
    $2x^2 + 3y = 1$

14. $x + y = 4$
    $x^2 + y^2 = 10$

15. $y = 3x$
    $2y^2 - xy = 15$

16. $x - 2y = 1$
    $4y^2 - 3x^2 = 1$

17. $3 + x + xy = 0$
    $2x + 5y = 8$

18. $xy = 12$
    $(x - 1)(y + 2) = 15$

19. Calculate the coordinates of the points where the line $y = 1 - 2x$ cuts the curve $x^2 + y^2 = 2$.

20. The sum of two numbers x and y is 11.
    The product of the two numbers is 21.25.
    a Write down two equations in x and y.
    b Solve your equations to find the possible values of x and y.

21. The sum of the areas of two squares is $818 \, \text{cm}^2$.
    The sum of the perimeters is 160 cm.
    Find the lengths of the sides of the squares.

22. The line $y = 2 - 2x$ cuts the curve $3x^2 - y^2 = 3$ at the points A and B.
    Find the length of the line AB.

23. The line $2x + 5y = 1$ meets the curve $x^2 + 5xy - 4y^2 + 10 = 0$ at the points A and B.
    Find the coordinates of the mid-point of AB.

24. The line $y = x - 10$ intersects the curve $x^2 + y^2 + 4x + 6y - 40 = 0$ at the points A and B.
    Find the length of the line AB.

25. The straight line $y = 2x - 2$ intersects the curve $x^2 - y = 5$ at the points A and B.
    Given that A lies below the x-axis and the point P lies on AB such that $AP : PB = 3 : 1$, find the coordinates of P.

26. The line $x - 2y = 2$ intersects the curve $x + y^2 = 10$ at two points A and B.
    Find the equation of the perpendicular bisector of the line AB.

3.2 Maximum and minimum values of a quadratic function

> **RECAP**
>
> The general equation of a quadratic function is $f(x) = ax^2 + bx + c$, where a, b and c are constants and $a \neq 0$.
>
> The graph of the function $y = ax^2 + bx + c$ is called a **parabola**. The orientation of the parabola depends on the value of a, the coefficient of x^2. 
>
> If $a > 0$, the curve has a **minimum point** which occurs at the lowest point of the curve.
>
> If $a < 0$, the curve has a **maximum point** which occurs at the highest point of the curve.
>
> The maximum and minimum points can also be called **turning points or stationary points**. Every parabola has a line of symmetry that passes through the maximum or minimum point.

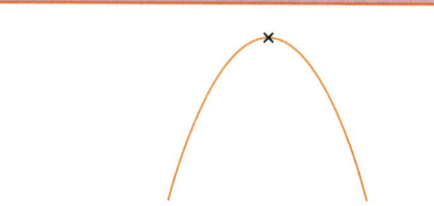

WORKED EXAMPLE 2

$f(x) = x^2 - 3x - 4 \qquad x \in \mathbb{R}$

a Find the axis crossing points for the graph of $y = f(x)$.

b Sketch the graph of $y = f(x)$ and use the symmetry of the curve to find the coordinates of the minimum point.

c State the range of the function $f(x)$.

Answers

a $y = x^2 - 3x - 4$

When $x = 0$, $y = -4$.

When $y = 0$,

$x^2 - 3x - 4 = 0$

$(x + 1)(x - 4) = 0$

$x = -1$ or $x = 4$

Axes crossing points are: $(0, -4)$, $(-1, 0)$ and $(4, 0)$.

b The line of symmetry cuts the x-axis midway between -1 and 4.

So the line of symmetry is $x = 1.5$

When $x = 1.5$, $y = (1.5)^2 - 3(1.5) - 4$.

$y = -6.25$.

Minimum point $= (1.5, -6.25)$.

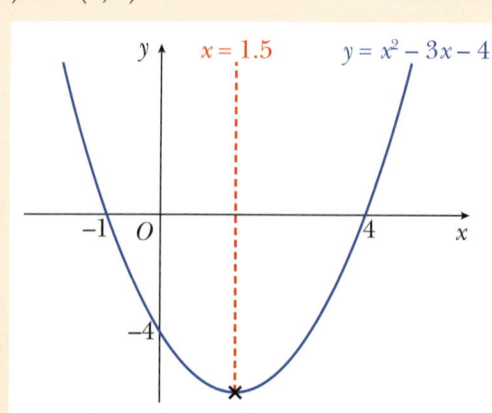

c The range is $f(x) \geq -6.25$.

Completing the square

If you expand the expressions $(x + d)^2$ and $(x - d)^2$ you obtain the results:
$$(x + d)^2 = x^2 + 2dx + d^2 \text{ and } (x - d)^2 = x^2 - 2dx + d^2$$

Rearranging these give the following important results:
$$x^2 + 2dx = (x + d)^2 - d^2$$
$$x^2 - 2dx = (x - d)^2 - d^2$$

This is known as **completing the square**.

To complete the square for $x^2 + 8x$:
$$8 \div 2 = 4$$
$$x^2 + 8x = (x + 4)^2 - 4^2$$
$$x^2 + 8x = (x + 4)^2 - 16$$

To complete the square for $x^2 + 10x - 3$:
$$10 \div 2 = 5$$
$$x^2 + 10x - 3 = (x + 5)^2 - 5^2 - 3$$
$$x^2 + 10x - 3 = (x + 5)^2 - 28$$

To complete the square for $2x^2 - 8x + 14$ you must first take a factor of 2 out of the expression:
$$2x^2 - 8x + 14 = 2[x^2 - 4x + 7]$$
$$4 \div 2 = 2$$
$$x^2 - 4x + 7 = (x - 2)^2 - 2^2 + 7$$
$$x^2 - 4x + 3 = (x - 2)^2 + 3$$
So, $2x^2 - 8x + 6 = 2[(x - 2)^2 + 3] = 2(x - 2)^2 + 6$

You can also use an algebraic method for completing the square, as shown in the following example.

WORKED EXAMPLE 3

Express $2x^2 - 4x + 5$ in the form $p(x - q)^2 + r$, where p, q and r are constants to be found.

Answers

$2x^2 - 4x + 5 = p(x - q)^2 + r$

Expanding the brackets and simplifying gives:

$2x^2 - 4x + 5 = px^2 - 2pqx + pq^2 + r$

Comparing coefficients of x^2, coefficients of x and the constant gives:

$2 = p$ --------(1) $-4 = -2pq$ -------(2) $5 = pq^2 + r$ -------(3)

Substituting $p = 2$ in equation (2) gives $q = 1$.
Substituting $p = 2$ and $q = 1$ in equation (3) gives $r = 3$.
So $2x^2 - 4x + 5 = 2(x - 1)^2 + 3$.

Completing the square for a quadratic expression or function enables you to:

- write down the maximum or minimum value of the expression
- write down the coordinates of the maximum or minimum point of the function
- sketch the graph of the function
- write down the line of symmetry of the function
- state the range of the function.

In **Worked example 3** you found that:

$$2x^2 - 4x + 5 = 2(x-1)^2 + 3$$

This part of the expression is a square so it will always be ≥ 0. The smallest value it can be is 0. This occurs when $x = 1$.

The minimum value of the expression is $2 \times 0 + 3 = 3$ and this minimum occurs when $x = 1$.

So the function $y = 2x^2 - 4x + 5$ will have a minimum point at the point $(1, 3)$.

When $x = 0$, $y = 5$.

The graph of $y = 2x^2 - 4x + 5$ can now be sketched:

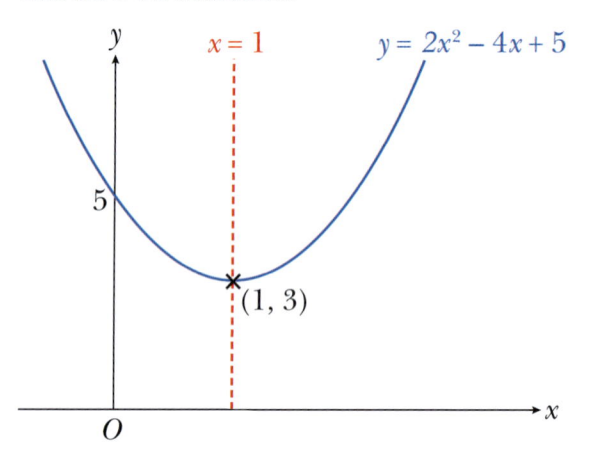

The line of symmetry is $x = 1$.

The range is $y \geq 3$.

The general rule is:

For a quadratic function $f(x) = ax^2 + bx + c$ that is written in the form $f(x) = a(x-h)^2 + k$,

i if $a > 0$, the minimum point is (h, k)
ii if $a < 0$, the maximum point is (h, k).

Chapter 3: Simultaneous equations and quadratics

WORKED EXAMPLE 4

$f(x) = 2 + 8x - 2x^2 \qquad x \in \mathbb{R}$

a Find the value of a, the value of b and the value of c for which $f(x) = a - b(x + c)^2$.

b Write down the coordinates of the maximum point on the curve $y = f(x)$.

c Sketch the graph of $y = f(x)$, showing the coordinates of the points where the graph intersects the x and y-axes.

d State the range of the function $f(x)$.

Answers

a $2 + 8x - 2x^2 = a - b(x + c)^2$

$2 + 8x - 2x^2 = a - b(x^2 + 2cx + c^2)$

$2 + 8x - 2x^2 = a - bx^2 - 2bcx - bc^2$

Comparing coefficients of x^2, coefficients of x and the constant gives:

$-2 = -b$ --------(1) $\qquad 8 = -2bc$ --------(2) $\qquad 2 = a - bc^2$ --------(3)

Substituting $b = 2$ in equation (2) gives $c = -2$.

Substituting $b = 2$ and $c = -2$ in equation (3) gives $a = 10$.

So $a = 10$, $b = 2$ and $c = -2$.

b $y = 10 - 2(x - 2)^2$

> This part of the expression is a square so it will always be $\geqslant 0$. The smallest value it can be is 0. This occurs when $x = 2$.

The maximum value of the expression is $10 - 2 \times 0 = 10$ and this maximum occurs when $x = 2$.

So the function $y = 2 + 8x - 2x^2$ will have maximum point at the point $(2, 10)$.

c $y = 2 + 8x - 2x^2$

When $x = 0$, $y = 2$.

When $y = 0$,

$10 - 2(x - 2)^2 = 0$

$2(x - 2)^2 = 10$

$(x - 2)^2 = 5$

$x - 2 = \pm\sqrt{5}$

$x = 2 \pm \sqrt{5}$

$x = 2 - \sqrt{5}$ or $x = 2 + \sqrt{5}$

$(x = -0.236$ or $x = 4.24$ to 3 sf$)$.

Axes crossing points are: $(0, 2)$, $(2 - \sqrt{5}, 0)$ and $(2 + \sqrt{5}, 0)$.

d The range is $f(x) \leqslant 10$.

Exercise 3.2

1 Use the symmetry of each quadratic function to find the maximum or minimum points.

Sketch each graph, showing all axis crossing points.
- **a** $y = x^2 - 5x - 6$
- **b** $y = x^2 - x - 20$
- **c** $y = x^2 + 4x - 21$
- **d** $y = x^2 + 3x - 28$
- **e** $y = x^2 + 4x + 1$
- **f** $y = 15 + 2x - x^2$

2 Express each of the following in the form $(x - m)^2 + n$.
- **a** $x^2 - 8x$
- **b** $x^2 - 10x$
- **c** $x^2 - 5x$
- **d** $x^2 - 3x$
- **e** $x^2 + 4x$
- **f** $x^2 + 7x$
- **g** $x^2 + 9x$
- **h** $x^2 + 3x$

3 Express each of the following in the form $(x - m)^2 + n$.
- **a** $x^2 - 8x + 15$
- **b** $x^2 - 10x - 5$
- **c** $x^2 - 6x + 2$
- **d** $x^2 - 3x + 4$
- **e** $x^2 + 6x + 5$
- **f** $x^2 + 6x + 9$
- **g** $x^2 + 4x - 17$
- **h** $x^2 + 5x + 6$

4 Express each of the following in the form $a(x - p)^2 + q$.
- **a** $2x^2 - 8x + 3$
- **b** $2x^2 - 12x + 1$
- **c** $3x^2 - 12x + 5$
- **d** $2x^2 - 3x + 2$
- **e** $2x^2 + 4x + 1$
- **f** $2x^2 + 7x - 3$
- **g** $2x^2 - 3x + 5$
- **h** $3x^2 - x + 6$

5 Express each of the following in the form $m - (x - n)^2$.
- **a** $6x - x^2$
- **b** $10x - x^2$
- **c** $3x - x^2$
- **d** $8x - x^2$

6 Express each of the following in the form $a - (x + b)^2$.
- **a** $5 - 2x - x^2$
- **b** $8 - 4x - x^2$
- **c** $10 - 5x - x^2$
- **d** $7 + 3x - x^2$

7 Express each of the following in the form $a - p(x + q)^2$.
- **a** $9 - 6x - 2x^2$
- **b** $1 - 4x - 2x^2$
- **c** $7 + 8x - 2x^2$
- **d** $2 + 5x - 3x^2$

8 a Express $4x^2 + 2x + 5$ in the form $a(x + b)^2 + c$, where a, b and c are constants.

b Does the function $y = 4x^2 + 2x + 5$ meet the x-axis? Explain your answer.

9 $f(x) = 2x^2 - 8x + 1$

a Express $2x^2 - 8x + 1$ in the form $a(x + b)^2 + c$, where a and b are integers.

b Find the coordinates of the stationary point on the graph of $y = f(x)$.

10 $f(x) = x^2 - x - 5$ for $x \in \mathbb{R}$

a Find the smallest value of $f(x)$ and the corresponding value of x.

b Hence write down a suitable domain for $f(x)$ in order that $f^{-1}(x)$ exists.

11 $f(x) = 5 - 7x - 2x^2$ for $x \in \mathbb{R}$

a Write $f(x)$ in the form $p - 2(x - q)^2$, where p and q are constants to be found.

b Write down the range of the function $f(x)$.

12 $f(x) = 14 + 6x - 2x^2$ for $x \in \mathbb{R}$

   a Express $14 + 6x - 2x^2$ in the form $a + b(x + c)^2$, where a, b and c are constants.

   b Write down the coordinates of the stationary point on the graph of $y = f(x)$.

   c Sketch the graph of $y = f(x)$.

13 $f(x) = 7 + 5x - x^2$ for $0 \leqslant x \leqslant 7$

   a Express $7 + 5x - x^2$ in the form $a - (x + b)^2$, where a, and b are constants.

   b Find the coordinates of the turning point of the function $f(x)$, stating whether it is a maximum or minimum point.

   c Find the range of f.

   d State, giving a reason, whether or not f has an inverse.

14 The function f is such that $f(x) = 2x^2 - 8x + 3$.

   a Write $f(x)$ in the form $2(x + a)^2 + b$, where a, and b are constants to be found.

   b Write down a suitable domain for f so that f^{-1} exists.

15 $f(x) = 4x^2 + 6x - 8$ where $x \geqslant m$

Find the smallest value of m for which f has an inverse.

16 $f(x) = 1 + 4x - x^2$ for $x \geqslant 2$

   a Express $1 + 4x - x^2$ in the form $a - (x + b)^2$, where a and b are constants to be found.

   b Find the coordinates of the turning point of the function $f(x)$, stating whether it is a maximum or minimum point.

   c Explain why $f(x)$ has an inverse and find an expression for $f^{-1}(x)$ in terms of x.

Cambridge IGCSE and O Level Additional Mathematics

3.3 Graphs of $y = |f(x)|$ where $f(x)$ is quadratic

To sketch the graph of the modulus function $y = |ax^2 + bx + c|$, you must:

- first sketch the graph of $y = ax^2 + bx + c$
- reflect in the x-axis the part of the curve $y = ax^2 + bx + c$ that is below the x-axis.

WORKED EXAMPLE 5

Sketch the graph of $y = |x^2 - 2x - 3|$.

Answers

First sketch the graph of $y = x^2 - 2x - 3$.
When $x = 0$, $y = -3$.
So the y-intercept is -3.
When $y = 0$,
$$x^2 - 2x - 3 = 0$$
$$(x + 1)(x - 3) = 0$$
$$x = -1 \text{ or } x = 3.$$

So the x-intercepts are -1 and 3.

The x-coordinate of the minimum point $= \dfrac{-1 + 3}{2} = 1$.

The y-coordinate of the minimum point $= (1)^2 - 2(1) - 3 = -4$.

The minimum point is $(1, -4)$.

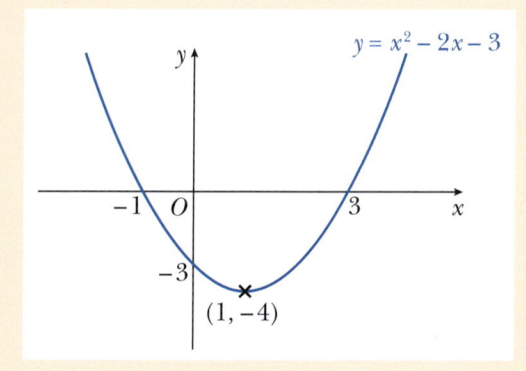

Now reflect in the x-axis the part of the curve $y = x^2 - 2x - 3$ that is below the x-axis.

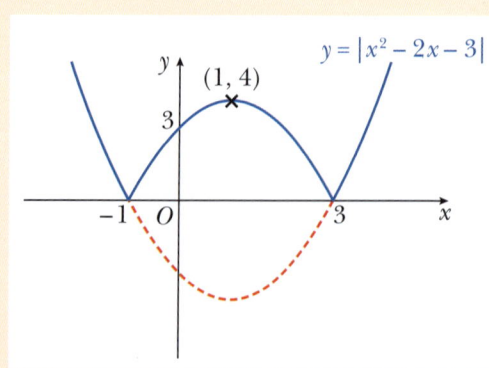

A sketch of the function $y = |x^2 + 4x - 12|$ is shown below.

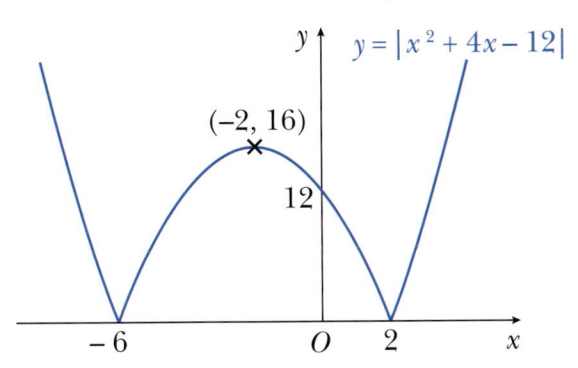

Now consider using this graph to find the number of solutions of the equation $|x^2 + 4x - 12| = k$ where $k \geqslant 0$.

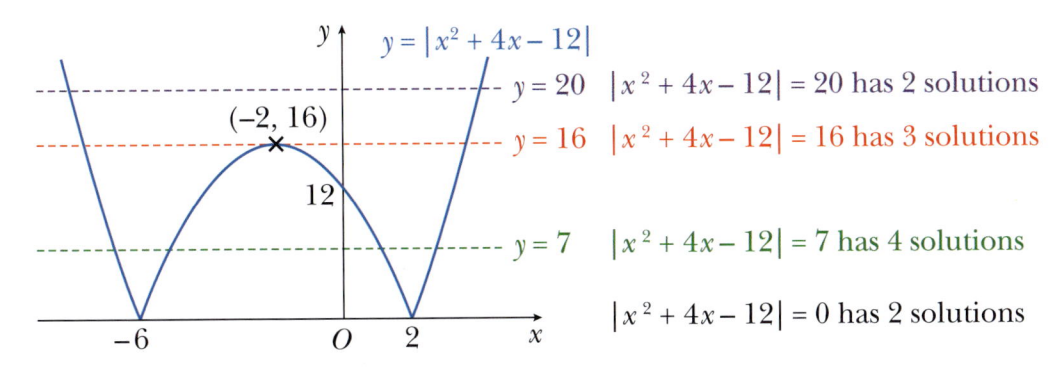

$y = 20$ $|x^2 + 4x - 12| = 20$ has 2 solutions
$y = 16$ $|x^2 + 4x - 12| = 16$ has 3 solutions
$y = 7$ $|x^2 + 4x - 12| = 7$ has 4 solutions
$|x^2 + 4x - 12| = 0$ has 2 solutions

The conditions for the number of solutions of the equation $|x^2 + 4x - 12| = k$ are:

Value of k	$k = 0$	$0 < k < 16$	$k = 16$	$k > 16$
Number of solutions	2	4	3	2

Equations involving $|f(x)|$, where f(x) is quadratic, can be solved algebraically:

To solve $|x^2 + 4x - 12| = 16$:

$x^2 + 4x - 12 = 16$ or $x^2 + 4x - 12 = -16$

$x^2 + 4x - 28 = 0$ or $x^2 + 4x + 4 = 0$

$x = \dfrac{-4 \pm \sqrt{4^2 - 4 \times 1 \times (-28)}}{2 \times 1}$ or $(x+2)(x+2) = 0$

$x = \dfrac{-4 \pm \sqrt{128}}{2}$ or $x = -2$

$x = -2 \pm 4\sqrt{2}$

($x = 3.66$ or $x = -7.66$ to 3 sf)

The exact solutions are $x = -2 - 4\sqrt{2}$ or $x = -2$ or $x = -2 + 4\sqrt{2}$.

> **Note:**
> The graph of $y = |x^2 + 4x - 12|$ is sketched below showing these three solutions.

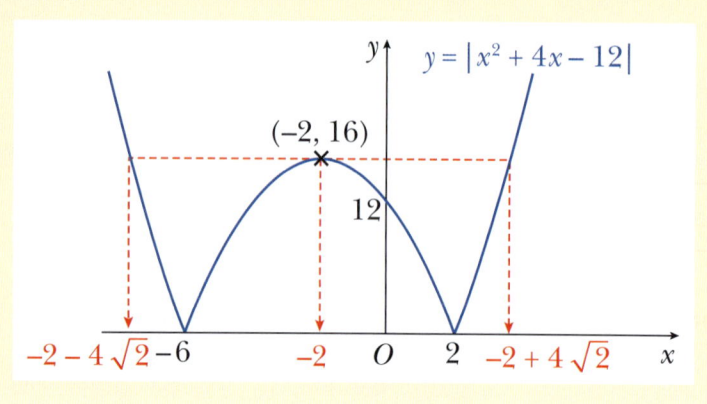

Exercise 3.3

1. Sketch the graphs of each of the following functions.
   a. $y = |x^2 - 4x + 3|$
   b. $y = |x^2 - 2x - 3|$
   c. $y = |x^2 - 5x + 4|$
   d. $y = |x^2 - 2x - 8|$
   e. $y = |2x^2 - 11x - 6|$
   f. $y = |3x^2 + 5x - 2|$

2. $f(x) = 1 - 4x - x^2$
   a. Write $f(x)$ in the form $a - (x + b)^2$, where a and b are constants.
   b. Sketch the graph of $y = f(x)$.
   c. Sketch the graph of $y = |f(x)|$.

3. $f(x) = 2x^2 + x - 3$
   a. Write $f(x)$ in the form $a(x + b)^2 + c$, where a, b and c are constants.
   b. Sketch the graph of $y = |f(x)|$.

4. a. Find the coordinates of the stationary point on the curve $y = |(x - 7)(x + 1)|$.
   b. Sketch the graph of $y = |(x - 7)(x + 1)|$.
   c. Find the set of values of k for which $|(x - 7)(x + 1)| = k$ has four solutions.

5. a. Find the coordinates of the stationary point on the curve $y = |(x + 5)(x + 1)|$.
   b. Find the set of values of k for which $|(x + 5)(x + 1)| = k$ has two solutions.

6. a. Find the coordinates of the stationary point on the curve $y = |(x - 8)(x - 3)|$.
   b. Find the value of k for which $|(x - 8)(x - 3)| = k$ has three solutions.

7. Solve these equations.
   a. $|x^2 - 6| = 10$
   b. $|x^2 - 2| = 2$
   c. $|x^2 - 5x| = 6$
   d. $|x^2 + 2x| = 24$
   e. $|x^2 - 5x + 1| = 3$
   f. $|x^2 + 3x - 1| = 3$
   g. $|x^2 + 2x - 4| = 5$
   h. $|2x^2 - 3| = 2x$
   i. $|x^2 - 4x + 7| = 4$

CHALLENGE Q

8 Solve these simultaneous equations.
   a $y = x + 1$
      $y = |x^2 - 2x - 3|$
   b $2y = x + 4$
      $y = \left|\dfrac{1}{2}x^2 - x - 3\right|$
   c $y = 2x$
      $y = |2x^2 - 4|$

3.4 Quadratic inequalities

RECAP

You should already know how to solve linear inequalities.

Two examples are shown below.

Solve $2(x - 5) < 9$	expand brackets
$2x - 10 < 9$	add 10 to both sides
$2x < 19$	divide both sides by 2
$x < 9.5$	

Solve $5 - 3x \geq 17$	subtract 5 from both sides
$-3x \geq 12$	divide both sides by -3
$x \leq -4$	

Note:
It is very important that you remember the rule that when you multiply or divide both sides of an inequality by a negative number then the inequality sign must be reversed. This is illustrated in the second example above, when both sides of the inequality were divided by -3.

CLASS DISCUSSION

Robert is asked to solve the inequality $\dfrac{7x + 12}{x} \geq 3$.

He writes: $7x + 12 \geq 3x$
$4x \geq -12$
So $x \geq -3$

Anna checks his answer using the number -4.

She writes: When $x = -4$,
$(7 \times (-4) + 12) \div (-4) = (-16) \div (-4) = 4$
Hence $x = -4$ is a value of x that satisfies the original inequality
So Robert's answer must be incorrect!

Discuss Robert's working out with your classmates and explain Robert's error.

Now solve the inequality $\dfrac{7x + 12}{x} \geq 3$ correctly.

Quadratic inequalities can be solved by sketching a graph and considering when the graph is above or below the x-axis.

WORKED EXAMPLE 6

Solve $x^2 - 3x - 4 > 0$.

Answers

Sketch the graph of $y = x^2 - 3x - 4$.
When $y = 0$, $x^2 - 3x - 4 = 0$
$$(x + 1)(x - 4) = 0$$
$x = -1$ or $x = 4$.
So the x-axis crossing points are -1 and 4.
For $x^2 - 3x - 4 > 0$ you need to find the range of values of x for which the curve is positive (above the x-axis).

The solution is $x < -1$ and $x > 4$.

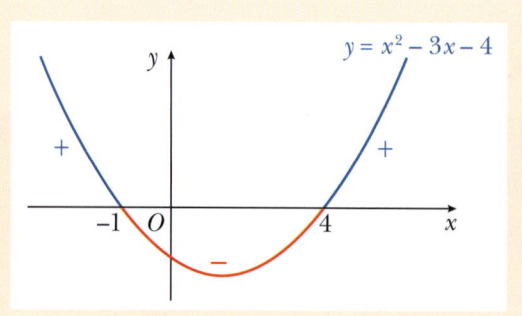

WORKED EXAMPLE 7

Solve $2x^2 \leqslant 15 - x$.

Answers

Rearranging: $2x^2 + x - 15 \leqslant 0$.
Sketch the graph of $y = 2x^2 + x - 15$.
When $y = 0$, $2x^2 + x - 15 = 0$
$$(2x - 5)(x + 3) = 0$$
$x = 2.5$ or $x = -3$.
So the x-axis crossing points are -3 and 2.5.
For $2x^2 + x - 15 \leqslant 0$ you need to find the range of values of x for which the curve is either zero or negative (below the x-axis).

The solution is $-3 \leqslant x \leqslant 2.5$.

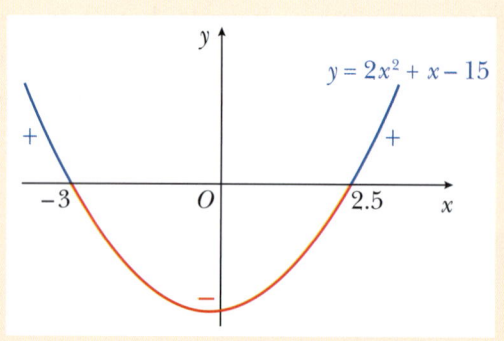

Exercise 3.4

1 Solve.

   a $(x + 3)(x - 4) > 0$ **b** $(x - 5)(x - 1) \leqslant 0$ **c** $(x - 3)(x + 7) \geqslant 0$
   d $x(x - 5) < 0$ **e** $(2x + 1)(x - 4) < 0$ **f** $(3 - x)(x + 1) \geqslant 0$
   g $(2x + 3)(x - 5) < 0$ **h** $(x - 5)^2 \geqslant 0$ **i** $(x - 3)^2 \leqslant 0$

2 Solve.

   a $x^2 + 5x - 14 < 0$ **b** $x^2 + x - 6 \geqslant 0$ **c** $x^2 - 9x + 20 \leqslant 0$
   d $x^2 + 2x - 48 > 0$ **e** $2x^2 - x - 15 \leqslant 0$ **f** $5x^2 + 9x + 4 > 0$

3 Solve.
   a $x^2 < 18 - 3x$
   b $12x < x^2 + 35$
   c $x(3 - 2x) \leq 1$
   d $x^2 + 4x < 3(x + 2)$
   e $(x + 3)(1 - x) < x - 1$
   f $(4x + 3)(3x - 1) < 2x(x + 3)$

4 Find the set of values of x for which
   a $x^2 - 11x + 24 < 0$ and $2x + 3 < 13$
   b $x^2 - 4x \leq 12$ and $4x - 3 > 1$
   c $x(2x - 1) < 1$ and $7 - 2x < 6$
   d $x^2 - 3x - 10 < 0$ and $x^2 - 10x + 21 < 0$
   e $x^2 + x - 2 > 0$ and $x^2 - 2x - 3 \geq 0$.

5 Solve.
   a $|x^2 + 2x - 2| < 13$
   b $|x^2 - 8x + 6| < 6$
   c $|x^2 - 6x + 4| < 4$

CHALLENGE Q

6 Find the range of values of x for which $\dfrac{4}{3x^2 - 2x - 8} < 0$.

3.5 Roots of quadratic equations

The answers to an equation are called the **roots** of the equation.

Consider solving the following three quadratic equations using the formula $x = \dfrac{-b \pm \sqrt{b^2 - 4ac}}{2a}$.

$x^2 + 2x - 8 = 0$	$x^2 + 6x + 9 = 0$	$x^2 + 2x + 6 = 0$
$x = \dfrac{-2 \pm \sqrt{2^2 - 4 \times 1 \times (-8)}}{2 \times 1}$	$x = \dfrac{-6 \pm \sqrt{6^2 - 4 \times 1 \times 9}}{2 \times 1}$	$x = \dfrac{-2 \pm \sqrt{2^2 - 4 \times 1 \times 6}}{2 \times 1}$
$x = \dfrac{-2 \pm \sqrt{36}}{2}$	$x = \dfrac{-2 \pm \sqrt{0}}{2}$	$x = \dfrac{-2 \pm \sqrt{-20}}{2}$
$x = 2$ or $x = -4$	$x = -1$ or $x = -1$	no solution
2 distinct roots	2 equal roots	0 roots

The part of the quadratic formula underneath the square root sign is called the **discriminant**.

discriminant $= b^2 - 4ac$

The sign (positive, zero or negative) of the discriminant tells you how many roots there are for a particular quadratic equation.

$b^2 - 4ac$	Nature of roots
> 0	2 real distinct roots
$= 0$	2 real equal roots
< 0	0 real roots

There is a connection between the roots of the quadratic equation $ax^2 + bx + c = 0$ and the corresponding curve $y = ax^2 + bx + c$.

$b^2 - 4ac$	Nature of roots of $ax^2 + bx + c = 0$	Shape of curve $y = ax^2 + bx + c$
> 0	2 real distinct roots	$a > 0$ or $a < 0$ The curve cuts the x-axis at 2 distinct points.
$= 0$	2 real equal roots	$a > 0$ or $a < 0$ The curve touches the x-axis at 1 point.
< 0	0 real roots	$a > 0$ or $a < 0$ The curve is entirely above or entirely below the x-axis.

WORKED EXAMPLE 8

Find the values of k for which $x^2 - 3x + 6 = k(x - 2)$ has two equal roots.

Answers

$$x^2 - 3x + 6 = k(x - 2)$$
$$x^2 - 3x + 6 - kx + 2k = 0$$
$$x^2 - (3 + k)x + 6 + 2k = 0$$

For two equal roots $b^2 - 4ac = 0$.

$$(3 + k)^2 - 4 \times 1 \times (6 + 2k) = 0$$
$$k^2 + 6k + 9 - 24 - 8k = 0$$
$$k^2 - 2k - 15 = 0$$
$$(k + 3)(k - 5) = 0$$

So $k = -3$ or $k = 5$.

Chapter 3: Simultaneous equations and quadratics

> **WORKED EXAMPLE 9**
>
> Find the values of k for which $x^2 + (k-2)x + 4 = 0$ has two distinct roots.
>
> **Answers**
>
> $x^2 + (k-2)x + 4 = 0$
>
> For two distinct roots $b^2 - 4ac > 0$
>
> $(k-2)^2 - 4 \times 1 \times 4 > 0$
>
> $k^2 - 4k + 4 - 16 > 0$
>
> $k^2 - 4k - 12 > 0$
>
> $(k+2)(k-6) > 0$
>
> Critical values are -2 and 6.
>
> So $k < -2$ or $k > 6$.

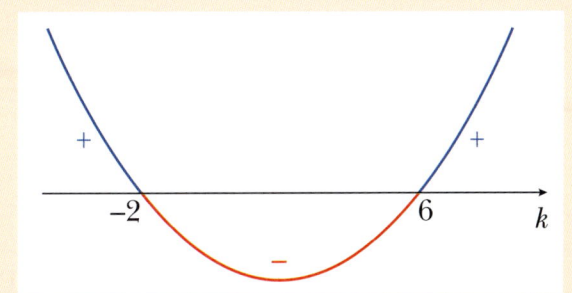

Exercise 3.5

1. State whether these equations have two distinct roots, two equal roots or no roots.

   a $x^2 + 4x + 4$ b $x^2 + 4x - 21$ c $x^2 + 9x + 1$ d $x^2 - 3x + 15$
   e $x^2 - 6x + 2$ f $4x^2 + 20x + 25$ g $3x^2 + 2x + 7$ h $5x^2 - 2x - 9$

2. Find the values of k for which $x^2 + kx + 9 = 0$ has two equal roots.

3. Find the values of k for which $kx^2 - 4x + 8 = 0$ has two distinct roots.

4. Find the values of k for which $3x^2 + 2x + k = 0$ has no real roots.

5. Find the values of k for which $(k+1)x^2 + kx - 2k = 0$ has two equal roots.

6. Find the values of k for which $kx^2 + 2(k+3)x + k = 0$ has two distinct roots.

7. Find the values of k for which $3x^2 - 4x + 5 - k = 0$ has two distinct roots.

8. Find the values of k for which $4x^2 - (k-2)x + 9 = 0$ has two equal roots.

9. Find the values of k for which $4x^2 + 4(k-2)x + k = 0$ has two equal roots.

10. Show that the roots of the equation $x^2 + (k-2)x - 2k = 0$ are real and distinct for all real values of k.

11. Show that the roots of the equation $kx^2 + 5x - 2k = 0$ are real and distinct for all real values of k.

3.6 Intersection of a line and a curve

When considering the intersection of a straight line and a parabola, there are three possible situations.

Situation 1	Situation 2	Situation 3
2 points of intersection	1 point of intersection	0 points of intersection
The line cuts the curve at two distinct points.	The line touches the curve at one point. This means that the line is a **tangent** to the curve.	The line does not intersect the curve.

You have already learnt that to find the points of intersection of the line $y = x - 6$ with the parabola $y = x^2 - 3x - 4$ you solve the two equations simultaneously.

This would give $x^2 - 3x - 4 = x - 6$

$x^2 - 4x + 2 = 0.$

The resulting quadratic equation can then be solved using the quadratic formula:

$$x = \frac{-b \pm \sqrt{b^2 - 4ac}}{2a}$$

The number of points of intersection will depend on the value of $b^2 - 4ac$.

The different situations are given in the table below.

$b^2 - 4ac$	Nature of roots	Line and curve
> 0	2 real distinct roots	2 distinct points of intersection
$= 0$	2 real equal roots	1 point of intersection (line is a tangent)
< 0	0 real roots	no points of intersection

The condition for a quadratic equation to have real roots is $b^2 - 4ac \geqslant 0$.

Chapter 3: Simultaneous equations and quadratics

WORKED EXAMPLE 10

Find the value of k for which $y = 2x + k$ is a tangent to the curve $y = x^2 - 4x + 4$.

Answers

$x^2 - 4x + 4 = 2x + k$

$x^2 - 6x + (4 - k) = 0$

Since the line is a tangent to the curve,
$b^2 - 4ac = 0.$

$(-6)^2 - 4 \times 1 \times (4 - k) = 0$

$36 - 16 + 4k = 0$

$k = -5$

WORKED EXAMPLE 11

Find the range of values of k for which $y = x - 5$ intersects the curve $y = kx^2 - 6$ at two distinct points.

Answers

$kx^2 - 6 = x - 5$

$kx^2 - x - 1 = 0$

Since the line intersects the curve at two distinct points,
$b^2 - 4ac > 0.$

$(-1)^2 - 4 \times k \times (-1) > 0$

$1 + 4k > 0$

$k > -\dfrac{1}{4}$

WORKED EXAMPLE 12

Find the values of k for which $y = kx - 3$ does not intersect the curve $y = x^2 - 2x + 1$.

Answers

$x^2 - 2x + 1 = kx - 3$

$x^2 - x(2 + k) + 4 = 0$

Since the line and curve do not intersect,
$b^2 - 4ac < 0.$

$(2 + k)^2 - 4 \times 1 \times 4 < 0$

$k^2 + 4k + 4 - 16 < 0$

$k^2 + 4k - 12 < 0$

$(k + 6)(k - 2) < 0$

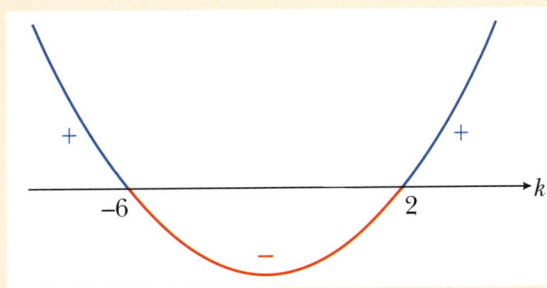

Critical values are -6 and 2.
So $-6 < k < 2$.

Exercise 3.6

1. Find the values of k for which $y = kx + 1$ is a tangent to the curve $y = 2x^2 + x + 3$.

2. Find the value of k for which the x-axis is a tangent to the curve $y = x^2 + (3 - k)x - (4k + 3)$.

3. Find the values of the constant c for which the line $y = x + c$ is a tangent to the curve $y = 3x + \dfrac{2}{x}$.

4. Find the set of values of k for which the line $y = 3x + 1$ cuts the curve $y = x^2 + kx + 2$ in two distinct points.

5. The line $y = 2x + k$ is a tangent to the curve $x^2 + 2xy + 20 = 0$.
   a. Find the possible values of k.
   b. For each of these values of k, find the coordinates of the point of contact of the tangent with the curve.

6. Find the set of values of k for which the line $y = k - x$ cuts the curve $y = x^2 - 7x + 4$ in two distinct points.

7. Find the values of k for which the line $y = kx - 10$ meets the curve $x^2 + y^2 = 10x$.

8. Find the set of values of m for which the line $y = mx - 5$ does not meet the curve $y = x^2 - 5x + 4$.

9. The line $y = mx + 6$ is a tangent to the curve $y = x^2 - 4x + 7$.
   Find the possible values of m..

Summary

Completing the square

For a quadratic function $f(x) = ax^2 + bx + c$ that is written in the form $f(x) = a(x - h)^2 + k$,

i if $a > 0$, the minimum point is (h, k) ii if $a < 0$, the maximum point is (h, k).

Chapter 3: Simultaneous equations and quadratics

Quadratic equation ($ax^2 + bx + c = 0$) and corresponding curve ($y = ax^2 + bx + c$)

$b^2 - 4ac$	Nature of roots of $ax^2 + bx + c = 0$	Shape of curve $y = ax^2 + bx + c$
> 0	2 real distinct roots	$a > 0$ or $a < 0$ The curve cuts the x-axis at 2 distinct points.
$= 0$	2 real equal roots	$a > 0$ or $a < 0$ The curve touches the x-axis at 1 point.
< 0	0 real roots	$a > 0$ or $a < 0$ The curve is entirely above or entirely below the x-axis.

Quadratic curve and straight line

Situation 1	Situation 2	Situation 3
2 points of intersection	1 point of intersection	0 points of intersection
The line cuts the curve at two distinct points.	The line touches the curve at one point. This means that the line is a **tangent** to the curve.	The line does not intersect the curve.

Solving simultaneously the equation of the curve with the equation of the line will give a quadratic equation of the form $ax^2 + bx + c = 0$. The discriminant $b^2 - 4ac$, gives information about the roots of the equation and also about the intersection of the curve with the line.

$b^2 - 4ac$	Nature of roots	Line and curve
> 0	2 real distinct roots	2 distinct points of intersection
$= 0$	2 real equal roots	1 point of intersection (line is a tangent)
< 0	no real roots	no points of intersection

The condition for a quadratic equation to have real roots is $b^2 - 4ac \geq 0$.

Cambridge IGCSE and O Level Additional Mathematics

Examination questions

Worked past paper example

The line $y = 2x - 8$ cuts the curve $2x^2 + y^2 - 5xy + 32 = 0$ at the points A and B.

Find the length of the line AB. [7]

Cambridge IGCSE Additional Mathematics 0606 Paper 21 Q8 Jun 2013

Answers

$y = 2x - 8$ ------------------------- (1)

$2x^2 + y^2 - 5xy + 32 = 0$ --------- (2)

Substitute for y from (1) in (2):

$2x^2 + (2x - 8)^2 - 5x(2x - 8) + 32 = 0$ expand brackets

$2x^2 + 4x^2 - 32x + 64 - 10x^2 + 40x + 32 = 0$ collect like terms

$-4x^2 + 8x + 96 = 0$ divide by -4

$x^2 - 2x - 24 = 0$ factorise

$(x - 6)(x + 4) = 0$

$x = 6$ or $x = -4$

When $x = 6$, $y = 2(6) - 8 = 4$.

When $x = -4$, $y = 2(-4) - 8 = -16$.

The points of intersection are $A(6, 4)$ and $B(-4, -16)$.

Using Pythagoras: $AB^2 = 20^2 + 10^2$

$AB^2 = 500$

$AB = \sqrt{500}$

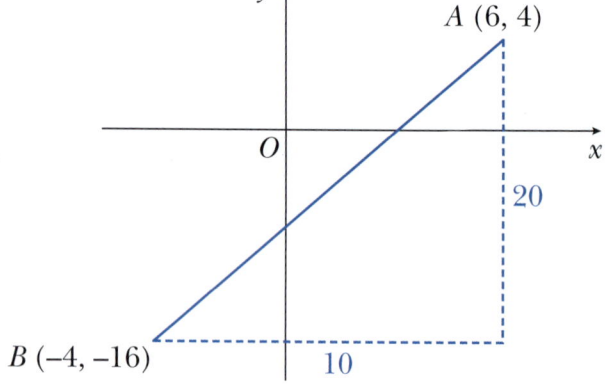

$AB = 22.4$ to 3 sf

Exercise 3.7

Exam Exercise

1. Find the set of values of k for which the line $y = k(4x - 3)$ does not intersect the curve $y = 4x^2 + 8x - 8$. [5]

   Cambridge IGCSE Additional Mathematics 0606 Paper 11 Q4 Jun 2014

2. Find the set of values of x for which $x(x + 2) < x$. [3]

   Cambridge IGCSE Additional Mathematics 0606 Paper 21 Q1 Jun 2014

3. **a** Express $2x^2 - x + 6$ in the form $p(x - q)^2 + r$, where p, q and r are constants to be found. [3]
   b Hence state the least value of $2x^2 - x + 6$ and the value of x at which this occurs. [2]

   Cambridge IGCSE Additional Mathematics 0606 Paper 21 Q5i,ii Jun 2014

Chapter 3: Simultaneous equations and quadratics

4 Find the set of values of k for which the curve $y = (k+1)x^2 - 3x + (k+1)$ lies below the x-axis. [4]

Cambridge IGCSE Additional Mathematics 0606 Paper 11 Q2 Nov 2013

5 Find the set of values of x for which $x^2 < 6 - 5x$. [3]

Cambridge IGCSE Additional Mathematics 0606 Paper 21 Q1 Nov 2013

6 Find the values of k for which the line $y = k - 6x$ is a tangent to the curve $y = x(2x + k)$. [4]

Cambridge IGCSE Additional Mathematics 0606 Paper 11 Q2 Nov 2012

7 It is given that $f(x) = 4 + 8x - x^2$.

    a Find the value of a and of b for which $f(x) = a - (x+b)^2$ and hence write down the coordinates of the stationary point of the curve $y = f(x)$. [3]

    b On the axes below, sketch the graph of $y = f(x)$, showing the coordinates of the point where your graph intersects the y-axis.

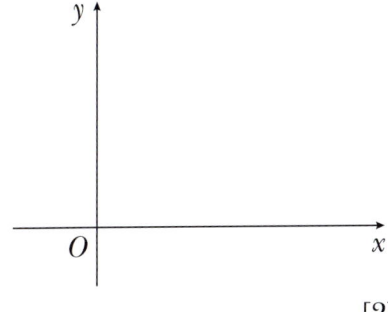

[2]

Cambridge IGCSE Additional Mathematics 0606 Paper 21 Q4i,ii Nov 2012

8 Given that the straight line $y = 3x + c$ is a tangent to the curve $y = x^2 + 9x + k$, express k in terms of c. [4]

Cambridge IGCSE Additional Mathematics 0606 Paper 21 Q2 Nov 2011

9 Find the set of values of k for which the line $y = 2x - 5$ cuts the curve $y = x^2 + kx + 11$ in two distinct points. [6]

Cambridge IGCSE Additional Mathematics 0606 Paper 21 Q4 Jun 2011

10 The equation of a curve is given by $y = 2x^2 + ax + 14$, where a is a constant.

Given that this equation can also be written as $y = 2(x - 3)^2 + b$, where b is a constant, find

    a the value of a and of b, [2]

    b the minimum value of y. [1]

Cambridge IGCSE Additional Mathematics 0606 Paper 11 Q1i,ii Nov 2010

11 Find the set of values of m for which the line $y = mx - 2$ cuts the curve $y = x^2 + 8x + 7$ in two distinct points. [6]

Cambridge IGCSE Additional Mathematics 0606 Paper 21 Q5 Nov 2010

12 a On a copy of the grid to the right, sketch the graph of $y = |(x-2)(x+3)|$ for $-5 \leq x \leq 4$, and state the coordinates of the points where the curve meets the coordinate axes. [4]

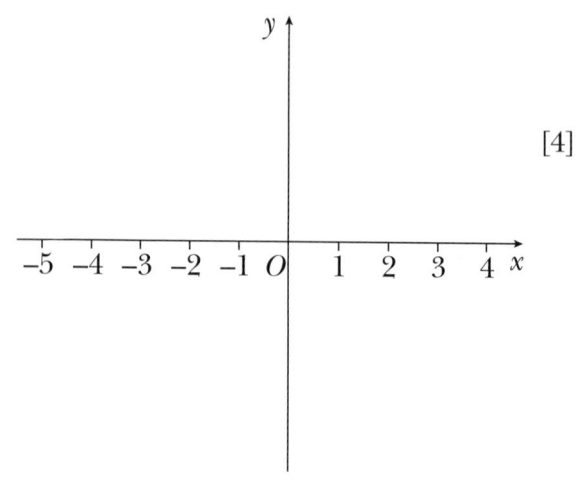

b Find the coordinates of the stationary point on the curve $y = |(x-2)(x+3)|$. [3]

c Given that k is a positive constant, state the set of values of k for which $|(x-2)(x+3)| = k$ has 2 solutions only. [3]

Cambridge IGCSE Additional Mathematics 0606 Paper 11 Q8i,ii,iii Nov 2013

Chapter 4
Indices and Surds

This section will show you how to:

- perform simple operations with indices and surds, including rationalising the denominator.

Cambridge IGCSE and O Level Additional Mathematics

> **RECAP**
>
> You should already know the meaning of the words index, power, exponent and base:
>
> $$2 \times 2 \times 2 \times 2 = 2^4$$
>
> where 4 is the index, exponent or power and 2 is the base.
>
> The plural of the word index is indices.
>
> You should also know and be able to apply the following rules of indices:
>
> | | | | | |
> |---|---|---|---|---|
> | RULE 1: | $a^m \times a^n = a^{m+n}$ | | RULE 6: | $a^0 = 1$ |
> | RULE 2: | $a^m \div a^n = a^{m-n}$ or $\dfrac{a^m}{a^n} = a^{m-n}$ | | RULE 7: | $a^{-n} = \dfrac{1}{a^n}$ |
> | RULE 3: | $(a^m)^n = a^{mn}$ | | RULE 8: | $a^{\frac{1}{n}} = \sqrt[n]{a}$ |
> | RULE 4: | $a^n \times b^n = (ab)^n$ | | RULE 9: | $a^{\frac{m}{n}} = (\sqrt[n]{a})^m = \sqrt[n]{a^m}$ |
> | RULE 5: | $\dfrac{a^n}{b^n} = \left(\dfrac{a}{b}\right)^n$ | | | |

4.1 Simplifying expressions involving indices

When simplifying expressions involving indices you often need to use more than one of the rules for indices.

WORKED EXAMPLE 1

Simplify $\dfrac{(4x^2y)^2 \times \sqrt{9x^6y^2}}{(x^3y^2)^{-2}}$.

Answers

$$\dfrac{(4x^2y)^2 \times \sqrt{9x^6y^2}}{(x^3y^2)^{-2}} = \dfrac{(4)^2(x^2)^2(y)^2 \times (9)^{\frac{1}{2}}(x^6)^{\frac{1}{2}}(y^2)^{\frac{1}{2}}}{(x^3)^{-2}(y^2)^{-2}}$$

$$= \dfrac{16x^4y^2 \times 3x^3y}{x^{-6}y^{-4}}$$

$$= \dfrac{48x^7y^3}{x^{-6}y^{-4}}$$

$$= 48x^{13}y^7$$

Exercise 4.1

1 Simplify each of the following.

a $(x^5)^3$ **b** $x^7 \times x^9$ **c** $x^5 \div x^8$

d $\sqrt{x^{10}}$ **e** $\sqrt{x^{-4}}$ **f** $(x^{-3})^5$

g $\sqrt[3]{x^6}$ **h** $(x^{-1})^2 \times \left(x^{\frac{1}{2}}\right)^8$ **i** $3x^2 y \times 5x^4 y^3$

j $\sqrt{25x^6 y^{-4}}$ **k** $\left(2x^3 y^{\frac{3}{2}}\right)^4$ **l** $\sqrt{9x^8 y^{-4}} \times \sqrt[3]{8x^6 y^{-3}}$

2 Simplify each of the following.

a $\dfrac{\sqrt[3]{x} \times \sqrt[3]{x^5}}{x^{-2}}$ **b** $\dfrac{x^2 \times \sqrt{x^5}}{x^{-\frac{1}{2}}}$

c $\dfrac{(\sqrt[3]{x})^2 \times \sqrt{x^6}}{x^{-\frac{1}{3}}}$ **d** $\dfrac{(3xy)^2 \times \sqrt{x^4 y^6}}{(2x^4 y^3)^2}$

3 Given that $\dfrac{(36x^4)^2}{8x^2 \times 3x} = 2^a \, 3^b \, x^c$, evaluate a, b and c.

4 Given that $\dfrac{\sqrt{x^{-1}} \times \sqrt[3]{y^2}}{\sqrt{x^6 y^{-\frac{2}{3}}}} = x^a \, y^b$, find the value of a and the value of b.

5 Given that $\dfrac{\sqrt{a^{\frac{4}{5}} b^{-\frac{2}{3}}}}{a^{-\frac{1}{5}} b^{\frac{2}{3}}} = a^x \, b^y$, find the value of x and the value of y.

6 Given that $\dfrac{(a^x)^2}{b^{5-x}} \times \dfrac{b^{y-4}}{a^y} = a^2 \, b^4$, find the value of x and the value of y.

7 Simplify $(1+x)^{\frac{3}{2}} - (1+x)^{\frac{1}{2}}$.

4.2 Solving equations involving indices

Consider the equation $2^x = 64$.

The equation has an unknown exponent (or index) and is called an **exponential equation**. You have already learnt how to solve simple exponential equations such as $2^x = 64$. In this section, you will learn how to solve more complicated exponential equations.

CLASS DISCUSSION

The diagram shows the graph of $y = 2^x$ for $-3 \leqslant x \leqslant 3$.

Discuss the following questions with your classmates:

- How does the graph behave when $x > 3$?
- How does the graph behave when $x < -3$?
- How does the graph of $y = 3^x$ compare with the graph of $y = 2^x$?
- How does the graph of $y = 4^x$ compare with the graphs of $y = 2^x$ and $y = 3^x$?

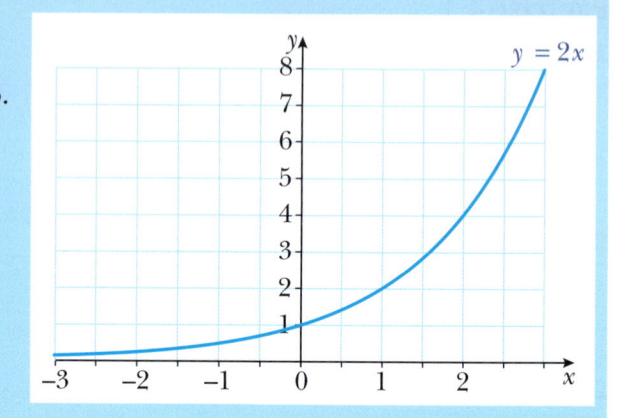

Now answer the following question:

- If $a > 0$, is it possible to find a value of x for which a^x is either 0 or negative?

WORKED EXAMPLE 2

Solve the equation $2^{3x+1} = 8$.

Answers

$2^{3x+1} = 8$ change 8 to 2^3

$2^{3x+1} = 2^3$ equate the indices

$3x + 1 = 3$ solve for x

$3x = 2$

$x = \dfrac{2}{3}$

WORKED EXAMPLE 3

Solve the equation $3^{2x-1} \times 9^{x-1} = 243$.

Answers

$3^{2x-1} \times 9^{x-1} = 243$ change to base 3

$3^{2x-1} \times (3^2)^{x-1} = 3^5$

$3^{2x-1} \times 3^{2x-2} = 3^5$ add the indices on the left hand side

$3^{4x-3} = 3^5$ equate the indices

$4x - 3 = 5$ solve for x

$4x = 8$

$x = 2$

WORKED EXAMPLE 4

Solve the simultaneous equations.
$9^x (27^y) = 1$
$4^x \div (\sqrt{2})^y = 128$

Answers

$9^x (27^y) = 1$ change to base 3
$4^x \div (\sqrt{2})^y = 128$ change to base 2

$3^{2x} \times 3^{3y} = 3^0$ add indices on the left hand side
$2^{2x} \div 2^{\frac{1}{2}y} = 2^7$ subtract indices on the left hand side

$3^{2x+3y} = 3^0$ equating the indices gives $2x + 3y = 0$
$2^{2x - \frac{1}{2}y} = 2^7$ equating the indices gives $2x - \frac{1}{2}y = 7$

$2x + 3y = 0$ subtract the two equations
$2x - \frac{1}{2}y = 7$

$3\frac{1}{2}y = -7$, so $y = -2$.

Substituting $y = -2$ into $2x + 3y = 0$ gives $x = 3$.
The solution is $x = 3$, $y = -2$.

WORKED EXAMPLE 5

a Solve the equation $4y^2 + 3y - 1 = 0$.

b Use your answer to **part a** to solve the equation $4(2^x)^2 + 3(2^x) - 1 = 0$.

Answers

a $4y^2 + 3y - 1 = 0$ factorise
$(4y - 1)(y + 1) = 0$
$4y - 1 = 0$ or $y + 1 = 0$
$y = \frac{1}{4}$ or $y = -1$

b $4(2^x)^2 + 3(2^x) - 1 = 0$ comparing with $4y^2 + 3y - 1 = 0$ gives $y = 2^x$

$2^x = \frac{1}{4}$ or $2^x = -1$ replace $\frac{1}{4}$ with 2^{-2}

$2^x = 2^{-2}$ or $2^x = -1$

Solving $2^x = 2^{-2}$, gives $x = -2$.
There is no solution to $2^x = -1$, since $2^x > 0$ for all real values of x.
The solution is $x = -2$.

Exercise 4.2

1 Solve each of the following equations.

  a $5^{2x} = 5^{7x-1}$ **b** $4^{2x+1} = 4^{3x-2}$

  c $7^{x^2} = 7^{6-x}$ **d** $3^{2x^2} = 3^{9x+5}$

2 Solve each of the following equations.

  a $2^{n+1} = 32$ **b** $4^{2n} = 256$ **c** $2^{n+2} = 128$

  d $3^{2n+1} = 27$ **e** $2^{n-1} = \dfrac{1}{4}$ **f** $2^{3n+2} = \dfrac{1}{128}$

  g $5^{n+1} = \dfrac{1}{125}$ **h** $5^{x^2-16} = 1$

3 Solve each of the following equations.

  a $2^x = 4^3$ **b** $3^{2x-1} = 27^x$ **c** $5^{3x-7} = 25^{2x}$

  d $3^x = 9^{x+5}$ **e** $4^{3x+4} = 8^{4x+12}$ **f** $25^{2x+1} = 125^{3x+2}$

  g $\left(\dfrac{1}{4}\right)^x = 64$ **h** $4^{5-3x} = \dfrac{1}{8^{x+1}}$ **i** $8^{4x-3} = \left(\dfrac{1}{16}\right)^{x+1}$

  j $5^{x^2+3} = 25^{2x}$ **k** $3^{x^2-4} = 27^x$ **l** $2^{2x^2-2} - 8^x = 0$

4 Solve each of the following equations.

  a $2^{3x} \times 4^{x+1} = 64$ **b** $2^{3x+1} \times 8^{x-1} = 128$

  c $(2^{2-x})(4^{2x+3}) = 8$ **d** $3^{x+1} \times 9^{2-x} = \dfrac{1}{27}$

5 Solve each of the following equations.

  a $\dfrac{27^{2x}}{3^{5-x}} = \dfrac{3^{2x+1}}{9^{x+3}}$ **b** $\dfrac{4^x}{2^{3-x}} = \dfrac{2^{3x}}{8^{x-2}}$

  c $\dfrac{2^{x+4}}{8^{-x}} = \dfrac{64}{4^{\frac{1}{2}x}}$ **d** $\dfrac{27^{2x}}{3^{6-x}} = \dfrac{3^{2x+1}}{9^{x+3}}$

6 Solve each of the following equations.

  a $3^{2x} \times 2^x = \dfrac{1}{18}$ **b** $2^{2x} \times 5^x = 8000$ **c** $5^{2x} \times 4^x = \dfrac{1}{1000}$

7 Solve each of the following pairs of simultaneous equations.

  a $4^x \div 2^y = 16$ **b** $27^x = 9(3^y)$ **c** $125^x \div 5^y = 25$

     $3^{2x} \times 9^y = 27$ $2^x \div 8^y = 1$ $2^{3x} \times \left(\dfrac{1}{8}\right)^{1-y} = 32$

8 a Solve the equation $2y^2 - 7y - 4 = 0$.

  b Use your answer to **part a** to solve the equation $2(2^x)^2 - 7(2^x) - 4 = 0$.

9 a Solve the equation $4y^2 = 15 + 7y$.

  b Use your answer to **part a** to solve the equation $4(9^x) = 15 + 7(3^x)$.

10 a Solve the equation $3y = 8 + \dfrac{3}{y}$.

  b Use your answer to **part a** to solve the equation $3x^{\frac{1}{2}} = 8 + 3x^{-\frac{1}{2}}$.

4.3 Surds

A surd is an irrational number of the form $\sqrt{n}$, where n is a positive integer that is not a perfect square.

$\sqrt{2}$, $\sqrt{5}$ and $\sqrt{12}$ are all surds.

$\sqrt{9}$ is not a surd because $\sqrt{9} = \sqrt{3^2} = 3$.

Other examples of surds are $2 + \sqrt{5}$, $\sqrt{7} - \sqrt{2}$ and $\dfrac{3 - \sqrt{2}}{5}$.

When an answer is given using a surd, it is an exact answer.

CLASS DISCUSSION

The frog can only hop onto lily pads that contain surds.

It is allowed to move along a row (west or east) or a column (north or south) but is not allowed to move diagonally.

Find the route that the frog must take to catch the fly.

frog	$\sqrt{5}$	$\sqrt{4}$	79	$\dfrac{2 - \sqrt{9}}{2}$
$\sqrt{400}$	$1 + \sqrt{6}$	$1 + \sqrt{25}$	$3\sqrt{4}$	$\sqrt{49}$
$\sqrt{3} + \sqrt{4}$	$\dfrac{\sqrt{5}}{3}$	$\sqrt{16} - \sqrt{9}$	$\sqrt{289}$	$\dfrac{\sqrt{4}}{3}$
$3\sqrt{5}$	$5 - \sqrt{9}$	$\dfrac{\sqrt{7}}{2}$	$5 + \sqrt{15}$	$\sqrt{4}\sqrt{3}$
$5 - \sqrt{10}$	$\dfrac{5\sqrt{7}}{2}$	$\sqrt{8} + 1$	$\dfrac{1 + \sqrt{4}}{3}$	fly

You can collect like terms together.

$6\sqrt{11} + 3\sqrt{11} = 9\sqrt{11}$ and $5\sqrt{7} - 2\sqrt{7} = 3\sqrt{7}$

WORKED EXAMPLE 6

Simplify $4(5 - \sqrt{3}) - 2(5\sqrt{3} - 1)$.

Answers

$4(5 - \sqrt{3}) - 2(5\sqrt{3} - 1)$ expand the brackets
$= 20 - 4\sqrt{3} - 10\sqrt{3} + 2$ collect like terms
$= 22 - 14\sqrt{3}$

Exercise 4.3

1 Simplify.

   a $\;3\sqrt{5}+7\sqrt{5}$ b $\;3\sqrt{10}+2\sqrt{10}$ c $\;8\sqrt{11}+\sqrt{11}$ d $\;6\sqrt{3}-\sqrt{3}$

2

   A $\;3\sqrt{5}+7\sqrt{3}$ B $\;2\sqrt{5}-3\sqrt{3}$ C $\;2\sqrt{3}-\sqrt{5}$

Simplify.

   a $\;A+B$ b $\;A-C$ c $\;2A+3B$ d $\;5A+2B-C$

3 The first 4 terms of a sequence are

   $2+3\sqrt{7}\quad 2+5\sqrt{7}\quad 2+7\sqrt{7}\quad 2+9\sqrt{7}$.

   a Write down the 6th term of this sequence.

   b Find the sum of the first 5 terms of this sequence.

   c Write down an expression for the nth term of this sequence.

4 a Find the exact length of AB.

   b Find the exact perimeter of the triangle.

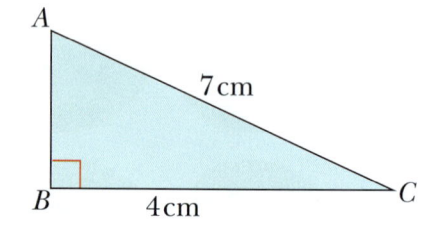

CHALLENGE Q

5 The number in the rectangle on the side of the triangle is the **sum** of the numbers at the adjacent vertices.

Find the value of x, the value of y and the value of z.

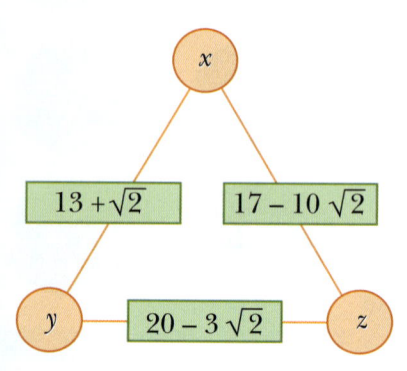

4.4 Multiplication, division and simplification of surds

You can multiply surds using the rule: $\sqrt{a} \times \sqrt{b} = \sqrt{ab}$

WORKED EXAMPLE 7

Simplify.
a $\sqrt{3} \times \sqrt{5}$ **b** $(\sqrt{8})^2$ **c** $2\sqrt{5} \times 3\sqrt{3}$

Answers
a $\sqrt{3} \times \sqrt{5} = \sqrt{3 \times 5} = \sqrt{15}$
b $(\sqrt{8})^2 = \sqrt{8} \times \sqrt{8} = \sqrt{64} = 8$ Note: $\sqrt{n} \times \sqrt{n} = n$
c $2\sqrt{5} \times 3\sqrt{3} = 6\sqrt{15}$

WORKED EXAMPLE 8

Expand and simplify.
a $(4 - \sqrt{3})^2$ **b** $(\sqrt{3} + 5\sqrt{2})(\sqrt{2} + \sqrt{3})$

Answers
a $(4 - \sqrt{3})^2$ square means multiply by itself
$= (4 - \sqrt{3})(4 - \sqrt{3})$ expand the brackets
$= 16 - 4\sqrt{3} - 4\sqrt{3} + 3$ collect like terms
$= 19 - 8\sqrt{3}$

b $(\sqrt{3} + 5\sqrt{2})(\sqrt{2} + \sqrt{3})$ expand the brackets
$= \sqrt{6} + 3 + 10 + 5\sqrt{6}$ collect like terms
$= 13 + 6\sqrt{6}$

$\sqrt{98}$ can be simplified using the multiplication rule.
$\sqrt{98} = \sqrt{49 \times 2} = \sqrt{49} \times \sqrt{2} = 7\sqrt{2}$

Cambridge IGCSE and O Level Additional Mathematics

WORKED EXAMPLE 9

Simplify $\sqrt{75} - \sqrt{12}$.

Answers

$\sqrt{75} - \sqrt{12}$ $75 = 25 \times 3$ and $12 = 4 \times 3$

$= \sqrt{25} \times \sqrt{3} - \sqrt{4} \times \sqrt{3}$ $\sqrt{25} = 5$ and $\sqrt{4} = 2$

$= 5 \times \sqrt{3} - 2 \times \sqrt{3}$ collect like terms

$= 3\sqrt{3}$

You can divide surds using the rule: $\dfrac{\sqrt{a}}{\sqrt{b}} = \sqrt{\dfrac{a}{b}}$

WORKED EXAMPLE 10

Simplify $\dfrac{\sqrt{77}}{\sqrt{11}}$.

Answers

$\dfrac{\sqrt{77}}{\sqrt{11}} = \sqrt{\dfrac{77}{11}} = \sqrt{7}$

Exercise 4.4

1 Simplify.

   a $\sqrt{18} \times \sqrt{2}$ **b** $\sqrt{2} \times \sqrt{72}$ **c** $\sqrt{5} \times \sqrt{6}$ **d** $(\sqrt{2})^2$

   e $(\sqrt{13})^2$ **f** $(\sqrt{5})^3$ **g** $3\sqrt{2} \times 5\sqrt{3}$ **h** $7\sqrt{5} \times 2\sqrt{7}$

2 Simplify.

   a $\dfrac{\sqrt{112}}{\sqrt{28}}$ **b** $\dfrac{\sqrt{52}}{\sqrt{26}}$ **c** $\dfrac{\sqrt{12}}{\sqrt{3}}$ **d** $\dfrac{\sqrt{17}}{\sqrt{68}}$

   e $\dfrac{\sqrt{12}}{\sqrt{108}}$ **f** $\dfrac{\sqrt{15}}{\sqrt{3}}$ **g** $\dfrac{\sqrt{54}}{\sqrt{6}}$ **h** $\dfrac{\sqrt{4}}{\sqrt{25}}$

   i $\dfrac{\sqrt{5}}{\sqrt{81}}$ **j** $\dfrac{\sqrt{88}}{2\sqrt{11}}$ **k** $\dfrac{9\sqrt{20}}{3\sqrt{5}}$ **l** $\dfrac{\sqrt{120}}{\sqrt{24}}$

3 Simplify.

   a $\sqrt{8}$ **b** $\sqrt{12}$ **c** $\sqrt{20}$ **d** $\sqrt{28}$

   e $\sqrt{50}$ **f** $\sqrt{72}$ **g** $\sqrt{18}$ **h** $\sqrt{32}$

   i $\sqrt{80}$ **j** $\sqrt{90}$ **k** $\sqrt{63}$ **l** $\sqrt{99}$

   m $\sqrt{44}$ **n** $\sqrt{125}$ **o** $\sqrt{117}$ **p** $\sqrt{200}$

q $\sqrt{75}$ r $\sqrt{3000}$ s $\dfrac{\sqrt{20}}{2}$ t $\dfrac{\sqrt{27}}{3}$

u $\dfrac{\sqrt{500}}{5}$ v $\sqrt{20} \times \sqrt{10}$ w $\sqrt{8} \times \sqrt{5}$ x $\sqrt{8} \times \sqrt{6}$

y $\sqrt{245} \times \sqrt{5}$

4 Simplify.
   a $5\sqrt{3} + \sqrt{48}$ b $\sqrt{12} + \sqrt{3}$ c $\sqrt{20} + 3\sqrt{5}$
   d $\sqrt{75} + 2\sqrt{3}$ e $\sqrt{32} - 2\sqrt{8}$ f $\sqrt{125} + \sqrt{80}$
   g $\sqrt{45} - \sqrt{5}$ h $\sqrt{20} - 5\sqrt{5}$ i $\sqrt{175} - \sqrt{28} + \sqrt{63}$
   j $\sqrt{50} + \sqrt{72} - \sqrt{18}$ k $\sqrt{200} - 2\sqrt{18} + \sqrt{72}$ l $5\sqrt{28} - 3\sqrt{63} - \sqrt{7}$
   m $\sqrt{80} + 2\sqrt{20} + 4\sqrt{45}$ n $5\sqrt{12} - 3\sqrt{48} + 2\sqrt{75}$ o $\sqrt{72} + \sqrt{8} - \sqrt{98} + \sqrt{50}$

5 Expand and simplify.
   a $\sqrt{2}(3 + \sqrt{2})$ b $\sqrt{3}(2\sqrt{3} + \sqrt{12})$ c $\sqrt{2}(5 - 2\sqrt{2})$
   d $\sqrt{3}(\sqrt{27} + 5)$ e $\sqrt{3}(\sqrt{3} - 1)$ f $\sqrt{5}(2\sqrt{5} + \sqrt{20})$
   g $(\sqrt{2} + 1)(\sqrt{2} - 1)$ h $(\sqrt{3} + 5)(\sqrt{3} - 1)$ i $(2 + \sqrt{5})(2\sqrt{5} + 1)$
   j $(3 - \sqrt{2})(3 + \sqrt{2})$ k $(4 + \sqrt{3})(4 - \sqrt{3})$ l $(1 + \sqrt{5})(1 - \sqrt{5})$
   m $(4 + 2\sqrt{3})(4 - 2\sqrt{3})$ n $(\sqrt{7} + \sqrt{5})(\sqrt{7} + 2\sqrt{5})$ o $(3 + 2\sqrt{2})(5 + 2\sqrt{2})$

6 Expand and simplify.
   a $(2 + \sqrt{5})^2$ b $(5 - \sqrt{3})^2$ c $(4 + 5\sqrt{3})^2$ d $(\sqrt{2} + \sqrt{3})^2$

7 A rectangle has sides of length $(2 + \sqrt{8})$ cm and $(7 - \sqrt{2})$ cm.
   Find the area of the rectangle.
   Express your answer in the form $a + b\sqrt{2}$, where a and b are integers.

8 a Find the value of AC^2.
   b Find the value of tan x.
      Write your answer in the form $\dfrac{a\sqrt{6}}{b}$,
      where a and b are integers.
   c Find the area of the triangle.
      Write your answer in the form $\dfrac{p\sqrt{6}}{q}$,
      where p and q are integers.

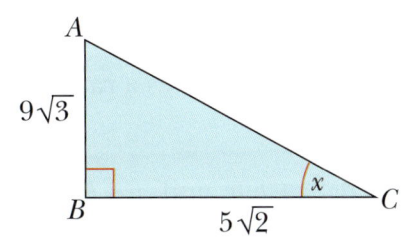

9 A cuboid has a square base.
   The sides of the square are of length $(1 + \sqrt{2})$ cm.
   The height of the cuboid is $(5 - \sqrt{2})$ cm.
   Find the volume of the cuboid.
   Express your answer in the form $a + b\sqrt{2}$, where a and b are integers.

CHALLENGE Q

10 Find the exact value of $\sqrt{2+\sqrt{3}} - \sqrt{2-\sqrt{3}}$.

(Hint: let $x = \sqrt{2+\sqrt{3}} - \sqrt{2-\sqrt{3}}$ and then square both sides of the equation.)

4.5 Rationalising the denominator of a fraction

CLASS DISCUSSION

Khadeeja says that:

'The product of two irrational numbers is irrational.'

Discuss this statement with your classmates and decide if this statement is:

| Always true | Sometimes true | Never true |

You must justify your decision.

You rationalise the denominator of a fraction when it is a surd.

To rationalise the denominator of a fraction means to turn an irrational denominator into a rational number.

In **Exercise 4.4, question 5m** you found that

$$(4 + 2\sqrt{3})(4 - 2\sqrt{3}) = (4)^2 - 8\sqrt{3} + 8\sqrt{3} - (2\sqrt{3})^2 = 16 - 12 = 4$$

This is an example of the product of two irrational numbers $(4 + 2\sqrt{3})$ and $(4 - 2\sqrt{3})$ giving a rational number (4).

$4 + 2\sqrt{3}$ and $4 - 2\sqrt{3}$ are called **conjugate surds**.

The product of two conjugate surds always gives a rational number.

The product of conjugate surds $a + b\sqrt{c}$ and $a - b\sqrt{c}$ is a rational number.

So you can rationalise the denominator of a fraction using these rules:

- For fractions of the form $\dfrac{1}{\sqrt{a}}$, multiply numerator and denominator by $\sqrt{a}$.

- For fractions of the form $\dfrac{1}{a + b\sqrt{c}}$, multiply numerator and denominator by $a - b\sqrt{c}$.

- For fractions of the form $\dfrac{1}{a - b\sqrt{c}}$, multiply numerator and denominator by $a + b\sqrt{c}$.

Chapter 4: Indices and Surds

> **Note:**
> To find products such as $(4 + 2\sqrt{3})(4 - 2\sqrt{3})$, it is quicker to use the algebraic identity:
> $(x + y)(x - y) = x^2 - y^2$
> So $(4 + 2\sqrt{3})(4 - 2\sqrt{3}) = 4^2 - (2\sqrt{3})^2 = 16 - 12 = 4$

WORKED EXAMPLE 11

Rationalise the denominators of

a $\dfrac{2}{\sqrt{5}}$ b $\dfrac{5}{2 + \sqrt{3}}$ c $\dfrac{\sqrt{7} + 3\sqrt{2}}{\sqrt{7} - \sqrt{2}}$.

Answers

a $\dfrac{2}{\sqrt{5}}$ multiply numerator and denominator by $\sqrt{5}$

$= \dfrac{2\sqrt{5}}{\sqrt{5}\,\sqrt{5}}$

$= \dfrac{2\sqrt{5}}{5}$

b $\dfrac{5}{2 + \sqrt{3}}$ multiply numerator and denominator by $(2 - \sqrt{3})$

$= \dfrac{5(2 - \sqrt{3})}{(2 + \sqrt{3})(2 - \sqrt{3})}$ use $(x + y)(x - y) = x^2 - y^2$ to expand the denominator

$= \dfrac{10 - 5\sqrt{3}}{(2)^2 - (\sqrt{3})^2}$

$= 10 - 5\sqrt{3}$

c $\dfrac{\sqrt{7} + 3\sqrt{2}}{\sqrt{7} - \sqrt{2}}$ multiply numerator and denominator by $(\sqrt{7} + \sqrt{2})$

$= \dfrac{(\sqrt{7} + 3\sqrt{2})(\sqrt{7} + \sqrt{2})}{(\sqrt{7} - \sqrt{2})(\sqrt{7} + \sqrt{2})}$ use $(x + y)(x - y) = x^2 - y^2$ to expand the denominator

$= \dfrac{7 + \sqrt{14} + 3\sqrt{14} + 6}{(\sqrt{7})^2 - (\sqrt{2})^2}$

$= \dfrac{13 + 4\sqrt{14}}{5}$

Exercise 4.5

1 Rationalise the denominators.

a $\dfrac{1}{\sqrt{5}}$ b $\dfrac{3}{\sqrt{2}}$ c $\dfrac{9}{\sqrt{3}}$ d $\dfrac{\sqrt{2}}{\sqrt{6}}$

e $\dfrac{4}{\sqrt{5}}$ f $\dfrac{12}{\sqrt{3}}$ g $\dfrac{4}{\sqrt{12}}$ h $\dfrac{10}{\sqrt{8}}$

i $\dfrac{3}{\sqrt{8}}$ j $\dfrac{\sqrt{2}}{\sqrt{32}}$ k $\dfrac{\sqrt{3}}{\sqrt{15}}$ l $\dfrac{\sqrt{12}}{\sqrt{156}}$

m $\dfrac{5}{2\sqrt{2}}$ n $\dfrac{7}{2\sqrt{3}}$ o $\dfrac{1 + \sqrt{5}}{\sqrt{5}}$ p $\dfrac{\sqrt{3} - 1}{\sqrt{3}}$

q $\dfrac{3 - \sqrt{2}}{\sqrt{2}}$ r $\dfrac{14 - \sqrt{7}}{\sqrt{7}}$

2 Rationalise the denominators and simplify.

a $\dfrac{1}{1+\sqrt{2}}$
b $\dfrac{1}{3+\sqrt{5}}$
c $\dfrac{1}{3+\sqrt{7}}$
d $\dfrac{4}{3-\sqrt{5}}$
e $\dfrac{5}{2+\sqrt{5}}$
f $\dfrac{\sqrt{7}}{2-\sqrt{7}}$
g $\dfrac{2}{2-\sqrt{3}}$
h $\dfrac{5}{2\sqrt{3}-3}$
i $\dfrac{1}{2\sqrt{3}-\sqrt{2}}$
j $\dfrac{8}{\sqrt{7}-\sqrt{5}}$

3 Rationalise the denominators and simplify.

a $\dfrac{2-\sqrt{3}}{2+\sqrt{3}}$
b $\dfrac{1+\sqrt{2}}{3-\sqrt{2}}$
c $\dfrac{\sqrt{2}+1}{2\sqrt{2}-1}$
d $\dfrac{\sqrt{7}-\sqrt{2}}{\sqrt{7}+\sqrt{2}}$
e $\dfrac{\sqrt{5}+1}{3-\sqrt{5}}$
f $\dfrac{\sqrt{17}-\sqrt{11}}{\sqrt{17}+\sqrt{11}}$
g $\dfrac{\sqrt{3}-\sqrt{7}}{\sqrt{3}+\sqrt{7}}$
h $\dfrac{\sqrt{23}+\sqrt{37}}{\sqrt{37}-\sqrt{23}}$

4 Write as a single fraction.

a $\dfrac{1}{\sqrt{3}+1}+\dfrac{1}{\sqrt{3}-1}$
b $\dfrac{2}{\sqrt{7}+\sqrt{2}}+\dfrac{1}{\sqrt{7}-\sqrt{2}}$
c $\dfrac{2}{4-\sqrt{3}}+\dfrac{1}{4+\sqrt{3}}$

5 The area of a rectangle is $(8+\sqrt{10})$ cm².

The length of one side is $(\sqrt{5}+\sqrt{2})$ cm.

Find the length of the other side in the form $a\sqrt{5}+b\sqrt{2}$, where a and b are integers.

6 A cuboid has a square base of length $(2+\sqrt{5})$ cm.

The volume of the cuboid is $(16+7\sqrt{5})$ cm³.

Find the height of the cuboid.

Express your answer in the form $a+b\sqrt{5}$, where a and b are integers.

7 A right circular cylinder has a volume of $(25+14\sqrt{3})\pi$ cm³ and a base radius of $(2+\sqrt{3})$ cm.

Find its height in the form $(a+b\sqrt{3})$ cm, where a and b are integers.

8 a Find the value of tan x.

Write your answer in the form $\dfrac{a+b\sqrt{2}}{c}$, where a, b and c are integers.

b Find the area of the triangle.

Write your answer in the form $\dfrac{p+q\sqrt{2}}{r}$, where p, q and r are integers.

9 Find the value of cos θ.

Write your answer in the form $\dfrac{a+b\sqrt{7}}{c}$, where a, b and c are integers.

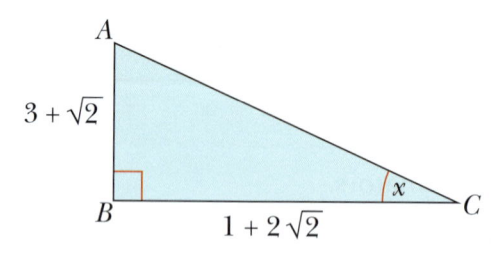

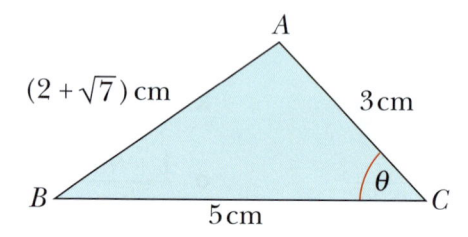

CHALLENGE Q

10 The blue circle has radius 2 and the green circle has radius 1. *AB* is a common tangent and all three circles touch each other.

Find the radius of the smaller circle.

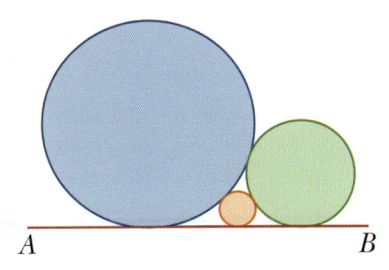

4.6 Solving equations involving surds

WORKED EXAMPLE 12

Solve $\sqrt{5}\,x = \sqrt{2}\,x + \sqrt{7}$.

Answers

$\sqrt{5}\,x = \sqrt{2}\,x + \sqrt{7}$ collect *x*'s on one side

$\sqrt{5}\,x - \sqrt{2}\,x = \sqrt{7}$ factorise

$x(\sqrt{5} - \sqrt{2}) = \sqrt{7}$ divide both sides by $(\sqrt{5} - \sqrt{2})$

$x = \dfrac{\sqrt{7}}{\sqrt{5} - \sqrt{2}}$ multiply numerator and denominator by $(\sqrt{5} + \sqrt{2})$

$x = \dfrac{\sqrt{7}\,(\sqrt{5} + \sqrt{2})}{(\sqrt{5} - \sqrt{2})(\sqrt{5} + \sqrt{2})}$ use $(x+y)(x-y) = x^2 - y^2$ to expand the denominator

$x = \dfrac{\sqrt{35} + \sqrt{14}}{(\sqrt{5})^2 - (\sqrt{2})^2}$

$x = \dfrac{\sqrt{35} + \sqrt{14}}{5 - 2}$

$x = \dfrac{\sqrt{35} + \sqrt{14}}{3}$

Cambridge IGCSE and O Level Additional Mathematics

WORKED EXAMPLE 13

Solve the simultaneous equations.
$$3x + 5y = 20$$
$$\sqrt{2}\, x - 5\sqrt{2}\, y = 8$$

Answers

$3x + 5y = 20$ multiply the first equation by $\sqrt{2}$
$\sqrt{2}\, x - 5\sqrt{2}\, y = 8$

$3\sqrt{2}\, x + 5\sqrt{2}\, y = 20\sqrt{2}$ add the two equations to eliminate y
$\sqrt{2}\, x - 5\sqrt{2}\, y = 8$

$4\sqrt{2}\, x = 20\sqrt{2} + 8$ divide both sides by $4\sqrt{2}$

$x = \dfrac{20\sqrt{2} + 8}{4\sqrt{2}}$ multiply numerator and denominator by $\sqrt{2}$

$x = \dfrac{(20\sqrt{2} + 8) \times \sqrt{2}}{4\sqrt{2} \times \sqrt{2}}$

$x = \dfrac{40 + 8\sqrt{2}}{8}$

$x = 5 + \sqrt{2}$

Substituting $x = 5 + \sqrt{2}$ in the first equation gives
$3(5 + \sqrt{2}) + 5y = 20$
$15 + 3\sqrt{2} + 5y = 20$
$5y = 5 - 3\sqrt{2}$
$y = \dfrac{5 - 3\sqrt{2}}{5}$

So the solution is $x = 5 + \sqrt{2}$, $y = \dfrac{5 - 3\sqrt{2}}{5}$.

CLASS DISCUSSION

Haroon writes:
$$x = 2$$
$$x + 2 = 4$$
$$x^2 + 4x + 4 = 16$$
$$x^2 + 4x - 12 = 0$$
$$(x + 6)(x - 2) = 0$$
$$\text{So } x = -6 \text{ or } x = 2$$

Discuss this with your classmates.

Explain why he now has two values for x.

In the class discussion you found that if you square both sides of an equation and then solve the resulting equation, you sometimes find that you have an answer that is not a valid solution of the original equation. Hence, it is always important to check your answers by substituting the answers back into the original equation.

WORKED EXAMPLE 14

Solve $\sqrt{x} = 2x - 6$.

Answers

$\sqrt{x} = 2x - 6$ square both sides
$x = (2x - 6)(2x - 6)$ expand the brackets
$x = 4x^2 - 24x + 36$ collect like terms
$4x^2 - 25x + 36 = 0$ factorise
$(4x - 9)(x - 4) = 0$
$x = \dfrac{9}{4}$ or $x = 4$

Check $x = \dfrac{9}{4}$ in the original equation:

$\sqrt{\dfrac{9}{4}} = \dfrac{3}{2}$ and $2 \times \dfrac{9}{4} - 6 = -\dfrac{3}{2}$, so $x = \dfrac{9}{4}$ is not a valid solution of the original equation.

Check $x = 4$ in the original equation:

$\sqrt{4} = 2$ and $2 \times 4 - 6 = 2$, so $x = 4$ is a solution of the original equation.

So the final answer is $x = 4$.

WORKED EXAMPLE 15

Solve $\sqrt{3x + 4} - \sqrt{2x + 1} = 1$

Answers

$\sqrt{3x + 4} - \sqrt{2x + 1} = 1$ isolate one of the square roots
$\sqrt{3x + 4} = 1 + \sqrt{2x + 1}$ square both sides
$3x + 4 = (1 + \sqrt{2x + 1})(1 + \sqrt{2x + 1})$ expand the brackets
$3x + 4 = 1 + 2\sqrt{2x + 1} + 2x + 1$ isolate the square root and collect like terms
$x + 2 = 2\sqrt{2x + 1}$ square both sides
$(x + 2)^2 = 4(2x + 1)$ expand the brackets
$x^2 + 4x + 4 = 8x + 4$ collect like terms
$x^2 - 4x = 0$ factorise
$x(x - 4) = 0$
$x = 0$ or $x = 4$

Check $x = 0$ in the original equation:
$\sqrt{3 \times 0 + 4} - \sqrt{2 \times 0 + 1} = \sqrt{4} - \sqrt{1} = 1$, so $x = 0$ is a solution of the original equation.

Check $x = 4$ in the original equation:
$\sqrt{3 \times 4 + 4} - \sqrt{2 \times 4 + 1} = \sqrt{16} - \sqrt{9} = 1$, so $x = 0$ is also a solution of the original equation.

So the final answer is $x = 0$ or $x = 4$.

Exercise 4.6

1 Solve these equations.

  a $\sqrt{12}\,x - \sqrt{5}\,x = \sqrt{3}$ **b** $\sqrt{10}\,x = \sqrt{5}\,x + \sqrt{2}$ **c** $\sqrt{17}\,x = 2\sqrt{3}\,x + \sqrt{5}$

2 Solve these simultaneous equations.

  a $3x - y = 5\sqrt{2}$ **b** $x + y = 5$ **c** $3x + y = 6$
      $2x + y = 5$ $\sqrt{6}\,x + 2y = 12$ $4x + 3y = 8 - 5\sqrt{5}$

  d $2x + y = 11$ **e** $x + \sqrt{2}\,y = 5 + 4\sqrt{2}$
      $5x - 3y = 11\sqrt{7}$ $x + y = 8$

3 Solve these equations.

  a $10\sqrt{x} - 4 = 7\sqrt{x} + 6$ **b** $6\sqrt{x} + 4 = 9\sqrt{x} + 3$ **c** $7\sqrt{x} + 9 = 10\sqrt{x} + 10$

  d $\sqrt{2x - 1} - 3 = 0$ **e** $\sqrt{2x - 3} = 6$ **f** $\sqrt{5x - 1} = \sqrt{x + 7}$

  g $3 + \sqrt{5x + 6} = 12$ **h** $\sqrt{5x^2 - 8} = 2x$ **i** $12 - \sqrt{x + 5} = 7$

4 Solve these equations.

  a $\sqrt{2x - 1} = x$ **b** $\sqrt{x + 6} = x$ **c** $\sqrt{2x + 3} - x = 0$

  d $\sqrt{10 - 2x} + x = 1$ **e** $\sqrt{x + 15} = x + 3$ **f** $\sqrt{x + 4} + 2 = x$

  g $\sqrt{x + 5} + 1 = x$ **h** $\sqrt{4x - 3} + 2x - 1 = 0$ **i** $\sqrt{x} = 2x - 6$

  j $\sqrt{3x + 1} - x - 1 = 0$ **k** $2x + 3 - \sqrt{20x + 9} = 0$

5 Solve these equations.

  a $\sqrt{2x + 7} = \sqrt{x + 3} + 1$ **b** $\sqrt{x} = \sqrt{x - 5} + 1$

  c $\sqrt{3x + 4} - \sqrt{2x + 1} = 1$ **d** $\sqrt{x + 1} - \sqrt{x} = 1$

  e $\sqrt{x + 1} + \sqrt{2x + 3} = 5$ **f** $\sqrt{16 - 2x} = 2 + \sqrt{36 + 6x}$

6 The roots of the equation $x^2 - 2\sqrt{6}\,x + 5 = 0$ are p and q, where $p > q$.

  Write $\dfrac{p}{q}$ in the form $\dfrac{a + b\sqrt{6}}{c}$, where a, b and c are integers.

7 Find the positive root of the equation $(4 - \sqrt{2})\,x^2 - (1 + 2\sqrt{2})\,x - 1 = 0$.

  Write your answer in the form $\dfrac{a + b\sqrt{2}}{c}$, where a, b and c are integers.

Summary

Rules of indices

RULE 1: $a^m \times a^n = a^{m+n}$

RULE 2: $a^m \div a^n = a^{(m-n)}$ or $\dfrac{a^m}{a^n} = a^{m-n}$

RULE 3: $(a^m)^n = a^{mn}$

RULE 4: $a^n \times b^n = (ab)^n$

RULE 5: $\dfrac{a^n}{b^n} = \left(\dfrac{a}{b}\right)^n$

RULE 6: $a^0 = 1$

RULE 7: $a^{-n} = \dfrac{1}{a^n}$

RULE 8: $a^{\frac{1}{n}} = \sqrt[n]{a}$

RULE 9: $a^{\frac{m}{n}} = (\sqrt[n]{a})^m = \sqrt[n]{a^m}$

Rules of surds

RULE 1: $\sqrt{ab} = \sqrt{a} \times \sqrt{b}$

RULE 2: $\sqrt{\dfrac{a}{b}} = \dfrac{\sqrt{a}}{\sqrt{b}}$

RULE 3: $\sqrt{a} \times \sqrt{a} = a$

The product of conjugate surds $a + b\sqrt{c}$ and $a - b\sqrt{c}$ is a rational number.

Examination questions

Worked past paper example

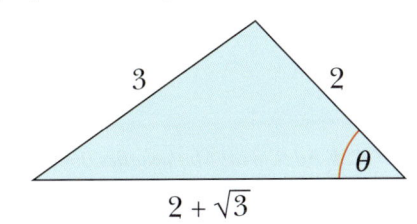

Without using a calculator, find the value of $\cos\theta$, giving your answer in the form $\dfrac{a + b\sqrt{3}}{c}$, where a, b and c are integers.

Cambridge IGCSE Additional Mathematics 0606 Paper 21 Q3 Nov 2011

Answers

Using the cosine rule:
$$3^2 = (2+\sqrt{3})^2 + 2^2 - 2\times(2+\sqrt{3})\times 2\times\cos\theta$$

Rearrange to make $\cos\theta$ the subject:

$\cos\theta = \dfrac{(2+\sqrt{3})^2 + 2^2 - 3^2}{2\times(2+\sqrt{3})\times 2}$ square brackets in the numerator
$(2+\sqrt{3})^2 = 4 + 2\sqrt{3} + 2\sqrt{3} + 3 = 7 + 4\sqrt{3}$

$\cos\theta = \dfrac{7+4\sqrt{3}+4-9}{4(2+\sqrt{3})}$ collect like terms in the numerator

$\cos\theta = \dfrac{2+4\sqrt{3}}{4(2+\sqrt{3})}$ multiply numerator and denominator by $(2-\sqrt{3})$

$\cos\theta = \dfrac{(2+4\sqrt{3})(2-\sqrt{3})}{4(2+\sqrt{3})(2-\sqrt{3})}$
$(2+4\sqrt{3})(2-\sqrt{3}) = 4 - 2\sqrt{3} + 8\sqrt{3} - 12 = -8 + 6\sqrt{3}$
$(2+\sqrt{3})(2-\sqrt{3}) = 2^2 - (\sqrt{3})^2 = 1$

$\cos\theta = \dfrac{-8+6\sqrt{3}}{4}$ divide numerator and denominator by 2

$\cos\theta = \dfrac{-4+3\sqrt{3}}{2}$

Exercise 4.7
Exam exercise

1 Solve $2^{x^2-5x} = \dfrac{1}{64}$. [4]

Cambridge IGCSE Additional Mathematics 0606 Paper 21 Q11a Jun 2014

2 Solve the simultaneous equations,
$\dfrac{4^x}{256^y} = 1024$
$3^{2x} \times 9^y = 243$ [5]

Cambridge IGCSE Additional Mathematics 0606 Paper 21 Q5 Nov 2013

3 Solve the equation $\dfrac{36^{2y-5}}{6^{3y}} = \dfrac{6^{2y-1}}{216^{y+6}}$. [4]

Cambridge IGCSE Additional Mathematics 0606 Paper 21 Q5b Jun 2012

4 Integers a and b are such that $(a+3\sqrt{5})^2 + a - b\sqrt{5} = 51$. Find the possible values of a and the corresponding values of b. [6]

Cambridge IGCSE Additional Mathematics 0606 Paper 21 Q9 Nov 2014

5 **Without using a calculator**, express $6(1+\sqrt{3})^{-2}$ in the form $a + b\sqrt{3}$, where a and b are integers to be found. [4]

Cambridge IGCSE Additional Mathematics 0606 Paper 21 Q2 Jun 2014

Chapter 4: Indices and Surds

6 Do not use a calculator in this question.

Express $\dfrac{(4\sqrt{5}-2)^2}{\sqrt{5}-1}$ in the form $p\sqrt{5}+q$, where p and q are integers. [4]

Cambridge IGCSE Additional Mathematics 0606 Paper 21 Q2 Nov 2013

7 Do not use a calculator in any part of this question.

   a i Show that $3\sqrt{5}-2\sqrt{2}$ is a square root of $53-12\sqrt{10}$. [1]

   ii State the other square root of $53-12\sqrt{10}$. [1]

   b Express $\dfrac{6\sqrt{3}+7\sqrt{2}}{4\sqrt{3}+5\sqrt{2}}$ in the form $a+b\sqrt{6}$, where a and b are integers to be found. [4]

Cambridge IGCSE Additional Mathematics 0606 Paper 11 Q7a,bi,ii Nov 2012

8 Calculators must not be used in this question.

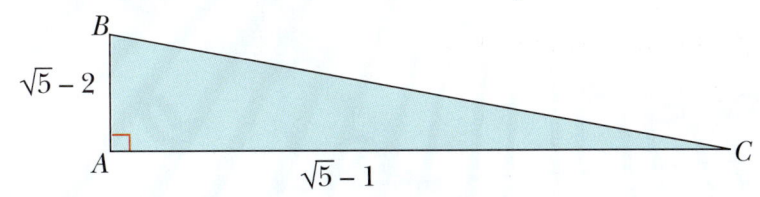

The diagram shows a triangle ABC in which angle $A = 90°$.

Sides AB and AC are $\sqrt{5}-2$ and $\sqrt{5}+1$ respectively.

Find $\tan B$ in the form $a+b\sqrt{5}$, where a and b are integers. [3]

Cambridge IGCSE Additional Mathematics 0606 Paper 11 Q7i Jun 2013

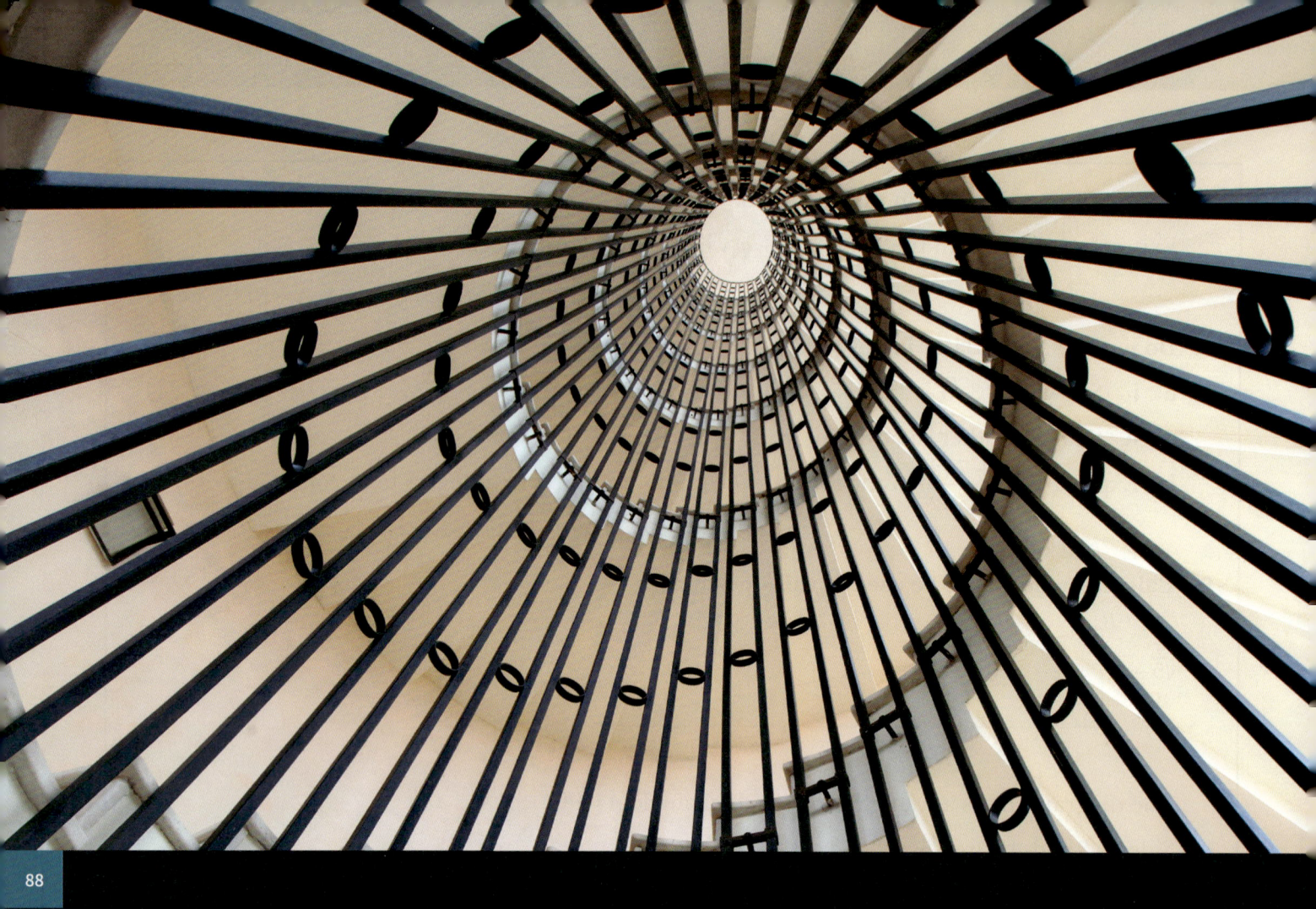

Chapter 5
Factors and polynomials

This section will show you how to:

- use the remainder and factor theorems
- find factors of polynomials
- solve cubic equations.

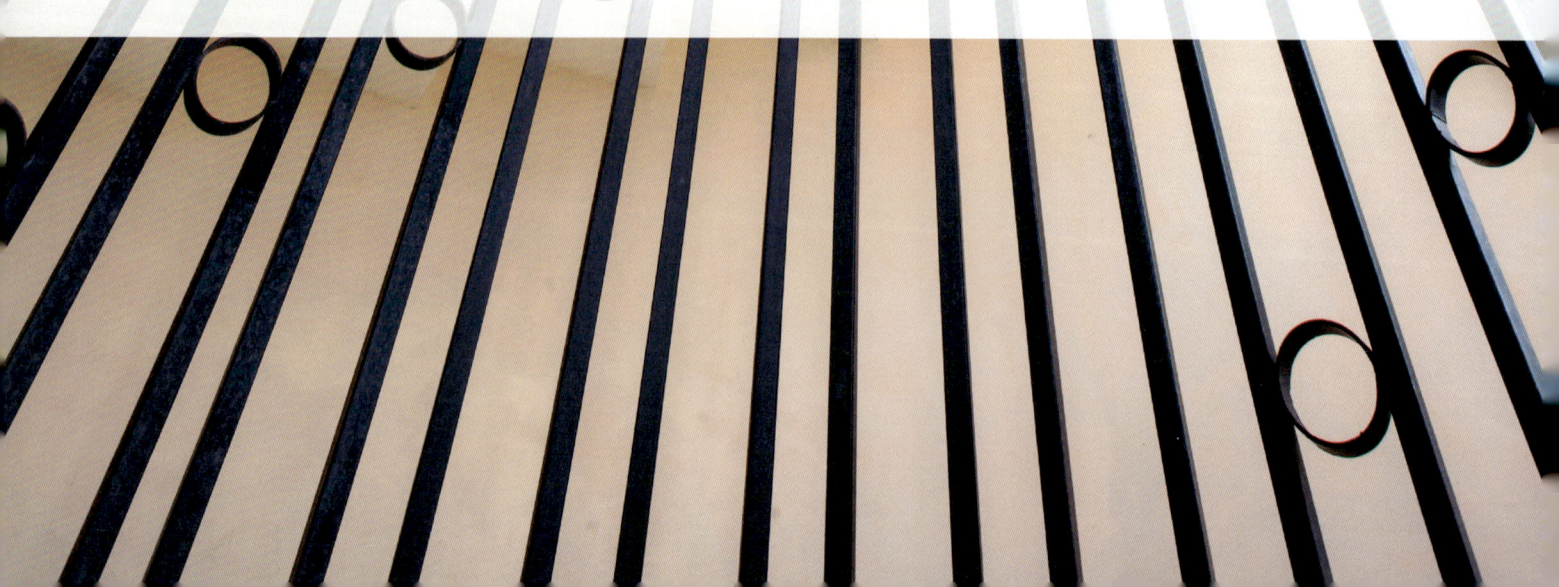

Chapter 5: Factors and polynomials

5.1 Adding, subtracting and multiplying polynomials

A **polynomial** is a an expression of the form
$$a_n x^n + a_{n-1} x^{n-1} + a_{n-2} x^{n-2} + \ldots + a_2 x^2 + a_1 x^1 + a_0$$
where:
- x is a variable
- n is a non-negative integer
- the coefficients $a_n, a_{n-1}, a_{n-2}, \ldots, a_2, a_1, a_0$ are constants
- a_n is called the leading coefficient and $a_n \neq 0$
- a_0 is called the constant term.

The highest power of x in the polynomial is called the **degree** of the polynomial.

You already know the special names for polynomials of degree 1, 2 and 3. These are shown in the table below together with the special name for a polynomial of degree 4.

Polynomial expression	Degree	Name
$ax + b, \quad a \neq 0$	1	linear
$ax^2 + bx + c, \quad a \neq 0$	2	quadratic
$ax^3 + bx^2 + cx + d, \quad a \neq 0$	3	cubic
$ax^4 + bx^3 + cx^2 + dx + e, \quad a \neq 0$	4	quartic

The next example is a recap on how to add, subtract and multiply polynomials.

WORKED EXAMPLE 1

If $P(x) = 2x^3 - 6x^2 - 5$ and $Q(x) = x^3 + 2x - 1$, find an expression for
a $P(x) + Q(x)$, **b** $P(x) - Q(x)$, **c** $2Q(x)$, **d** $P(x)Q(x)$.

Answers

a $P(x) + Q(x) = 2x^3 - 6x^2 - 5 + x^3 + 2x - 1$ collect like terms
$= 3x^3 - 6x^2 + 2x - 6$

b $P(x) - Q(x) = (2x^3 - 6x^2 - 5) - (x^3 + 2x - 1)$ remove brackets
$= 2x^3 - 6x^2 - 5 - x^3 - 2x + 1$ collect like terms
$= x^3 - 6x^2 - 2x - 4$

c $2Q(x) = 2(x^3 + 2x - 1)$
$= 2x^3 + 4x - 2$

d $P(x)Q(x) = (2x^3 - 6x^2 - 5)(x^3 + 2x - 1)$
$= 2x^3(x^3 + 2x - 1) - 6x^2(x^3 + 2x - 1) - 5(x^3 + 2x - 1)$
$= 2x^6 + 4x^4 - 2x^3 - 6x^5 - 12x^3 + 6x^2 - 5x^3 - 10x + 5$
$= 2x^6 - 6x^5 + 4x^4 - 19x^3 + 6x^2 - 10x + 5$

Cambridge IGCSE and O Level Additional Mathematics

CLASS DISCUSSION

$P(x)$ is a polynomial of degree p and $Q(x)$ is a polynomial of degree q, where $p > q$.
Discuss with your classmates what the degree of each of the following polynomials is:

$P(x) + Q(x)$	$2P(x)$	$Q(x) + 5$
$-3Q(x)$	$P^2(x)$	$[Q(x)]^2$
$P(x)Q(x)$	$QP(x)$	$Q(x) - P(x)$

Exercise 5.1

1. If $P(x) = 3x^4 + 2x^2 - 1$ and $Q(x) = 2x^3 + x^2 + 1$, find an expression for
   a $P(x) + Q(x)$
   b $3P(x) + Q(x)$
   c $P(x) - 2Q(x)$
   d $P(x)Q(x)$.

2. Find the following products.
   a $(2x - 1)(4x^3 + x + 2)$
   b $(x^3 + 2x^2 - 1)(3x + 2)$
   c $(3x^2 + 2x - 5)(x^3 + x^2 + 4)$
   d $(x + 2)^2(3x^3 + x - 1)$
   e $(x^2 - 5x + 2)^2$
   f $(3x - 1)^3$

3. Simplify each of the following.
   a $(2x - 3)(x + 2) + (x + 1)(x - 1)$
   b $(3x + 1)(x^2 + 5x + 2) - (x^2 - 4x + 2)(x + 3)$
   c $(2x^3 + x - 1)(x^2 + 3x - 4) - (x + 2)(x^3 - x^2 + 5x + 2)$

4. If $f(x) = 2x^2 - x - 4$ and $g(x) = x^2 + 5x + 2$, find an expression for
   a $f(x) + xg(x)$
   b $[f(x)]^2$
   c $f^2(x)$
   d $gf(x)$.

5.2 Division of polynomials

To be able to divide a polynomial by another polynomial you first need to remember how to do long division with numbers.

The steps for calculating $5508 \div 17$ are:

$$
\begin{array}{r}
324 \\
17{\overline{\smash{\big)}\,5508}} \\
\underline{51} \\
40 \\
\underline{34} \\
68 \\
\underline{68} \\
0
\end{array}
$$

Divide 55 by 17
$3 \times 17 = 51$
$55 - 51 = 4$, bring down the 0 from the next column
Divide 40 by 17, $2 \times 17 = 34$
$40 - 34 = 6$, bring down the 8 from the next column
Divide 68 by 17, $4 \times 17 = 68$
$68 - 68 = 0$

So $\quad 5508 \div 17 = 324$

dividend   divisor   quotient

The same process can be applied to the division of polynomials.

WORKED EXAMPLE 2

Divide $x^3 - 5x^2 + 8x - 4$ by $x - 2$.

Answers

Step 1:

$$
\begin{array}{r}
x^2 \\
x-2{\overline{\smash{\big)}\,x^3 - 5x^2 + 8x - 4}} \\
\underline{x^3 - 2x^2} \\
-3x^2 + 8x
\end{array}
$$

divide the first term of the polynomial by x, $x^3 \div x = x^2$
multiply $(x-2)$ by x^2, $x^2(x-2) = x^3 - 2x^2$
subtract, $(x^3 - 5x^2) - (x^3 - 2x^2) = -3x^2$
bring down the $8x$ from the next column

Step 2: Repeat the process

$$
\begin{array}{r}
x^2 - 3x \\
x-2{\overline{\smash{\big)}\,x^3 - 5x^2 + 8x - 4}} \\
\underline{x^3 - 2x^2} \\
-3x^2 + 8x \\
\underline{-3x^2 + 6x} \\
2x - 4
\end{array}
$$

divide $-3x^2$ by x, $-3x^2 \div x = -3x$
multiply $(x-2)$ by $-3x$, $-3x(x-2) = -3x^2 + 6x$
subtract, $(-3x^2 + 8x) - (-3x^2 + 6x) = 2x$
bring down the -4 from the next column

Step 3: Repeat the process

$$
\begin{array}{r}
x^2 - 3x + 2 \\
x-2{\overline{\smash{\big)}\,x^3 - 5x^2 + 8x - 4}} \\
\underline{x^3 - 2x^2} \\
-3x^2 + 8x \\
\underline{-3x^2 + 6x} \\
2x - 4 \\
\underline{2x - 4} \\
0
\end{array}
$$

divide $2x$ by x, $2x \div x = 2$
multiply $(x-2)$ by 2, $2(x-2) = 2x - 4$
subtract, $(2x - 4) - (2x - 4) = 0$

So $(x^3 - 5x^2 + 8x - 4) \div (x - 2) = x^2 - 3x + 2$.

Cambridge IGCSE and O Level Additional Mathematics

WORKED EXAMPLE 3

Divide $2x^3 - x + 51$ by $x + 3$.

There are no x^2 terms in $2x^3 - x + 51$ so we write it as $2x^3 + 0x^2 - x + 51$.

Answers

Step 1:

$$
\begin{array}{r}
2x^2 \\
x+3 \overline{)\, 2x^3 + 0x^2 - x + 51} \\
\underline{2x^3 + 6x^2 } \\
-6x^2 - x
\end{array}
$$

divide the first term of the polynomial by x, $2x^3 \div x = 2x^2$
multiply $(x+3)$ by $2x^2$, $2x^2(x+3) = 2x^3 + 6x^2$
subtract, $(2x^3 + 0x^2) - (2x^3 + 6x^2) = -6x^2$
bring down the $-x$ from the next column

Step 2: Repeat the process

$$
\begin{array}{r}
2x^2 - 6x \\
x+3 \overline{)\, 2x^3 + 0x^2 - x + 51} \\
\underline{2x^3 + 6x^2 } \\
-6x^2 - x \\
\underline{-6x^2 - 18x } \\
17x + 51
\end{array}
$$

divide $-6x^2$ by x, $-6x^2 \div x = -6x$
multiply $(x+3)$ by $-6x$, $-6x(x+3) = -6x^2 - 18x$
subtract, $(-6x^2 - x) - (-6x^2 - 18x) = 17x$
bring down the 51 from the next column

Step 3: Repeat the process

$$
\begin{array}{r}
x^2 - 6x + 17 \\
x+3 \overline{)\, 2x^3 + 0x^2 - x + 51} \\
\underline{2x^3 + 6x^2 } \\
-6x^2 - x \\
\underline{-6x^2 - 18x } \\
17x + 51 \\
\underline{17x + 51} \\
0
\end{array}
$$

divide $17x$ by x, $17x \div x = 17$
multiply $(x+3)$ by 17, $17(x+3) = 17x + 51$
subtract, $(17x + 51) - (17x + 51) = 0$

So $(2x^3 - x + 51) \div (x+3) = 2x^2 - 6x + 17$.

Exercise 5.2

1 Simplify each of the following.

   a $(x^3 + 3x^2 - 46x - 48) \div (x+1)$
   b $(x^3 - x^2 - 3x + 2) \div (x-2)$
   c $(x^3 - 20x^2 + 100x - 125) \div (x-5)$
   d $(x^3 - 3x - 2) \div (x-2)$
   e $(x^3 - 3x^2 - 33x + 35) \div (x-7)$
   f $(x^3 + 2x^2 - 9x - 18) \div (x+2)$

2 Simplify each of the following.

   a $(3x^3 + 8x^2 + 3x - 2) \div (x+2)$
   b $(6x^3 + 11x^2 - 3x - 2) \div (3x+1)$
   c $(3x^3 - 11x^2 + 20) \div (x-2)$
   d $(3x^3 - 21x^2 + 4x - 28) \div (x-7)$

3 Simplify.

a $\dfrac{3x^3 - 3x^2 - 4x + 4}{x - 1}$

b $\dfrac{2x^3 + 9x^2 + 25}{x + 5}$

c $\dfrac{3x^3 - 50x + 8}{3x^2 + 12x - 2}$

d $\dfrac{x^3 - 14x - 15}{x^2 - 3x - 5}$

4 a Divide $x^4 - 1$ by $(x + 1)$. **b** Divide $x^3 - 8$ by $(x - 2)$.

5.3 The factor theorem

In **Worked example 2** you found that $x - 2$ divided exactly into $(x^3 - 5x^2 + 8x - 4)$.

$$(x^3 - 5x^2 + 8x - 4) \div (x - 2) = x^2 - 3x + 2$$

This can also be written as:

$$(x^3 - 5x^2 + 8x - 4) = (x - 2)(x^2 - 3x + 2)$$

If a polynomial $P(x)$ is divided exactly by a linear factor $a - c$ to give the polynomial $Q(x)$, then

$$P(x) = (x - c)Q(x).$$

Substituting $a - c$ into this formula gives $P(c) = 0$.

Hence:

> If for a polynomial $P(x)$, $P(c) = 0$ then $x - c$ is a factor of $P(x)$.

This is known as the **factor theorem**.

For example, when $x = 2$,

$$4x^3 - 8x^2 - x + 2 = 4(2)^3 - 8(2)^2 - 2 + 2 = 32 - 32 - 2 + 2 = 0.$$

Therefore $x - 2$ is a factor of $4x^3 - 8x^2 - x + 2$.

The factor theorem can be extended to:

> If for a polynomial $P(x)$, $P\left(\dfrac{b}{a}\right) = 0$ then $ax - b$ is a factor of $P(x)$.

For example, when $x = \dfrac{1}{2}$,

$$4x^3 - 2x^2 + 8x - 4 = 4\left(\dfrac{1}{2}\right)^3 - 2\left(\dfrac{1}{2}\right)^2 + 8\left(\dfrac{1}{2}\right) - 4 = \dfrac{1}{2} - \dfrac{1}{2} + 4 - 4 = 0.$$

Therefore $2x - 1$ is a factor of $4x^3 - 2x^2 + 8x - 4$.

CLASS DISCUSSION

Discuss with your classmates which of the following expressions are exactly divisible by $x - 2$.

$x^3 - x^2 - x - 2$	$2x^3 + 5x^2 - 4x - 3$	$x^3 - 4x^2 + 8x - 8$
$2x^4 - x^3 + 3x^2 - 2x - 5$	$x^3 - 8$	$3x^3 - 8x - 8$
$6x^3 - 10x^2 - 18$	$x^3 + x^2 - 4x - 4$	$x^3 + x + 10$

WORKED EXAMPLE 4

Show that $x - 3$ is a factor of $x^3 - 6x^2 + 11x - 6$ by
a algebraic division
b the factor theorem.

Answers

a Divide $x^3 - 6x^2 + 11x - 6$ by $x - 3$.

$$\begin{array}{r} x^2 - 3x + 2 \\ x-3{\overline{\smash{\big)}\,x^3 - 6x^2 + 11x - 6}} \\ \underline{x^3 - 3x^2} \\ -3x^2 + 11x \\ \underline{-3x^2 + 9x} \\ 2x - 6 \\ \underline{2x - 6} \\ 0 \end{array}$$

The remainder $= 0$, so $x - 3$ is a factor of $x^3 - 6x^2 + 11x - 6$.

b Let $f(x) = x^3 - 6x^2 + 11x - 6$ if $f(3) = 0$, then $x - 3$ is a factor.

$f(3) = (3)^3 - 6(3)^2 + 11(3) - 6$

$ = 27 - 54 + 33 - 6$

$ = 0$

So $x - 3$ is a factor of $x^3 - 6x^2 + 11x - 6$.

Chapter 5: Factors and polynomials

WORKED EXAMPLE 5

$2x^2 + x - 1$ is a factor of $2x^3 - x^2 + ax + b$.

Find the value of a and the value of b.

Answers

Let $f(x) = 2x^3 - x^2 + ax + b$.

If $2x^2 + x - 1 = (2x - 1)(x + 1)$ is a factor of $f(x)$, then $2x - 1$ and $x + 1$ are also factors of $f(x)$.

Using the factor theorem $f\left(\dfrac{1}{2}\right) = 0$ and $f(-1) = 0$.

$f\left(\dfrac{1}{2}\right) = 0$ gives $2\left(\dfrac{1}{2}\right)^3 - \left(\dfrac{1}{2}\right)^2 + a\left(\dfrac{1}{2}\right) + b = 0$

$$\dfrac{1}{4} - \dfrac{1}{4} + \dfrac{a}{2} + b = 0$$

$$a = -2b \qquad \text{--------(1)}$$

$f(-1) = 0$ gives $2(-1)^3 - (-1)^2 + a(-1) + b = 0$

$$-2 - 1 - a + b = 0$$

$$a = b - 3 \qquad \text{--------(2)}$$

$(2) = (1)$ gives $b - 3 = -2b$

$$3b = 3$$

$$b = 1$$

Substituting in (2) gives $a = -2$.

So $a = -2$, $b = 1$.

Exercise 5.3

1 Use the factor theorem to show:

 a $x - 4$ is a factor of $x^3 - 3x^2 - 6x + 8$

 b $x + 1$ is a factor of $x^3 - 3x - 2$

 c $x - 2$ is a factor of $5x^3 - 17x^2 + 28$

 d $3x + 1$ is a factor of $6x^3 + 11x^2 - 3x - 2$.

2 Find the value of a in each of the following.

 a $x + 1$ is a factor of $6x^3 + 27x^2 + ax + 8$.

 b $x + 7$ is a factor of $x^3 - 5x^2 - 6x + a$.

 c $2x + 3$ is a factor of $4x^3 + ax^2 + 29x + 30$.

3 $x - 2$ is a factor of $x^3 + ax^2 + bx - 4$.

 Express b in terms of a.

4 Find the value of a and the value of b in each of the following.

 a $x^2 + 3x - 10$ is a factor of $x^3 + ax^2 + bx + 30$.

 b $2x^2 - 11x + 5$ is a factor of $ax^3 - 17x^2 + bx - 15$.

 c $4x^2 - 4x - 15$ is a factor of $4x^3 + ax^2 + bx + 30$.

5 It is given that $x^2 - 5x + 6$ and $x^3 - 6x^2 + 11x + a$ have a common factor. Find the possible value of a.

6 $x - 2$ is a common factor of $3x^3 - (a-b)x - 8$ and $x^3 - (a+b)x + 30$. Find the value of a and the value of b.

7 $x - 3$ and $2x - 1$ are factors of $2x^3 - px^2 - 2qx + q$.
   a Find the value of p and the value of q.
   b Explain why $x + 3$ is also a factor of the expression.

8 $x + a$ is a factor of $x^3 + 8x^2 + 4ax - 3a$.
   a Show that $a^3 - 4a^2 + 3a = 0$.
   b Find the possible values of a.

5.4 Cubic expressions and equations

Consider factorising $x^3 - 5x^2 + 8x - 4$ completely.
In **Worked example 2** you found that $(x^3 - 5x^2 + 8x - 4) \div (x - 2) = x^2 - 3x + 2$.
This can be rewritten as: $x^3 - 5x^2 + 8x - 4 = (x - 2)(x^2 - 3x + 2)$.
Factorising completely gives: $x^3 - 5x^2 + 8x - 4 = (x - 2)(x - 2)(x - 1)$.

Hence if you know one factor of a cubic expression it is possible to then factorise the expression completely. The next example illustrates three different methods for doing this.

WORKED EXAMPLE 6

Factorise $x^3 - 3x^2 - 13x + 15$ completely.

Answers
Let $f(x) = x^3 - 3x^2 - 13x + 15$.
The positive and negative factors of 15 are ± 1, ± 3 and ± 5.
$f(1) = (1)^3 - 3 \times (1)^2 - 13 \times (1) + 15 = 0$
So $x - 1$ is a factor of $f(x)$.
The other factors can be found by any of the following methods.

Method 1 (by trial and error)
$f(x) = x^3 - 3x^2 - 13x + 15$

$f(1) = (1)^3 - 3 \times (1)^2 - 13 \times (1) + 15 = 0$
So $x - 1$ is a factor of $f(x)$.

$f(-3) = (-3)^3 - 3 \times (-3)^2 - 13 \times (-3) + 15 = 0$
So $x + 3$ is a factor of $f(x)$.

$f(5) = (5)^3 - 3 \times (5)^2 - 13 \times (5) + 15 = 0$
So $x - 5$ is a factor of $f(x)$.
Hence $f(x) = (x - 1)(x - 5)(x + 3)$

Method 2 (by long division)

$$\require{enclose}\begin{array}{r}x^2-2x-15\\x-1\enclose{longdiv}{x^3-3x^2-13x+15}\\\underline{x^3-x^2}\\-2x^2-13x\\\underline{-2x^2+2x}\\-15x+15\\\underline{-15x+15}\\0\end{array}$$

$$f(x) = (x-1)(x^2 - 2x - 15)$$
$$= (x-1)(x-5)(x+3)$$

Method 3 (by equating coefficients)

Since $x - 1$ is a factor, $x^3 - 3x^2 - 13x + 15$ can be written as:
$$x^3 - 3x^2 - 13x + 15 = (x-1)(ax^2 + bx + c)$$

coefficient of x^3 is 1, so $a = 1$ since $1 \times 1 = 1$	constant term is −15, so $c = -15$ since $-1 \times -15 = 15$

$x^3 - 3x^2 - 13x + 15 = (x-1)(x^2 + bx - 15)$ **expand and collect like terms**
$x^3 - 3x^2 - 13x + 15 = x^3 + (b-1)x^2 + (-b-15)x + 15$

Equating coefficients of x^2: $b - 1 = -3$
$$b = -2$$

$$f(x) = (x-1)(x^2 - 2x - 15)$$
$$= (x-1)(x-5)(x+3)$$

WORKED EXAMPLE 7

Solve $2x^3 - 3x^2 - 18x - 8 = 0$.

Answers

Let $f(x) = 2x^3 - 3x^2 - 18x - 8$.

The positive and negative factors of 8 are ±1, ±2, ±4 and ±8.
$f(-2) = 2(-2)^3 - 3 \times (-2)^2 - 18 \times (-2) - 8 = 0$

So $x + 2$ is a factor of $f(x)$.
$$2x^3 - 3x^2 - 18x - 8 = (x+2)(ax^2 + bx + c)$$

coefficient of x^3 is 2, so $a = 2$ since $1 \times 2 = 2$	constant term is −8, so $c = -4$ since $2 \times -4 = -8$

$2x^3 - 3x^2 - 18x - 8 = (x+2)(2x^2 + bx - 4)$ **expand and collect like terms**
$2x^3 - 3x^2 - 18x - 8 = 2x^3 + (b+4)x^2 + (2b-4)x - 8$

Equating coefficients of x^2: $b + 4 = -3$
$$b = -7$$
$$f(x) = (x + 2)(2x^2 - 7x - 4)$$
$$= (x + 2)(2x + 1)(x - 4)$$
Hence $(x + 2)(2x + 1)(x - 4) = 0$.
So $x = -2$ or $x = -\dfrac{1}{2}$ or $x = 4$.

WORKED EXAMPLE 8

Solve $2x^3 + 7x^2 - 2x - 1 = 0$.

Answers

Let $f(x) = 2x^3 + 7x^2 - 2x - 1$.
The positive and negative factors of -1 are ± 1.
$f(-1) = 2(-1)^3 + 7 \times (-1)^2 - 2 \times (-1) - 1 \neq 0$
$f(1) = 2(1)^3 + 7 \times (1)^2 - 2 \times (1) - 1 \neq 0$
So $x - 1$ and $x + 1$ are not factors of $f(x)$.
By inspection, $f\left(\dfrac{1}{2}\right) = 2\left(\dfrac{1}{2}\right)^3 + 7 \times \left(\dfrac{1}{2}\right)^2 - 2 \times \left(\dfrac{1}{2}\right) - 1 = 0$.
So $2x - 1$ is a factor of:
$$2x^3 + 7x^2 - 2x - 1 = (2x - 1)(ax^2 + bx + c)$$

coefficient of x^3 is 2, so $a = 1$ since $2 \times 1 = 2$	constant term is -1, so $c = 1$ since $-1 \times 1 = -1$

$$2x^3 + 7x^2 - 2x - 1 = (2x - 1)(x^2 + bx + 1)$$
$$2x^3 + 7x^2 - 2x - 1 = 2x^3 + (2b - 1)x^2 + (2 - b)x - 1$$

Equating coefficients of x^2: $2b - 1 = 7$
$$b = 4$$
So $2x^3 + 7x^2 - 2x - 1 = (2x - 1)(x^2 + 4x + 1)$.
$$x = \dfrac{1}{2} \text{ or } x = \dfrac{-4 \pm \sqrt{4^2 - 4 \times 1 \times 1}}{2 \times 1}$$
$$x = \dfrac{1}{2} \text{ or } x = \dfrac{-4 \pm 2\sqrt{3}}{2}$$
$$x = \dfrac{1}{2} \text{ or } x = -2 + \sqrt{3} \text{ or } x = -2 - \sqrt{3}$$

Not all cubic expressions can be factorised into 3 linear factors.

Consider the cubic expression $x^3 + x^2 - 36$.

Let $f(x) = x^3 + x^2 - 36$.
$f(3) = (3)^3 + (3)^2 - 36 = 0$

So $x - 3$ is a factor of $f(x)$.

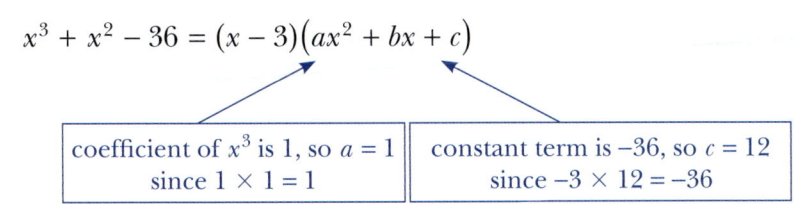

$$x^3 + x^2 - 36 = (x - 3)(ax^2 + bx + c)$$

| coefficient of x^3 is 1, so $a = 1$ since $1 \times 1 = 1$ | constant term is -36, so $c = 12$ since $-3 \times 12 = -36$ |

$x^3 + x^2 - 36 = (x - 3)(x^2 + bx + 12)$
$x^3 + x^2 - 36 = x^3 + (b - 3)x^2 + (12 - 3b)x - 36$

Equating coefficients of x^2: $b - 3 = 1$
$b = 4$

So $x^3 + x^2 - 36 = (x - 3)(x^2 + 4x + 12)$

(Note: $x^2 + 4x + 12$ cannot be factorised into two further linear factors, since the discriminant < 0.)

Exercise 5.4

1. **a** Show that $x - 1$ is a factor of $2x^3 - x^2 - 2x + 1$.
   b Hence factorise $2x^3 - x^2 - 2x + 1$ completely.

2. Factorise these cubic expressions completely.
   a $x^3 + 2x^2 - 3x - 10$
   b $x^3 + 4x^2 - 4x - 16$
   c $2x^3 - 9x^2 - 18x$
   d $x^3 - 8x^2 + 5x + 14$
   e $2x^3 - 13x^2 + 17x + 12$
   f $3x^3 + 2x^2 - 19x + 6$
   g $4x^3 - 8x^2 - x + 2$
   h $2x^3 + 3x^2 - 32x + 15$

3. Solve the following equations.
   a $x^3 - 3x^2 - 33x + 35 = 0$
   b $x^3 - 6x^2 + 11x - 6 = 0$
   c $3x^3 + 17x^2 + 18x - 8 = 0$
   d $2x^3 + 3x^2 - 17x + 12 = 0$
   e $2x^3 - 3x^2 - 11x + 6 = 0$
   f $2x^3 + 7x^2 - 5x - 4 = 0$
   g $4x^3 + 12x^2 + 5x - 6 = 0$
   h $2x^3 - 3x^2 - 29x + 60 = 0$

4. Solve the following equations.
   Express roots in the form $a \pm b\sqrt{c}$, where necessary.
   a $x^3 + 5x^2 - 4x - 2 = 0$
   b $x^3 + 8x^2 + 12x - 9 = 0$
   c $x^3 + 2x^2 - 7x - 2 = 0$
   d $2x^3 + 3x^2 - 17x + 12 = 0$

5. Solve the equation $2x^3 + 9x^2 - 14x - 9 = 0$.
   Express roots in the form $a \pm b\sqrt{c}$, where necessary.

6 Solve the equation $x^3 + 8x^2 + 12x = 9$.
  Write your answers correct to 2 decimal places where necessary.

7 a Show that $x - 2$ is a factor of $x^3 - x^2 - x - 2$.
  b Hence show that $x^3 - x^2 - x - 2 = 0$ has only one real root and state the value of this root.

8 f(x) is a cubic polynomial where the coefficient of x^3 is 1.
  Find f(x) when the roots of f(x) = 0 are:
  a −2, 1 and 5   b −5, −2 and 4   c −3, 0 and 2.

9 f(x) is a cubic polynomial where the coefficient of x^3 is 2.
  Find f(x) when the roots of f(x) = 0 are:
  a −0.5, 2 and 4   b 0.5, 1 and 2   c −1.5, 1 and 5.

10 f(x) is a cubic polynomial where the coefficient of x^3 is 1.
   The roots of $f(x) = 0$ are $-3, 1 + \sqrt{2}$ and $1 - \sqrt{2}$.
   Express f(x) as a cubic polynomial in x with integer coefficients.

11 f(x) is a cubic polynomial where the coefficient of x^3 is 2.
   The roots of $f(x) = 0$ are $\frac{1}{2}, 2 + \sqrt{3}$ and $2 - \sqrt{3}$.
   Express f(x) as a cubic polynomial in x with integer coefficients.

12 $2x + 3$ is a factor of $2x^4 + (a^2 + 1)x^3 - 3x^2 + (1 - a^3)x + 3$.
   a Show that $4a^3 - 9a^2 + 4 = 0$.
   b Find the possible values of a.

5.5 The remainder theorem

Consider $f(x) = 2x^3 - 4x^2 + 7x - 37$.

Substituting $x = 3$ in the polynomial gives $f(3) = 2(3)^3 - 4(3)^2 + 7(3) - 37 = 2$.

When $2x^3 - 4x^2 + 7x - 37$ is divided by $x - 3$, there is a remainder.

$$\begin{array}{r}
2x^2 + 2x + 13 \\
x - 3 \overline{\smash{)}2x^3 - 4x^2 + 7x - 37} \\
\underline{2x^3 - 6x^2 } \\
2x^2 + 7x \\
\underline{2x^2 - 6x } \\
13x - 37 \\
\underline{13x - 39} \\
2
\end{array}$$

The remainder is 2. This is the same value as f(3).

$f(x) = 2x^3 - 4x^2 + 7x - 36$, can be written as
$f(x) = (x - 3)(2x^2 + 2x + 13) + 2$.

In general:

If a polynomial P(x) is divided by $x - c$ to give the polynomial Q(x) and a remainder R, then

$P(x) = (x - c)Q(x) + R.$

Substituting $x = c$ into this formula gives $P(c) = R$.

This leads to the **remainder theorem**:

> If a polynomial P(x) is divided by $x - c$, the remainder is P(c).

The Remainder Theorem can be extended to:

> If a polynomial P(x) is divided by $ax - b$, the remainder is $P\left(\dfrac{b}{a}\right)$.

WORKED EXAMPLE 9

Find the remainder when $7x^3 + 6x^2 - 40x + 17$ is divided by $(x + 3)$ by using

a algebraic division   **b** the factor theorem.

Answers

a Divide $7x^3 + 6x^2 - 40x + 17$ by $(x + 3)$.

$$
\begin{array}{r}
7x^2 + 15x + 5 \\
x + 3 \overline{\smash{)}7x^3 + 6x^2 - 40x + 17} \\
\underline{7x^3 + 21x^2 } \\
-15x^2 - 40x \\
\underline{-15x^2 - 45x } \\
5x + 17 \\
\underline{5x + 15} \\
2
\end{array}
$$

The remainder is 2.

b Let $f(x) = 7x^3 + 6x^2 - 40x + 17$.

Remainder = $f(-3)$
$= 7(-3)^3 + 6(-3)^2 - 40(-3) + 17$
$= -189 + 54 + 120 + 17$
$= 2$

WORKED EXAMPLE 10

$f(x) = 2x^3 + ax^2 - 9x + b$

When $f(x)$ is divided by $x - 1$, the remainder is 1.
When $f(x)$ is divided by $x + 2$, the remainder is 19.
Find the value of a and of b.

Answers

$f(x) = 2x^3 + ax^2 - 9x + b$

When $f(x)$ is divided by $x - 1$, the remainder is 1 means that: $f(1) = 1$.
$$2(1)^3 + a(1)^2 - 9(1) + b = 1$$
$$2 + a - 9 + b = 1$$
$$a + b = 8 \quad \text{-----------(1)}$$

When $f(x)$ is divided by $x + 2$, the remainder is 19 means that: $f(-2) = 19$.
$$2(-2)^3 + a(-2)^2 - 9(-2) + b = 19$$
$$-16 + 4a + 18 + b = 19$$
$$4a + b = 17 \quad \text{------(2)}$$

(2) − (1) gives $3a = 9$
$$a = 3$$
Substituting $a = 3$ in equation (2) gives $b = 5$.
$a = 3$ and $b = 5$

Exercise 5.5

1 Find the remainder when

   a $x^3 + 2x^2 - x + 3$ is divided by $x - 1$

   b $x^3 - 6x^2 + 11x - 7$ is divided by $x - 2$

   c $x^3 - 3x^2 - 33x + 30$ is divided by $x + 2$

   d $2x^3 - x^2 - 18x + 11$ is divided by $2x - 1$.

2 **a** When $x^3 + x^2 + ax - 2$ is divided by $x - 1$, the remainder is 5.
      Find the value of a.

   b When $2x^3 - 6x^2 + 7x + b$ is divided by $x + 2$, the remainder is 3.
      Find the value of b.

   c When $2x^3 + x^2 + cx - 10$ is divided by $2x - 1$, the remainder is -4.
      Find the value of c.

3 $f(x) = x^3 + ax^2 + bx - 5$

   $f(x)$ has a factor of $x - 1$ and leaves a remainder of 3 when divided by $x + 2$.
   Find the value of a and of b.

4 $f(x) = x^3 + ax^2 + 11x + b$

   $f(x)$ has a factor of $x - 2$ and leaves a remainder of 24 when divided by $x - 5$.
   Find the value of a and of b.

5 f(x) = $x^3 - 2x^2 + ax + b$

f(x) has a factor of $x - 3$ and leaves a remainder of 15 when divided by $x + 2$.

a Find the value of a and of b.
b Solve the equation f(x) = 0.

6 f(x) = $4x^3 + 8x^2 + ax + b$

f(x) has a factor of $2x - 1$ and leaves a remainder of 48 when divided by $x - 2$.

a Find the value of a and of b.
b Find the remainder when f(x) is divided by $x - 1$.

7 f(x) = $2x^3 + (a + 1)x^2 - ax + b$

When f(x) is divided by $x - 1$, the remainder is 5.
When f(x) is divided by $x - 2$, the remainder is 14.
Show that $a = -4$ and find the value of b.

8 f(x) = $ax^3 + bx^2 + 5x - 2$

When f(x) is divided by $x - 1$, the remainder is 6.
When f(x) is divided by $2x + 1$, the remainder is -6.
Find the value of a and of b.

9 f(x) = $x^3 - 5x^2 + ax + b$

f(x) has a factor of $x - 2$.

a Express b in terms of a.
b When f(x) is divided by $x + 1$, the remainder is -9.
Find the value of a and of b.

10 f(x) = $x^3 + ax^2 + bx + c$

The roots of f(x) = 0 are 2, 3, and k.
When f(x) is divided by $x - 1$, the remainder is -8.

a Find the value of k.
b Find the remainder when f(x) is divided by $x + 1$.

11 f(x) = $4x^3 + ax^2 + 13x + b$

f(x) has a factor of $2x - 1$ and leaves a remainder of 21 when divided by $x - 2$.

a Find the value of a and of b.
b Find the remainder when the expression is divided by $x + 1$.

12 f(x) = $x^3 - 8x^2 + kx - 20$

When f(x) is divided by $x - 1$, the remainder is R.
When f(x) is divided by $x - 2$, the remainder is $4R$.
Find the value of k.

13 f(x) = $x^3 + 2x^2 - 6x + 9$

When f(x) is divided by $x + a$, the remainder is R.
When f(x) is divided by $x - a$, the remainder is $2R$.

a Show that $3a^3 - 2a^2 - 18a - 9 = 0$.
b Solve the equation in **part a** completely.

14 f(x) = $x^3 + 6x^2 + kx - 15$

When f(x) is divided by $x - 1$, the remainder is R.

When f(x) is divided by $x + 4$, the remainder is $-R$.

a Find the value of k.

b Hence find the remainder when the expression is divided by $x + 2$.

CHALLENGE Q

15 f(x) = $x^3 + ax^2 + bx + c$

The roots of f(x) = 0 are 1, k, and $k + 1$.

When f(x) is divided by $x - 2$, the remainder is 20.

a Show that $k^2 - 3k - 18 = 0$.

b Hence find the possible values of k.

Summary

The factor theorem:

If, for a polynomial P(x), P(c) = 0 then $x - c$ is a factor of P(x).

If, for a polynomial P(x), $P\left(\dfrac{b}{a}\right) = 0$ then $ax - b$ is a factor of P(x).

The remainder theorem:

If a polynomial P(x) is divided by $x - c$, the remainder is P(c).

If a polynomial P(x) is divided by $ax - b$, the remainder is $P\left(\dfrac{b}{a}\right)$.

Examination questions

Worked past paper example

The function f is such that $f(x) = 4x^3 - 8x^2 + ax + b$, where a and b are constants. It is given that $2x - 1$ is a factor of $f(x)$ and that when $f(x)$ is divided by $x + 2$ the remainder is 20. Find the remainder when $f(x)$ is divided by $x - 1$. [6]

Cambridge IGCSE Additional Mathematics 0606 Paper 11 Q2 Nov 2011

Answer

$f(x) = 4x^3 - 8x^2 + ax + b$

If $2x - 1$ is a factor, then $f\left(\dfrac{1}{2}\right) = 0$.

$$4\left(\dfrac{1}{2}\right)^3 - 8\left(\dfrac{1}{2}\right)^2 + a\left(\dfrac{1}{2}\right) + b = 0$$

$$\dfrac{1}{2} - 2 + a\left(\dfrac{1}{2}\right) + b = 0$$

$$a\left(\dfrac{1}{2}\right) + b = 1\dfrac{1}{2}$$

$$a + 2b = 3 \quad \text{----------------(1)}$$

Remainder = 20 when divided by $x + 2$, means that $f(-2) = 20$.

$$4(-2)^3 - 8(-2)^2 + a(-2) + b = 20$$

$$-32 - 32 - 2a + b = 20$$

$$-2a + b = 84 \quad \text{----------------(2)}$$

From (1) $a = 3 - 2b$.

Substituting in (2), gives: $-2(3 - 2b) + b = 84$

$$-6 + 4b + b = 84$$

$$5b = 90$$

$$b = 18$$

So $a = -33$, $b = 18$.

Remainder when $f(x) = 4x^3 - 8x^2 - 33x + 18$ is divided by $(x - 1)$ is $f(1)$.

remainder $= 4(1)^3 - 8(1)^2 - 33(1) + 18$

$= 4 - 8 - 33 + 18$

$= -19$

Exercise 5.6

Exam Exercise

1. **a** Show that $x - 2$ is a factor of $3x^3 - 14x^2 + 32$. [1]
   b Hence factorise $3x^3 - 14x^2 + 32$ completely. [4]

   Cambridge IGCSE Additional Mathematics 0606 Paper 21 Q12i,ii Nov 2012

2. The function $f(x) = ax^3 + 4x^2 + bx - 2$, where a and b are constants, is such that $2x - 1$ is a factor. Given that the remainder when $f(x)$ is divided by $x - 2$ is twice the remainder when $f(x)$ is divided by $x + 1$, find the value of a and of b. [6]

   Cambridge IGCSE Additional Mathematics 0606 Paper 11 Q6 Nov 2013

3. **a** The remainder when the expression $x^3 + 9x^2 + bx + c$ is divided by $x - 2$ is twice the remainder when the expression is divided by $x - 1$. Show that $c = 24$. [5]
   b Given that $x + 8$ is a factor of $x^3 + 9x^2 + bx + 24$, show that the equation $x^3 + 9x^2 + bx + 24 = 0$ has only one real root. [4]

   Cambridge IGCSE Additional Mathematics 0606 Paper 21 Q10i,ii Nov 2012

4. The expression $x^3 + 8x^2 + px - 25$ leaves a remainder of R when divided by $x - 1$ and a remainder of $-R$ when divided by $x + 2$.
   a Find the value of p. [4]
   b Hence find the remainder when the expression is divided by $x + 3$. [2]

   Cambridge IGCSE Additional Mathematics 0606 Paper 21 Q5i,ii Jun 2011

5. Factorise completely the expression $2x^3 - 11x^2 - 20x - 7$. [5]

   Cambridge IGCSE Additional Mathematics 0606 Paper 11 Q4 Nov 2010

6. The expression $x^3 + ax^2 - 15x + b$ has a factor of $x - 2$ and leaves a remainder 75 when divided by $x + 3$. Find the value of a and of b. [5]

   Cambridge IGCSE Additional Mathematics 0606 Paper 21 Q2 Nov 2010

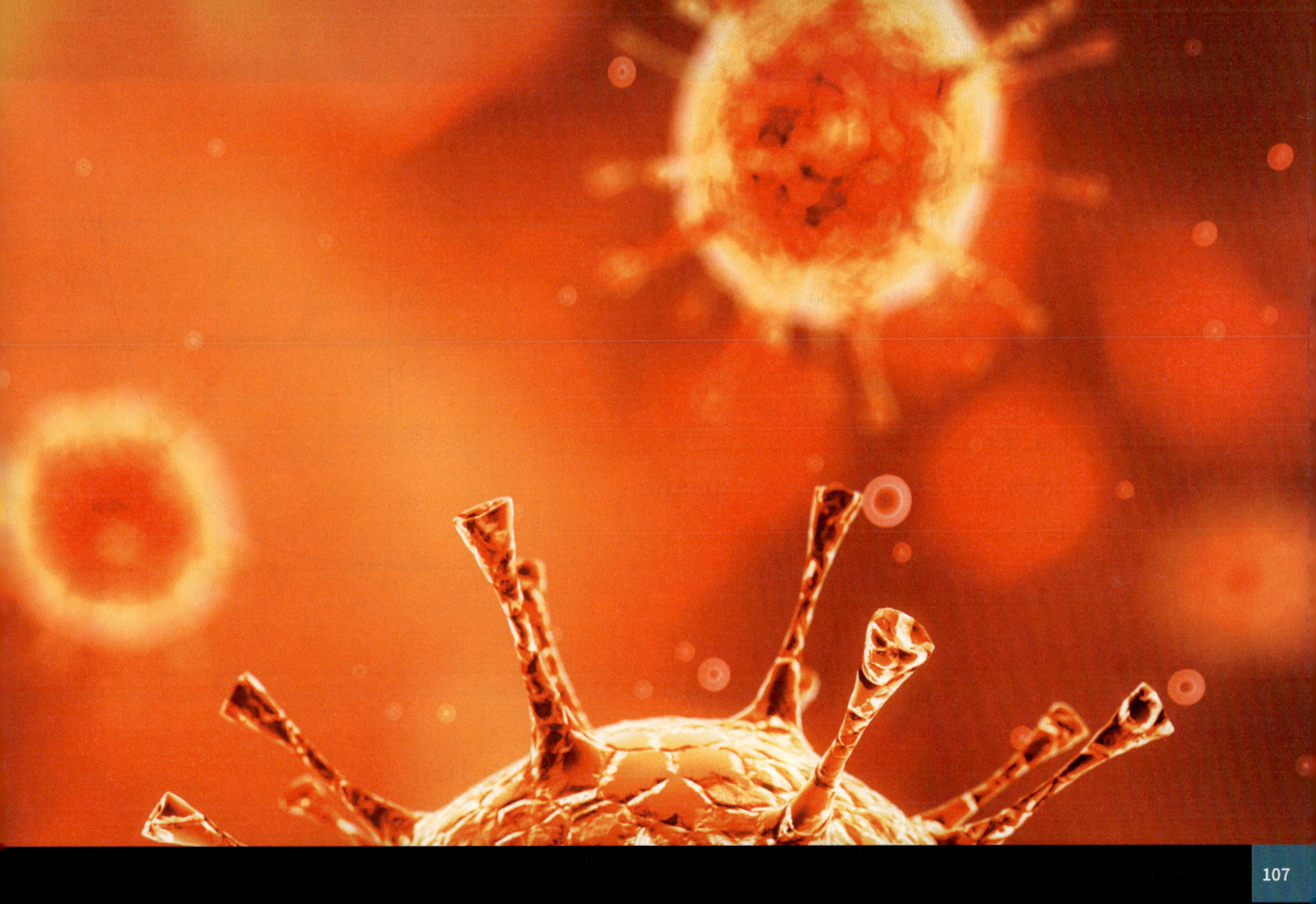

Chapter 6
Logarithmic and exponential functions

This section will show you how to:

- use simple properties of the logarithmic and exponential functions including $\ln x$ and e^x
- use graphs of the logarithmic and exponential functions including $\ln x$ and e^x and graphs of $ke^{nx} + a$ and $k \ln(ax + b)$ where n, k, a and b are integers
- use the laws of logarithms, including change of base of logarithms
- solve equations of the form $a^x = b$.

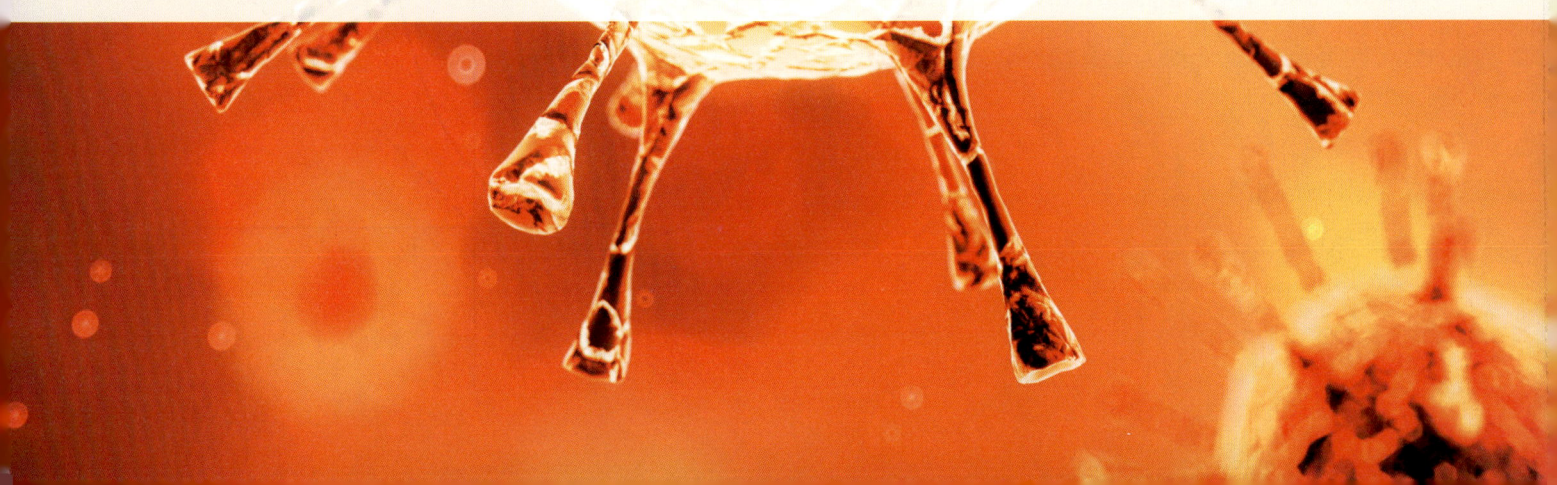

6.1 Logarithms to base 10

Consider the exponential function $f(x) = 10^x$.

To solve $\quad 10^x = 30$.
You can say $\quad 10^1 = 10$ and $10^2 = 100$.
So $\qquad 1 < x < 2$.

The graph of $y = 10^x$ could be used to give a more accurate value for x when $10^x = 30$:
From the graph, $x \approx 1.48$.

There is a function that gives the value of x directly:

If $10^x = 30$ then $x = \log_{10} 30$.
$\log_{10} 30$ is read as 'log 30 to base 10'.
log is short for **logarithm**.

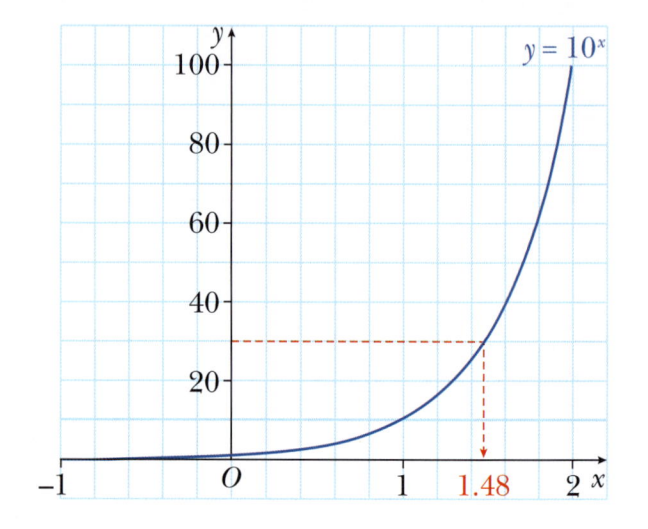

> **Note:**
> $\log_{10} 30$ can also be written as $\lg 30$ or $\log 30$.

On your calculator, for logs to the base 10, you use the (log) or (lg) key.

So if $10^x = 30$
then $\quad x = \log_{10} 30$
$\qquad x = 1.477$ to 4 sf.

Hence the rule for base 10 is:

$$\text{If } y = 10^x \text{ then } x = \log_{10} y.$$

This rule can be described in words as:

$\log_{10} y$ is the power that 10 must be raised to in order to obtain y.

For example, $\log_{10} 100 = 2$ since $100 = 10^2$.

$y = 10^x$ and $y = \log_{10} x$ are inverse functions.

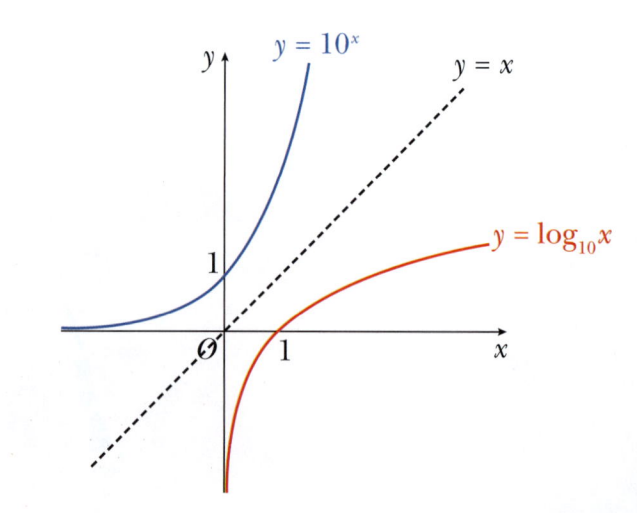

Chapter 6: Logarithmic and exponential functions

CLASS DISCUSSION

Discuss with your classmates why each of these four statements is true.

$\log_{10} 10 = 1$ $\log_{10} 1 = 0$ $\log_{10} 10^x = x$ for $x \in \mathbb{R}$ $x = 10^{\log_{10} x}$ for $x > 0$

WORKED EXAMPLE 1

a Convert $10^x = 45$ to logarithmic form.
b Solve $10^x = 45$ giving your answer correct to 3 sf.

a Method 1
$10^x = 45$
Step 1: Identify the base and index: The base is 10. The index is x.
Step 2: Start to write in log form: In log form the index always goes on its own and the base goes at the base of the logarithm. So $x = \log_{10}?$
Step 3: Complete the log form: Fill in the last number. $x = \log_{10} 45$
So $x = \log_{10} 45$.

Method 2
$10^x = 45$
$\log_{10} 10^x = \log_{10} 45$ Take logs to base 10 of both sides. $\log_{10} 10^x = x$
$x = \log_{10} 45$

b $10^x = 45$
$x = \log_{10} 45$
$x \approx 1.65$

Cambridge IGCSE and O Level Additional Mathematics

WORKED EXAMPLE 2

a Convert $\log_{10} x = 2.9$ to exponential form.
b Solve $\log_{10} x = 2.9$ giving your answer correct to 3 sf.

Answers

a Method 1
$\log_{10} x = 2.9$

Step 1: Identify the base and index: The base is 10. The index is 2.9.
(In log form the index is always on its own.)

Step 2: Start to write in exponential form: Write the base and the index first.
So $10^{2.9} = ?$

Step 3: Complete the exponential form: $x = 10^{2.9}$
So $x = 10^{2.9}$

Method 2
$\log_{10} x = 2.9$
$10^{\log_{10} x} = 10^{2.9}$ $\quad 10^{\log_{10} x} = x$
$x = 10^{2.9}$

b $\log_{10} x = 2.9$
$x = 10^{2.9}$
$x \approx 794$

WORKED EXAMPLE 3

Find the value of
a $\log_{10} 100\,000$ **b** $\log_{10} 0.001$ **c** $\log_{10} 100\sqrt{10}$.

Answers

a $\log_{10} 100\,000 = \log_{10} 10^5$ write 100 000 as a power of 10, $100\,000 = 10^5$
$\qquad\qquad\quad = 5$

b $\log_{10} 0.001 = \log_{10} 10^{-3}$ write 0.001 as a power of 10, $0.001 = 10^{-3}$
$\qquad\qquad = -3$

c $\log_{10} 100\sqrt{10} = \log_{10} 10^{2.5}$ write $100\sqrt{10}$ as a power of 10
$\qquad\qquad\quad = 2.5$ $100\sqrt{10} = 10^2 \times 10^{0.5} = 10^{2.5}$

Exercise 6.1

1 Convert from exponential form to logarithmic form.
  a $10^3 = 1000$
  b $10^2 = 100$
  c $10^6 = 1\,000\,000$
  d $10^x = 2$
  e $10^x = 15$
  f $10^x = 0.06$

2 Solve each of these equations, giving your answers correct to 3 sf.
  a $10^x = 75$
  b $10^x = 300$
  c $10^x = 720$
  d $10^x = 15.6$
  e $10^x = 0.02$
  f $10^x = 0.005$

3 Convert from logarithmic form to exponential form.
  a $\lg 100\,000 = 5$
  b $\lg 10 = 1$
  c $\lg \dfrac{1}{1000} = -3$
  d $\lg x = 7.5$
  e $\lg x = 1.7$
  f $\lg x = -0.8$

4 Solve each of these equations, giving your answers correct to 3 sf.
  a $\lg x = 5.1$
  b $\lg x = 3.16$
  c $\lg x = 2.16$
  d $\lg x = -0.3$
  e $\lg x = -1.5$
  f $\lg x = -2.84$

5 Without using a calculator, find the value of
  a $\lg 10\,000$
  b $\lg 0.01$
  c $\lg \sqrt{10}$
  d $\lg \left(\sqrt[3]{10}\right)$
  e $\lg \left(10\sqrt{10}\right)$
  f $\lg \left(\dfrac{1000}{\sqrt{10}}\right)$.

6.2 Logarithms to base a

In the last section you learnt about logarithms to the base of 10.

The same principles can be applied to define logarithms in other bases.

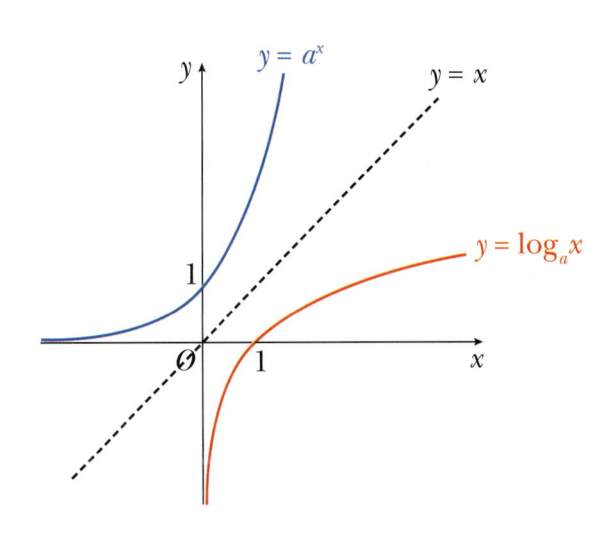

If $y = a^x$ then $x = \log_a y$.
$\log_a a = 1$ $\log_a 1 = 0$
$\log_a a^x = x$ $x = a^{\log_a x}$

The conditions for $\log_a x$ to be defined are:
- $a > 0$ and $a \neq 1$
- $x > 0$

Cambridge IGCSE and O Level Additional Mathematics

WORKED EXAMPLE 4

Convert $2^4 = 16$ to logarithmic form.

Answers

Method 1

$2^4 = 16$

Step 1: Identify the base and index: The base is 2. The index is 4.

Step 2: Start to write in log form: In log form the index always goes on its own and the base goes at the base of the logarithm. So $4 = \log_2 ?$

Step 3: Complete the log form: Fill in the last number. $4 = \log_2 16$

So $4 = \log_2 16$.

Method 2

$2^4 = 16$
$\log_2 2^4 = \log_2 16$ Take logs to base 2 of both sides, $\log_2 2^4 = 4$.
$4 = \log_2 16$

WORKED EXAMPLE 5

Convert $\log_7 49 = 2$ to exponential form.

Answers

Method 1

$\log_7 49 = 2$

Step 1: Identify the base and index: The base is 7. The index is 2.
     (In log form the index is always on its own.)

Step 2: Start to write in exponential form: Write the base and the index first. So $7^2 = ?$

Step 3: Complete the exponential form: $7^2 = 49$

So $7^2 = 49$

Method 2

$\log_7 49 = 2$
$7^{\log_7 49} = 7^2$ $7^{\log_7 49} = 49$
$49 = 7^2$

Chapter 6: Logistic and exponential functions

> **WORKED EXAMPLE 6**
>
> Find the value of
> **a** $\log_3 81$ **b** $\log_2 128$ **c** $\log_4 \dfrac{1}{16}$.
>
> **Answers**
>
> **a** $\log_3 81 = \log_3 3^4$ write 81 as a power of 3, $81 = 3^4$
> $= 4$
>
> **b** $\log_2 128 = \log_2 2^7$ write 128 as a power of 2, $128 = 2^7$
> $= 7$
>
> **c** $\log_4 \dfrac{1}{16} = \log_4 4^{-2}$ write $\dfrac{1}{16}$ as a power of 4, $\dfrac{1}{16} = 4^{-2}$
> $= -2$

Exercise 6.2

1 Convert from exponential form to logarithmic form.
    a $4^3 = 64$ **b** $2^5 = 32$ **c** $5^3 = 125$
    d $6^2 = 36$ **e** $2^{-5} = \dfrac{1}{32}$ **f** $3^{-4} = \dfrac{1}{81}$
    g $a^2 = b$ **h** $x^y = 4$ **i** $a^b = c$

2 Convert from logarithmic form to exponential form.
    a $\log_2 4 = 2$ **b** $\log_2 64 = 6$ **c** $\log_5 1 = 0$
    d $\log_3 9 = 2$ **e** $\log_{36} 6 = \dfrac{1}{2}$ **f** $\log_8 2 = \dfrac{1}{3}$
    g $\log_x 1 = 0$ **h** $\log_x 8 = y$ **i** $\log_a b = c$

3 Solve.
    a $\log_2 x = 4$ **b** $\log_3 x = 2$ **c** $\log_5 x = 4$
    d $\log_3 x = \dfrac{1}{2}$ **e** $\log_x 144 = 2$ **f** $\log_x 27 = 3$
    g $\log_2(x-1) = 4$ **h** $\log_3(2x+1) = 2$ **i** $\log_5(2-3x) = 3$

4 Find the value of:
    a $\log_4 16$ **b** $\log_3 81$ **c** $\log_4 64$ **d** $\log_2 0.25$
    e $\log_3 243$ **f** $\log_2(8\sqrt{2})$ **g** $\log_5(25\sqrt{5})$ **h** $\log_2\left(\dfrac{1}{\sqrt{8}}\right)$
    i $\log_{64} 8$ **j** $\log_7\left(\dfrac{\sqrt{7}}{7}\right)$ **k** $\log_5 \sqrt[3]{5}$ **l** $\log_3 \dfrac{1}{\sqrt{3}}$

5 Simplify.
    a $\log_x x^2$ **b** $\log_x \sqrt[3]{x}$ **c** $\log_x(x\sqrt{x})$ **d** $\log_x \dfrac{1}{x^2}$
    e $\log_x\left(\dfrac{1}{x^2}\right)^3$ **f** $\log_x(\sqrt{x^7})$ **g** $\log_x\left(\dfrac{x}{\sqrt[3]{x}}\right)$ **h** $\log_x\left(\dfrac{x\sqrt{x}}{\sqrt[3]{x}}\right)$

6 Solve.
    a $\log_3(\log_2 x) = 1$ **b** $\log_2(\log_5 x) = 2$

Cambridge IGCSE and O Level Additional Mathematics

6.3 The laws of logarithms

If x and y are both positive and $a > 0$ and $a \neq 1$, then the following **laws of logarithms** can be used:

Multiplication law

$$\log_a(xy) = \log_a x + \log_a y$$

Division law

$$\log_a\left(\frac{x}{y}\right) = \log_a x - \log_a y$$

Power law

$$\log_a(x)^m = m \log_a x$$

Proofs:

$\log_a(xy)$
$= \log_a\left(a^{\log_a x} \times a^{\log_a y}\right)$
$= \log_a\left(a^{\log_a x + \log_a y}\right)$
$= \log_a x + \log_a y$

$\log_a\left(\dfrac{x}{y}\right)$
$= \log_a\left(\dfrac{a^{\log_a x}}{a^{\log_a y}}\right)$
$= \log_a\left(a^{\log_a x - \log_a y}\right)$
$= \log_a x - \log_a y$

$\log_a(x)^m$
$= \log_a\left(\left(a^{\log_a x}\right)^m\right)$
$= \log_a\left(a^{m \log_a x}\right)$
$= m \log_a x$

Using the power law, $\log_a\left(\dfrac{1}{x}\right) = \log_a x^{-1}$

$\qquad\qquad\qquad\qquad\qquad = -\log_a x$

This gives another useful rule to remember:

$$\log_a\left(\frac{1}{x}\right) = -\log_a x$$

WORKED EXAMPLE 7

Use the laws of logarithms to simplify these expressions.

a $\lg 3 + \lg 2$
b $\log_4 15 \div \log_4 5$
c $2\log_3 4 + 5 \log_3 2$

Answers

a $\lg 3 + \lg 2$
$= \lg(3 \times 2)$
$= \lg 6$

b $\log_4 15 \div \log_4 5$
$= \log_4\left(\dfrac{15}{5}\right)$
$= \log_4 3$

c $2\log_3 4 + 5 \log_3 2$
$= \log_3 4^2 + \log_3 2^5$
$= \log_3(16 \times 32)$
$= \log_3 512$

Chapter 6: Logarithmic and exponential functions

> **WORKED EXAMPLE 8**
>
> Given that $\log_5 p = x$ and $\log_5 q = y$, express in terms of x and/or y
>
> **a** $\log_5 p + \log_5 q^3$ **b** $\log_5 p^2 - \log_5 \sqrt{q}$ **c** $\log_5\left(\dfrac{q}{5}\right)$
>
> **Answers**
>
> **a** $\log_5 p + \log_5 q^3$
> $= \log_5 p + 3\log_5 q$
> $= x + 3y$
>
> **b** $\log_5 p^2 - \log_5 \sqrt{q}$
> $= 2\log_5 p - \dfrac{1}{2}\log_5 q$
> $= 2x - \dfrac{1}{2}y$
>
> **c** $\log_5\left(\dfrac{q}{5}\right)$
> $= \log_5 q - \log_5 5$
> $= y - 1$

Exercise 6.3

1 Write as a single logarithm.
   a $\log_2 5 + \log_2 3$ **b** $\log_3 12 - \log_3 2$ **c** $3\log_5 2 + \log_5 8$
   d $2\log_7 4 - 3\log_7 2$ **e** $\dfrac{1}{2}\log_3 25 + \log_3 4$ **f** $2\log_7\left(\dfrac{1}{4}\right) + \log_7 8$
   g $1 + \log_4 3$ **h** $\lg 5 - 2$ **i** $3 - \log_4 10$

2 Write as a single logarithm, then simplify your answer.
   a $\log_2 56 - \log_2 7$ **b** $\log_6 12 + \log_6 3$ **c** $\dfrac{1}{2}\log_2 36 - \log_2 3$
   d $\log_3 15 - \dfrac{1}{2}\log_3 25$ **e** $\log_4 40 - \dfrac{1}{3}\log_4 125$ **f** $\dfrac{1}{2}\log_3 16 - 2\log_3 6$

3 Simplify.
   a $2\log_5 3 - \dfrac{1}{2}\log_5 4 + \log_5 8$ **b** $2 + \dfrac{1}{2}\log_2 49 - \log_2 21$

4 **a** Express 16 and 0.25 as powers of 2.
   b Hence, simplify $\dfrac{\log_3 16}{\log_3 0.25}$.

5 Simplify.
   a $\dfrac{\log_7 4}{\log_7 2}$ **b** $\dfrac{\log_7 27}{\log_7 3}$ **c** $\dfrac{\log_3 64}{\log_3 0.25}$ **d** $\dfrac{\log_5 100}{\log_5 0.01}$

6 Given that $u = \log_5 x$, find, in simplest form in terms of u
   a x **b** $\log_5\left(\dfrac{x}{25}\right)$ **c** $\log_5(5\sqrt{x})$ **d** $\log_5\left(\dfrac{x\sqrt{x}}{125}\right)$.

7 Given that $\log_4 p = x$ and $\log_4 q = y$, express in terms of x and/or y
   a $\log_4(4p)$ **b** $\log_4\left(\dfrac{16}{p}\right)$ **c** $\log_4 p + \log_4 q^2$ **d** pq.

8 Given that $\log_a x = 5$ and $\log_a y = 8$, find
   a $\log_a\left(\dfrac{1}{y}\right)$ **b** $\log_a\left(\dfrac{\sqrt{x}}{y}\right)$ **c** $\log_a(xy)$ **d** $\log_a(x^2 y^3)$.

9 Given that $\log_a x = 12$ and $\log_a y = 4$, find the value of
   a $\log_a\left(\dfrac{x}{y}\right)$ **b** $\log_a\left(\dfrac{x^2}{y}\right)$ **c** $\log_a(x\sqrt{y})$ **d** $\log_a\left(\dfrac{y}{\sqrt[3]{x}}\right)$.

6.4 Solving logarithmic equations

You have already learnt how to solve simple logarithmic equations.

In this section you will learn how to solve more complicated equations.

It is essential, when solving equations involving logs, that all roots are checked in the original equation.

> **WORKED EXAMPLE 9**
>
> Solve.
>
> **a** $2\log_8(x+2) = \log_8(2x+19)$ **b** $4\log_x 2 - \log_x 4 = 8$
>
> **Answers**
>
> **a** $2\log_8(x+2) = \log_8(2x+19)$ use the power law
> $\log_8(x+2)^2 = \log_8(2x+19)$ use equality of logarithms
> $(x+2)^2 = 2x+19$ expand brackets
> $x^2 + 4x + 4 = 2x + 19$
> $x^2 + 2x - 15 = 0$
> $(x-3)(x+5) = 0$
> $x = 3$ or $x = -5$
>
> Check when $x = 3$: $2\log_8(x+2) = 2\log_8 5 = \log_8 25$ is defined
> $\log_8(2x+19) = \log_8 25$ is defined
>
> So $x = 3$ is a solution, since both sides of the equation are defined and equivalent in value.
>
> Check when $x = -5$: $2\log_8(x+2) = 2\log_8(-3)$ is not defined
> So $x = -5$ is not a solution of the original equation.
> Hence, the solution is $x = 3$.
>
> **b** $4\log_x 2 - \log_x 4 = 2$ use the power law
> $\log_x 2^4 - \log_x 2^2 = 2$ use the division law
> $\log_x 2^{4-2} = 2$
> $\log_x 2^2 = 2$
> $\log_x 4 = 2$ convert to exponential form
> $x^2 = 4$
> $x = \pm 2$
>
> Since logarithms only exist for positive bases, $x = -2$ is not a solution.
>
> Check when $x = 2$: $4\log_2 2 - \log_2 4 = 4 - 2\log_2 2$
> $= 4 - 2$
> $= 2$
>
> So $x = 2$ satisfies the original equation.
> Hence, the solution is $x = 2$.

Exercise 6.4

1 Solve.

  a $\log_2 x + \log_2 4 = \log_2 20$ **b** $\log_4 2x - \log_4 5 = \log_4 3$

  c $\log_4(x-5) + \log_4 5 = 2\log_4 10$ **d** $\log_3(x+3) = 2\log_3 4 + \log_3 5$

2 Solve.

  a $\log_6 x + \log_6 3 = 2$ **b** $\lg(5x) - \lg(x-4) = 1$

  c $\log_2(x+4) = 1 + \log_2(x-3)$ **d** $\log_3(2x+3) = 2 + \log_3(2x-5)$

  e $\log_5(10x+3) - \log_5(2x-1) = 2$ **f** $\lg(4x+5) + 2\lg 2 = 1 + \lg(2x-1)$

3 Solve.

  a $\log_5(x+8) + \log_5(x+2) = \log_5 20x$ **b** $\log_3 x + \log_3(x-2) = \log_3 15$

  c $2\log_4 x - \log_4(x+3) = 1$ **d** $\lg x + \lg(x+1) = \lg 20$

  e $\log_3 x + \log_3(2x-5) = 1$ **f** $3 + 2\log_2 x = \log_2(14x-3)$

  g $\lg(x+5) + \lg 2x = 2$ **h** $\lg x + \lg(x-15) = 2$

4 Solve.

  a $\log_x 64 - \log_x 4 = 1$ **b** $\log_x 16 + \log_x 4 = 3$

  c $\log_x 4 - 2\log_x 3 = 2$ **d** $\log_x 15 = 2 + \log_x 5$

5 Solve.

  a $(\log_5 x)^2 - 3\log_5(x) + 2 = 0$ **b** $(\log_5 x)^2 - \log_5(x^2) = 15$

  c $(\log_5 x)^2 - \log_5(x^3) = 18$ **d** $2(\log_2 x)^2 + 5\log_2(x^2) = 72$

CHALLENGE Q

6 Solve the simultaneous equations.

  a $xy = 64$ **b** $2^x = 4^y$
       $\log_x y = 2$ $2\lg y = \lg x + \lg 5$

  c $\log_4(x+y) = 2\log_4 x$ **d** $xy = 640$
       $\log_4 y = \log_4 3 + \log_4 x$ $2\log_{10} x - \log_{10} y = 2$

  e $\log_{10} a = 2\log_{10} b$ **f** $4^{xy} = 2^{x+5}$
       $\log_{10}(2a-b) = 1$ $\log_2 y - \log_2 x = 1$

CHALLENGE Q

7 **a** Show that $\lg(x^2 y) = 18$ can be written as $2\lg x + \lg y = 18$.

   b $\lg(x^2 y) = 18$ and $\lg\left(\dfrac{x}{y^3}\right) = 2$.

   Find the value of $\lg x$ and $\lg y$.

6.5 Solving exponential equations

In Chapter 4 you learnt how to solve exponential equations whose terms could be converted to the same base. In this section you will learn how to solve exponential equations whose terms cannot be converted to the same base.

> **WORKED EXAMPLE 10**
>
> Solve, giving your answers correct to 3 sf.
> **a** $3^x = 40$ **b** $5^{2x+1} = 200$
>
> **Answers**
>
> **a** $\quad 3^x = 40$ $\qquad$ take logs of both sides
> $\quad \lg 3^x = \lg 40$ $\qquad$ use the power rule
> $\quad x \lg 3 = \lg 40$ $\qquad$ divide both sides by $\lg 3$
> $\quad x = \dfrac{\lg 40}{\lg 3}$
> $\quad x \approx 3.36$
>
> **b** $\quad 5^{2x+1} = 200$ $\qquad$ take logs of both sides
> $\quad \lg 5^{2x+1} = \lg 200$ $\qquad$ use the power rule
> $\quad (2x+1) \lg 5 = \lg 200$ $\qquad$ divide both sides by $\lg 5$
> $\quad 2x + 1 = \dfrac{\lg 200}{\lg 5}$
> $\quad 2x + 1 = 3.292\ldots$
> $\quad 2x = 2.292\ldots$
> $\quad x \approx 1.15$

> **WORKED EXAMPLE 11**
>
> Solve $3(2^{2x}) - 2^{x+1} - 8 = 0$.
>
> **Answers**
>
> $3(2^{2x}) - 2^{x+1} - 8 = 0$ $\qquad$ replace 2^{x+1} with $2(2^x)$
> $3(2^{2x}) - 2(2^x) - 8 = 0$ $\qquad$ use the substitution $y = 2^x$
> $3y^2 - 2y - 8 = 0$ $\qquad$ factorise
> $(y - 2)(3y + 4) = 0$
>
> When $y = 2$
> $\quad 2 = 2^x$
> $\quad x = 1$
>
> When $y = -\dfrac{4}{3}$
> $\quad -\dfrac{4}{3} = 2^x$ $\qquad$ there are no solutions to this equation since 2^x is always positive
>
> Hence, the solution is $x = 1$.

Chapter 6: Logarithmic and exponential functions

Exercise 6.5

1 Solve, giving your answers correct to 3 sf.
   - **a** $2^x = 70$
   - **b** $3^x = 20$
   - **c** $5^x = 4$
   - **d** $2^{3x} = 150$
   - **e** $3^{x+1} = 55$
   - **f** $2^{2x+1} = 20$
   - **g** $7^{x-5} = 40$
   - **h** $7^x = 3^{x+4}$
   - **i** $5^{x+1} = 3^{x+2}$
   - **j** $4^{x-1} = 5^{x+1}$
   - **k** $3^{2x+3} = 5^{3x+1}$
   - **l** $3^{4-5x} = 2^{x+4}$

2 **a** Show that $2^{x+1} - 2^{x-1} = 15$ can be written as $2(2^x) - \frac{1}{2}(2^x) = 15$.
   b Hence find the value of 2^x.
   c Find the value of x.

3 Solve, giving your answers correct to 3 sf.
   - **a** $2^{x+2} - 2^x = 4$
   - **b** $2^{x+1} - 2^{x-1} - 8 = 0$
   - **c** $3^{x+1} - 8(3^{x-1}) - 5 = 0$
   - **d** $2^{x+2} - 2^{x-3} = 12$
   - **e** $5^x - 5^{x+2} + 125 = 0$

4 Use the substitution $y = 3^x$ to solve the equation $3^{2x} + 2 = 5(3^x)$.

5 Solve, giving your answers correct to 3 sf.
   - **a** $3^{2x} - 6 \times 3^x + 5 = 0$
   - **b** $4^{2x} - 6 \times 4^x - 7 = 0$
   - **c** $2^{2x} - 2^x - 20 = 0$
   - **d** $5^{2x} - 2(5^x) - 3 = 0$

6 Use the substitution $u = 5^x$ to solve the equation $5^{2x} - 2(5^{x+1}) + 21 = 0$.

7 Solve, giving your answers correct to 3 sf.
   - **a** $2^{2x} + 2^{x+1} - 15 = 0$
   - **b** $6^{2x} - 6^{x+1} + 7 = 0$
   - **c** $3^{2x} - 2(3^{x+1}) + 8 = 0$
   - **d** $4^{2x+1} = 17(4^x) - 15$

8 Solve, giving your answers correct to 3 sf.
   - **a** $4^x - 3(2^x) - 10 = 0$
   - **b** $16^x + 2(4^x) - 35 = 0$
   - **c** $9^x - 2(3^{x+1}) + 8 = 0$
   - **d** $25^x + 20 = 12(5^x)$

CHALLENGE Q

9 $3^{2x+1} \times 5^{x-1} = 27^x \times 5^{2x}$

Find the value of **a** 15^x **b** x.

6.6 Change of base of logarithms

You sometimes need to change the base of a logarithm.

A logarithm in base b can be written with a different base c using the **change of base rule**.

If $a, b, c > 0$ and $b, c \neq 1$, then:

$$\log_b a = \frac{\log_c a}{\log_c b}$$

Proof:

If $x = \log_b a$, then $b^x = a$ take logs of both sides

$\log_c b^x = \log_c a$ use the power rule

$x \log_c b = \log_c a$ divide both sides by $\log_c b$

$$x = \frac{\log_c a}{\log_c b}$$

$$\log_b a = \frac{\log_c a}{\log_c b}$$

If $c = a$ in the change of base rule, then the rule gives:

$$\log_b a = \frac{1}{\log_a b}$$

WORKED EXAMPLE 12

Change $\log_2 7$ to base 10. Hence evaluate $\log_2 7$ correct to 3 sf.

Answers

$\log_2 7 = \dfrac{\lg 7}{\lg 2} \approx 2.81$

Note:
Some calculators have a $\boxed{\log_\blacksquare \square}$ key.
This can be used to evaluate $\log_2 7$ directly.

The change of base rule can be used to solve equations involving logarithms with different bases.

WORKED EXAMPLE 13

Solve $\log_3 x = \log_9(x+6)$.

Answers

$\log_3 x = \log_9(x+6)$ change $\log_9(x+6)$ to base 3

$\log_3 x = \dfrac{\log_3(x+6)}{\log_3 9}$ $\log_3 9 = \log_3 3^2 = 2$

$\log_3 x = \dfrac{\log_3(x+6)}{2}$ multiply both sides by 2

$2\log_3 x = \log_3(x+6)$ use the power rule

$\log_3 x^2 = \log_3(x+6)$ use equality of logs

$x^2 = x+6$

$x^2 - x - 6 = 0$

$(x-3)(x+2) = 0$

$x = 3$ or $x = -2$

Check when $x = 3$: $\log_3 3$ is defined and is equal to 1

                     $\log_9(3+6) = \log_9 9$ is defined and is equal to 1

So $x = 3$ is a solution, since both sides of the equation are defined and equivalent in value.

Check when $x = -2$: $\log_3(-2)$ is not defined

So $x = -2$ is not a solution of the original equation.

Hence, the solution is $x = 3$.

Exercise 6.6

1 Use the rule $\log_b a = \dfrac{\log_{10} a}{\log_{10} b}$ to evaluate these correct to 3 sf.

    a $\log_2 10$ **b** $\log_3 33$ **c** $\log_5 8$ **d** $\log_7 0.0025$

2 Given that $u = \log_4 x$, find, in simplest form in terms of u.

    a $\log_x 4$,   **b** $\log_x 16$,   **c** $\log_x 2$,   **d** $\log_x 8$.

3 Given that $\log_9 y = x$, express in terms of x.

    a $\log_y 9$,   **b** $\log_9(9y)$,   **c** $\log_3 y$,   **d** $\log_3(81y)$.

4 **a** Given that $\log_p x = 20$ and $\log_p y = 5$, find $\log_y x$.

    b Given that $\log_p X = 15$ and $\log_p Y = 6$, find the value of $\log_X Y$.

5 Evaluate $\log_p 2 \times \log_8 p$.

6 Solve.

    a $\log_9 3 + \log_9(x+4) = \log_5 25$ **b** $2\log_4 2 + \log_7(2x+3) = \log_3 27$

7 **a** Express $\log_4 x$ in terms of $\log_2 x$.

    b Using your answer of **part a**, and the substitution $u = \log_2 x$, solve the equation $\log_4 x + \log_2 x = 12$.

8 Solve.

   a $\log_2 x + 5\log_4 x = 14$
   b $\log_3 x + 2\log_9 x = 4$
   c $5\log_2 x - \log_4 x = 3$
   d $4\log_3 x = \log_9 x + 2$

9 a Express $\log_x 3$ in terms of a logarithm to base 3.

   b Using your answer of **part a**, and the substitution $u = \log_3 x$, solve the equation $\log_3 x = 3 - 2\log_x 3$.

10 Solve.

   a $\log_3 x = 9\log_x 3$
   b $\log_5 x + \log_x 5 = 2$
   c $\log_4 x - 4\log_x 4 + 3 = 0$
   d $\log_4 x + 6\log_x 4 - 5 = 0$
   e $\log_2 x - 9\log_x 2 = 8$
   f $\log_5 y = 4 - 4\log_y 5$

11 a Express $\log_4 x$ in terms of $\log_2 x$.

   b Express $\log_8 y$ in terms of $\log_2 y$.

   c Hence solve, the simultaneous equations
   $6\log_4 x + 3\log_8 y = 16$
   $\log_2 x - 2\log_4 y = 4$.

> **CHALLENGE Q**
>
> 12 Solve the simultaneous equations
> $2\log_3 y = \log_5 125 + \log_3 x$
> $2^y = 4^x$.

6.7 Natural logarithms

There is another type of logarithm to a special base called e.

The number e is an irrational number and $e \approx 2.718$.

The number e is a very important number in mathematics as it has very special properties. You will learn about these special properties in Chapters 15 and 16.

Logarithms to the base of e are called **natural logarithms**.

ln x is used to represent $\log_e x$.

If $y = e^x$ then $x = \ln y$.

$y = \ln x$ is the reflection of $y = e^x$ in the line $y = x$.
$y = \ln x$ and $y = e^x$ are inverse functions.

All the rules of logarithms that you have learnt so far also apply for natural logarithms.

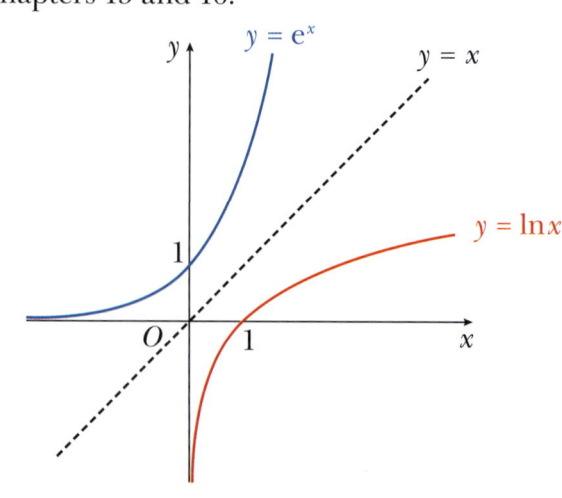

Exercise 6.7

1. Use a calculator to evaluate correct to 3 sf.
   a e^2 b $e^{1.5}$ c $e^{0.2}$ d e^{-3}

2. Use a calculator to evaluate correct to 3 sf.
   a $\ln 4$ b $\ln 2.1$ c $\ln 0.7$ d $\ln 0.39$

3. Without using a calculator find the value of
   a $e^{\ln 5}$ b $e^{\frac{1}{2}\ln 64}$ c $3e^{\ln 2}$ d $-e^{-\ln \frac{1}{2}}$

4. Solve.
   a $e^{\ln x} = 7$ b $\ln e^x = 2.5$ c $e^{2\ln x} = 36$ d $e^{-\ln x} = 20$

5. Solve, giving your answers correct to 3 sf.
   a $e^x = 70$ b $e^{2x} = 28$ c $e^{x+1} = 16$ d $e^{2x-1} = 5$

6. Solve, giving your answers in terms of natural logarithms.
   a $e^x = 7$ b $2e^x + 1 = 7$ c $e^{2x-5} = 3$ d $\frac{1}{2}e^{3x-1} = 4$

7. Solve, giving your answers correct to 3 sf.
   a $\ln x = 3$ b $\ln x = -2$ c $\ln(x+1) = 7$ d $\ln(2x-5) = 3$

8. Solve, giving your answers correct to 3 sf.
   a $\ln x^3 + \ln x = 5$ b $e^{3x+4} = 2e^{x-1}$ c $\ln(x+5) - \ln x = 3$

9. Solve, giving your answers in exact form.
   a $\ln(x-3) = 2$ b $e^{2x-1} = 7$ c $e^{2x} - 4e^x = 0$
   d $e^x = 2e^{-x}$ e $e^{2x} - 9e^x + 20 = 0$ f $e^x + 6e^{-x} = 5$

10. Solve, giving your answers correct to 3 sf.
    a $e^{2x} - 2e^x - 24 = 0$ b $e^{2x} - 5e^x + 4 = 0$ c $e^x + 2e^{-x} = 80$

11. Solve the simultaneous equations, giving your answers in exact form.
    a $\ln x = 2\ln y$
    $\ln y - \ln x = 1$
    b $e^{5x-y} = 3e^{3x}$
    $e^{2x} = 5e^{x+y}$

6.8 Practical applications of exponential equations

In this section you will see how exponential equations can be applied to real-life situations.

> **WORKED EXAMPLE 14**
>
> The temperature, $T\,°C$, of a hot drink, t minutes after it is made, is given by
> $$T = 75e^{-0.02t} + 20.$$
> **a** Find the temperature of the drink when it was made.
> **b** Find the temperature of the drink when $t = 6$.
> **c** Find the value of t when $T = 65$.
>
> **Answers**
>
> **a** When $t = 0$, $\quad T = 75e^{-0.02 \times 0} + 20$
> $\qquad\qquad\qquad\; = 75e^0 + 20 \qquad$ use $e^0 = 1$
> $\qquad\qquad\qquad\; = 95$
> Temperature of the drink when first made is 95 °C.
>
> **b** When $t = 6$, $\quad T = 75e^{-0.02 \times 6} + 20$
> $\qquad\qquad\qquad\; = 86.5$
> Temperature of the drink when $t = 6$ is 86.5 °C.
>
> **c** When $T = 65$, $\quad 65 = 75e^{-0.02t} + 20 \qquad$ subtract 20 from both sides
> $\qquad\qquad\qquad\; 45 = 75e^{-0.02t} \qquad\qquad\;$ divide both sides by 75
> $\qquad\qquad\qquad\; 0.6 = e^{-0.02t} \qquad\qquad\;\;$ take ln of both sides
> $\qquad\qquad\ln 0.6 = -0.02t \qquad\qquad\;\;$ divide both sides by -0.02
> $\qquad\qquad\qquad\;\; t = \dfrac{\ln 0.6}{-0.02}$
> $\qquad\qquad\qquad\;\; t = 25.5$ to 3 sf

Exercise 6.8

1 At the start of an experiment the number of bacteria was 100.

This number increases so that after t minutes the number of bacteria, N, is given by the formula
$$N = 100 \times 2^t.$$

a Estimate the number of bacteria after 12 minutes.

b Estimate the time, in minutes, it takes for the number of bacteria to exceed 10 000 000.

2 At the beginning of 2015, the population of a species of animals was estimated at 50 000.

This number decreased so that, after a period of n years, the population was
$$50000e^{-0.03n}.$$

a Estimate the population at the beginning of 2020.

b Estimate the year in which the population would be expected to have first decreased to 5000.

3 The volume of water in a container, $V\,\text{cm}^3$, at time t minutes, is given by the formula
$$V = 2000\,e^{-kt}.$$
When $V = 1000$, $t = 15$.
   a Find the value of k.
   b Find the value of V when $t = 22$.

4 A species of fish is introduced to a lake.
The population, N, of this species of fish after t weeks is given by the formula
$$N = 500\,e^{-0.3t}.$$
   a Find the initial population of these fish.
   b Estimate the number of these fish after 6 weeks.
   c Estimate the number of weeks it takes for the number of these fish to have fallen to $\dfrac{1}{2}$ of the number introduced.

5 The value, $\$V$, of a house n years after it was built is given by the formula
$$V = 250\,000\,e^{an}.$$
When $n = 3$, $V = 350\,000$.
   a Find the initial value of this house.
   b Find the value of a.
   c Estimate the number of years for this house to double in value.

6 The area, $A\,\text{cm}^2$, of a patch of mould is measured daily.
The area, n days after the measurements started, is given by the formula
$$A = A_0 b^n.$$
When $n = 2$, $A = 1.8$ and when $n = 3$, $A = 2.4$.
   a Find the value of b.
   b Find the value of A_0 and explain what A_0 represents.
   c Estimate the number of days for the area of this patch of mould to exceed $7\,\text{cm}^2$.

6.9 The graphs of simple logarithmic and exponential functions

You should already know the properties of the graphs $y = e^x$ and $y = \ln x$.

The graph of $y = e^x$

- $y = e^x$ intercepts the y-axis at $(0, 1)$.
- $e^x > 0$ for all values of x.
- When x gets closer to $-\infty$, then y gets closer to 0.
- This can be written as: As $x \to -\infty$, then $y \to 0$.
- The graph is said to be asymptotic to the negative x-axis.
- Also, as $x \to +\infty$, then $y \to +\infty$.

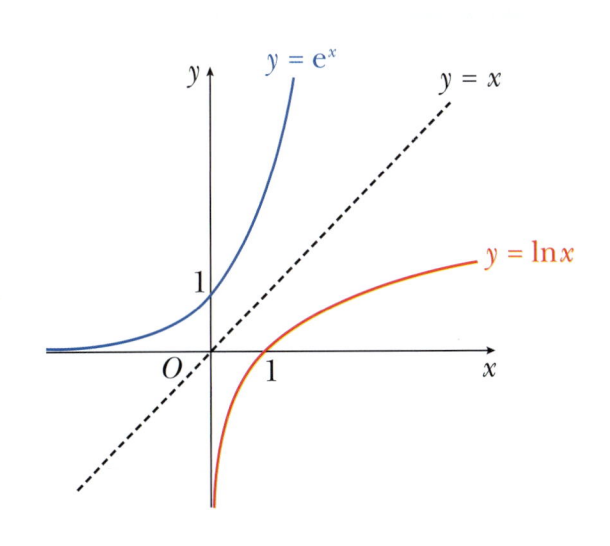

The graph of $y = \ln x$

- $y = \ln x$ intercepts the x-axis at $(1, 0)$.
- $\ln x$ only exists for positive values of x.
- As $x \to 0$, then $y \to -\infty$.
- The graph is asymptotic to the negative y-axis.
- As $x \to +\infty$, then $y \to +\infty$.

$y = e^x$ and $y = \ln x$ are inverse functions, so they are mirror images of each other in the line $y = x$.

Exercise 6.9

1 Use a graphing software package to plot each of the following family of curves for $k = 3, 2, 1, -1, -2$ and -3.

  a $y = e^{kx}$ **b** $y = ke^x$ **c** $y = e^x + k$

  Describe the properties of each family of curves.

2 Use a graphing software package to plot each of the following family of curves for $k = 3, 2, 1, -1, -2$ and -3.

  a $y = \ln kx$ **b** $y = k \ln x$ **c** $y = \ln(x + k)$

  Describe the properties of each family of curves.

6.10 The graphs of $y = ke^{nx} + a$ and $y = k\ln(ax + b)$ where n, k, a and b are integers

> **CLASS DISCUSSION**
>
> Consider the function $y = 2e^{3x} + 1$.
>
> Discuss the following and decide on the missing answers:
>
> 1 When $x = 0$, $y = \ldots$ 4 As $x \to +\infty$, $y \to \ldots$
> 2 The y-intercept is $(\ldots, \ldots)$ 5 As $x \to -\infty$, $y \to \ldots$
> 3 When $y = 0$, x is $\ldots$ 6 The line $y = \ldots$ is an $\ldots$
>
> Now sketch the graph of $y = 2e^{3x} + 1$ and compare your answer with your classmates.
>
> (Remember to show any axis crossing points and asymptotes on your sketch graph.)

WORKED EXAMPLE 15

Sketch the graph of $y = 3e^{-2x} - 5$.

Answers

When $x = 0$, $y = 3e^0 - 5$
$= 3 - 5$
$= -2$ hence the y-intercept is $(0, -2)$

When $y = 0$, $0 = 3e^{-2x} - 5$

$$\frac{5}{3} = e^{-2x}$$

$$\ln\left(\frac{5}{3}\right) = -2x$$

$$x = -\frac{1}{2}\ln\left(\frac{5}{3}\right)$$

$x \approx -0.255$ hence the x-intercept is $(-0.255, 0)$

As $x \to +\infty$, $e^{-2x} \to 0$ so $y \to -5$ hence the asymptote is $y = -5$

As $x \to -\infty$, $e^{-2x} \to \infty$ so $y \to \infty$

The sketch graph of $y = 3e^{-2x} - 5$ is:

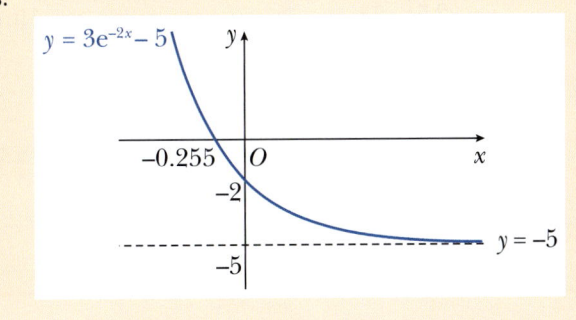

Cambridge IGCSE and O Level Additional Mathematics

WORKED EXAMPLE 16

Sketch the graph of $y = 4\ln(2x + 5)$.

Answers

When $x = 0$, $y = 4\ln 5$,
≈ 6.44 hence the y-intercept is $(0, 4\ln 5)$

When $y = 0$, $0 = 4\ln(2x + 5)$
$0 = \ln(2x + 5)$
$e^0 = 2x + 5$
$1 = 2x + 5$
$x = -2$ hence the x-intercept is $(-2, 0)$

$\ln x$ only exists for positive values of x.
So $4\ln(2x + 5)$ only exists for $2x + 5 > 0$
$x > -2.5$.

As $x \to +\infty$, $y \to \infty$
As $x \to -2.5$, $y \to -\infty$ hence the asymptote is $x = -2.5$

The sketch graph of $y = 4\ln(2x + 5)$ is:

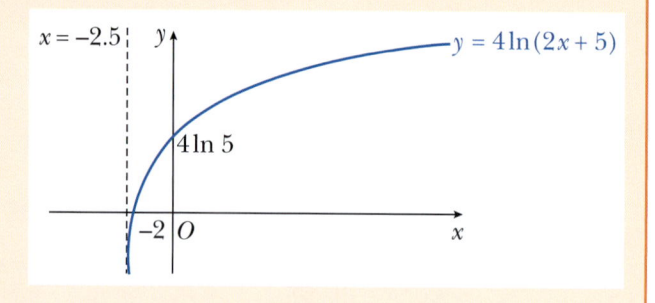

Exercise 6.10

1 Sketch the graphs of each of the following exponential functions.
[Remember to show the axis crossing points and the asymptotes.]

     a $y = 2e^x - 4$ **b** $y = 3e^x + 6$ **c** $y = 5e^x + 2$

     d $y = 2e^{-x} + 6$ **e** $y = 3e^{-x} - 1$ **f** $y = -2e^{-x} + 4$

     g $y = 4e^{2x} + 1$ **h** $y = 2e^{-5x} + 8$ **i** $y = -e^{4x} + 2$

2 Sketch the graphs of each of the following logarithmic functions.
[Remember to show the axis crossing points and the asymptotes.]

     a $y = \ln(2x + 4)$ **b** $y = \ln(3x - 6)$ **c** $y = \ln(8 - 2x)$

     d $y = 2\ln(2x + 2)$ **e** $y = 4\ln(2x - 4)$ **f** $y = -3\ln(6x - 9)$

6.11 The inverse of logarithmic and exponential functions

In Chapter 2 you learnt how to find the inverse of a one-one function.

This section shows you how to find the inverse of exponential and logarithmic functions.

> **WORKED EXAMPLE 17**
>
> Find the inverse of each function and state its domain.
> **a** $f(x) = 2e^{-4x} + 3$ for $x \in \mathbb{R}$ **b** $f(x) = 3\ln(2x - 4)$ for $x > 2$
>
> **Answers**
>
> **a** $f(x) = 2e^{-4x} + 3$ for $x \in \mathbb{R}$
>
> Step 1: Write the function as $y = \longrightarrow \quad y = 2e^{-4x} + 3$
>
> Step 2: Interchange the x and y variables. $\longrightarrow \quad x = 2e^{-4y} + 3$
>
> Step 3: Rearrange to make y the subject. $\longrightarrow \quad x - 3 = 2e^{-4y}$
>
> $$\frac{x-3}{2} = e^{-4y}$$
>
> $$\ln\left(\frac{x-3}{2}\right) = -4y$$
>
> $$y = -\frac{1}{4}\ln\left(\frac{x-3}{2}\right)$$
>
> $f^{-1}(x) = -\frac{1}{4}\ln\left(\frac{x-3}{2}\right)$ for $x > 3$
>
> **b** $f(x) = 3\ln(2x - 4),\ x > 2$
>
> Step 1: Write the function as $y = \longrightarrow \quad y = 3\ln(2x - 4)$
>
> Step 2: Interchange the x and y variables. $\longrightarrow \quad x = 3\ln(2y - 4)$
>
> Step 3: Rearrange to make y the subject. $\longrightarrow \quad \frac{x}{3} = \ln(2y - 4)$
>
> $$e^{\frac{x}{3}} = 2y - 4$$
>
> $$2y = e^{\frac{x}{3}} + 4$$
>
> $$y = \frac{1}{2}e^{\frac{x}{3}} + 2$$
>
> $f^{-1}(x) = \frac{1}{2}e^{\frac{x}{3}} + 2$ for $x \in \mathbb{R}$

Exercise 6.11

1 The following functions are each defined for $x \in \mathbb{R}$.

Find $f^{-1}(x)$ for each function and state its domain.

a $f(x) = e^x + 4$ **b** $f(x) = e^x - 2$ **c** $f(x) = 5e^x - 1$

d $f(x) = 3e^{2x} + 1$ **e** $f(x) = 5e^{2x} + 3$ **f** $f(x) = 4e^{-3x} + 5$

g $f(x) = 2 - e^x$ **h** $f(x) = 5 - 2e^{-2x}$

2 Find $f^{-1}(x)$ for each function.
  a $f(x) = \ln(x+1), x > -1$
  b $f(x) = \ln(x-3), x > 3$
  c $f(x) = 2\ln(x+2), x > -2$
  d $f(x) = 2\ln(2x+1), x > -\frac{1}{2}$
  e $f(x) = 3\ln(2x-5), x > \frac{5}{2}$
  f $f(x) = -5\ln(3x-1), x > \frac{1}{3}$

3 $f(x) = e^{2x} + 1$ for $x \in \mathbb{R}$
  a State the range of $f(x)$.
  b Find $f^{-1}(x)$.
  c State the domain of $f^{-1}(x)$.
  d Find $f^{-1}f(x)$.

4 $f(x) = e^x$ for $x \in \mathbb{R}$ $g(x) = \ln 5x$ for $x > 0$
  a Find **i** $fg(x)$ **ii** $gf(x)$.
  b Solve $g(x) = 3f^{-1}(x)$.

5 $f(x) = e^{3x}$ for $x \in \mathbb{R}$ $g(x) = \ln x$ for $x > 0$
  a Find **i** $fg(x)$ **ii** $gf(x)$.
  b Solve $f(x) = 2g^{-1}(x)$.

6 $f(x) = e^{2x}$ for $x \in \mathbb{R}$ $g(x) = \ln(2x+1)$ for $x > -\frac{1}{2}$
  a Find $fg(x)$.
  b Solve $f(x) = 8g^{-1}(x)$.

Summary

The rules of logarithms
If $y = a^x$ then $x = \log_a y$.

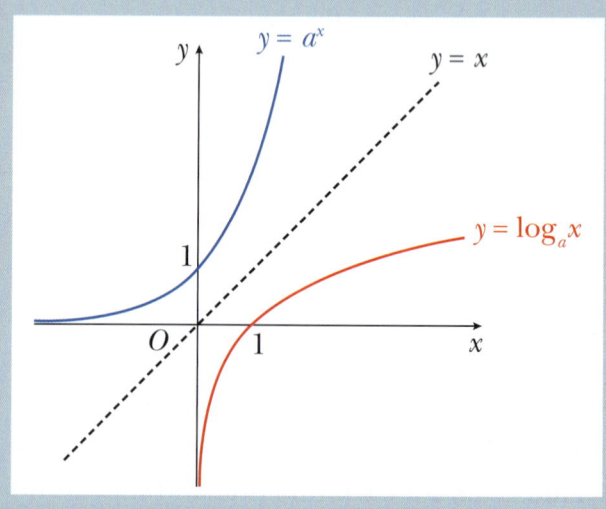

$\log_a a = 1$ $\log_a 1 = 0$

$\log_a a^x = x$ $x = a^{\log_a x}$

Product rule: $\log_a(xy) = \log_a x + \log_a y$

Division rule: $\log_a\left(\dfrac{x}{y}\right) = \log_a x - \log_a y$

Power rule: $\log_a(x)^m = m\log_a x$ $\left[\text{special case: } \log_a\left(\dfrac{1}{x}\right) = -\log_a x\right]$

Change of base: $\log_b a = \dfrac{\log_c a}{\log_c b}$ $\left[\text{special case: } \log_b a = \dfrac{1}{\log_a b}\right]$

Chapter 6: Logarithmic and exponential functions

Natural logarithms

Logarithms to the base of e are called natural logarithms.
ln x is used to represent $\log_e x$.

If $y = e^x$ then $x = \ln y$.

All the rules of logarithms apply for natural logarithms.

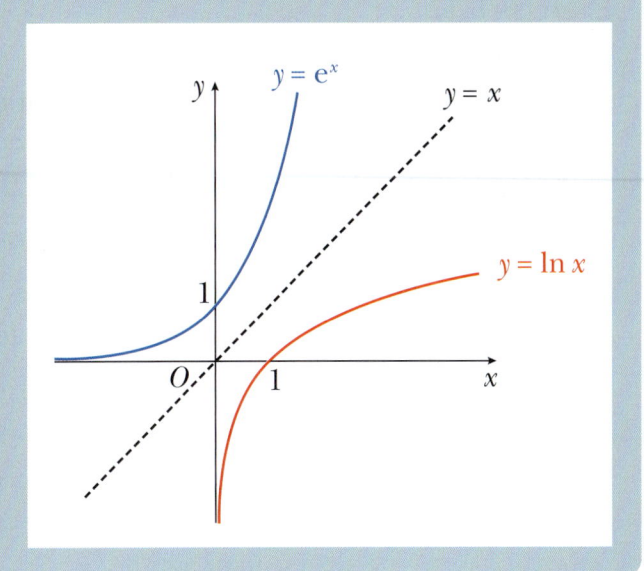

Examination questions

Worked past paper example

By changing the base of $\log_{2a} 4$, express $(\log_{2a} 4)(1 + \log_a 2)$ as a single logarithm to base a. [4]

Cambridge IGCSE Additional Mathematics 0606 Paper 21 Q11b Jun 2014

Answer

$\log_{2a} 4 = \dfrac{\log_a 4}{\log_a 2a}$ use the product rule on the denominator

$= \dfrac{\log_a 4}{\log_a 2 + \log_a a}$ remember that $\log_a a = 1$

$= \dfrac{\log_a 4}{1 + \log_a 2}$

$(\log_{2a} 4)(1 + \log_a 2) = \left(\dfrac{\log_a 4}{1 + \log_a 2}\right)(1 + \log_a 2)$

$= \dfrac{(\log_a 4)(1 + \log_a 2)}{1 + \log_a 2}$ divide numerator and denominator by $(1 + \log_a 2)$

$= \log_a 4$

131

Exercise 6.12
Exam Exercise

1. **a** Using the substitution $y = 5^x$, show that the equation $5^{2x+1} - 5^{x+1} + 2 = 2(5^x)$ can be written in the form $ay^2 + by + 2 = 0$, where a and b are constants to be found. [2]
   b Hence solve the equation $5^{2x+1} - 5^{x+1} + 2 = 2(5^x)$. [4]

   Cambridge IGCSE Additional Mathematics 0606 Paper 11 Q4i,ii Nov 2014

2. Solve the following simultaneous equations.
$$\log_2(x+3) = 2 + \log_2 y$$
$$\log_2(x+y) = 3$$ [5]

   Cambridge IGCSE Additional Mathematics 0606 Paper 21 Q3 Nov 2014

3. Functions g and h are defined by
$$g(x) = 4e^x - 2 \text{ for } x \in \mathbb{R},$$
$$h(x) = \ln 5x \text{ for } x > 0.$$
   a Find $g^{-1}(x)$. [2]
   b Solve $gh(x) = 18$. [3]

   Cambridge IGCSE Additional Mathematics 0606 Paper 11 Q12bi,ii Nov 2013

4. Given that $\log_p X = 5$ and $\log_p Y = 2$, find
   a $\log_p X^2$, [1]
   b $\log_p \dfrac{1}{X}$, [1]
   c $\log_{XY} p$. [2]

   Cambridge IGCSE Additional Mathematics 0606 Paper 21 Q4i,ii,iii Nov 2013

5. **a** Given that $\log_4 x = \dfrac{1}{2}$, find the value of x. [1]
   b Solve $2\log_4 y - \log_4(5y - 12) = \dfrac{1}{2}$. [4]

   Cambridge IGCSE Additional Mathematics 0606 Paper 11 Q4i,ii Jun 2013

6. Solve the equation $3^{2x} = 1000$, giving your answer to 2 decimal places. [2]

   Cambridge IGCSE Additional Mathematics 0606 Paper 21 Q5a Jun 2012

7. Express $\lg a + 3\lg b - 3$ as a single logarithm. [3]

   Cambridge IGCSE Additional Mathematics 0606 Paper 11 Q2 Jun 2011

8. Using the substitution $u = 5^x$, or otherwise, solve
$$5^{2x+1} = 7(5^x) - 2.$$ [5]

   Cambridge IGCSE Additional Mathematics 0606 Paper 11 Q4 Nov 2012

9 The temperature, $T°$ Celsius, of an object, t minutes after it is removed from a heat source, is given by
$$T = 55\,e^{-0.1t} + 15.$$
a Find the temperature of the object at the instant it is removed from the heat source. [1]
b Find the temperature of the object when $t = 8$. [1]
c Find the value of t when $T = 25$. [3]

Cambridge IGCSE Additional Mathematics 0606 Paper 21 Q8i,ii,iii Jun 2011

Chapter 7
Straight-line graphs

This section will show you how to:

- solve questions involving mid-point and length of a line
- use the condition for two lines to be parallel or perpendicular
- interpret the equation of a straight-line graph in the form $y = mx + c$
- transform given relationships, including $y = ax^n$ and $y = ab^x$, to straight-line form and hence determine unknown constants by calculating the gradient or intercept of the transformed graph.

Chapter 7: Straight-line graphs

> **RECAP**
>
> You should already be familiar with the following coordinate geometry work:
>
> **Length of a line, gradient and mid-point**
>
> P is the point (x_1, y_1) and Q is the point (x_2, y_2).
> M is the mid-point of the line PQ.
>
> The length of the line $PQ = \sqrt{(x_2 - x_1)^2 + (y_2 - y_1)^2}$.
>
> The gradient of the line $PQ = \dfrac{y_2 - y_1}{x_2 - x_1}$.
>
> The coordinates of M are $\left(\dfrac{x_1 + x_2}{2}, \dfrac{y_1 + y_2}{2}\right)$. 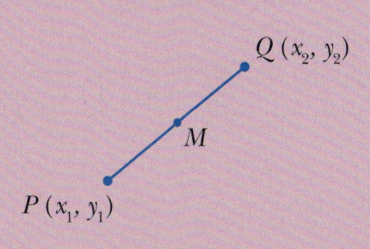
>
> **Gradients of parallel lines**
>
> If two lines are parallel then their gradients are equal. 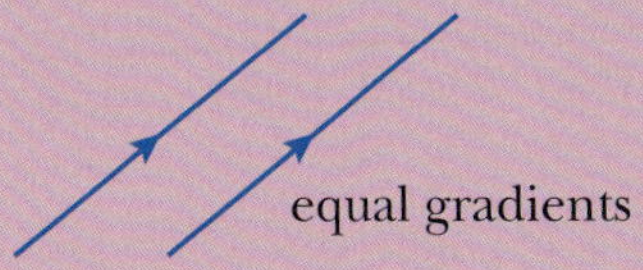
>
> equal gradients
>
> **Gradients of perpendicular lines** 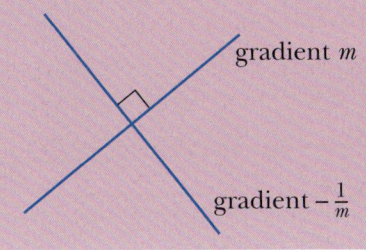
>
> gradient m
>
> gradient $-\dfrac{1}{m}$
>
> If a line has a gradient of m, a line perpendicular to it has a gradient of $-\dfrac{1}{m}$.
>
> This rule can also be written as:
>
> If the gradients of the two perpendicular lines are m_1 and m_2, then $m_1 \times m_2 = -1$.
>
> **The equation of a straight line**
>
> The equation of a straight line is $y = mx + c$ where $m =$ the gradient and $c =$ the y-intercept.

Cambridge IGCSE and O Level Additional Mathematics

7.1 Problems involving length of a line and mid-point

You need to know how to apply the formulae for the mid-point and the length of a line segment to solve problems.

WORKED EXAMPLE 1

A is the point $(-3, 7)$ and B is the point $(6, 2)$.
a Find the length of AB.
b Find the mid-point of AB.

Answers

a $(-3, 7)$ $(6, -2)$ decide which values to use for x_1, y_1, x_2, y_2
    (x_1, y_1) (x_2, y_2)

$AB = \sqrt{(x_2 - x_1)^2 + (y_2 - y_1)^2}$
$= \sqrt{(6--3)^2 + (-2-7)^2}$
$= 9\sqrt{2}$

b Midpoint $= \left(\dfrac{x_1 + x_2}{2}, \dfrac{y_1 + y_2}{2}\right)$

$= \left(\dfrac{-3 + 6}{2}, \dfrac{7 + -2}{2}\right)$

$= (1.5, 2.5)$

WORKED EXAMPLE 2

The distance between two points $P(7, a)$ and $Q(a + 1, 9)$ is 15.
Find the two possible values of a.

Answers

$(7, a)$ $(a + 1, 9)$ decide which values to use for
(x_1, y_1) (x_2, y_2) x_1, y_1, x_2, y_2

Using $PQ = \sqrt{(x_2 - x_1)^2 + (y_2 - y_1)^2}$ and $PQ = 15$.

$\sqrt{(a + 1 - 7)^2 + (9 - a)^2} = 15$
$\sqrt{(a - 6)^2 + (9 - a)^2} = 15$ square both sides
$(a - 6)^2 + (9 - a)^2 = 225$
$a^2 - 12a + 36 + 81 - 18a + a^2 = 225$ collect terms on one side
$2a^2 - 30a - 108 = 0$ divide both sides by 2
$a^2 - 15a - 54 = 0$ factorise
$(a - 18)(a + 3) = 0$ solve
$a - 18 = 0$ or $a + 3 = 0$

Hence $a = 18$ or $a = -3$.

Chapter 7: Straight-line graphs

WORKED EXAMPLE 3

The coordinates of the mid-point of the line segment joining $A(-5, 11)$ and $B(p, q)$, are $(2.5, -6)$.

Find the value of p and the value of q.

Answers

$(-5, 11)$ (p, q) decide which values to use for x_1, y_1, x_2, y_2
 ↑↑   ↑↑
(x_1, y_1) (x_2, y_2)

Using $\left(\dfrac{x_1 + x_2}{2}, \dfrac{y_1 + y_2}{2}\right)$ and mid-point $= (2.5, -6)$.

$\left(\dfrac{x_1 + x_2}{2}, \dfrac{y_1 + y_2}{2}\right) = (2.5, -6)$

$\left(\dfrac{-5 + p}{2}, \dfrac{11 + q}{2}\right) = (2.5, -6)$

Equating the x-coordinates gives: $\dfrac{-5 + p}{2} = 2.5$

$-5 + p = 5$

$p = 10$

Equating the y-coordinates gives: $\dfrac{11 + q}{2} = -6$

$11 + q = -12$

$q = -23$

Hence $p = 10$ and $q = -23$.

WORKED EXAMPLE 4

Three of the vertices of a parallelogram $ABCD$ are $A(-10, 1)$, $B(6, -2)$ and $C(14, 4)$.

a Find the mid-point of AC.

b Find the coordinates of D.

Answers

a Mid-point of $AC = \left(\dfrac{-10 + 14}{2}, \dfrac{1 + 4}{2}\right) = (2, 2.5)$.

b Let the coordinates of D be (m, n).

Since $ABCD$ is a parallelogram, the mid-point of BD is the same as the mid-point of AC.

Mid-point of $BD = \left(\dfrac{6 + m}{2}, \dfrac{-2 + n}{2}\right) = (2, 2.5)$

Equating the x-coordinates gives: $\dfrac{6 + m}{2} = 2$

$6 + m = 4$

$m = -2$

Equating the y-coordinates gives: $\dfrac{-2 + n}{2} = 2.5$

$-2 + n = 7$

$n = 5$

Cambridge IGCSE and O Level Additional Mathematics

The coordinates of D are (−2, 7).

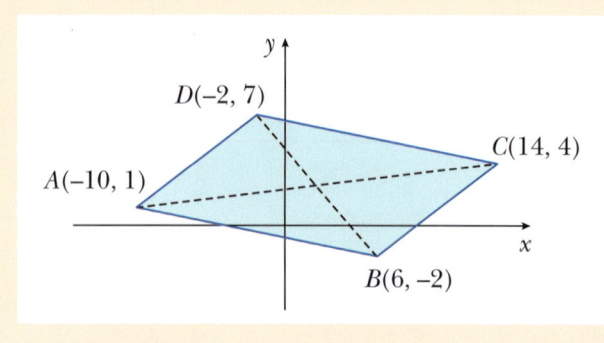

(Diagram: parallelogram with vertices A(−10, 1), B(6, −2), C(14, 4), D(−2, 7), with diagonals shown dashed)

CLASS DISCUSSION

This triangle has sides of length $5\sqrt{3}$ cm, $2\sqrt{6}$ cm and $7\sqrt{2}$ cm.
Priya says that the triangle is right-angled.
Discuss whether she is correct.
Explain your reasoning.

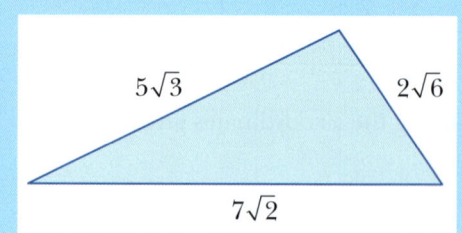

(Diagram: triangle with sides labelled $5\sqrt{3}$, $2\sqrt{6}$, $7\sqrt{2}$)

Exercise 7.1

1 Find the length of the line segment joining
   a (2, 0) and (5, 0)   **b** (−7, 4) and (−7, 8)   **c** (2, 1) and (8, 9)
   d (−3, 1) and (2, 13)   **e** (5, −2) and (2, −6)   **f** (4, 4) and (−20, −3)
   g (6, −5) and (1, 2)   **h** (−3, −2) and (−1, −5)   **i** (−7, 7) and (5, −5).

2 Calculate the lengths of the sides of the triangle PQR.
   Use your answers to determine whether or not the triangle is right-angled.
   a P(3, 11), Q(5, 7), R(11, 10)
   b P(−7, 8), Q(−1, 4), R(5, 12)
   c P(−8, −3), Q(−4, 5), R(−2, −6)

3 A(−1, 0), B(1, 6) and C(7, 4).
   Show that triangle ABC is a right-angled isosceles triangle.

4 The distance between two points P(10, 2b) and Q(b, −5) is $5\sqrt{10}$.
   Find the two possible values of b.

5 The distance between two points P(6, −2) and Q(2a, a) is 5.
   Find the two possible values of a.

6 Find the coordinates of the mid-point of the line segment joining
   a (5, 2) and (7, 6)   **b** (4, 3) and (9, 11)   **c** (8, 6) and (−2, 10)
   d (−1, 7) and (2, −4)   **e** (−7, −8) and (−2, 3)   **f** (2a, −3b) and (4a, 5b).

7 The coordinates of the mid-point of the line segment joining $P(-8, 2)$ and $Q(a, b)$, are $(5, -3)$.

Find the value of a and the value of b.

8 Three of the vertices of a parallelogram $ABCD$ are $A(-7, 6)$, $B(-1, 8)$ and $C(7, 3)$.

  a Find the mid-point of AC.

  b Find the coordinates of D.

9 The point $P(2k, k)$ is equidistant from $A(-2, 4)$ and $B(7, -5)$.

Find the value of k.

10 In triangle ABC, the mid-points of the sides AB, BC and AC are $P(2, 3)$, $Q(3, 5)$ and $R(-4, 4)$ respectively. Find the coordinates of A, B and C.

7.2 Parallel and perpendicular lines

You need to know how to apply the rules for gradients to solve problems involving parallel and perpendicular lines.

WORKED EXAMPLE 5

The coordinates of 3 points are $A(8 - k, 2)$, $B(-2, k)$ and $C(-8, 2k)$.

Find the possible values of k if A, B and C are collinear.

Answers

If A, B and C are collinear then they lie on the same line.

gradient of AB = gradient of BC

$$\frac{k-2}{-2-(8-k)} = \frac{2k-k}{-8-(-2)}$$

$$\frac{k-2}{k-10} = \frac{k}{-6} \quad \text{cross multiply}$$

$-6(k-2) = k(k-10)$ expand brackets

$-6k + 12 = k^2 - 10k$ collect terms on one side

$k^2 - 4k - 12 = 0$ factorise

$(k-6)(k+2) = 0$ solve

$k - 6 = 0$ or $k + 2 = 0$

Hence $k = 6$ or $k = -2$.

WORKED EXAMPLE 6

The vertices of triangle ABC are $A(-4, 2)$, $B(5, -5)$ and $C(k, k+2)$.
Find the possible values of k if angle ACB is $90°$.

Answers

Since angle ACB is $90°$,
gradient of AC × gradient of $BC = -1$.

$$\frac{(k+2)-2}{k-(-4)} \times \frac{(k+2)-(-5)}{k-5} = -1$$

$$\frac{k}{k+4} \times \frac{k+7}{k-5} = -1$$

$$k(k+7) = -(k+4)(k-5)$$

$$k^2 + 7k = -(k^2 - k - 20)$$

$$k^2 + 7k = -k^2 + k + 20$$

$$2k^2 + 6k - 20 = 0$$

$$k^2 + 3k - 10 = 0$$

$$(k+5)(k-2) = 0$$

$$k + 5 = 0 \text{ or } k - 2 = 0$$

Hence $k = -5$ or $k = 2$.

The two possible situations are:

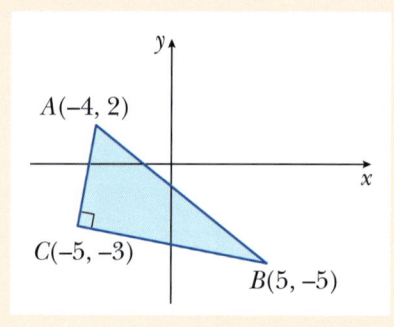

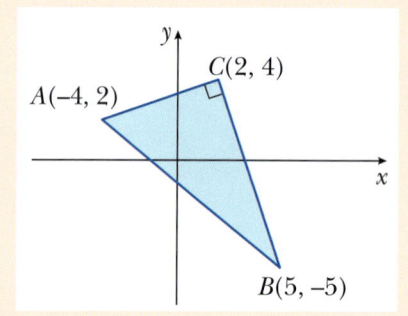

Exercise 7.2

1 Find the gradient of the line AB for each of the following pairs of points.
   a $A(1, 2)$ $B(3, -2)$
   b $A(4, 3)$ $B(5, 0)$
   c $A(-4, 4)$ $B(7, 4)$
   d $A(1, -9)$ $B(4, 1)$
   e $A(-4, -3)$ $B(5, 0)$
   f $A(6, -7)$ $B(2, -4)$

2 Write down the gradient of lines perpendicular to a line with gradient:
   a 3
   b $-\frac{1}{2}$
   c $\frac{2}{5}$
   d $1\frac{1}{4}$
   e $-2\frac{1}{2}$

3 Two vertices of a rectangle $ABCD$ are $A(3, -5)$ and $B(6, -3)$.
   a Find the gradient of CD.
   b Find the gradient of BC.

4 $A(-1, -5)$, $B(5, -2)$ and $C(1, 1)$.

   $ABCD$ is a trapezium.

   AB is parallel to DC and angle BAD is 90°.

   Find the coordinates of D.

5 The mid-point of the line segment joining $P(-2, 3)$ and $Q(4, -1)$ is M.

   The point C has coordinates $(-1, -2)$.

   Show that CM is perpendicular to PQ.

6 $A(-2, 2)$, $B(3, -1)$ and $C(9, -4)$.

   a Find the gradient of AB and the gradient of BC.

   b Use your answer to **part a** to decide whether or not the points A, B and C are collinear.

7 The coordinates of 3 points are $A(-4, 4)$, $B(k, -2)$ and $C(2k + 1, -6)$.

   Find the value of k if A, B and C are collinear.

8 The vertices of triangle ABC are $A(-k, -2)$, $B(k, -4)$ and $C(4, k-2)$.

   Find the possible values of k if angle ABC is 90°.

CHALLENGE Q

9 A is the point $(-2, 0)$ and B is the point $(2, 6)$.

   Find the point C on the x-axis such that angle ABC is 90°.

7.3 Equations of straight lines

You should already know that the equation of a straight line is

$$y = mx + c$$

where m = the gradient and c = the y-intercept.

There is an alternative formula that can be used when you know the gradient of the straight line and a point on the line.

Consider a line, with gradient m, which passes through the known point $A(x_1, y_1)$ and whose general point is $P(x, y)$.

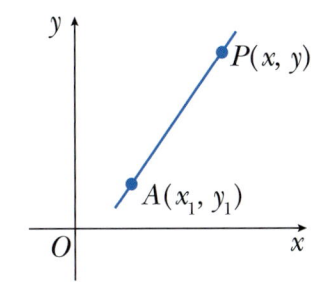

Gradient of $AP = m$, hence $\dfrac{y - y_1}{x - x_1} = m$ multiply both sides by $(x - x_1)$

$$y - y_1 = m(x - x_1).$$

The equation of a straight line, with gradient m, which passes through the point (x_1, y_1) is:

$$y - y_1 = m(x - x_1)$$

WORKED EXAMPLE 7

Find the equation of the straight line
- **a** with gradient 2 and passing through the point $(4, 7)$
- **b** passing through the points $(-5, 8)$ and $(1, -4)$.

Answers

a Using $y - y_1 = m(x - x_1)$ with $m = 2$, $x_1 = 4$ and $y_1 = 7$

$$y - 7 = 2(x - 4)$$
$$y - 7 = 2x - 8$$
$$y = 2x - 1$$

b $(-5, 8)$ $(1, -4)$ decide which values to use for x_1, y_1, x_2, y_2
     ↑↑   ↑↑
   (x_1, y_1) (x_2, y_2)

Gradient $= m = \dfrac{y_2 - y_1}{x_2 - x_1} = \dfrac{(-4) - 8}{1 - (-5)} = -2$

Using $y - y_1 = m(x - x_1)$ with $m = -2$, $x_1 = -5$ and $y_1 = 8$.

$$y - 8 = -2(x + 5)$$
$$y - 8 = -2x - 10$$
$$y = -2x - 2$$

WORKED EXAMPLE 8

Find the equation of the perpendicular bisector of the line joining $A(3, 2)$ and $B(7, 10)$.

Answers

Gradient of $AB = \dfrac{10-2}{7-3} = \dfrac{8}{4} = 2$. using $\dfrac{y_2 - y_1}{x_2 - x_1}$

Gradient of the perpendicular is $-\dfrac{1}{2}$. using $m_1 \times m_2 = -1$

Mid-point of $AB = \left(\dfrac{3+7}{2}, \dfrac{2+10}{2}\right) = (5, 6)$. using $\left(\dfrac{x_1 + x_2}{2}, \dfrac{y_1 + y_2}{2}\right)$

So the perpendicular bisector is the line passing through the point $(5, 6)$ with gradient $-\dfrac{1}{2}$.

Using $y - y_1 = m(x - x_1)$ with $x_1 = 5$, $y_1 = 6$ and $m = -\dfrac{1}{2}$.

$$y - 6 = -\dfrac{1}{2}(x - 5)$$

$$y - 6 = -\dfrac{1}{2}x + \dfrac{5}{2}$$

$$y = -\dfrac{1}{2}x + 8.5 \quad \text{multiply both sides by 2 and rearrange}$$

$$x + 2y = 17$$

Exercise 7.3

1. Find the equation of the line with
   a. gradient 3 and passing through the point $(6, 5)$
   b. gradient -4 and passing through the point $(2, -1)$
   c. gradient $-\dfrac{1}{2}$ and passing through the point $(8, -3)$.

2. Find the equation of the line passing through
   a. $(3, 2)$ and $(5, 7)$ b. $(-1, 6)$ and $(5, -3)$ c. $(5, -2)$ and $(-7, 4)$.

3. Find the equation of the line
   a. parallel to the line $y = 2x + 4$, passing through the point $(6, 2)$
   b. parallel to the line $x + 2y = 5$, passing through the point $(2, -5)$
   c. perpendicular to the line $2x + 3y = 12$, passing through the point $(7, 3)$
   d. perpendicular to the line $4x - y = 6$, passing through the point $(4, -1)$.

4. P is the point $(2, 5)$ and Q is the point $(6, 0)$.
   A line l is drawn through P perpendicular to PQ to meet the y-axis at the point R.
   a. Find the equation of the line l.
   b. Find the coordinates of the point R.
   c. Find the area of triangle OPR where O is the origin.

5. Find the equation of the perpendicular bisector of the line segment joining the points
   a. $(1, 3)$ and $(-3, 1)$ b. $(-1, -5)$ and $(5, 3)$ c. $(0, -9)$ and $(5, -2)$.

6 The perpendicular bisector of the line joining $A(-1, 4)$ and $B(2, 2)$ intersects the x-axis at P and the y-axis at Q.
   a Find the coordinates of P and of Q.
   b Find the length of PQ.
   c Find the area of triangle OPQ where O is the origin.

7 The line l_1 has equation $3x + 2y = 12$.
  The line l_2 has equation $y = 2x - 1$.
  The lines l_1 and l_2 intersect at the point A.
   a Find the coordinates of A.
   b Find the equation of the line through A which is perpendicular to the line l_1.

8 The coordinates of three points are $A(1, 5)$, $B(9, 7)$ and $C(k, -6)$.
  M is the mid-point of AB and MC is perpendicular to AB.
   a Find the coordinates of M.
   b Find the value of k.

9 The coordinates of triangle ABC are $A(2, -1)$, $B(3, 7)$ and $C(14, 5)$.
  P is the foot of the perpendicular from B to AC.
   a Find the equation of BP.
   b Find the coordinates of P.
   c Find the lengths of AC and BP.
   d Use your answers to **part c** to find the area of triangle ABC.

CHALLENGE Q

10 The coordinates of triangle PQR are $P(-3, -2)$, $Q(5, 10)$ and $R(11, -2)$.
   a Find the equation of the perpendicular bisectors of **i** PQ **ii** QR.
   b Find the coordinates of the point which is equidistant from P, Q and R.

Hint:
The point is where the perpendicular bisectors of the sides intersect.

7.4 Areas of rectilinear figures

CLASS DISCUSSION

Discuss with your classmates, how you can find the area of triangle ABC.
Try to find as many different methods as possible.
Compare the ease of use of each of these methods.

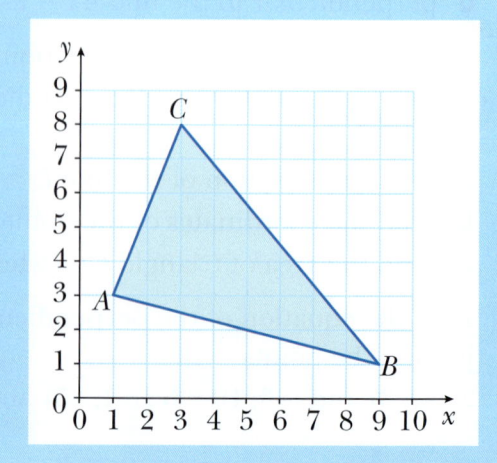

Chapter 7: Straight-line graphs

There is a method that you might not have seen before. It is often referred to as the 'shoestring' or 'shoelace' method. You do not have to know this method for the examination, but you may find it useful to know.

If the vertices of triangle ABC are $A(x_1, y_1)$, $B(x_2, y_2)$ and $C(x_3, y_3)$, then:

$$\text{Area of triangle } ABC = \frac{1}{2} | x_1 y_2 + x_2 y_3 + x_3 y_1 - x_2 y_1 - x_3 y_2 - x_1 y_3 |$$

This complicated formula can be written as: $\frac{1}{2} \begin{vmatrix} x_1 & x_2 & x_3 & x_1 \\ y_1 & y_2 & y_3 & y_1 \end{vmatrix}$

The products in the direction ↘ are given positive signs and the products in the direction ↗ are given negative signs.

For the triangle in the class discussion $A(1, 3)$, $B(9, 1)$ and $C(3, 8)$: $\frac{1}{2} \begin{vmatrix} 1 & 9 & 3 & 1 \\ 3 & 1 & 8 & 3 \end{vmatrix}$

area of triangle $ABC = \frac{1}{2} | 1 \times 1 + 9 \times 8 + 3 \times 3 - 3 \times 9 - 1 \times 3 - 8 \times 1 |$

$= \frac{1}{2} | 1 + 72 + 9 - 27 - 3 - 8 |$

$= \frac{1}{2} | 44 |$

$= 22 \text{ units}^2$

This method can be extended for use with polygons with more than 3 sides.

Note:
If you take the vertices in an anticlockwise direction around a shape, then the inside of the modulus sign will be positive. If you take the vertices in a clockwise direction, then the inside of the modulus sign will be negative.

WORKED EXAMPLE 9

The vertices of a pentagon $ABCDE$ are $A(0, -1)$, $B(5, 1)$, $C(3, 4)$, $B(-1, 6)$ and $C(-3, 2)$.
a Find the area of the pentagon using the 'shoestring' method.
b Find the area of the pentagon using the 'boxing in' method.

Answers

a $\frac{1}{2} \begin{vmatrix} 0 & 5 & 3 & -1 & -3 & 0 \\ -1 & 1 & 4 & 6 & 2 & -1 \end{vmatrix}$

Area of pentagon $= \frac{1}{2} | 0 + 20 + 18 + (-2) + 3 - (-5) - 3 - (-4) - (-18) - 0 |$

$= \frac{1}{2} | 63 |$

$= 31.5 \text{ units}^2$

b For the 'boxing in' method, you draw a rectangle around the outside of the pentagon.

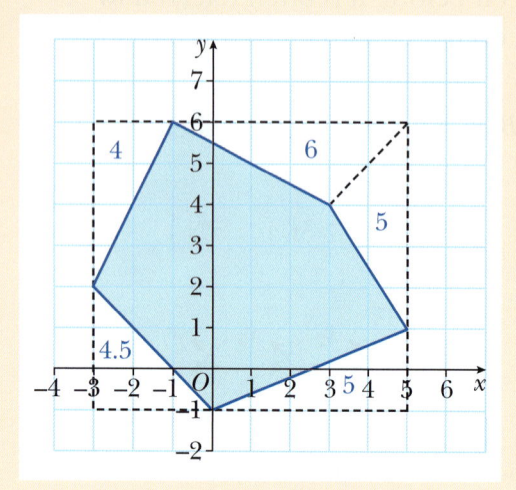

Area of pentagon = area of rectangle − sum of the outside areas
= (8 × 7) − (4 + 6 + 5 + 5 + 4.5)
= 56 − 24.5
= 31.5 units²

Exercise 7.4

1 Find the area of these triangles.
  a $A(-2, 3)$, $B(0, -4)$, $C(5, 6)$
  b $P(-3, 1)$, $Q(5, -3)$, $R(2, 4)$

2 Find the area of these quadrilaterals.
  a $A(1, 8)$, $B(-4, 5)$, $C(-2, -3)$, $D(4, -2)$
  b $P(2, 7)$, $Q(-5, 6)$, $R(-3, -4)$, $S(7, 2)$

3 Triangle PQR where $P(1, 4)$, $Q(-3, -4)$ and $R(7, k)$ is right-angled at Q.
  a Find the value of k.
  b Find the area of triangle PQR.

4 A is the point $(-4, 0)$ and B is the point $(2, 3)$.
  M is the mid-point of the line AB.
  Point C is such that $\overrightarrow{MC} = \begin{pmatrix} 3 \\ -6 \end{pmatrix}$.
  a Find the coordinates of M and C.
  b Show that CM is perpendicular to AB.
  c Find the area of triangle ABC.

5 Angle ABC is 90° and M is the mid-point of the line AB.
  The point C lies on the y-axis.
  a Find the coordinates of B and C.
  b Find the area of triangle ABC.

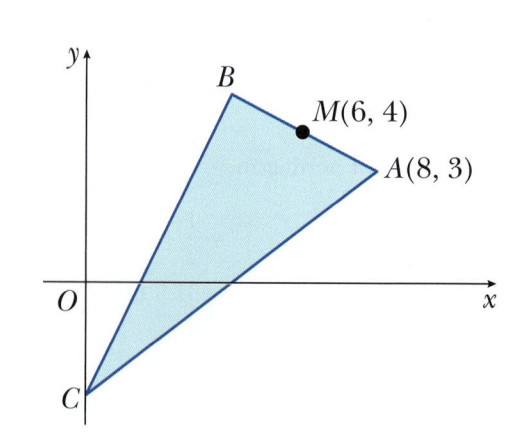

6 A is the point $(-4, 5)$ and B is the point $(5, 8)$.

The perpendicular to the line AB at the point A crosses the y-axis at the point C.

  a Find the coordinates of C.

  b Find the area of triangle ABC.

7 AB is parallel to DC and BC is perpendicular to AB.

  a Find the coordinates of C.

  b Find the area of trapezium $ABCD$.

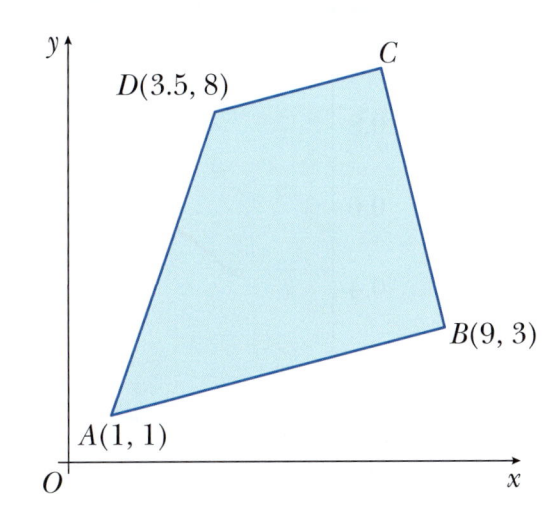

8 $ABCD$ is a square.

A is the point $(-2, 0)$ and C is the point $(6, 4)$.

AC and BD are diagonals of the square, which intersect at M.

  a Find the coordinates of M, B and D.

  b Find the area of $ABCD$.

9 The coordinates of 3 of the vertices of a parallelogram $ABCD$ are $A(-4, 3)$, $B(5, -5)$ and $C(15, -1)$.

  a Find the coordinates of the points of intersection of the diagonals.

  b Find the coordinates of the point D.

  c Find the area of parallelogram $ABCD$.

7.5 Converting from a non-linear equation to linear form

Some situations in the real world can be modelled using an equation.

Consider an experiment where a simple pendulum, of length L cm, travels from A to B and back to A in a time of T seconds. The table shows the time taken, T, for different lengths L.

L	5	10	15	20	25	30
T	0.45	0.63	0.78	0.90	1.00	1.10

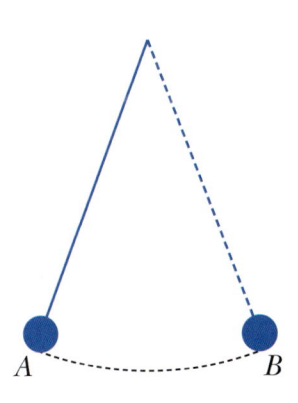

When the graph of T against L is drawn, the points lie on a curve.
They do not lie on a straight line.

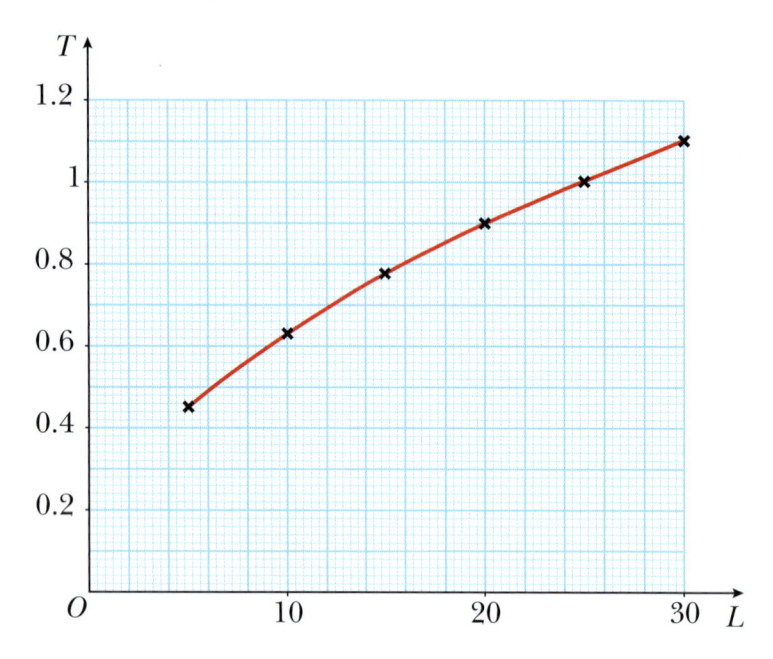

So how can you find the equation of the curve?

If you are told that the rule connecting the variables T and L is believed to be $T = a\sqrt{L}$, you should draw the graph of T against $\sqrt{L}$. To do this, you must first make a table of values for T and $\sqrt{L}$.

$\sqrt{L}$	2.24	3.16	3.87	4.47	5.00	5.48
T	0.45	0.63	0.78	0.90	1.00	1.10

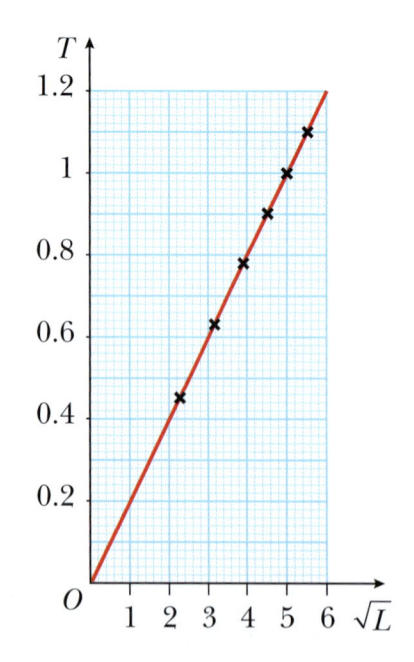

The fact that the points now lie on a straight line confirms the belief that the rule connecting the variables T and L is $T = a\sqrt{L}$.

The gradient of the straight line tells you the value of a.

Using the two end points, gradient $= \dfrac{1.1 - 0.45}{5.48 - 2.24} \approx 0.2$.

Hence the approximate rule connecting T and L is
$$T = 0.2\sqrt{L}$$

In the example above you have converted from a non-linear graph to a linear graph.

Before you can model more complicated relationships, you must first learn how to choose suitable variables for Y and X to convert from a non-linear equation into the linear form $Y = mX + c$ where m is the gradient of the straight line and c is the Y-intercept.

WORKED EXAMPLE 10

Convert $y = ax + \dfrac{b}{x}$, where a and b are constants, into the form $Y = mX + c$.

Answers

Method 1 $y = ax + \dfrac{b}{x}$

Multiplying both sides of the equation by x gives:
$$xy = ax^2 + b$$
Now compare $xy = ax^2 + b$ with $Y = mX + c$:

$$\underset{Y}{(xy)} = \underset{m}{a}\underset{X}{(x^2)} + \underset{c}{b}$$

The non-linear equation $y = ax + \dfrac{b}{x}$ becomes the linear equation:

$Y = mX + c$, where $Y = xy$, $X = x^2$, $m = a$ and $c = b$

Method 2 $y = ax + \dfrac{b}{x}$

Dividing both sides of the equation by x gives:
$$\dfrac{y}{x} = a + \dfrac{b}{x^2}$$
Now compare $\dfrac{y}{x} = a + \dfrac{b}{x^2}$ with $Y = mX + c$:

$$\underset{Y}{\left(\dfrac{y}{x}\right)} = \underset{m}{b}\underset{X}{\left(\dfrac{1}{x^2}\right)} + \underset{c}{a}$$

The non-linear equation $y = ax + \dfrac{b}{x}$ becomes the linear equation:

$Y = mX + c$, where $Y = \dfrac{y}{x}$, $X = \dfrac{1}{x^2}$, $m = b$ and $c = a$

It is important to note that the variables X and Y in $Y = mX + c$ must contain only the original variables x and y. They must not contain the unknown constants a and b.

Similarly the constants m and c must contain only the original unknown constants a and b. They must not contain the variables x and y.

> **WORKED EXAMPLE 11**
>
> Convert $y = ae^{-bx}$, where a and b are constants, into the form $Y = mX + c$.
>
> **Answers**
>
> $$y = ae^{-bx}$$
>
> Taking natural logarithms of both sides gives
>
> $$\ln y = \ln(ae^{-bx})$$
> $$\ln y = \ln a + \ln e^{-bx}$$
> $$\ln y = \ln a - bx$$
> $$\ln y = -bx + \ln a$$
>
> Now compare $\ln y = -bx + \ln a$ with $Y = mX + c$:
>
> $$\underbrace{\ln y}_{Y} = \underbrace{-b}_{m} \underbrace{x}_{X} + \underbrace{\ln a}_{c}$$
>
> The non-linear equation $y = ae^{-bx}$ becomes the linear equation:
>
> $Y = mX + c$, where $Y = \ln y$, $X = x$, $m = -b$ and $c = \ln a$

Exercise 7.5

1 Convert each of these non-linear equations into the form $Y = mX + c$, where a and b are constants. State clearly what the variables X and Y and the constants m and c represent.

(Note: there may be more than one way to do this.)

a $y = ax^2 + b$ **b** $y = ax + \dfrac{b}{x}$ **c** $y = ax^2 - bx$

d $y(a - x) = bx$ **e** $y = a\sqrt{x} + \dfrac{b}{\sqrt{x}}$ **f** $y = \dfrac{a}{x^2} + b$

g $x = axy + by$ **h** $\dfrac{1}{y} = a\sqrt{x} - \dfrac{b}{\sqrt{x}}$

2 Convert each of these non-linear equations into the form $Y = mX + c$, where a and b are constants. State clearly what the variables X and Y and the constants m and c represent.

(Note: there may be more than one way to do this.)

a $y = 10^{ax+b}$ **b** $y = e^{ax-b}$ **c** $y = ax^b$

d $y = ab^x$ **e** $x^a y^b = e^2$ **f** $xa^y = b$

g $a = e^{x^2 + by}$ **h** $y = ae^{bx}$

7.6 Converting from linear form to a non-linear equation

WORKED EXAMPLE 12

Find y in terms of x.

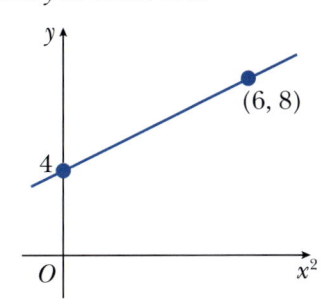

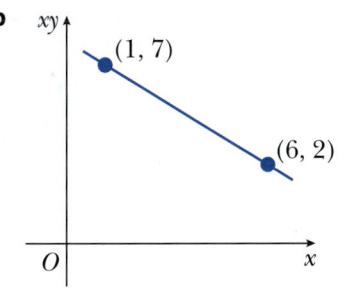

a [Graph showing line on y vs x^2 axes, passing through $(0, 4)$ and $(6, 8)$]

b [Graph showing line on xy vs x axes, passing through $(1, 7)$ and $(6, 2)$]

Answers

a The linear equation is $Y = mX + c$, where $Y = y$ and $X = x^2$.

Gradient $= m = \dfrac{8 - 4}{6 - 0} = \dfrac{2}{3}$

Y-intercept $= c = 4$

Hence $Y = \dfrac{2}{3}X + 4$.

The non-linear equation is $y = \dfrac{2}{3}x^2 + 4$.

b The linear equation is $Y = mX + c$, where $Y = xy$ and $X = x$.

Gradient $= m = \dfrac{2 - 7}{6 - 1} = -1$

Using $Y = mX + c$, $m = -1$, $X = 6$ and $Y = 2$

$2 = -1 \times 6 + c$

$c = 8$

Hence $Y = -X + 8$.

The non-linear equation is $xy = -x + 8$

$y = -1 + \dfrac{8}{x}$.

WORKED EXAMPLE 13

Variables x and y are such that $y = a \times b^x$, where a and b are constants.

The diagram shows the graph of $\lg y$ against x, passing through the points $(2, 5)$ and $(6, 13)$.

Find the value of a and the value of b.

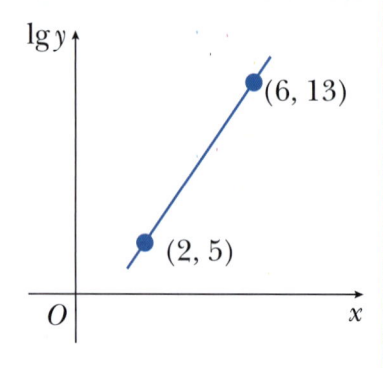

Answers

$$y = a \times b^x$$

Taking logarithms of both sides gives:

$$\lg y = \lg (a \times b^x)$$
$$\lg y = \lg a + \ln b^x$$
$$\lg y = x \lg b + \lg a$$

Now compare $\lg y = x \lg b + \lg a$ with $Y = mX + c$:

$$\underset{Y}{(\ln y)} = \underset{m}{\lg b} \; \underset{X}{(x)} + \underset{c}{\ln a}$$

Gradient $= m = \dfrac{13 - 5}{6 - 2} = 2$

$$\lg b = 2$$
$$b = 10^2$$

Using $Y = mX + c$, $m = 2$, $X = 2$ and $Y = 5$

$$5 = 2 \times 2 + c$$
$$c = 1$$
$$\lg a = 1$$
$$a = 10^1$$

Hence $a = 10$ and $b = 100$.

Exercise 7.6

1 The graphs show part of a straight line obtained by plotting y against some function of x.

For each graph, express y in terms of x.

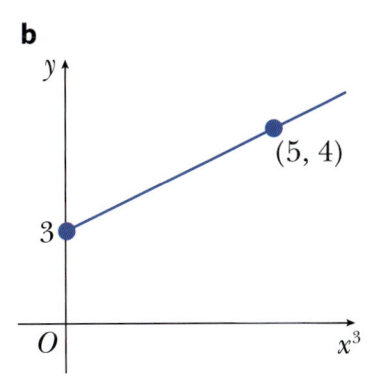

a Graph of y against x, passing through origin and $(3, 6)$.

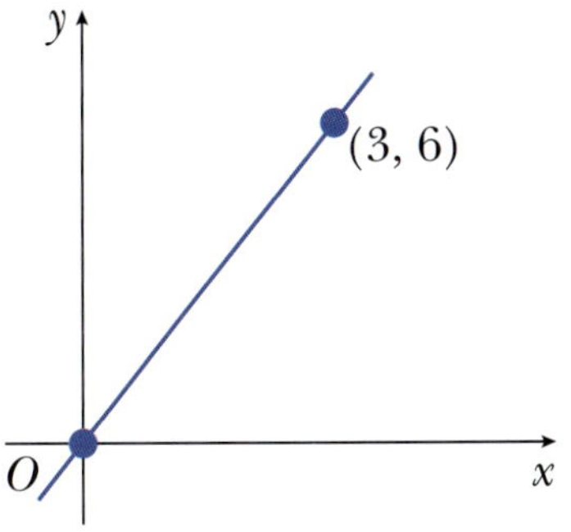

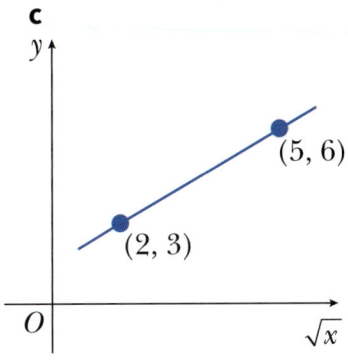

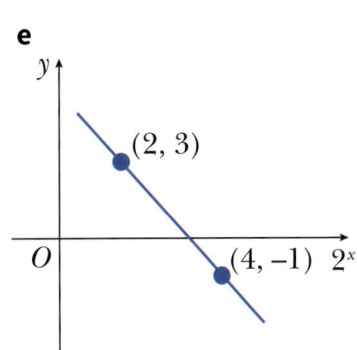

b Graph of y against x^3, passing through $(0, 3)$ and $(5, 4)$.

c Graph of y against $\sqrt{x}$, passing through $(2, 3)$ and $(5, 6)$.

d Graph of y against x^4, passing through $(1, 5)$ and $(5, 3)$.

e Graph of y against 2^x, passing through $(2, 3)$ and $(4, -1)$.

f Graph of y against $\ln x$, passing through $(3, 3)$ and $(7, -2)$.

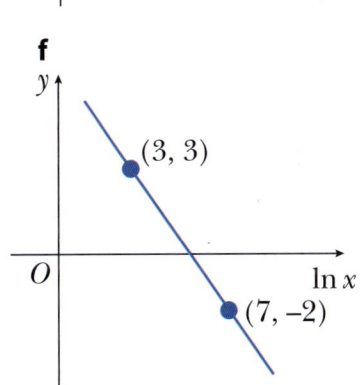

2 For each of the following relations
   i express y in terms of x
   ii find the value of y when $x = 2$.

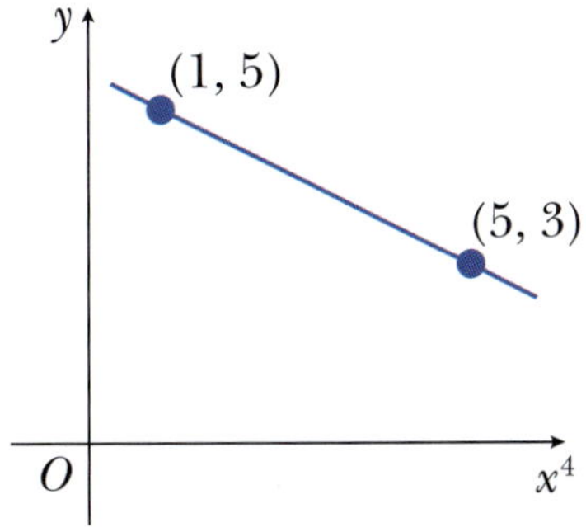

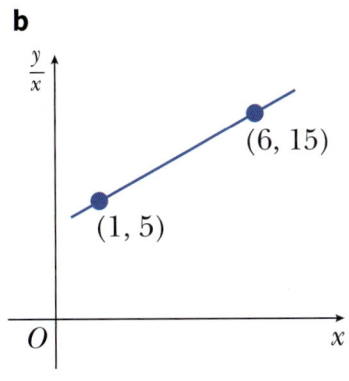

a Graph of $\dfrac{1}{y}$ against x^2, passing through $(1, 2)$ and $(5, 6)$.

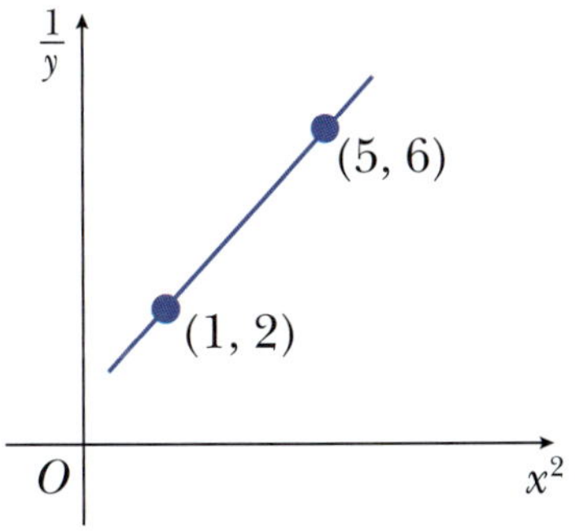

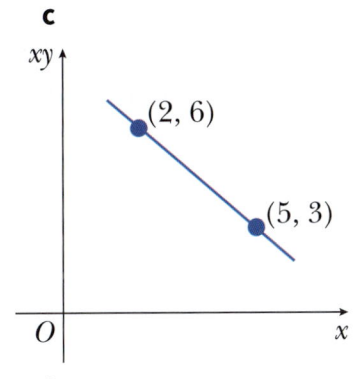

b Graph of $\dfrac{y}{x}$ against x, passing through $(1, 5)$ and $(6, 15)$.

c Graph of xy against x, passing through $(2, 6)$ and $(5, 3)$.

d Graph of $\sqrt{y}$ against x^2, passing through $(2, 9)$ and $(6, 1)$.

e Graph of $x + y$ against x^2, passing through $(2, -2)$ and $(10, 8)$.

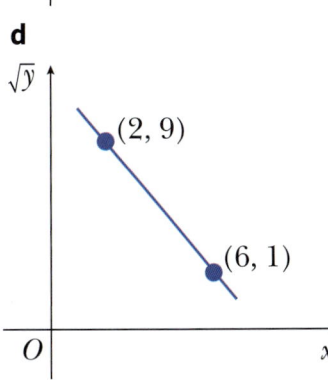

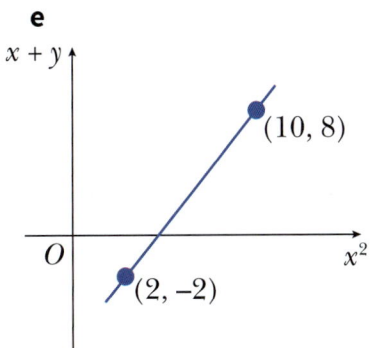

f Graph of $y\sqrt{x}$ against x, passing through $(1, 2)$ and $(5, 6)$.

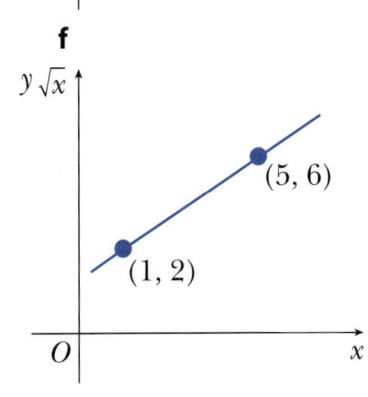

3 Variables x and y are related so that, when $\dfrac{y}{x^2}$ is plotted on the vertical axis and x^3 is plotted on the horizontal axis, a straight-line graph passing through (2, 12) and (6, 4) is obtained.

Express y in terms of x.

4 Variables x and y are related so that, when y^2 is plotted on the vertical axis and 2^x is plotted on the horizontal axis, a straight-line graph which passes through the point (8, 49) with gradient 3 is obtained.

   a Express y^2 in terms of 2^x.
   b Find the value of x when $y = 11$.

5 Variables x and y are related so that, when $\dfrac{y}{x}$ is plotted on the vertical axis and x is plotted on the horizontal axis, a straight-line graph passing through the points (2, 4) and (5, −2) is obtained.

   a Express y in terms of x.
   b Find the value of x and the value of y such that $\dfrac{y}{x} = 3$.

6 Variables x and y are related so that, when e^y is plotted on the vertical axis and x^2 is plotted on the horizontal axis, a straight-line graph passing through the points (3, 4) and (8, 9) is obtained.

   a Express e^y in terms of x.
   b Express y in terms of x.

7 Variables x and y are related so that, when $\lg y$ is plotted on the vertical axis and x is plotted on the horizontal axis, a straight-line graph passing through the points (6, 2) and (10, 8) is obtained.

   a Express $\lg y$ in terms of x.
   b Express y in terms of x, giving your answer in the form $y = a \times 10^{bx}$.

8 Variables x and y are related so that, when $\lg y$ is plotted on the vertical axis and $\lg x$ is plotted on the horizontal axis, a straight-line graph passing through the points (4, 8) and (8, 14) is obtained.

   a Express y in terms of x, giving your answer in the form $y = a \times x^b$.
   b Find the value of x when $y = 51.2$.

9 Variables x and y are related so that, when $\ln y$ is plotted on the vertical axis and $\ln x$ is plotted on the horizontal axis, a straight-line graph passing through the points (1, 2) and (4, 11) is obtained.

   a Express $\ln y$ in terms of x.
   b Express y in terms of x.

10 Variables x and y are such that, when $\ln y$ is plotted on the vertical axis and $\ln x$ is plotted on the horizontal axis, a straight-line graph passing through the points (2.5, 7.7) and (3.7, 5.3) is obtained.

   a Find the value of $\ln y$ when $\ln x = 0$.
   b Given that $y = a \times x^b$, find the value of a and the value of b.

7.7 Finding relationships from data

When experimental data is collected for two variables, it is useful if you can then establish the mathematical relationship connecting the two variables.

If the data forms a straight-line when a graph is plotted, it is easy to establish the connection using the equation $y = mx + c$.

It is more usual, however, for the data to lie on a curve and to be connected by a non-linear equation.

In this section, you will learn how to apply what you have just learnt in sections **7.5** and **7.6** to find the non-linear equation connecting two variables.

WORKED EXAMPLE 14

x	5	10	20	40	80
y	2593	1596	983	605	372

The table shows experimental values of the variables x and y.

a By plotting a suitable straight-line graph, show that x and y are related by the equation $y = k \times x^n$, where k and n are constants.

b Use your graph to estimate the value of k and the value of n.

Answers

a
$$y = k \times x^n \quad \text{take logs of both sides}$$
$$\lg y = \lg (k \times x^n) \quad \text{use the multiplication law}$$
$$\lg y = \lg k + \lg x^n \quad \text{use the power law}$$
$$\lg y = n \lg x + \lg k$$

Now compare $\lg y = n \lg x + \lg k$ with $Y = mX + c$:

$$\underset{Y}{\boxed{\lg y}} = \underset{m}{n} \underset{X}{\boxed{\lg x}} + \underset{c}{\lg k}$$

Hence the graph of $\lg y$ against $\lg x$ needs to be drawn where
- gradient = n
- intercept on vertical axis = $\lg k$.

Table of values is

lg x	0.699	1.000	1.301	1.602	1.903
lg y	3.414	3.203	2.993	2.782	2.571

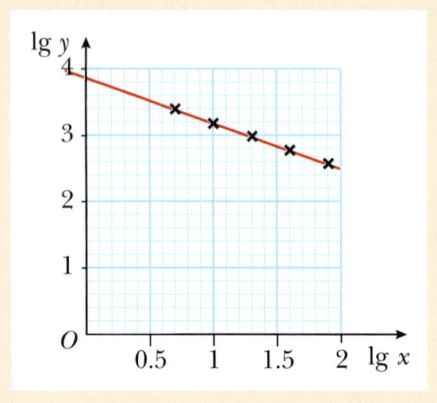

The points form an approximate straight line, so x and y are related by the equation $y = k \times x^n$.

n = gradient

$\approx \dfrac{2.571 - 3.414}{1.903 - 0.699}$

≈ -0.7

$\lg k$ = intercept on vertical axis

$\lg k \approx 3.9$

$k \approx 10^{3.9}$

$k \approx 7943$

Chapter 7: Straight-line graphs

WORKED EXAMPLE 15

x	2	4	6	8	10
y	4.75	2.19	1.42	1.05	0.83

The table shows experimental values of the variables x and y.
The variables are known to be related by the equation $y = \dfrac{a + bx}{x^2}$, where a and b are constants.

a Draw the graph of x^2y against x.
b Use your graph to estimate the value of a and the value of b.

An alternate method for obtaining a straight-line graph for the equation $y = \dfrac{a + bx}{x^2}$ is to plot xy on the vertical axis and $\dfrac{1}{x}$ on the horizontal axis.

c Without drawing a second graph, estimate the gradient and the intercept on the vertical axis of this graph.

Answers

a First make a table of values for of x^2y and x:

x	2	4	6	8	10
x^2y	19	35.0	51.1	67.2	83

The graph of x^2y against x is:

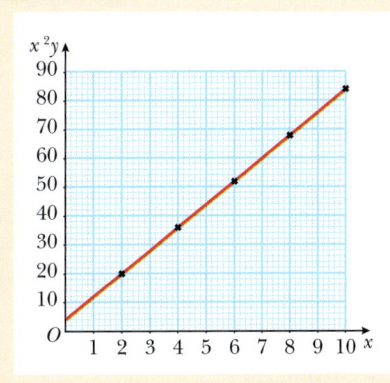

b Using $\quad y = \dfrac{a + bx}{x^2}$

$\quad\quad\quad\quad x^2y = bx + a$

Now compare $x^2y = bx + a$ with $Y = mX + c$:

$\quad\quad\quad (x^2y) = b(x) + a$
$\quad\quad\quad\uparrow\quad\quad\uparrow\quad\uparrow\quad\uparrow$
$\quad\quad\quad Y = m\ X + c$

Hence, $b =$ gradient $= \dfrac{83 - 19}{10 - 2} = 8$ and $a = y$-intercept $= 3$

$a = 3$ and $b = 8$

c Using $\quad y = \dfrac{a + bx}{x^2}$

$\quad\quad\quad\quad xy = \dfrac{a + bx}{x}$

$\quad\quad\quad\quad xy = \dfrac{a}{x} + b$

Now compare $xy = \dfrac{a}{x} + b$ with $Y = mX + c$:

$\quad\quad\quad (xy) = a \times \left(\dfrac{1}{x}\right) + b$
$\quad\quad\quad\uparrow\quad\quad\uparrow\quad\quad\uparrow\quad\quad\uparrow$
$\quad\quad\quad Y = m\quad X + c$

Gradient $= a = 3$ and intercept on vertical axis $= b = 8$.

Cambridge IGCSE and O Level Additional Mathematics

Exercise 7.7

1

x	0.5	1.0	1.5	2.0	2.5
y	1.00	3.00	3.67	4.00	4.20

The table shows experimental values of the variables x and y.

a Copy and complete the following table.

x					
xy					

b Draw the graph of xy against x.

c Express y in terms of x.

d Find the value of x and the value of y for which $xy = 2$.

2

x	0.1	0.2	0.3	0.4	0.5
y	0.111	0.154	0.176	0.189	0.200

The table shows experimental values of the variables x and y.

a Copy and complete the following table.

$\dfrac{1}{x}$					
$\dfrac{1}{y}$					

b Draw the graph of $\dfrac{1}{y}$ against $\dfrac{1}{x}$.

c Express y in terms of x.

d Find the value of x when $y = 0.16$.

3

x	1	2	3	4	5
y	12.8	7.6	6.4	6.2	6.4

The table shows experimental values of the variables x and y.

a Draw the graph of xy against x^2.

b Use your graph to express y in terms of x.

c Find the value of x and the value of y for which $xy = 12.288$.

Chapter 7: Straight-line graphs

4 The mass, m grams, of a radioactive substance is given by the formula $m = m_0 e^{-kt}$, where t is the time in days after the mass was first recorded and m_0 and k are constants.
The table below shows experimental values of t and m.

t	10	20	30	40	50
m	40.9	33.5	27.4	22.5	18.4

a Draw the graph of $\ln m$ against t.
b Use your graph to estimate the value of m_0 and k.
c Estimate the value of m when $t = 27$.

5

x	10	100	1000	10 000
y	15	75	378	1893

The table shows experimental values of the variables x and y.
The variables are known to be related by the equation $y = kx^n$ where k and n are constants.

a Draw the graph of $\lg y$ against $\lg x$.
b Use your graph to estimate the value of k and n.

6

x	2	4	6	8	10
y	12.8	32.8	83.9	214.7	549.8

The table shows experimental values of the variables x and y.
The variables are known to be related by the equation $y = a \times b^x$ where a and b are constants.

a Draw the graph of $\lg y$ against x.
b Use your graph to estimate the value of a and the value of b.

7

x	2	4	6	8	10
y	4.9	13.3	36.2	98.3	267.1

The table shows experimental values of the variables x and y.
The variables are known to be related by the equation $y = a \times e^{nx}$ where a and n are constants.

a Draw the graph of $\ln y$ against x.
b Use your graph to estimate the value of a and the value of n.

8

x	2	4	6	8	10
y	30.0	44.7	66.7	99.5	148.4

The table shows experimental values of the variables x and y.

The variables are known to be related by the equation $y = e^{ax+b}$ where a and b are constants.

a Draw the graph of $\ln y$ against x.

b Use your graph to estimate the value of a and the value of b.

c Estimate the value of x when $y = 50$.

9

x	2	4	6	8	10
y	0.10	0.33	1.08	3.48	11.29

The table shows experimental values of the variables x and y.

The variables are known to be related by the equation $y = 10^a \times b^x$, where a and b are constants.

a Draw the graph of $\lg y$ against x.

b Use your graph to estimate the value of a and the value of b.

c Estimate the value of x when $y = 5$.

10

x	0.2	0.4	0.5	0.7	0.9
y	36	12	9	6	4.5

The table shows experimental values of the variables x and y.

The variables are known to be related by the equation $y = \dfrac{a}{x+b}$, where a and b are constants.

a Draw the graph of y against xy.

b Use your graph to estimate the value of a and the value of b.

An alternate method for obtaining a straight-line graph for the equation $y = \dfrac{a}{x+b}$ is to plot x on the vertical axis and $\dfrac{1}{y}$ on the horizontal axis.

c Without drawing a second graph, estimate the gradient and the intercept on the vertical axis of this graph.

11

x	2	5	15	25	60
y	11.5	5.54	2.30	1.53	0.76

The table shows experimental values of the variables x and y.

a Draw the graph of $\ln y$ against $\ln x$.

b Express y in terms of x.

An alternate method for obtaining the relationship between x and y is to plot $\lg y$ on the vertical axis and $\lg x$ on the horizontal axis.

c Without drawing a second graph, find the gradient and the intercept on the vertical axis of this graph.

Summary

Length of a line segment, gradient and mid-point

Length of $PQ = \sqrt{(x_2 - x_1)^2 + (y_2 - y_1)^2}$

Gradient of $PQ = \dfrac{y_2 - y_1}{x_2 - x_1}$

Mid-point of $PQ = \left(\dfrac{x_1 + x_2}{2}, \dfrac{y_1 + y_2}{2} \right)$

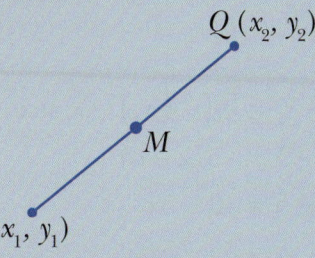

Parallel and perpendicular lines

If two lines are parallel then their gradients are equal.

If a line has a gradient of m, a line perpendicular to it has a gradient of $-\dfrac{1}{m}$.

If the gradients of the two perpendicular lines are m_1 and m_2, then $m_1 \times m_2 = -1$.

The equation of a straight line

$y = mx + c$ where m = the gradient and c = the y-intercept.

$y - y_1 = m(x - x_1)$ where m = the gradient and (x_1, y_1) is a known point on the line.

Non-linear equations

To convert a non-linear equation involving x and y into a linear equation, express the equation in the form $Y = mX + c$, where X and Y are expressions in x and/or y.

Examination questions

Worked example exam question

Solutions to this question by accurate drawing will not be accepted.

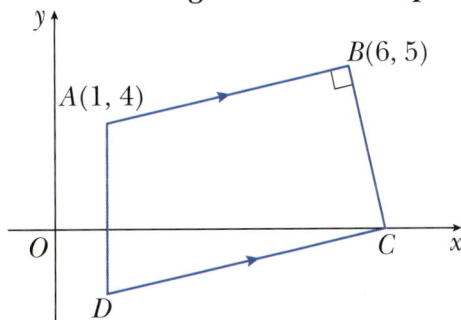

The diagram shows a quadrilateral $ABCD$ in which A is the point $(1, 4)$, and B is the point $(6, 5)$. Angle ABC is a right angle and the point C lies on the x-axis. The line AD is parallel to the y-axis and the line CD is parallel to BA. Find

a the equation of the line CD, [5]

b the area of the quadrilateral $ABCD$. [4]

Cambridge IGCSE Additional Mathematics 0606 Paper 21 Q10i,ii Nov 2010

Answers

a Gradient of $AB = \dfrac{5-4}{6-1} = \dfrac{1}{5}$ use $m_1 m_2 = -1$ to find gradient of BC

Gradient of $BC = -5$

Equation of BC: $y - y_1 = m(x - x_1)$ use $m = -5$, $x_1 = 6$ and $y_1 = 5$

$y - 5 = -5(x - 6)$

$y - 5 = 30 - 5x$

$y = 35 - 5x$

When $y = 0$, $0 = 35 - 5x$

$x = 7$

C is the point $(7, 0)$

Equation of CD: $y - y_1 = m(x - x_1)$ use $m = \dfrac{1}{5}$, $x_1 = 7$ and $y_1 = 0$

$y - 0 = \dfrac{1}{5}(x - 7)$

Equation of CD is $y = \dfrac{1}{5}(x - 7)$

b AD is parallel to the y-axis, hence the x-coordinate of D is 1.

Substituting $x = 1$ into the equation $y = \dfrac{1}{5}(x - 7)$ gives $y = -1.2$.

Use the 'shoestring' method with $A(1, 4)$, $B(6, 5)$, $C(7, 0)$ and $D(1, -1.2)$.

Area of $ABCD = \dfrac{1}{2} \left| \begin{array}{ccccc} 1 & 6 & 7 & 1 & 1 \\ 4 & 5 & 0 & -1.2 & 4 \end{array} \right|$

$= \dfrac{1}{2} |5 + 0 + (-8.4) + 4 - 24 - 35 - 0 - (-1.2)|$

$= \dfrac{1}{2} |-57.2|$

$= 28.6$ units^2

Exercise 7.8

Exam exercise

1. The point P lies on the line joining $A(-2, 3)$ and $B(10, 19)$ such that $AP:PB = 1:3$.
   a Show that the x-coordinate of P is 1 and find the y-coordinate of P. [2]
   b Find the equation of the line through P which is perpendicular to AB. [3]
   The line through P which is perpendicular to AB meets the y-axis at the point Q.
   c Find the area of the triangle AQB. [3]

   Cambridge IGCSE Additional Mathematics 0606 Paper 11 Q8 Nov 2014

2 The table shows values of variables V and p.

V	10	50	100	200
p	95.0	8.5	3.0	1.1

   a By plotting a suitable straight line graph, show that V and p are related by the equation $p = kV^n$, where k and n are constants. [4]

   Use your graph to find

   b the value of n, [2]

   c the value of p when $V = 35$. [2]

   Cambridge IGCSE Additional Mathematics 0606 Paper 11 Q8i,ii,iii Jun 2014

3 **Solutions to this question by accurate drawing will not be accepted**.

   The points $A(-3, 2)$ and $B(1, 4)$ are vertices of an isosceles triangle ABC, where angle $B = 90°$.

   a Find the length of the line AB. [1]

   b Find the equation of the line BC. [3]

   c Find the coordinates of each of the two possible positions of C. [6]

   Cambridge IGCSE Additional Mathematics 0606 Paper 11 Q10i,ii,iii Nov 2013

4 Variables x and y are such that $y = Ab^x$, where A and b are constants. The diagram shows the graph of $\ln y$ against x, passing through the points $(2, 4)$ and $(8, 10)$.

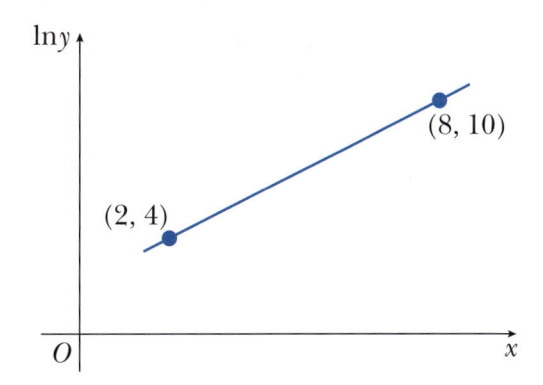

   Find the value of A and of b. [5]

   Cambridge IGCSE Additional Mathematics 0606 Paper 11 Q2 Jun 2013

5 Solutions to this question by accurate drawing will not be accepted.

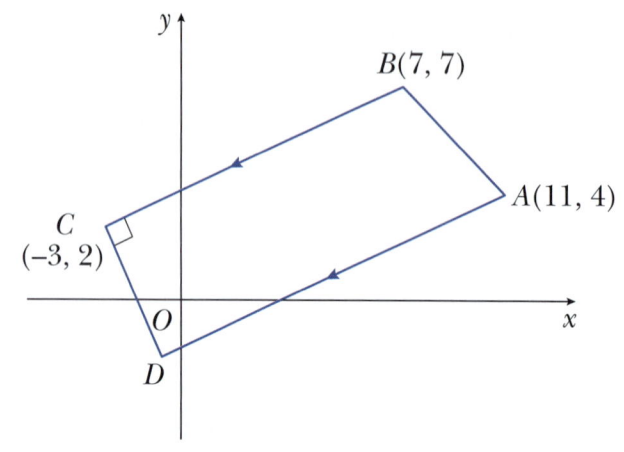

The diagram shows a trapezium $ABCD$ with vertices $A(11, 4)$, $B(7, 7)$, $C(-3, 2)$ and D.
The side AD is parallel to BC and the side CD is perpendicular to BC.
Find the area of the trapezium $ABCD$. [9]

Cambridge IGCSE Additional Mathematics 0606 Paper 21 Q10 Jun 2012

6 The table shows experimental values of two variables x and y.

x	1	2	3	4	5
y	3.40	2.92	2.93	3.10	3.34

It is known that x and y are related by the equation $y = \dfrac{a}{\sqrt{x}} + bx$, where a and b are constants.

a Complete the following table.

$x\sqrt{x}$					
$y\sqrt{x}$					

[1]

b On a grid plot $y\sqrt{x}$ against $x\sqrt{x}$ and draw a straight line graph. [2]
c Use your graph to estimate the value of a and of b. [3]
d Estimate the value of y when x is 1.5. [1]

Cambridge IGCSE Additional Mathematics 0606 Paper 21 Q9i-iv Nov 2011

7 The points A and B have coordinates $(-2, 15)$ and $(3, 5)$ respectively.
The perpendicular to the line AB at the point $A(-2, 15)$ crosses the y-axis at the point C.
Find the area of triangle ABC. [6]

Cambridge IGCSE Additional Mathematics 0606 Paper 11 Q7 Jun 2011

8 Variables x and y are such that, when $\ln y$ is plotted against $\ln x$, a straight line graph passing through the points $(2, 5.8)$ and $(6, 3.8)$ is obtained.

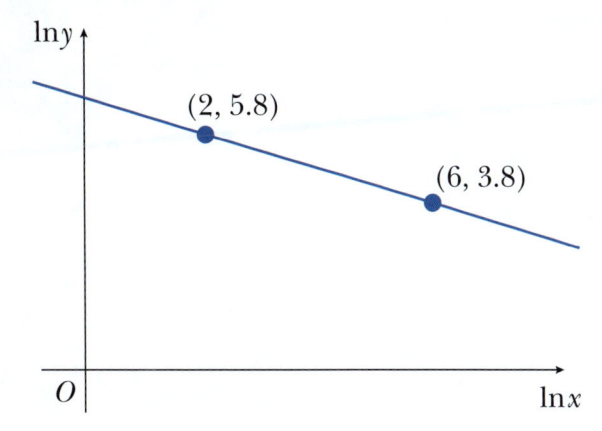

i Find the value of $\ln y$ when $\ln x = 0$. [2]

ii Given that $y = Ax^b$, find the value of A and of b. [5]

Cambridge IGCSE Additional Mathematics 0606 Paper 11 Q8i,ii Nov 2010

Chapter 8
Circular measure

This section will show you how to:

- use radian measure
- solve problems involving the arc length and sector area of a circle.

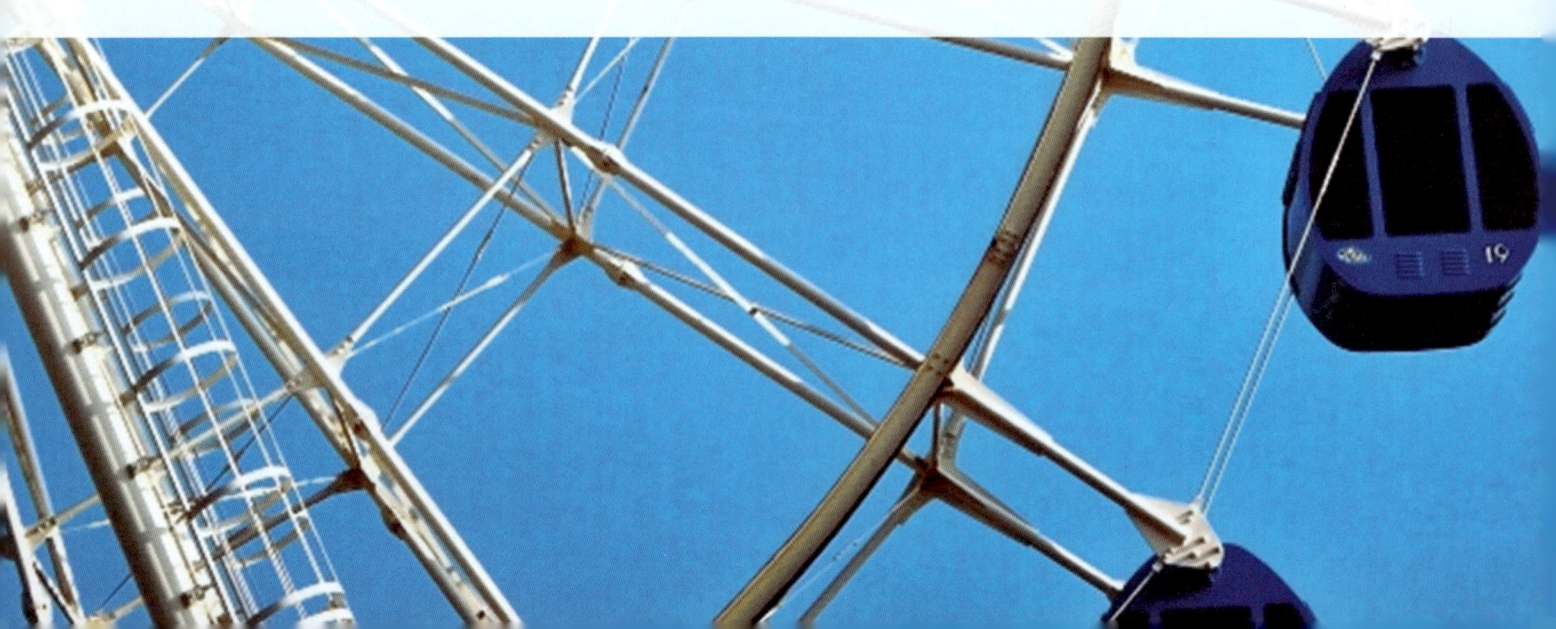

8.1 Circular measure

Have you ever wondered why there are 360 degrees in one complete revolution?

The original reason for choosing the degree as a unit of angular measure is actually unknown but there are a number of different theories:

- ancient astronomers claimed that the Sun advanced in its path by one degree each day and that a solar year consisted of 360 days
- the ancient Babylonians divided the circle into 6 equilateral triangles and then subdivided each angle at O into 60 further parts, resulting in 360 divisions in one complete revolution
- 360 has many factors which makes division of the circle so much easier.

Degrees are not the only way in which you can measure angles. In this section you will learn how to use **radian** measure. This is sometimes referred to as the natural unit of angular measure and it is used extensively in mathematics because it can simplify many formulae and calculations.

In the diagram below, the magnitude of angle AOB is 1 radian (1 radian is written as 1 rad or 1^c).

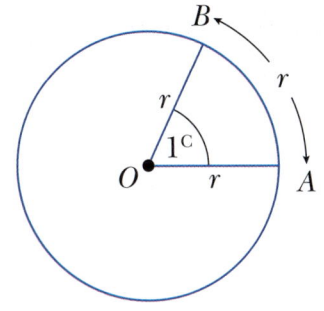

> An arc equal in length to the radius of a circle subtends an angle of 1 radian at the centre.

It follows that the circumference (an arc of length $2\pi r$) subtends an angle of 2π radians at the centre.

$$2\pi \text{ radians} = 360°$$

> π radians = 180°

When an angle is written in terms of π, the radian symbol is usually omitted. Hence, $\pi = 180°$.

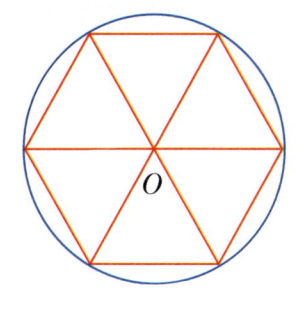

Cambridge IGCSE and O Level Additional Mathematics

Converting from degrees to radians

Since $180° = \pi$, then $90° = \dfrac{\pi}{2}$, $45° = \dfrac{\pi}{4}$ etc.

Angles that are not simple fractions of 180° can be converted using the following rule:

> To change from degrees to radians, multiply by $\dfrac{\pi}{180}$.

Converting from radians to degrees

Since $\pi = 180°$, $\dfrac{\pi}{6} = 30°$, $\dfrac{\pi}{10} = 18°$ etc.

Angles that are not simple fractions of π can be converted using the following rule:

> To change from radians to degrees, multiply by $\dfrac{180}{\pi}$.

(It is useful to remember that 1 radian $= 1 \times \dfrac{180}{\pi} \approx 57°$.)

WORKED EXAMPLE 1

a Change 60° to radians, giving your answer in terms of π.

b Change $\dfrac{3\pi}{5}$ radians to degrees.

Answers

a Method 1:

$180° = \pi$ radians

$\left(\dfrac{180}{3}\right)° = \dfrac{\pi}{3}$ radians

$60° = \dfrac{\pi}{3}$ radians

Method 2:

$60° = \left(60 \times \dfrac{\pi}{180}\right)$ radians

$60° = \dfrac{\pi}{3}$ radians

b Method 1:

π radians $= 180°$

$\dfrac{\pi}{5}$ radians $= 36°$

$\dfrac{3\pi}{5}$ radians $= 108°$

Method 2:

$\dfrac{3\pi}{5}$ radians $= \left(\dfrac{3\pi}{5} \times \dfrac{180}{\pi}\right)°$

$\dfrac{3\pi}{5}$ radians $= 108°$

Chapter 8: Circular measure

Exercise 8.1

1 Change these angles to radians, in terms of π.
  a 10°   b 20°   c 40°   d 50°   e 15°
  f 120°   g 135°   h 225°   i 360°   j 720°
  k 80°   l 300°   m 9°   n 75°   o 210°

2 Change these angles to degrees.
  a $\dfrac{\pi}{2}$ b $\dfrac{\pi}{6}$ c $\dfrac{\pi}{12}$ d $\dfrac{\pi}{9}$ e $\dfrac{2\pi}{3}$
  f $\dfrac{4\pi}{5}$ g $\dfrac{7\pi}{10}$ h $\dfrac{5\pi}{12}$ i $\dfrac{3\pi}{20}$ j $\dfrac{9\pi}{10}$
  k $\dfrac{6\pi}{5}$ l 3π m $\dfrac{7\pi}{4}$ n $\dfrac{8\pi}{3}$ o $\dfrac{9\pi}{2}$

3 Write each of these angles in radians correct to 3 sf.
  a 32°   b 55°   c 84°   d 123°   e 247°

4 Write each of these angles in degrees correct to 1 decimal place.
  a 1.3 rad   b 2.5 rad   c 1.02 rad   d 1.83 rad   e 0.58 rad

5 Copy and complete the tables, giving your answers in terms of π.

a
Degrees	0	45	90	135	180	225	270	315	360
Radians	0				π				2π

b
Degrees	0	30	60	90	120	150	180	210	240	270	300	330	360
Radians	0						π						2π

6 Use your calculator to find
  a sin 1.3 rad   b tan 0.8 rad   c sin 1.2 rad
  d $\sin \dfrac{\pi}{2}$ e $\cos \dfrac{\pi}{3}$ f $\tan \dfrac{\pi}{4}$.

> **Note:**
> You do not need to change the angle to degrees. You should set the angle mode on your calculator to radians.

CLASS DISCUSSION

You should already be familiar with the following mathematical words that are used in circle questions:

- chord
- arc
- sector
- segment

Discuss and explain, with the aid of diagrams, the meaning of each of these words.

Explain what is meant by:

- minor arc and major arc
- minor sector and major sector
- minor segment and major segment.

If you know the radius, r cm, and the angle θ (in degrees) at the centre of the circle, describe how you would find:

- arc length
- area of sector
- perimeter of sector
- length of chord
- perimeter of segment
- area of segment.

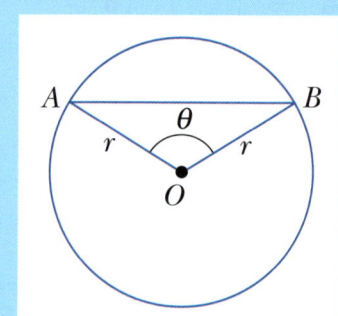

8.2 Length of an arc

From the definition of a radian, the arc that subtends an angle of 1 radian at the centre of the circle is of length r. Hence, if an arc subtends an angle of θ radians at the centre, the length of the arc is $r\theta$.

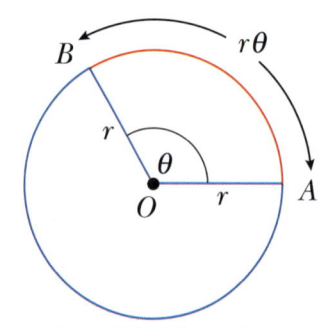

$$\text{Arc length} = r\theta$$

WORKED EXAMPLE 2

An arc subtends an angle of $\dfrac{\pi}{6}$ radians at the centre of a circle with radius 8 cm. Find the length of the arc in terms of π.

Answers

$$\begin{aligned}
\text{Arc length} &= r\theta \\
&= 8 \times \frac{\pi}{6} \\
&= \frac{4\pi}{3} \text{ cm}
\end{aligned}$$

Chapter 8: Circular measure

WORKED EXAMPLE 3

A sector has an angle of 2 radians and an arc length of 9.6 cm.
Find the radius of the sector.

Answers

Arc length $= r\theta$
$9.6 = r \times 2$
$r = 4.8$ cm

WORKED EXAMPLE 4

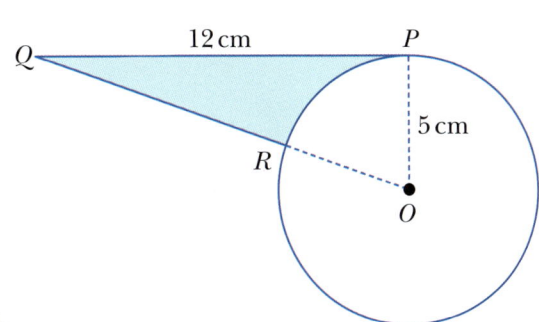

The circle has radius 5 cm and centre O.

PQ is a tangent to the circle at the point P.

QRO is a straight line. Find:

a angle POQ, in radians
b QR
c the perimeter of the shaded region.

Answers

a $\tan POQ = \dfrac{12}{5}$ triangle QPO is right-angled since PQ is a tangent

Angle $POQ = \tan^{-1}\left(\dfrac{12}{5}\right)$ remember to have your calculator in radian mode

$= 1.176...$
$= 1.18$ radians

b $OQ^2 = 12^2 + 5^2$ using Pythagoras
$OQ^2 = 169$
$OQ = 13$
Hence $QR = 8$ cm.

c Perimeter $= PQ + QR +$ arc PR use arc $PR = r\theta$
$= 12 + 8 + (5 \times 1.176...)$
$= 25.9$ cm

Exercise 8.2

1 Find, in terms of π, the arc length of a sector of:

  a radius 6 cm and angle $\dfrac{\pi}{4}$
  b radius 5 cm and angle $\dfrac{2\pi}{5}$
  c radius 10 cm and angle $\dfrac{3\pi}{8}$
  d radius 18 cm and angle $\dfrac{5\pi}{6}$.

2   Find the arc length of a sector of:
    a radius 8 cm and angle 1.2 radians   b radius 2.5 cm and angle 0.8 radians.

3   Find, in radians, the angle of a sector of:
    a radius 4 cm and arc length 5 cm   b radius 9 cm and arc length 13.5 cm.

4   Find the perimeter of each of these sectors.
    a 1.1 rad, 4 cm
    b 2 rad, 8 cm
    c 4.2 rad, 5 cm

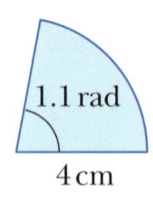

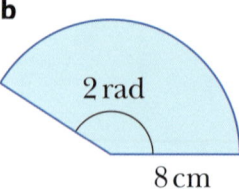

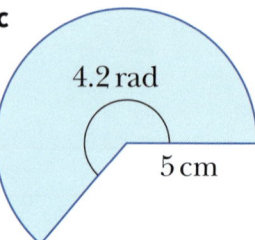

5   $ABCD$ is a rectangle with $AB = 6$ cm and $BC = 16$ cm.
    O is the mid-point of BC.
    $OAED$ is a sector of a circle, centre O. Find:
    a AO
    b angle AOD, in radians
    c the perimeter of the shaded region.

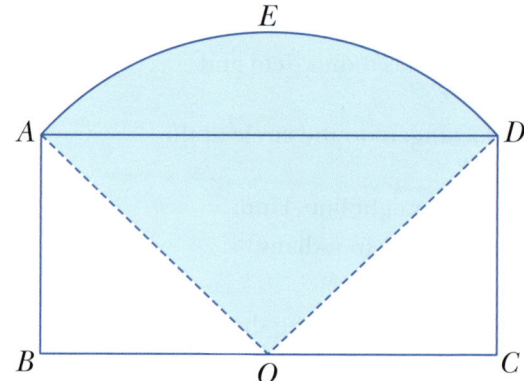

6   Find:
    a the length of arc AB
    b the length of chord AB
    c the perimeter of the shaded segment.

7   Triangle EFG is isosceles with $EG = FG = 16$ cm.
    GH is an arc of a circle, centre F, with angle $HFG = 0.85$ radians. Find:
    a the length of arc GH
    b the length of EF
    c the perimeter of the shaded region.

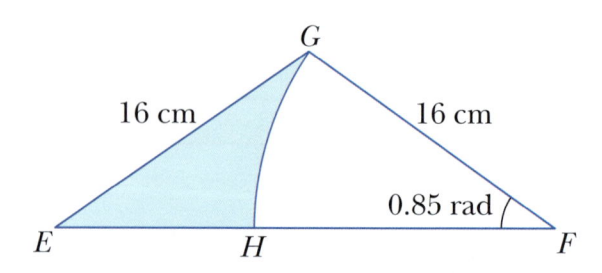

8.3 Area of a sector

To find the formula for the area of a sector you use the ratio:

$$\frac{\text{area of sector}}{\text{area of circle}} = \frac{\text{angle in the sector}}{\text{complete angle at the centre}}$$

When θ is measured in radians, the ratio becomes

$$\frac{\text{area of sector}}{\pi r^2} = \frac{\theta}{2\pi}$$

$$\text{area of sector} = \frac{\theta}{2\pi} \times \pi r^2$$

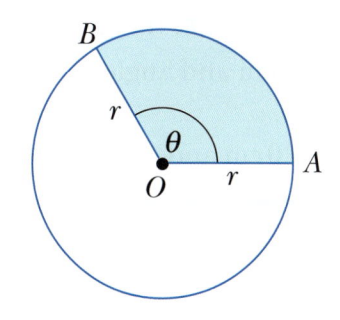

$$\text{area of sector} = \frac{1}{2} r^2 \theta$$

WORKED EXAMPLE 5

Find the area of a sector of a circle with radius 6 cm and angle $\frac{2\pi}{3}$ radians. Give your answer in terms of π.

Answers

$$\text{Area of sector} = \frac{1}{2} r^2 \theta$$

$$= \frac{1}{2} \times 6^2 \times \frac{2\pi}{3}$$

$$= 12\pi \, \text{cm}^2$$

WORKED EXAMPLE 6

Calculate the area of the shaded segment correct to 3 sf.

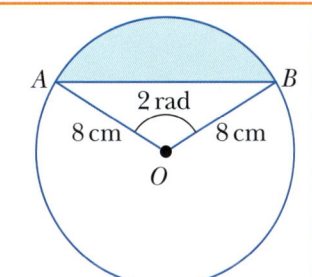

Answers

Area of triangle $AOB = \frac{1}{2} \times 8 \times 8 \times \sin(2^c)$ using area of triangle $= \frac{1}{2} ab \sin C$

$$= 29.0975...$$
$$= 29.0975...$$

Area of sector $AOB = \frac{1}{2} \times 8 \times 8 \times 2$ using area of sector $= \frac{1}{2} r^2 \theta$

$$= 64$$

Area of segment = area of sector AOB − area of triangle AOB

$$= 64 - 29.0975...$$
$$= 34.9 \, \text{cm}^2$$

Exercise 8.3

1. Find, in terms of π, the area of a sector of:
   - **a** radius 6 cm and angle $\dfrac{\pi}{3}$
   - **b** radius 15 cm and angle $\dfrac{3\pi}{5}$
   - **c** radius 10 cm and angle $\dfrac{7\pi}{10}$
   - **d** radius 9 cm and angle $\dfrac{5\pi}{6}$.

2. Find the area of a sector of:
   - **a** radius 4 cm and angle 1.3 radians
   - **b** radius 3.8 cm and angle 0.6 radians.

3. Find, in radians, the angle of a sector of:
   - **a** radius 3 cm and area 5 cm²
   - **b** radius 7 cm and area 30 cm².

4. *POQ* is the sector of a circle, centre *O*, radius 10 cm.
   The length of arc *PQ* is 8 cm. Find:
   - **a** angle *POQ*, in radians
   - **b** the area of the sector *POQ*.

5. A sector of a circle, radius *r* cm, has a perimeter of 150 cm.
   Find an expression, in terms of *r*, for the area of the sector.

6. *ABCD* is a rectangle with *AB* = 9 cm and *BC* = 18 cm.
   O is the mid-point of *BC*.
   OAED is a sector of a circle, centre *O*. Find:
   - **a** *AO*
   - **b** angle *AOD*, in radians
   - **c** the area of the shaded region.

7. The circle has radius 12 cm and centre *O*.
   PQ is a tangent to the circle at the point *P*.
   QRO is a straight line. Find:
   - **a** angle *POQ*, in radians
   - **b** the area of sector *POR*
   - **c** the area of the shaded region.

8. *AOB* is the sector of a circle, centre *O*, radius 8 cm.
   AC is a tangent to the circle at the point *A*.
   CBO is a straight line and the area of sector *AOB* is 32 cm².
   Find:
   - **a** angle *AOB*, in radians
   - **b** the area of triangle *AOC*
   - **c** the area of the shaded region.

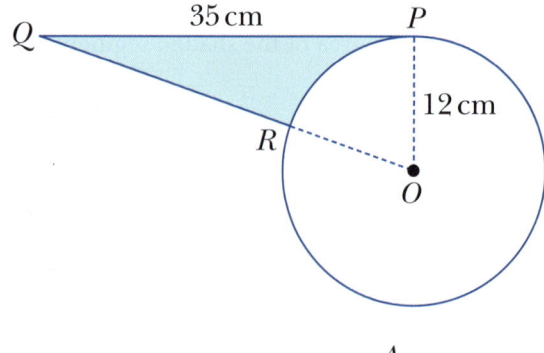

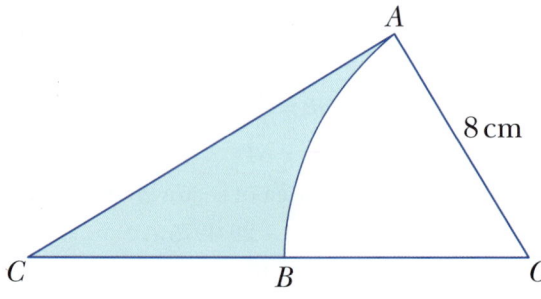

Chapter 8: Circular measure

9 Triangle *EFG* is isosceles with *EG* = *FG* = 9 cm.
  GH is an arc of a circle, centre *F*, with angle
  HFG = 0.6 radians. Find:
  a the area of sector of *HFG*
  b the area of triangle *EFG*
  c the area of the shaded region.

10 The diagram shows a circle, centre *O*, radius 12 cm.
   Angle *AOB* = θ radians.
   Arc *AB* = 9π cm.
   a Show that $\theta = \dfrac{3\pi}{4}$.
   b Find the area of the shaded region.

11 *AOD* is a sector of a circle, centre *O*, radius 4 cm.
   BOC is a sector of a circle, centre *O*, radius 10 cm.
   The shaded region has a perimeter of 18 cm. Find:
   a angle *AOD*, in radians
   b the area of the shaded region.

12 *AOB* is a sector of a circle, centre *O*, with radius 9 cm.
   Angle *COD* = 0.5 radians and angle *ODC* is a right angle.
   OC = 5 cm. Find:
   a *OD*
   b *CD*
   c the perimeter of the shaded region
   d the area of the shaded region.

13 *FOG* is a sector of a circle, centre *O*, with angle
   FOG = 1.2 radians.
   EOH is a sector of a circle, centre *O*, with radius 5 cm.
   The shaded region has an area of 71.4 cm².
   Find the perimeter of the shaded region.

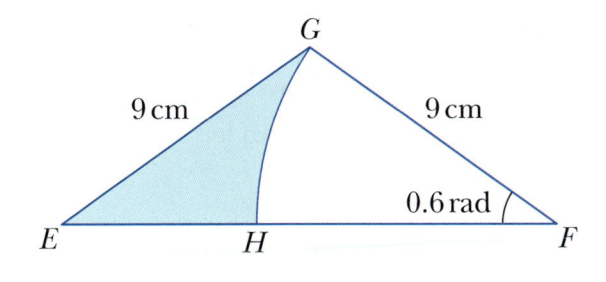

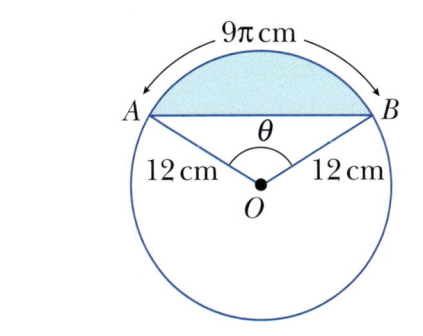

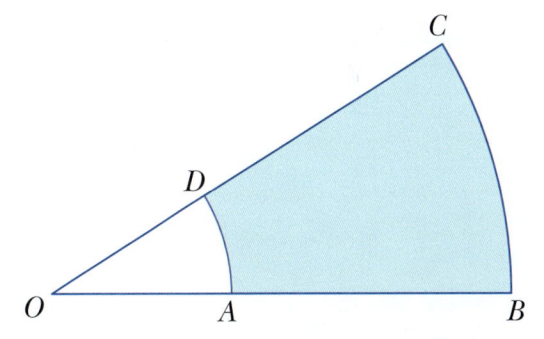

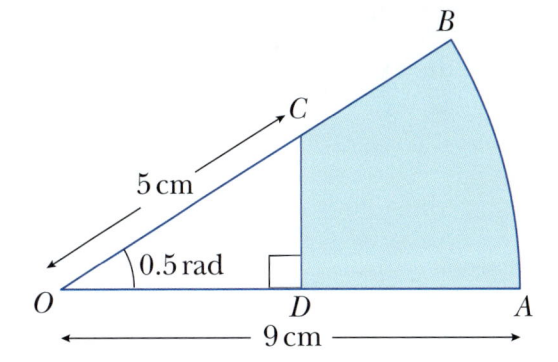

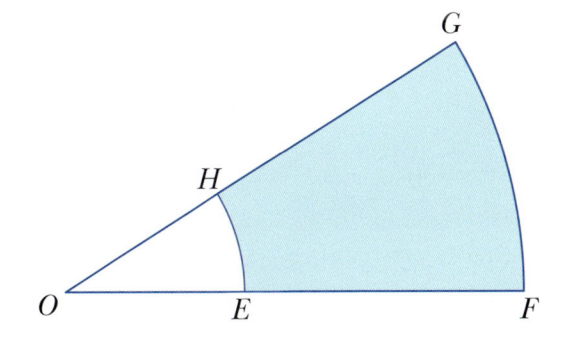

CHALLENGE Q

14 The diagram shows a semi-circle, centre O, radius 10 cm.

FH is the arc of a circle, centre E.

Find the area of:

a triangle EOF

b sector FOG

c sector FEH

d the shaded region.

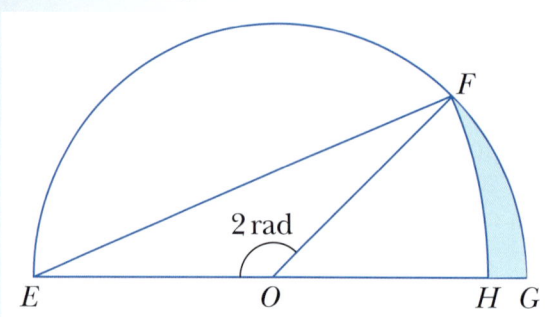

Summary

One radian (1^c) is the size of the angle subtended at the centre of a circle, radius r, by an arc of length r.

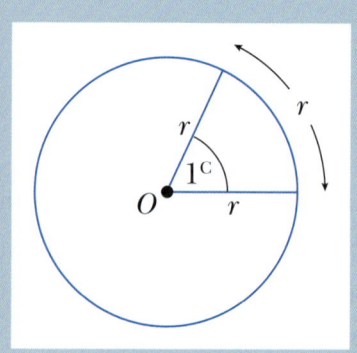

When θ is measured in radians:

- the length of arc $AB = r\theta$
- the area of sector $AOB = \dfrac{1}{2}r^2\theta$.

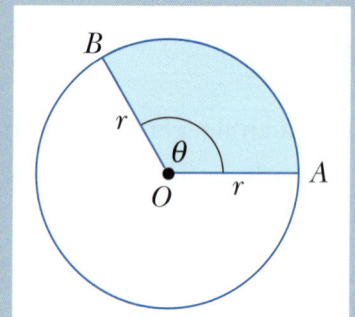

Chapter 8: Circular measure

Examination questions

Worked example

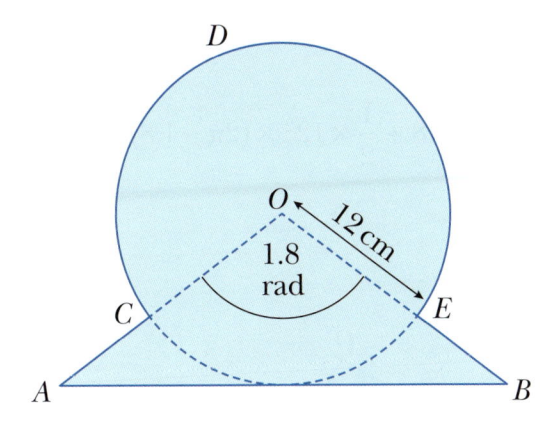

The diagram shows an isosceles triangle AOB and a sector $OCDEO$ of a circle with centre O.
The line AB is a tangent to the circle.
Angle $AOB = 1.8$ radians and the radius of the circle is 12 cm.

a Show that the distance $AC = 7.3$ cm to 1 decimal place. [2]
b Find the perimeter of the shaded region. [6]
c Find the area of the shaded region. [4]

Cambridge IGCSE Additional Mathematics 0606 Paper 21 Q11 Jun 2011

Answer

a $\cos 0.9 = \dfrac{12}{OA}$

$OA = \dfrac{12}{\cos 0.9} = 19.3047...$

$AC = OA - 12 = 7.3047...$

$= 7.3$ to 1 dp

b Perimeter = arc CDE + EB + BA + AC hence need to find arc CDE, EB and BA
  arc CDE: arc $CDE = r\theta$ where θ is the angle in the major sector $= 2\pi - 1.8$
  $= 12 \times (2\pi - 1.8)$
  $= 53.798...$

  EB: $\cos 0.9 = \dfrac{12}{OB}$ using half of the isosceles triangle

  $OB = \dfrac{12}{\cos 0.9} = 19.3047...$

  $EB = OB - OE = 19.3047 - 12 = 7.3047...$

  BA: $BA = 2 \times (OA \times \sin 0.9) = 30.24378...$

  Perimeter = arc CDE + EB + BA + AC
  $= 53.798... + 7.3047... + 30.24378... + 7.3047...$
  $= 98.7$ cm

c area of shaded region = area of triangle OAB + area of major sector CDE

$$= \frac{1}{2}ab\sin C + \frac{1}{2}r^2\theta$$

$$= \frac{1}{2} \times 19.307^2 \times \sin 1.8 + \frac{1}{2} \times 12^2 \times (2\pi - 1.8)$$

$$= 504 \text{ cm}^2$$

Exercise 8.4
Exam Exercise

1

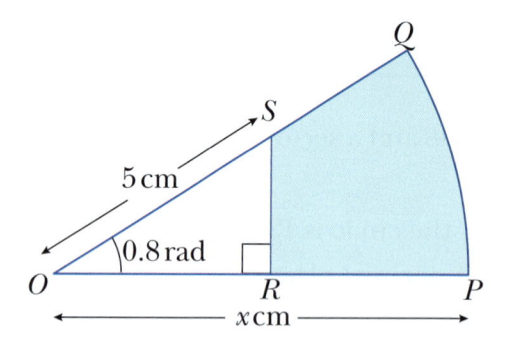

The diagram shows a sector OPQ of a circle with centre O and radius x cm.
Angle POQ is 0.8 radians. The point S lies on OQ such that $OS = 5$ cm.
The point R lies on OP such that angle ORS is a right angle.
Given that the area of triangle ORS is one-fifth of the area of sector OPQ, find

   a the area of sector OPQ in terms of x and hence show that the value of x is 8.837 correct to 4 significant figures, [5]
   b the perimeter of $PQSR$, [3]
   c the area of $PQSR$. [2]

Cambridge IGCSE Additional Mathematics 0606 Paper 21 Q11a,b Nov 2014

2

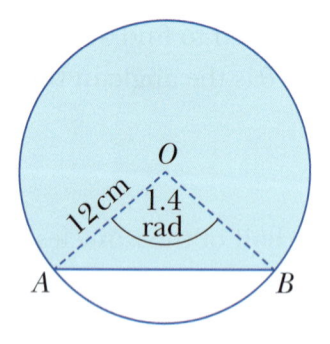

The diagram shows a circle with centre O and a chord AB.
The radius of the circle is 12 cm and angle AOB is 1.4 radians.

   a Find the perimeter of the shaded region. [5]
   b Find the area of the shaded region. [4]

Cambridge IGCSE Additional Mathematics 0606 Paper 21 Q10i,ii Nov 2013

3

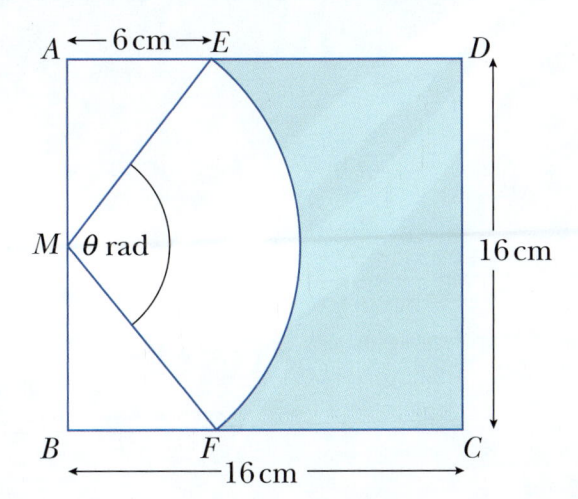

The diagram shows a square *ABCD* of side 16 cm. *M* is the mid-point of *AB*.
The points *E* and *F* are on *AD* and *BC* respectively such that *AE* = *BF* = 6 cm.
EF is an arc of the circle centre *M*, such that angle *EMF* is θ radians.

a Show that $\theta = 1.855$ radians, correct to 3 decimal places. [2]
b Calculate the perimeter of the shaded region. [4]
c Calculate the area of the shaded region. [3]

Cambridge IGCSE Additional Mathematics 0606 Paper 11 Q8i,ii,iii Jun 2013

4

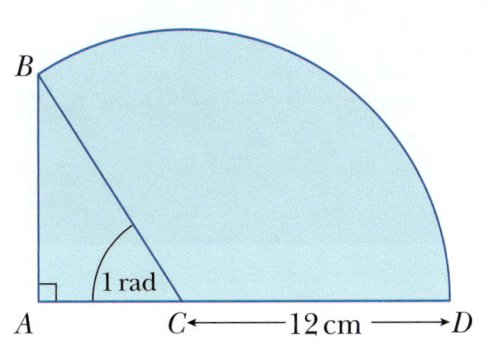

The diagram shows a right-angled triangle *ABC* and a sector *CBDC* of a circle with centre *C* and radius 12 cm. Angle *ACB* = 1 radian and *ACD* is a straight line.

a Show that the length of *AB* is approximately 10.1 cm. [1]
b Find the perimeter of the shaded region. [5]
c Find the area of the shaded region. [4]

Cambridge IGCSE Additional Mathematics 0606 Paper 21 Q11i,ii,iii Jun 2012

Chapter 9
Trigonometry

This section will show you how to:

- find the trigonometric ratios of angles of any magnitude
- determine the amplitude and period of trigonometric functions
- describe the relationship between trigonometric graphs
- sketch graphs of $y = |f(x)|$, where f(x) is a trigonometric function
- draw and use the graphs of $y = a\sin bx + c$, $y = a\cos bx + c$, $y = a\tan bx + c$
- use trigonometric relationships
- solve simple trigonometric equations
- prove simple trigonometric identities.

Chapter 9: Trigonometry

> **RECAP**
>
> You should already know the following trigonometric ratios:
>
> $\sin\theta = \dfrac{\text{opposite}}{\text{hypotenuse}}$ $\cos\theta = \dfrac{\text{adjacent}}{\text{hypotenuse}}$ $\tan\theta = \dfrac{\text{opposite}}{\text{adjacent}}$
>
> $\sin\theta = \dfrac{y}{r}$ $\cos\theta = \dfrac{x}{r}$ $\tan\theta = \dfrac{y}{x}$

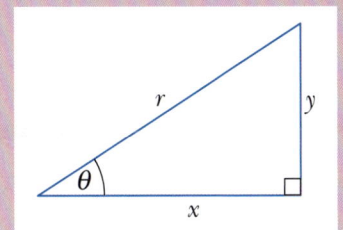

9.1 Angles between 0° and 90°

WORKED EXAMPLE 1

Given that $\sin\theta = \dfrac{2}{\sqrt{5}}$ and that θ is acute, find the exact values of

a $\sin^2\theta$ **b** $\cos\theta$ **c** $\tan\theta$ **d** $\dfrac{\sin\theta}{\tan\theta - \cos\theta}$.

Answers

a $\sin^2\theta = \sin\theta \times \sin\theta$ $\sin^2\theta$ means $(\sin\theta)^2$

$= \dfrac{2}{\sqrt{5}} \times \dfrac{2}{\sqrt{5}}$

$= \dfrac{4}{5}$

b $\sin\theta = \dfrac{2}{\sqrt{5}}$

The right-angled triangle to represent θ is:

Using Pythagoras' theorem, $x = \sqrt{(\sqrt{5})^2 - 2^2}$

$x = 1$

Hence, $\cos\theta = \dfrac{1}{\sqrt{5}} = \dfrac{\sqrt{5}}{5}$.

c $\tan\theta = \dfrac{2}{1} = 2$

d $\dfrac{\sin\theta}{\tan\theta - \cos\theta} = \dfrac{\frac{2}{\sqrt{5}}}{2 - \frac{1}{\sqrt{5}}}$ multiply numerator and denominator by $\sqrt{5}$

$= \dfrac{2}{2\sqrt{5} - 1}$ multiply numerator and denominator by $(2\sqrt{5} + 1)$

$= \dfrac{2(2\sqrt{5} + 1)}{(2\sqrt{5} - 1)(2\sqrt{5} + 1)}$

$= \dfrac{2(2\sqrt{5} + 1)}{19}$

$= \dfrac{2 + 4\sqrt{5}}{19}$

The sine, cosine and tangent of 30°, 45° and 60° (or $\frac{\pi}{6}$, $\frac{\pi}{4}$ and $\frac{\pi}{3}$) can be obtained exactly from the following two triangles:

Consider a right-angled isosceles triangle whose two equal sides are of length 1 unit.

The third side is found using Pythagoras' theorem: $\sqrt{1^2 + 1^2} = \sqrt{2}$

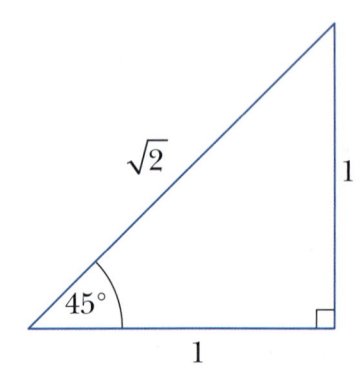

$$\sin 45° = \frac{1}{\sqrt{2}} \left(= \frac{\sqrt{2}}{2}\right) \qquad \sin \frac{\pi}{4} = \frac{1}{\sqrt{2}} \left(= \frac{\sqrt{2}}{2}\right)$$

$$\cos 45° = \frac{1}{\sqrt{2}} \left(= \frac{\sqrt{2}}{2}\right) \qquad \cos \frac{\pi}{4} = \frac{1}{\sqrt{2}} \left(= \frac{\sqrt{2}}{2}\right)$$

$$\tan 45° = 1 \qquad \tan \frac{\pi}{4} = 1$$

Consider an equilateral triangle whose sides are of length 2 units.

The perpendicular bisector to the base splits the equilateral triangle into two congruent right-angled triangles.

The height of the triangle can be found using Pythagoras' theorem: $\sqrt{2^2 - 1^2} = \sqrt{3}$

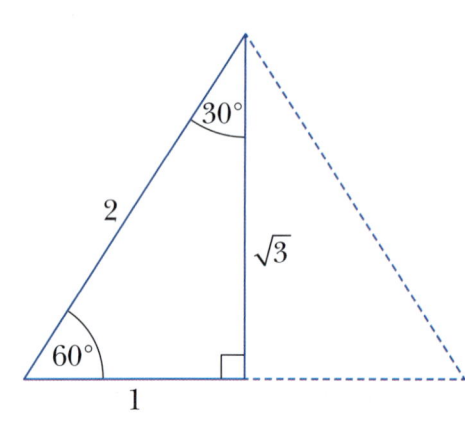

$$\sin 60° = \frac{\sqrt{3}}{2} \qquad \sin \frac{\pi}{3} = \frac{\sqrt{3}}{2}$$

$$\cos 60° = \frac{1}{2} \qquad \cos \frac{\pi}{3} = \frac{1}{2}$$

$$\tan 60° = \sqrt{3} \qquad \tan \frac{\pi}{3} = \sqrt{3}$$

$$\sin 30° = \frac{1}{2} \qquad \sin \frac{\pi}{6} = \frac{1}{2}$$

$$\cos 30° = \frac{\sqrt{3}}{2} \qquad \cos \frac{\pi}{6} = \frac{\sqrt{3}}{2}$$

$$\tan 30° = \frac{1}{\sqrt{3}} \left(= \frac{\sqrt{3}}{3}\right) \qquad \tan \frac{\pi}{6} = \frac{1}{\sqrt{3}} \left(= \frac{\sqrt{3}}{3}\right)$$

Note:
You do not need to learn these triangles and ratios for the examination, but you may find it useful to know them.

WORKED EXAMPLE 2

Find the exact value of

a $\sin 45° \sin 60°$ **b** $\cos^2 45°$ **c** $\dfrac{\tan \dfrac{\pi}{3} + \sin \dfrac{\pi}{4}}{1 - \cos \dfrac{\pi}{3}}$.

Answers

a $\sin 45° \sin 60° = \dfrac{1}{\sqrt{2}} \times \dfrac{\sqrt{3}}{2}$

$= \dfrac{\sqrt{3}}{2\sqrt{2}}$ rationalise the denominator

$= \dfrac{\sqrt{3} \times \sqrt{2}}{2\sqrt{2} \times \sqrt{2}}$

$= \dfrac{\sqrt{6}}{4}$

b $\cos^2 45° = \cos 45° \times \cos 45°$ $\cos^2 45°$ means $(\cos 45°)^2$

$= \dfrac{1}{\sqrt{2}} \times \dfrac{1}{\sqrt{2}}$

$= \dfrac{1}{2}$

c $\dfrac{\tan \dfrac{\pi}{3} + \sin \dfrac{\pi}{4}}{1 - \cos \dfrac{\pi}{3}} = \dfrac{\sqrt{3} + \dfrac{1}{\sqrt{2}}}{1 - \dfrac{1}{2}}$ the denominator simplifies to $\dfrac{1}{2}$

$= \left(\sqrt{3} + \dfrac{1}{\sqrt{2}}\right) \times 2$ expand brackets

$= 2\sqrt{3} + \dfrac{2}{\sqrt{2}}$ rationalise the denominator

$= 2\sqrt{3} + \sqrt{2}.$

Exercise 9.1

1 Given that $\tan \theta = \dfrac{2}{3}$ and that θ is acute, find the exact values of
   a $\sin \theta$ **b** $\cos \theta$ **c** $\sin^2 \theta$
   d $\sin^2 \theta + \cos^2 \theta$ **e** $\dfrac{2 + \sin \theta}{3 - \cos \theta}$.

2 Given that $\sin \theta = \dfrac{\sqrt{2}}{5}$ and that θ is acute, find the exact values of
   a $\cos \theta$ **b** $\tan \theta$ **c** $1 - \sin^2 \theta$
   d $\sin \theta + \cos \theta$ **e** $\dfrac{\cos \theta - \sin \theta}{\tan \theta}$.

3 Given that $\cos \theta = \dfrac{1}{7}$ and that θ is acute, find the exact values of
   a $\sin \theta$ **b** $\tan \theta$ **c** $\tan \theta \cos \theta$
   d $\sin^2 \theta + \cos^2 \theta$ **e** $\dfrac{\cos \theta - \tan \theta}{1 - \cos^2 \theta}$.

4 Find the exact value of each of the following.

a $\tan 45° \cos 60°$ **b** $\tan^2 60°$ **c** $\dfrac{\tan 30°}{\cos 30°}$

d $\sin 45° + \cos 30°$ **e** $\dfrac{\cos^2 30°}{\cos 45° + \cos 60°}$ **f** $\dfrac{\tan 45° - \sin 30°}{1 + \sin^2 60°}$.

5 Find the exact value of each of the following.

a $\sin\dfrac{\pi}{4}\cos\dfrac{\pi}{3}$ **b** $\sin^2\dfrac{\pi}{4}$ **c** $\dfrac{\tan\dfrac{\pi}{6}}{\cos\dfrac{\pi}{4}}$

d $\dfrac{5 - \tan\dfrac{\pi}{3}}{\sin\dfrac{\pi}{3}}$ **e** $\dfrac{1}{\sin\dfrac{\pi}{6}} - \dfrac{1}{\cos\dfrac{\pi}{4}}$ **f** $\dfrac{\tan\dfrac{\pi}{4} - \sin\dfrac{\pi}{4}}{\tan\dfrac{\pi}{6} \cdot \sin\dfrac{\pi}{6}}$.

9.2 The general definition of an angle

You need to be able to use the three basic trigonometric functions for any angle.

To do this you need a general definition for an angle:

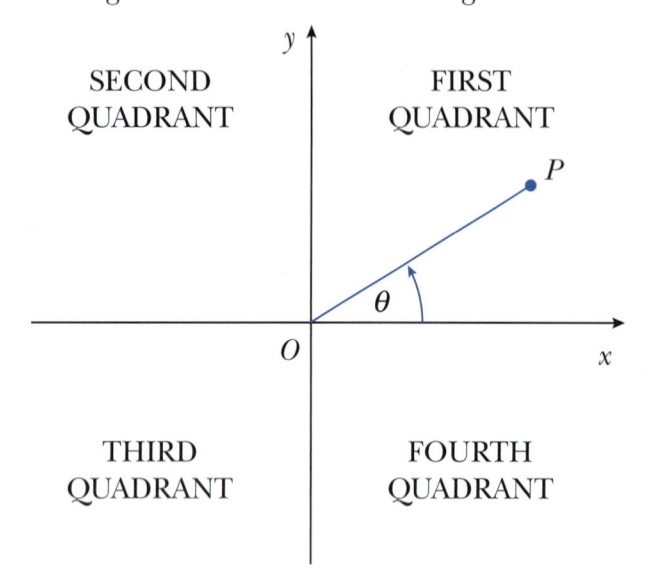

An angle is a measure of the rotation of a line OP about a fixed point O.

The angle is measured from the positive x-direction.

An anticlockwise rotation is taken as positive and a clockwise rotation is taken as negative.

The Cartesian plane is divided into four quadrants and the angle θ is said to be in the quadrant where OP lies. In the diagram above, θ is in the first quadrant.

WORKED EXAMPLE 3

Draw a diagram showing the quadrant in which the rotating line *OP* lies for each of the following angles. In each case find the acute angle that the line *OP* makes with the *x*-axis.

a 240°   b −70°   c 490°   d $\dfrac{2\pi}{3}$

Answers

a 240° is an anticlockwise rotation   b −70° is a clockwise rotation

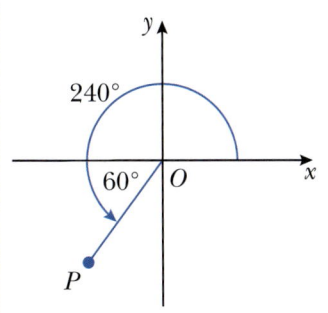

acute angle = 60°   acute angle = 70°

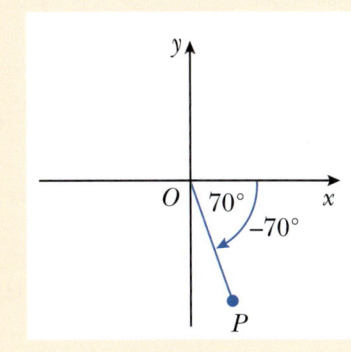

c 490° is an anticlockwise rotation   d $\dfrac{2\pi}{3}$ is an anticlockwise rotation
   490° = 360° + 130°

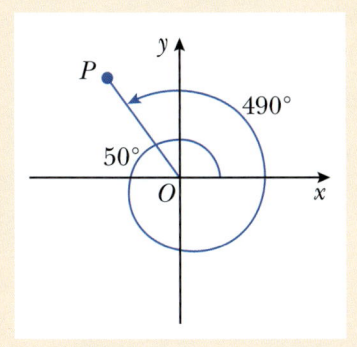

acute angle = 50°   acute angle = $\dfrac{\pi}{3}$

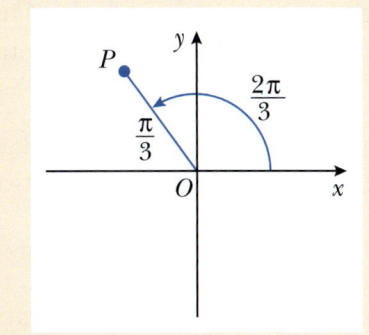

Exercise 9.2

1 Draw a diagram showing the quadrant in which the rotating line *OP* lies for each of the following angles. In each question indicate clearly the direction of rotation and find the acute angle that the line *OP* makes with the *x*-axis.

   a 110°   b −60°   c 220°   d −135°   e −300°
   f $\dfrac{3\pi}{4}$ g $\dfrac{7\pi}{6}$ h $-\dfrac{5\pi}{3}$ i $\dfrac{13\pi}{9}$ j $-\dfrac{5\pi}{8}$

2 State the quadrant that *OP* lies in when the angle that *OP* makes with the positive *x*-axis is:

   a 110°   b 300°   c −160°   d 245°   e −500°
   f $\dfrac{\pi}{4}$ g $\dfrac{11\pi}{6}$ h $-\dfrac{5\pi}{6}$ i $\dfrac{13\pi}{6}$ j $\dfrac{9\pi}{4}$

9.3 Trigonometric ratios of general angles

In general, trigonometric ratios of any angle θ in any quadrant are defined as:

$$\sin\theta = \frac{y}{r}, \quad \cos\theta = \frac{x}{r}, \quad \tan\theta = \frac{y}{x}, \quad x \neq 0$$

where x and y are the coordinates of the point P and r is the length of OP and $r = \sqrt{x^2 + y^2}$.

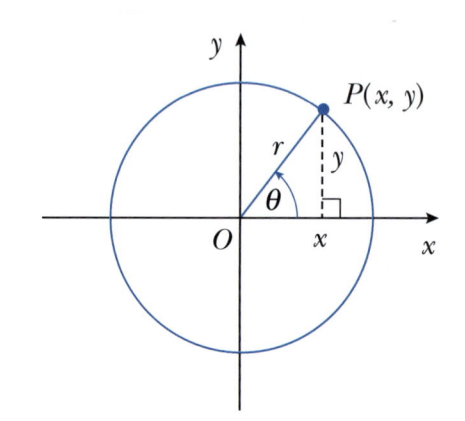

You need to know the signs of the three trigonometric ratios in the four quadrants.

In the first quadrant sin, cos and tan are positive. (Since x, y and r are all positive.)

By considering the sign of x and y you can find the sign of each of the three trigonometric ratios in the other three quadrants.

> **CLASS DISCUSSION**
>
> $\sin\theta = \frac{y}{r}$ By considering the sign of y in the second, third and fourth quadrants, determine the signs of the sine ratio in each of these quadrants.
>
> $\cos\theta = \frac{x}{r}$ By considering the sign of x in the second, third and fourth quadrants, determine the signs of the cosine ratio in each of these quadrants.
>
> $\tan\theta = \frac{y}{x}$ By considering the sign of x and y in the second, third and fourth quadrants, determine the signs of the tangent ratio in each of these quadrants. What happens to the tangent ratio when $x = 0$?
>
> On a copy of the diagram, record which ratios are positive in each quadrant.
>
> The first quadrant has been completed for you.
> (All three ratios are positive in the first quadrant.)

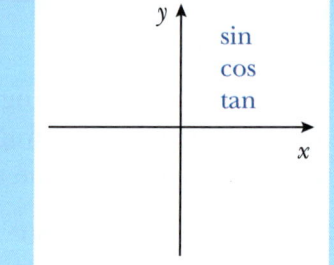

Chapter 9: Trigonometry

The results of the class discussion, can be summarised as:

You can memorise this diagram using a mnemonic such as '**A**ll **S**tudents **T**rust **C**ambridge'.

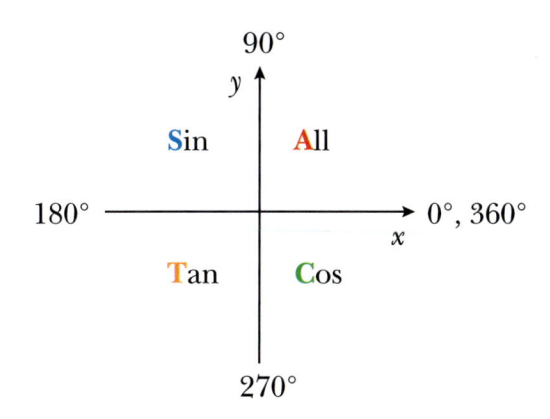

```
         90°
          y
    Sin  |  All
         |
  180° —-+—-> 0°, 360°
         |     x
    Tan  |  Cos
         |
        270°
```

WORKED EXAMPLE 4

Express in terms of trigonometric ratios of acute angles.

a $\cos(-110°)$ **b** $\sin 125°$

Answers

a The acute angle made with the *x*-axis is 70°.

In the third quadrant only tan is positive, so cos is negative.

$\cos(-110°) = -\cos 70°$

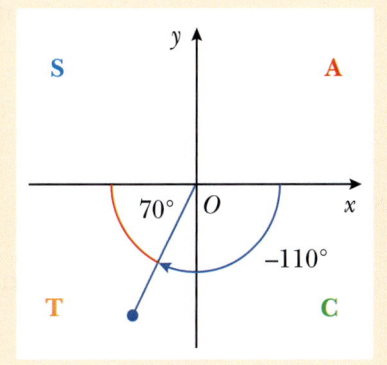

```
       y
   S   |   A
       |
   70° | O      x
    \  |
     \ | -110°
   T   |   C
```

b The acute angle made with the *x*-axis is 55°.
In the second quadrant sin is positive.
$\sin 125° = \sin 55°$

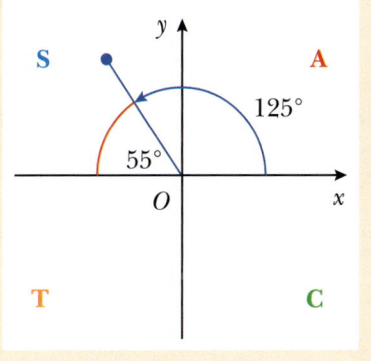

```
       y
   S   |   A
    \  |
     \ | 125°
   55° |
       O        x
   T   |   C
```

Cambridge IGCSE and O Level Additional Mathematics

WORKED EXAMPLE 5

Given that $\sin\theta = -\dfrac{3}{5}$ and that $180° \leq \theta \leq 270°$, find the value of $\tan\theta$ and the value of $\cos\theta$.

Answers

θ is in the third quadrant.

tan is positive and cos is negative in this quadrant.

$x^2 + (-3)^2 = 5^2$

$x^2 = 25 - 9 = 16$

Since $x < 0$, $x = -4$

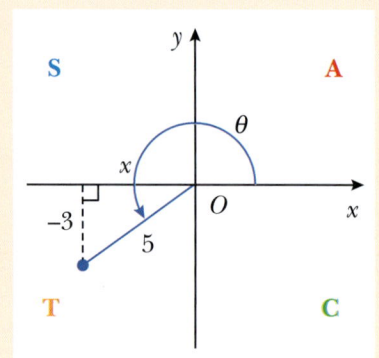

$\tan\theta = \dfrac{-3}{-4} = \dfrac{3}{4}$ and $\cos\theta = \dfrac{-4}{5} = -\dfrac{4}{5}$

Exercise 9.3

1. Express the following as trigonometric ratios of acute angles.

   a $\sin 220°$ b $\cos 325°$ c $\tan 140°$ d $\cos(-25°)$

   e $\tan 600°$ f $\sin\dfrac{4\pi}{5}$ g $\tan\dfrac{7\pi}{4}$ h $\cos\left(-\dfrac{11\pi}{6}\right)$

   i $\tan\dfrac{2\pi}{3}$ j $\sin\dfrac{9\pi}{4}$

2. Given that $\cos\theta = \dfrac{2}{5}$ and that $270° \leq \theta \leq 360°$, find the value of

   a $\tan\theta$ b $\sin\theta$.

3. Given that $\tan\theta = -\sqrt{3}$ and that $90° \leq \theta \leq 180°$, find the value of

   a $\sin\theta$ b $\cos\theta$.

4. Given that $\sin\theta = \dfrac{5}{13}$ and that θ is obtuse, find the value of

   a $\cos\theta$ b $\tan\theta$.

5. Given that $\tan\theta = \dfrac{2}{3}$ and that θ is reflex find the value of

   a $\sin\theta$ b $\cos\theta$.

6. Given that $\tan A = \dfrac{4}{3}$ and $\cos B = -\dfrac{1}{\sqrt{3}}$, where A and B are in the same quadrant, find the value of

   a $\sin A$ b $\cos A$ c $\sin B$ d $\tan B$.

7. Given that $\sin A = -\dfrac{12}{13}$ and $\cos B = \dfrac{3}{5}$, where A and B are in the same quadrant, find the value of

   a $\cos A$ b $\tan A$ c $\sin B$ d $\tan B$.

9.4 Graphs of trigonometric functions

CLASS DISCUSSION

Consider taking a ride on a Ferris wheel, with radius 50 metres, which rotates at a constant speed.

You enter the ride from a platform that is level with the centre of the wheel and the wheel turns in an anticlockwise direction.

Sketch the following two graphs and discuss their properties:
- a graph of your **vertical displacement from the centre of the wheel** plotted against **angle turned through**
- a graph of your **horizontal displacement from the centre of the wheel** plotted against **angle turned through**.

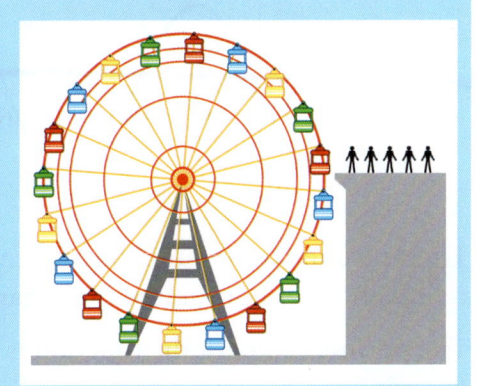

The graphs of $y = \sin x$ and $y = \cos x$

Suppose that OP makes an angle of x with the positive horizontal axis and that P moves around the unit circle, through one complete revolution. The coordinates of P will be $(\cos x, \sin x)$.

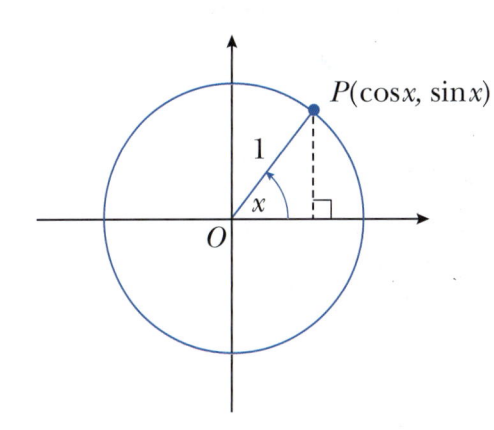

The height of P above the horizontal axis changes from $0 \to 1 \to 0 \to -1 \to 0$.

The graph of $\sin x$ against x for $0° \leq x \leq 360°$ is:

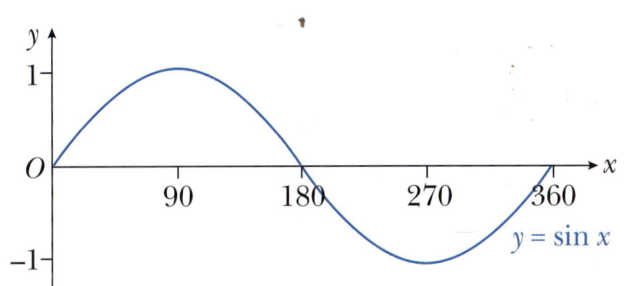

The distance of P from the vertical axis changes from $1 \to 0 \to -1 \to 0 \to 1$.

The graph of $\cos x$ against x for $0° \leq x \leq 360°$ is:

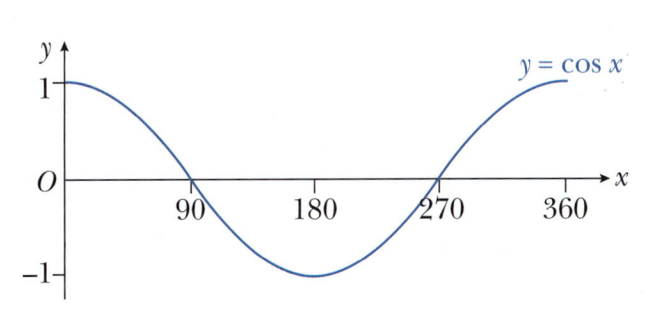

The graphs of $y = \sin x$ and $y = \cos x$ can be continued beyond $0° \leq x \leq 360°$:

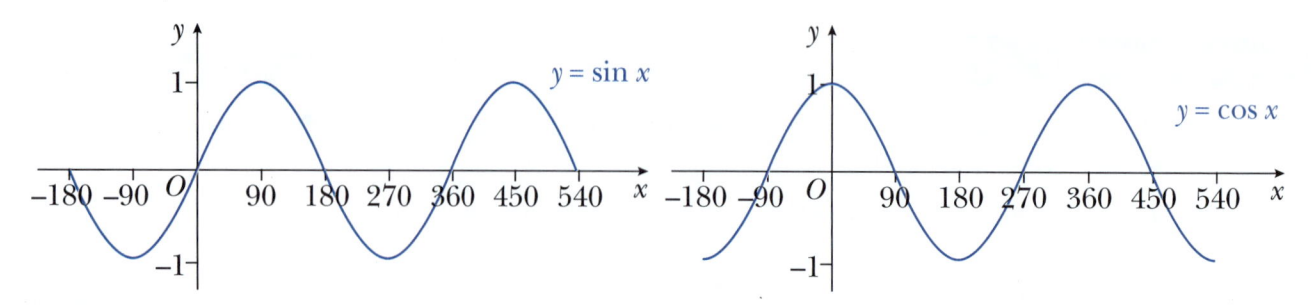

The sine and cosine functions are called **periodic functions** because they repeat themselves over and over again.

The **period** of a periodic function is defined as the length of one repetition or cycle.

The basic sine and cosine functions repeat every 360°.

We say they have a **period** of 360°. (Period = 2π, if working in radians.)

The **amplitude** of a periodic function is defined as the distance between a maximum (or minimum) point and the principal axis.

The basic sine and cosine functions have amplitude 1.

The graph of $y = \tan x$

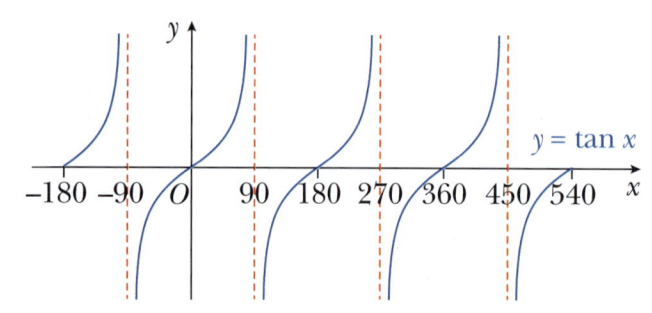

The tangent function behaves very differently to the sine and cosine functions.

The tangent function repeats its cycle every 180° so its period is 180°.

The red dashed lines at $x = \pm 90°$, $x = 270°$ and $x = 450°$ are asymptotes. The branches of the graph get closer and closer to the asymptotes without ever reaching them.

The tangent function does not have an amplitude.

The graphs of $y = a \sin bx + c$, $y = a \cos bx + c$ and $y = a \tan bx + c$

You have already learnt about the graphs of $y = \sin x$, $y = \cos x$ and $y = \tan x$.

In this section you will learn how to sketch the graphs of $y = a \sin bx + c$, $y = a \cos bx + c$ and $y = a \tan bx + c$ where a and b are positive integers and c is an integer.

You can use graphing software to observe how the values of a, b and c affect the trigonometric functions.

The graph of $y = a \sin x$

Using graphing software, the graphs of $y = \sin x$ and $y = 2\sin x$ are:

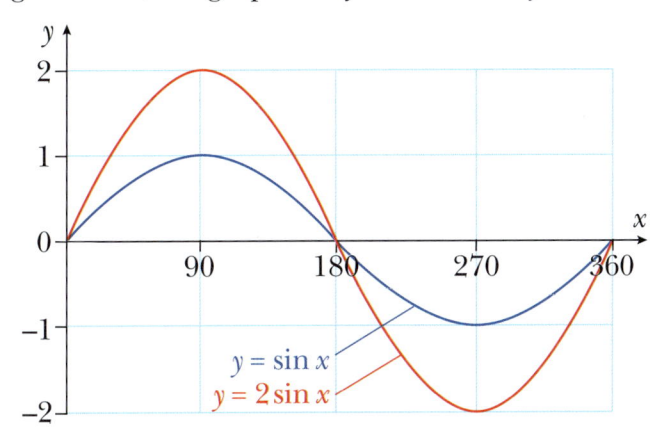

The graph of $y = 2\sin x$ is a stretch of the graph of $y = \sin x$.

It has been stretched from the x-axis with a stretch factor of 2.

The amplitude of $y = 2\sin x$ is 2 and the period is 360°.

Similarly, it can be shown that graph of $y = 3\sin x$ is a stretch of $y = \sin x$ from the x-axis with stretch factor 3. The amplitude of $y = 3\sin x$ is 3 and the period is 360°.

ACTIVITY

Use graphing software to confirm that:

- $y = 2\cos x$ is a stretch of $y = \cos x$ from the x-axis with stretch factor 2
- $y = 3\cos x$ is a stretch of $y = \cos x$ from the x-axis with stretch factor 3

and

- $y = 2\tan x$ is a stretch of $y = \tan x$ from the x-axis with stretch factor 2
- $y = 3\tan x$ is a stretch of $y = \tan x$ from the x-axis with stretch factor 3.

The graph of $y = \sin bx$

Using graphing software, the graphs of $y = \sin x$ and $y = \sin 2x$ are:

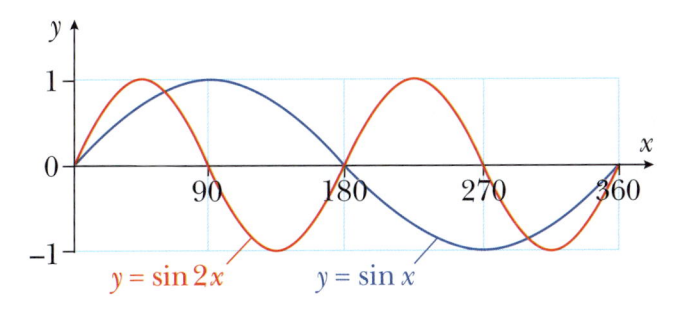

The graph of $y = \sin 2x$ is a stretch of the graph of $y = \sin x$.

It has been stretched from the y-axis with a stretch factor of $\frac{1}{2}$.

The amplitude of $y = \sin 2x$ is 1 and the period is 180°.

Similarly, the graph of $y = \sin 3x$ is a stretch, from the y-axis, of $y = \sin x$ with stretch factor $\frac{1}{3}$.

The amplitude of $y = \sin 3x$ is 1 and the period is 120°.

> ### ACTIVITY
>
> Use graphing software to confirm that:
>
> - $y = \cos 2x$ is a stretch of $y = \cos x$ from the y-axis with stretch factor $\frac{1}{2}$
>
> - $y = \cos 3x$ is a stretch of $y = \cos x$ from the y-axis with stretch factor $\frac{1}{3}$
>
> and
>
> - $y = \tan 2x$ is a stretch of $y = \tan x$ from the y-axis with stretch factor $\frac{1}{2}$
>
> - $y = \tan 3x$ is a stretch of $y = \tan x$ from the y-axis with stretch factor $\frac{1}{3}$

The graph of $y = \sin x + c$

Using graphing software, the graphs of $y = \sin x$ and $y = \sin x + 1$ are:

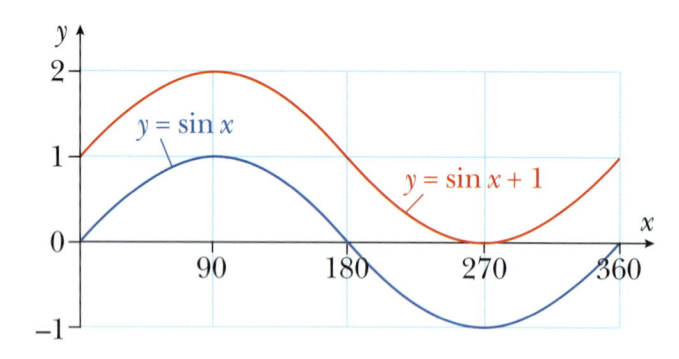

The graph of $y = \sin x + 1$ is a translation of the graph of $y = \sin x$.

It has been translated by the vector $\begin{pmatrix} 0 \\ 1 \end{pmatrix}$.

The amplitude of $y = \sin x + 1$ is 1 and the period is 360°.

Similarly, the graph of $y = \sin x + 2$ is a translation of $y = \sin x$ by the vector $\begin{pmatrix} 0 \\ 2 \end{pmatrix}$.

The amplitude of $y = \sin x + 2$ is 1 and the period is 360°.

Chapter 9: Trigonometry

> **ACTIVITY**
>
> Use graphing software to confirm that:
> - $y = \cos x + 1$ is a translation of $y = \cos x$ by the vector $\begin{pmatrix} 0 \\ 1 \end{pmatrix}$
> - $y = \cos x + 2$ is a translation of $y = \cos x$ by the vector $\begin{pmatrix} 0 \\ 2 \end{pmatrix}$
> - $y = \cos x - 3$ is a translation of $y = \cos x$ by the vector $\begin{pmatrix} 0 \\ -3 \end{pmatrix}$
>
> and
>
> - $y = \tan x + 1$ is a translation of $y = \tan x$ by the vector $\begin{pmatrix} 0 \\ 1 \end{pmatrix}$
> - $y = \tan x - 2$ is a translation of $y = \tan x$ by the vector $\begin{pmatrix} 0 \\ -2 \end{pmatrix}$

In conclusion,

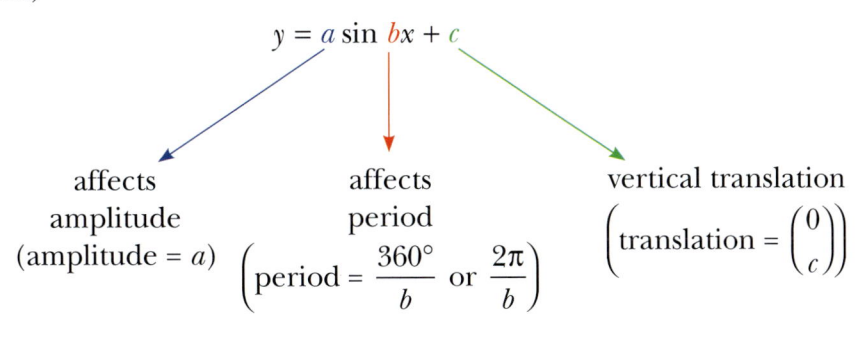

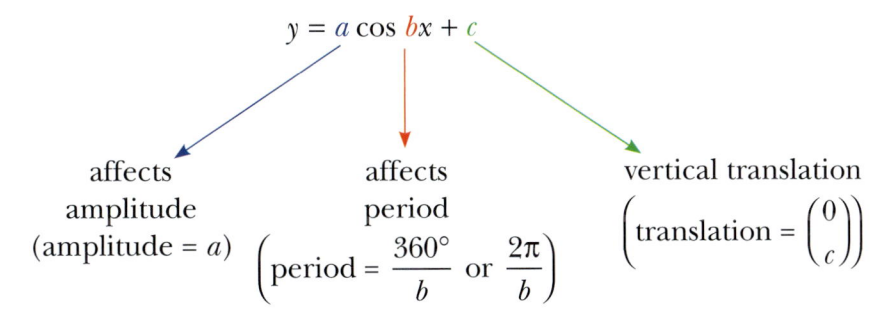

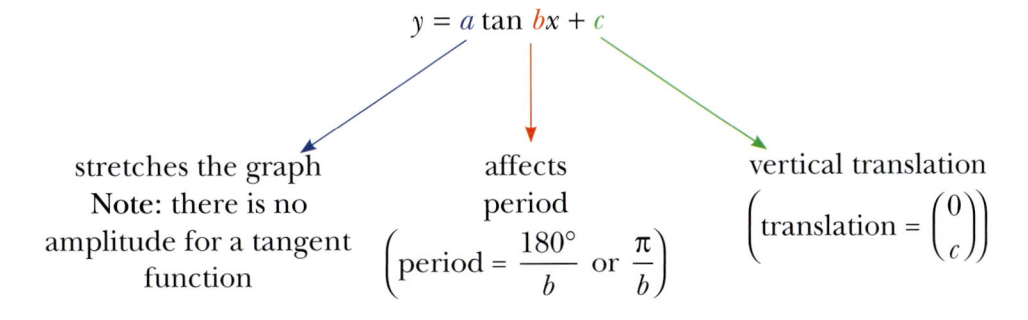

$$y = a \sin bx + c$$

- affects amplitude (amplitude = a)
- affects period $\left(\text{period} = \dfrac{360°}{b} \text{ or } \dfrac{2\pi}{b}\right)$
- vertical translation $\left(\text{translation} = \begin{pmatrix} 0 \\ c \end{pmatrix}\right)$

$$y = a \cos bx + c$$

- affects amplitude (amplitude = a)
- affects period $\left(\text{period} = \dfrac{360°}{b} \text{ or } \dfrac{2\pi}{b}\right)$
- vertical translation $\left(\text{translation} = \begin{pmatrix} 0 \\ c \end{pmatrix}\right)$

$$y = a \tan bx + c$$

- stretches the graph
  Note: there is no amplitude for a tangent function
- affects period $\left(\text{period} = \dfrac{180°}{b} \text{ or } \dfrac{\pi}{b}\right)$
- vertical translation $\left(\text{translation} = \begin{pmatrix} 0 \\ c \end{pmatrix}\right)$

Sketching trigonometric functions

The sketch graph of a trigonometric function, such as
$y = 2\cos 3x - 1$ for $0° \leq x \leq 360°$, can be built up in steps.

Step 1: Start with a sketch of $y = \cos x$:

Period = 360°

Amplitude = 1

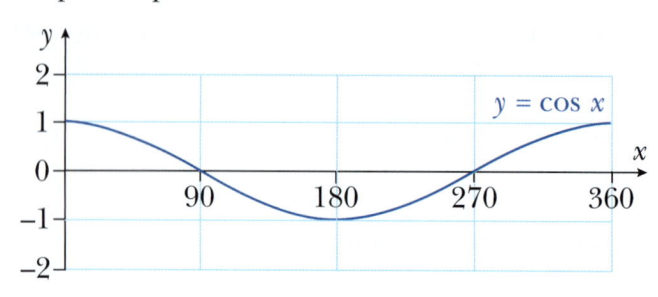

Step 2: Sketch the graph of $y = \cos 3x$:

Stretch $y = \cos x$ from the y-axis with stretch factor $\dfrac{1}{3}$.

Period = $\dfrac{360°}{3} = 120°$

Amplitude = 1

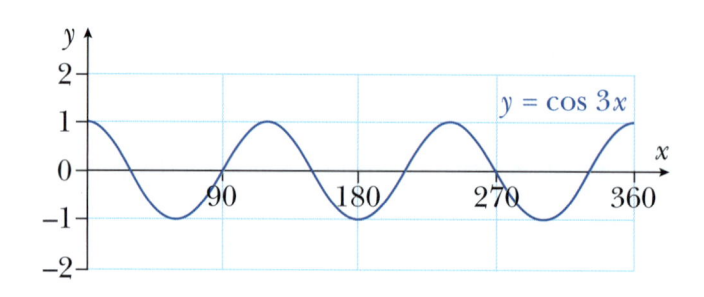

Step 3: Sketch the graph of $y = 2\cos 3x$:

Stretch $y = \cos 3x$ from the y-axis with stretch factor 2.

Period = $\dfrac{360°}{3} = 120°$

Amplitude = 2

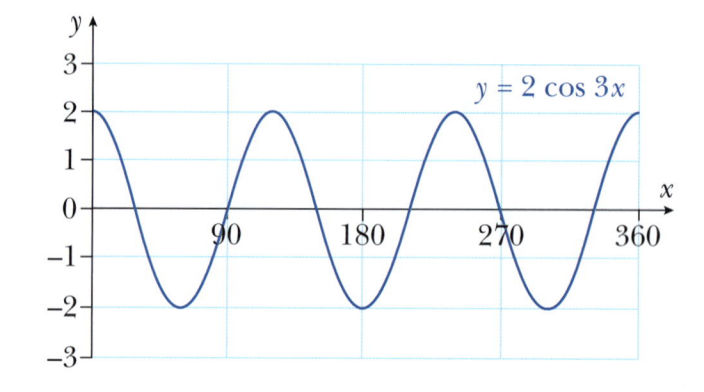

Step 4: Sketch the graph of $y = 2\cos 3x - 1$:

Translate $y = 2\cos 3x$ by $\begin{pmatrix} 0 \\ -1 \end{pmatrix}$.

Period = $\dfrac{360°}{3} = 120°$

Amplitude = 2

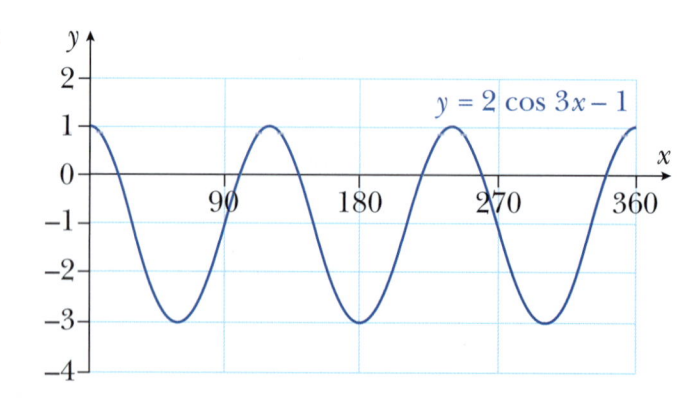

WORKED EXAMPLE 6

$f(x) = 3 \sin 2x$ for $0° \leqslant x \leqslant 360°$

a Write down the period of f.

b Write down the amplitude of f.

c Write down the coordinates of the maximum and minimum points on the curve $y = f(x)$.

d Sketch the graph of $y = f(x)$.

e Use your answer to **part d** to sketch the graph of $y = 3 \sin 2x + 1$.

Answers

a Period $= \dfrac{360°}{2} = 180°$

b Amplitude $= 3$

c $y = \sin x$ has its maximum and minimum points at:

$(90°, 1), (270°, -1), (450°, 1)$ and $(630°, -1)$

Hence, $f(x) = 3 \sin 2x$ has its maximum and minimum points at:

$(45°, 3), (135°, -3), (225°, 3)$ and $(315°, -3)$

d

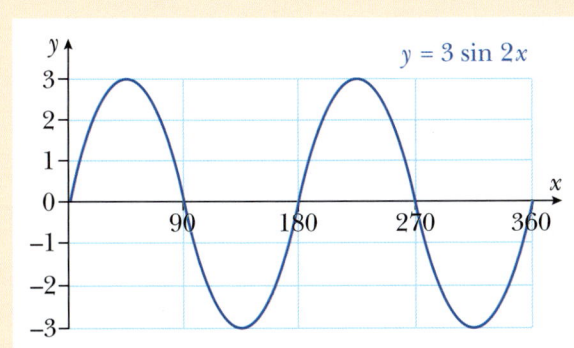

e $y = 3 \sin 2x + 1$ is a translation of the graph $y = 3 \sin 2x$ by the vector $\begin{pmatrix} 0 \\ 1 \end{pmatrix}$.

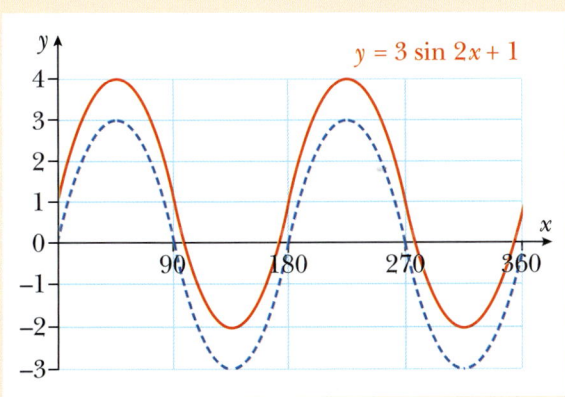

Cambridge IGCSE and O Level Additional Mathematics

> **WORKED EXAMPLE 7**
>
> **a** On the same grid, sketch the graphs of $y = \sin 2x$ and $y = 1 + \cos 2x$ for $0° \leqslant x \leqslant 360°$.
>
> **b** State the number of roots of the equation $\sin 2x = 1 + \cos 2x$ for $0° \leqslant x \leqslant 360°$.
>
> **Answers**
>
> **a**
>
> *(Graph showing $y = 1 + \cos 2x$ and $y = \sin 2x$ plotted on the interval $0°$ to $360°$, with intersection points marked.)*
>
> **b** The graphs of $y = \sin 2x$ and $y = 1 + \cos 2x$ intersect each other at 4 points in the interval.
>
> Hence, the number of roots of $\sin 2x = 1 + \cos 2x$ is 4.

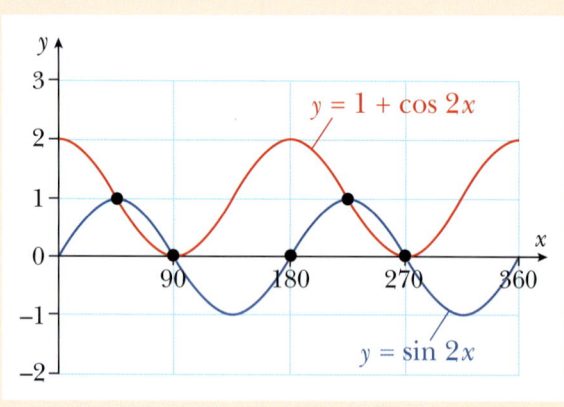

Exercise 9.4

1 a The following functions are defined for $0° \leqslant x \leqslant 360°$.

For each function, write down the amplitude, the period and the coordinates of the maximum and minimum points.

    i $f(x) = 7 \cos x$ **ii** $f(x) = 2 \sin 2x$ **iii** $f(x) = 2 \cos 3x$

    iv $f(x) = 3 \sin \frac{1}{2} x$ **v** $f(x) = 4 \cos x + 1$ **vi** $f(x) = 5 \sin 2x - 2$

b Sketch the graph of each function in **part a** and use graphing software to check your answers.

2 a The following functions are defined for $0 \leqslant x \leqslant 2\pi$.

For each function, write down the amplitude, the period and the coordinates of the maximum and minimum points.

    i $f(x) = 4 \sin x$ **ii** $f(x) = \cos 3x$ **iii** $f(x) = 2 \sin 3x$

    iv $f(x) = 3 \cos \frac{1}{2} x$ **v** $f(x) = \sin 2x + 3$ **vi** $f(x) = 4 \cos 2x - 1$

b Sketch the graph of each function in **part a** and use graphing software to check your answers.

3

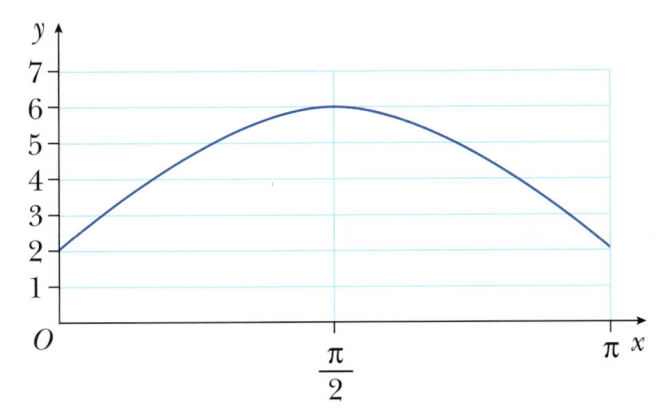

The graph of $y = a + b\sin cx$, for $0 \leq x \leq \pi$, is shown above.

Write down the value of a, the value of b and the value of c.

4

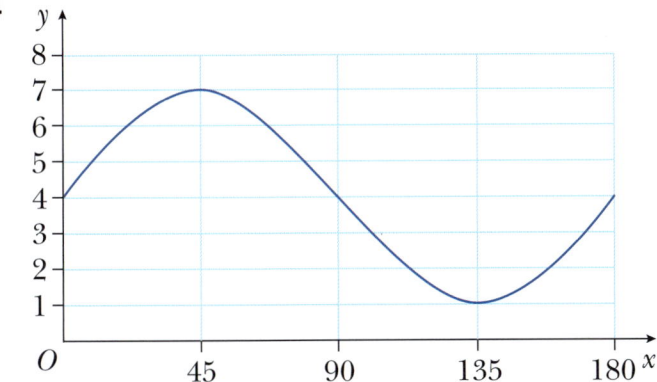

Part of the graph of $y = a\sin bx + c$ is shown above.

Write down the value of a, the value of b and the value of c.

5

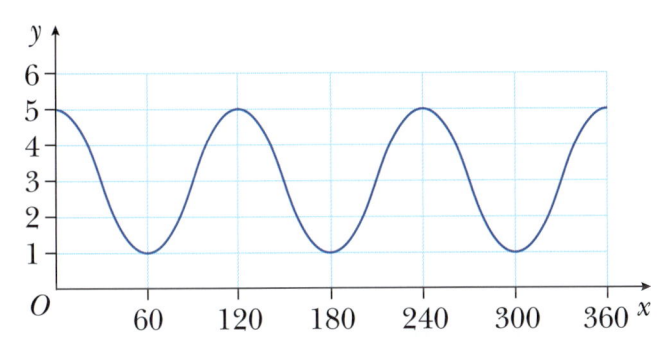

The graph of $y = a + b\cos cx$, for $0° \leq x \leq 360°$, is shown above.

Write down the value of a, the value of b and the value of c.

6 a The following functions are defined for $0° \leq x \leq 360°$.

For each function, write down the period and the equations of the asymptotes.

  i $f(x) = \tan 2x$ **ii** $f(x) = 3\tan\dfrac{1}{2}x$ **iii** $f(x) = 2\tan 3x + 1$

  b Sketch the graph of each function and use graphing software to check your answers.

7 a The following functions are defined for $0 \leq x \leq 2\pi$.

For each function, write down the period and the equations of the asymptotes.

   i $f(x) = \tan 4x$ ii $f(x) = 2\tan 3x$ iii $f(x) = 5\tan 2x - 3$

b Sketch the graph of each function and use graphing software to check your answers.

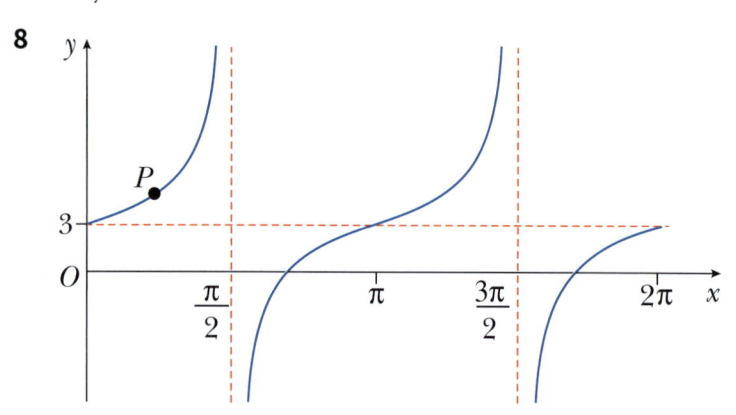

8

Part of the graph of $y = A \tan Bx + C$ is shown above.

The graph passes through the point $P\left(\dfrac{\pi}{4},\ 4\right)$.

Find the value of A, the value of B and the value of C.

9 $f(x) = a + b \sin cx$

The maximum value of f is 13, the minimum value of f is 5 and the period is 60°.

Find the value of a, the value of b and the value of c.

10 $f(x) = A + 3\cos Bx$ for $0° \leq x \leq 360°$

The maximum value of f is 5 and the period is 72°.

a Write down the value of A and the value of B.

b Write down the amplitude of f.

c Sketch the graph of f.

11 $f(x) = A + B \sin Cx$ for $0° \leq x \leq 360°$

The amplitude of f is 3, the period is 90° and the minimum value of f is −2.

a Write down the value of A, the value of B and the value of C.

b Sketch the graph of f.

12 a On the same grid, sketch the graphs of $y = \sin x$ and $y = 1 + \sin 2x$ for $0° \leq x \leq 360°$.

b State the number of roots of the equation $\sin 2x - \sin x + 1 = 0$ for $0° \leq x \leq 360°$.

13 a On the same grid, sketch the graphs of $y = \sin x$ and $y = 1 + \cos 2x$ for $0° \leq x \leq 360°$.

 b State the number of roots of the equation $\sin x = 1 + \cos 2x$ for $0° \leq x \leq 360°$.

14 a On the same grid, sketch the graphs of $y = 3\cos 2x$ and $y = 2 + \sin x$ for $0° \leq x \leq 360°$.

 b State the number of roots of the equation $3\cos 2x = 2 + \sin x$ for $0° \leq x \leq 360°$.

9.5 Graphs of $y = |f(x)|$, where $f(x)$ is a trigonometric function

You have already learnt how to sketch graphs of $y = |f(x)|$ where $f(x)$ is either linear or quadratic.

In this section you will learn how to sketch graphs of $y = |f(x)|$ where $f(x)$ is a trigonometric function.

WORKED EXAMPLE 8

a Sketch the graph of $f(x) = |\sin x|$ for $0 \leq x \leq 2\pi$.
b State the range of the function f.

Answers

a Step 1: Sketch the graph of $y = \sin x$

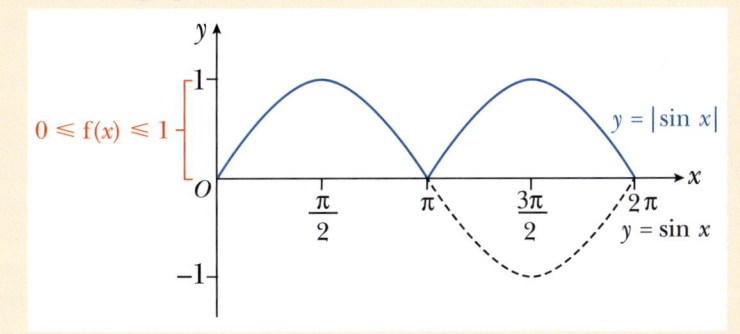

Step 2: Reflect in the x-axis the part of the curve $y = \sin x$ that is below the x-axis.

b The range of the function f is $0 \leq f(x) \leq 1$.

Cambridge IGCSE and O Level Additional Mathematics

> **WORKED EXAMPLE 9**
>
> **a** On the same grid, sketch the graphs of $y = |\sin 2x|$ and $y = \cos x$ for $0° \leq x \leq 360°$.
>
> **b** State the number of roots of the equation $|\sin 2x| = \cos x$ for $0° \leq x \leq 360°$.
>
> **Answers**
>
> **a** For $y = |\sin 2x|$ sketch the graph of $y = \sin 2x$ and then reflect in the x-axis the part of the curve $y = \sin 2x$ that is below the x-axis. 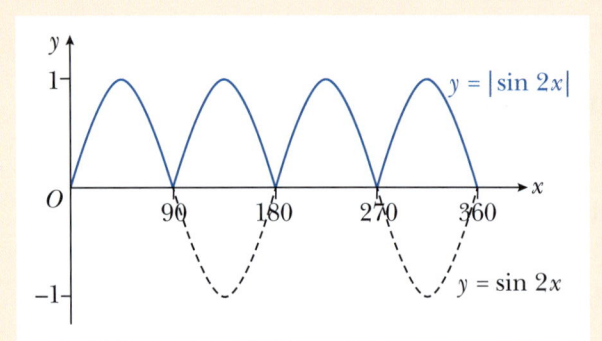
>
> Hence, the graphs of $y = |\sin 2x|$ and $y = \cos x$ are: 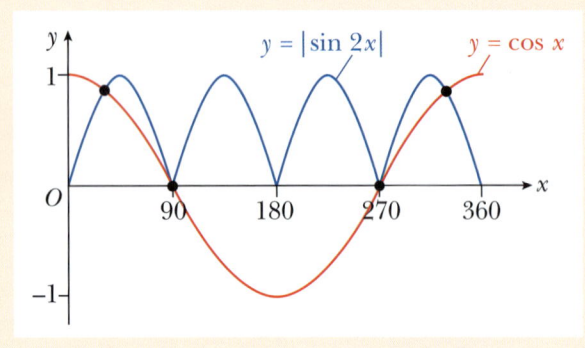
>
> **b** The graphs of $y = |\sin 2x|$ and $y = \cos x$ intersect each other at 4 points in the interval.
>
> Hence, the number of roots of $|\sin 2x| = \cos x$ is 4.

Exercise 9.5

Use graphing software to check your graphs in this exercise.

1. Sketch the graphs of each of the following functions, for $0° \leq x \leq 360°$, and state the range of each function.

   a $f(x) = |\tan x|$ **b** $f(x) = |\cos 2x|$ **c** $f(x) = |3 \sin x|$

   d $f(x) = \left|\sin \dfrac{1}{2}x\right|$ **e** $f(x) = \left|2 \cos \dfrac{1}{2}x\right|$ **f** $f(x) = |2 \sin 2x|$

   g $f(x) = |\sin x - 2|$ **h** $f(x) = |5 \sin x + 1|$ **i** $f(x) = |4 \cos x - 3|$

2. **a** Sketch the graph of $y = 2\sin x - 1$ for $0° \leq x \leq 180°$.

   b Sketch the graph of $y = |2\sin x - 1|$ for $0° \leq x \leq 180°$.

   c Write down the number of solutions of the equation $|2\sin x - 1| = 0.5$ for $0° \leq x \leq 180°$.

3 a Sketch the graph of $y = 2 + 5\cos x$ for $0° \leq x \leq 180°$.

   b Sketch the graph of $y = |2 + 5\cos x|$ for $0° \leq x \leq 180°$.

   c Write down the number of solutions of the equation $|2 + 5\cos x| = 1$ for $0° \leq x \leq 180°$.

4 a Sketch the graph of $y = 2 + 3\cos x$ for $0° \leq x \leq 180°$.

   b Sketch the graph of $y = |2 + 3\cos x|$ for $0° \leq x \leq 180°$.

   c Write down the number of solutions of the equation $|2 + 3\sin 2x| = 1$ for $0° \leq x \leq 180°$.

5 a On the same grid, sketch the graphs of $y = |\tan x|$ and $y = \cos x$ for $0° \leq x \leq 360°$.

   b State the number of roots of the equation $|\tan x| = \cos x$ for $0° \leq x \leq 360°$.

6 a On the same grid, sketch the graphs of $y = |\sin 2x|$ and $y = \tan x$ for $0 \leq x \leq 2\pi$.

   b State the number of roots of the equation $|\sin 2x| = \tan x$ for $0 \leq x \leq 2\pi$.

7 a On the same grid, sketch the graphs of $y = |0.5 + \sin x|$ and $y = \cos x$ for $0° \leq x \leq 360°$.

   b State the number of roots of the equation $|0.5 + \sin x| = \cos x$ for $0° \leq x \leq 360°$.

8 a On the same grid, sketch the graphs of $y = |1 + 4\cos x|$ and $y = 2 + \cos x$ for $0° \leq x \leq 360°$.

   b State the number of roots of the equation $|1 + 4\cos x| = 2 + \cos x$ for $0° \leq x \leq 360°$.

9 The equation $|3\cos x - 2| = k$, has 2 roots for the interval $0 \leq x \leq 2\pi$. Find the possible values of k.

CHALLENGE Q

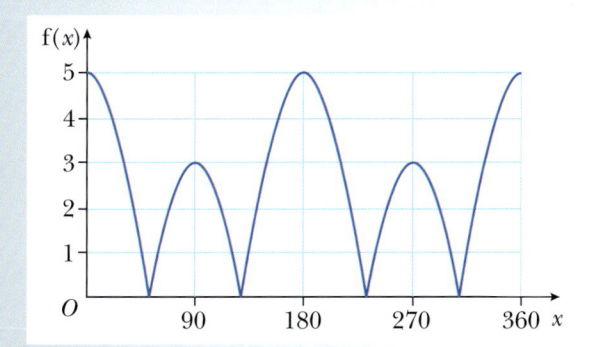

10 The diagram shows the graph of $f(x) = |a + b\cos cx|$, where a, b and c are positive integers.

Find the value of a, the value of b and the value of c.

9.6 Trigonometric equations

Consider the right-angled triangle:

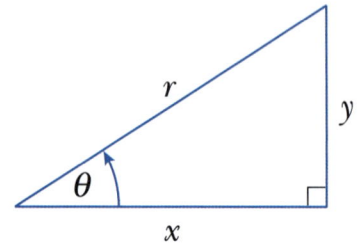

$$\sin\theta = \frac{y}{r} \qquad \cos\theta = \frac{x}{r} \qquad \tan\theta = \frac{y}{x}$$

The following rules can be found from this triangle:

$$\tan\theta = \frac{y}{x} \qquad \text{divide numerator and denominator by } r$$

$$= \frac{\frac{y}{r}}{\frac{x}{r}} \qquad \text{use } \frac{y}{r} = \sin\theta \text{ and } \frac{x}{r} = \cos\theta$$

$$\tan\theta = \frac{\sin\theta}{\cos\theta}$$

$$x^2 + y^2 = r^2 \qquad \text{divide both sides by } r^2$$

$$\left(\frac{x}{r}\right)^2 + \left(\frac{y}{r}\right)^2 = 1 \qquad \text{use } \frac{x}{r} = \cos\theta \text{ and } \frac{y}{r} = \sin\theta$$

$$\cos^2\theta + \sin^2\theta = 1$$

These two important rules will be needed to solve some trigonometric equations later in this section.

Consider solving the equation: $\quad \sin x = 0.5$

$$x = \sin^{-1}(0.5)$$

A calculator will give the answer: $\quad x = 30°$

There are, however, many more values of x for which $\sin x = 0.5$.

Consider the graph of $y = \sin x$ for $-360° \leqslant x \leqslant 360°$:

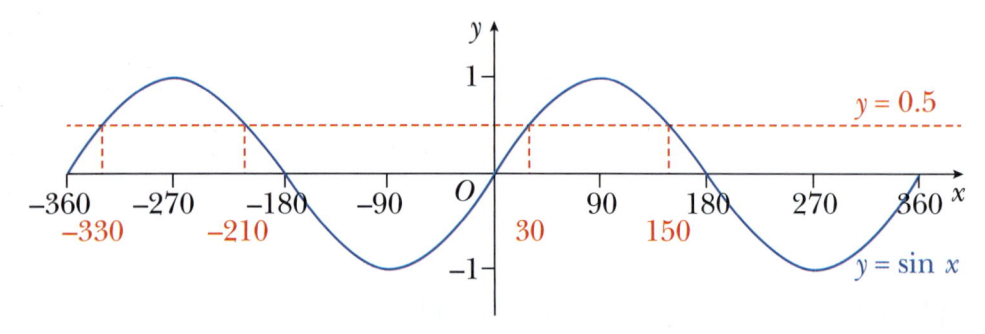

The sketch graph shows there are four values of x, between $-360°$ and $360°$, for which $\sin x = 0.5$.

You can use the calculator value of $x = 30°$, together with the symmetry of the curve to find the remaining answers.

Hence the solution of $\sin x = 0.5$ for $-360° \leq x \leq 360°$ is:
$$x = -330°, -210°, 30° \text{ or } 150°$$

WORKED EXAMPLE 10

Solve $\cos x = -0.4$ for $0° \leq x \leq 360°$.

Answers

$\cos x = -0.4$ use a calculator to find $\cos^{-1}(-0.4)$ to 1 decimal place

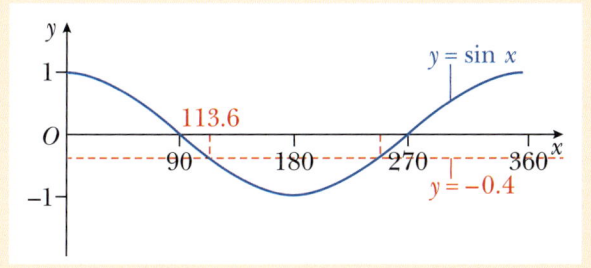

$x = 113.6°$

[Graph showing $y = \sin x$ with horizontal line $y = -0.4$ intersecting the curve at $x = 113.6$, with axis markings at 90, 180, 270, 360]

The sketch graph shows there are two values of x, between $0°$ and $360°$, for which $\cos x = -0.4$.

Using the symmetry of the curve, the second value is $(360° - 113.6°) = 246.4°$.

Hence the solution of $\cos x = -0.4$ for $0° \leq x \leq 360°$ is
$$x = 113.6° \text{ or } 246.4°.$$

WORKED EXAMPLE 11

Solve $\tan 2A = -1.8$ for $0° \leq A \leq 180°$.

Answers

$\tan 2A = -1.8$ let $x = 2A$
$\tan x = -1.8$ use a calculator to find $\tan^{-1}(-1.8)$
$x = -60.95°$

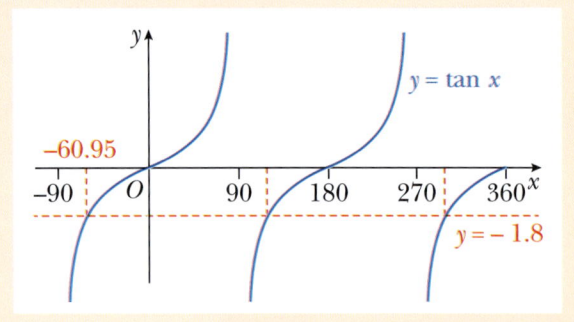

Using the symmetry of the curve:

$x = -60.95$ $x = (-60.95 + 180)$ $x = (119.05 + 180)$
                 $= 119.05$ $= 299.05$

Using $x = 2A$,

$2A = -60.95$ $2A = 119.05$ $2A = 299.05$
$A = -30.5$ $A = 59.5$ $A = 149.5$

Hence the solution of $\tan 2A = -1.8$ for $0° \leq x \leq 180°$ is
$A = 59.5°$ or $A = 149.5°$.

WORKED EXAMPLE 12

Solve $\sin\left(2A - \dfrac{\pi}{3}\right) = 0.6$ for $0 \leqslant A \leqslant \pi$.

Answers

$\sin\left(2A - \dfrac{\pi}{3}\right) = 0.6$ let $x = 2A - \dfrac{\pi}{3}$

$\sin x = 0.6$ use a calculator to find $\sin^{-1} 0.6$

$x = 0.6435$ radians

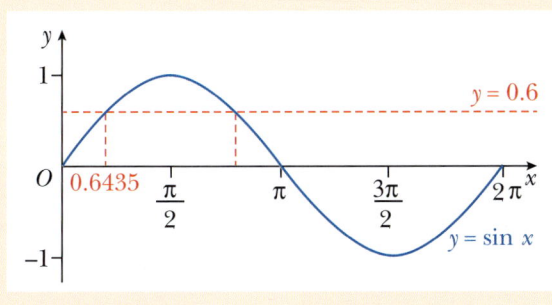

Using the symmetry of the curve:

$x = 0.6435$ $x = \pi - 0.6435$
                           $= 2.498$

Using $x = 2A - \dfrac{\pi}{3}$

$2A - \dfrac{\pi}{3} = 0.6435$ $2A - \dfrac{\pi}{3} = 2.498$

$A = \dfrac{1}{2}\left(0.6435 + \dfrac{\pi}{3}\right)$ $A = \dfrac{1}{2}\left(2.498 + \dfrac{\pi}{3}\right)$

$A = 0.845$ $A = 1.77$

Hence the solution of $\sin\left(2A - \dfrac{\pi}{3}\right) = 0.6$ for $0 \leqslant A \leqslant \pi$ is

$A = 0.845$ or 1.77 radians.

Cambridge IGCSE and O Level Additional Mathematics

WORKED EXAMPLE 13

Solve $\sin^2 x - 2\sin x \cos x = 0$ for $0° \leq x \leq 360°$.

Answers

$\sin^2 x - 2\sin x \cos x = 0$ factorise
$\sin x (\sin x - 2\cos x) = 0$

$\sin x = 0$ or $\sin x - 2\cos x = 0$
$x = 0°, 180°, 360°$ $\sin x = 2\cos x$
                            $\tan x = 2$
                            $x = 63.4$ or $180 + 63.4$
                            $x = 63.4°$ or $243.4°$

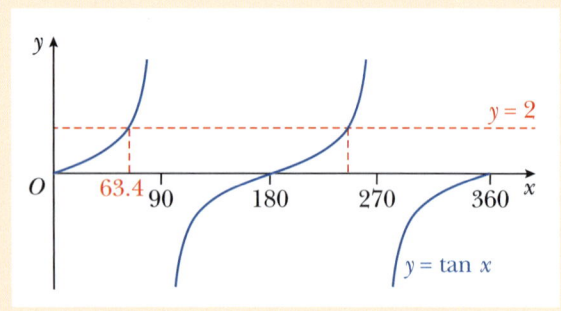

The solution of $\sin^2 x - 2\sin x \cos x = 0$ for $0° \leq x \leq 360°$ is
$x = 0°, 63.4°, 180°, 243.4°$ or $360°$.

WORKED EXAMPLE 14

Solve $1 + \cos x = 3\sin^2 x$ for $0° \leq x \leq 360°$.

Answers

$1 + \cos x = 3\sin^2 x$ use $\sin^2 x = 1 - \cos^2 x$
$1 + \cos x = 3(1 - \cos^2 x)$ expand brackets and collect terms
$3\cos^2 x + \cos x - 2 = 0$ factorise
$(3\cos x - 2)(\cos x + 1) = 0$

$3\cos x - 2 = 0$ or $\cos x + 1 = 0$
$\cos x = \dfrac{2}{3}$ $\cos x = -1$
$x = 48.2°$ or $360 - 48.2$ $x = 180°$
$x = 48.2°$ or $311.8°$

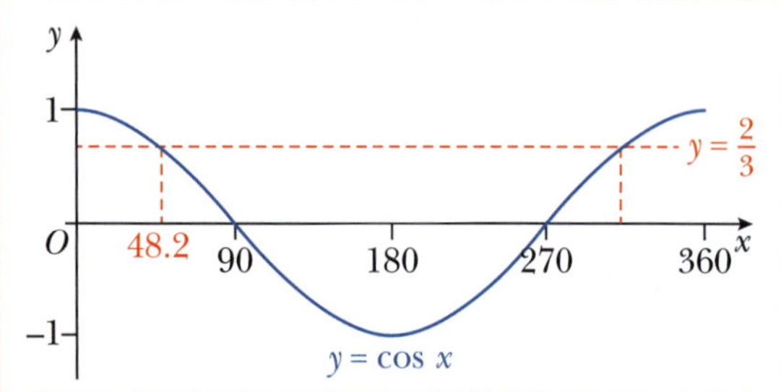

The solution of $1 + \cos x = 3\sin^2 x$ for $0° \leq x \leq 360°$ is
$x = 48.2°, 180°$ or $311.8°$.

Exercise 9.6

1 Solve each of these equations for $0° \leqslant x \leqslant 360°$.
  a $\sin x = 0.3$
  b $\cos x = 0.2$
  c $\tan x = 2$
  d $\sin x = -0.6$
  e $\tan x = -1.4$
  f $\sin x = -0.8$
  g $4\sin x - 3 = 0$
  h $2\cos x + 1 = 0$

2 Solve each of the these equations for $0 \leqslant x \leqslant 2\pi$.
  a $\cos x = 0.5$
  b $\tan x = 0.2$
  c $\sin x = 2$
  d $\tan x = -3$
  e $\sin x = -0.75$
  f $\cos x = -0.55$
  g $4\sin x = 1$
  h $5\sin x + 2 = 0$

3 Solve each of these equations for $0° \leqslant x \leqslant 180°$.
  a $\sin 2x = 0.8$
  b $\cos 2x = -0.6$
  c $\tan 2x = 2$
  d $\sin 2x = -0.6$
  e $5\cos 2x = 4$
  f $7\sin 2x = -2$
  g $1 + 3\tan 2x = 0$
  h $2 - 3\sin 2x = 0$

4 Solve each of these equations for the given domains.
  a $\cos(x - 30°) = -0.5$ for $0° \leqslant x \leqslant 360°$.
  b $6\sin(2x + 45°) = -5$ for $0° \leqslant x \leqslant 180°$.
  c $2\cos\left(\dfrac{2x}{3}\right) + \sqrt{3} = 0$ for $0° \leqslant x \leqslant 540°$.
  d $\cos\left(x + \dfrac{\pi}{6}\right) = -0.5$ for $0 < x < 2\pi$.
  e $\sin(2x - 3) = 0.6$ for $0 < x < \pi$ radians.
  f $\sqrt{2}\sin\left(\dfrac{x}{2} + \dfrac{\pi}{6}\right) = 1$ for $0 < x < 4\pi$ radians.

5 Solve each of these equations for $0° \leqslant x \leqslant 360°$.
  a $4\sin x = \cos x$
  b $3\sin x + 4\cos x = 0$
  c $5\sin x - 3\cos x = 0$
  d $5\cos 2x - 4\sin 2x = 0$

6 Solve $4\sin(2x - 0.4) - 5\cos(2x - 0.4) = 0$ for $0 \leqslant x \leqslant \pi$.

7 Solve each of these equations for $0° \leqslant x \leqslant 360°$.
  a $\sin x \tan(x - 30°) = 0$
  b $5\tan^2 x - 4\tan x = 0$
  c $3\cos^2 x = \cos x$
  d $\sin^2 x + \sin x \cos x = 0$
  e $5\sin x \cos x = \cos x$
  f $\sin x \tan x = \sin x$

8 Solve each of these equations for $0° \leqslant x \leqslant 360°$.
  a $4\sin^2 x = 1$
  b $25\tan^2 x = 9$

9 Solve each of these equations for $0° \leqslant x \leqslant 360°$.
  a $\tan^2 x + 2\tan x - 3 = 0$
  b $2\sin^2 x + \sin x - 1 = 0$
  c $3\cos^2 x - 2\cos x - 1 = 0$
  d $2\sin^2 x - \cos x - 1 = 0$
  e $3\cos^2 x - 3 = \sin x$
  f $\sin x + 5 = 6\cos^2 x$
  g $2\cos^2 x - \sin^2 x - 2\sin x - 1 = 0$
  h $1 + \tan x \cos x = 2\cos^2 x$
  i $3\cos x = 8\tan x$

10 $f(x) = \sin x$ for $0 \leqslant x \leqslant \dfrac{\pi}{2}$ $\qquad$ $g(x) = 2x - 1$ for $x \in \mathbb{R}$
  Solve $gf(x) = 0.5$.

9.7 Trigonometric identities

$\sin^2 x + \cos^2 x = 1$ is called a **trigonometric identity** because it is true for all values of x.

In this section you will learn how to prove more complicated identities involving $\sin x$, $\cos x$ and $\tan x$.

When proving an identity, it is usual to start with the more complicated side of the identity and prove that it simplifies to the less complicated side. This is illustrated in the next example.

> **Note:**
> LHS means left-hand side and RHS means right-hand side.

WORKED EXAMPLE 15

Prove the identity $(1 + \sin x)^2 + (1 - \sin x)^2 + 2\cos^2 x = 4$.

Answers

$\begin{aligned}
\text{LHS} &= (1 + \sin x)^2 + (1 - \sin x)^2 + 2\cos^2 x \\
&= (1 + \sin x)(1 + \sin x) + (1 - \sin x)(1 - \sin x) + 2\cos^2 x &&\text{expand brackets} \\
&= 1 + 2\sin x + \sin^2 x + 1 - 2\sin x + \sin^2 x + 2\cos^2 x &&\text{collect like terms} \\
&= 2 + 2\sin^2 x + 2\cos^2 x \\
&= 2 + 2(\sin^2 x + \cos^2 x) &&\text{use } \sin^2 x + \cos^2 x = 1 \\
&= 2 + 2 \times 1 \\
&= 4 \\
&= \text{RHS}
\end{aligned}$

WORKED EXAMPLE 16

Prove the identity $\dfrac{1}{\cos x} - \cos x = \sin x \tan x$.

Answers

$\begin{aligned}
\text{LHS} &= \dfrac{1}{\cos x} - \cos x \\
&= \dfrac{1}{\cos x} - \dfrac{\cos^2 x}{\cos x} \\
&= \dfrac{1 - \cos^2 x}{\cos x} &&\text{use } 1 - \cos^2 x = \sin^2 x \\
&= \dfrac{\sin^2 x}{\cos x} \\
&= \sin x \times \dfrac{\sin x}{\cos x} &&\text{use } \dfrac{\sin x}{\cos x} = \tan x \\
&= \sin x \tan x \\
&= \text{RHS}
\end{aligned}$

CLASS DISCUSSION

Equivalent trigonometric expressions

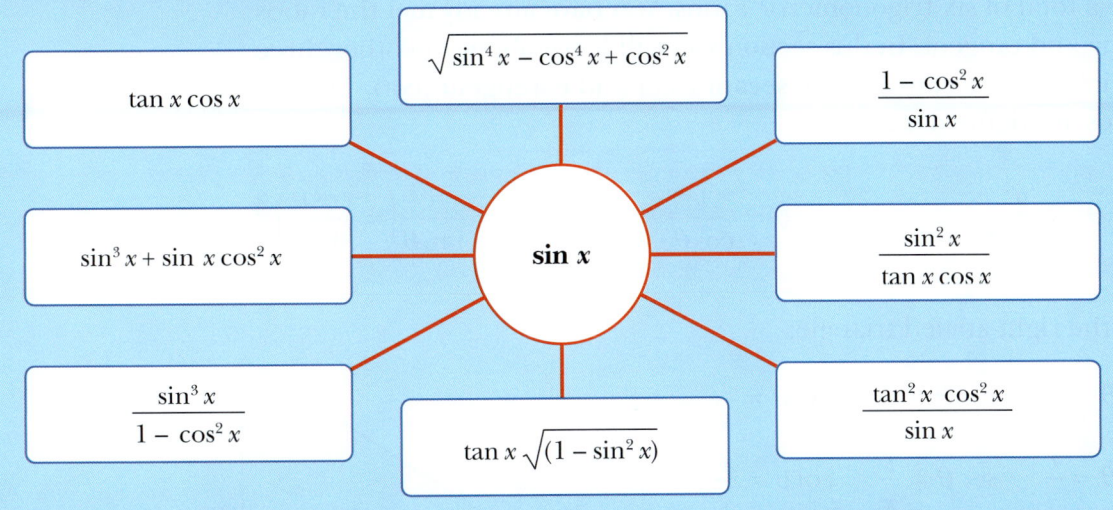

Central node: **sin x**

Connected expressions:
- $\tan x \cos x$
- $\sqrt{\sin^4 x - \cos^4 x + \cos^2 x}$
- $\dfrac{1 - \cos^2 x}{\sin x}$
- $\sin^3 x + \sin x \cos^2 x$
- $\dfrac{\sin^2 x}{\tan x \cos x}$
- $\dfrac{\sin^3 x}{1 - \cos^2 x}$
- $\tan x \sqrt{(1 - \sin^2 x)}$
- $\dfrac{\tan^2 x \; \cos^2 x}{\sin x}$

Discuss why each of the trigonometric expressions in the blue boxes simplify to sin x.

Create as many trigonometric expressions of your own which simplify to tan x.

(Your expressions must contain at least two different trigonometric ratios.)

Compare your answers with your classmates.

Exercise 9.7

1 Prove each of these identities.

a $\dfrac{\sin x}{\tan x} = \cos x$

b $\dfrac{\cos^2 x}{\sqrt{1 - \sin^2 x}} = \cos x$

c $\dfrac{1 - \sin^2 x}{\cos x} = \cos x$

d $\dfrac{\cos^2 x - \sin^2 x}{\cos x + \sin x} + \sin x = \cos x$

e $(\sin x + \cos x)^2 = 1 + 2 \sin x \cos x$

f $\sqrt{4 - 4\sin^2 x} = 2 \cos x$

2 Prove each of these identities.

a $\cos^2 x - \sin^2 x = 2\cos^2 x - 1$

b $\cos^2 x - \sin^2 x = 1 - 2\sin^2 x$

c $\cos^4 x + \sin^2 x \cos^2 x = \cos^2 x$

d $2(1 + \cos x) - (1 + \cos x)^2 = \sin^2 x$

e $2 - (\sin x + \cos x)^2 = (\sin x - \cos x)^2$

f $\cos^4 x + \sin^2 x = \sin^4 x + \cos^2 x$

3 Prove each of these identities.

a $\dfrac{\cos^2 x - \sin^2 x}{\cos x - \sin x} = \cos x + \sin x$

b $\dfrac{\sin x}{1 + \cos x} + \dfrac{1 + \cos x}{\sin x} = \dfrac{2}{\sin x}$

c $\dfrac{\cos^4 x - \sin^4 x}{\cos^2 x} = 1 - \tan^2 x$

d $\dfrac{\sin^2 x \left(1 - \cos^2 x\right)}{\cos^2 x \left(1 - \sin^2 x\right)} = \tan^4 x$

9.8 Further trigonometric equations

The cosecant, secant and cotangent ratios

There are a total of six trigonometric ratios. You have already met the ratios sine, cosine and tangent. In this section you will learn about the other three ratios, which are **cosecant** (cosec), **secant** (sec) and **cotangent** (cot). These three ratios are defined as:

$$\csc\theta = \frac{1}{\sin\theta} \qquad \sec\theta = \frac{1}{\cos\theta} \qquad \cot\theta = \frac{1}{\tan\theta}\left(=\frac{\cos\theta}{\sin\theta}\right)$$

Consider the right-angled triangle:

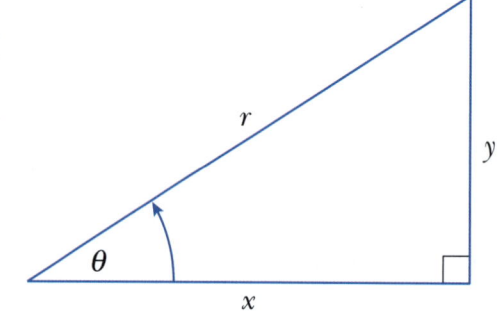

$$\sin\theta = \frac{y}{r} \qquad \cos\theta = \frac{x}{r} \qquad \tan\theta = \frac{y}{x}$$

$$\csc\theta = \frac{r}{y} \qquad \sec\theta = \frac{r}{x} \qquad \cot\theta = \frac{x}{y}$$

The following rules can be found from this triangle:

$$x^2 + y^2 = r^2 \qquad \text{divide both sides by } x^2$$

$$1 + \left(\frac{y}{x}\right)^2 = \left(\frac{r}{x}\right)^2 \qquad \text{use } \frac{y}{x} = \tan\theta \text{ and } \frac{r}{x} = \sec\theta$$

$$1 + \tan^2\theta = \sec^2\theta$$

$$x^2 + y^2 = r^2 \qquad \text{divide both sides by } y^2$$

$$\left(\frac{x}{y}\right)^2 + 1 = \left(\frac{r}{y}\right)^2 \qquad \text{use } \frac{x}{y} = \cot\theta \text{ and } \frac{r}{y} = \csc\theta$$

$$\cot^2\theta + 1 = \csc^2\theta$$

These important identities will be needed to solve trigonometric equations in this section.

WORKED EXAMPLE 17

Solve $2\csc^2 x + \cot x - 8 = 0$ for $0° \leq x \leq 360°$.

Answers

$2\csc^2 x + \cot x - 8 = 0$ use $1 + \cot^2 x = \csc^2 x$
$2(1 + \cot^2 x) + \cot x - 8 = 0$ expand brackets and collect terms
$2\cot^2 x + \cot x - 6 = 0$ factorise
$(2\cot x - 3)(\cot x + 2) = 0$
$2\cot x - 3 = 0$ or $\cot x + 2 = 0$
$\cot x = \dfrac{3}{2}$ $\cot x = -2$
$\tan x = \dfrac{2}{3}$ $\tan x = -\dfrac{1}{2}$

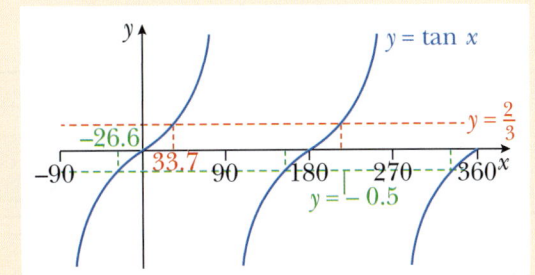

$x = 33.7$ or $33.7 + 180$ $x = -26.6$ or $-26.6 + 180$ or $-26.6 + 360$
$x = 33.7°$ or $213.7°$ $x = -153.4°$ or $333.4°$ (since $-26.6°$ is out of range)

The solution of $2\csc^2 x + \cot x - 8 = 0$ for $0° \leq x \leq 360°$ is
$x = 33.7°, 153.4°, 213.7°$ or $333.4°$.

Exercise 9.8

1. Solve each of these equations for $0° \leq x \leq 360°$.
   a. $\cot x = 0.3$
   b. $\sec x = 4$
   c. $\csc x = -2$
   d. $3\sec x - 5 = 0$

2. Solve each of the these equations for $0 \leq x \leq 2\pi$.
   a. $\csc x = 5$
   b. $\cot x = 0.8$
   c. $\sec x = -4$
   d. $2\cot x + 3 = 0$

3. Solve each of these equations for $0° \leq x \leq 180°$.
   a. $\sec 2x = 1.6$
   b. $\csc 2x = 5$
   c. $\cot 2x = -1$
   d. $5\csc 2x = -7$

4. Solve each of these equations for the given domains.
   a. $\sec(x - 30°) = 3$ for $0° \leq x \leq 360°$
   b. $\csc(2x + 45°) = -5$ for $0° \leq x \leq 180°$
   c. $\cot\left(x + \dfrac{\pi}{3}\right) = 2$ for $0 < x < 2\pi$
   d. $3\sec(2x + 3) = 4$ for $0 < x < \pi$

5. Solve each of these equations for $0° \leq x \leq 360°$.
   a. $\sec^2 x = 4$
   b. $9\cot^2 x = 4$
   c. $16\cot^2 \dfrac{1}{2}x = 9$

6. Solve each of these equations for $0° \leq x \leq 360°$.
   a. $3\tan^2 x - \sec x - 1 = 0$
   b. $4\tan^2 x + 8\sec x = 1$
   c. $2\sec^2 x = 5\tan x + 5$
   d. $2\cot^2 x - 5\csc x - 1 = 0$
   e. $6\cos x + 6\sec x = 13$
   f. $\cot x + 6\sin x - 2\cos x = 3$
   g. $3\cot x = 2\sin x$
   h. $12\sec x - 10\cos x - 9\tan x = 0$

Cambridge IGCSE and O Level Additional Mathematics

9.9 Further trigonometric identities

In this section you will learn how to prove trigonometric identities that involve any of the six trigonometric ratios.

CLASS DISCUSSION

Odd one out

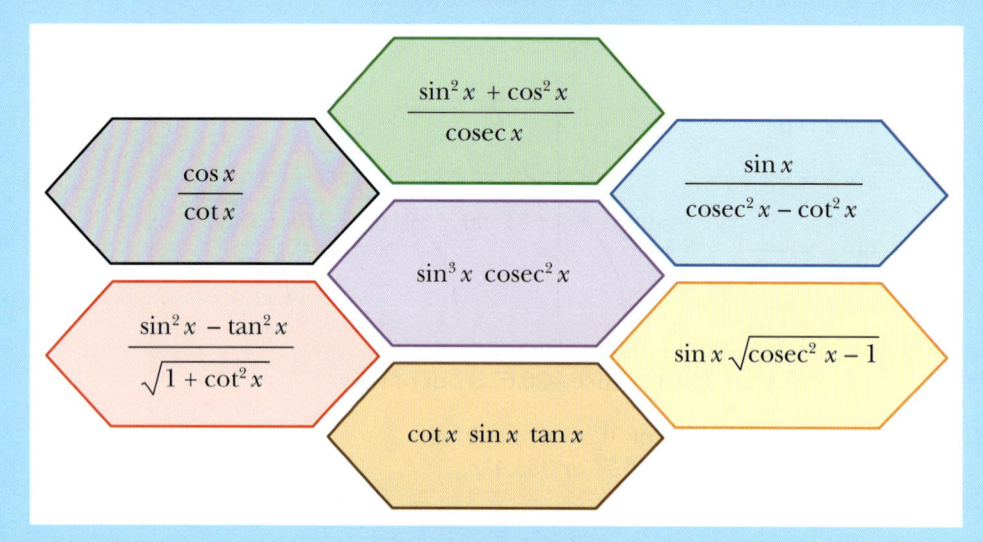

$$\frac{\sin^2 x + \cos^2 x}{\operatorname{cosec} x}$$

$$\frac{\cos x}{\cot x}$$

$$\frac{\sin x}{\operatorname{cosec}^2 x - \cot^2 x}$$

$$\sin^3 x \ \operatorname{cosec}^2 x$$

$$\frac{\sin^2 x - \tan^2 x}{\sqrt{1 + \cot^2 x}}$$

$$\sin x \sqrt{\operatorname{cosec}^2 x - 1}$$

$$\cot x \ \sin x \ \tan x$$

Find the trigonometric expression that does not match the other six expressions.
Create as many expressions of your own to match the 'odd one out'.
(Your expressions must contain at least two different trigonometric ratios.)
Compare your answers with your classmates.

WORKED EXAMPLE 18

Prove the identity $\dfrac{1 + \sec x}{\tan x + \sin x} = \operatorname{cosec} x$.

Answers

$\text{LHS} = \dfrac{1 + \sec x}{\tan x + \sin x}$ use $\sec x = \dfrac{1}{\cos x}$ and $\tan x = \dfrac{\sin x}{\cos x}$

$= \dfrac{1 + \dfrac{1}{\cos x}}{\dfrac{\sin x}{\cos x} + \sin x}$ multiply numerator and denominator by $\cos x$

$= \dfrac{\cos x + 1}{\sin x + \sin x \cos x}$ factorise the denominator

$= \dfrac{\cos x + 1}{\sin x (\cos x + 1)}$ divide numerator and denominator by $(\cos x + 1)$

$= \dfrac{1}{\sin x}$ use $\operatorname{cosec} x = \dfrac{1}{\sin x}$

$= \operatorname{cosec} x$

$= \text{RHS}$

Exercise 9.9

1 Prove each of these identities.

   a $\tan x + \cot x = \sec x \operatorname{cosec} x$
   b $\sin x + \cos x \cot x = \operatorname{cosec} x$
   c $\operatorname{cosec} x - \sin x = \cos x \cot x$
   d $\sec x \operatorname{cosec} x - \cot x = \tan x$

2 Prove each of these identities.

   a $(1 + \sec x)(\operatorname{cosec} x - \cot x) = \tan x$
   b $(1 + \sec x)(1 - \cos x) = \sin x \tan x$
   c $\tan^2 x - \sec^2 x + 2 = \operatorname{cosec}^2 x - \cot^2 x$
   d $(\cot x + \tan x)(\cot x - \tan x) = \operatorname{cosec}^2 x - \sec^2 x$

3 Prove each of these identities.

   a $\dfrac{1}{\tan x + \cot x} = \sin x \cos x$
   b $\dfrac{\sin^2 x + \cos^2 x}{\cos^2 x} = \sec^2 x$

   c $\dfrac{\sin^2 x \cos x + \cos^3 x}{\sin x} = \cot x$
   d $\dfrac{1 - \cos^2 x}{\sec^2 x - 1} = 1 - \sin^2 x$

   e $\dfrac{1 + \tan^2 x}{\tan x} = \sec x \operatorname{cosec} x$
   f $\dfrac{\sin x}{1 - \cos^2 x} = \operatorname{cosec} x$

   g $\dfrac{\sin x \tan^2 x}{1 + \tan^2 x} = \sin^3 x$
   h $\dfrac{1 - \sec^2 x}{1 - \operatorname{cosec}^2 x} = \tan^4 x$

   i $\dfrac{1 + \sin x}{1 - \sin x} = (\tan x + \sec x)^2$
   j $\dfrac{\cos x \cot x}{\cos x + \cot x} = \sec x - \tan x$

4 Prove each of these identities.

   a $\dfrac{\sin x}{\cos x} + \dfrac{\cos x}{\sin x} = \sec x \operatorname{cosec} x$
   b $\dfrac{1}{1 - \sin x} - \dfrac{1}{1 + \sin x} = 2 \tan x \sec x$

   c $\dfrac{1}{1 + \cos x} + \dfrac{1}{1 - \cos x} = 2 \operatorname{cosec}^2 x$
   d $\dfrac{\cos x}{1 - \tan x} + \dfrac{\sin x}{1 - \cot x} = \sin x + \cos x$

   e $\dfrac{\cos x}{1 + \sin x} + \dfrac{\cos x}{1 - \sin x} = 2 \sec x$
   f $\dfrac{\cos x}{\operatorname{cosec} x + 1} + \dfrac{\cos x}{\operatorname{cosec} x - 1} = 2 \tan x$

Summary

Positive and negative angles

Angles measured anticlockwise from the positive x-direction are positive.

Angles measured clockwise from the positive x-direction are negative.

Diagram showing where sin, cos and tan are positive

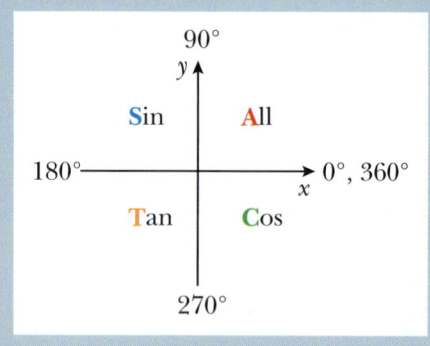

Useful mnemonic: '**A**ll **S**tudents **T**rust **C**ambridge'

Cosecant, secant and cotangent

$$\text{cosec}\,\theta = \frac{1}{\sin\theta} \qquad \sec\theta = \frac{1}{\cos\theta} \qquad \cot\theta = \frac{1}{\tan\theta}$$

Trigonometric identities

$\tan x = \dfrac{\sin x}{\cos x}$

$\sin^2 x + \cos^2 x = 1$

$1 + \tan^2 x = \sec^2 x$

$1 + \cot^2 x = \text{cosec}^2 x$

Examination questions

Worked past paper example

The diagram shows the graph of $y = a\sin(bx) + c$ for $0 \leq x \leq 2\pi$, where a, b and c are positive integers.

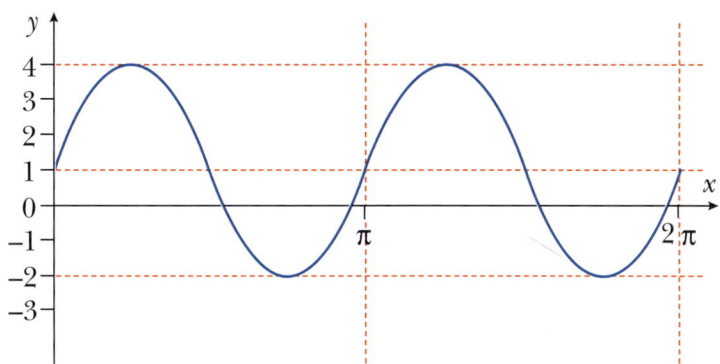

State the value of a, of b and of c. [3]

Cambridge IGCSE Additional Mathematics 0606 Paper 11 Q1 Nov 2013

Answer

$y = a\sin(bx) + c$
a = amplitude   period = $\pi = \dfrac{2\pi}{b}$
$a = 3$ $b = 2$

The graph of $y = 3\sin 2x$ has been translated by the vector $\begin{pmatrix} 0 \\ 1 \end{pmatrix}$, hence $c = 1$.

$a = 3$, $b = 2$, $c = 1$

Exercise 9.10

Exam Exercise

1. **a** Sketch the curve $y = 3\cos 2x - 1$ for $0° \leq x \leq 180°$. [3]
   b i State the amplitude of $1 - 4\sin 2x$. [1]
   ii State the period of $5\tan 3x + 1$. [1]

   Cambridge IGCSE Additional Mathematics 0606 Paper 11 Q2 Nov 2014

2. **a** Solve $2\cos 3x = \cot 3x$ for $0° \leq x \leq 90°$. [5]
   b Solve $\sec\left(y + \dfrac{\pi}{2}\right) = -2$ for $0 \leq y \leq \pi$ radians. [4]

   Cambridge IGCSE Additional Mathematics 0606 Paper 11 Q11a,b Nov 2014

3. **a** Prove that $\sec x \csc x - \cot x = \tan x$. [4]
   b Use the result from **part a** to solve the equation $\sec x \csc x = 3\cot x$ for $0° < x < 360°$. [4]

   Cambridge IGCSE Additional Mathematics 0606 Paper 21 Q10i,ii Nov 2014

4 Show that $\dfrac{1+\sin\theta}{\cos\theta} + \dfrac{\cos\theta}{1+\sin\theta} = 2\sec\theta$. [4]

Cambridge IGCSE Additional Mathematics 0606 Paper 21 Q12a,b Nov 2013

5 **a** Solve the equation $2\cosec x + \dfrac{7}{\cos x} = 0$ for $0° \leq x \leq 360°$. [4]

b Solve the equation $7\sin(2y-1) = 5$ for $0 \leq y \leq 5$ radians. [5]

Cambridge IGCSE Additional Mathematics 0606 Paper 11 Q1i,ii,iii Jun 2013

6 On a copy of the axes below sketch, for $0 \leq x \leq 2\pi$, the graph of

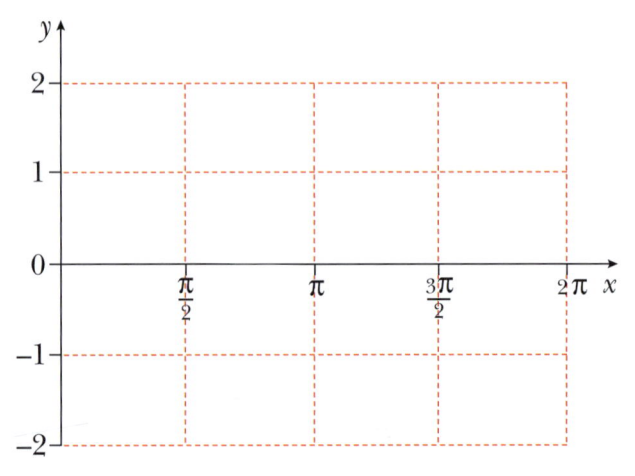

a $y = \cos x - 1$ [2]

b $y = \sin 2x$. [2]

c State the number of solutions of the equation $\cos x - \sin 2x = 1$, for $0 \leq x \leq 2\pi$. [1]

Cambridge IGCSE Additional Mathematics 0606 Paper 11 Q1i,ii,iii Jun 2013

7 Prove that $\left(\dfrac{1+\sin\theta}{\cos\theta}\right)^2 + \left(\dfrac{1-\sin\theta}{\cos\theta}\right)^2 = 2 + 4\tan^2\theta$. [4]

Cambridge IGCSE Additional Mathematics 0606 Paper 21 Q1 Jun 2013

8 **a** Given that $15\cos^2\theta + 2\sin^2\theta = 7$, show that $\tan^2\theta = \dfrac{8}{5}$. [4]

b Solve $15\cos^2\theta + 2\sin^2\theta = 7$ for $0 \leq \theta \leq \pi$ radians. [3]

Cambridge IGCSE Additional Mathematics 0606 Paper 11 Q6i,ii Jun 2012

9

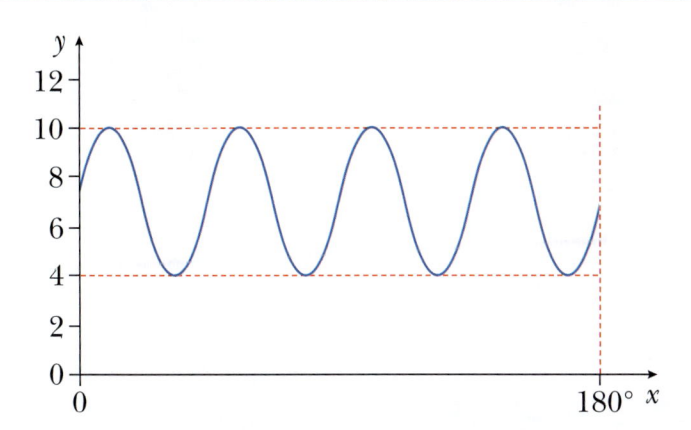

a The diagram shows a sketch of the curve $y = a\sin(bx) + c$ for $0° \leq x \leq 180°$.

Find the values of a, b and c. [3]

b Given that $f(x) = 5\cos 3x + 1$, for all x, state

i the period of f, [1]

ii the amplitude of f. [1]

Cambridge IGCSE Additional Mathematics 0606 Paper 21 Q3a,bi,ii Jun 2012

Chapter 10
Permutations and combinations

This section will show you how to:

- find the number of arrangements of *n* distinct items
- find the number of permutations of *r* items from *n* distinct items
- find the number of combinations of *r* items from *n* distinct items
- solve problems using permutations and combinations.

Chapter 10: Permutations and Combinations

10.1 Factorial notation

$5 \times 4 \times 3 \times 2 \times 1$ is called 5 factorial and is written as 5!

It is useful to remember that $n! = n \times (n-1)!$

For example $5! = 5 \times 4!$

WORKED EXAMPLE 1

Find the value of:

a $\dfrac{8!}{5!}$

b $\dfrac{11!}{8!3!}$

Answers

a $\dfrac{8!}{5!} = \dfrac{8 \times 7 \times 6 \times 5 \times 4 \times 3 \times 2 \times 1}{5 \times 4 \times 3 \times 2 \times 1}$

$= 8 \times 7 \times 6$

$= 336$

b $\dfrac{11!}{8!3!} = \dfrac{11 \times 10 \times 9 \times 8 \times 7 \times 6 \times 5 \times 4 \times 3 \times 2 \times 1}{8 \times 7 \times 6 \times 5 \times 4 \times 3 \times 2 \times 1 \times 3 \times 2 \times 1}$

$= \dfrac{990}{6}$

$= 165$

Exercise 10.1

1 Without using a calculator, find the value of each of the following. Use the *x*! key on your calculator to check your answers.

a $7!$
b $\dfrac{4!}{2!}$
c $\dfrac{7!}{3!}$
d $\dfrac{8!}{5!}$

d $\dfrac{4!}{2!2!}$
e $\dfrac{6!}{3!2!}$
f $\dfrac{6!}{(3!)^2}$
g $\dfrac{5!}{3!} \times \dfrac{7!}{4!}$

2 Rewrite each of the following using factorial notation.

a 2×1
b $6 \times 5 \times 4 \times 3 \times 2 \times 1$
c $5 \times 4 \times 3$

d $17 \times 16 \times 15 \times 14$
e $\dfrac{10 \times 9 \times 8}{3 \times 2 \times 1}$
f $\dfrac{12 \times 11 \times 10 \times 9 \times 8}{4 \times 3 \times 2 \times 1}$

CHALLENGE Q

3 Rewrite each of the following using factorial notation.

a $n(n-1)(n-2)(n-3)$
b $n(n-1)(n-2)(n-3)(n-4)(n-5)$

c $\dfrac{n(n-1)(n-2)}{5 \times 4 \times 3 \times 2 \times 1}$
d $\dfrac{n(n-1)(n-2)(n-3)(n-4)}{3 \times 2 \times 1}$

Cambridge IGCSE and O Level Additional Mathematics

10.2 Arrangements

CLASS DISCUSSION

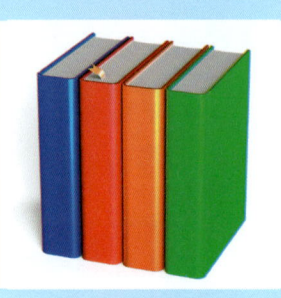

These books are arranged in the order **BROG**. (**B**lue, **R**ed, **O**range, **G**reen).

The books could be arranged in the order **OGBR**.

Find the number of different ways that the 4 books can be arranged in a line.

You will need to be systematic.

How many ways are there of arranging five different books in a line?

To find the number of ways of arranging the letters A, B and C in a line you can use two methods.

Method 1
List all the possible arrangements.
These are: ABC   ACB   BAC   BCA   CAB and CBA.
There are 6 different arrangements.

Method 2
Consider filling 3 spaces.

The first space can be filled in **3** ways with either A or B or C.
For each of these **3** ways of filling the first space there are 2 ways of filling the second space.
There are **3 × 2** ways of filling the first and second spaces.
For each of the ways of filling the first and second spaces there is just **1** way of filling the third space.
There are **3 × 2 × 1** ways of filling the three spaces.
The number of arrangements = 3 × 2 × 1 = 6.
3 × 2 × 1 is called 3 factorial and can be written as 3!.

In the class discussion, you should have found that there were 24 different ways of arranging the 4 books.
4! = 4 × 3 × 2 × 1 = 24

> The number of ways of arranging n distinct items in a line = $n!$.

WORKED EXAMPLE 2

G R A D I E N T S

a Find the number of different arrangements of these nine cards if there are no restrictions.
b Find the number of arrangements that begin with **GRAD**.
c Find the number of arrangements that begin with **G** and end with **S**.

Chapter 10: Permutations and Combinations

Answers

a There are 9 different cards.
number of arrangements = 9! = 362 880

b The first four letters are **GRAD**, so there are now only 5 letters left to be arranged.
number of arrangements = 5! = 120

c The first and last letters are fixed, so there are now 7 letters to arrange between the **G** and the **S**.
number of arrangements = 7! = 5040

WORKED EXAMPLE 3

a Find the number of different arrangements of these seven objects if there are no restrictions.
b Find the number of arrangements where the squares and circles alternate.
c Find the number of arrangements where all the squares are together.
d Find the number of arrangements where the squares are together and the circles are together.

Answers

a There are 7 different objects.
number of arrangements = 7! = 5040

b If the squares and circles alternate, a possible arrangement is:

There are 4! different ways of arranging the four squares.
There are 3! different ways of arranging the three circles.
So the total number of possible arrangements = 4! × 3! = 24 × 6 = 144.

c If the squares are all together, a possible arrangement is:

The number of ways of arranging the 1 block of four squares and the 3 circles = 4!
There are 4! ways of arranging the four squares within the block of squares.
So the total number of possible arrangements = 4! × 4! = 24 × 24 = 576.

d If the squares are together and the circles are together, a possible arrangement is:

There are 4! × 3! ways of having the squares at the start and the circles at the end.
Another possible arrangement is:

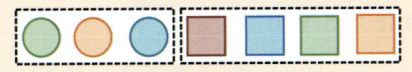

There are 3! × 4! ways of having the circles at the start and the squares at the end.
total number of arrangements = 4! × 3! + 3! × 4! = 144 + 144 = 288

221

Exercise 10.2

1. Find the number of different arrangements of
   a 4 people sitting in a row on a bench
   b 7 different books on a shelf.

2. Find the number of different arrangements of letters in each of the following words.
   a TIGER b OLYMPICS c PAINTBRUSH

3. a Find the number of different four-digit numbers that can be formed using the digits 3, 5, 7 and 8 without repetition.
   b How many of these four-digit numbers are
   i even
   ii greater than 8000?

4. A shelf holds 7 different books.
   4 of the books are cookery books and 3 of the books are history books.
   a Find the number of ways the books can be arranged if there are no restrictions.
   b Find the number of ways the books can be arranged if the 4 cookery books are kept together.

5. Five-digit numbers are to be formed using the digits 2, 3, 4, 5 and 6.
   Each digit may only be used once in any number.
   a Find how many different five-digit numbers can be formed.
   How many of these five-digit numbers are
   b even
   c greater than 40 000
   d even and greater than 40 000?

6. Three girls and two boys are to be seated in a row.
   Find the number of different ways that this can be done if
   a the girls and boys sit alternately
   b a girl sits at each end of the row
   c the girls sit together and the boys sit together.

7. a Find the number of different arrangements of the letters in the word ORANGE.
   Find the number of these arrangements that
   b begin with the letter O
   c have the letter O at one end and the letter E at the other end.

8. a Find the number of different six-digit numbers which can be made using the digits 0, 1, 2, 3, 4 and 5 without repetition. Assume that a number cannot begin with 0.
   b How many of the six-digit numbers in **part a** are even?

9 6 girls and 2 boys are to be seated in a row.

Find the number of ways that this can be done if the 2 boys must have exactly 4 girls seated between them.

10.3 Permutations

In the last section, you learnt that if you had three letters A, B and C and 3 spaces to fill, then the number of ways of filling the spaces was $3 \times 2 \times 1 = 3!$

Now consider having 8 letters A, B, C, D, E, F, G, H and 3 spaces to fill.

The first space can be filled in **8** ways.

For each of these **8** ways of filling the first space there are **7** ways of filling the second space.

There are 8×7 ways of filling the first and second spaces.

For each of the ways of filling the first and second spaces there are **6** ways of filling the third space.

There are $8 \times 7 \times 6$ ways of filling the three spaces.

The number of different ways of arranging three letters chosen from eight letters $= 8 \times 7 \times 6 = 336$.

The different arrangements of the letters are called **permutations**.

The notation $^8P_3$ is used to represent the number of permutations of 3 items chosen from 8 items.

Note that $8 \times 7 \times 6$ can also be written as $\dfrac{8 \times 7 \times 6 \times 5 \times 4 \times 3 \times 2 \times 1}{5 \times 4 \times 3 \times 2 \times 1} = \dfrac{8!}{5!} = \dfrac{8!}{(8-3)!}$

So $^8P_3 = \dfrac{8!}{(8-3)!} = \dfrac{8!}{5!} = 336$.

> The general rule for finding the number of **permutations** of r items from n distinct items is $^nP_r = \dfrac{n!}{(n-r)!}$.

- In permutations, **order matters**.
- By definition, $0! = 1$.

Cambridge IGCSE and O Level Additional Mathematics

To explain why 0! = 1, consider finding the number of permutations of 5 letters taken from 5 letters.

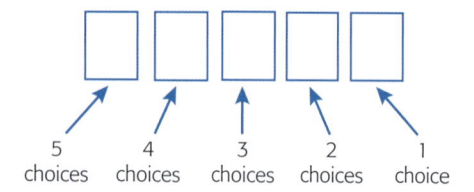

5 choices   4 choices   3 choices   2 choices   1 choice

The number of ways of filling the 5 spaces with the 5 letters = $5 \times 4 \times 3 \times 2 \times 1 = 120$.

But, $^5P_5 = \dfrac{5!}{(5-5)!} = \dfrac{5!}{0!} = \dfrac{120}{0!}$.

So $\dfrac{120}{0!} = 120$. Hence 0! must be equal to 1.

WORKED EXAMPLE 4

A security code consists of 3 letters selected from A, B, C, D, E, F followed by 2 digits selected from 5, 6, 7, 8, 9.

Find the number of possible security codes if no letter or number can be repeated.

Answers

Method 1

There are 6 letters and 5 digits to select from.

Number of arrangements of 3 letters from 6 letters = $^6P_3$

Number of arrangements of 2 digits from 5 digits = $^5P_2$

So number of possible security codes = $^6P_3 \times ^5P_2 = 120 \times 20 = 2400$.

Method 2

There are 6 letters and 5 digits to select from.

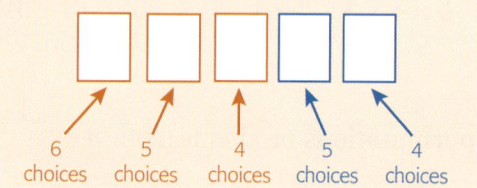

6 choices   5 choices   4 choices   5 choices   4 choices

The first three spaces must be filled with three of the six letters.

There is a choice of 6 for the first space, 5 for the second space and 4 for the third space.

The last two spaces must be filled with two of the 5 digits.

There is a choice of 5 for the first space and 4 for the second space.

So number of possible security codes = $6 \times 5 \times 4 \times 5 \times 4 = 2400$.

Chapter 10: Permutations and Combinations

WORKED EXAMPLE 5

Find how many even numbers between 3000 and 4000 can be formed using the digits 1, 3, 5, 6, 7 and 9 if no number can be repeated.

Answers

Method 1

The first number must be a 3 and the last number must be a 6.

$$\boxed{3}\ \boxed{*}\ \boxed{*}\ \boxed{6}$$

There are now two spaces to fill using two of the remaining four digits 1, 5, 7 and 9.

Number of ways of filling the remaining two spaces = $^4P_2 = \dfrac{4!}{(4-2)!} = \dfrac{4!}{2!} = 12$.

There are 12 different numbers that satisfy the conditions.

Method 2

Consider the number of choices for filling each of the four spaces.

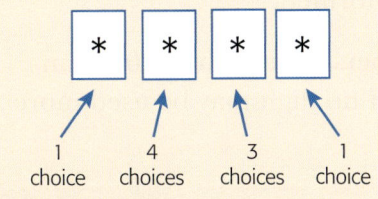

$$\boxed{*}\ \boxed{*}\ \boxed{*}\ \boxed{*}$$

1 choice   4 choices   3 choices   1 choice

Number of ways of filling the four spaces = $1 \times 4 \times 3 \times 1$

There are 12 different numbers that satisfy the conditions.

Method 3

In this example it is not impractical to list all the possible permutations.

These are: 3156 3516 3176 3716 3196 3916
           3576 3756 3196 3916 3796 3976

There are 12 different numbers that satisfy the conditions.

Exercise 10.3

1. Without using a calculator, find the value of each of the following.
   Use the ^nP_r key on you calculator to check your answers.

   a $^8P_5$ **b** $^6P_4$ **c** $^{11}P_8$ **d** $^7P_7$

2. Find the number of different ways that 4 books, chosen from 6 books be arranged on a shelf.

3. How many different five-digit numbers can be formed from the digits 1, 2, 3, 4, 5, 6, 7, 8, 9 if no digit can be repeated?

4. There are 8 competitors in a long jump competition.
   In how many different ways can the first, second and third prizes be awarded?

5 Find how many different four-digit numbers greater than 4000 that can be formed using the digits 1, 2, 3, 4, 5, 6 and 7 if no digit can be used more than once.

6 Find how many even numbers between 5000 and 6000 can be formed from the digits 2, 4, 5, 7, 8, if no digit can be used more than once.

7 A four-digit number is formed using four of the eight digits 1, 2, 3, 4, 5, 6, 7 and 8. No digit can be used more than once.

Find how many different four-digit numbers can be formed if

 a there are no restrictions **b** the number is odd

 c the number is greater than 6000 **d** the number is odd and greater than 6000.

8 Numbers are formed using the digits 3, 5, 6, 8 and 9.

No digit can be used more than once.

Find how many different

 a three-digit numbers can be formed

 b numbers using three or more digits can be formed.

9 Find how many different even four-digit numbers greater than 2000 can be formed using the digits 1, 2, 3, 4, 5, 6, 7, 8 if no digit may be used more than once.

CLASS DISCUSSION

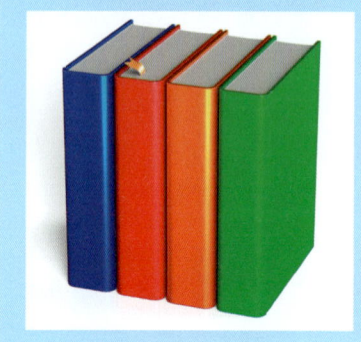

You have already investigated the number of ways of arranging 4 different books in a line.

You are now going to consider the number of ways you can select 3 books from the 4 books where the order of selection does not matter.

If the order does not matter, then the selection **BRO** is the same as **OBR**.

Find the number of different ways of selecting 3 books from the 4 books.

A combination is a selection of some items where the order of selection does not matter.

So for **combinations order does not matter**.

Consider the set of 5 crayons.

To find the number of different ways of choosing 3 crayons from the set of 5 crayons you can use two methods.

Method 1

List all the possible selections.

So there are 10 different ways of choosing 3 crayons from 5.

Method 2
The number of combinations of 3 from 5 = $\dfrac{5!}{3!2!} = \dfrac{5 \times 4}{2!} = 10$.

10.4 Combinations

> The general rule for finding the number of **combinations** of r items from n distinct items is:
> $$^nC_r = \dfrac{n!}{r!(n-r)!}$$

- In combinations, **order does not matter**.
- ^nC_r is read as 'n choose r'.
  So $^5C_3$ is read as '5 choose 3'.
- ^nC_r can also br written as $\binom{n}{r}$.
- $^{10}C_3$ is the same as $^{10}C_7$.
  So the number of ways of choosing 3 from 10 is the same as the number of ways of choosing 7 from 10. This is because when you choose a group of 3 from 10, you are automatically left with a group of 7.

WORKED EXAMPLE 6

A team of 6 swimmers is to be selected from a group of 20 swimmers.
Find the number of different ways in which the team can be selected.

Answers
Number of ways of selecting the team = $^{20}C_6 = \dfrac{20!}{6!14!} = 38\,760$.

WORKED EXAMPLE 7

A   B

The diagram shows 2 different tents A and B.
Tent A holds 3 people and tent B holds 4 people.
Find the number of ways in which 7 people can be assigned to the two tents.

Answers

Number of ways of choosing 3 people from 7 for tent A = $^7C_3$ = 35.
So, the number of ways of assigning the 7 people to the two tents = 35.

WORKED EXAMPLE 8

3 coats and 2 dresses are to be selected from 9 coats and 7 dresses.
Find the number of different selections that can be made.

Answers

Number of ways of choosing 3 coats from 9 coats = $^9C_3$.
Number of ways of choosing 2 dresses from 7 dresses = $^7C_2$.
So, the number of possible selections = $^9C_3 \times {}^7C_2$ = 84 × 21 = 1764.

WORKED EXAMPLE 9

A quiz team of 5 students is to be selected from 6 boys and 4 girls.
Find the number of possible teams that can be selected in which there are more boys than girls.

Answers

If there are more boys than girls there could be:
5 boys   0 girls   number of ways = $^6C_5 \times {}^4C_0$ = 6 × 1 = 6
4 boys   1 girl   number of ways = $^6C_4 \times {}^4C_1$ = 15 × 4 = 60
3 boys   2 girls   number of ways = $^6C_3 \times {}^4C_2$ = 20 × 6 = 120
So, the total number of possible teams = 6 + 60 + 120 = 186.

Chapter 10: Permutations and Combinations

WORKED EXAMPLE 10

Sofia has to play 5 pieces of music for her music examination.

She has 13 pieces of music to choose from.

There are 7 pieces written by Chopin, 4 written by Mozart and 2 written by Bach.

Find the number of ways the 5 pieces can be chosen if

a there are no restrictions

b there must be 2 pieces by Chopin, 2 pieces by Mozart and 1 piece by Bach

c there must be at least one piece by each composer.

Answers

a Number of ways of choosing 5 from 13 = $^{13}C_5$ = 1287

b Number of ways of choosing 2 from 7 pieces by Chopin = $^7C_2$
Number of ways of choosing 2 from 4 pieces by Mozart = $^4C_2$
Number of ways of choosing 1 from 2 pieces by Bach = $^2C_1$
So, number of possible selections = $^7C_2 \times {}^4C_2 \times {}^2C_1 = 21 \times 6 \times 2 = 252$.

c If there is at least one piece by each composer there could be:

3 Chopin   1 Mozart   1 Bach   number of ways = $^7C_3 \times {}^4C_1 \times {}^2C_1 = 35 \times 4 \times 2 = 280$
1 Chopin   3 Mozart   1 Bach   number of ways = $^7C_1 \times {}^4C_3 \times {}^2C_1 = 7 \times 4 \times 2 = 56$
2 Chopin   2 Mozart   1 Bach   number of ways = $^7C_2 \times {}^4C_2 \times {}^2C_1 = 21 \times 6 \times 2 = 252$
2 Chopin   1 Mozart   2 Bach   number of ways = $^7C_2 \times {}^4C_1 \times {}^2C_2 = 21 \times 4 \times 1 = 84$
1 Chopin   2 Mozart   2 Bach   number of ways = $^7C_1 \times {}^4C_2 \times {}^2C_2 = 7 \times 6 \times 1 = 42$

So, total number of ways = 280 + 56 + 252 + 84 + 42 = 714.

Exercise 10.4

1 Without using a calculator find the value of each of the following, and then use the ^nC_r key on your calculator to check your answers.

  a $^5C_1$ b $^6C_3$ c $^4C_4$ d $\binom{8}{4}$ e $\binom{5}{5}$ f $\binom{7}{4}$

2 Show that $^8C_3 = {}^8C_5$.

3 How many different ways are there of selecting

  a 3 photographs from 10 photographs

  b 5 books from 7 books

  c a team of 11 footballers from 14 footballers?

4 How many different combinations of 3 letters can be chosen from the letters P, Q, R, S, T?

5 The diagram shows 2 different boxes, A and B.

8 different toys are to be placed in the boxes.

Find the number of ways in which the 8 toys can be placed in the boxes so that 5 toys are in box A and 3 toys are in box B.

6 4 pencils and 3 pens are to be selected from a collection of 8 pencils and 5 pens.

Find the number of different selections that can be made.

7 Four of the letters of the word PAINTBRUSH are selected at random.

Find the number of different combinations if

 a there is no restriction on the letters selected

 b the letter T must be selected.

8 A test consists of 30 questions.

Each answer is either correct or incorrect.

Find the number of different ways in which it is possible to answer

 a exactly 10 questions correctly

 b exactly 25 questions correctly.

9 An athletics club has 10 long distance runners, 8 sprinters and 5 jumpers.

A team of 3 long distance runners, 5 sprinters and 2 jumpers is to be selected.

Find the number of ways in which the team can be selected.

10 A team of 5 members is to be chosen from 5 men and 3 women.

Find the number of different teams that can be chosen

 a if there are no restrictions

 b that consist of 3 men and 2 women

 c that consist of no more than 1 woman.

11 A committee of 5 people is to be chosen from 6 women and 7 men.

Find the number of different committees that can be chosen

 a if there are no restrictions

 b if there are more men than women.

12 A committee of 6 people is to be chosen from 6 men and 7 women.

The committee must contain at least 1 man.

Find the number of different committees that can be formed.

13 A school committee of 5 people is to be selected from a group of 4 teachers and 7 students.

Find the number of different ways that the committee can be selected if

 a there are no restrictions

 b there must be at least 1 teacher and there must be more students than teachers.

14 A test consists of 10 different questions.

4 of the questions are on trigonometry and 6 questions are on algebra.

Students are asked to answer 8 questions.

  a Find the number of ways in which students can select 8 questions if there are no restrictions.

  b Find the number of these selections which contain at least 4 algebra questions.

15 Rafiu has a collection of 10 CDs.

4 of the CDs are classical, 3 are jazz and 3 are rock.

He selects 5 of the CDs from his collection.

Find the number of ways he can make his selection if

  a there are no restrictions

  b his selection must contain his favourite jazz CD

  c his selection must contain at least 3 classical CDs.

16 In a group of 15 entertainers, there are 6 singers, 5 guitarists and 4 comedians.

A show is to be given by 6 of these entertainers.

In the show there must be at least 1 guitarist and 1 comedian.

There must also be more singers than guitarists.

Find the number of ways that the 6 entertainers can be selected.

Summary

Arrangements in a line

The number of ways of arranging n distinct items in a line is
$$n \times (n-1) \times (n-2) \times \ldots \times 3 \times 2 \times 1 = n!$$

Permutations

The number of **permutations** of r items from n distinct items is
$$^nP_r = \frac{n!}{(n-r)!}.$$
In permutations, **order matters**.

Combinations

The number of **combinations** of r items from n distinct items is
$$^nC_r = \binom{n}{r} = \frac{n!}{r!(n-r)!}.$$
In combinations, **order does not matter**.

Cambridge IGCSE and O Level Additional Mathematics

Examination questions

Worked past paper example

1 a i Find how many different 4-digit numbers can be formed using the digits 1, 2, 3, 4, 5 and 6 if no digit is repeated. [1]

  ii How many of the 4-digit numbers found in **part i** are greater than 6000? [1]

  iii How many of the 4-digit numbers found in **part i** are greater than 6000 and are odd? [1]

b A quiz team of 10 players is to be chosen from a class of 8 boys and 12 girls.

  i Find the number of different teams that can be chosen if the team has to have equal numbers of girls and boys. [3]

  ii Find the number of different teams that can be chosen if the team has to include the youngest and oldest boy and the youngest and oldest girl. [2]

Cambridge IGCSE Additional Mathematics 0606 Paper 11 Q10ai,ii,iii,bi,ii Nov 2014

Answers

1 a i Number of 4-digit numbers = $^6P_4 = 360$.

  ii **Method 1**

  The first number must be a 6.

  | 6 | * | * | * |

  There are now three spaces to fill using three of the remaining five digits 1, 2, 3, 4 and 5.

  Number of ways of filling the remaining three spaces = $^5P_3 = \dfrac{5!}{(5-3)!} = \dfrac{5!}{2!} = 60$.

  There are 60 different numbers that satisfy the conditions.

  Method 2

  Consider the number of choices for filling each of the four spaces.

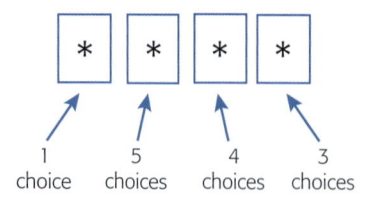

  | * | * | * | * |

  1 choice, 5 choices, 4 choices, 3 choices

  Number of ways of filling the four spaces = $1 \times 5 \times 4 \times 3$.

  There are 60 different numbers that satisfy the conditions.

iii Method 1

The first number must be a 6.

| 6 | * | * | * |

The last number must be a 1, 3 or 5.

The middle two spaces must then be filled using two of the remaining four numbers.

Number of ways of filling the four spaces = $1 \times {}^4P_2 \times 3 = 1 \times \dfrac{4!}{(4-2)!} \times 3 = 3 \times \dfrac{4!}{2!} = 36$.

There are 36 different numbers that satisfy the conditions.

Method 2

Consider the number of choices for filling each of the four spaces.

The first number must be a 6.

The last number must be a 1, 3 or 5.

When the first and last spaces have been filled there will be four numbers left to choose from.

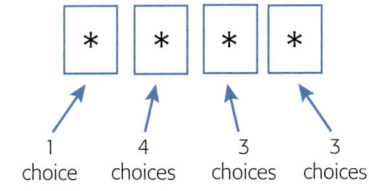

| * | * | * | * |
 1 choice, 4 choices, 3 choices, 3 choices

Number of ways of filling the four spaces = $1 \times 4 \times 3 \times 3$.

There are 36 different numbers that satisfy the conditions.

b i There must be 5 boys and 5 girls.

Number of ways of choosing 5 boys from 8 = ${}^8C_5$.

Number of ways of choosing 5 girls from 12 = ${}^{12}C_5$.

Number of possible teams = ${}^8C_5 \times {}^{12}C_5 = 56 \times 792 = 44\,352$.

ii The team includes the youngest and oldest boy and the youngest and oldest girl.

There are now 6 places left to fill and 16 people left to choose from.

Number of ways of choosing 6 from 16 = ${}^{16}C_6 = 8008$.

Number of possible teams = 8008.

Exercise 10.5
Exam Exercise

1 a How many even numbers less than 500 can be formed using the digits 1, 2, 3, 4 and 5?
Each digit may be used only once in any number. [4]

b A committee of 8 people is to be chosen from 7 men and 5 women.

Find the number of different committees that could be selected if

   i the committee contains at least 3 men and at least 3 women, [4]

   ii the oldest man or the oldest woman, but not both, must be included in the committee. [2]

Cambridge IGCSE Additional Mathematics 0606 Paper 11 Q10a,bi,ii Jun 2014

2 a An art gallery displays 10 paintings in a row.

Of these paintings, 5 are by Picasso, 4 by Monet and 1 by Turner.

   i Find the number of different ways the paintings can be displayed if there are no restrictions. [1]

   ii Find the number of different ways the paintings can be displayed if the paintings by each of the artists are kept together. [3]

b A committee of 4 senior students and 2 junior students is to be selected from a group of 6 senior students and 5 junior students.

   i Calculate the number of different committees that can be selected. [3]

One of the 6 senior students is a cousin of one of the 5 junior students.

   ii Calculate the number of different committees which can be selected if at most one of these cousins is included. [3]

Cambridge IGCSE Additional Mathematics 0606 Paper 21 Q9ai,ii,bi,ii Nov 2012

3 a Arrangements containing 5 different letters from the word AMPLITUDE are to be made.

Find

   i the number of 5-letter arrangements if there are no restrictions, [1]

   ii the number of 5-letter arrangements which start with the letter A and end with the letter E. [1]

b Tickets for a concert are given out randomly to a class containing 20 students.

No student is given more than one ticket. There are 15 tickets.

   i Find the number of ways in which this can be done. [1]

There are 12 boys and 8 girls in the class. Find the number of different ways in which

   ii 10 boys and 5 girls get tickets, [3]

   iii all the boys get tickets. [1]

Cambridge IGCSE Additional Mathematics 0606 Paper 11 Q4ai,ii,bi,ii,iii Jun 2012

4 Six-digit numbers are to be formed using the digits 3, 4, 5, 6, 7 and 9.

Each digit may only be used once in any number.

  a Find how many different six-digit numbers can be formed. [1]

Find how many of these six-digit numbers are

  b even, [1]

  c greater than 500 000, [1]

  d even and greater than 500 000. [3]

Cambridge IGCSE Additional Mathematics 0606 Paper 11 Q4i-iv Nov 2011

5 **a** A shelf contains 8 different travel books, of which 5 are about Europe and 3 are about Africa.

    i Find the number of different ways the books can be arranged if there are no restrictions. [2]

    ii Find the number of different ways the books can be arranged if the 5 books about Europe are kept together. [2]

  b 3 DVDs and 2 videotapes are to be selected from a collection of 7 DVDs and 5 videotapes. Calculate the number of different selections that could be made. [3]

Cambridge IGCSE Additional Mathematics 0606 Paper 21 Q6ai,ii,b Jun 2011

6 A 4-digit number is formed by using four of the seven digits 1, 3, 4, 5, 7, 8 and 9.

No digit can be used more than once in any number.

Find how many different 4-digit numbers can be formed if

  a there are no restrictions, [2]

  b the number is less than 4000, [2]

  c the number is even and less than 4000. [2]

Cambridge IGCSE Additional Mathematics 0606 Paper 21 Q6i,ii,iii Nov 2010

Chapter 11
Binomial expansions

This section will show you how to:

- expand expressions of the form $(a + b)^n$ where n is a positive integer.

Chapter 11: Binomial expansions

11.1 Pascal's triangle

The word 'binomial' means 'two terms'.

The word is used in algebra for expressions such as $x + 5$ and $2x - 3y$.

You should already know that $(a + b)^2 = (a + b)(a + b) = a^2 + 2ab + b^2$.

The expansion of $(a + b)^2$ can be used to expand $(a + b)^3$.

$$\begin{aligned}(a + b)^3 &= (a + b)(a + b)^2 \\ &= (a + b)(a^2 + 2ab + b^2) \\ &= a^3 + 2a^2b + ab^2 + a^2b + 2ab^2 + b^3 \\ &= a^3 + 3a^2b + 3ab^2 + b^3\end{aligned}$$

Similarly it can be shown that $(a + b)^4 = a^4 + 4a^3b + 6a^2b^2 + 4ab^3 + b^4$.

Writing the expansions of $(a + b)^n$ out in order:

$(a + b)^1 = 1a + 1b$
$(a + b)^2 = 1a^2 + 2ab + 1b^2$
$(a + b)^3 = 1a^3 + 3a^2b + 3ab^2 + 1b^3$
$(a + b)^4 = 1a^4 + 4a^3b + 6a^2b^2 + 4ab^3 + 1b^4$

If you look at the expansion of $(a + b)^4$, you should notice that the powers of a and b form a pattern.

- The first term is a^4 and then the power of a decreases by 1 whilst the power of b increases by 1 in each successive term.
- All of the terms have a total index of 4 (a^4, a^3b, a^2b^2, ab^3 and b^4).

There is a similar pattern in the other expansions.

The coefficients also form a pattern that is known as **Pascal's triangle**.

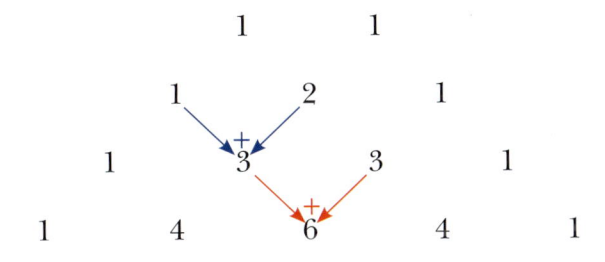

$$\begin{array}{ccccccccc} & & & & 1 & & 1 & & \\ & & & 1 & & 2 & & 1 & \\ & & 1 & & 3 & & 3 & & 1 \\ & 1 & & 4 & & 6 & & 4 & & 1 \end{array}$$

Note:
- Each row always starts and finishes with a 1.
- Each number is the sum of the two numbers in the row above it.

The next row would be:

$$1 \quad 5 \quad 10 \quad 10 \quad 5 \quad 1$$

This row can then be used to write down the expansion of $(a + b)^5$.

$(a + b)^5 = 1a^5 + 5a^4b + 10a^3b^2 + 10a^2b^3 + 5ab^4 + 1b^5$

Cambridge IGCSE and O Level Additional Mathematics

> **CLASS DISCUSSION**
>
> ```
>           1   1
>         1   2   1
>       1   3   3   1
>     1   4   6   4   1
>   1   5  10  10   5   1
> 1   6  15  20  15   6   1
> ```
>
> There are many number patterns in Pascal's triangle.
>
> For example, the numbers 1, 4, 10 and 20 have been highlighted.
>
> 1   4   10   20
>
> These numbers are called tetrahedral numbers.
>
> Which other number patterns can you find in Pascal's triangle?
>
> What do you notice if you find the total of each row in Pascal's triangle?

> **WORKED EXAMPLE 1**
>
> Use Pascal's triangle to find the expansion of:
> **a** $(2 + 5x)^3$ **b** $(2x - 3)^4$
>
> **Answers**
>
> **a** $(2 + 5x)^3$
>
> The index = 3 so use the 3rd row in Pascal's triangle.
>
> The 3rd row of Pascal's triangle is 1, 3, 3 and 1.
>
> $(2 + 5x)^3 = 1(2)^3 + 3(2)^2(5x) + 3(2)(5x)^2 + 1(5x)^3$ Use the expansion of $(a + b)^3$.
>
> $\qquad\qquad = 8 + 60x + 150x^2 + 125x^3$
>
> **b** $(2x - 3)^4$
>
> The index = 4 so use the 4th row in Pascal's triangle.
>
> The 4th row of Pascal's triangle is 1, 4, 6, 4 and 1.
>
> $(2x - 3)^4 = 1(2x)^4 + 4(2x)^3(-3) + 6(2x)^2(-3)^2$ Use the expansion of $(a + b)^4$.
>
> $\qquad\qquad\quad + 4(2x)(-3)^3 + 1(-3)^4$
>
> $\qquad\qquad = 16x^4 - 96x^3 + 216x^2 - 216x^3 + 81$

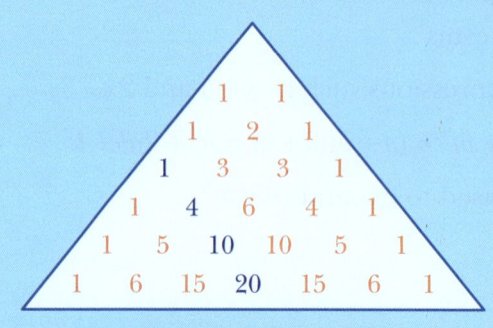

Chapter 11: Binomial expansions

> **WORKED EXAMPLE 2**
>
> **a** Expand $(2-x)^5$.
> **b** Find the coefficient of x^3 in the expansion of $(1+3x)(2-x)^5$.
>
> **Answers**
>
> **a** $(2-x)^5$
> The index = 5 so use the 5th row in Pascal's triangle.
> The 5th row of Pascal's triangle is 1, 5, 10, 10, 5 and 1.
> $(2-x)^5 = 1(2)^5 + 5(2)^4(-x) + 10(2)^3(-x)^2 + 10(2)^2(-x)^3 + 5(2)(-x)^4 + 1(-x)^5$
> $= 32 - 80x + 80x^2 - 40x^3 + 10x^4 - x^5$
>
> **b** $(1+3x)(2-x)^5 = (1+3x)(32 - 80x + 80x^2 - 40x^3 + 10x^4 - x^5)$
> The term in x^3 comes from the products:
>
> $(1+3x)(32 - 80x + 80x^2 - 40x^3 + 10x^4 - x^5)$
> $1 \times (-40x^3) = -40x^3$ and $3x \times 80x^2 = 240x^3$
> So the coefficient of x^3 is $-40 + 240 = 200$.

Exercise 11.1

1 Write down the 6th and 7th rows of Pascal's triangle.

2 Use Pascal's triangle to find the expansions of:

    a $(1+x)^3$ **b** $(1-x)^4$ **c** $(p+q)^4$ **d** $(2+x)^3$

    e $(x+y)^5$ **f** $(y+4)^3$ **g** $(a-b)^3$ **h** $(2x+y)^4$

    i $(x-2y)^3$ **j** $(3x-4)^4$ **k** $\left(x+\dfrac{2}{x}\right)^3$ **l** $\left(x^2-\dfrac{1}{2x^3}\right)^3$

3 Find the coefficient of x^3 in the expansions of:

    a $(x+4)^4$ **b** $(1+x)^5$ **c** $(3-x)^4$ **d** $(3+2x)^3$

    e $(x-2)^5$ **f** $(2x+5)^4$ **g** $(4x-3)^5$ **h** $\left(3-\dfrac{1}{2}x\right)^4$

4 $(4+x)^5 + (4-x)^5 = A + Bx^2 + Cx^4$

Find the value of A, the value of B and the value of C.

5 Expand $(1+2x)(1+3x)^4$.

6 The coefficient of x in the expansion of $(2+ax)^3$ is 96.

Find the value of the constant a.

7 a Expand $(3+x)^4$.

   b Use your answer to **part a** to express $(3+\sqrt{5})^4$ in the form $a+b\sqrt{5}$.

8 a Expand $(1+x)^5$.
  b Use your answer to **part a** to express
    i $(1+\sqrt{3})^5$ in the form $a+b\sqrt{3}$, ii $(1-\sqrt{3})^5$ in the form $c+d\sqrt{3}$.
  c Use your answers to **part b** to simplify $(1+\sqrt{3})^5 + (1-\sqrt{3})^5$.

9 a Expand $(2-x^2)^4$.
  b Find the coefficient of x^6 in the expansion of $(1+3x^2)(2-x^2)^4$.

10 Find the coefficient of x in the expansion $\left(x - \dfrac{3}{x}\right)^5$.

11 Find the term independent of x in the expansion of $\left(x^2 + \dfrac{1}{2x}\right)^3$.

CHALLENGE Q

12 a Find the first three terms, in ascending powers of y, in the expansion of $(2+y)^5$.
   b By replacing y with $3x - 4x^2$, find the coefficient of x^2 in the expansion of $(2 + 3x - 4x^2)^5$.

CHALLENGE Q

13 The coefficient of x^3 in the expansion of $(3+ax)^5$ is 12 times the coefficient of x^2 in the expansion of $\left(1 + \dfrac{ax}{2}\right)^4$. Find the value of a.

Chapter 11: Binomial expansions

CLASS DISCUSSION

The stepping stone game

The rules are that you can move East → or South ↓ from any stone.

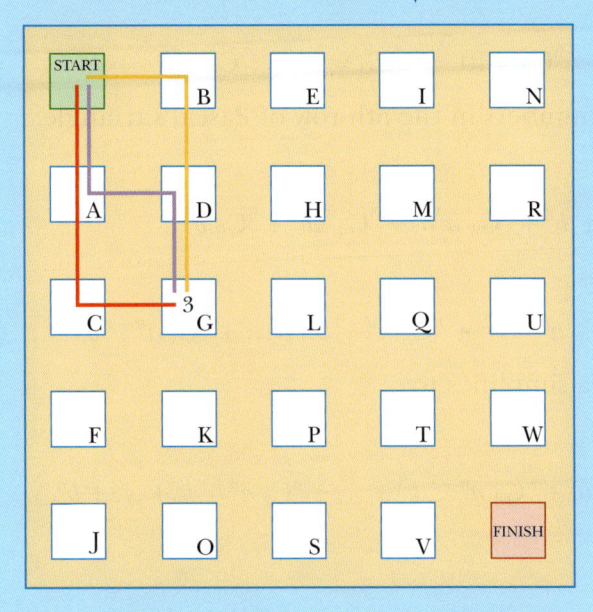

The diagram shows there are 3 routes from the START stone to stone G.

1. Find the number of routes from the START stone to each of the following stones:
   - **a** i A   ii B
   - **b** i C   ii D   iii E
   - **c** i F   ii G   iii H   iv I

   What do you notice about your answers to **parts a, b** and **c**?

2. There are 6 routes from the START to stone L.

   How could you have calculated that there are 6 routes without drawing or visualising them?

3. What do you have to do to find the number of routes to any stone?

4. How many routes are there from the START stone to the FINISH stone?

In the class discussion you should have found that the number of routes from the START stone to stone Q is 10.

To move from START to Q you must move East (E) 3 and South (S) 2, in any order.

Hence the number of routes is the same as the number of different combinations of 3 E's and 2 S's.

The combinations are:

| EEESS | EESES | EESSE | ESESE | ESEES |
| ESSEE | SSEEE | SESEE | SEESE | SEEES |

So the number of routes is 10.

This is the same as $^5C_3$ (or $^5C_2$).

Cambridge IGCSE and O Level Additional Mathematics

11.2 The binomial theorem

Pascal's triangle can be used to expand $(a + b)^n$ for any positive integer n, but if n is large it can take a long time. Combinations can be used to help expand binomial expressions more quickly.

Using a calculator:

$^5C_0 = 1$ $\quad ^5C_1 = 5$ $\quad ^5C_2 = 10$ $\quad ^5C_3 = 10$ $\quad ^5C_4 = 5$ $\quad ^5C_5 = 1$

These numbers are the same as the numbers in the 5th row of Pascal's triangle.

So the expansion of $(a + b)^5$ is:

$$(a + b)^5 = {}^5C_0\, a^5 + {}^5C_1\, a^4 b + {}^5C_2\, a^3 b^2 + {}^5C_3\, a^2 b^3 + {}^5C_4\, ab^4 + {}^5C_5\, b^5$$

This can be written more generally as:

$$(a + b)^n = {}^nC_0\, a^n + {}^nC_1\, a^{n-1} b + {}^nC_2\, a^{n-2} b^2 + {}^nC_3\, a^{n-3} b^3 + \ldots + {}^nC_r\, a^{n-r} b^r + \ldots + {}^nC_n\, b^n$$

But $^nC_0 = 1$ and $^nC_n = 1$, so the formula simplifies to:

$$(a + b)^n = a^n + {}^nC_1\, a^{n-1} b + {}^nC_2\, a^{n-2} b^2 + {}^nC_3\, a^{n-3} b^3 + \ldots + {}^nC_r\, a^{n-r} b^r + \ldots + b^n$$

or

$$(a + b)^n = a^n + \binom{n}{1} a^{n-1} b + \binom{n}{2} a^{n-2} b^2 + \binom{n}{3} a^{n-3} b^3 + \ldots + \binom{n}{r} a^{n-r} b^r + \ldots + b^n$$

The formulae above are known as the **binomial theorem**.

WORKED EXAMPLE 3

Use the binomial theorem to expand $(3 + 4x)^5$.

Answers

$(3 + 4x)^5 = 3^5 + {}^5C_1\, 3^4(4x) + {}^5C_2\, 3^3(4x)^2 + {}^5C_3\, 3^2(4x)^3 + {}^5C_4\, 3(4x)^4 + (4x)^5$

$\qquad\quad = 243 + 1620x + 4320x^2 + 5760x^3 + 3840x^4 + 1024x^5$

WORKED EXAMPLE 4

Find the coefficient of x^{20} in the expansion of $(2 - x)^{25}$.

Answers

$(2 - x)^{25} = 2^{25} + {}^{25}C_1\, 2^{24}(-x) + {}^{25}C_2\, 2^{23}(-x)^2 + \ldots + {}^{25}C_{20}\, 2^5 (-x)^{20} + \ldots + (-x)^{25}$

The term containing x^{20} is $^{25}C_{20} \times 2^5 \times (-x)^{20}$.

$\qquad = 53\,130 \times 32 \times x^{20}$

$\qquad = 1\,700\,160 x^{20}$

So the coefficient of x^{20} is $1\,700\,160$.

Using the binomial theorem,

$(1 + x)^7 = 1^7 + {}^7C_1\, 1^6\, x + {}^7C_2\, 1^5\, x^2 + {}^7C_3\, 1^4\, x^3 + {}^7C_4\, 1^3 x^4 + \ldots$

$= 1 + {}^7C_1\, x + {}^7C_2\, x^2 + {}^7C_3\, x^3 + {}^7C_4\, x^4 + \ldots$

But ${}^7C_1, {}^7C_2, {}^7C_3$ and ${}^7C_4$ can also be written as:

$${}^7C_1 = \frac{7!}{1!6!} = 7 \qquad {}^7C_2 = \frac{7!}{2!5!} = \frac{7 \times 6}{2!} \qquad {}^7C_3 = \frac{7!}{3!4!} = \frac{7 \times 6 \times 5}{3!}$$

$${}^7C_4 = \frac{7!}{4!3!} = \frac{7 \times 6 \times 5 \times 4}{4!}$$

So, $(1 + x)^7 = 1 + 7x + \dfrac{7 \times 6}{2!} x^2 + \dfrac{7 \times 6 \times 5}{3!} x^3 + \dfrac{7 \times 6 \times 5 \times 4}{4!} x^4 + \ldots$

This leads to an alternative formula for binomial expansions:

$$(1 + x)^n = 1 + nx + \frac{n(n-1)}{2!} x^2 + \frac{n(n-1)(n-2)}{3!} x^3 + \frac{n(n-1)(n-2)(n-3)}{4!} x^4 + \ldots$$

The following example illustrates how this alternative formula can be applied.

WORKED EXAMPLE 5

Find the first four terms of the binomial expansion to
a $(1 + 3y)^7$ **b** $(2 - y)^6$

Answers

a $(1 + 3y)^7 = 1 + 7(3y) + \dfrac{7 \times 6}{2!}(3y)^2 + \dfrac{7 \times 6 \times 5}{3!}(3y)^3 + \ldots$ Replace x by $3y$ and n by 7 in the formula.

$= 1 + 21y + 189y^2 + 945y^3 + \ldots$

b $(2 - y)^6 = \left[2\left(1 - \dfrac{y}{2}\right)\right]^6$ The formula is for $(1 + x)^n$ so take out a factor of 2.

$= 2^6 \left(1 - \dfrac{y}{2}\right)^6$

$= 2^6 \left[1 + 6\left(-\dfrac{y}{2}\right) + \dfrac{6 \times 5}{2!}\left(-\dfrac{y}{2}\right)^2 + \dfrac{6 \times 5 \times 4}{3!}\left(-\dfrac{y}{2}\right)^3 + \ldots\right]$ Replace x by $\left(-\dfrac{y}{2}\right)$ and n by 6 in the formula.

$= 2^6 \left[1 - 3y + \dfrac{15}{4} y^2 - \dfrac{5}{2} y^3 + \ldots\right]$ Multiply terms in brackets by 2^6.

$= 64 - 192y + 240y^2 - 160y^3 + \ldots$

Cambridge IGCSE and O Level Additional Mathematics

Exercise 11.2

1 Write the following rows of Pascal's triangle using combination notation.

   a row 3   **b** row 4   **c** row 5

2 Use the binomial theorem to find the expansions of:

   a $(1+x)^4$ **b** $(1-x)^5$ **c** $(1+2x)^4$ **d** $(3+x)^3$

   e $(x+y)^4$ **f** $(2-x)^5$ **g** $(a-2b)^4$ **h** $(2x+3y)^4$

   i $\left(\dfrac{1}{2}x-3\right)^4$ **j** $\left(1-\dfrac{x}{10}\right)^5$ **k** $\left(x-\dfrac{3}{x}\right)^5$ **l** $\left(x^2+\dfrac{1}{2x^2}\right)^6$.

3 Find the term in x^3 for each of the following expansions:

   a $(2+x)^5$ **b** $(5+x)^8$ **c** $(1+2x)^6$ **d** $(3+2x)^5$

   e $(1-x)^6$ **f** $(2-x)^9$ **g** $(10-3x)^7$ **h** $(4-5x)^{15}$.

4 Use the binomial theorem to find the first three terms in each of these expansions:

   a $(1+x)^{10}$ **b** $(1+2x)^8$ **c** $(1-3x)^7$ **d** $(3+2x)^6$

   e $(3-x)^9$ **f** $\left(2+\dfrac{1}{2}x\right)^8$ **g** $(5-x^2)^9$ **h** $(4x-5y)^{10}$.

5 **a** Write down, in ascending powers of x, the first 4 terms in the expansion of $(1+2x)^6$.

   b Find the coefficient of x^3 in the expansions of $\left(1-\dfrac{x}{3}\right)(1+2x)^6$.

6 **a** Write down, in ascending powers of x, the first 4 terms in the expansion of $\left(1+\dfrac{x}{2}\right)^{13}$.

   b Find the coefficient of x^3 in the expansions of $(1+3x)\left(1+\dfrac{x}{2}\right)^{13}$.

7 **a** Write down, in ascending powers of x, the first 4 terms in the expansion of $(1-3x)^{10}$.

   b Find the coefficient of x^3 in the expansions of $(1-4x)(1-3x)^{10}$.

8 **a** Find, in ascending powers of x, the first 3 terms of the expansion of $(1+2x)^7$.

   b Hence find the coefficient of x^2 in the expansion of $(1+2x)^7(1-3x+5x^2)$.

9 **a** Find, in ascending powers of x, the first 4 terms of the expansion of $(1+x)^7$.

   b Hence find the coefficient of y^3 in the expansion of $(1+y-y^2)^7$.

10 Find the coefficient of x in the binomial expansion of $\left(x-\dfrac{3}{x}\right)^7$.

11 Find the term independent of x in the binomial expansion of $\left(x+\dfrac{1}{2x^2}\right)^9$.

CHALLENGE Q

12 When $(1+ax)^n$ is expanded the coefficients of x^2 and x^3 are equal.

   Find a in terms of n.

Summary

If n is a positive integer then $(a+b)^n$ can be expanded using the formula

$$(a+b)^n = a^n + {}^nC_1 a^{n-1}b + {}^nC_2 a^{n-2}b^2 + {}^nC_3 a^{n-3}b^3 + \ldots + {}^nC_r a^{n-r}b^r + \ldots + b^n$$

or

$$(a+b)^n = a^n + \binom{n}{1} a^{n-1}b + \binom{n}{2} a^{n-2}b^2 + \binom{n}{3} a^{n-3}b^3 + \ldots + \binom{n}{r} a^{n-r}b^r + \ldots + b^n$$

and where ${}^nC_r = \binom{n}{r} = \dfrac{n!}{(n-r)!\,r!}$.

In particular,

$$(1+x)^n = 1 + nx + \frac{n(n-1)}{2!}x^2 + \frac{n(n-1)(n-2)}{3!}x^3 + \frac{n(n-1)(n-2)(n-3)}{4!}x^4 + \ldots + x^n.$$

Examination questions

Worked past paper example

a Find the first 4 terms in the expansion of $(2+x^2)^6$ in ascending powers of x. [3]

b Find the term independent of x in the expansion of $(2+x^2)^6\left(1 - \dfrac{3}{x^2}\right)^2$. [3]

Cambridge IGCSE Additional Mathematics 0606 Paper 11 Q3i,ii Jun 2015

Answer

a Expanding $(2+x^2)^6$ using the binomial theorem gives

$$2^6 + {}^6C_1\, 2^5 x^2 + {}^6C_2\, 2^4 (x^2)^2 + {}^6C_3\, 2^3 (x^2)^3 = 64 + 192x^2 + 240x^4 + 160x^6 \ldots$$

b $(2+x^2)^6\left(1 - \dfrac{2}{x^2}\right)^2 = (64 + 192x^2 + 240x^4 + 160x^6 \ldots)\left(1 - \dfrac{6}{x^2} + \dfrac{9}{x^4}\right)$

Term independent of x = $(64 \times 1) + \left(192x^2 \times -\dfrac{6}{x^2}\right) + \left(240x^4 \times \dfrac{9}{x^4}\right)$

$= 64 - 1152 + 2160$
$= 1072$

Exercise 11.3
Exam Exercise

1 a Find the first four terms in the expansion of $(2 + x)^6$ in ascending powers of x. [3]

b Hence find the coefficient of x^3 in the expansion of $(1 + 3x)(1 - x)(2 + x)^6$. [4]

Cambridge IGCSE Additional Mathematics 0606 Paper 21 Q7i,ii Jun 2013

2 a Find the first 3 terms, in descending powers of x, in the expansion of $\left(x + \dfrac{2}{x^2}\right)^6$. [3]

b Hence find the term independent of x in the expansion of $\left(2 - \dfrac{4}{x^3}\right)\left(x + \dfrac{2}{x^2}\right)^6$. [2]

Cambridge IGCSE Additional Mathematics 0606 Paper 11 Q6i,ii Nov 2012

3 The coefficient of x^2 in the expansion of $\left(1 + \dfrac{x}{5}\right)^n$, where n is a positive integer is $\dfrac{3}{5}$.

a Find the value of n. [4]

b Using this value of n, find the term independent of x in the expansion of
$\left(1 + \dfrac{x}{5}\right)^n \left(2 - \dfrac{3}{x}\right)^2$. [4]

Cambridge IGCSE Additional Mathematics 0606 Paper 11 Q7i,ii Nov 2011

4 a Find the coefficient of x^3 in the expansion of $\left(1 - \dfrac{x}{2}\right)^{12}$. [2]

b Find the coefficient of x^3 in the expansion of $(1 + 4x)\left(1 - \dfrac{x}{2}\right)^{12}$. [3]

Cambridge IGCSE Additional Mathematics 0606 Paper 21 Q2i,ii Jun 2011

5 a Find, in ascending powers of x, the first 3 terms in the expansion of $(2 - 5x)^6$, giving your answer in the form $a + bx + cx^2$, where a, b and c are integers. [3]

b Find the coefficient of x in the expansion of $(2 - 5x)^6 \left(1 + \dfrac{x}{2}\right)^{10}$. [3]

Cambridge IGCSE Additional Mathematics 0606 Paper 11 Q6i,ii Nov 2010

Chapter 12
Differentiation 1

This section will show you how to:

- use the notations $f'(x)$, $f''(x)$, $\dfrac{dy}{dx}$, $\dfrac{d^2y}{dx^2}$, $\left[\dfrac{d}{dx}\left(\dfrac{dy}{dx}\right)\right]$
- use the derivative of x^n (for any rational n), together with constant multiples, sums and composite functions of these
- differentiate products and quotients of functions
- apply differentiation to gradients, tangents and normals, stationary points, connected rates of change, small increments and approximations and practical maxima and minima problems
- use the first and second derivative tests to discriminate between maxima and minima.

Cambridge IGCSE and O Level Additional Mathematics

> **RECAP**
>
> You have learnt how to find the gradient of a straight line joining the two points (x_1, y_1) and (x_2, y_2) using the formula:
>
> $$\text{Gradient} = \frac{y_2 - y_1}{x_2 - x_1}$$
>
> You should also have learnt how to estimate the gradient of a curve at a particular point.
>
> For example, to find the gradient of the curve $y = x^2$ at the point $(1, 1)$:
>
> **Step 1:** Draw the graph of $y = x^2$.
>
> **Step 2:** Draw a tangent to the curve at the point $(1, 1)$.
>
> **Step 3:** Find the gradient of the tangent using $\dfrac{y_2 - y_1}{x_2 - x_1}$.
>
> This method only gives an approximate answer (because of the inaccuracy of drawing the tangent) and it is also very time consuming.
>
> In this chapter you will learn an accurate method for finding the gradient of a curve, which does not involve drawing the curve first. This accurate method is called **differentiation**.

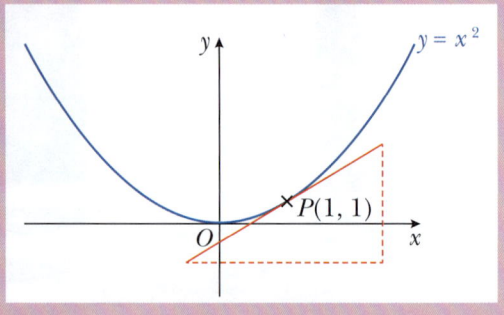

12.1 The gradient function

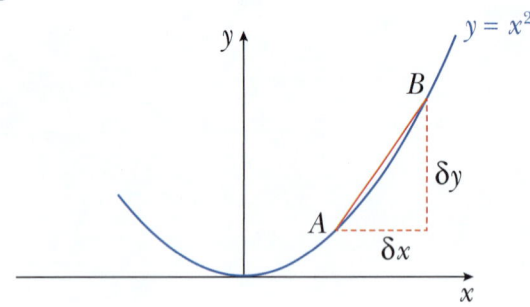

The diagram shows a point $A(x, y)$ on the curve $y = x^2$ and a point B which is close to the point A.

The coordinates of B are $(x + \delta x, y + \delta y)$ where δx is a small increase in the value of x and δy is a small increase in the value of y.

The coordinates of A and B can also be written as (x, x^2) and $(x + \delta x, (x + \delta x)^2)$.

$$\begin{aligned}
\text{gradient of chord } AB &= \frac{y_2 - y_1}{x_2 - x_1} \\
&= \frac{(x + \delta x)^2 - x^2}{(x + \delta x) - x} \\
&= \frac{x^2 + 2x\delta x + (\delta x)^2 - x^2}{\delta x} \\
&= \frac{2x\delta x + (\delta x)^2}{\delta x} \\
&= 2x + \delta x
\end{aligned}$$

As $B \to A$, $\delta x \to 0$ and the gradient of the chord $AB \to$ the gradient of the curve at A.

Hence, gradient of curve $= 2x$.

This process of finding the gradient of a curve at any point is called **differentiation** from first principles.

Notation

There are three different notations that can be used to describe the rule above.

1. If $y = x^2$, then $\dfrac{dy}{dx} = 2x$.
2. If $f(x) = x^2$, then $f'(x) = 2x$.
3. $\dfrac{d}{dx}(x^2) = 2x$.

$\dfrac{dy}{dx}$ is called the **derivative** of y with respect to x.

$f'(x)$ is called the **gradient function** of the curve $y = f(x)$.

$\dfrac{d}{dx}(x^2) = 2x$ means 'if you differentiate x^2 with respect to x, the result is $2x$'.

You do not need to be able to differentiate from first principles for the examination but you are expected to know the rules of differentiation.

Differentiation of power functions

The rule for differentiating power functions is:

$$\text{If } y = x^n, \text{ then } \dfrac{dy}{dx} = nx^{n-1}.$$

It is easier to remember this rule as:

'multiply by the power n and then subtract one from the power'

So for the earlier example where $y = x^2$,

$$\dfrac{dy}{dx} = 2 \times x^{2-1}$$
$$= 2x^1$$
$$= 2x.$$

Cambridge IGCSE and O Level Additional Mathematics

WORKED EXAMPLE 1

Differentiate with respect to x.

a x^5 **b** $\dfrac{1}{x^3}$ **c** $\sqrt{x}$ **d** 3

Answers

a $\dfrac{d}{dx}(x^5) = 5x^{5-1}$
$= 5x^4$

b $\dfrac{d}{dx}\left(\dfrac{1}{x^3}\right) = \dfrac{d}{dx}(x^{-3})$
$= -3x^{-3-1}$
$= -3x^{-4}$
$= -\dfrac{3}{x^4}$

c $\dfrac{d}{dx}(\sqrt{x}) = \dfrac{d}{dx}\left(x^{\frac{1}{2}}\right)$
$= \dfrac{1}{2}x^{\frac{1}{2}-1}$
$= \dfrac{1}{2}x^{-\frac{1}{2}}$
$= \dfrac{1}{2\sqrt{x}}$

d $\dfrac{d}{dx}(3) = \dfrac{d}{dx}(3x^0)$
$= 0x^{0-1}$
$= 0$

You need to know and be able to use the following two rules:

Scalar multiple rule:

$$\dfrac{d}{dx}[k\,\mathrm{f}(x)] = k\dfrac{d}{dx}[\mathrm{f}(x)]$$

Addition/subtraction rule:

$$\dfrac{d}{dx}[\mathrm{f}(x) \pm \mathrm{g}(x)] = \dfrac{d}{dx}[\mathrm{f}(x)] \pm \dfrac{d}{dx}[\mathrm{g}(x)]$$

WORKED EXAMPLE 2

Differentiate $2x^5 - 3x^2 + \dfrac{1}{2x^3} + \dfrac{5}{\sqrt{x}}$ with respect to x.

Answers

$\dfrac{d}{dx}\left(2x^5 - 3x^2 + \dfrac{1}{2x^3} + \dfrac{5}{\sqrt{x}}\right) = \dfrac{d}{dx}\left(2x^5 - 3x^2 + \dfrac{1}{2}x^{-3} + 5x^{-\frac{1}{2}}\right)$

$= 2\dfrac{d}{dx}(x^5) - 3\dfrac{d}{dx}(x^2) + \dfrac{1}{2}\dfrac{d}{dx}(x^{-3}) + 5\dfrac{d}{dx}\left(x^{-\frac{1}{2}}\right)$

$= 2(5x^4) - 3(2x) + \dfrac{1}{2}(-3x^{-4}) + 5\left(-\dfrac{1}{2}x^{-\frac{3}{2}}\right)$

$= 10x^4 - 6x - \dfrac{3}{2}x^{-4} - \dfrac{5}{2}x^{-\frac{3}{2}}$

WORKED EXAMPLE 3

Find the gradient of the curve $y = (3x + 2)(2x - 1)$ at the point $(-1, 3)$.

Answers

$y = (3x + 2)(2x - 1)$

$y = 6x^2 + x - 2$

$\dfrac{dy}{dx} = 12x + 1$

When $x = -1$, $\dfrac{dy}{dx} = 12(-1) + 1$

$= -11$

Gradient of curve at $(-1, 3)$ is -11.

Exercise 12.1

1 Differentiate with respect to x.

- **a** x^4
- **b** x^9
- **c** x^{-3}
- **d** x^{-6}
- **e** $\dfrac{1}{x}$
- **f** $\dfrac{1}{x^5}$
- **g** $\sqrt{x}$
- **h** $\sqrt{x^5}$
- **i** $x^{-\frac{1}{5}}$
- **j** $x^{\frac{1}{3}}$
- **k** $\sqrt[3]{x^2}$
- **l** $\dfrac{1}{\sqrt{x}}$
- **m** x
- **n** $x^{\frac{3}{2}}$
- **o** $\sqrt[3]{x^5}$
- **p** $x^2 \times x^4$
- **q** $x^2 \times x$
- **r** $\dfrac{x^4}{x^2}$
- **s** $\dfrac{x}{\sqrt{x}}$
- **t** $\dfrac{x\sqrt{x}}{x^3}$

2 Differentiate with respect to x.

  a $2x^3 - 5x + 4$
  b $8x^5 - 3x^2 - 2$
  c $7 - 2x^3 + 4x$
  d $3x^2 + \dfrac{2}{x} - \dfrac{1}{x^2}$
  e $2x - \dfrac{1}{x} - \dfrac{1}{\sqrt{x}}$
  f $\dfrac{x+5}{\sqrt{x}}$
  g $\dfrac{x^2 - 3}{x}$
  h $\dfrac{5x^2 - \sqrt{x}}{x}$
  i $\dfrac{x^2 - x - 1}{\sqrt{x}}$
  j $5x^2(x+1)$
  k $x^{-2}(2x - 5)$
  l $\dfrac{1}{x}(x^2 - 2)$
  m $(3x+1)^2$
  n $(1 - x^3)^2$
  o $(2x-1)(3x+4)$

3 Find the value of $\dfrac{dy}{dx}$ at the given point on the curve.

  a $y = 3x^2 - 4$ at the point $(1, -1)$
  b $y = 4 - 2x^2$ at the point $(-1, 2)$
  c $y = 2 + \dfrac{8}{x}$ at the point $(-2, -2)$
  d $y = 5x^3 - 2x^2 - 3$ at the point $(0, -3)$
  e $y = \dfrac{x+5}{x}$ at the point $(5, 2)$
  f $y = \dfrac{x-3}{\sqrt{x}}$ at the point $(9, 2)$

4 Find the coordinates of the point on the curve $y = 2x^2 - x - 1$ at which the gradient is 7.

5 Find the gradient of the curve $y = \dfrac{x-4}{x}$ at the point where the curve crosses the x-axis.

6 Find the gradient of the curve $y = x^3 - 2x^2 + 5x - 3$ at the point where the curve crosses the y-axis.

7 The curve $y = 2x^2 + 7x - 4$ and the line $y = 5$ meet at the points P and Q.

  Find the gradient of the curve at the point P and at the point Q.

8 The curve $y = ax^2 + bx$ has gradient 8 when $x = 2$ and has gradient -10 when $x = -1$.

  Find the value of a and the value of b.

9 The gradient of the curve $y = ax + \dfrac{b}{x}$ at the point $(-1, -3)$ is -7.
Find the value of a and the value of b.

10 Find the coordinates of the points on this curve $y = \dfrac{x^3}{3} - \dfrac{5x^2}{2} + 6x - 1$ where the gradient is 2.

11 The curve $y = \dfrac{1}{3}x^3 - 2x^2 - 8x + 5$ and the line $y = x + 5$ meet at the points A, B and C.

   a Find the coordinates of the points A, B and C.

   b Find the gradient of the curve at the points A, B and C.

12 $y = 4x^3 + 3x^2 - 6x - 1$

   a Find $\dfrac{dy}{dx}$.

   b Find the range of values of x for which $\dfrac{dy}{dx} \geqslant 0$.

13 $y = x^3 + x^2 - 16x - 16$

   a Find $\dfrac{dy}{dx}$.

   b Find the range of values of x for which $\dfrac{dy}{dx} \leqslant 0$.

12.2 The chain rule

To differentiate $y = (2x + 3)^8$, you could expand the brackets and then differentiate each term separately. This would take a long time to do. There is a more efficient method available that allows you to find the derivative without expanding:

Let $u = 2x + 3$, then $y = (2x + 3)^8$ becomes $y = u^8$.

The derivative of the composite function $y = (2x + 3)^8$ can then be found using the **chain rule**:

$$\dfrac{dy}{dx} = \dfrac{dy}{du} \times \dfrac{du}{dx}$$

Cambridge IGCSE and O Level Additional Mathematics

> **WORKED EXAMPLE 4**
>
> Find the derivative of $y = (2x + 3)^8$.
>
> **Answers**
>
> $y = (2x + 3)^8$
>
> Let $u = 2x + 3$ so $y = u^8$
>
> $\dfrac{du}{dx} = 2$ and $\dfrac{dy}{du} = 8u^7$
>
> Using $\dfrac{dy}{dx} = \dfrac{dy}{du} \times \dfrac{du}{dx}$
>
> $= 8u^7 \times 2$
>
> $= 8(2x + 3)^7 \times 2$
>
> $= 16(2x + 3)^7$

With practice you will find that you can do this mentally:

Consider the 'inside' of $(2x + 3)^8$ to be $2x + 3$.

To differentiate $(2x + 3)^8$:

Step 1: Differentiate the 'outside' first: $8(2x + 3)^7$

Step 2: Then differentiate the 'inside': 2

Step 3: Multiply these two expressions: $16(2x + 3)^7$

> **WORKED EXAMPLE 5**
>
> Find the derivative of $y = \dfrac{2}{(5x^2 - 1)^4}$.
>
> **Answers**
>
> $y = \dfrac{2}{(5x^2 - 1)^4}$
>
> let $u = 5x^2 - 1$ so $y = 2u^{-4}$
>
> $\dfrac{du}{dx} = 10x$ and $\dfrac{dy}{du} = -8u^{-5}$
>
> Using $\dfrac{dy}{dx} = \dfrac{dy}{du} \times \dfrac{du}{dx}$
>
> $= -8u^{-5} \times 10x$
>
> $= -8(5x^2 - 1)^{-5} \times 10x$
>
> $= \dfrac{-80x}{(5x^2 - 1)^5}$
>
> Alternatively, to differentiate the expression mentally:
>
> Write $\dfrac{2}{(5x^2 - 1)^4}$ as $2(5x^2 - 1)^{-4}$.
>
> **Step 1:** Differentiate the 'outside' first: $-8(5x^2 - 1)^{-5}$
>
> **Step 2:** Then differentiate the 'inside': $10x$
>
> **Step 3:** Multiply the two expressions: $-80x(5x^2 - 1)^{-5} = \dfrac{-80x}{(5x^2 - 1)^5}$

Exercise 12.2

1 Differentiate with respect to x.

   a $(x+2)^9$ **b** $(3x-1)^7$ **c** $(1-5x)^6$ **d** $\left(\dfrac{1}{2}x-7\right)^4$

   e $\dfrac{(2x+1)^6}{3}$ **f** $2(x-4)^6$ **g** $6(5-x)^5$ **h** $\dfrac{1}{2}(2x+5)^8$

   i $(x^2+2)^4$ **j** $(1-2x^2)^7$ **k** $(x^2-3x)^5$ **l** $\left(x^2+\dfrac{2}{x}\right)^4$

2 Differentiate with respect to x.

   a $\dfrac{1}{(x+4)}$ **b** $\dfrac{3}{(2x-1)}$ **c** $\dfrac{5}{(2-3x)}$ **d** $\dfrac{16}{(2x^2-5)}$

   e $\dfrac{4}{(x^2-2x)}$ **f** $\dfrac{1}{(x-1)^5}$ **g** $\dfrac{2}{(5x+1)^3}$ **h** $\dfrac{1}{2(3x-2)^4}$

3 Differentiate with respect to x.

   a $\sqrt{x+2}$ **b** $\sqrt{5x-1}$ **c** $\sqrt{2x^2-3}$ **d** $\sqrt{x^3+2x}$

   e $\sqrt[3]{3-2x}$ **f** $4\sqrt{2x-1}$ **g** $\dfrac{1}{\sqrt{3x-1}}$ **h** $\dfrac{3}{\sqrt[3]{2-5x}}$

4 Find the gradient of the curve $y = (2x-5)^4$ at the point $(3, 1)$.

5 Find the gradient of the curve $y = \dfrac{8}{(x-2)^2}$ at the point where the curve crosses the y-axis.

6 Find the gradient of the curve $y = x + \dfrac{4}{x-5}$ at the points where the curve crosses the x-axis.

7 Find the coordinates of the point on the curve $y = \sqrt{(x^2-6x+13)}$ where the gradient is 0.

8 The curve $y = \dfrac{a}{\sqrt{bx+1}}$ passes through the point $(1, 4)$ and has gradient $-\dfrac{3}{2}$ at this point.

Find the value of a and the value of b.

12.3 The product rule

Consider the function $\quad y = x^2(x^5+1)$.

$$y = x^7 + x^2$$

$$\dfrac{dy}{dx} = 7x^6 + 2x$$

The function $y = x^2(x^5+1)$ can also be considered as the product of two separate functions $y = uv$ where $u = x^2$ and $v = x^5 + 1$.

To differentiate the product of two functions you can use the **product rule**:

$$\dfrac{d}{dx}(uv) = u\dfrac{dv}{dx} + v\dfrac{du}{dx}$$

It is easier to remember this rule as

'(first function × derivative of second function) + (second function × derivative of first function)'

So for $y = x^2(x^5 + 1)$, $\dfrac{dy}{dx} = \underbrace{(x^2)}_{\text{first}} \underbrace{\dfrac{d}{dx}(x^5 + 1)}_{\substack{\text{differentiate} \\ \text{second}}} + \underbrace{(x^5 + 1)}_{\text{second}} \underbrace{\dfrac{d}{dx}(x^2)}_{\substack{\text{differentiate} \\ \text{first}}}$

$= (x^2)(5x^4) + (x^5 + 1)(2x)$

$= 5x^6 + 2x^6 + 2x$

$= 7x^6 + 2x$

WORKED EXAMPLE 6

Find the derivative of $y = (5x + 1)\sqrt{6x - 1}$.

Answers

$y = (5x + 1)\sqrt{6x - 1}$

$= (5x + 1)(6x - 1)^{\frac{1}{2}}$

$\dfrac{dy}{dx} = \underbrace{(5x + 1)}_{\text{first}} \underbrace{\dfrac{d}{dx}\left[(6x - 1)^{\frac{1}{2}}\right]}_{\substack{\text{differentiate} \\ \text{second}}} + \underbrace{\left[(6x - 1)^{\frac{1}{2}}\right]}_{\text{second}} \underbrace{\dfrac{d}{dx}(5x + 1)}_{\substack{\text{differentiate} \\ \text{first}}}$

$= (5x + 1)\underbrace{\left[\dfrac{1}{2}(6x - 1)^{-\frac{1}{2}}(6)\right]}_{\text{use the chain rule}} + \left(\sqrt{6x - 1}\right)(5)$

$= \dfrac{3(5x + 1)}{\sqrt{6x - 1}} + 5\sqrt{6x - 1}$ write as a single fraction

$= \dfrac{3(5x + 1) + 5(6x - 1)}{\sqrt{6x - 1}}$ simplify the numerator

$= \dfrac{45x - 2}{\sqrt{6x - 1}}$

Chapter 12: Differentiation 1

> **WORKED EXAMPLE 7**
>
> Find the x-coordinate of the points on the curve $y = (x+2)^2(2x-5)^3$ where the gradient is 0.
>
> **Answers**
>
> $y = (x+2)^2(2x-5)^3$
>
> $\dfrac{dy}{dx} = \underbrace{(x+2)^2}_{\text{first}} \underbrace{\dfrac{d}{dx}[(2x-5)^3]}_{\text{differentiate second}} + \underbrace{(2x-5)^3}_{\text{second}} \underbrace{\dfrac{d}{dx}[(x+2)^2]}_{\text{differentiate first}}$
>
> $= (x+2)^2 \underbrace{[3(2x-5)^2(2)]}_{\text{use the chain rule}} + (2x-5)^3 \underbrace{[2(x+2)^1(1)]}_{\text{use the chain rule}}$
>
> $= 6(x+2)^2(2x-5)^2 + 2(x+2)(2x-5)^3$ factorise
>
> $= 2(x+2)(2x-5)^2[3(x+2) + (2x-5)]$ simplify
>
> $= 2(x+2)(2x-5)^2(5x+1)$
>
> $\dfrac{dy}{dx} = 0$ when $2(x+2)(2x-5)^2(5x+1) = 0$
>
> $x + 2 = 0$ $2x - 5 = 0$ $5x + 1 = 0$
>
> $x = -2$ $x = 2.5$ $x = -0.2$

Exercise 12.3

1. Use the product rule to differentiate each of the following with respect to x:

   a $x(x+4)$ b $2x(3x+5)$ c $x(x+2)^3$

   d $x^2(x-1)^3$ e $x\sqrt{x-5}$ f $(x+2)\sqrt{x}$

   g $x^2\sqrt{x+3}$ h $\sqrt{x}(3-x^2)^3$ i $(2x+1)(x^2+5)$

   j $(x+4)(x-3)^3$ k $(x-1)^2(x+2)^2$ l $(2x+1)^3(x-3)^4$

2. Find the gradient of the curve $y = x^2\sqrt{x+2}$ at the point $(2, 8)$.

3. Find the gradient of the curve $y = (x-1)^3(x+3)^2$ at the point where $x = 2$.

4. Find the gradient of the curve $y = (x+2)(x-5)^2$ at the points where the curve meets the x-axis.

5. Find the x-coordinate of the points on the curve $y = (2x-3)^3(x+2)^4$ where the gradient is zero.

6. Find the x-coordinate of the point on the curve $y = (x+3)\sqrt{4-x}$ where the gradient is zero.

Cambridge IGCSE and O Level Additional Mathematics

12.4 The quotient rule

The function $y = \dfrac{x^3 + 1}{(2x - 3)}$ can be differentiated by writing the function in the form $y = (x^3 + 1)(2x - 3)^{-1}$ and then by applying the product rule.

Alternatively, $y = \dfrac{x^3 + 1}{(2x - 3)}$ can be considered as the division (quotient) of two separate functions:

$$y = \frac{u}{v} \text{ where } u = x^3 + 1 \text{ and } v = 2x - 3.$$

To differentiate the quotient of two functions you can use the **quotient rule**:

$$\frac{d}{dx}\left(\frac{u}{v}\right) = \frac{v\dfrac{du}{dx} - u\dfrac{dv}{dx}}{v^2}$$

It is easier to remember this rule as:

$$\frac{(\text{denominator} \times \text{derivative of numerator}) - (\text{numerator} \times \text{derivative of denominator})}{(\text{denominator})^2}$$

WORKED EXAMPLE 8

Use the quotient rule to find the derivative of $y = \dfrac{x^3 + 1}{(2x - 3)}$.

Answers

$y = \dfrac{x^3 + 1}{(2x - 3)}$

$$\frac{dy}{dx} = \frac{\overbrace{(2x - 3)}^{\text{denominator}} \times \overbrace{\dfrac{d}{dx}(x^3 + 1)}^{\substack{\text{differentiate}\\ \text{numerator}}} - \overbrace{(x^3 + 1)}^{\text{numerator}} \times \overbrace{\dfrac{d}{dx}(2x - 3)}^{\substack{\text{differentiate}\\ \text{denometer}}}}{\underbrace{(2x - 3)^2}_{\text{denominator squared}}}$$

$= \dfrac{(2x - 3)(3x^2) - (x^3 + 1)(2)}{(2x - 3)^2}$

$= \dfrac{6x^3 - 9x^2 - 2x^3 - 2}{(2x - 3)^2}$

$= \dfrac{4x^3 - 9x^2 - 2}{(2x - 3)^2}$

Chapter 12: Differentiation 1

> **CLASS DISCUSSION**
>
> An alternative method for finding $\dfrac{dy}{dx}$ in the example above is to express y in the form
> $$y = (x^3 + 1)(2x - 3)^{-1}$$
> and to then differentiate using the product rule.
>
> Try this method and then discuss with your classmates which method you prefer.

WORKED EXAMPLE 9

Find the derivative of $y = \dfrac{(x+1)^2}{\sqrt{x+2}}$.

Answers

$y = \dfrac{(x+1)^2}{\sqrt{x+2}}$

$\dfrac{dy}{dx} = \dfrac{\overbrace{\sqrt{x+2}}^{\text{denominator}} \times \overbrace{\dfrac{d}{dx}\left[(x+1)^2\right]}^{\substack{\text{differentiate}\\\text{numerator}}} - \overbrace{(x+1)^2}^{\text{numerator}} \times \overbrace{\dfrac{d}{dx}\left[\sqrt{x+2}\right]}^{\substack{\text{differentiate}\\\text{denometer}}}}{\underbrace{\left(\sqrt{x+2}\right)^2}_{\text{denominator squared}}}$

$= \dfrac{\left(\sqrt{x+2}\right)\left[2(x+1)^1(1)\right] - (x+1)^2\left[\dfrac{1}{2}(x+2)^{-\frac{1}{2}}(1)\right]}{x+2}$

$= \dfrac{2(x+1)\sqrt{x+2} - \dfrac{(x+1)^2}{2\sqrt{x+2}}}{x+2}$ multiply numerator and denominator by $2\sqrt{x+2}$

$= \dfrac{4(x+1)(x+2) - (x+1)^2}{2(x+2)\sqrt{x+2}}$ factorise the numerator

$= \dfrac{(x+1)\left[4(x+2) - (x+1)\right]}{2(x+2)^{\frac{3}{2}}}$

$= \dfrac{(x+1)(3x+7)}{2(x+2)^{\frac{3}{2}}}$

Exercise 12.4

1 Use the quotient rule to differentiate each of the following with respect to x:

a $\dfrac{1+2x}{5-x}$ b $\dfrac{3x+2}{x+4}$ c $\dfrac{x-1}{3x+4}$ d $\dfrac{5x-2}{3-8x}$

e $\dfrac{x^2}{5x-2}$ f $\dfrac{x}{x^2-1}$ g $\dfrac{5}{3x-1}$ h $\dfrac{x+4}{x^2-2}$

2 Find the gradient of the curve $y = \dfrac{x+3}{x-1}$ at the point $(2, 5)$.

3 Find the coordinates of the points on the curve $y = \dfrac{x^2}{2x-1}$ where $\dfrac{dy}{dx} = 0$.

4 Find the gradient of the curve $y = \dfrac{7x-2}{2x+3}$ at the point where the curve crosses the y-axis.

5 Differentiate with respect to x:

a $\dfrac{\sqrt{x}}{2x+1}$ b $\dfrac{x}{\sqrt{1-2x}}$ c $\dfrac{x^2}{\sqrt{x^2+2}}$ d $\dfrac{5\sqrt{x}}{3+x}$

6 Find the gradient of the curve $y = \dfrac{x-2}{\sqrt{x+5}}$ at the point $(-4, -6)$.

7 Find the coordinates of the point on the curve $y = \dfrac{2(x-5)}{\sqrt{x+1}}$ where the gradient is $\dfrac{5}{4}$.

8 The line $5x - 5y = 2$ intersects the curve $x^2y - 5x + y + 2 = 0$ at three points.

a Find the coordinates of the points of intersection.

b Find the gradient of the curve at each of the points of intersection.

12.5 Tangents and normals

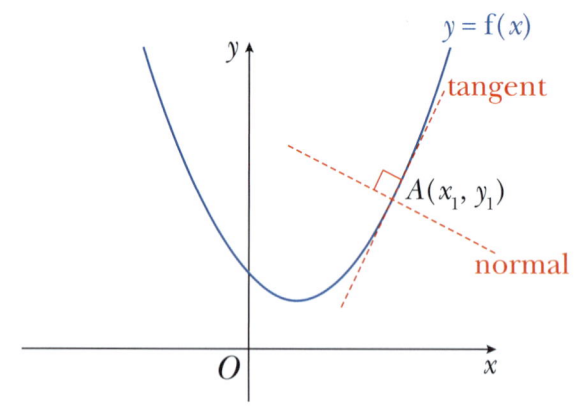

The line perpendicular to the tangent at the point A is called the **normal** at A.

If the value of $\dfrac{dy}{dx}$ at the point (x_1, y_1) is m, then the equation of the tangent is given by:

$$y - y_1 = m(x - x_1)$$

The normal at the point (x_1, y_1) is perpendicular to the tangent, so the gradient of the normal is $-\dfrac{1}{m}$ and the equation of the normal is given by:

$$y - y_1 = -\dfrac{1}{m}(x - x_1), \ m \neq 0$$

WORKED EXAMPLE 10

Find the equation of the tangent and the normal to the curve $y = 3x^2 - x + \dfrac{8}{x}$ at the point where $x = 2$.

Answers

$y = 3x^2 - x + 8x^{-1}$

$\dfrac{dy}{dx} = 6x - 1 - 8x^{-2}$

When $x = 2$, $y = 3(2)^2 - (2) + 8(2)^{-1} = 14$

and $\dfrac{dy}{dx} = 6(2) - 1 - 8(2)^{-2} = 9$

Tangent: passes through the point $(2, 14)$ and gradient $= 9$

$y - 14 = 9(x - 2)$
$y = 9x - 4$

Normal: passes through the point $(2, 14)$ and gradient $= -\dfrac{1}{9}$

$y - 14 = -\dfrac{1}{9}(x - 2)$
$9y + x = 128$

Cambridge IGCSE and O Level Additional Mathematics

> **WORKED EXAMPLE 11**
>
> The normals to the curve $y = x^3 - 5x^2 + 3x + 1$, at the points $A(4, -3)$ and $B(1, 0)$, meet at the point C.
>
> **a** Find the coordinates of C.
>
> **b** Find the area of triangle ABC.
>
> **Answers**
>
> **a** $\dfrac{dy}{dx} = 3x^2 - 10x + 3$
>
> When $x = 4$, $\dfrac{dy}{dx} = 3(4)^2 - 10(4) + 3 = 11$
>
> When $x = 1$, $\dfrac{dy}{dx} = 3(1)^2 - 10(1) + 3 = -4$
>
> Normal at A: passes through the point $(4, -3)$ and gradient $= -\dfrac{1}{11}$
>
> $y - (-3) = -\dfrac{1}{11}(x - 4)$
>
> $11y = -x - 29$ ----------(1)
>
> Normal at B: passes through the point $(1, 0)$ and gradient $= \dfrac{1}{4}$
>
> $y - 0 = \dfrac{1}{4}(x - 1)$
>
> $4y = x - 1$ ----------(2)
>
> Adding equations (1) and (2) gives $15y = -30$
>
> $y = -2$
>
> When $y = -2$, $11(-2) = -x - 29$
>
> $x = -7$
>
> Hence, C is the point $(-7, -2)$.
>
> **b**
>
> Area of triangle $ABC = \dfrac{1}{2} \left| \begin{matrix} 4 & 1 & -7 & 4 \\ -3 & 0 & -2 & -3 \end{matrix} \right|$
>
> $= \dfrac{1}{2} |0 + (-2) + 21 - (-3) - 0 - (-8)|$
>
> $= \dfrac{1}{2} |30|$
>
> $= 15$ units^2

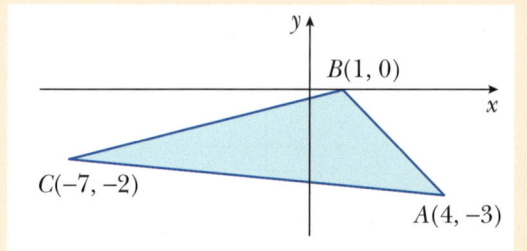

Exercise 12.5

1. Find the equation of the tangent to the curve at the given value of x:

   a $y = x^4 - 3$ at $x = 1$
   b $y = x^2 + 3x + 2$ at $x = -2$

   c $y = 2x^3 + 5x^2 - 1$ at $x = 1$
   d $y = 5 + \dfrac{2}{x}$ at $x = -2$

   e $y = (x - 3)(2x - 1)^2$ at $x = 2$
   f $y = \dfrac{x}{x + 1}$ at $x = -3$

2. Find the equation of the normal to the curve at the given value of x:

   a $y = x^2 + 5x$ at $x = -1$
   b $y = 3x^2 - 4x + 1$ at $x = 2$

   c $y = 5x^4 - 7x^2 + 2x$ at $x = -1$
   d $y = 4 - \dfrac{2}{x^2}$ at $x = -2$

   e $y = 2x(x - 3)^3$ at $x = 2$
   f $y = \dfrac{x + 2}{x - 2}$ at $x = 6$

3. Find the equation of the tangent and the normal to the curve $y = 5x - \dfrac{3}{x}$ at the point where $x = 1$.

4. The normal to the curve $y = x^3 - 2x + 1$ at the point $(2, 5)$ intersects the y-axis at the point P.

   Find the coordinates of P.

5. Find the equation of the tangent and the normal to the curve $y = \dfrac{x - 1}{\sqrt{x + 4}}$ at the point where the curve intersects the y-axis.

6. The tangents to the curve $y = x^2 - 5x + 4$, at the points $(1, 0)$ and $(3, -2)$, meet at the point Q.

   Find the coordinates of Q.

7. The tangent to the curve $y = 3x^2 - 10x - 8$ at the point P is parallel to the line $y = 2x - 5$.

   Find the equation of the tangent at P.

8. A curve has equation $y = x^3 - x + 6$.

   a Find the equation of the tangent to this curve at the point $P(-1, 6)$.

   The tangent at the point Q is parallel to the tangent at P.

   b Find the coordinates of Q.

   c Find the equation of the normal at Q.

9. A curve has equation $y = 4 + (x - 1)^4$.

   The normal at the point $P(1, 4)$ and the normal at the point $Q(2, 5)$ intersect at the point R.

   Find the coordinates of R.

10. A curve has equation $y = (2 - \sqrt{x})^4$.

    The normal at the point $P(1, 1)$ and the normal at the point $Q(9, 1)$ intersect at the point R.

    a Find the coordinates of R.

    b Find the area of triangle PQR.

11 A curve has equation $y = \sqrt{x}(x-2)^3$.

The tangent at the point $P(3, \sqrt{3})$ and the normal at the point $Q(9, 1)$ intersect at the point R.

a Show that the equation of the tangent at the point $P(3, \sqrt{3})$ is
$$y = \frac{19\sqrt{3}}{6}x - \frac{17\sqrt{3}}{2}.$$

b Find the equation of the normal at the point $Q(1, -1)$.

12 The equation of a curve is $y = \dfrac{x^2}{x+2}$.

The tangent to the curve at the point where $x = -3$ meets the y-axis at M.

The normal to the curve at the point where $x = -3$ meets the x-axis at N.

Find the area of the triangle MNO, where O is the origin.

13 The equation of a curve is $y = \dfrac{x-3}{x+2}$.

The curve intersects the x-axis at the point P.

The normal to the curve at P meets the y-axis at the point Q.

Find the area of the triangle POQ, where O is the origin.

12.6 Small increments and approximations

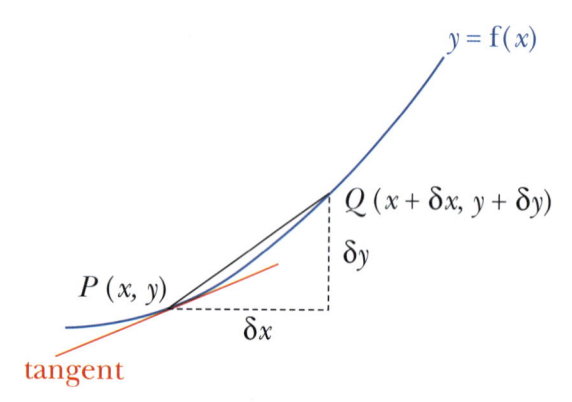

The diagram shows the tangent to the curve $y = f(x)$ at the point $P(x, y)$.

The gradient of the tangent at the point P is $\dfrac{dy}{dx}$.

The point $Q(x + \delta x, y + \delta y)$ is a point on the curve close to the point P.

The gradient of the chord PQ is $\dfrac{\delta y}{\delta x}$.

If P and Q are sufficiently close then:

$$\frac{\delta y}{\delta x} \approx \frac{dy}{dx}$$

Chapter 12: Differentiation 1

WORKED EXAMPLE 12

Variables x and y are connected by the equation $y = x^3 + x^2$.

Find the approximate increase in y as x increases from 2 to 2.05.

Answers

$y = x^3 + x^2$

$\dfrac{dy}{dx} = 3x^2 + 2x$

When $x = 2$, $\dfrac{dy}{dx} = 3(2)^2 + 2(2) = 16$

Using $\dfrac{\delta y}{\delta x} \approx \dfrac{dy}{dx}$

$\dfrac{\delta y}{0.05} \approx 16$

$\delta y \approx 16 \times 0.05$

$\delta y \approx 0.8$

WORKED EXAMPLE 13

The volume, $V\,\text{cm}^3$, of a sphere with radius r cm is $V = \dfrac{4}{3}\pi r^3$.

Find, in terms of p, the approximate change in V as r increases from 10 to $10 + p$, where p is small.

Answers

$V = \dfrac{4}{3}\pi r^3$

$\dfrac{dV}{dr} = 4\pi r^2$

When $r = 10$, $\dfrac{dV}{dr} = 4\pi(10)^2 = 400\pi$

Using $\dfrac{\delta V}{\delta r} \approx \dfrac{dV}{dr}$

$\dfrac{\delta V}{p} \approx 400\pi$

$\delta V \approx 400\pi p$

Cambridge IGCSE and O Level Additional Mathematics

Exercise 12.6

1. Variables x and y are connected by the equation $y = 2x^3 - 3x$.
   Find the approximate change in y as x increases from 2 to 2.01.

2. Variables x and y are connected by the equation $y = 5x^2 - \dfrac{8}{x^3}$.
   Find the approximate change in y as x increases from 1 to 1.02.

3. Variables x and y are connected by the equation $x^2 y = 400$.
   Find, in terms of p, the approximate change in y as x increases from 10 to $10 + p$, where p is small.

4. Variables x and y are connected by the equation $y = \left(\dfrac{1}{3}x - 2\right)^6$.
   Find, in terms of p, the approximate change in y as x increases from 9 to $9 + p$, where p is small.

5. A curve has equation $y = (x+1)(2x-3)^4$.
   Find, in terms of p, the approximate change in y as x increases from 2 to $2 + p$, where p is small.

6. A curve has equation $y = (x-2)\sqrt{2x+1}$.
   Find, in terms of p, the approximate change in y as x increases from 4 to $4 + p$, where p is small.

7. The periodic time, T seconds, for a pendulum of length L cm is
   $T = 2\pi\sqrt{\dfrac{L}{10}}$.
   Find the approximate increase in T as L increases from 40 to 41.

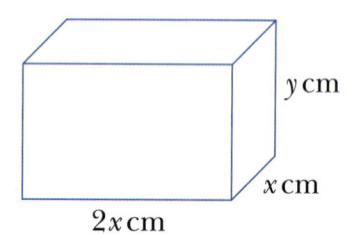

8.

   The volume of the solid cuboid is $360\,\text{cm}^3$ and the surface area is $A\,\text{cm}^2$.

   a Express y in terms of x.

   b Show that $A = 4x^2 + \dfrac{1080}{x}$.

   c Find, in terms of p, the approximate change in A as x increases from 2 to $2 + p$, where p is small. State whether the change is an increase or decrease.

Chapter 12: Differentiation 1

12.7 Rates of change

CLASS DISCUSSION

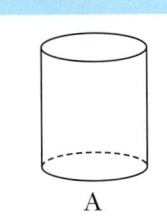

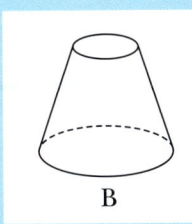

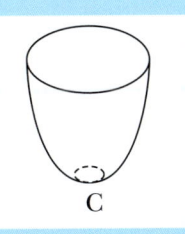

A   B   C

Consider pouring water at a constant rate of $10\,\text{cm}^3\,\text{s}^{-1}$ into each of these three large containers.

1 Discuss how the height of water in container A changes with time.
2 Discuss how the height of water in container B changes with time.
3 Discuss how the height of water in container C changes with time.

On copies of the axes below, sketch graphs to show how the height (h cm) varies with time (t seconds) for each container.

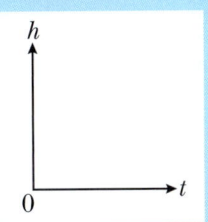

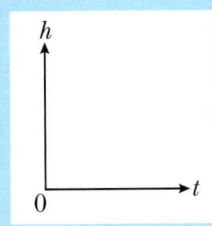

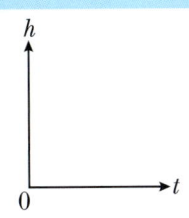

You already know that $\dfrac{dy}{dx}$ represents the rate of change of y with respect to x.
There are many situations where the rate of change of one quantity depends on the changing value of a second quantity.

In the class discussion, the **rate of change** of the height of water at a particular time, t, can be found by finding the value of $\dfrac{dh}{dt}$ at time t. (The gradient of the tangent at time t.)

WORKED EXAMPLE 14

Variables V and t are connected by the equation $V = 5t^2 - 8t + 3$.
Find the rate of change of V with respect to t when $t = 4$.

Answers

$V = 5t^2 - 8t + 3$

$\dfrac{dV}{dt} = 10t - 8$

When $t = 4$, $\dfrac{dV}{dt} = 10(4) - 8 = 32$

Connected rates of change

When two variables x and y both vary with a third variable t, the three variables can be connected using the chain rule:

$$\frac{dy}{dt} = \frac{dy}{dx} \times \frac{dx}{dt}$$

You may also need to use the rule that:

$$\frac{dx}{dy} = \frac{1}{\frac{dy}{dx}}$$

WORKED EXAMPLE 15

Variables x and y are connected by the equation $y = x^3 - 5x^2 + 15$.

Given that x increases at a rate of 0.1 units per second, find the rate of change of y when $x = 4$.

Answers

$y = x^3 - 5x^2 + 15$ and $\frac{dx}{dt} = 0.1$

$\frac{dy}{dx} = 3x^2 - 10x$

When $x = 4$, $\frac{dy}{dx} = 3(4)^2 - 10(4)$

$= 8$

Using the chain rule, $\frac{dy}{dt} = \frac{dy}{dx} \times \frac{dx}{dt}$

$= 8 \times 0.1$

$= 0.8$

Rate of change of y is 0.8 units per second.

WORKED EXAMPLE 16

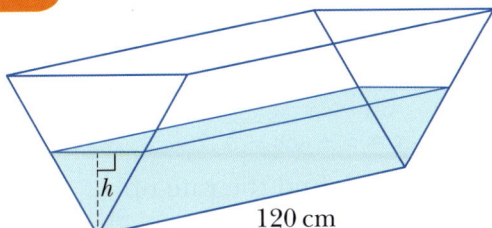

The diagram shows a water container in the shape of a triangular prism of length 120 cm.

The vertical cross-section is an equilateral triangle.

Water is poured into the container at a rate of $24 \text{ cm}^3 \text{s}^{-1}$.

a Show that the volume of water in the container, $V \text{ cm}^3$, is given by $V = 40\sqrt{3} \, h^2$, where h cm is the height of the water in the container.

b Find the rate of change of h when $h = 12$.

Answers

a Length of side of triangle $= \dfrac{h}{\sin 60°}$

$= \dfrac{2\sqrt{3}h}{3}$

Area of triangle $= \dfrac{1}{2} \times \dfrac{2\sqrt{3}h}{3} \times h$

$= \dfrac{\sqrt{3}h^2}{3}$

$V = $ area of triangle $\times 120$

$= \dfrac{\sqrt{3}h^2}{3} \times 120$

$= 40\sqrt{3} \, h^2$

b $\dfrac{dV}{dh} = 80\sqrt{3} \, h$ and $\dfrac{dV}{dt} = 24$

When $h = 12$, $\dfrac{dV}{dh} = 80\sqrt{3} \, (12)$

$= 960\sqrt{3}$

Using the chain rule, $\dfrac{dh}{dt} = \dfrac{dh}{dV} \times \dfrac{dV}{dt}$

$= \dfrac{1}{960\sqrt{3}} \times 24$

$= \dfrac{\sqrt{3}}{120}$

Rate of change of h is $\dfrac{\sqrt{3}}{120}$ cm per second.

Exercise 12.7

1. Variables x and y are connected by the equation $y = x^2 - 5x$.

   Given that x increases at a rate of 0.05 units per second, find the rate of change of y when $x = 4$.

2. Variables x and y are connected by the equation $y = x + \sqrt{x-5}$.

   Given that x increases at a rate of 0.1 units per second, find the rate of change of y when $x = 9$.

3. Variables x and y are connected by the equation $y = (x-3)(x+5)^3$.

   Given that x increases at a rate of 0.2 units per second, find the rate of change of y when $x = -4$.

4. Variables x and y are connected by the equation $y = \dfrac{5}{2x-1}$.

   Given that y increases at a rate of 0.1 units per second, find the rate of change of x when $x = -2$.

5. Variables x and y are connected by the equation $y = \dfrac{2x}{x^2+3}$.

   Given that x increases at a rate of 2 units per second, find the rate of increase of y when $x = 1$.

6. Variables x and y are connected by the equation $y = \dfrac{2x-5}{x-1}$.

   Given that x increases at a rate of 0.02 units per second, find the rate of change of y when $y = 1$.

7. Variables x and y are connected by the equation $\dfrac{1}{y} = \dfrac{1}{8} - \dfrac{2}{x}$.

   Given that x increases at a rate of 0.01 units per second, find the rate of change of y when $x = 8$.

8. A square has sides of length x cm and area A cm^2.

   The area is increasing at a constant rate of 0.2 cm^{2}s^{-1}.

   Find the rate of increase of x when $A = 16$.

9. A cube has sides of length x cm and volume V cm^3.

   The volume is increasing at a rate of 2 cm^{3}s^{-1}.

   Find the rate of increase of x when $V = 512$.

10. A sphere has radius r cm and volume V cm^3.

    The radius is increasing at a rate of $\dfrac{1}{\pi}$ cm s^{-1}.

    Find the rate of increase of the volume when $V = 972\pi$.

11. A solid metal cuboid has dimensions x cm by x cm by $5x$ cm.

    The cuboid is heated and the volume increases at a rate of 0.5 cm^{3}s^{-1}.

    Find the rate of increase of x when $x = 4$.

12. A cone has base radius r cm and a fixed height 18 cm.

    The radius of the base is increasing at a rate of 0.1 cm s^{-1}.

    Find the rate of change of the volume when $r = 10$.

13 Water is poured into the conical container at a rate of $5\,\text{cm}^3\,\text{s}^{-1}$.

After t seconds, the volume of water in the container, $V\,\text{cm}^3$, is given by $V = \dfrac{1}{12}\pi h^3$, where h cm is the height of the water in the container.

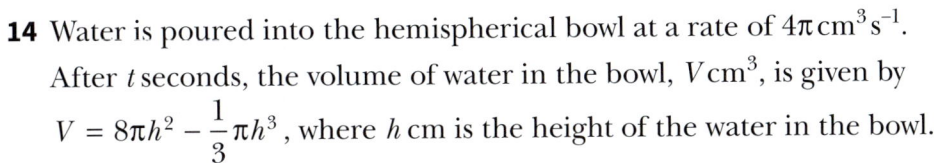

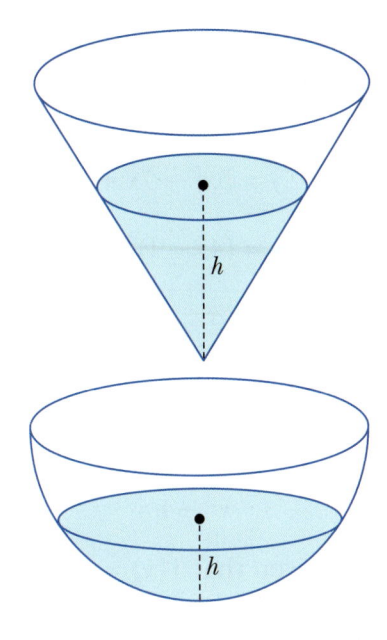

a Find the rate of change of h when $h = 5$.

b Find the rate of change of h when $h = 10$.

14 Water is poured into the hemispherical bowl at a rate of $4\pi\,\text{cm}^3\,\text{s}^{-1}$.

After t seconds, the volume of water in the bowl, $V\,\text{cm}^3$, is given by $V = 8\pi h^2 - \dfrac{1}{3}\pi h^3$, where h cm is the height of the water in the bowl.

a Find the rate of change of h when $h = 2$.

b Find the rate of change of h when $h = 4$.

12.8 Second derivatives

If you differentiate y with respect to x you obtain $\dfrac{dy}{dx}$.

$\dfrac{dy}{dx}$ is called the **first derivative** of y with respect to x.

If you differentiate $\dfrac{dy}{dx}$ with respect to x you obtain $\dfrac{d}{dx}\left(\dfrac{dy}{dx}\right)$ which can also be written as $\dfrac{d^2y}{dx^2}$.

$\dfrac{d^2y}{dx^2}$ is called the **second derivative** of y with respect to x.

So for $y = x^3 - 7x^2 + 2x + 1$ or $f(x) = x^3 - 7x^2 + 2x + 1$

$\dfrac{dy}{dx} = 3x^2 - 14x + 2$ or $f'(x) = 3x^2 - 14x + 2$

$\dfrac{d^2y}{dx^2} = 6x - 14$ or $f''(x) = 6x - 14$

WORKED EXAMPLE 17

Given that $y = 3x^2 - \dfrac{5}{x}$, find $\dfrac{d^2y}{dx^2}$.

Answers

$y = 3x^2 - 5x^{-1}$

$\dfrac{dy}{dx} = 6x + 5x^{-2}$

$\dfrac{d^2y}{dx^2} = 6 - 10x^{-3}$

$\phantom{\dfrac{d^2y}{dx^2}} = 6 - \dfrac{10}{x^3}$

Exercise 12.8

1 Find $\dfrac{d^2y}{dx^2}$ for each of the following functions.

   a $y = 5x^2 - 7x + 3$ **b** $y = 2x^3 + 3x^2 - 1$ **c** $y = 4 - \dfrac{3}{x^2}$

   d $y = (4x+1)^5$ **e** $y = \sqrt{2x+1}$ **f** $y = \dfrac{4}{\sqrt{x+3}}$

2 Find $\dfrac{d^2y}{dx^2}$ for each of the following functions.

   a $y = x(x-4)^3$ **b** $y = \dfrac{4x-1}{x^2}$ **c** $y = \dfrac{x+1}{x-3}$

   d $y = \dfrac{x+2}{x^2-1}$ **e** $y = \dfrac{x^2}{x-5}$ **f** $y = \dfrac{2x+5}{3x-1}$

3 Given that $f(x) = x^3 - 7x^2 + 2x + 1$, find

   a $f(1)$ **b** $f'(1)$ **c** $f''(1)$.

4 A curve has equation $y = 4x^3 + 3x^2 - 6x - 1$.

   a Show that $\dfrac{dy}{dx} = 0$ when $x = -1$ and when $x = 0.5$.

   b Find the value of $\dfrac{d^2y}{dx^2}$ when $x = -1$ and when $x = 0.5$.

5 A curve has equation $y = 2x^3 - 15x^2 + 24x + 6$.

Copy and complete the table to show whether $\dfrac{dy}{dx}$ and $\dfrac{d^2y}{dx^2}$ are positive (+), negative (−) or zero (0) for the given values of x.

x	0	1	2	3	4	5
$\dfrac{dy}{dx}$						
$\dfrac{d^2y}{dx^2}$						

12.9 Stationary points

Consider the graph of the function $y = f(x)$ shown below.

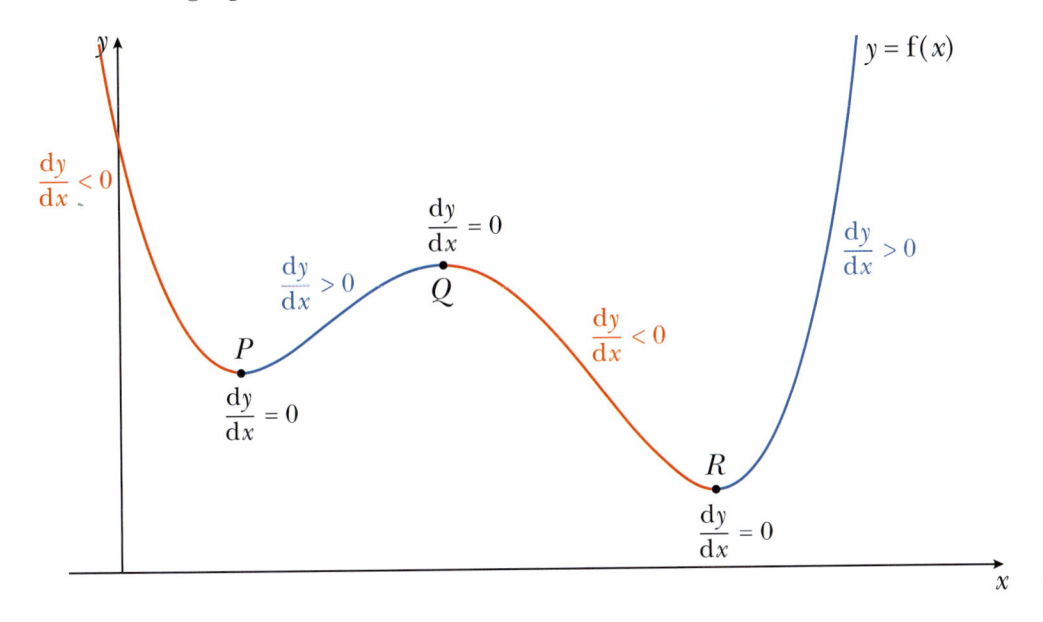

The red sections of the curve show where the gradient is negative (where f(x) is a decreasing function) and the blue sections show where the gradient is positive (where f(x) is an increasing function). The gradient of the curve is zero at the points P, Q and R.

A point where the gradient is zero is called a **stationary point** or a **turning point**.

Maximum points

The stationary point Q is called a **maximum point** because the value of y at this point is greater than the value of y at other points close to Q.

At a maximum point:
- $\dfrac{dy}{dx} = 0$
- the gradient is positive to the left of the maximum and negative to the right

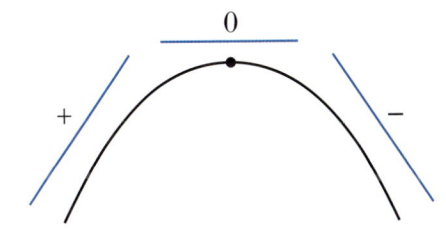

Minimum points

The stationary points P and R are called **minimum points**.

At a minimum point:
- $\dfrac{dy}{dx} = 0$
- the gradient is negative to the left of the minimum and positive to the right

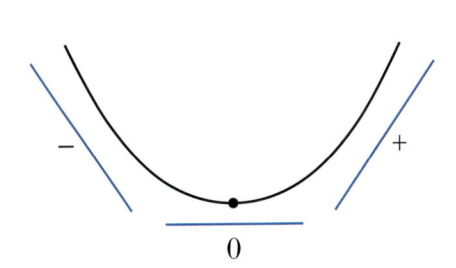

Stationary points of inflexion

There is a third type of stationary point (turning point) called a **point of inflexion**.

At a stationary point of inflexion:
- $\dfrac{dy}{dx} = 0$
- the gradient changes $\begin{cases} \text{from positive to zero and then to positive again} \\ \text{or} \\ \text{from negative to zero and then to negative again} \end{cases}$

You do not need to know about points of inflexion for the examination. They have been included here for completeness.

WORKED EXAMPLE 18

Find the coordinates of the stationary points on the curve $y = x^3 - 3x + 1$ and determine the nature of these points. Sketch the graph of $y = x^3 - 3x + 1$.

Answers

$y = x^3 - 3x + 1$

$\dfrac{dy}{dx} = 3x^2 - 3$

For stationary points, $\dfrac{dy}{dx} = 0$.

$3x^2 - 3 = 0$

$x^2 - 1 = 0$

$(x+1)(x-1) = 0$

$x = -1$ or $x = 1$

When $x = -1$, $y = (-1)^3 - 3(-1) + 1 = 3$

When $x = 1$, $y = (1)^3 - 3(1) + 1 = -1$

The stationary points are $(-1, 3)$ and $(1, -1)$.

Now consider the gradient on either side of the points $(-1, 3)$ and $(1, -1)$:

x	-1.1	-1	-0.9
$\dfrac{dy}{dx}$	$3(-1.1)^2 - 3 =$ positive	0	$3(-0.9)^2 - 3 =$ negative
direction of tangent	/	—	\
shape of curve	⌒		

x	0.9	1	1.1
$\dfrac{dy}{dx}$	$3(0.9)^2 - 3 =$ negative	0	$3(1.1)^2 - 3 =$ positive
direction of tangent	\	—	/
shape of curve	⌣		

So (−1, 3) is a maximum point and (1, −1) is a minimum point.

The sketch graph of $y = x^3 − 3x + 1$ is:

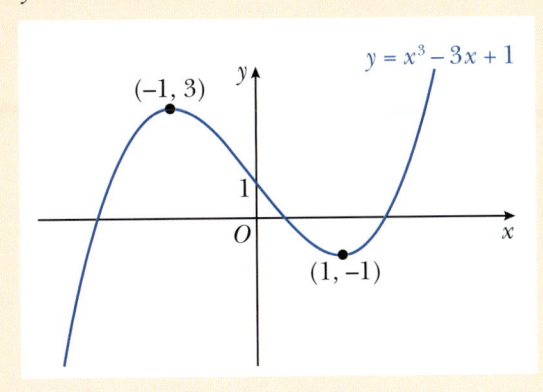

Second derivatives and stationary points

Consider moving from left to right along a curve, passing through a maximum point:

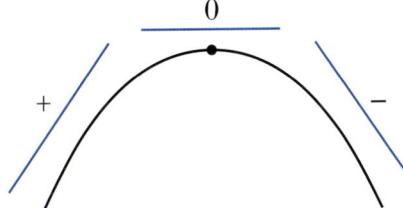

The gradient, $\dfrac{dy}{dx}$, starts as a positive value, decreases to zero at the maximum point and then decreases to a negative value.

Since $\dfrac{dy}{dx}$ decreases as x increases, then the rate of change of $\dfrac{dy}{dx}$ is negative.

[The rate of change of $\dfrac{dy}{dx}$ is written as $\dfrac{d}{dx}\left(\dfrac{dy}{dx}\right) = \dfrac{d^2y}{dx^2}$.]

This leads to the rule:

> If $\dfrac{dy}{dx} = 0$ and $\dfrac{d^2y}{dx^2} < 0$, then the point is a maximum point.

Now, consider moving from left to right along a curve, passing through a minimum point:

The gradient, $\dfrac{dy}{dx}$, starts as a negative value, increases to zero at the minimum point and then increases to a positive value.

Since $\dfrac{dy}{dx}$ increases as x increases, then the rate of change of $\dfrac{dy}{dx}$ is positive.

This leads to the rule:

> If $\dfrac{dy}{dx} = 0$ and $\dfrac{d^2y}{dx^2} > 0$, then the point is a minimum point.

WORKED EXAMPLE 19

Find the coordinates of the stationary points on the curve $y = 2x^3 - 15x^2 + 24x + 6$ and determine the nature of these points. Sketch the graph of $y = 2x^3 - 15x^2 + 24x + 6$.

Answers

$y = 2x^3 - 15x^2 + 24x + 6$

$\dfrac{dy}{dx} = 6x^2 - 30x + 24$

For stationary points, $\dfrac{dy}{dx} = 0$.

$6x^2 - 30x + 24 = 0$

$x^2 - 5x + 4 = 0$

$(x - 1)(x - 4) = 0$

$x = 1$ or $x = 4$

When $x = 1$, $y = 2(1)^3 - 15(1)^2 + 24(1) + 6 = 17$

When $x = 4$, $y = 2(4)^3 - 15(4)^2 + 24(4) + 6 = -10$

The stationary points are $(1, 17)$ and $(4, -10)$.

$\dfrac{d^2y}{dx^2} = 12x - 30$

When $x = 1$, $\dfrac{d^2y}{dx^2} = -18$ which is < 0

When $x = 4$, $\dfrac{d^2y}{dx^2} = 18$ which is > 0

So $(1, 17)$ is a maximum point and $(4, -10)$ is a minimum point.

The sketch graph of $y = 2x^3 - 15x^2 + 24x + 6$ is:

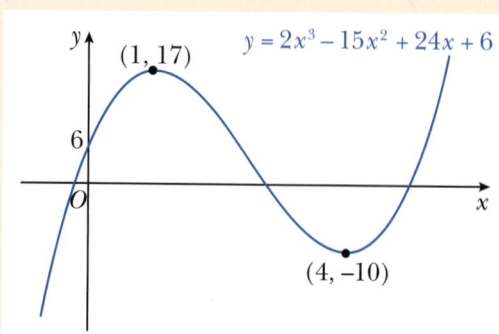

Exercise 12.9

1 Find the coordinates of the stationary points on each of the following curves and determine the nature of each of the stationary points.

   a $y = x^2 - 12x + 8$
   b $y = (5 + x)(1 - x)$
   c $y = x^3 - 12x + 2$
   d $y = x^3 + x^2 - 16x - 16$
   e $y = x(3 - 4x - x^2)$
   f $y = (x - 1)(x^2 - 6x + 2)$

2 Find the coordinates of the stationary points on each of the following curves and determine the nature of each of the stationary points.

   a $y = \sqrt{x} + \dfrac{4}{\sqrt{x}}$
   b $y = x^2 - \dfrac{2}{x}$
   c $y = \dfrac{4}{x} + \sqrt{x}$
   d $y = \dfrac{2x}{x^2 + 9}$
   e $y = \dfrac{x^2}{x + 1}$
   f $y = \dfrac{x^2 - 5x + 3}{x + 1}$

3 The equation of a curve is $y = \dfrac{2x + 5}{x + 1}$.
   Find $\dfrac{dy}{dx}$ and hence explain why the curve has no turning points.

4 The curve $y = 2x^3 + ax^2 - 12x + 7$ has a maximum point at $x = -2$.
   Find the value of a.

5 The curve $y = x^3 + ax + b$ has a stationary point at $(1, 3)$.
   a Find the value of a and the value of b.
   b Determine the nature of the stationary point $(1, 3)$.
   c Find the coordinates of the other stationary point on the curve and determine the nature of this stationary point.

6 The curve $y = x^2 + \dfrac{a}{x} + b$ has a stationary point at $(1, -1)$.
   a Find the value of a and the value of b.
   b Determine the nature of the stationary point $(1, -1)$.

7 The curve $y = ax + \dfrac{b}{x^2}$ has a stationary point at $(-1, -12)$.
   a Find the value of a and the value of b.
   b Determine the nature of the stationary point $(-1, -12)$.

Cambridge IGCSE and O Level Additional Mathematics

12.10 Practical maximum and minimum problems

There are many problems for which you need to find the maximum or minimum value of a function, such as the maximum area that can be enclosed within a shape or the minimum amount of material that can be used to make a container.

WORKED EXAMPLE 20

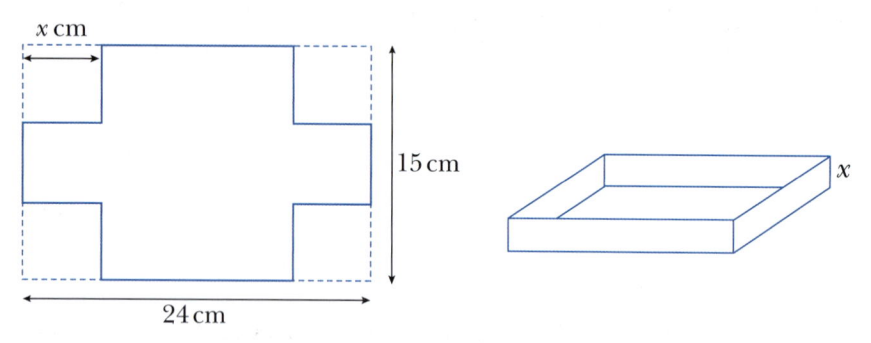

The diagram shows a 24 cm by 15 cm sheet of metal with a square of side x cm removed from each corner. The metal is then folded to make an open rectangular box of depth x cm and volume V cm^3.

a Show that $V = 4x^3 - 78x^2 + 360x$.

b Find the stationary value of V and the value of x for which this occurs.

c Determine the nature of this stationary value.

Answers

a V = length × breadth × height
$= (24 - 2x)(15 - 2x)x$
$= (360 - 78x + 4x^2)x$
$= 4x^3 - 78x^2 + 360x$

b $\dfrac{dV}{dx} = 12x^2 - 156x + 360$

Stationary values occur when $\dfrac{dy}{dx} = 0$.

$12x^2 - 156x + 360 = 0$
$x^2 - 13x + 30 = 0$
$(x - 10)(x - 3) = 0$
$x = 10$ or $x = 3$

The dimensions of the box must be positive so $x = 3$.
When $x = 3$, $V = 4(3)^3 - 78(3)^2 + 360(3) = 486$.
The stationary value of V is 486 and occurs when $x = 3$.

c $\dfrac{d^2V}{dx^2} = 24x - 156$

When $x = 3$, $\dfrac{d^2V}{dx^2} = 24(3) - 156 = -84$ which is < 0

The stationary value is a maximum value.

WORKED EXAMPLE 21

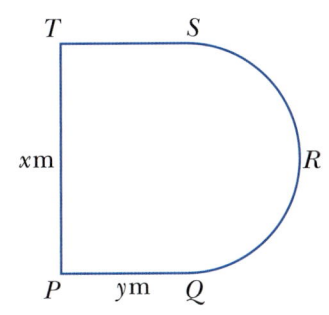

A piece of wire, of length 2 m, is bent to form the shape $PQRST$.
$PQST$ is a rectangle and QRS is a semi-circle with diameter SQ.
$PT = x$ m and $PQ = ST = y$ m.
The total area enclosed by the shape is A m^2.

a Express y in terms of x.

b Show that $A = x - \dfrac{1}{2}x^2 - \dfrac{1}{8}\pi x^2$.

c Find $\dfrac{dA}{dx}$ and $\dfrac{d^2A}{dx^2}$.

d Find the value for x for which there is a stationary value of A.

e Determine the magnitude and nature of this stationary value.

Answers

a Perimeter = PQ + arc QRS + ST + TP

$$2 = y + \frac{1}{2} \times 2\pi\left(\frac{x}{2}\right) + y + x$$

$$2 = 2y + \frac{1}{2}\pi x + x$$

$$2y = 2 - x - \frac{1}{2}\pi x$$

$$y = 1 - \frac{1}{2}x - \frac{1}{4}\pi x$$

b A = area of rectangle + area of semi-circle

$$= xy + \frac{1}{2}\pi\left(\frac{x}{2}\right)^2$$

$$= x\left(1 - \frac{1}{2}x - \frac{1}{4}\pi x\right) + \frac{1}{8}\pi x^2$$

$$= x - \frac{1}{2}x^2 - \frac{1}{4}\pi x^2 + \frac{1}{8}\pi x^2$$

$$= x - \frac{1}{2}x^2 - \frac{1}{8}\pi x^2$$

c $\dfrac{dA}{dx} = 1 - x - \dfrac{1}{4}\pi x$

$\dfrac{d^2A}{dx^2} = -1 - \dfrac{1}{4}\pi$

d Stationary values occur when $\dfrac{dA}{dx} = 0$.

$$1 - x - \dfrac{1}{4}\pi x = 0$$
$$4 - 4x - \pi x = 0$$
$$x(4 + \pi) = 4$$

Stationary value occurs when $x = \dfrac{4}{(4 + \pi)}$.

e when $x = \dfrac{4}{(4 + \pi)}$, $A = \dfrac{4}{(4 + \pi)} - \dfrac{1}{2}\left[\dfrac{4}{(4 + \pi)}\right]^2 - \dfrac{1}{8}\pi\left[\dfrac{4}{(4 + \pi)}\right]^2$

$$= \dfrac{4(4 + \pi) - 8 - 2\pi}{(4 + \pi)^2}$$

$$= \dfrac{8 + 2\pi}{(4 + \pi)^2}$$

$$= \dfrac{2(4 + \pi)}{(4 + \pi)^2}$$

$$= \dfrac{2}{(4 + \pi)}$$

when $x = \dfrac{4}{(4 + \pi)}$, $\dfrac{d^2A}{dx^2} = -1 - \dfrac{1}{4}\pi$ which is < 0

The stationary value of A is $\dfrac{2}{(4 + \pi)}$ m² and it is a maximum value.

Exercise 12.10

1 The sum of two numbers x and y is 8.
  a Express y in terms of x.
  b i Given that $P = xy$, write down an expression for P in terms of x.
  ii Find the maximum value of P.
  c i Given that $S = x^2 + y^2$, write down an expression for S, in terms of x.
  ii Find the minimum value of S.

2 The diagram shows a rectangular garden with a fence on three of its sides and a wall on its fourth side. The total length of the fence is 100 m and the area enclosed is A m².
  a Show that $A = \dfrac{1}{2}x(100 - x)$.
  b Find the maximum area of the garden enclosed and the value of x for which this occurs.

3 The volume of the solid cuboid is 576 cm³ and the surface area is A cm².
  a Express y in terms of x.
  b Show that $A = 4x^2 + \dfrac{1728}{x}$.
  c Find the maximum value of A and state the dimensions of the cuboid for which this occurs.

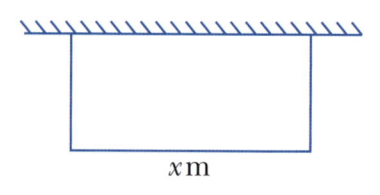

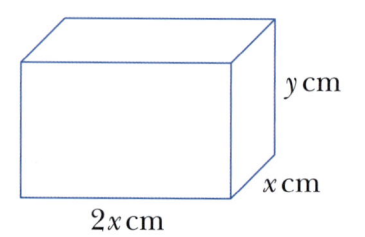

4 A cuboid has a total surface area of $400\,\text{cm}^2$ and a volume of $V\,\text{cm}^3$.

The dimensions of the cuboid are $4x\,\text{cm}$ by $x\,\text{cm}$ by $h\,\text{cm}$.

   a Express h in terms of V and x.

   b Show that $V = 160x - \dfrac{16}{5}x^3$.

   c Find the value of x when V is a maximum.

5 A piece of wire, of length $60\,\text{cm}$, is bent to form a sector of a circle with radius $r\,\text{cm}$ and sector angle θ radians. The total area enclosed by the shape is $A\,\text{cm}^2$.

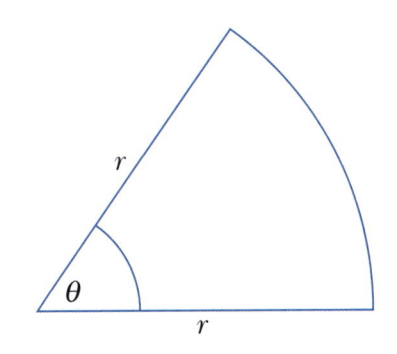

   a Express θ in terms of r.

   b Show that $A = 30r - r^2$.

   c Find $\dfrac{dA}{dr}$ and $\dfrac{d^2A}{dr^2}$.

   d Find the value for r for which there is a stationary value of A.

   e Determine the magnitude and nature of this stationary value.

6 The diagram shows a window made from a rectangle with base $2r\,\text{m}$ and height $h\,\text{m}$ and a semicircle of radius $r\,\text{m}$. The perimeter of the window is $6\,\text{m}$ and the surface area is $A\,\text{m}^2$.

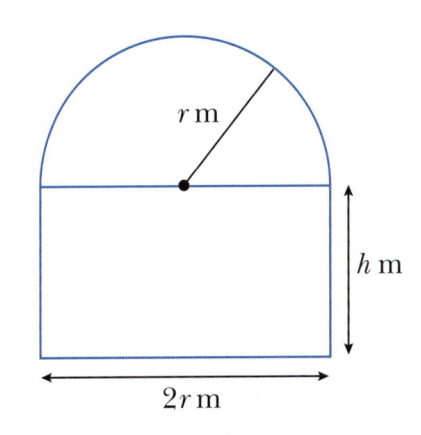

   a Express h in terms of r.

   b Show that $A = 6r - 2r^2 - \dfrac{1}{2}\pi r^2$.

   c Find $\dfrac{dA}{dr}$ and $\dfrac{d^2A}{dr^2}$.

   d Find the value for r for which there is a stationary value of A.

   e Determine the magnitude and nature of this stationary value.

7 $ABCD$ is a rectangle with base length $2p$ units, and area A units^2.

The points A and B lie on the x-axis and the points C and D lie on the curve $y = 4 - x^2$.

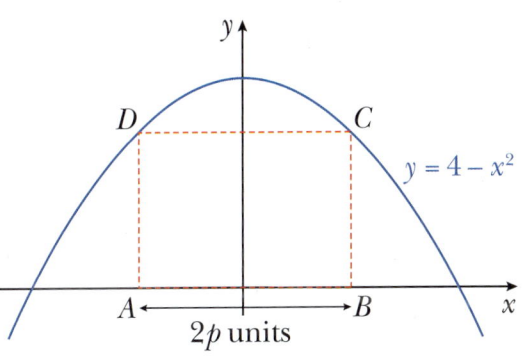

   a Express BC in terms of p.

   b Show that $A = 2p(4 - p^2)$.

   c Find the value of p for which A has a stationary value.

   d Find this stationary value and determine its nature.

8 A solid cylinder has radius $r\,\text{cm}$ and height $h\,\text{cm}$.

The volume of this cylinder is $250\pi\,\text{cm}^3$ and the surface area is $A\,\text{cm}^2$.

   a Express h in terms of r.

   b Show that $A = 2\pi r^2 + \dfrac{500\pi}{r}$.

   c Find $\dfrac{dA}{dr}$ and $\dfrac{d^2A}{dr^2}$.

   d Find the value for r for which there is a stationary value of A.

   e Determine the magnitude and nature of this stationary value.

9 The diagram shows a solid formed by joining a hemisphere of radius r cm to a cylinder of radius r cm and height h cm. The surface area of the solid is 288π cm^2 and the volume is V cm^3.

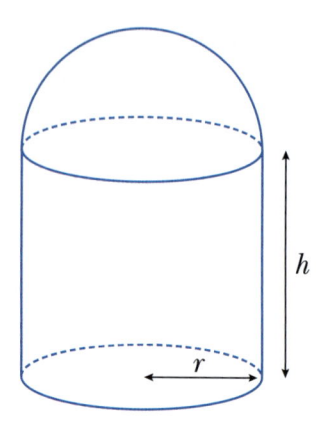

  a Express h in terms of r.
  b Show that $V = 144\pi r - \dfrac{5}{6}\pi r^3$.
  c Find the exact value of r such that V is a maximum.

10 A piece of wire, of length 50 cm, is cut into two pieces.

One piece is bent to make a square of side x cm and the other is bent to make a circle of radius r cm. The total area enclosed by the two shapes is A cm^2.

  a Express r in terms of x.
  b Show that $A = \dfrac{(\pi + 4)x^2 - 100x + 625}{\pi}$.
  c Find the stationary value of A and the value of x for which this occurs. Give your answers correct to 3 sf.

11 The diagram shows a solid cylinder of radius r cm and height $2h$ cm cut from a solid sphere of radius 5 cm. The volume of the cylinder is V cm^3.

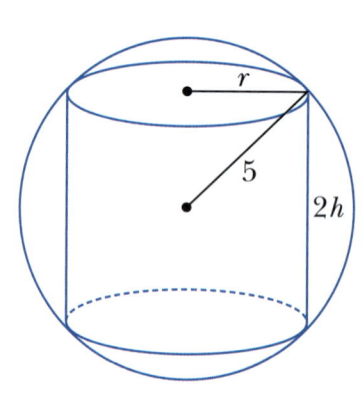

  a Express r in terms of h.
  b Show that $V = 2\pi h(25 - h^2)$.
  c Find the value for h for which there is a stationary value of V.
  d Determine the nature of this stationary value.

CHALLENGE

12 The diagram shows a hollow cone with base radius 12 cm and height 24 cm.

A solid cylinder stands on the base of the cone and the upper edge touches the inside of the cone.

The cylinder has base radius r cm, height h cm and volume V cm^3.

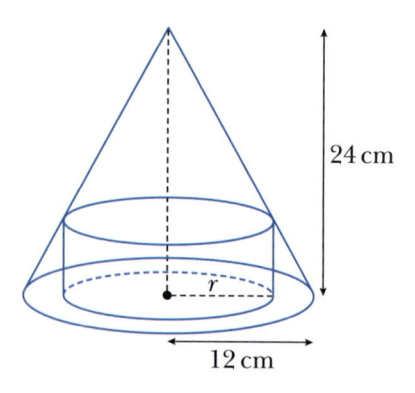

  a Express h in terms of r.
  b Show that $V = 2\pi r^2 (12 - r)$.
  c Find the volume of the largest cylinder which can stand inside the cone.

CHALLENGE

13 The diagram shows a right circular cone of base radius r cm and height h cm cut from a solid sphere of radius 10 cm. The volume of the cone is V cm^3.

  a Express r in terms of h.
  b Show that $V = \dfrac{1}{3}\pi h^2 (20 - h)$.
  c Find the value for h for which there is a stationary value of V.
  d Determine the magnitude and nature of this stationary value.

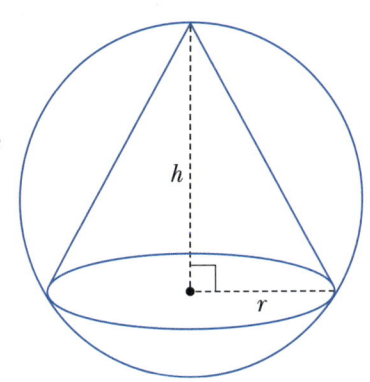

Summary

Rules of differentiation

Power rule: If $y = x^n$, then $\dfrac{dy}{dx} = nx^{n-1}$

Scalar multiple rule: $\dfrac{d}{dx}\big[kf(x)\big] = k\dfrac{d}{dx}\big[f(x)\big]$

Addition/subtraction rule: $\dfrac{d}{dx}\big[f(x) \pm g(x)\big] = \dfrac{d}{dx}\big[f(x)\big] \pm \dfrac{d}{dx}\big[g(x)\big]$

Chain rule: $\dfrac{dy}{dx} = \dfrac{dy}{du} \times \dfrac{du}{dx}$

Product rule: $\dfrac{d}{dx}(uv) = u\dfrac{dv}{dx} + v\dfrac{du}{dx}$

Quotient rule: $\dfrac{d}{dx}\left(\dfrac{u}{v}\right) = \dfrac{v\dfrac{du}{dx} - u\dfrac{dv}{dx}}{v^2}$

Tangents and normals

If the value of $\dfrac{dy}{dx}$ at the point (x_1, y_1) is m, then:

- the equation of the tangent is given by $y - y_1 = m(x - x_1)$
- the equation of the normal is given by $y - y_1 = -\dfrac{1}{m}(x - x_1)$

Small increments and approximations

If δx and δy are sufficiently small then $\dfrac{\delta y}{\delta x} \approx \dfrac{dy}{dx}$.

Stationary points

Stationary points (turning points) of a function $y = f(x)$ occur when $\dfrac{dy}{dx} = 0$.

First derivative test for maximum and minimum points

At a maximum point:
- $\dfrac{dy}{dx} = 0$
- the gradient is positive to the left of the maximum and negative to the right

At a minimum point:
- $\dfrac{dy}{dx} = 0$
- the gradient is negative to the left of the minimum and positive to the right

Second derivative test for maximum and minimum points

If $\dfrac{dy}{dx} = 0$ and $\begin{cases} \dfrac{d^2y}{dx^2} < 0, \text{ then the point is a maximum point} \\ \dfrac{d^2y}{dx^2} > 0, \text{ then the point is a minimum point} \end{cases}$

Examination questions

Worked past paper example

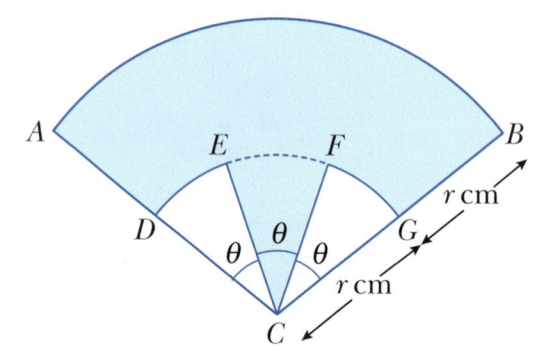

The figure shows a sector ABC of a circle centre C, radius $2r$ cm, where angle ACB is 3θ radians. The points D, E, F and G lie on an arc of a circle centre C, radius r cm. The points D and G are the mid-points of CA and CB respectively. Angles DCE and FCG are each θ radians. The area of the shaded region is $5\,\text{cm}^2$.

a By first expressing θ in terms of r, show that the perimeter, P cm, of the shaded region is given by $P = 4r + \dfrac{8}{r}$. [6]

b Given that r can vary, show that the stationary value of P can be written in the form $k\sqrt{2}$, where k is a constant to be found. [4]

c Determine the nature of this stationary value and find the value of θ for which it occurs. [2]

Cambridge IGCSE Additional Mathematics 0606 Paper 11 Q10(part) Nov 2011

Answers

a Area of sector ABC − (area of sector DCE + area of sector FCG) = 5

$$\frac{1}{2}(2r)^2(3\theta) - \left(\frac{1}{2}r^2\theta + \frac{1}{2}r^2\theta\right) = 5$$

$$6r^2\theta - r^2\theta = 5$$

$$5r^2\theta = 5$$

$$\theta = \frac{1}{r^2}$$

$P = CE + \text{arc } ED + DA + \text{arc } AB + BG + \text{arc } GF + FC$

$= r + r\theta + r + (2r)(3\theta) + r + r\theta + r$

$= 4r + 8r\theta$

$= 4r + 8r \times \dfrac{1}{r^2}$

$= 4r + \dfrac{8}{r}$

b $P = 4r + 8r^{-1}$

$\dfrac{dP}{dr} = 4 - 8r^{-2}$

Stationary values occur when $\dfrac{dP}{dr} = 0$.

$4 - \dfrac{8}{r^2} = 0$

$r^2 = 2$

$r = \sqrt{2}$

When $r = \sqrt{2}$, $P = 4(\sqrt{2}) + \dfrac{8}{\sqrt{2}} = 8\sqrt{2}$

Stationary value of P is $8\sqrt{2}$.

c When $r = \sqrt{2}$, $\theta = \dfrac{1}{(\sqrt{2})^2} = \dfrac{1}{2}$

$\dfrac{dP}{dr} = 4 - 8r^{-2}$

$\dfrac{d^2P}{dr^2} = 16r^{-3}$

When $r = \sqrt{2}$, $\dfrac{d^2P}{dr^2} = \dfrac{16}{(\sqrt{2})^3} = $ positive

The stationary value is a minimum and occurs when $\theta = \dfrac{1}{2}$.

Cambridge IGCSE and O Level Additional Mathematics

Exercise 12.11
Exam Exercise

1. Find the coordinates of the stationary point on the curve $y = x^2 + \dfrac{16}{x}$. [4]

   Cambridge IGCSE Additional Mathematics 0606 Paper 11 Q1 Nov 2014

2. Given that $y = \dfrac{x^2}{2+x^2}$, show that $\dfrac{dy}{dx} = \dfrac{kx}{(2+x)^2}$, where k is a constant to be found. [3]

   Cambridge IGCSE Additional Mathematics 0606 Paper 21 Q8i Nov 2014

3. Given that a curve has equation $y = \dfrac{1}{x} + 2\sqrt{x}$, where $x > 0$, find

   a $\dfrac{dy}{dx}$, [2]

   b $\dfrac{d^2y}{dx^2}$. [2]

   Hence or otherwise, find

   c the coordinates and nature of the stationary point on the curve. [4]

   Cambridge IGCSE Additional Mathematics 0606 Paper 21 Q7i,ii,iii Jun 2014

4. A sector of a circle of radius r cm has an angle θ radians, where $\theta < \pi$. The perimeter of the sector is 30 cm.

   a Show that the area, A cm², of the sector is given by $A = 15r - r^2$. [3]

   b Given that r can vary, find the maximum area of the sector. [3]

   Cambridge IGCSE Additional Mathematics 0606 Paper 21 Q8i,ii Jun 2014

5. a Given that $y = \left(\dfrac{1}{4}x - 5\right)^8$, find $\dfrac{dy}{dx}$. [2]

   b Hence find the approximate change in y as x increases from 12 to $12 + p$, where p is small. [2]

   Cambridge IGCSE Additional Mathematics 0606 Paper 21 Q3i,ii Nov 2013

6. Find the equation of the normal to the curve $y = \dfrac{x^2 + 8}{x - 2}$ at the point on the curve where $x = 4$. [6]

   Cambridge IGCSE Additional Mathematics 0606 Paper 21 Q6 Jun 2013

7. a Find the equation of the tangent to the curve $y = x^3 + 2x^2 - 3x + 4$ at the point where the curve crosses the y-axis. [4]

   b Find the coordinates of the point where the tangent meets the curve again. [3]

   Cambridge IGCSE Additional Mathematics 0606 Paper 11 Q5i,ii Jun 2012

8. The normal to the curve $y = x^3 + 6x^2 - 34x + 44$ at the point $P(2, 8)$ cuts the x-axis at A and the y-axis at B. Show that the mid-point of the line AB lies on the line $4y = x + 9$. [8]

   Cambridge IGCSE Additional Mathematics 0606 Paper 21 Q6 Nov 2012

9 Given that $f(x) = x^2 - \dfrac{648}{\sqrt{x}}$, find the value of x for which $f''(x) = 0$. [6]

Cambridge IGCSE Additional Mathematics 0606 Paper 21 Q7 Jun 2012

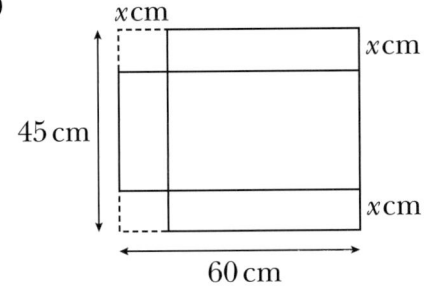

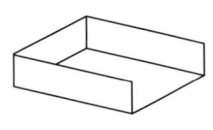

10

A rectangular sheet of metal measures 60 cm by 45 cm. A scoop is made by cutting out squares, of side x cm, from two corners of the sheet and folding the remainder as shown.

a Show that the volume, V cm^3 of the scoop is given by

$$V = 2700x - 165x^2 + 2x^3.$$ [2]

b Given that x can vary, find the value of x for which V has a stationary value. [4]

Cambridge IGCSE Additional Mathematics 0606 Paper 21 Q7i,ii Nov 2010

Chapter 13
Vectors

This section will show you how to:

- use vectors in any form, e.g. $\begin{pmatrix} a \\ b \end{pmatrix}$, $\overrightarrow{AB}$, **p**, $a\mathbf{i} + b\mathbf{j}$
- use position vectors and unit vectors
- find the magnitude of a vector; add and subtract vectors and multiply vectors by scalars
- compose and resolve velocities
- use relative velocity, including solving problems on interception.

> **RECAP**
>
> You should already be familiar with the following vector work:
>
> Quantities that have both magnitude and direction are called **vectors**.
>
> Quantities that have only magnitude are called **scalars**. 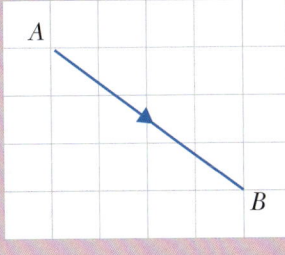
>
> $\overrightarrow{AB}$ means the displacement from the point A to the point B.
>
> For the diagram, $\overrightarrow{AB} = \begin{pmatrix} 4 \\ -3 \end{pmatrix}$.
>
> The 'magnitude' of the vector $\overrightarrow{AB}$ means the 'length' of the vector $\overrightarrow{AB}$ and is denoted by $|\overrightarrow{AB}|$.
>
> $|\overrightarrow{AB}|$ is called the **modulus** of the vector $\overrightarrow{AB}$.
>
> Using Pythagoras for the diagram, $|\overrightarrow{AB}| = \sqrt{(4)^2 + (-3)^2} = 5$. 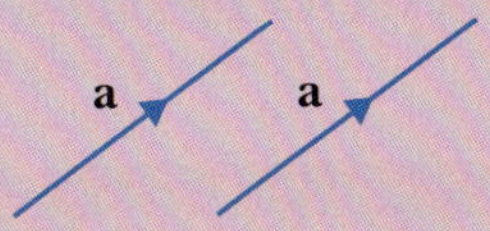
>
> Two vectors are said to be equal if they are the same length and are in the same direction. 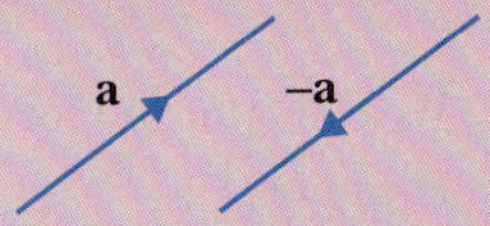
>
> The vector $-\mathbf{a}$ is the same length as the vector $\mathbf{a}$ but is in the opposite direction.
>
> ## Addition and subtraction of vectors
>
> The vector $\mathbf{a} + \mathbf{b}$ means the vector $\mathbf{a}$ followed by the vector $\mathbf{b}$.
>
> The vector $\mathbf{a} - \mathbf{b}$ means the vector $\mathbf{a}$ followed by the vector $-\mathbf{b}$.
>
> The resultant vector is often shown with a double arrow.
>
> It is drawn from the starting point to the finishing point.
>
> For example, if $\mathbf{a} = \begin{pmatrix} 2 \\ 3 \end{pmatrix}$ and $\mathbf{b} = \begin{pmatrix} 4 \\ 1 \end{pmatrix}$, then $\mathbf{a} + \mathbf{a}$ and $\mathbf{a} - \mathbf{b}$ can be shown on a vector diagram as: 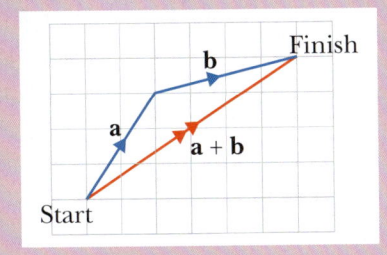 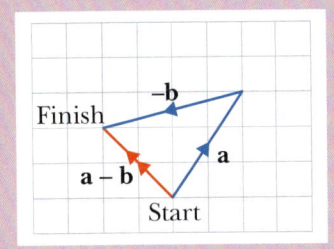
>
> $\mathbf{a} + \mathbf{b}$ and $\mathbf{a} - \mathbf{b}$ can also be found as follows:
>
> $\mathbf{a} + \mathbf{b} = \begin{pmatrix} 2 \\ 3 \end{pmatrix} + \begin{pmatrix} 4 \\ 1 \end{pmatrix} = \begin{pmatrix} 2+4 \\ 3+1 \end{pmatrix} = \begin{pmatrix} 6 \\ 4 \end{pmatrix}$ $\mathbf{a} - \mathbf{b} = \begin{pmatrix} 2 \\ 3 \end{pmatrix} - \begin{pmatrix} 4 \\ 1 \end{pmatrix} = \begin{pmatrix} 2-4 \\ 3-1 \end{pmatrix} = \begin{pmatrix} -2 \\ 2 \end{pmatrix}$
>
> ## Multiplication by a scalar 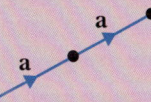
>
> The vector $\mathbf{a} + \mathbf{a}$ can be written as $2\mathbf{a}$. 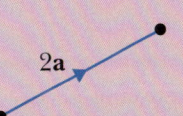
>
> The vectors $\mathbf{a}$ and $2\mathbf{a}$ are examples of parallel vectors.
>
> Two vectors are parallel if one vector can be written as a multiple of the other vector.
>
> For example:
>
> $\begin{pmatrix} -1 \\ 3 \end{pmatrix}$ and $\begin{pmatrix} -5 \\ 15 \end{pmatrix}$ are parallel and in the same direction because $\begin{pmatrix} -5 \\ 15 \end{pmatrix} = 5\begin{pmatrix} -1 \\ 3 \end{pmatrix}$.
>
> $\begin{pmatrix} 2 \\ -4 \end{pmatrix}$ and $\begin{pmatrix} -6 \\ 12 \end{pmatrix}$ are parallel and in opposite directions because $\begin{pmatrix} -6 \\ 12 \end{pmatrix} = -3\begin{pmatrix} 2 \\ -4 \end{pmatrix}$.
>
> ## Collinear points
>
> If $\overrightarrow{AB} = k\overrightarrow{AC}$ then the points A, B and C are **collinear**.
>
> (This is because the lines AB and AC must be parallel and the point A lies on both lines.)

13.1 Further vector notation

The vector $\overrightarrow{AB}$ in the diagram can be written in component form as $\begin{pmatrix} 4 \\ 3 \end{pmatrix}$.

$\overrightarrow{AB}$ can also be written as $4\mathbf{i} + 3\mathbf{j}$, where:

i is a vector of length 1 unit in the positive x-direction

and **j** is a vector of length 1 unit in the positive y-direction.

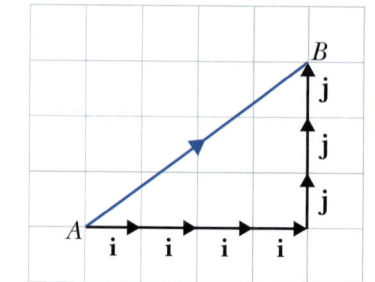

> **Note:**
> A vector of length 1 unit is called a **unit vector**.

WORKED EXAMPLE 1

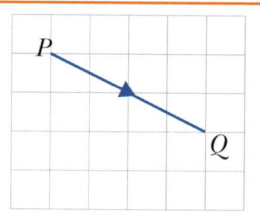

a Write $\overrightarrow{PQ}$ in the form $a\mathbf{i} + b\mathbf{j}$.
b Find $|\overrightarrow{PQ}|$.

Answers

a $\overrightarrow{PQ} = 4\mathbf{i} - 2\mathbf{j}$
b Using Pythagoras, $|\overrightarrow{PQ}| = \sqrt{(4)^2 + (-2)^2} = \sqrt{20} = 2\sqrt{5}$.

You could be asked to find the unit vector in the direction of a given vector. The method is outline in the following example.

WORKED EXAMPLE 2

$\overrightarrow{EF} = 4\mathbf{i} + 3\mathbf{j}$

Find the unit vector in the direction of the vector $\overrightarrow{EF}$.

Answers

First find the length of the vector $\overrightarrow{EF}$:

$EF^2 = 4^2 + 3^2$ using Pythagoras

$EF = 5$

Hence the unit vector in the direction of $\overrightarrow{EF}$ is:

$\dfrac{1}{5}(4\mathbf{i} + 3\mathbf{j})$

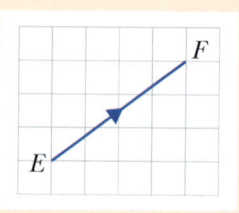

Chapter 13: Vectors

WORKED EXAMPLE 3

$\mathbf{a} = -2\mathbf{i} + 3\mathbf{j}$, $\mathbf{b} = 4\mathbf{i} - \mathbf{j}$ and $\mathbf{c} = -22\mathbf{i} + 18\mathbf{j}$.

Find λ and μ such that $\lambda\mathbf{a} + \mu\mathbf{b} = \mathbf{c}$.

Answers

$\lambda\mathbf{a} + \mu\mathbf{b} = \mathbf{c}$

$\lambda(-2\mathbf{i} + 3\mathbf{j}) + \mu(4\mathbf{i} - \mathbf{j}) = -22\mathbf{i} + 18\mathbf{j}$

Equating the **i**'s gives
$-2\lambda + 4\mu = -22$
$-\lambda + 2\mu = -11$ ------------(1)

Equating the **j**'s gives
$3\lambda - \mu = 18$
$6\lambda - 2\mu = 36$ ------------(2)

Adding equations (1) and (2) gives
$5\lambda = 25$
$\lambda = 5$

Substituting for λ in equation (1) gives
$-5 + 2\mu = -11$
$2\mu = -6$
$\mu = -3$

So $\lambda = 5$, $\mu = -3$.

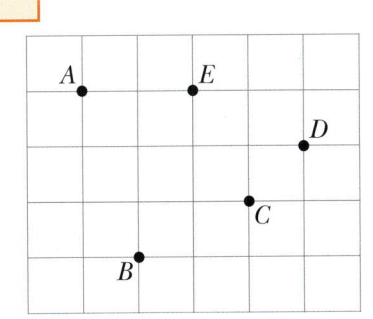

Exercise 13.1

1 Write each vector in the form $a\mathbf{i} + b\mathbf{j}$.

    a $\overrightarrow{AB}$ **b** $\overrightarrow{AC}$ **c** $\overrightarrow{AD}$
    d $\overrightarrow{AE}$ **e** $\overrightarrow{BE}$ **f** $\overrightarrow{DE}$
    g $\overrightarrow{EA}$ **h** $\overrightarrow{DB}$ **i** $\overrightarrow{DC}$

2 Find the magnitude of each of these vectors.

    a $-2\mathbf{i}$ **b** $4\mathbf{i} + 3\mathbf{j}$ **c** $5\mathbf{i} - 12\mathbf{j}$ **d** $-8\mathbf{i} - 6\mathbf{j}$
    e $7\mathbf{i} + 24\mathbf{j}$ **f** $15\mathbf{i} - 8\mathbf{j}$ **g** $-4\mathbf{i} + 4\mathbf{j}$ **h** $5\mathbf{i} - 10\mathbf{j}$

3 The vector $\overrightarrow{AB}$ has a magnitude of 20 units and is parallel to the vector $4\mathbf{i} + 3\mathbf{j}$.
   Find $\overrightarrow{AB}$.

4 The vector $\overrightarrow{PQ}$ has a magnitude of 39 units and is parallel to the vector $12\mathbf{i} - 5\mathbf{j}$.
   Find $\overrightarrow{PQ}$.

5 Find the unit vector in the direction of each of these vectors.

    a $6\mathbf{i} + 8\mathbf{j}$ **b** $5\mathbf{i} + 12\mathbf{j}$ **c** $-4\mathbf{i} - 3\mathbf{j}$ **d** $8\mathbf{i} - 15\mathbf{j}$ **e** $3\mathbf{i} + 3\mathbf{j}$

6 $\mathbf{p} = 8\mathbf{i} - 6\mathbf{j}$, $\mathbf{q} = -2\mathbf{i} + 3\mathbf{j}$ and $\mathbf{r} = 10\mathbf{i}$

   Find:

    a $2\mathbf{q}$ **b** $2\mathbf{p} + \mathbf{q}$ **c** $\frac{1}{2}\mathbf{p} - 3\mathbf{r}$ **d** $\frac{1}{2}\mathbf{r} - \mathbf{p} - \mathbf{q}$.

7 $p = 9i + 12j$, $q = 3i - 3j$ and $r = 7i + j$
   Find:
   a $|p + q|$ b $|p + q + r|$.

8 $p = 7i - 2j$ and $q = i + \mu j$.
   Find λ and μ such that $\lambda p + q = 36i - 13j$.

9 $a = 5i - 6j$, $b = -i + 2j$ and $c = -13i + 18j$.
   Find λ and μ such that $\lambda a + \mu b = c$.

13.2 Position vectors

The position vector of a point P relative to an origin, O, means the displacement of the point P from O.

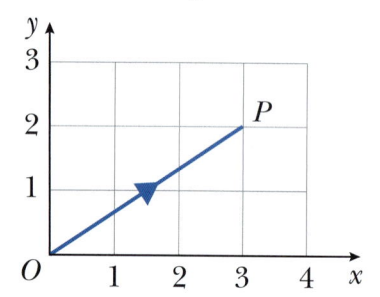

For this diagram, the position vector of P is

$$\overrightarrow{OP} = \begin{pmatrix} 3 \\ 2 \end{pmatrix} \quad \text{or} \quad \overrightarrow{OP} = 3i + 2j$$

Now consider two points A and B with position vectors a and b.

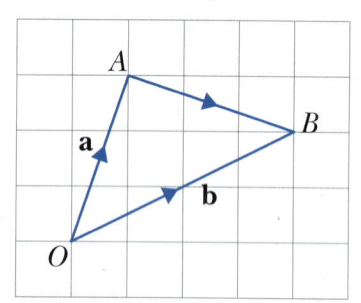

$\overrightarrow{AB}$ means the position vector of B relative to A.

$$\overrightarrow{AB} = \overrightarrow{AO} + \overrightarrow{OB}$$
$$= -\overrightarrow{OA} + \overrightarrow{OB}$$

Hence:

$$\overrightarrow{AB} = \overrightarrow{OB} - \overrightarrow{OA} \quad \text{or} \quad \overrightarrow{AB} = b - a$$

Chapter 13: Vectors

WORKED EXAMPLE 5

Relative to an origin O, the position vector of P is $4\mathbf{i} + 5\mathbf{j}$ and the position vector of Q is $10\mathbf{i} - 3\mathbf{j}$.

a Find $\overrightarrow{PQ}$.

The point R lies on PQ such that $\overrightarrow{PR} = \dfrac{1}{4}\overrightarrow{PQ}$.

b Find the position vector of R.

Answers

a $\overrightarrow{PQ} = \overrightarrow{OQ} - \overrightarrow{OP}$ $\qquad \overrightarrow{OQ} = 10\mathbf{i} - 3\mathbf{j}$ and $\overrightarrow{OP} = 4\mathbf{i} + 5\mathbf{j}$

$\phantom{\overrightarrow{PQ}} = (10\mathbf{i} - 3\mathbf{j}) - (4\mathbf{i} + 5\mathbf{j})$ $\qquad$ collect $\mathbf{i}$'s and $\mathbf{j}$'s

$\overrightarrow{PQ} = 6\mathbf{i} - 8\mathbf{j}$

b $\overrightarrow{PR} = \dfrac{1}{4}\overrightarrow{PQ}$

$\phantom{\overrightarrow{PR}} = \dfrac{1}{4}(6\mathbf{i} - 8\mathbf{j})$

$\phantom{\overrightarrow{PR}} = 1.5\mathbf{i} - 2\mathbf{j}$

$\overrightarrow{OR} = \overrightarrow{OP} + \overrightarrow{PR}$

$\phantom{\overrightarrow{OR}} = (4\mathbf{i} + 5\mathbf{j}) + (1.5\mathbf{i} - 2\mathbf{j})$

$\overrightarrow{OR} = 5.5\mathbf{i} + 3\mathbf{j}$

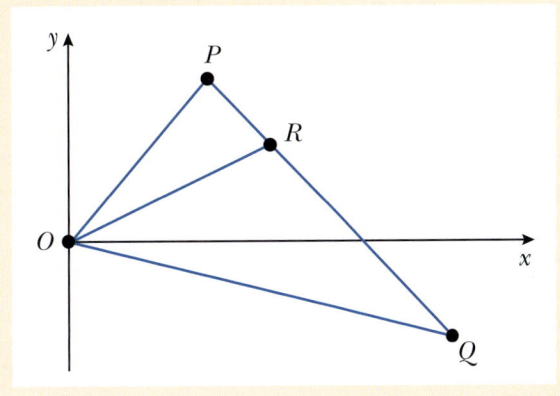

WORKED EXAMPLE 6

Relative to an origin O, the position vectors of points A, B and C are $-2\mathbf{i} + 5\mathbf{j}$, $10\mathbf{i} - \mathbf{j}$ and $\lambda(2\mathbf{i} + \mathbf{j})$ respectively. Given that C lies on the line AB, find the value of λ.

Answers

$\overrightarrow{AB} = \overrightarrow{OB} - \overrightarrow{OA}$ $\qquad \overrightarrow{OB} = 10\mathbf{i} - \mathbf{j}$ and $\overrightarrow{OA} = -2\mathbf{i} + 5\mathbf{j}$

$\phantom{\overrightarrow{AB}} = (10\mathbf{i} - \mathbf{j}) - (-2\mathbf{i} + 5\mathbf{j})$ $\qquad$ collect $\mathbf{i}$'s and $\mathbf{j}$'s

$\phantom{\overrightarrow{AB}} = 12\mathbf{i} - 6\mathbf{j}$

If C lies on the line AB, then $\overrightarrow{AC} = k\overrightarrow{AB}$.

$\overrightarrow{AC} = \overrightarrow{OC} - \overrightarrow{OA}$ $\qquad \overrightarrow{OC} = \lambda(2\mathbf{i} + \mathbf{j})$ and $\overrightarrow{OA} = -2\mathbf{i} + 5\mathbf{j}$

$\phantom{\overrightarrow{AC}} = \lambda(2\mathbf{i} + \mathbf{j}) - (-2\mathbf{i} + 5\mathbf{j})$ $\qquad$ collect $\mathbf{i}$'s and $\mathbf{j}$'s

$\phantom{\overrightarrow{AC}} = (2\lambda + 2)\mathbf{i} - (5 - \lambda)\mathbf{j}$

$k\overrightarrow{AB} = k(12\mathbf{i} - 6\mathbf{j})$

$\phantom{k\overrightarrow{AB}} = 12k\mathbf{i} - 6k\mathbf{j}$

Hence, $(2\lambda + 2)\mathbf{i} - (5 - \lambda)\mathbf{j} = 12k\mathbf{i} - 6k\mathbf{j}$

Equating the $\mathbf{i}$'s gives: $\quad 2\lambda + 2 = 12k$ ----------------(1)

Equating the $\mathbf{j}$'s gives: $\quad 5 - \lambda = 6k$ $\qquad\qquad\qquad\qquad$ multiply both sides by 2

$\phantom{\text{Equating the j's gives: }} 10 - 2\lambda = 12k$ ----------------(2)

Using equation (1) and equation (2) gives

$\qquad\qquad 2\lambda + 2 = 10 - 2\lambda$

$\qquad\qquad\qquad 4\lambda = 8$

$\qquad\qquad\qquad\lambda = 2$

Exercise 13.2

1 Find $\overrightarrow{AB}$, in the form $a\mathbf{i} + b\mathbf{j}$, for each of the following:
   a $A(4, 7)$ and $B(3, 4)$ b $A(0, 6)$ and $B(2, -4)$
   c $A(3, -3)$ and $B(6, -2)$ d $A(7, 0)$ and $B(-5, 3)$
   e $A(-4, -2)$ and $B(-3, 5)$ f $A(5, -6)$ and $B(-1, -7)$.

2   a O is the origin, P is the point $(1, 5)$ and $\overrightarrow{PQ} = \begin{pmatrix} 3 \\ 5 \end{pmatrix}$. Find $\overrightarrow{OQ}$.

   b O is the origin, E is the point $(-3, 4)$ and $\overrightarrow{EF} = \begin{pmatrix} -2 \\ 7 \end{pmatrix}$.
   Find the position vector of F.

   c O is the origin, M is the point $(4, -2)$ and $\overrightarrow{NM} = \begin{pmatrix} 3 \\ -5 \end{pmatrix}$.
   Find the position vector of N.

3 The vector $\overrightarrow{OA}$ has a magnitude of 25 units and is parallel to the vector $-3\mathbf{i} + 4\mathbf{j}$.

   The vector $\overrightarrow{OB}$ has a magnitude of 26 units and is parallel to the vector $12\mathbf{i} + 5\mathbf{j}$.

   Find:
   a $\overrightarrow{OA}$ b $\overrightarrow{OB}$ c $\overrightarrow{AB}$ d $|\overrightarrow{AB}|$.

4 Relative to an origin O, the position vector of A is $-7\mathbf{i} - 7\mathbf{j}$ and the position vector of B is $9\mathbf{i} + 5\mathbf{j}$.
   The point C lies on AB such that $\overrightarrow{AC} = 3\overrightarrow{CB}$.
   a Find $\overrightarrow{AB}$.
   b Find the unit vector in the direction of $\overrightarrow{AB}$.
   c Find the position vector of C.

5 Relative to an origin O, the position vector of P is $-2\mathbf{i} - 4\mathbf{j}$ and the position vector of Q is $8\mathbf{i} + 20\mathbf{j}$.
   a Find $\overrightarrow{PQ}$.
   b Find $|\overrightarrow{PQ}|$.
   c Find the unit vector in the direction of $\overrightarrow{PQ}$.
   d Find the position vector of M, the mid-point of PQ.

6 Relative to an origin O, the position vector of A is $4\mathbf{i} - 2\mathbf{j}$ and the position vector of B is $\lambda \mathbf{i} + 2\mathbf{j}$.
   The unit vector in the direction of $\overrightarrow{AB}$ is $0.3\mathbf{i} + 0.4\mathbf{j}$. Find the value of λ.

7 Relative to an origin O, the position vector of A is $\begin{pmatrix} -10 \\ 10 \end{pmatrix}$ and the position vectors of B is $\begin{pmatrix} 10 \\ -11 \end{pmatrix}$.
   a Find $\overrightarrow{AB}$.

   The points A, B and C lie on a straight line such that $\overrightarrow{AC} = 2\overrightarrow{AB}$.
   b Find the position vector of the point C.

8 Relative to an origin O, the position vector of A is $\begin{pmatrix} 21 \\ -20 \end{pmatrix}$ and the position vectors of B is $\begin{pmatrix} 24 \\ 18 \end{pmatrix}$.

   a Find:

   i $|\overrightarrow{OA}|$ ii $|\overrightarrow{OB}|$ iii $|\overrightarrow{AB}|$.

   The points A, B and C lie on a straight line such that $\overrightarrow{AC} = \overrightarrow{CB}$.

   b Find the position vector of the point C.

9 Relative to an origin O, the position vector of A is $3\mathbf{i} - 2\mathbf{j}$ and the position vector of B is $15\mathbf{i} + 7\mathbf{j}$.

   a Find $\overrightarrow{AB}$.

   The point C lies on AB such that $\overrightarrow{AC} = \frac{1}{3}\overrightarrow{AB}$.

   b Find the position vector of C.

10 Relative to an origin O, the position vector of A is $6\mathbf{i} + 6\mathbf{j}$ and the position vector of B is $12\mathbf{i} - 2\mathbf{j}$.

   a Find $\overrightarrow{AB}$.

   The point C lies on AB such that $\overrightarrow{AC} = \frac{3}{4}\overrightarrow{AB}$.

   b Find the position vector of C.

11 Relative to an origin O, the position vector of A is $\begin{pmatrix} 3 \\ 4 \end{pmatrix}$ and the position vector of B is $\begin{pmatrix} 5 \\ 5 \end{pmatrix}$.

   The points A, B and C are such that $\overrightarrow{BC} = 2\overrightarrow{AB}$. Find the position vector of C.

12 Relative to an origin O, the position vectors of points A, B and C are $-5\mathbf{i} - 11\mathbf{j}$, $23\mathbf{i} - 4\mathbf{j}$ and $\lambda(\mathbf{i} - 3\mathbf{j})$ respectively.
   Given that C lies on the line AB, find the value of λ.

13 Relative to an origin O, the position vectors of A, B and C are $-2\mathbf{i} + 7\mathbf{j}$, $2\mathbf{i} - \mathbf{j}$ and $6\mathbf{i} + \lambda\mathbf{j}$ respectively.

   a Find the value of λ when $AC = 17$.

   b Find the value of λ when ABC is a straight line.

   c Find the value of λ when ABC is a right-angle.

14 Relative to an origin O, the position vector of A is $-6\mathbf{i} + 4\mathbf{j}$ and the position vector of B is $18\mathbf{i} + 6\mathbf{j}$. C lies on the y-axis and $\overrightarrow{OC} = \overrightarrow{OA} + \lambda\overrightarrow{OB}$.
   Find $\overrightarrow{OC}$.

15 Relative to an origin O, the position vector of P is $8\mathbf{i} + 3\mathbf{j}$ and the position vector of Q is $-12\mathbf{i} - 7\mathbf{j}$. R lies on the x-axis and $\overrightarrow{OR} = \overrightarrow{OP} + \mu\overrightarrow{OQ}$.
   Find $\overrightarrow{OR}$.

Cambridge IGCSE and O Level Additional Mathematics

CHALLENGE Q

16 Relative to an origin O, the position vectors of points P, Q and R are $-6\mathbf{i} + 8\mathbf{j}$, $-4\mathbf{i} + 2\mathbf{j}$ and $5\mathbf{i} + 5\mathbf{j}$ respectively.

a Find the magnitude of:
 i $\overrightarrow{PQ}$ ii $\overrightarrow{PR}$ iii $\overrightarrow{QR}$.

b Show that angle PQR is $90°$.

c If $\overrightarrow{OP} = \lambda \overrightarrow{OQ} + \mu \overrightarrow{OR}$, find the value of λ and the value of μ.

13.3 Vector geometry

WORKED EXAMPLE 7

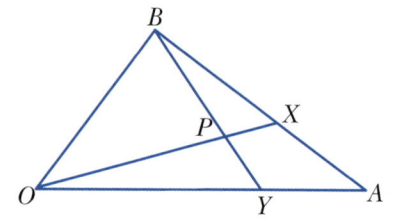

$\overrightarrow{OA} = \mathbf{a}$, $\overrightarrow{OB} = \mathbf{b}$, $\overrightarrow{BX} = \dfrac{3}{5} = \overrightarrow{BA}$ and $\overrightarrow{OY} = \dfrac{3}{4} \overrightarrow{OA}$.

a Find in terms of $\mathbf{a}$ and $\mathbf{b}$:
 i $\overrightarrow{BA}$ ii $\overrightarrow{BX}$ iii $\overrightarrow{OX}$ iv $\overrightarrow{BY}$

b Given that $\overrightarrow{OP} = \lambda \overrightarrow{OX}$, find $\overrightarrow{OP}$ in terms of λ, $\mathbf{a}$ and $\mathbf{b}$.

c Given that $\overrightarrow{BP} = \mu \overrightarrow{BY}$, find $\overrightarrow{OP}$ in terms of μ, $\mathbf{a}$ and $\mathbf{b}$.

d Find the value of λ and the value of μ.

Answers

a i $\overrightarrow{BA} = \overrightarrow{OA} - \overrightarrow{OB} = \mathbf{a} - \mathbf{b}$

ii $\overrightarrow{BX} = \dfrac{3}{5} \overrightarrow{BA} = \dfrac{3}{5}(\mathbf{a} - \mathbf{b})$

iii $\overrightarrow{OX} = \overrightarrow{OB} + \overrightarrow{BX} = \mathbf{b} + \dfrac{3}{5}(\mathbf{a} - \mathbf{b}) = \dfrac{3}{5}\mathbf{a} + \dfrac{2}{5}\mathbf{b}$

iv $\overrightarrow{BY} = \overrightarrow{BO} + \overrightarrow{OY} = -\mathbf{b} + \dfrac{3}{4}\overrightarrow{OA} = \dfrac{3}{4}\mathbf{a} - \mathbf{b}$

b $\overrightarrow{OP} = \lambda \overrightarrow{OX}$

$= \lambda \left(\dfrac{3}{5}\mathbf{a} + \dfrac{2}{5}\mathbf{b} \right)$

$= \dfrac{3\lambda}{5}\mathbf{a} + \dfrac{2\lambda}{5}\mathbf{b}$

c $\overrightarrow{OP} = \overrightarrow{OB} + \overrightarrow{BP}$

$= \mathbf{b} + \mu \overrightarrow{BY}$

$= \mathbf{b} + \mu\left(\dfrac{3}{4}\mathbf{a} - \mathbf{b}\right)$

$= \dfrac{3\mu}{4}\mathbf{a} + (1 - \mu)\mathbf{b}$

d Equating the coefficients of **a** for $\overrightarrow{OP}$ gives:

$\dfrac{3\lambda}{5} = \dfrac{3\mu}{4}$ divide both sides by 3

$\dfrac{\lambda}{5} = \dfrac{\mu}{4}$ multiply both sides by 20

$4\lambda = 5\mu$ ----------------(1)

Equating the coefficients of **b** for $\overrightarrow{OP}$ gives:

$\dfrac{2\lambda}{5} = 1 - \mu$ multiply both sides by 5

$2\lambda = 5 - 5\mu$ ----------(2)

Adding equation (1) and equation (2) gives:

$6\lambda = 5$

$\lambda = \dfrac{5}{6}$

Substituting $\lambda = \dfrac{5}{6}$ in equation (1) gives $\mu = \dfrac{2}{3}$.

Hence, $\lambda = \dfrac{5}{6}$ and $\mu = \dfrac{2}{3}$.

WORKED EXAMPLE 8

$\overrightarrow{OA} = 3\mathbf{a}$, $\overrightarrow{OB} = 4\mathbf{b}$ and M is the mid-point of OB.

$OP : PA = 4 : 3$ and $\overrightarrow{BX} = \lambda \overrightarrow{BP}$.

a Find in terms of **a** and **b**:

  i $\overrightarrow{AB}$ **ii** $\overrightarrow{MA}$.

b Find in terms of λ, **a** and **b**:

  i $\overrightarrow{BX}$ **ii** $\overrightarrow{MX}$.

c If M, X and A are collinear, find the value of λ.

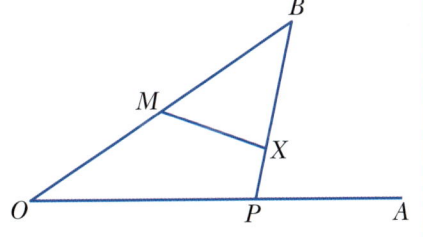

Answers

a **i** $\overrightarrow{AB} = \overrightarrow{AO} + \overrightarrow{OB}$

          $= -3\mathbf{a} + 4\mathbf{b}$

  ii $\overrightarrow{MA} = \overrightarrow{MO} + \overrightarrow{OA}$

          $= -2\mathbf{b} + 3\mathbf{a}$

          $= 3\mathbf{a} - 2\mathbf{b}$

b i $\overrightarrow{BX} = \lambda \overrightarrow{BP}$

$= \lambda(\overrightarrow{BO} + \overrightarrow{OP})$

$= \lambda\left(-4\mathbf{b} + \dfrac{4}{7}\overrightarrow{OA}\right)$ use $\overrightarrow{OA} = 3\mathbf{a}$

$= \dfrac{12\lambda}{7}\mathbf{a} - 4\lambda\mathbf{b}$

ii $\overrightarrow{MX} = \overrightarrow{MB} + \overrightarrow{BX}$ use $\overrightarrow{BX} = \dfrac{12\lambda}{7}\mathbf{a} - 4\lambda\mathbf{b}$

$= 2\mathbf{b} + \dfrac{12\lambda}{7}\mathbf{a} - 4\lambda\mathbf{b}$ collect **a**'s and **b**'s

$= \dfrac{12\lambda}{7}\mathbf{a} + (2 - 4\lambda)\mathbf{b}$

c If M, X and A are collinear, then $\overrightarrow{MX} = k\overrightarrow{MA}$.

$\dfrac{12\lambda}{7}\mathbf{a} + (2 - 4\lambda)\mathbf{b} = k(3\mathbf{a} - 2\mathbf{b})$

Equating the coefficients of **a** gives:

$3k = \dfrac{12\lambda}{7}$ divide both sides by 3

$k = \dfrac{4\lambda}{7}$ ----------------(1)

Equating the coefficients of **b** gives:

$-2k = 2 - 4\lambda$ divide both sides by −2

$k = 2\lambda - 1$ ----------(2)

Using equation (1) and equation (2) gives:

$2\lambda - 1 = \dfrac{4\lambda}{7}$

$14\lambda - 7 = 4\lambda$

$10\lambda = 7$

$\lambda = 0.7$

Exercise 13.3

1 $\overrightarrow{OA} = \mathbf{a}$, $\overrightarrow{OB} = \mathbf{b}$.

R is the mid-point of OA and $\overrightarrow{OP} = 3\overrightarrow{OB}$.

$\overrightarrow{AQ} = \lambda\overrightarrow{AB}$ and $\overrightarrow{RQ} = \mu\overrightarrow{RP}$.

  a Find $\overrightarrow{OQ}$ in terms of λ, **a** and **b**.

  b Find $\overrightarrow{OQ}$ in terms of μ, **a** and **b**.

  c Find the value of λ and the value of μ.

2 $\overrightarrow{AB} = 5\mathbf{a}$, $\overrightarrow{DC} = 3\mathbf{a}$ and $\overrightarrow{CB} = \mathbf{b}$.

$\overrightarrow{AX} = \lambda\overrightarrow{AC}$ and $\overrightarrow{DX} = \mu\overrightarrow{DB}$.

  a Find in terms of **a** and **b**,   **i** $\overrightarrow{AD}$,   **ii** $\overrightarrow{DB}$.

  b Find in terms of λ, μ, **a** and/or **b**,   **i** $\overrightarrow{AX}$,   **ii** $\overrightarrow{DX}$.

  c Find the value of λ and the value of μ.

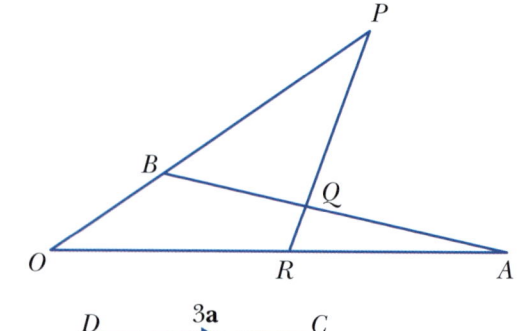

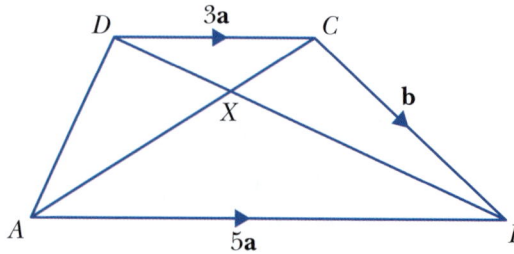

Chapter 13: Vectors

3 $\overrightarrow{OP} = \mathbf{a}$, $\overrightarrow{PY} = 2\mathbf{b}$, and $\overrightarrow{OQ} = 3\mathbf{b}$.
$\overrightarrow{OX} = \lambda\overrightarrow{OY}$ and $\overrightarrow{QX} = \mu\overrightarrow{QP}$.

a Find $\overrightarrow{OX}$ in terms of λ, $\mathbf{a}$ and $\mathbf{b}$,
b Find $\overrightarrow{OX}$ in terms of μ, $\mathbf{a}$ and $\mathbf{b}$,
c Find the value of λ and the value of μ.

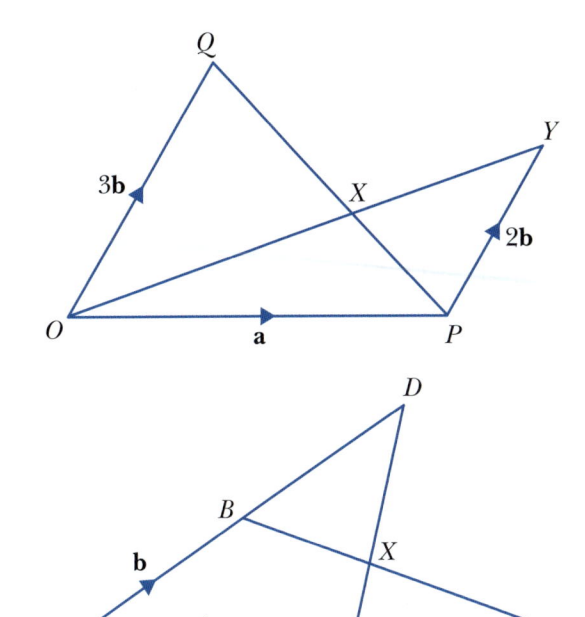

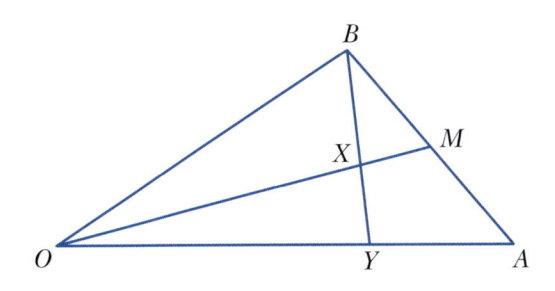

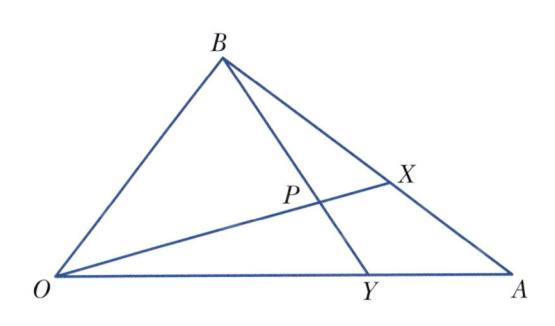

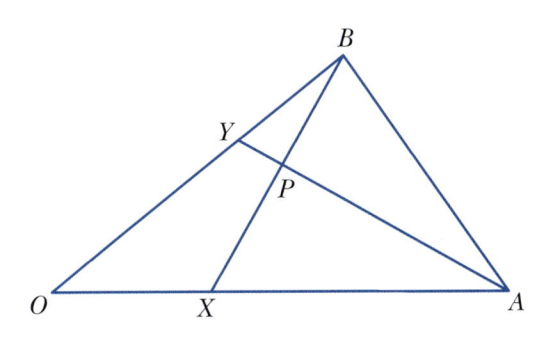

4 $\overrightarrow{OA} = \mathbf{a}$, $\overrightarrow{OB} = \mathbf{b}$.
B is the mid-point of OD and $\overrightarrow{AC} = \dfrac{2}{3}\overrightarrow{OA}$.
$\overrightarrow{AX} = \lambda\overrightarrow{AD}$ and $\overrightarrow{BX} = \mu\overrightarrow{BC}$.

a Find $\overrightarrow{OX}$ in terms of λ, $\mathbf{a}$ and $\mathbf{b}$.
b Find $\overrightarrow{OX}$ in terms of μ, $\mathbf{a}$ and $\mathbf{b}$.
c Find the value of λ and the value of μ.

5 $\overrightarrow{OA} = \mathbf{a}$, $\overrightarrow{OB} = \mathbf{b}$.
M is the mid-point of AB and $\overrightarrow{OY} = \dfrac{3}{4}\overrightarrow{OA}$.
$\overrightarrow{OX} = \lambda\overrightarrow{OM}$ and $\overrightarrow{BX} = \mu\overrightarrow{BY}$.

a Find in terms of $\mathbf{a}$ and $\mathbf{b}$,
   i $\overrightarrow{AB}$ **ii** $\overrightarrow{OM}$.
b Find $\overrightarrow{OX}$ in terms of λ, $\mathbf{a}$ and $\mathbf{b}$.
c Find $\overrightarrow{OX}$ in terms of μ, $\mathbf{a}$ and $\mathbf{b}$.
d Find the value of λ and the value of μ.

6 $\overrightarrow{OA} = \mathbf{a}$, $\overrightarrow{OB} = \mathbf{b}$, $\overrightarrow{BX} = \dfrac{3}{5}\overrightarrow{BA}$ and $\overrightarrow{OY} = \dfrac{5}{7}\overrightarrow{OA}$.

$\overrightarrow{OP} = \lambda\overrightarrow{OX}$ and $\overrightarrow{BP} = \mu\overrightarrow{BY}$.

a Find $\overrightarrow{OP}$ in terms of λ, $\mathbf{a}$ and $\mathbf{b}$.
b Find $\overrightarrow{OP}$ in terms of μ, $\mathbf{a}$ and $\mathbf{b}$.
c Find the value of λ and the value of μ.

7 $\overrightarrow{OA} = \mathbf{a}$, $\overrightarrow{OB} = \mathbf{b}$ and O is the origin.
$\overrightarrow{OX} = \lambda\overrightarrow{OA}$ and $\overrightarrow{OY} = \mu\overrightarrow{OB}$.

a i Find $\overrightarrow{BX}$ in terms of λ, $\mathbf{a}$ and $\mathbf{b}$.
   ii Find $\overrightarrow{AY}$ in terms of μ, $\mathbf{a}$ and $\mathbf{b}$.
b $5\overrightarrow{BP} = 2\overrightarrow{BX}$ and $\overrightarrow{AY} = 4\overrightarrow{PY}$.
   i Find $\overrightarrow{OP}$ in terms of λ, $\mathbf{a}$ and $\mathbf{b}$.
   ii Find $\overrightarrow{OP}$ in terms of μ, $\mathbf{a}$ and $\mathbf{b}$.
   iii Find the value of λ and the value of μ.

8 O, A, B and C are four points such that
   $\overrightarrow{OA} = 7\mathbf{a} - 5\mathbf{b}$, $\overrightarrow{OB} = 2\mathbf{a} + 5\mathbf{b}$ and $\overrightarrow{OC} = -2\mathbf{a} + 13\mathbf{b}$.

   a Find i $\overrightarrow{AC}$ ii $\overrightarrow{AB}$.

   b Use your answers to **part a** to explain why B lies on the line AC.

CHALLENGE Q

9 $\overrightarrow{OA} = \mathbf{a}$ and $\overrightarrow{OB} = \mathbf{b}$.
   $OA : AE = 1 : 3$ and $AB : BC = 1 : 2$.
   $OB = BD$

   a Find, in terms of $\mathbf{a}$ and/or $\mathbf{b}$,
      i $\overrightarrow{OE}$ ii $\overrightarrow{OD}$ iii $\overrightarrow{OC}$.

   b Find, in terms of $\mathbf{a}$ and/or $\mathbf{b}$,
      i $\overrightarrow{CE}$ ii $\overrightarrow{CD}$ iii $\overrightarrow{DE}$.

   c Use your answers to **part b** to explain why C, D and E are collinear.

   d Find the ratio $CD : DE$.

13.4 Constant velocity problems

If an object moves with a constant velocity, **v**, where $\mathbf{v} = (4\mathbf{i} - 2\mathbf{j})$ m s^{-1}, the velocity can be represented on a diagram as:

Velocity is a quantity that has both magnitude and direction.

The magnitude of the velocity is the speed.

If $\mathbf{v} = (4\mathbf{i} - 2\mathbf{j})$ m s^{-1} then,

$$\text{speed} = \sqrt{(4)^2 + (-2)^2}$$
$$= \sqrt{20}$$
$$= 2\sqrt{5} \text{ m s}^{-1}.$$

You should already know the formula for an object moving with constant speed:

$$\text{speed} = \frac{\text{distance travelled}}{\text{time taken}}$$

Similarly, the formula for an object moving with constant velocity is:

$$\text{velocity} = \frac{\text{displacement}}{\text{time taken}}$$

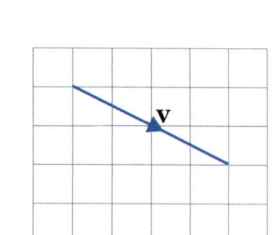

Splitting a velocity into its components

The velocity of a particle travelling north-east at $4\sqrt{2}\,\text{m s}^{-1}$ can be written in the form $(a\mathbf{i} + b\mathbf{j})\,\text{m s}^{-1}$:

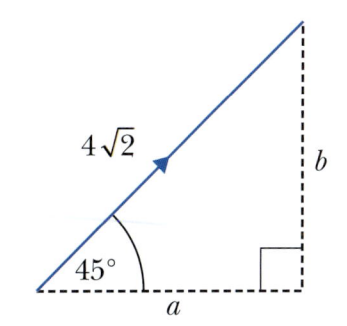

$\cos 45° = \dfrac{a}{4\sqrt{2}}$ and $\sin 45° = \dfrac{b}{4\sqrt{2}}$

$a = 4\sqrt{2} \times \cos 45°$ $\qquad b = 4\sqrt{2} \times \sin 45°$

$a = 4$ $\qquad\qquad\qquad\quad b = 4$

Hence the velocity vector is $(4\mathbf{i} + 4\mathbf{j})\,\text{m s}^{-1}$.

The velocity of a particle travelling on a bearing of 120° at $20\,\text{m s}^{-1}$ can be written in the form $(x\mathbf{i} + y\mathbf{j})\,\text{m s}^{-1}$:

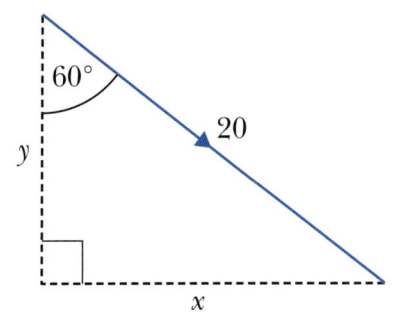

$\sin 60° = \dfrac{x}{20}$ and $\cos 60° = \dfrac{y}{20}$

$x = 20 \times \sin 60°$ $\qquad y = 20 \times \cos 60°$

$x = 10\sqrt{3}$ $\qquad\qquad\quad y = 10$

Hence the velocity vector is $(10\sqrt{3}\mathbf{i} - 10\mathbf{j})\,\text{m s}^{-1}$.

WORKED EXAMPLE 9

An object travels at a constant velocity from point A to point B.
$\overrightarrow{AB} = (32\mathbf{i} - 24\mathbf{j})\,\text{m}$ and the time taken is 4s. Find:

a the velocity **b** the speed.

Answers

a velocity $= \dfrac{\text{displacement}}{\text{time taken}} = \dfrac{32\mathbf{i} - 24\mathbf{j}}{4} = (8\mathbf{i} - 6\mathbf{j})\,\text{m s}^{-1}$

b speed $= \sqrt{(8)^2 + (-6)^2} = 10\,\text{m s}^{-1}$

Consider a boat sailing with velocity $\begin{pmatrix} 3 \\ -2 \end{pmatrix}\,\text{km h}^{-1}$.

At 12 00 hours the boat is at the point A with position vector $\begin{pmatrix} 3 \\ 13 \end{pmatrix}\,\text{km}$ relative to an origin O.

The diagram shows the positions of the boat at 12 00 hours, 1 pm, 2 pm, 3 pm, 4 pm …

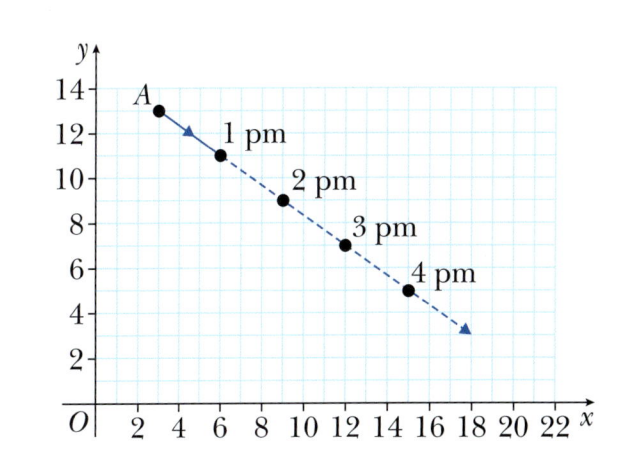

The position at 1 pm $= \begin{pmatrix} 3 \\ 13 \end{pmatrix} + 1\begin{pmatrix} 3 \\ -2 \end{pmatrix} = \begin{pmatrix} 6 \\ 11 \end{pmatrix}$

The position at 2 pm $= \begin{pmatrix} 3 \\ 13 \end{pmatrix} + 2\begin{pmatrix} 3 \\ -2 \end{pmatrix} = \begin{pmatrix} 9 \\ 9 \end{pmatrix}$

The position at 3 pm $= \begin{pmatrix} 3 \\ 13 \end{pmatrix} + 3\begin{pmatrix} 3 \\ -2 \end{pmatrix} = \begin{pmatrix} 12 \\ 7 \end{pmatrix}$

The position at 4 pm $= \begin{pmatrix} 3 \\ 13 \end{pmatrix} + 4\begin{pmatrix} 3 \\ -2 \end{pmatrix} = \begin{pmatrix} 15 \\ 5 \end{pmatrix}$

Hence the position vector, **r**, of the boat t hours after 12 00 hours is given by the expression:

$$\mathbf{r} = \begin{pmatrix} 3 \\ 13 \end{pmatrix} + t\begin{pmatrix} 3 \\ -2 \end{pmatrix}.$$

This leads to the general rule:

> If an object has initial position **a** and moves with a constant velocity **v**, the position vector **r**, at time t, is given by the formula: $\mathbf{r} = \mathbf{a} + t\mathbf{v}$.

Exercise 13.4

1. **a** Displacement = $(21\mathbf{i} + 54\mathbf{j})$ m, time taken = 6 seconds. Find the velocity.
   b Velocity = $(5\mathbf{i} - 6\mathbf{j})\,\text{m s}^{-1}$, time taken = 6 seconds. Find the displacement.
   c Velocity = $(-4\mathbf{i} + 4\mathbf{j})\,\text{km h}^{-1}$, displacement = $(-50\mathbf{i} + 50\mathbf{j})$ km.
   Find the time taken.

2. A car travels from a point A with position vector $(60\mathbf{i} - 40\mathbf{j})$ km to a point B with position vector $(-50\mathbf{i} + 18\mathbf{j})$ km.
   The car travels with constant velocity and takes 5 hours to complete the journey.
   Find the velocity vector.

3. A helicopter flies from a point P with position vector $(50\mathbf{i} + 100\mathbf{j})$ km to a point Q.
   The helicopter flies with a constant velocity of $(30\mathbf{i} - 40\mathbf{j})\,\text{km h}^{-1}$ and takes 2.5 hours to complete the journey. Find the position vector of the point Q.

4. **a** A car travels north-east with a speed of $18\sqrt{2}\,\text{km h}^{-1}$.
   Find the velocity vector of the car.
   b A boat sails on a bearing of $030°$ with a speed of $20\,\text{km h}^{-1}$.
   Find the velocity vector of the boat.
   c A plane flies on a bearing of $240°$ with a speed of $100\,\text{m s}^{-1}$.
   Find the velocity vector of the plane.

5. A particle starts at a point P with position vector $(-80\mathbf{i} + 60\mathbf{j})$ m relative to an origin O.
   The particle travels with velocity $(12\mathbf{i} - 16\mathbf{j})\,\text{m s}^{-1}$.
   a Find the speed of the particle.
   b Find the position vector of the particle after
      i 1 second   **ii** 2 seconds   **iii** 3 seconds.
   c Find the position vector of the particle t seconds after leaving P.

6 At 12 00 hours, a ship leaves a point Q with position vector $(10\mathbf{i} + 38\mathbf{j})$ km relative to an origin O. The ship travels with velocity $(6\mathbf{i} - 8\mathbf{j})$ km h^{-1}.
   a Find the speed of the ship.
   b Find the position vector of the ship at 3 pm.
   c Find the position vector of the ship t hours after leaving Q.
   d Find the time when the ship is at the point with position vector $(61\mathbf{i} - 30\mathbf{j})$ km.

7 At 12 00 hours, a tanker sails from a point P with position vector $(5\mathbf{i} + 12\mathbf{j})$ km relative to an origin O. The tanker sails south-east with a speed of $12\sqrt{2}$ km h^{-1}.
   a Find the velocity vector of the tanker.
   b Find the position vector of the tanker at
      i 14 00 hours   ii 12 45 hours.
   c Find the position vector of the tanker t hours after leaving P.

8 At 12 00 hours, a boat sails from a point P.
   The position vector, $\mathbf{r}$ km, of the boat relative to an origin O, t hours after 12 00 is given by $\mathbf{r} = \begin{pmatrix} 10 \\ 6 \end{pmatrix} + t\begin{pmatrix} 5 \\ 12 \end{pmatrix}$.
   a Write down the position vector of the point P.
   b Write down the velocity vector of the boat.
   c Find the speed of the boat.
   d Find the distance of the boat from P after 4 hours.

9 At 15 00 hours, a submarine departs from point A and travels a distance of 120 km to a point B.
   The position vector, $\mathbf{r}$ km, of the submarine relative to an origin O, t hours after 15 00 is given by $\mathbf{r} = \begin{pmatrix} 15 + 8t \\ 20 + 6t \end{pmatrix}$.
   a Write down the position vector of the point A.
   b Write down the velocity vector of the submarine.
   c Find the position vector of the point B.

10 At 12 00 hours two boats, A and B, have position vectors $(-10\mathbf{i} + 40\mathbf{j})$ km and $(70\mathbf{i} + 10\mathbf{j})$ km and are moving with velocities $(20\mathbf{i} + 10\mathbf{j})$ km h^{-1} and $(-10\mathbf{i} + 30\mathbf{j})$ km h^{-1} respectively.
   a Find the position vectors of A and B at 15 00 hours.
   b Find the distance between A and B at 15 00 hours.

11 At time $t = 0$, boat P leaves the origin and travels with velocity $(3\mathbf{i} + 4\mathbf{j})$ km h^{-1}.
   Also at time $t = 0$, boat Q leaves the point with position vector $(-10\mathbf{i} + 17\mathbf{j})$ km and travels with velocity $(5\mathbf{i} + 2\mathbf{j})$ km h^{-1}.
   a Write down the position vectors of boats A and B after 2 hours.
   b Find the distance between boats P and Q when $t = 2$.

13.5 Interception problems

Vectors can be used to show whether or not two objects meet.

WORKED EXAMPLE 10

At 12 00 hours two objects, A and B, have position vectors $(8\mathbf{i} + 14\mathbf{j})$ m and $(-\mathbf{i} + 2\mathbf{j})$ m and are moving with velocities $(\mathbf{i} - 3\mathbf{j})\,\text{m s}^{-1}$ and $(4\mathbf{i} + \mathbf{j})\,\text{m s}^{-1}$ respectively.

a Show that A and B meet and find the time that they meet.
b Find the position vector of the point where they meet.

Answers

a $\mathbf{r}_A = \begin{pmatrix} 8 \\ 14 \end{pmatrix} + t \begin{pmatrix} 1 \\ -3 \end{pmatrix}$ and $\mathbf{r}_B = \begin{pmatrix} -1 \\ 2 \end{pmatrix} + t \begin{pmatrix} 4 \\ 1 \end{pmatrix}$

If A and B meet $\mathbf{r}_A = \mathbf{r}_B$ for one particular value of t.

$$\begin{pmatrix} 8 \\ 14 \end{pmatrix} + t \begin{pmatrix} 1 \\ -3 \end{pmatrix} = \begin{pmatrix} -1 \\ 2 \end{pmatrix} + t \begin{pmatrix} 4 \\ 1 \end{pmatrix}$$

Using the top row of the vector equation: $8 + t = -1 + 4t$
$$3t = 9$$
$$t = 3$$

Using the bottom row of the vector equation: $14 - 3t = 2 + t$
$$4t = 12$$
$$t = 3$$

Since the vector equation has the solution $t = 3$ the objects A and B meet after 3 hours.

Hence, they meet at 15 00 hours.

b Substituting $t = 3$ into $\mathbf{r}_A = \begin{pmatrix} 8 \\ 14 \end{pmatrix} + t \begin{pmatrix} 1 \\ -3 \end{pmatrix}$ gives

$$\mathbf{r}_A = \begin{pmatrix} 8 \\ 14 \end{pmatrix} + 3 \begin{pmatrix} 1 \\ -3 \end{pmatrix}$$

$$\mathbf{r}_A = \begin{pmatrix} 11 \\ 5 \end{pmatrix}$$

Position vector of point where they meet is $(11\mathbf{i} + 5\mathbf{j})$ m.

WORKED EXAMPLE 11

At 12 00 hours, C is at the point with position vector $(15\mathbf{i} + 2\mathbf{j})$ m and is moving with a velocity of $(-3\mathbf{i} + 2\mathbf{j})\,\text{m s}^{-1}$. At 14 00 hours D is at the point with position vector $(4\mathbf{i} + 12\mathbf{j})$ m and is moving with velocity $(\mathbf{i} - 2\mathbf{j})\,\text{m s}^{-1}$. Show that C and D do not meet.

Answers

When C has been moving for t hours, D has been moving for $(t - 2)$ hours.

$$\mathbf{r}_C = \begin{pmatrix} 15 \\ 2 \end{pmatrix} + t \begin{pmatrix} -3 \\ 2 \end{pmatrix} \quad \text{and} \quad \mathbf{r}_D = \begin{pmatrix} 4 \\ 12 \end{pmatrix} + (t - 2) \begin{pmatrix} 1 \\ -2 \end{pmatrix}$$

If C and D meet $\mathbf{r}_C = \mathbf{r}_D$ for one particular value of t.

$$\begin{pmatrix} 15 \\ 2 \end{pmatrix} + t \begin{pmatrix} -3 \\ 2 \end{pmatrix} = \begin{pmatrix} 4 \\ 12 \end{pmatrix} + (t - 2) \begin{pmatrix} 1 \\ -2 \end{pmatrix}$$

Using the top row of the vector equation: $\quad 15 - 3t = 4 + t - 2$

$$4t = 13$$
$$t = 3.25$$

Using the bottom row of the vector equation: $\quad 2 + 2t = 12 - 2t + 4$

$$4t = 14$$
$$t = 3.5$$

Since there is no value of t that satisfies both rows of the vector equation, the objects do not meet.

Some intercept problems require the use of trigonometry, as shown in the next example.

WORKED EXAMPLE 12

A ship that is travelling at $18\,\text{km h}^{-1}$ on a bearing of $060°$ sends out a distress call.

A lifeboat that is 20 km from the ship and on a bearing of $160°$ from the ship receives the call and sets off immediately. The lifeboat travels in a straight line at constant speed and takes 45 minutes to reach the ship.

a Find the speed of the lifeboat.

b Find the bearing on which the lifeboat travelled.

Answers

a 45 minutes = 0.75 hours

Distance travelled by ship = $0.75 \times 18 = 13.5$ km

Let x = distance travelled by the lifeboat in km

Using the cosine rule:

$x^2 = 20^2 + 13.5^2 - 2 \times 20 \times 13.5 \times \cos 100°$

$x^2 = 676.02\ldots$

$x = 26.0\ldots$

$\text{speed} = \dfrac{\text{distance travelled}}{\text{time taken}}$

$= \dfrac{26.0}{0.75}$

Hence, the speed of the lifeboat is 34.7 km h^{-1}.

b Using the sine rule:

$\dfrac{\sin \theta}{13.5} = \dfrac{\sin 100°}{26.0}$

$\sin \theta = \dfrac{13.5 \times \sin 100°}{26.0}$

$\theta = 30.8°$

The angle made by the direction of the lifeboat with the north line = $30.8 - 20 = 10.8°$.

Hence, the bearing on which the lifeboat travelled is $011°$ (correct to the nearest degree).

Exercise 13.5

1 Determine whether the following pairs of objects meet. If they do meet, find the position vector of the point where they meet and the time at which they meet.

a At 12 00 hours, objects A and B are at points with position vectors $(\mathbf{i} + 2\mathbf{j})$ m and $(11\mathbf{i} + 6\mathbf{j})$ m and are moving with velocities $(5\mathbf{i} + 3\mathbf{j})$ m s^{-1} and $(\mathbf{j})$ m s^{-1} respectively.

b At 12 00 hours, objects C and D, are at points with position vectors $(\mathbf{i} + \mathbf{j})$ m and $(2\mathbf{j})$ m and are moving with velocities $(2\mathbf{i} + 3\mathbf{j})$ m s^{-1} and $(\mathbf{i} + \mathbf{j})$ m s^{-1} respectively.

c At 14 00 hours, ships E and F are at points with position vectors $30\mathbf{j}$ km and $(80\mathbf{i} - 10\mathbf{j})$ km and are travelling with velocities $(20\mathbf{i} + 10\mathbf{j})$ km h^{-1} and $(-10\mathbf{i} + 30\mathbf{j})$ km h^{-1} respectively.

d At 12 00 hours, G is at the point with position vector $(3\mathbf{i} + 3\mathbf{j})$ km and travels with velocity $(4\mathbf{i} + \mathbf{j})$ km h^{-1}. One hour later H leaves the point with position vector $(7\mathbf{i} - 17\mathbf{j})$ km and travels with velocity $(4\mathbf{i} + 8\mathbf{j})$ km h^{-1}.

e At 08 00 hours, M is at the point with position vector $(-5\mathbf{i} + 7\mathbf{j})$ km and travels with a velocity of $(10\mathbf{i} + 10\mathbf{j})$ km h^{-1}. Two hours later N leaves the point with position vector $(18\mathbf{i} + 33\mathbf{j})$ km and travels with velocity $(8\mathbf{i} + 6\mathbf{j})$ km h^{-1}.

2 At 12 00 hours, objects P and Q, are at points with position vectors $(40\mathbf{i} + 10\mathbf{j})$ m and $(-4\mathbf{i} + 54\mathbf{j})$ m and are moving with velocities $(\lambda\mathbf{i} + 8\mathbf{j})$ m s^{-1} and $(2\mathbf{i} + 4\mathbf{j})$ m s^{-1} respectively.

Given that P and Q meet, find the value of λ.

CHALLENGE Q

3 A cargo ship that is travelling due east at 28 km h^{-1} sends out a distress call.

A lifeboat that is 125 km from the cargo ship and on a bearing of 200° from the cargo ship receives the call and sets off immediately. The lifeboat travels in a straight line at constant speed and takes 3 hours to reach the cargo ship.

  a Find the speed of the lifeboat.
  b Find the bearing on which the lifeboat travelled.

13.6 Relative velocity

You have probably heard the saying that 'motion is relative'. The velocity of an object only really has meaning when it is expressed relative to some 'frame of reference'. It is usual to consider objects moving relative to the Earth.

The velocity of one body relative to another is called its relative velocity.

Cambridge IGCSE and O Level Additional Mathematics

CLASS DISCUSSION

Discuss the following three situations with your classmates:

Situation 1
Consider sitting next to the driver of a car that is travelling at $40\,\text{m s}^{-1}$ relative to the Earth. What is the velocity of the driver relative to you?

Situation 2
Consider two cars travelling in the same direction along a motorway at $35\,\text{m s}^{-1}$ and $25\,\text{m s}^{-1}$ relative to the Earth.

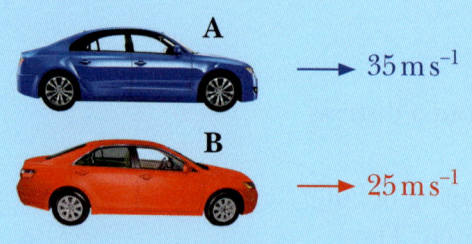

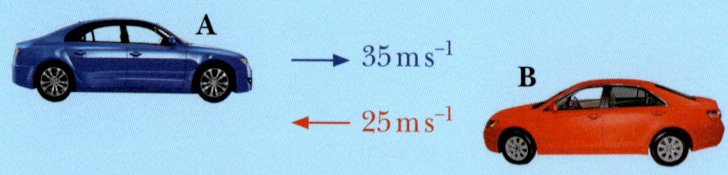

A → $35\,\text{m s}^{-1}$

B → $25\,\text{m s}^{-1}$

What is the velocity of car A relative to car B?
What is the velocity of car B relative to car A?

Situation 3
Consider two cars travelling in opposite directions along a motorway at $35\,\text{m s}^{-1}$ and $25\,\text{m s}^{-1}$ relative to the Earth.

A → $35\,\text{m s}^{-1}$

← $25\,\text{m s}^{-1}$ B

What is the velocity of car A relative to car B?
What is the velocity of car B relative to car A?

Sian can swim at $1\,\text{m s}^{-1}$ in a river where there is no current. (No current means that she is swimming in still water.) If there is no current, Sian will experience no difficulty swimming from a point P on one bank of the river to a point Q directly opposite on the other bank. Sian will simply have to aim directly for the point Q.

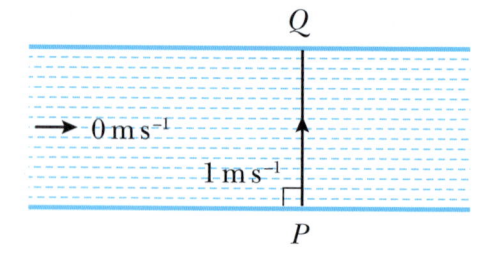

Now consider Sian swimming in the river when a current is flowing at $0.8\,\text{m s}^{-1}$. If Sian starts at point P and aims for the point Q on the opposite bank, she will get carried downstream to a point R because of the current.

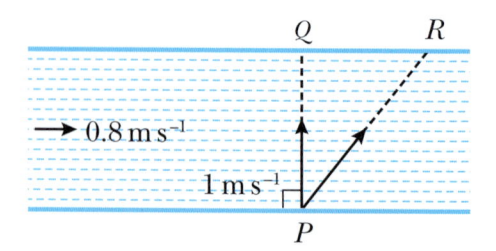

Let $_W\mathbf{v}_E$ = the velocity of the water relative to the Earth

$_S\mathbf{v}_E$ = the velocity of Sian relative to the Earth

$_S\mathbf{v}_W$ = the velocity of Sian relative to the water (i.e. the velocity of Sian in still water).

These vectors can be represented on a vector triangle as:

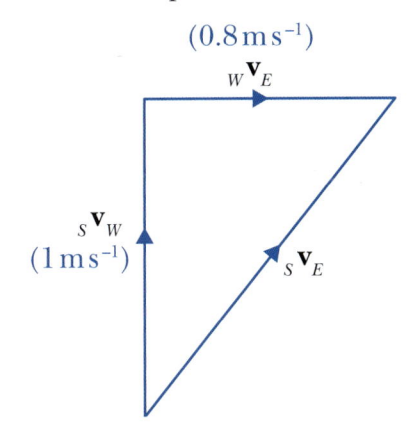

$(0.8\,\text{m}\,\text{s}^{-1})$
$_W\mathbf{v}_E$

$_S\mathbf{v}_W$
$(1\,\text{m}\,\text{s}^{-1})$

$_S\mathbf{v}_E$

using Pythagoras
$|_S\mathbf{v}_E| = \sqrt{1^2 + 0.8^2}$
$|_S\mathbf{v}_E| = 1.28\,\text{m}\,\text{s}^{-1}$ to 3 sf

Now consider Sian swimming directly to the opposite bank of the river when a current is flowing at $0.8\,\text{m}\,\text{s}^{-1}$. Sian will need to aim upstream in order to achieve this.

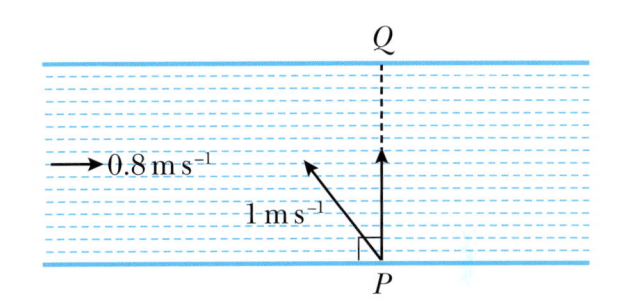

The vector triangle for the velocities is:

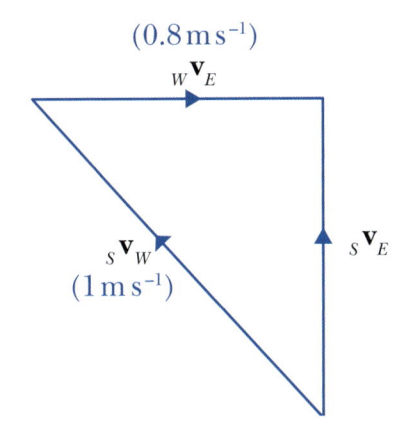

$(0.8\,\text{m}\,\text{s}^{-1})$
$_W\mathbf{v}_E$

$_S\mathbf{v}_W$
$(1\,\text{m}\,\text{s}^{-1})$

$_S\mathbf{v}_E$

using Pythagoras
$|_S\mathbf{v}_E| = \sqrt{1^2 - 0.8^2}$
$|_S\mathbf{v}_E| = 0.6\,\text{m}\,\text{s}^{-1}$

Using the vector triangles above you can write down the rule:

$$_S\mathbf{v}_W + {_W\mathbf{v}_E} = {_S\mathbf{v}_E} \quad \text{or} \quad _S\mathbf{v}_W = {_S\mathbf{v}_E} - {_W\mathbf{v}_E}$$

(This is sometimes written more briefly as: $_S\mathbf{v}_W = \mathbf{v}_S - \mathbf{v}_W$)

The general rule for relative velocity is:

$$_A\mathbf{v}_B = \mathbf{v}_A - \mathbf{v}_B$$

where $_A\mathbf{v}_B$ = the velocity of A relative to B
$\mathbf{v}_A$ = the velocity of A relative to the Earth
$\mathbf{v}_B$ = the velocity of B relative to the Earth.

Cambridge IGCSE and O Level Additional Mathematics

> **WORKED EXAMPLE 13** 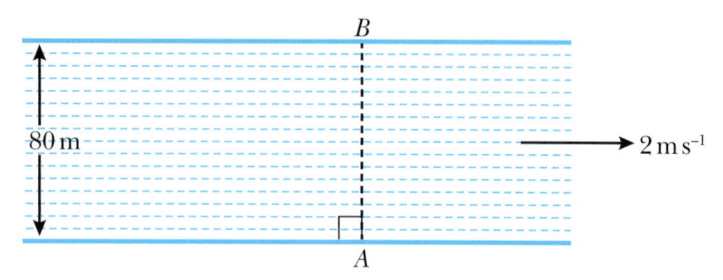
>
> The diagram shows a river 80 m wide, flowing at $2\,\text{m s}^{-1}$ between parallel banks. A motorboat travels in a straight line from a point A to a point B directly opposite A. The motorboat takes 2 minutes to cross the river.
>
> **a** Find the speed of the motorboat in still water.
>
> **b** Find the angle to the bank at which the motorboat was steered.
>
> **Answers**
>
> **a** Distance travelled = 80 m   Time taken = 120 seconds
>
> $$\text{Speed} = \frac{\text{distance travelled}}{\text{time taken}} = \frac{80}{120} = \frac{2}{3}\,\text{m s}^{-1}$$
>
> The velocity vector for the motorboat (M) relative to the Earth (E) is: $_M\mathbf{v}_E$ $(\tfrac{2}{3}\,\text{m s}^{-1})$
>
> The velocity vector for the water (W) relative to the Earth (E) is: $(2\,\text{m s}^{-1})$ $_W\mathbf{v}_E$
>
> The velocity of the motorboat (M) in still water (W) = $_M\mathbf{v}_W$.
>
> Using $_M\mathbf{v}_W + {}_W\mathbf{v}_E = {}_M\mathbf{v}_E$, a vector triangle can be drawn: 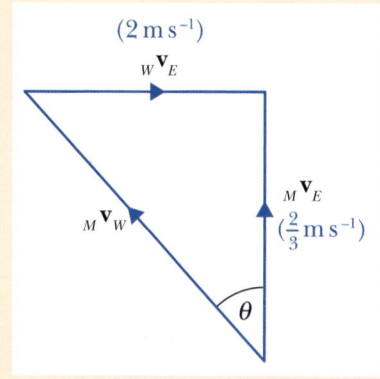
>
> Using Pythagoras $|_M\mathbf{v}_W| = \sqrt{2^2 + \left(\tfrac{2}{3}\right)^2}$
>
> $|_M\mathbf{v}_W| = 2.108\ldots$
>
> Speed of the motorboat in still water = $2.11\,\text{m s}^{-1}$ to 3 sf.
>
> **b** $\theta = \tan^{-1}\left(\dfrac{2}{2/3}\right) = 71.6°$
>
> Hence angle made with bank = $90° - 71.6° = 18.4°$.

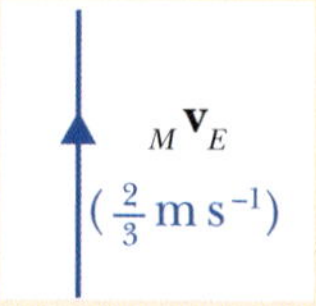

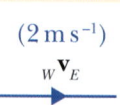

WORKED EXAMPLE 14

A plane, whose speed in still air is 230 km h^{-1}, flies directly from F to G.

G is 460 km from F on a bearing of 060°.

There is a wind of 75 km h^{-1} blowing from the west.

Find the time taken for the flight.

Answers

Using $_P\mathbf{v}_W + {_W}\mathbf{v}_E = {_P}\mathbf{v}_E$, a vector triangle can be drawn:

where $_P\mathbf{v}_W$ = velocity of plane relative to wind

$_W\mathbf{v}_E$ = velocity of wind relative to Earth

$_P\mathbf{v}_E$ = velocity of plane relative to Earth.

Using the sine rule

$$\frac{\sin \theta}{75} = \frac{\sin 30°}{230}$$

$$\theta = \sin^{-1}\left(\frac{75 \times \sin 30°}{230}\right)$$

$$\theta = 9.3835...$$

So third angle of triangle $= 180 - (30 + 9.3835) = 140.6164... = 141°$ to 3 sf.

Using the cosine rule

$$|_P\mathbf{v}_E| = \sqrt{(75)^2 + (230)^2 - 2 \times 75 \times 230 \times \cos 140.6°} = 291.874...$$

$$= 292 \text{ km h}^{-1} \text{ to 3 sf}$$

Time taken $= \dfrac{\text{distance travelled}}{\text{speed}} = \dfrac{460}{291.874...} = 1.576$ hours

Time taken is 1 hour 35 minutes.

Exercise 13.6

1. Arti cycles due north at 15 km h^{-1}.

   Dian runs due east at 12 km h^{-1}.

   Find the speed of Dian relative to Arti.

2. Aroon walks at 4 km h^{-1} on a bearing of 090°.

   Mali runs at 10 km h^{-1} on a bearing of 135°.

   Find the speed of Mali relative to Aroon.

3. A car is travelling due north along a road at 90 km h^{-1}.

   A truck is travelling on a bearing of 300° along a second road at 70 km h^{-1}.

   Find the speed of the truck relative to the car.

4. A river flows at a speed of 4 m s^{-1} between two parallel banks.

   A canoe, whose speed in still water is 3 m s^{-1}, is steered at right angles to the riverbank.

   a Find the resultant speed of the canoe.

   b Find the direction that the canoe travels.

Cambridge IGCSE and O Level Additional Mathematics

5   A river flows at a speed of $7\,\text{m}\,\text{s}^{-1}$ between two parallel banks.

   A boat, whose speed in still water is $4\,\text{m}\,\text{s}^{-1}$, is steered downstream at an angle of 60° to the riverbank.

   a Find the resultant speed of the boat.

   b Find the direction that the boat travels.

6   A river flows between parallel banks.

   The river is 50 m wide and flows at a speed of $1.5\,\text{m}\,\text{s}^{-1}$.

   A boat travels in a straight line from a point P on one bank to a point Q directly opposite to P.

   The boat takes 15 seconds to cross the river.

   a Find the speed of the boat in still water.

   b Find the angle to the bank at which the boat was steered.

7   Raju can row his boat at $6\,\text{m}\,\text{s}^{-1}$ in still water.

   He crosses a river that is 70 m wide and is flowing at a speed of $3\,\text{m}\,\text{s}^{-1}$.

   a Find the angle to the bank at which Raju must steer his boat if he is to reach the point on the opposite bank directly opposite to his starting position.

   b Find the time Raju takes to cross the river.

8   Sakda can paddle his canoe at $5\,\text{m}\,\text{s}^{-1}$ in still water.

   He paddles with his canoe pointing in a direction at an angle of 70° to a riverbank in the upstream direction. The river is flowing at $4\,\text{m}\,\text{s}^{-1}$.

   Find the speed and direction in which he actually travels.

9   Babu can swim at $4\,\text{m}\,\text{s}^{-1}$ in still water.

   He wants to cross a river by the shortest possible route.

   The river is 80 m wide and flows at a speed of $1.5\,\text{m}\,\text{s}^{-1}$.

   a Find the direction in which he must swim.

   b Find the time Babu takes to cross the river.

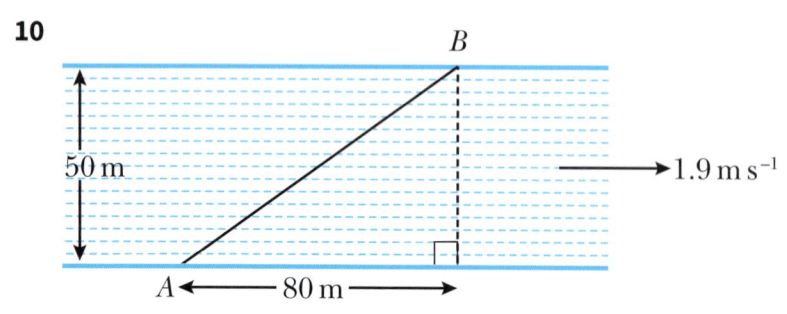

10

   The diagram shows a river 50 m wide, flowing at $1.9\,\text{m}\,\text{s}^{-1}$ between parallel banks.

   A canoe travels in a straight line from a point A on one bank to a point B on the opposite bank 80 m downstream from A. The canoe takes 15 s to cross the river.

a Find the speed of the canoe in still water.

b Find the angle to the bank that the canoe was steered.

11 A river flows between parallel banks.

The river is 150 m wide and flows at a speed of $2.5\,\text{m s}^{-1}$.

A ferry that has a speed of $4\,\text{m s}^{-1}$ in still water travels in a straight line across the river.

It travels from a point A on one bank to a point B, 80 m downstream of A, on the opposite bank. Find the time it takes to travel from A to B.

12 A cyclist travels due north on a straight horizontal road at $6\,\text{m s}^{-1}$.

To the cyclist the wind appears to be blowing from the south-west.

The wind has a constant speed of $15\,\text{m s}^{-1}$.

Find the direction from which the wind is blowing.

13 A plane flies due north from P to Q, a distance of 1200 km, in a time of 2 hours.

A steady wind blows from the south-west at a speed of $160\,\text{km h}^{-1}$.

a Find the speed of the plane in still air.

b Find the direction in which the plane must be headed.

14 An aircraft is steered in the direction 060°.

A steady wind blows from the east at $100\,\text{km h}^{-1}$.

The speed of the aircraft in still air is $300\,\text{km h}^{-1}$.

Find the true velocity of the aircraft.

15 A plane, whose speed in still air is $350\,\text{km h}^{-1}$, flies directly from A to B.

B is 600 km from A on a bearing of 200°.

There is a wind of $100\,\text{km h}^{-1}$ blowing from the south.

Find the time taken for the flight.

16 To a passenger on a boat sailing on a bearing of 040° at $30\,\text{km h}^{-1}$, a jet ski appears to be travelling on a bearing of 135° at $50\,\text{km h}^{-1}$.

Find the true velocity of the jet ski.

17 A car travels due east at $45\,\text{km h}^{-1}$.

The car driver observes a train which is travelling due south at $125\,\text{km h}^{-1}$.

Find the speed and direction of the train relative to the car.

Cambridge IGCSE and O Level Additional Mathematics

13.7 Relative velocity using i, j notation

Relative velocity calculations are often much simpler when working with vectors in component form as demonstrated in the next example.

WORKED EXAMPLE 15

Yacht A has a velocity of $(6\mathbf{i} + 4\mathbf{j})$ km h^{-1} and yacht B has a velocity of $(2\mathbf{i} + 8\mathbf{j})$ km h^{-1}.

a Find the velocity of yacht A relative to yacht B.

b Find the speed of yacht A relative to yacht B.

Answers

a $_A\mathbf{v}_B = \mathbf{v}_A - \mathbf{v}_B$

$= (6\mathbf{i} + 4\mathbf{j}) - (2\mathbf{i} + 8\mathbf{j})$

$= 4\mathbf{i} - 4\mathbf{j}$

Velocity of yacht A relative to yacht $B = (4\mathbf{i} - 4\mathbf{j})$ km h^{-1}.

b using Pythagoras $|_A\mathbf{v}_B| = \sqrt{4^2 + (-4)^2}$

$|_A\mathbf{v}_B| = 4\sqrt{2}$

Speed of yacht A relative to yacht $B = 5.66$ km h^{-1} to 3 sf.

Exercise 13.7

1 $\mathbf{v}_A$ and $\mathbf{v}_B$ are the velocity vectors of two objects A and B.

Find $_A\mathbf{v}_B$ (the velocity of A relative to B) and the speed of A relative to B for each of the following:

a $\mathbf{v}_A = 15\mathbf{i}$ m s^{-1} $\qquad$ $\mathbf{v}_B = 10\mathbf{i}$ m s^{-1}

b $\mathbf{v}_A = 18\mathbf{i}$ m s^{-1} $\qquad$ $\mathbf{v}_B = -8\mathbf{i}$ m s^{-1}

c $\mathbf{v}_A = (18\mathbf{i} + 5\mathbf{j})$ m s^{-1} $\qquad$ $\mathbf{v}_B = (7\mathbf{i} + 3\mathbf{j})$ m s^{-1}

d $\mathbf{v}_A = (2\mathbf{i} - 5\mathbf{j})$ m s^{-1} $\qquad$ $\mathbf{v}_B = (4\mathbf{i} + 8\mathbf{j})$ m s^{-1}

e $\mathbf{v}_A = (-5\mathbf{i} + 5\mathbf{j})$ km h^{-1} $\qquad$ $\mathbf{v}_B = (6\mathbf{i} - 2\mathbf{j})$ km h^{-1}.

2 Ship S sails with a velocity of $(15\mathbf{i} + 12\mathbf{j})$ km h^{-1}.

Ship T sails with a velocity of $(10\mathbf{i} + 7\mathbf{j})$ km h^{-1}.

Find the velocity of S relative to T.

3 Aircraft A has a velocity of $(-5\mathbf{i} + 5\mathbf{j})$ m s^{-1}.

To a passenger on aircraft A, aircraft B appears to be travelling with a velocity of $(8\mathbf{i} - 2\mathbf{j})$ m s^{-1}.

Find the velocity of aircraft B.

4 A ship is sailing south-west with a speed of $16\sqrt{2}$ km h^{-1} and a submarine is travelling with velocity $(20\mathbf{i} + 15\mathbf{j})$ km h^{-1}.

a Find the velocity vector of the ship.

b Find the velocity of the ship relative to the submarine.

5 A plane takes 3 hours to fly from X to Y where $\overrightarrow{XY} = (600\mathbf{i} + 450\mathbf{j})$ km.

A wind is blowing with velocity $(-40\mathbf{i} + 30\mathbf{j})$ km h^{-1}.

  a Find the velocity vector of the plane in still air.

  b Find the bearing on which the plane must be directed.

6 A plane flies from P to Q where $PQ = 280$ km.

The velocity of the plane in still air is $(250\mathbf{i} - 45\mathbf{j})$ km h^{-1}.

A constant wind blows with velocity $(60\mathbf{i} - 60\mathbf{j})$ km h^{-1}.

  a Find the bearing of Q from P.

  b Find the time of flight.

7 A plane flies from an airport A to an airport B.

The position vector of B relative to A is $(1200\mathbf{i} + 240\mathbf{j})$ km.

The velocity of the plane in still air is $(240\mathbf{i} + 120\mathbf{j})$ km h^{-1}.

There is a constant wind blowing and the flight takes 4 hours.

  a Find the velocity vector of the wind.

  b Find the speed of the wind.

  c Find the bearing of the direction from which the wind is blowing.

Summary

Position vectors

$\overrightarrow{AB}$ means the position vector of B relative to A.

$\overrightarrow{AB} = \overrightarrow{OB} - \overrightarrow{OA}$ or $\overrightarrow{AB} = \mathbf{b} - \mathbf{a}$

If an object has initial position $\mathbf{a}$ and moves with a constant velocity $\mathbf{v}$, the position vector $\mathbf{r}$, at time t, is given by the formula: $\mathbf{r} = \mathbf{a} + t\mathbf{v}$.

Velocity

$$\text{Velocity} = \frac{\text{displacement}}{\text{time taken}}$$

Relative velocity

The velocity of one body relative to another is called its relative velocity.

$_A\mathbf{v}_B = \mathbf{v}_A - \mathbf{v}_B$ where $_A\mathbf{v}_B$ = the velocity of A relative to B

$\mathbf{v}_A$ = the velocity of A relative to the Earth

$\mathbf{v}_B$ = the velocity of B relative to the Earth

Examination questions

Worked past paper example

In this question $\begin{pmatrix} 1 \\ 0 \end{pmatrix}$ is a unit vector due east and $\begin{pmatrix} 0 \\ 1 \end{pmatrix}$ is a unit vector due north.

At 12:00 a coastguard, at point O, observes a ship with position vector $\begin{pmatrix} 16 \\ 12 \end{pmatrix}$ km relative to O. The ship is moving at a steady speed of $10\,km\,h^{-1}$ on a bearing of 330°.

a Find the value of p such that $\begin{pmatrix} -5 \\ p \end{pmatrix}$ km h^{-1} represents the velocity of the ship. [2]

b Write down, in terms of t, the position vector of the ship, relative to O, t hours after 12 00. [2]

c Find the time when the ship is due north of O. [2]

d Find the distance of the ship from O at this time. [2]

Cambridge IGCSE Additional Mathematics 0606 Paper 21 Q7i-iv Nov 2012

Answers

a $\cos 60° = \dfrac{x}{10}$ and $\sin 60° = \dfrac{y}{10}$

$x = 10 \times \cos 60°$ $\qquad y = 10 \times \sin 60°$

$x = 5$ $\qquad\qquad\qquad y = 5\sqrt{3}$

The velocity vector of the ship is $\begin{pmatrix} -5 \\ 5\sqrt{3} \end{pmatrix}$ m s^{-1}.

Hence, $p = 5\sqrt{3}$.

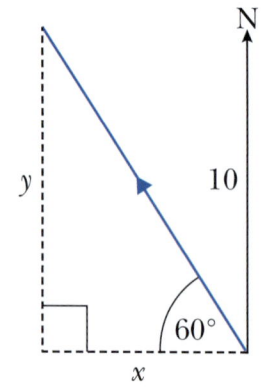

b $\mathbf{r} = \begin{pmatrix} 16 \\ 12 \end{pmatrix} + t\begin{pmatrix} -5 \\ 5\sqrt{3} \end{pmatrix} = \begin{pmatrix} 16 - 5t \\ 12 + 5\sqrt{3}t \end{pmatrix}$

c $\mathbf{r} = \begin{pmatrix} 16 - 5t \\ 12 + 5\sqrt{3}t \end{pmatrix}$

Ship is due north of O when

$16 - 5t = 0$

$t = 3.2$

Time $= 15\ 12$

d When $t = 3.2$, $\mathbf{r} = \begin{pmatrix} 16 - 5 \times 3.2 \\ 12 + 5\sqrt{3} \times 3.2 \end{pmatrix} = \begin{pmatrix} 0 \\ 12 + 16\sqrt{3} \end{pmatrix}$

Distance of ship from $O = 12 + 16\sqrt{3} = 39.7$ km to 3 sf.

Exercise 13.8
Exam Exercise

1

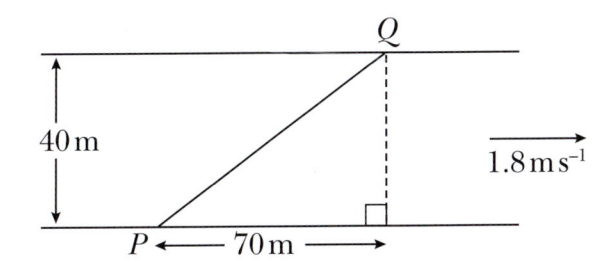

The diagram shows a river with parallel banks. The river is 40 m wide and is flowing with a speed of $1.8\,\mathrm{m\,s^{-1}}$. A canoe travels in a straight line from a point P on one bank to a point Q on the opposite bank 70 m downstream from P. Given that the canoe takes 12 s to travel from P to Q, calculate the speed of the canoe in still water and the angle to the bank that the canoe was steered. [8]

Cambridge IGCSE Additional Mathematics 0606 Paper 21 Q9 Nov 2013

2 Relative to an origin O, the position vectors of the points A and B are $2\mathbf{i} - 3\mathbf{j}$ and $11\mathbf{i} + 42\mathbf{j}$ respectively.

   a Write down an expression for $\overrightarrow{AB}$. [2]

   The point C lies on AB such that $\overrightarrow{AC} = \frac{1}{3}\overrightarrow{AB}$.

   b Find the length of $\overrightarrow{OC}$. [4]

   The point D lies on $\overrightarrow{OA}$ such that $\overrightarrow{DC}$ is parallel to $\overrightarrow{OB}$.

   c Find the position vector of D. [2]

Cambridge IGCSE Additional Mathematics 0606 Paper 21 Q8i,ii,iii Jun 2012

3

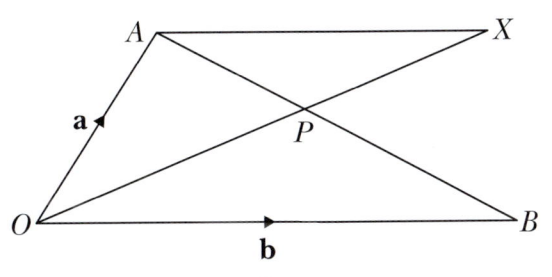

In the diagram $\overrightarrow{OA} = \mathbf{a}$, $\overrightarrow{OB} = \mathbf{b}$ and $\overrightarrow{AP} = \frac{2}{5}\overrightarrow{AB}$.

   a Given that $\overrightarrow{OX} = \mu\overrightarrow{OP}$, where μ is a constant, express $\overrightarrow{OX}$ in terms of μ, $\mathbf{a}$ and $\mathbf{b}$. [3]

   b Given also that $\overrightarrow{AX} = \lambda\overrightarrow{OB}$, where λ is a constant, use a vector method to find the value of μ and of λ. [5]

Cambridge IGCSE Additional Mathematics 0606 Paper 21 Q8i,ii Nov 2011

Cambridge IGCSE and O Level Additional Mathematics

4 Relative to an origin O, the position vectors of the points A and B are $\mathbf{i} - 4\mathbf{j}$ and $7\mathbf{i} + 20\mathbf{j}$ respectively. The point C lies on AB and is such that $\overrightarrow{AC} = \frac{2}{3}\overrightarrow{AB}$. Find the position vector of C and the magnitude of this vector. [5]

Cambridge IGCSE Additional Mathematics 0606 Paper 21 Q3 Jun 2011

5 A plane, whose speed in still air is $250\,\text{km}\,\text{h}^{-1}$ flies directly from A to B, where B is $500\,\text{km}$ from A on a bearing of $060°$. There is a constant wind of $80\,\text{km}\,\text{h}^{-1}$ blowing from the south. Find, to the nearest minute, the time taken for the flight. [7]

Cambridge IGCSE Additional Mathematics 0606 Paper 21 Q9 Nov 2010

Chapter 14
Matrices

This section will show you how to:

- display information in the form of a matrix of any order and interpret the data in a given matrix
- solve problems involving the calculation of the sum and product (where appropriate) of two matrices and interpret the results
- calculate the product of a scalar quantity and a matrix
- use the algebra of 2×2 matrices (including the zero and identity matrix)
- calculate the determinant and inverse of a non-singular 2×2 matrix and solve simultaneous linear equations.

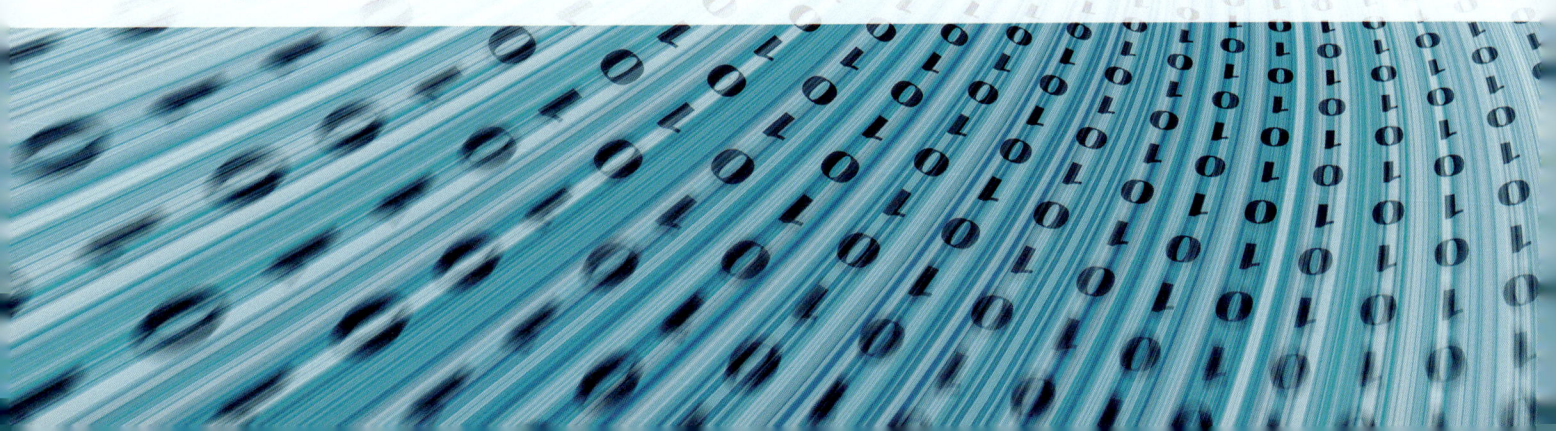

Cambridge IGCSE and O Level Additional Mathematics

14.1 Addition, subtraction and multiplication by a scalar

You have already learnt how to add, subtract and multiply matrices by a scalar.

You should know that it is only possible to add or subtract two matrices when the **order** of the two matrices is the same.

The matrix $\begin{pmatrix} 5 & 1 & 0 \\ 2 & 4 & 3 \end{pmatrix}$ has order 2×3. (2 **rows** and 3 **columns**)

WORKED EXAMPLE 1

Write down the order of the matrix $\begin{pmatrix} 4 & 1 & 3 & 4 \\ 1 & 5 & 0 & 7 \end{pmatrix}$.

Answers

$\begin{pmatrix} 4 & 1 & 3 & 4 \\ 1 & 5 & 0 & 7 \end{pmatrix}$ The matrix has 2 rows and 4 columns.

The order is 2×4.

WORKED EXAMPLE 2

$A = \begin{pmatrix} 1 & -3 & 7 \\ -1 & 2 & 6 \end{pmatrix} \qquad B = \begin{pmatrix} 5 & 2 & 1 \\ 0 & -1 & 3 \end{pmatrix}$

Find **a** $3A$,   **b** $A + B$,   **c** $B - A$.

Answers

a $3A = 3\begin{pmatrix} 1 & -3 & 7 \\ -1 & 2 & 6 \end{pmatrix}$ multiply each number inside **A** by 3

$= \begin{pmatrix} 3 & -9 & 21 \\ -3 & 6 & 18 \end{pmatrix}$

b $A + B = \begin{pmatrix} 1 & -3 & 7 \\ -1 & 2 & 6 \end{pmatrix} + \begin{pmatrix} 5 & 2 & 1 \\ 0 & -1 & 3 \end{pmatrix}$ add corresponding numbers

$= \begin{pmatrix} 6 & -1 & 8 \\ -1 & 1 & 9 \end{pmatrix}$

c $A - B = \begin{pmatrix} 1 & -3 & 7 \\ -1 & 2 & 6 \end{pmatrix} - \begin{pmatrix} 5 & 2 & 1 \\ 0 & -1 & 3 \end{pmatrix}$ subtract corresponding numbers

$= \begin{pmatrix} -4 & -5 & 6 \\ -1 & 3 & 3 \end{pmatrix}$

> **CLASS DISCUSSION**
>
> **A**, **B**, **C** are matrices of the same order.
> Discuss with your classmates whether the following statements are always true.
> - **A** + **B** = **B** + **A**
> - **A** − **B** = **B** − **A**
> - **A** + (**B** + **C**) = (**A** + **B**) + **C**

Exercise 14.1

1 Write down the order of these matrices.

a $\begin{pmatrix} 5 & 1 \\ 0 & -1 \end{pmatrix}$
b $\begin{pmatrix} 2 \\ 5 \end{pmatrix}$
c $\begin{pmatrix} 3 & 2 & 4 \\ 1 & 0 & 1 \\ 0 & 5 & 0 \end{pmatrix}$
d $\begin{pmatrix} 6 & 4 & 1 & 3 & 7 \end{pmatrix}$

2 $\mathbf{A} = \begin{pmatrix} 3 & 4 \\ 1 & 5 \end{pmatrix}$ $\mathbf{B} = \begin{pmatrix} -2 & 0 \\ 1 & 2 \end{pmatrix}$

Find

a 2**A**
b 5**B**
c **A** + **B**
d **A** − **B**
e 2**A** + 5**B**
f 3(**A** + **B**)
g $\mathbf{A} - \frac{1}{2}\mathbf{B}$
h $2\mathbf{A} + \frac{1}{2}\mathbf{B}$.

3 $\begin{pmatrix} 2 & 0 & 1 \\ 4 & 3 & x \end{pmatrix} - \begin{pmatrix} -1 & -3 & 0 \\ 2 & 4 & 5 \end{pmatrix} = \begin{pmatrix} 3 & y & 1 \\ 2 & -1 & 2 \end{pmatrix}$

4 $\mathbf{A} = \begin{pmatrix} 7 & -2 \\ 3 & 5 \end{pmatrix}$ $\mathbf{B} = \begin{pmatrix} 4 & 1 \\ -1 & 0 \end{pmatrix}$ $\mathbf{C} = \begin{pmatrix} 5 & 0 \\ 3 & -2 \end{pmatrix}$

Find

a **A** + **B**
b **B** + **A**
c **A** − **B**
d **B** − **A**
e **A** + (**B** + **C**)
f (**A** + **B**) + **C**.

Comment on your results.

5 A shop sells electric kettles and toasters.

The table below shows the number of sales over a three-day period.

	Day 1	Day 2	Day 3
kettle	20	15	18
toaster	15	20	14

a Write down 3 matrices whose sum shows the total number of sales for kettles and the total number of sales for toasters.

b Calculate this sum.

14.2 Matrix products

You have already learnt how to multiply matrices.

You should know that it is only possible to multiply two matrices when the number of columns in the first matrix is the same as the number of rows in the second matrix.

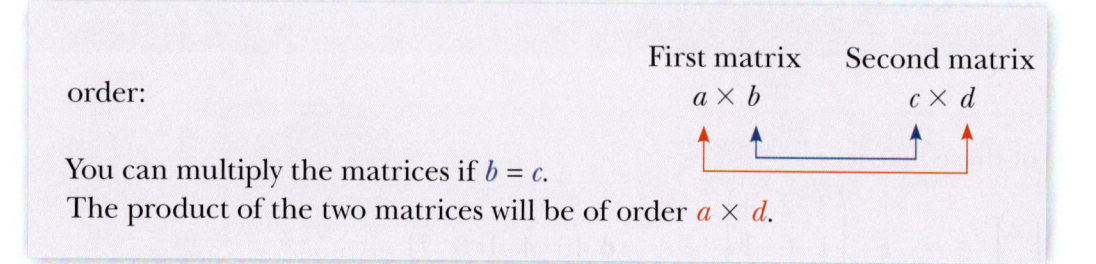

order: First matrix   Second matrix
                         $a \times b$ $c \times d$

You can multiply the matrices if $b = c$.
The product of the two matrices will be of order $a \times d$.

CLASS DISCUSSION

A, B, C, D and **E** are matrices.

The order of each of these five matrices is shown in the table.

A	B	C	D	E
1×2	3×4	2×3	3×1	4×2

It is possible to obtain a 4×4 matrix by performing the matrix product **ECB**:

         E   C   B
      4×2 2×3 3×4

Find which of the following are possible using the matrices **A, B, C, D** and **E** and matrix multiplication. [You must use 2 or more matrices and you may use a matrix more than once.]

1×1	1×2	1×3	1×4
2×1	2×2	2×3	2×4
3×1	3×2	3×3	3×4
4×1	4×2	4×3	4×4

WORKED EXAMPLE 3

Work out $\begin{pmatrix} 5 & 1 & 0 \\ 2 & 4 & 3 \end{pmatrix} \begin{pmatrix} 1 & 2 \\ 6 & 3 \\ 1 & 0 \end{pmatrix}$.

Answers

First consider the order of the matrices: $2 \times 3 \quad 3 \times 2$. The answer will be 2×2.

$\begin{pmatrix} 5 & 1 & 0 \\ 2 & 4 & 3 \end{pmatrix} \begin{pmatrix} 1 & 2 \\ 6 & 3 \\ 1 & 0 \end{pmatrix} = \begin{pmatrix} * & * \\ * & * \end{pmatrix}$

You must now multiply each row in the first matrix with each column in the second matrix to find the missing numbers.

$5 \times 1 + 1 \times 6 + 0 \times 1 = 11$ $5 \times 2 + 1 \times 3 + 0 \times 0 = 13$

$2 \times 1 + 4 \times 6 + 3 \times 1 = 29$ $2 \times 2 + 4 \times 3 + 3 \times 0 = 16$

$\begin{pmatrix} 5 & 1 & 0 \\ 2 & 4 & 3 \end{pmatrix} \begin{pmatrix} 1 & 2 \\ 6 & 3 \\ 1 & 0 \end{pmatrix} = \begin{pmatrix} 11 & 13 \\ 29 & 16 \end{pmatrix}$

CLASS DISCUSSION

For 2×2 matrix multiplication, discuss and decide which of the following statements are always true:

- **AB = BA**
- **A(B + C) = AB + AC**
- **A(B + C) = BA + CA**
- **A(BC) = (AB)C**
- if **O** is the zero matrix $\begin{pmatrix} 0 & 0 \\ 0 & 0 \end{pmatrix}$, then **AO = OA = O**
- if **I** is the identity matrix $\begin{pmatrix} 1 & 0 \\ 0 & 1 \end{pmatrix}$, then **AI = IA = A**
- if k is a constant then $\mathbf{A}(k\mathbf{B}) = k(\mathbf{AB})$.

Exercise 14.2

1. $A = \begin{pmatrix} 2 & 2 \\ 1 & 3 \end{pmatrix}$ $B = \begin{pmatrix} 3 & 0 \\ 1 & -2 \\ 2 & 4 \end{pmatrix}$ $C = \begin{pmatrix} 0 & 0 \\ 0 & 0 \end{pmatrix}$ $D = \begin{pmatrix} 1 \\ 4 \end{pmatrix}$ $E = \begin{pmatrix} 1 & 0 \\ 0 & 1 \end{pmatrix}$

   Find, where possible:

   a AB   b BA   c BC   d BD

   e BE   f ED   g BAD   h ACED

2. $A = \begin{pmatrix} -3 & 1 \\ 1 & 2 \\ 2 & -5 \end{pmatrix}$ $B = \begin{pmatrix} 4 & 1 & 3 \\ 1 & 5 & 0 \end{pmatrix}$ $C = \begin{pmatrix} 3 \\ 2 \end{pmatrix}$

   Write down, but do not evaluate, matrix products that may be calculated from the matrices **A**, **B** and **C**.
   [You may use a matrix only once in each product.]

3. $A = \begin{pmatrix} 3 & 2 \\ 1 & -5 \end{pmatrix}$ $B = \begin{pmatrix} 1 & 4 \\ -2 & 3 \end{pmatrix}$

   Find **BA**.

4. $A = \begin{pmatrix} -2 & 1 & 3 \end{pmatrix}$ $B = \begin{pmatrix} 3 & 1 \\ 2 & 0 \\ -1 & -6 \end{pmatrix}$

   Find **AB**.

5. $A = \begin{pmatrix} 4 & 1 \\ 1 & -2 \end{pmatrix}$ $B = \begin{pmatrix} 2 & -12 \\ -3 & 60 \end{pmatrix}$ $C = \begin{pmatrix} 3 \\ 2 \\ -5 \end{pmatrix}$

   a Calculate **AB**.   b Calculate **BC**.

6. $A = \begin{pmatrix} 3 & -1 \\ 5 & -2 \end{pmatrix}$ $B = \begin{pmatrix} 4 & 0 \\ -2 & 3 \end{pmatrix}$

   Find matrix **X** such that $X = B^2 + 4A$.

7. $A = \begin{pmatrix} 5 & 1 \\ 3 & 2 \end{pmatrix}$ $B = \begin{pmatrix} 1 & -2 \\ 3 & 0 \end{pmatrix}$ $C = \begin{pmatrix} 2 \\ 5 \end{pmatrix}$

   Calculate   a AB   b BA   c BC.

8. $A = \begin{pmatrix} 1 & -3 & 7 \\ -1 & 2 & 6 \end{pmatrix}$ $B = \begin{pmatrix} 4 & 1 \\ -1 & 2 \end{pmatrix}$

   Calculate   a 5A   b B^2 c BA.

9. $A = \begin{pmatrix} 0 & 1 \\ -1 & 2 \end{pmatrix}$

   Find the value of p and the value of q for which $pA^2 + qA = I$, where **I** is the identity matrix.

Chapter 14: Matrices

14.3 Practical applications of matrix products

Matrix multiplication can be used in practical situations, as shown in the next two examples.

WORKED EXAMPLE 4

A shop sells TVs and radios.

The table below shows the sales on a particular day.

TV	Radio
8	15

A TV costs $600 and a radio costs $150.

a Write down 2 matrices whose product shows the total value of the sales that day.

b Calculate this product.

Answers

a $\begin{pmatrix} 8 & 15 \end{pmatrix} \begin{pmatrix} 600 \\ 150 \end{pmatrix} = (*)$ the orders are $1 \times 2 \quad 2 \times 1 = 1 \times 1$

Where $* =$ total value of the sales.

b $\begin{pmatrix} 8 & 15 \end{pmatrix} \begin{pmatrix} 600 \\ 150 \end{pmatrix} = (*)$ multiply the row by the column to find the missing number

$8 \times 600 + 15 \times 150 = 7050$

$\begin{pmatrix} 8 & 15 \end{pmatrix} \begin{pmatrix} 600 \\ 15 \end{pmatrix} = (7050)$

So, total value of the sales = $7050.

WORKED EXAMPLE 5

An airline company has 3 types of aircraft, A, B and C.

It has 10 of type A, 6 of type B and 4 of type C.

Each aircraft has Economy, Premium Economy, Business and First class seats.

The table shows the number of each type on the aircrafts.

	Economy	Premium Economy	Business	First class
type A	390	40	80	10
type B	240	40	50	15
type C	120	40	50	15

a i Write down 2 matrices whose product shows the total number of seats available in each class.

  ii Calculate this product.

Each day the aircrafts make one flight.

The table below shows the percentage of seats empty in each class on a particular day.

Economy	Premium Economy	Business	First class
5%	10%	15%	20%

b i Write down a matrix whose product with the matrix in **part a ii** gives the total number of empty seats on that day.

  ii Calculate this product.

Answers

a i $(10 \ 6 \ 4) \begin{pmatrix} 390 & 40 & 80 & 10 \\ 240 & 40 & 50 & 15 \\ 120 & 40 & 50 & 15 \end{pmatrix} = (* \ * \ * \ *)$

the orders are $1 \times 3 \qquad 3 \times 4 = 1 \times 4$

  ii $10 \times 390 + 6 \times 240 + 4 \times 120 = 5820$ Economy
$10 \times 40 \ + 6 \times 40 \ + 4 \times 40 \ = 800$ Premium Economy
$10 \times 80 \ + 6 \times 50 \ + 4 \times 50 \ = 1300$ Business
$10 \times 10 \ + 6 \times 15 \ + 4 \times 15 \ = 250$ First class

$(10 \ 6 \ 4) \begin{pmatrix} 390 & 40 & 80 & 10 \\ 240 & 40 & 50 & 15 \\ 120 & 40 & 50 & 15 \end{pmatrix} = (5820 \ 800 \ 1300 \ 250)$

b i $\begin{pmatrix} 0.05 \\ 0.1 \\ 0.15 \\ 0.2 \end{pmatrix}$

  ii $(5820 \ 800 \ 1300 \ 250) \begin{pmatrix} 0.05 \\ 0.1 \\ 0.15 \\ 0.2 \end{pmatrix} = (*)$ multiply the row by the column to find *

the orders are $1 \times 4 \qquad 4 \times 1 = 1 \times 1$

$5820 \times 0.05 + 800 \times 0.1 + 1300 \times 0.15 + 250 \times 0.2 = 616$

$(5820 \ 800 \ 1300 \ 250) \begin{pmatrix} 0.05 \\ 0.1 \\ 0.15 \\ 0.2 \end{pmatrix} = (616)$

So, there were a total of 616 empty seats.

Exercise 14.3

1 Kiera buys 2 dresses, 5 blouses and 1 coat.

The table below shows the cost of each of these items.

Dress	Blouse	Coat
$60	$30	$100

a Write down 2 matrices whose product shows the total cost of the clothes.

b Calculate this product.

2 In an athletics competition, a team won 5 gold medals, 9 silver medals and 14 bronze medals.

The table below shows the number of points scored for each medal.

Gold	Silver	Bronze
5	3	1

a Write down 2 matrices whose product shows the total points scored by the team.

b Calculate this product.

3 Four football teams each play ten matches.

The teams are called the Reds, the Blues, the Greens and the Yellows.

The table shows their results.

	Won	Drawn	Lost
Reds	5	3	2
Blues	4	3	3
Greens	3	4	3
Yellows	2	4	4

A win earns 3 points, a draw earns 1 point and a loss earns 0 points.

a Write down 2 matrices whose product shows the total number of points earned by each team.

b Calculate this product.

4 A model shop sells three model-making kits, A, B and C.

The table shows the number of kits sold over a two-week period.

	A	B	C
week 1	19	20	15
week 2	18	18	16

Kit A costs $50, kit B costs $60 and kit C costs $80.

a Write down 2 matrices whose product shows the total amount of money taken each week.

b Calculate this product.

Cambridge IGCSE and O Level Additional Mathematics

5 Rafiu takes two multiple choice tests, each with 20 questions.

A correct answer scores 2 marks, an incorrect answer loses 1 mark and if no answer is given, 0 marks is scored.

His responses are summarised in the table.

	Test 1	Test 2
correct answer	14	13
incorrect answer	4	2
no answer	2	5

a Write down 2 matrices whose product shows his score for each test.

b Calculate this product.

6 A classic car event is held over 2 days.

The first table shows the ticket price, in $, for adults, students and children.

The second table shows the number of tickets sold for adults, students and children.

	Ticket prices ($)	
	Day 1	Day 2
adult	20	15
student	12	10
child	6	5

	Tickets sold	
	Day 1	Day 2
adult	500	600
student	100	150
child	50	50

a i Write down 2 matrices whose product shows the amount of ticket money taken on Day 1.

  ii Calculate this product.

b i Write down 2 matrices whose product shows the amount of ticket money taken on Day 2.

  ii Calculate this product.

c Find the total amount of money taken over the two days.

7 A company produces three different wooden figures: an elephant, a hippopotamus and a giraffe.

Each wooden figure has to be carved, sanded and then polished.

The number of minutes required for each of these three stages and the cost, in $ per minute, are shown in the table.

	Number of minutes required			Cost per minute ($)
	Elephant	Hippopotamus	Giraffe	
carving	70	60	80	0.40
sanding	15	15	20	0.15
polishing	12	10	15	0.15

One day the company makes 60 elephants, 40 hippopotamuses and 50 giraffes.

a Write down 3 matrices whose product shows the total cost of producing all of these wooden figures.

b Calculate this product.

8 A company produces two types of biscuits: X and Y.

The biscuits are made from butter, sugar and flour.

The percentages of butter, sugar and flour needed to produce each biscuit are shown in the table.

	Percentage		
	Butter	Sugar	Flour
biscuit X	25	35	40
biscuit Y	20	30	50

Each day 800 kg of biscuit X and 600 kg of biscuit Y are produced.

Butter costs $2.30 per kg, sugar costs $1.50 per kg and flour costs $1.20 per kg.

a Write down 3 matrices whose product shows the total cost of the daily products.

b Calculate this product.

9 A clothing factory produces skirts, dresses, shirts and trousers.

Each item of clothing has to be cut, sewn and pressed.

The number of minutes required for each of these three stages and the cost, in $ per minute, are shown in the table.

	Number of minutes required				Cost per minute ($)
	Skirt	Dress	Shirt	Trousers	
cutting	10	12	15	12	0.40
sewing	50	160	180	100	0.60
pressing	2	4	4	3	0.30

One day the factory produces 100 skirts, 200 dresses, 200 shirts and 150 trousers.

a Write down 3 matrices whose product shows the total cost of producing all of these items.

b Calculate this product.

10 Farrida takes two multiple choice tests, each with 10 questions.

A correct answer scores 5 marks, an incorrect answer loses 1 mark and if no answer is given, 0 marks are scored.

Her final total mark is the sum of 60% of her mark for Test 1 and 40% of her mark for Test 2.

Farrida's responses are summarised in the table.

	Test 1	Test 2
correct answer	4	5
incorrect answer	4	2
no answer	2	3

a Write down 3 matrices whose product shows Farrida's final total score.

b Calculate this product.

14.4 The inverse of a 2 × 2 matrix

If $\mathbf{AB} = \mathbf{I}$, where $\mathbf{I}$ is the identity matrix then $\mathbf{A}$ and $\mathbf{B}$ are said to be **inverse** matrices.

The inverse of matrix $\mathbf{A}$ is denoted by $\mathbf{A}^{-1}$.

So, $\mathbf{AA}^{-1} = \mathbf{A}^{-1}\mathbf{A} = \mathbf{I}$.

The inverse matrix is calculated using the following formula:

$$\text{If } \mathbf{A} = \begin{pmatrix} a & b \\ c & d \end{pmatrix} \text{ then } \mathbf{A}^{-1} = \frac{1}{|\mathbf{A}|}\begin{pmatrix} d & -b \\ -c & a \end{pmatrix}, \text{ where } |\mathbf{A}| = ad - bc.$$

$|\mathbf{A}|$ is called the **determinant** of the matrix.

The steps to find the determinant of the matrix $\mathbf{A} = \begin{pmatrix} 3 & 5 \\ 2 & 4 \end{pmatrix}$ are:

- Multiply the numbers on the leading diagonal. 3×4
- Multiply the numbers on the other diagonal. 2×5
- Subtract. $|\mathbf{A}| = 3 \times 4 - 2 \times 5 = 2$.

The steps for finding the inverse of the matrix $\mathbf{A} = \begin{pmatrix} 3 & 5 \\ 2 & 4 \end{pmatrix}$ are:

Step 1: Calculate the determinant $|\mathbf{A}| = 3 \times 4 - 2 \times 5 = 2$.

Step 2: Swap the numbers on the leading diagonal to give $\begin{pmatrix} 4 & 5 \\ 2 & 3 \end{pmatrix}$.

Step 3: Change the signs of the numbers on the other diagonal to give $\begin{pmatrix} 4 & -5 \\ -2 & 3 \end{pmatrix}$.

Step 4: Divide by the determinant $\mathbf{A}^{-1} = \frac{1}{2}\begin{pmatrix} 4 & -5 \\ -2 & 3 \end{pmatrix}$ or $\mathbf{A}^{-1} = \begin{pmatrix} 2 & -2\frac{1}{2} \\ -1 & 1\frac{1}{2} \end{pmatrix}$.

> **Hint:**
> $|\mathbf{A}|$ can also be written as det $\mathbf{A}$.

A matrix has no inverse when the determinant is zero because you cannot divide by zero.

A matrix with no inverse is called a **singular** matrix.

A matrix with an inverse is called a **non-singular** matrix.

WORKED EXAMPLE 6

a Given that $\mathbf{A} = \begin{pmatrix} 2 & -5 \\ -3 & 9 \end{pmatrix}$, find $\mathbf{A}^{-1}$.

b Hence find the matrix $\mathbf{M}$ such that $\mathbf{AM} = \begin{pmatrix} 6 & 0 \\ 9 & -3 \end{pmatrix}$.

Answers

a $\mathbf{A} = \begin{pmatrix} 2 & -5 \\ -3 & 9 \end{pmatrix}$

$|\mathbf{A}| = (2 \times 9) - (-3 \times -5) = 18 - 15 = 3$

$\mathbf{A}^{-1} = \dfrac{1}{3}\begin{pmatrix} 9 & 5 \\ 3 & 2 \end{pmatrix}$
- swap the numbers on the leading diagonal
- change the signs of the numbers on the other diagonal
- divide by the determinant

$\mathbf{A}^{-1} = \begin{pmatrix} 3 & 1\frac{2}{3} \\ 1 & \frac{2}{3} \end{pmatrix}$

b $\mathbf{AM} = \begin{pmatrix} 6 & 0 \\ 9 & -3 \end{pmatrix}$

pre-multiply both sides by $\mathbf{A}^{-1}$

$\mathbf{A}^{-1}\mathbf{AM} = \mathbf{A}^{-1}\begin{pmatrix} 6 & 0 \\ 9 & -3 \end{pmatrix}$

$\mathbf{AA}^{-1} = \mathbf{I}$ and $\mathbf{A}^{-1} = \dfrac{1}{3}\begin{pmatrix} 9 & 5 \\ 3 & 2 \end{pmatrix}$

$\mathbf{M} = \dfrac{1}{3}\begin{pmatrix} 9 & 5 \\ 3 & 2 \end{pmatrix}\begin{pmatrix} 6 & 0 \\ 9 & -3 \end{pmatrix}$

$\mathbf{M} = \dfrac{1}{3}\begin{pmatrix} 99 & -15 \\ 36 & -6 \end{pmatrix}$

$\mathbf{M} = \begin{pmatrix} 33 & -5 \\ 12 & -2 \end{pmatrix}$

WORKED EXAMPLE 7

$$P = \begin{pmatrix} 2 & 3 \\ 1 & 4 \end{pmatrix} \quad Q = \begin{pmatrix} 12 & 23 \\ 2 & 13 \end{pmatrix}$$

a Find the inverse matrix P^{-1}.

b Find the matrix X such that $XP = Q$.

Answers

a $P = \begin{pmatrix} 2 & 3 \\ 1 & 4 \end{pmatrix}$

$|P| = (2 \times 4) - (1 \times 3) = 8 - 3 = 5$

$P^{-1} = \dfrac{1}{5}\begin{pmatrix} 4 & -3 \\ -1 & 2 \end{pmatrix}$
- swap the numbers on the leading diagonal

$P^{-1} = \dfrac{1}{5}\begin{pmatrix} 4 & -3 \\ -1 & 2 \end{pmatrix}$
- change the signs of the numbers on the other diagonal
- divide by the determinant

b Find the matrix X such that $XP = Q$.

$XP = Q$ post-multiply both sides by P^{-1}

$XPP^{-1} = QP^{-1}$ $PP^{-1} = I$

$X = \begin{pmatrix} 12 & 23 \\ 2 & 13 \end{pmatrix} \dfrac{1}{5}\begin{pmatrix} 4 & -3 \\ -1 & 2 \end{pmatrix}$ use $A(kB) = k(AB)$

$X = \dfrac{1}{5}\begin{pmatrix} 12 & 23 \\ 2 & 13 \end{pmatrix}\begin{pmatrix} 4 & -3 \\ -1 & 2 \end{pmatrix}$

$X = \dfrac{1}{5}\begin{pmatrix} 25 & 10 \\ -5 & 20 \end{pmatrix}$

$X = \begin{pmatrix} 5 & 2 \\ -1 & 4 \end{pmatrix}$

Exercise 14.4

1 Find the inverse matrix for each of these matrices.

a $\begin{pmatrix} 3 & 4 \\ 2 & 3 \end{pmatrix}$ **b** $\begin{pmatrix} 7 & -4 \\ -3 & 2 \end{pmatrix}$ **c** $\begin{pmatrix} 1 & -1 \\ 1 & 2 \end{pmatrix}$ **d** $\begin{pmatrix} 5 & 2 \\ 6 & 3 \end{pmatrix}$

e $\begin{pmatrix} 7 & 3 \\ 2 & 1 \end{pmatrix}$ **f** $\begin{pmatrix} 2 & 2 \\ -1 & 1 \end{pmatrix}$ **g** $\begin{pmatrix} 7 & -2 \\ 5 & -1 \end{pmatrix}$ **h** $\begin{pmatrix} 6 & -1 \\ -2 & -1 \end{pmatrix}$

2 The matrix $\begin{pmatrix} 2 & -4 \\ 5 & 3x \end{pmatrix}$ has no inverse. Find the value of x.

3 Given that $A = \begin{pmatrix} 2 & 0 \\ 1 & 1 \end{pmatrix}$, find $(A^2)^{-1}$.

4 The matrices **A** and **B** are given that $\mathbf{A} = \begin{pmatrix} 2 & 1 \\ -6 & -2 \end{pmatrix}$ and $\mathbf{B} = \begin{pmatrix} 5 & -1 \\ 0 & 2 \end{pmatrix}$.

Find matrix **Q** such that $\mathbf{Q} = \mathbf{B}(\mathbf{A}^{-1})$.

5 a Given that $\mathbf{A} = \begin{pmatrix} -1 & 4 \\ -2 & 3 \end{pmatrix}$, find $\mathbf{A}^{-1}$.

b Hence find the matrix **B** such that $\begin{pmatrix} -1 & 4 \\ -2 & 3 \end{pmatrix} \mathbf{B} = \begin{pmatrix} 0 & 1 \\ 5 & -2 \end{pmatrix}$.

6 $\mathbf{A} = \begin{pmatrix} 3 & -1 \\ -5 & 2 \end{pmatrix}$

Find the matrix **B** such that $\mathbf{BA} = \begin{pmatrix} 7 & -1 \\ 5 & 2 \end{pmatrix}$.

7 $\mathbf{A} = \begin{pmatrix} 4 & 1 \\ 2 & 3 \end{pmatrix}$ $\qquad$ $\mathbf{B} = \begin{pmatrix} 6 & -13 \\ 8 & -9 \end{pmatrix}$

Find the matrix **X** such that $\mathbf{AX} = \mathbf{B}$.

8 $\mathbf{A} = \begin{pmatrix} 2 & 7 \\ 1 & 6 \end{pmatrix}$ $\qquad$ $\mathbf{B} = \begin{pmatrix} 1 & -9 \\ -2 & -7 \end{pmatrix}$

a Find the inverse matrix $\mathbf{A}^{-1}$.

b Find the matrix **X** such that $\mathbf{XA} = \mathbf{B}$.

9 $\mathbf{A} = \begin{pmatrix} 2 & 1 \\ -3 & 4 \end{pmatrix}$ $\qquad$ $\mathbf{B} = \begin{pmatrix} 10 & 4 \\ -15 & 5 \end{pmatrix}$

a Find the inverse matrix $\mathbf{A}^{-1}$.

b Find the matrix **X** such that $\mathbf{AX} = \mathbf{B}$.

10 $\mathbf{A} = \begin{pmatrix} 4 & 2 \\ 2 & 3 \end{pmatrix}$ $\qquad$ $\mathbf{B} = \begin{pmatrix} -10 & -3 \\ 10 & 7 \end{pmatrix}$

Find the matrix **X** such that $\mathbf{XA} = \mathbf{B}$.

11 $\mathbf{A} = \begin{pmatrix} 3 & -2 \\ 1 & 1 \end{pmatrix}$

a Find the inverse of the matrix $\mathbf{A} + \mathbf{I}$, where **I** is the identity matrix.

b Use your answer to **part a** to find the matrix **X** such that $\mathbf{AX} + \mathbf{X} = \mathbf{B}$, where $\mathbf{B} = \begin{pmatrix} 3 \\ 4 \end{pmatrix}$.

12 $\mathbf{A} = \begin{pmatrix} -1 & 2 \\ -2 & 5 \end{pmatrix}$

a Find the inverse of the matrix $\mathbf{A} - \mathbf{I}$, where **I** is the identity matrix.

b Use your answer to **part a** to find the matrix **Y** such that $\mathbf{YA} - \mathbf{Y} = \mathbf{B}$, where $\mathbf{B} = \begin{pmatrix} 5 & 2 \\ -1 & 3 \end{pmatrix}$.

CHALLENGE Q

13 If $\mathbf{A} = \begin{pmatrix} a & b \\ c & d \end{pmatrix}$, and $\mathbf{A}$ is non-singular, prove that $\mathbf{A}^{-1} = \dfrac{1}{ad-bc}\begin{pmatrix} d & -b \\ -c & a \end{pmatrix}$.

Hint:
Let $\mathbf{A}^{-1} = \begin{pmatrix} e & f \\ g & h \end{pmatrix}$ and use the fact that $\mathbf{AA}^{-1} = \mathbf{I}$ to obtain two pairs of simultaneous equations to solve for e, f, g and h.

14.5 Simultaneous equations

You have already learnt algebraic methods for solving equations such as $\begin{cases} 3x - y = 10 \\ x + y = -2 \end{cases}$

In this section you will learn how to use inverse matrices to solve simultaneous linear equations.

The equations $\begin{cases} 3x - y = 10 \\ x + y = -2 \end{cases}$ can be written in matrix form as $\begin{pmatrix} 3 & -1 \\ 1 & 1 \end{pmatrix}\begin{pmatrix} x \\ y \end{pmatrix} = \begin{pmatrix} 10 \\ -2 \end{pmatrix}$.

If you let $\mathbf{A} = \begin{pmatrix} 3 & -1 \\ 1 & 1 \end{pmatrix}$ the matrix equation becomes $\mathbf{A}\begin{pmatrix} x \\ y \end{pmatrix} = \begin{pmatrix} 10 \\ -2 \end{pmatrix}$.

Pre-multiplying both sides by $\mathbf{A}^{-1}$, you obtain $\quad \mathbf{A}^{-1}\mathbf{A}\begin{pmatrix} x \\ y \end{pmatrix} = \mathbf{A}^{-1}\begin{pmatrix} 10 \\ -2 \end{pmatrix}$

But since $\mathbf{A}^{-1}\mathbf{A} = \mathbf{I}$, this becomes $\quad \begin{pmatrix} x \\ y \end{pmatrix} = \mathbf{A}^{-1}\begin{pmatrix} 10 \\ -2 \end{pmatrix}$

Hence to solve the equations $\begin{cases} 3x - y = 10 \\ x + y = -2 \end{cases}$

Step 1: Write in matrix form. $\quad\longrightarrow\quad \begin{pmatrix} 3 & -1 \\ 1 & 1 \end{pmatrix}\begin{pmatrix} x \\ y \end{pmatrix} = \begin{pmatrix} 10 \\ -2 \end{pmatrix}$

Step 2: Find the inverse of $\begin{pmatrix} 3 & -1 \\ 1 & 1 \end{pmatrix}$. $\quad\longrightarrow\quad$ Inverse $= \dfrac{1}{4}\begin{pmatrix} 1 & 1 \\ -1 & 3 \end{pmatrix}$

Step 3: Multiply both sides by the inverse. $\quad\longrightarrow\quad \begin{pmatrix} x \\ y \end{pmatrix} = \dfrac{1}{4}\begin{pmatrix} 1 & 1 \\ -1 & 3 \end{pmatrix}\begin{pmatrix} 10 \\ -2 \end{pmatrix}$

Step 4: Simplify. $\quad\longrightarrow\quad \begin{pmatrix} x \\ y \end{pmatrix} = \dfrac{1}{4}\begin{pmatrix} 8 \\ -16 \end{pmatrix} = \begin{pmatrix} 2 \\ -4 \end{pmatrix}$

So the solution is $x = 2, y = -4$.

WORKED EXAMPLE 8

Solve the equations $\begin{cases} 8x + 3y - 7 = 0 \\ 3x + 5y + 9 = 0 \end{cases}$

Answers

$\begin{cases} 8x + 3y - 7 = 0 \\ 3x + 5y + 9 = 0 \end{cases}$ rearrange the two equations

$\begin{cases} 8x + 3y = 7 \\ 3x + 5y = -9 \end{cases}$ write in matrix form

$\begin{pmatrix} 8 & 3 \\ 3 & 5 \end{pmatrix} \begin{pmatrix} x \\ y \end{pmatrix} = \begin{pmatrix} 7 \\ -9 \end{pmatrix}$ pre-multiply by the inverse of $\begin{pmatrix} 8 & 3 \\ 3 & 5 \end{pmatrix}$

$\begin{pmatrix} x \\ y \end{pmatrix} = \frac{1}{31} \begin{pmatrix} 5 & -3 \\ -3 & 8 \end{pmatrix} \begin{pmatrix} 7 \\ -9 \end{pmatrix}$ simplify

$\begin{pmatrix} x \\ y \end{pmatrix} = \frac{1}{31} \begin{pmatrix} 62 \\ -93 \end{pmatrix} = \begin{pmatrix} 2 \\ -3 \end{pmatrix}$

So the solution is $x = 2$, $y = -3$.

There are three possible situations when solving simultaneous linear equations:

Intersecting lines	Parallel lines	Coincident lines
one unique solution	no solution	infinite solutions

If the determinant is zero when using matrices to solve simultaneous linear equations, then this indicates that the lines must be either parallel or coincident.

Exercise 14.5

1 Write in matrix form.

    a $x + 3y = 21$ **b** $3x + 7y = 22$ **c** $2x - 3y = 1$ **d** $2x - 5y = 1$
        $5x - 2y = 10$ $5x - 2y = 2$ $x + 5y = 0$ $7x + 8y = 4$

2 Solve.

    a $2x + 3y = 21$ **b** $4x + 2y = 22$ **c** $7x + 8y = 1$ **d** $2x + y = -3$
        $5x - y = 10$ $6x - y = 2$ $x + 4y = -7$ $3x - 2y = -8$

    e $x + 2y = 8$ **f** $x - 5y = 18$ **g** $x - y + 2 = 0$ **h** $y = 2x - 7$
        $3x + 4y = 6$ $x + 3y = 2$ $3x + 2y - 14 = 0$ $y = x - 3$

3 $A = \begin{pmatrix} 1 & -2 \\ 5 & 3 \end{pmatrix}$.

   a Find the inverse matrix, A^{-1}.

   b Use your answer to **part a** to solve the simultaneous equations.
   $$x - 2y = 7$$
   $$5x + 3y = -4$$

4 $A = \begin{pmatrix} 1 & -2 \\ 4 & -3 \end{pmatrix}$.

   a Find the inverse matrix of **A**.

   b Solve the simultaneous equations.
   $$2y - x + 13 = 0$$
   $$3y + 4x - 8 = 0$$

   c Find the matrix **B** such that $BA = \begin{pmatrix} 13 & -4 \\ -3 & -5 \end{pmatrix}$.

> **CHALLENGE Q**
>
> 5 a Write in matrix form.
> $$kx + 4y = 7$$
> $$9x + ky = 4$$
>
>   b Find the values of k for which the equations do not have a unique solution.

Summary

Order of a matrix

$\begin{pmatrix} 4 & 1 & 3 & 4 \\ 1 & 5 & 0 & 7 \end{pmatrix}$ The matrix has 2 rows and 4 columns. The order is 2×4.

Addition and subtraction of matrices

To add two matrices of the same order, you add corresponding elements.

To subtract two matrices of the same order, you subtract corresponding elements.

If matrices **A** and **B** are of the same order:

A + **B** = **B** + **A**

A + (**B** + **C**) = (**A** + **B**) + **C**

Multiplication by a scalar

To evaluate $k\mathbf{A}$, where k is a scalar, you multiply each element inside matrix **A** by k.

Multiplication of matrices
The rule for deciding whether two matrices can be multiplied is:

order: First matrix Second matrix
         $a \times b$ $c \times d$

You can multiply the matrices if $b = c$.
The product of the two matrices will be of order $a \times d$.

It is important to remember that: **AB ≠ BA**.

The following rules apply for matrix multiplication.
A(B + C) = AB + AC
A(BC) = (AB)C
If k is a scalar then **A**$(k$**B**$) = k($**AB**$)$.

The zero matrix
$\mathbf{O} = \begin{pmatrix} 0 & 0 \\ 0 & 0 \end{pmatrix}$, is called the zero matrix for 2×2 matrices.
AO = OA = O

The identity matrix
$\mathbf{I} = \begin{pmatrix} 1 & 0 \\ 0 & 1 \end{pmatrix}$, is called the identity matrix for 2×2 matrices.
AI = IA = A

Inverse matrices
If $\mathbf{A} = \begin{pmatrix} a & b \\ c & d \end{pmatrix}$ then $\mathbf{A}^{-1} = \dfrac{1}{|\mathbf{A}|}\begin{pmatrix} d & -b \\ -c & a \end{pmatrix}$, where $|\mathbf{A}| = ad - bc$.

$|\mathbf{A}|$ is called the **determinant** of the matrix.
$\mathbf{A}^{-1}$ is called the **inverse** matrix.
AA⁻¹ = A⁻¹A = I
A matrix with no inverse is called a **singular** matrix.
A matrix with an inverse is called a **non-singular** matrix.

Cambridge IGCSE and O Level Additional Mathematics

Examination questions

Worked past paper example

Matrices **A** and **B** are such that $\mathbf{A} = \begin{pmatrix} 3a & 2b \\ -a & b \end{pmatrix}$ and $\mathbf{B} = \begin{pmatrix} -a & b \\ 2a & 2b \end{pmatrix}$ where a and b are non-zero constants.

a Find $\mathbf{A}^{-1}$. [2]

b Using your answer to **part a**, find the matrix **X** such that $\mathbf{XA} = \mathbf{B}$. [4]

Cambridge IGCSE Additional Mathematics 0606 Paper 11 Q7i,ii Nov 2014

Answer

a $\mathbf{A} = \begin{pmatrix} 3a & 2b \\ -a & b \end{pmatrix}$

$|\mathbf{A}| = (3a \times b) - (-a \times 2b) = 3ab - (-2ab) = 5ab$

$\mathbf{A}^{-1} = \dfrac{1}{5ab}\begin{pmatrix} b & -2b \\ a & 3a \end{pmatrix}$

- swap the numbers on the leading diagonal
- change the signs of the numbers on the other diagonal

$\mathbf{A}^{-1} = \dfrac{1}{5ab}\begin{pmatrix} b & -2b \\ a & 3a \end{pmatrix}$

- divide by the determinant

b $\mathbf{XA} = \mathbf{B}$

$\mathbf{XAA}^{-1} = \mathbf{BA}^{-1}$ post-multiply both sides by $\mathbf{A}^{-1}$

$\mathbf{X} = \mathbf{BA}^{-1}$ $\mathbf{AA}^{-1} = \mathbf{I}$

$= \begin{pmatrix} -a & b \\ 2a & 2b \end{pmatrix} \dfrac{1}{5ab}\begin{pmatrix} b & -2b \\ a & 3a \end{pmatrix}$

$= \dfrac{1}{5ab}\begin{pmatrix} -a & b \\ 2a & 2b \end{pmatrix}\begin{pmatrix} b & -2b \\ a & 3a \end{pmatrix}$

$= \dfrac{1}{5ab}\begin{pmatrix} 0 & 5ab \\ 4ab & 2ab \end{pmatrix}$

So, $\mathbf{X} = \begin{pmatrix} 0 & 1 \\ \frac{4}{5} & \frac{2}{5} \end{pmatrix}$

Exercise 14.6
Exam Exercise

1 Matrices **A** and **B** are such that $\mathbf{A} = \begin{pmatrix} -1 & 4 \\ 7 & 6 \\ 4 & 2 \end{pmatrix}$ and $\mathbf{B} = \begin{pmatrix} 2 & 1 \\ 3 & 5 \end{pmatrix}$.

  a Find **AB**. [2]

  b Find $\mathbf{B}^{-1}$. [2]

  c Using your answer to **part b**, solve the simultaneous equations.
  $$4x + 2y = -3$$
  $$6x + 10y = -22$$ [3]

  Cambridge IGCSE Additional Mathematics 0606 Paper 11 Q6i,ii,iii Jun 2014

2 It is given that matrix $\mathbf{A} = \begin{pmatrix} 2 & 3 \\ 4 & 1 \end{pmatrix}$.

  a Find $\mathbf{A} + 2\mathbf{I}$. [1]

  b Find $\mathbf{A}^2$. [2]

  c Using your answer to **part b**, find the matrix **B** such that $\mathbf{A}^2\mathbf{B} = \mathbf{I}$. [2]

  Cambridge IGCSE Additional Mathematics 0606 Paper 11 Q11ai,ii,iii Nov 2013

3 **a** Given that $\mathbf{A} = \begin{pmatrix} 2 & -1 \\ 3 & 5 \end{pmatrix}$, find $\mathbf{A}^{-1}$. [2]

  b Using your answer to **part a**, or otherwise find the values of a, b, c and d such that
  $$\mathbf{A}\begin{pmatrix} a & b \\ c & -1 \end{pmatrix} = \begin{pmatrix} 7 & 5 \\ 17 & d \end{pmatrix}.$$ [5]

  Cambridge IGCSE Additional Mathematics 0606 Paper 11 Q6i,ii Jun 2013

4 **a** Given that $\mathbf{A} = \begin{pmatrix} 4 & -3 \\ 2 & 5 \end{pmatrix}$, find the inverse matrix $\mathbf{A}^{-1}$. [2]

  b Use your answer to **part a** to solve the simultaneous equations
  $$4x - 3y = -10$$
  $$2x + 5y = 21$$ [2]

  Cambridge IGCSE Additional Mathematics 0606 Paper 21 Q1i,ii Jun 2012

5 It is given that $\mathbf{A} = \begin{pmatrix} 3 & 2 \\ 1 & -5 \end{pmatrix}$ and $\mathbf{B} = \begin{pmatrix} 1 & 4 \\ -2 & 3 \end{pmatrix}$.

  a Find $2\mathbf{A} - \mathbf{B}$. [2]

  b Find **BA**. [2]

  c Find the inverse matrix, $\mathbf{A}^{-1}$. [2]

  d Use your answer to **part c** solve the simultaneous equations.
  $$3x + 2y = 23$$
  $$x - 5y = 19$$ [2]

  Cambridge IGCSE Additional Mathematics 0606 Paper 21 Q10i-iv Nov 2011

Cambridge IGCSE and O Level Additional Mathematics

6 **a** Matrices **A**, **B** and **C** are given by $\mathbf{A} = \begin{pmatrix} 2 & 1 \\ 1 & 3 \\ 2 & 5 \end{pmatrix}$, $\mathbf{B} = \begin{pmatrix} 2 & 1 & 3 & 4 \\ 1 & 5 & 6 & 7 \end{pmatrix}$ and $\mathbf{C} = \begin{pmatrix} 9 \\ 10 \end{pmatrix}$.

Write down, but do not evaluate, matrix products which may be calculated from the matrices **A**, **B** and **C**. [2]

b Given that $\mathbf{X} = \begin{pmatrix} 2 & 4 \\ 3 & 5 \end{pmatrix}$ and $\mathbf{Y} = \begin{pmatrix} 2x & 3y \\ x & 4y \end{pmatrix}$, find the value of x and y such that

$\mathbf{X}^{-1}\mathbf{Y} = \begin{pmatrix} -12x + 3y & 6 \\ -7x + 3y & 6 \end{pmatrix}$. [6]

Cambridge IGCSE Additional Mathematics 0606 Paper 11 Q8a,b Jun 2011

7 Students take three multiple-choice tests, each with ten questions. A correct answer earns 5 marks. If no answer is given 1 mark is scored. An incorrect answer loses 2 marks. A student's final total mark is the sum of 20% of the mark in test 1, 30% of the mark in test 2 and 50% of the mark in test 3. One student's responses are summarised in the table below.

	Test 1	Test 2	Test 3
correct answer	7	6	5
no answer	1	3	5
incorrect answer	2	1	0

Write down three matrices such that matrix multiplication will give this student's final total mark and hence find this total mark. [5]

Cambridge IGCSE Additional Mathematics 0606 Paper 21 Q4 Nov 2010

Chapter 15
Differentiation 2

This section will show you how to:

- differentiate $\sin x$, $\cos x$, $\tan x$, e^x and $\ln x$ together with constant multiples, sums and composite functions of these.

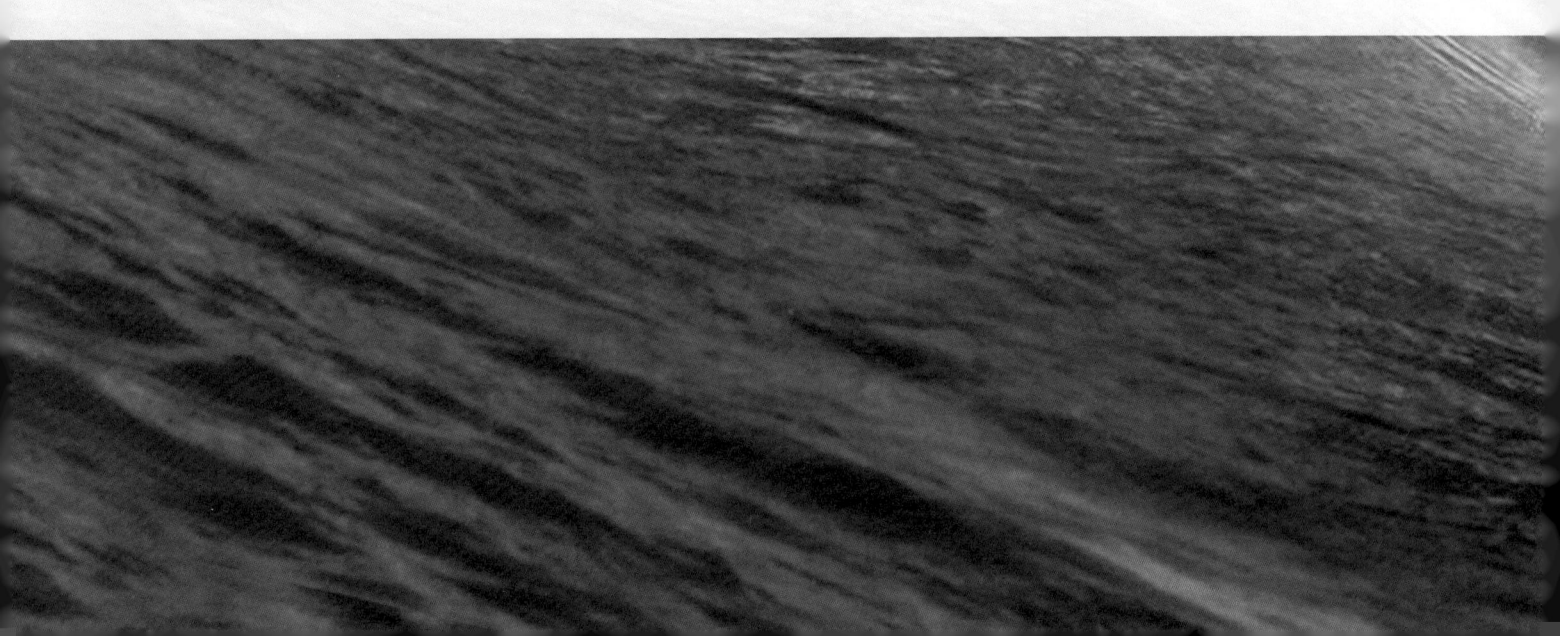

Cambridge IGCSE and O Level Additional Mathematics

> **RECAP**
>
> In Chapter 12 you learnt that if $y = x^2$, then $\dfrac{dy}{dx} = 2x$.
>
> This can also be written as: if $f(x) = x^2$, then $f'(x) = 2x$.
>
> Graphing software can be used to show the function $f(x) = x^2$ and its gradient (derived) function $f'(x)$.

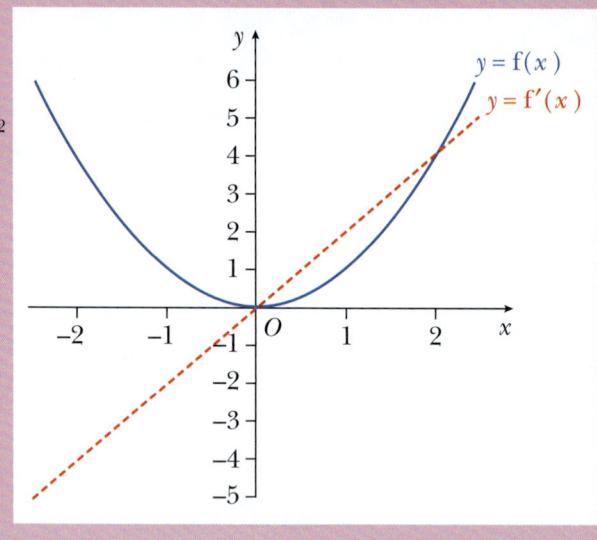

15.1 Derivatives of exponential functions

CLASS DISCUSSION

Graphing software has been used to draw the graphs of $y = 2^x$ and $y = 3^x$ together with their gradient (derived) functions.

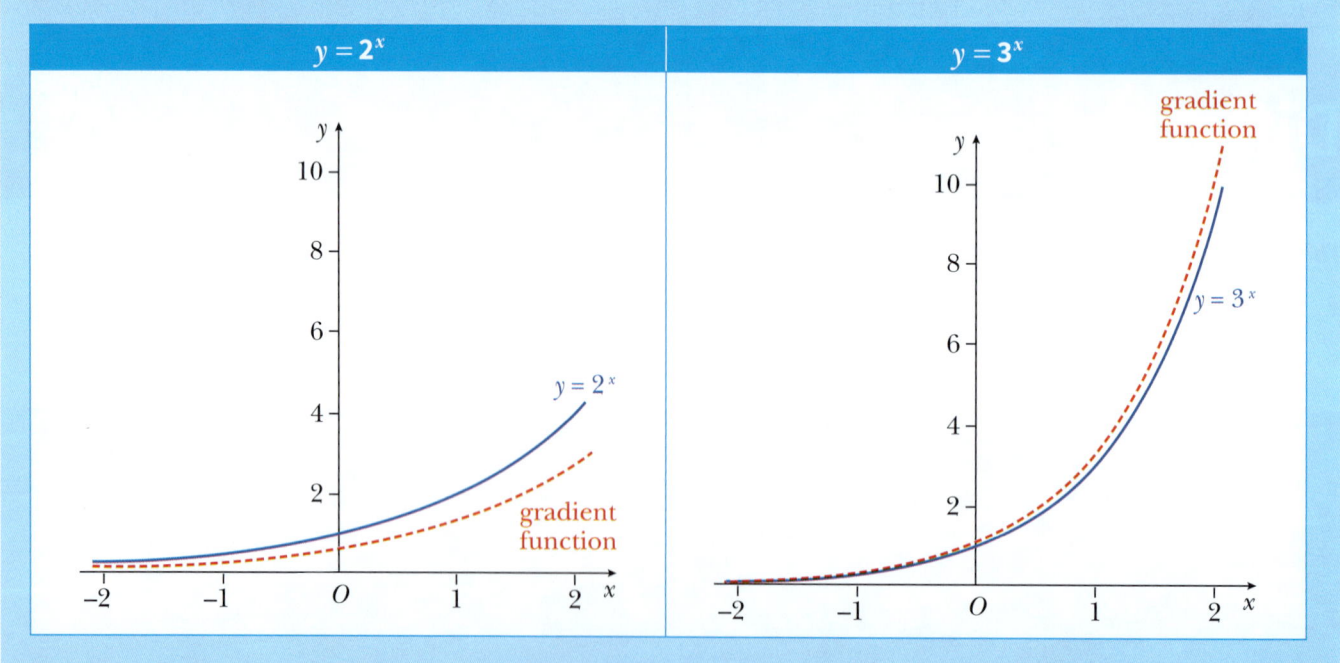

Discuss with your classmates what conclusions can be made from these two graphs.

In Chapter 6 you learnt about the exponential function $y = e^x$ where $e \approx 2.718$.

This function has the very special property that the gradient function is identical to the original function. This leads to the rule:

$$\frac{d}{dx}(e^x) = e^x$$

The derivative of $e^{f(x)}$

Consider the function $y = e^{f(x)}$.

Let $y = e^u$ where $u = f(x)$

$\dfrac{dy}{du} = e^u \qquad \dfrac{du}{dx} = f'(x)$

Using the chain rule: $\dfrac{dy}{dx} = \dfrac{dy}{du} \times \dfrac{du}{dx}$

$\qquad\qquad\qquad\qquad = e^u \times f'(x)$

$\qquad\qquad\qquad\qquad = f'(x) \times e^{f(x)}$

$$\frac{d}{dx}\left[e^{f(x)}\right] = f'(x) \times e^{f(x)}$$

In particular:

$$\frac{d}{dx}\left[e^{ax+b}\right] = a \times e^{ax+b}$$

WORKED EXAMPLE 1

Differentiate with respect to x.

a e^{5x} **b** e^{x^2-3x} **c** $x^2 e^{-3x}$ **d** $\dfrac{e^{2x}}{x}$

Answers

a $\dfrac{d}{dx}(e^{5x}) = \underbrace{5}_{\text{differentiate index}} \times \underbrace{e^{5x}}_{\text{original function}} = 5e^{5x}$

b $\dfrac{d}{dx}(e^{x^2-3x}) = \underbrace{(2x-3)}_{\text{differentiate index}} \times \underbrace{e^{x^2-3x}}_{\text{original function}} = (2x-3)e^{x^2-3x}$

c $\dfrac{d}{dx}(x^2 e^{-3x}) = x^2 \times \dfrac{d}{dx}(e^{-3x}) + e^{-3x} \times \dfrac{d}{dx}(x^2)$ product rule

$= x^2 \times (-3e^{-3x}) + e^{-3x} \times 2x$

$= -3x^2 e^{-3x} + 2x e^{-3x}$

$= x\, e^{-3x}(2 - 3x)$

d $\dfrac{d}{dx}\left(\dfrac{e^{2x}}{x}\right) = \dfrac{x \times \dfrac{d}{dx}(e^{2x}) - e^{2x} \times \dfrac{d}{dx}(x)}{x^2}$ quotient rule

$= \dfrac{x \times 2e^{2x} - e^{2x} \times 1}{x^2}$

$= \dfrac{e^{2x}(2x-1)}{x^2}$

WORKED EXAMPLE 2

A curve has equation $y = (e^{2x} + e^{3x})^5$.

Find the value of $\dfrac{dy}{dx}$ when $x = 0$.

Answers

$y = (e^{2x} + e^{3x})^5$

$\dfrac{dy}{dx} = 5(e^{2x} + e^{3x})^4 \times (2e^{2x} + 3e^{3x})$ chain rule

when $x = 0$, $\dfrac{dy}{dx} = 5(e^0 + e^0)^4 \times (2e^0 + 3e^0)$

$= 5 \times 2 \times 5$

$= 50$

Chapter 15: Differentiation 2

> **CLASS DISCUSSION**
>
> By writing 2 as $e^{\ln 2}$ find an expression for $\dfrac{d}{dx}(2^x)$.
>
> Discuss with your classmates whether you can find similar expressions for $\dfrac{d}{dx}(3^x)$ and $\dfrac{d}{dx}(4^x)$.

Exercise 15.1

1 Differentiate with respect to x.

　a e^{7x} 　　　　b e^{3x} 　　　　c $3e^{5x}$

　d $2e^{-4x}$ 　　e $6e^{-\frac{x}{2}}$ 　　f e^{3x+1}

　g e^{x^2+1} 　　h $5x - 3e^{\sqrt{x}}$ 　　i $2 + \dfrac{1}{e^{3x}}$

　j $2(3 - e^{2x})$ 　k $\dfrac{e^x + e^{-x}}{2}$ 　l $5\left(x^2 + e^{x^2}\right)$

2 Differentiate with respect to x.

　a xe^x 　　　　b $x^2 e^{2x}$ 　　c $3xe^{-x}$

　d $\sqrt{x}\, e^x$ 　　e $\dfrac{e^x}{x}$ 　　f $\dfrac{e^{2x}}{\sqrt{x}}$

　g $\dfrac{e^x + 1}{e^x - 1}$ 　h $xe^{2x} - \dfrac{e^{2x}}{2}$ 　i $\dfrac{x^2 e^x - 5}{e^x + 1}$

3 Find the equation of the tangent to

　a $y = \dfrac{5}{e^{2x} + 3}$ at $x = 0$

　b $y = \sqrt{e^{2x} + 1}$ at $x = \ln 5$

　c $y = x^2(1 + e^x)$ at $x = 1$.

4 A curve has equation $y = 5e^{2x} - 4x - 3$.

　The tangent to the curve at the point $(0, 2)$ meets the x-axis at the point A.

　Find the coordinates of A.

15.2 Derivatives of logarithmic functions

CLASS DISCUSSION

Graphing software has been used to draw the graph of $y = \ln x$ together with its gradient (derived) function.

The gradient function passes through the points $\left(\dfrac{1}{2}, 2\right)$, $(1, 1)$, $\left(2, \dfrac{1}{2}\right)$ and $\left(5, \dfrac{1}{5}\right)$.

Discuss with your classmates what conclusions you can make about the gradient function.

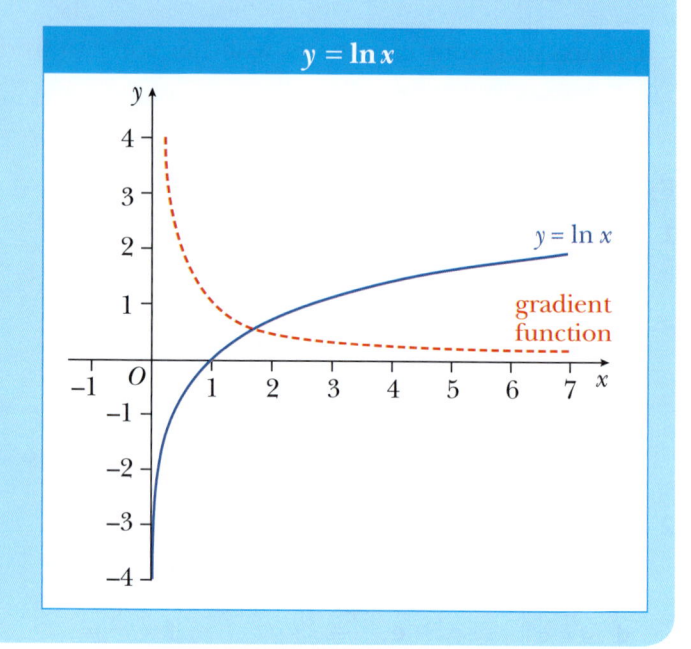

From the class discussion you should have concluded that:

$$\dfrac{d}{dx}(\ln x) = \dfrac{1}{x}$$

The derivative of ln f(x)

Consider the function $y = \ln f(x)$.

Let $y = \ln u$ where $u = f(x)$.

$$\dfrac{dy}{du} = \dfrac{1}{u} \qquad \dfrac{du}{dx} = f'(x)$$

Using the chain rule:
$$\dfrac{dy}{dx} = \dfrac{dy}{du} \times \dfrac{du}{dx}$$
$$= \dfrac{1}{u} \times f'(x)$$
$$= \dfrac{f'(x)}{f(x)}$$

$$\dfrac{d}{dx}\left[\ln f(x)\right] = \dfrac{f'(x)}{f(x)}$$

Chapter 15: Differentiation 2

In particular:

$$\frac{d}{dx}[\ln(ax+b)] = \frac{a}{ax+b}$$

WORKED EXAMPLE 3

Differentiate with respect to x.

a $\ln 8x$ **b** $\ln(5x-7)$ **c** $\ln(2x^2+5)$ **d** $\ln\sqrt{x-10}$

a $\dfrac{d}{dx}(\ln 8x) = \dfrac{8}{8x}$ ← 'inside' differentiated / 'inside'

$= \dfrac{1}{x}$

b $\dfrac{d}{dx}[\ln(5x-7)] = \dfrac{5}{5x-7}$ ← 'inside' differentiated / 'inside'

c $\dfrac{d}{dx}[\ln(2x^2+5)] = \dfrac{4x}{2x^2+5}$ ← 'inside' differentiated / 'inside'

d Method 1: $\dfrac{d}{dx}[\ln\sqrt{x-10}] = \dfrac{\frac{1}{2}(x-10)^{-\frac{1}{2}}(1)}{\sqrt{x-10}}$ ← 'inside' differentiated / 'inside'

$= \dfrac{1}{2(x-10)}$

Method 2: using the rules of logarithms before differentiating.

$\dfrac{d}{dx}[\ln\sqrt{x-10}] = \dfrac{d}{dx}\left[\ln(x-10)^{\frac{1}{2}}\right]$ use $\ln a^m = m \ln a$

$= \dfrac{d}{dx}\left[\dfrac{1}{2}\ln(x-10)\right]$

$= \dfrac{1}{2} \times \dfrac{d}{dx}[\ln(x-10)]$

$= \dfrac{1}{2} \times \dfrac{1}{x-10}$ ← 'inside' differentiated / 'inside'

$= \dfrac{1}{2(x-10)}$

WORKED EXAMPLE 4

Differentiate with respect to x.

a $5x^6 \ln 2x$ **b** $\dfrac{\ln x}{3x}$

Answers

a $\dfrac{d}{dx}(5x^6 \ln 2x) = 5x^6 \times \dfrac{d}{dx}(\ln 2x) + \ln 2x \times \dfrac{d}{dx}(5x^6)$ product rule

$= 5x^6 \times \dfrac{2}{2x} + \ln 2x \times 30x^5$

$= 5x^5 + 30x^5 \ln 2x$

b $\dfrac{d}{dx}\left(\dfrac{\ln x}{3x}\right) = \dfrac{3x \times \dfrac{d}{dx}(\ln x) - \ln x \times \dfrac{d}{dx}(3x)}{(3x)^2}$ quotient rule

$= \dfrac{3x \times \dfrac{1}{x} - \ln x \times 3}{9x^2}$

$= \dfrac{1 - \ln x}{3x^2}$

WORKED EXAMPLE 5

A curve has equation $y = \ln\left[\dfrac{\sqrt{2x-1}}{x^2+1}\right]$.

a Show that $y = \dfrac{1}{2}\ln(2x-1) - \ln(x^2+1)$.

b Hence, find the value of $\dfrac{dy}{dx}$ when $x = 1$.

Answers

a $y = \ln\left[\dfrac{\sqrt{2x-1}}{x^2+1}\right]$ use $\log_a\left(\dfrac{x}{y}\right) = \log_a x - \log_a y$

$= \ln(2x-1)^{\frac{1}{2}} - \ln(x^2+1)$ use $\log_a(x)^m = m\log_a x$

$= \dfrac{1}{2}\ln(2x-1) - \ln(x^2+1)$

b $\dfrac{dy}{dx} = \dfrac{d}{dx}\left[\dfrac{1}{2}\ln(2x-1)\right] - \dfrac{d}{dx}\left[\ln(x^2+1)\right]$

$= \dfrac{1}{2} \times \dfrac{d}{dx}[\ln(2x-1)] - \dfrac{d}{dx}[\ln(x^2+1)]$

$= \dfrac{1}{2} \times \dfrac{2}{2x-1} - \dfrac{2x}{x^2+1}$

$= \dfrac{1}{2x-1} - \dfrac{2x}{x^2+1}$

$= \dfrac{x^2+1 - 2x(2x-1)}{(2x-1)(x^2+1)}$

$= \dfrac{-3x^2+2x+1}{(2x-1)(x^2+1)}$

When $x = 1$, $\dfrac{dy}{dx} = 0$.

> **WORKED EXAMPLE 6**
>
> A curve has equation $y = \log_2(5x - 2)$.
> **a** Show that $y = \dfrac{1}{\ln 2}[\ln(5x-2)]$.
> **b** Hence, find the value of $\dfrac{dy}{dx}$ when $x = 2$.
>
> **Answers**
> **a** $y = \log_2(5x-2)$ 　　　use $\log_b a = \dfrac{\log_c a}{\log_c b}$
>
> $= \dfrac{\ln(5x-2)}{\ln 2}$
>
> $= \dfrac{1}{\ln 2}[\ln(5x-2)]$
>
> **b** $\dfrac{dy}{dx} = \dfrac{1}{\ln 2} \times \dfrac{d}{dx}[\ln(5x-2)]$
>
> $= \dfrac{1}{\ln 2} \times \dfrac{5}{5x-2}$
>
> $= \dfrac{5}{(5x-2)\ln 2}$
>
> When $x = 2$, $\dfrac{dy}{dx} = \dfrac{5}{8\ln 2}$.

Exercise 15.2

1 Differentiate with respect to x.

　a $\ln 5x$ 　　　**b** $\ln 12x$ 　　　**c** $\ln(2x+3)$

　d $2 + \ln(1-x^2)$ 　　**e** $\ln(3x+1)^2$ 　　**f** $\ln\sqrt{x+2}$

　g $\ln(2-5x)^4$ 　　**h** $2x + \ln\left(\dfrac{4}{x}\right)$ 　　**i** $5 - \ln\dfrac{3}{(2-3x)}$

　j $\ln(\ln x)$ 　　**k** $\ln(\sqrt{x}+1)^2$ 　　**l** $\ln(x^2 + \ln x)$

2 Differentiate with respect to x.

　a $x \ln x$ 　　　**b** $2x^2 \ln x$ 　　　**c** $(x-1)\ln x$

　d $5x \ln x^2$ 　　**e** $x^2 \ln(\ln x)$ 　　**f** $\dfrac{\ln 2x}{x}$

　g $\dfrac{4}{\ln x}$ 　　**h** $\dfrac{\ln(2x+1)}{x^2}$ 　　**i** $\dfrac{\ln(x^3-1)}{2x+3}$

3 A curve has equation $y = x^2 \ln 3x$.

　Find the value of $\dfrac{dy}{dx}$ and $\dfrac{d^2y}{dx^2}$ at the point where $x = 2$.

4 Use the laws of logarithms to help differentiate these expressions with respect to x.

   a $\ln\sqrt{3x+1}$
   b $\ln\dfrac{1}{(2x-5)}$
   c $\ln\left[x(x-5)^4\right]$
   d $\ln\left(\dfrac{2x+1}{x-1}\right)$
   e $\ln\left(\dfrac{2-x}{x^2}\right)$
   f $\ln\left[\dfrac{x(x+1)}{x+2}\right]$
   g $\ln\left[\dfrac{2x+3}{(x-5)(x+1)}\right]$
   h $\ln\left[\dfrac{2}{(x+3)^2(x-1)}\right]$
   i $\ln\left[\dfrac{(x+1)(2x-3)}{x(x-1)}\right]$

5 Find $\dfrac{dy}{dx}$ for each of the following.

   a $y = \log_3 x$
   b $y = \log_2 x^2$
   c $y = \log_4 (5x - 1)$

   Hint:
   Use change of base of logarithms before differentiating.

6 Find $\dfrac{dy}{dx}$ for each of the following.

   a $e^y = 4x^2 - 1$
   b $e^y = 5x^3 - 2x$
   c $e^y = (x+3)(x-4)$

   Hint:
   Take the natural logarithm of both sides of the equation before differentiating.

7 A curve has equation $x = \dfrac{1}{2}\left[e^{y(3x+7)} + 1\right]$.
   Find the value of $\dfrac{dy}{dx}$ when $x = 1$.

15.3 Derivatives of trigonometric functions

CLASS DISCUSSION

Graphing software has been used to draw the graphs of $y = \sin x$ and $y = \cos x$ together with their gradient (derived) functions.

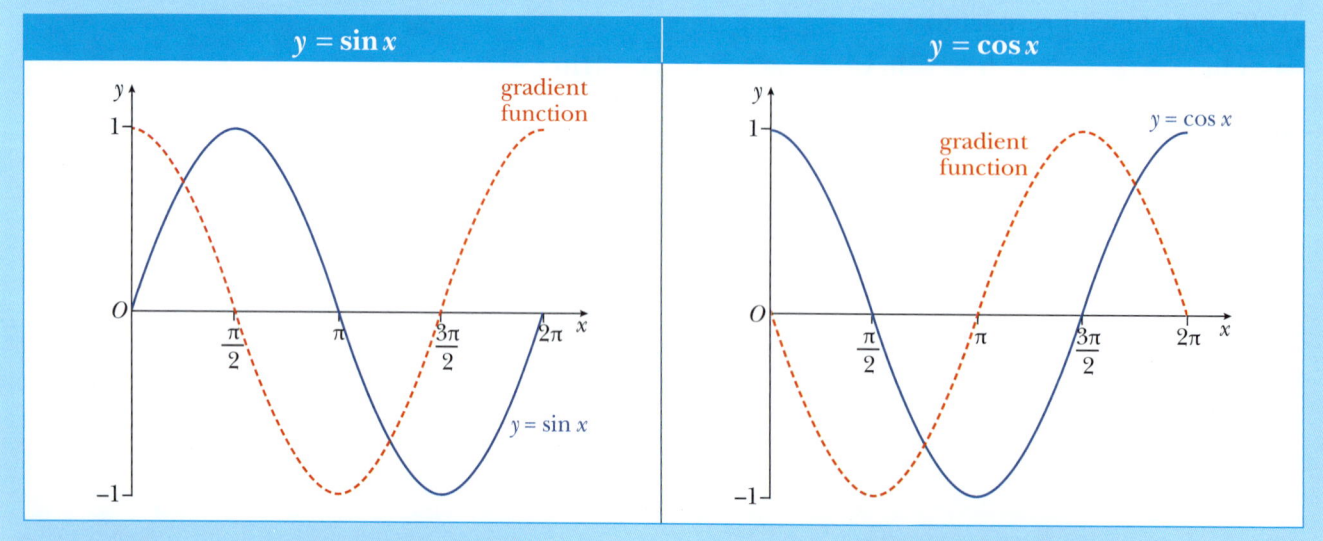

Discuss with your classmates what conclusions you can make from these two graphs.

From the class discussion you should have concluded that if x is measured in radians then:

$$\frac{d}{dx}(\sin x) = \cos x$$

$$\frac{d}{dx}(\cos x) = -\sin x$$

The derivative of $\tan x$ can be found using these two results together with the quotient rule.

$$\frac{d}{dx}(\tan x) = \frac{d}{dx}\left(\frac{\sin x}{\cos x}\right) \qquad \text{use the quotient rule}$$

$$= \frac{\cos x \times \frac{d}{dx}(\sin x) - \sin x \times \frac{d}{dx}(\cos x)}{(\cos x)^2}$$

$$= \frac{\cos x \times \cos x - \sin x \times (-\sin x)}{\cos^2 x}$$

$$= \frac{\cos^2 x + \sin^2 x}{\cos^2 x} \qquad \text{use } \cos^2 x + \sin^2 x = 1$$

$$= \frac{1}{\cos^2 x} \qquad \text{use } \frac{1}{\cos x} = \sec x$$

$$= \sec^2 x$$

$$\frac{d}{dx}(\tan x) = \sec^2 x$$

> **WORKED EXAMPLE 7**
>
> Differentiate with respect to x.
> **a** $7\cos x$ **b** $x^2 \sin x$ **c** $\dfrac{3\tan x}{x}$ **d** $(5 - 3\cos x)^8$
>
> **Answers**
>
> **a** $\dfrac{d}{dx}(7\cos x) = 7\dfrac{d}{dx}(\cos x)$
> $\phantom{\dfrac{d}{dx}(7\cos x)} = -7\sin x$
>
> **b** $\dfrac{d}{dx}(x^2 \sin x) = x^2 \times \dfrac{d}{dx}(\sin x) + \sin x \times \dfrac{d}{dx}(x^2)$ product rule
> $\phantom{\dfrac{d}{dx}(x^2 \sin x)} = x^2 \cos x + 2x \sin x$
>
> **c** $\dfrac{d}{dx}\left(\dfrac{3\tan x}{x}\right) = \dfrac{x \times \dfrac{d}{dx}(3\tan x) - 3\tan x \times \dfrac{d}{dx}(x)}{x^2}$ quotient rule
> $\phantom{\dfrac{d}{dx}\left(\dfrac{3\tan x}{x}\right)} = \dfrac{x \times 3\sec^2 x - 3\tan x \times 1}{x^2}$
> $\phantom{\dfrac{d}{dx}\left(\dfrac{3\tan x}{x}\right)} = \dfrac{3x \sec^2 x - 3\tan x}{x^2}$
>
> **d** $\dfrac{d}{dx}\left[(5 - 3\cos x)^8\right] = 8(5 - 3\cos x)^7 \times 3\sin x$ chain rule
> $\phantom{\dfrac{d}{dx}\left[(5 - 3\cos x)^8\right]} = 24\sin x(5 - 3\cos x)^7$

Derivatives of $\sin(ax + b)$, $\cos(ax + b)$ and $\tan(ax + b)$

Consider the function $y = \sin(ax + b)$ where x is measured in radians.

Let $y = \sin u$ where $u = ax + b$.

$\dfrac{dy}{du} = \cos u$ $\dfrac{du}{dx} = a$

Using the chain rule: $\dfrac{dy}{dx} = \dfrac{dy}{du} \times \dfrac{du}{dx}$
$\phantom{\text{Using the chain rule: }\dfrac{dy}{dx}} = \cos u \times a$
$\phantom{\text{Using the chain rule: }\dfrac{dy}{dx}} = a \cos(ax + b)$

$$\dfrac{d}{dx}[\sin(ax + b)] = a\cos(ax + b)$$

Similarly, it can be shown that:

$$\dfrac{d}{dx}[\cos(ax + b)] = -a\sin(ax + b)$$

$$\dfrac{d}{dx}[\tan(ax + b)] = a\sec^2(ax + b)$$

> **Note:**
> It is important to remember that, in calculus, all angles are measured in radians unless a question tells you otherwise.

WORKED EXAMPLE 8

Differentiate with respect to x.

a $5\sin\left(\dfrac{\pi}{3} - 2x\right)$ **b** $x\cos 3x$ **c** $\dfrac{x^2}{\sin\left(2x + \dfrac{\pi}{4}\right)}$ **d** $(1 + 3\tan 2x)^5$

Answers

a $\dfrac{d}{dx}\left[5\sin\left(\dfrac{\pi}{3} - 2x\right)\right] = 5\dfrac{d}{dx}\left[\sin\left(\dfrac{\pi}{3} - 2x\right)\right]$

$\qquad = 5 \times \cos\left(\dfrac{\pi}{3} - 2x\right) \times (-2)$

$\qquad = -10\cos\left(\dfrac{\pi}{3} - 2x\right)$

b $\dfrac{d}{dx}(x\cos 3x) = x \times \dfrac{d}{dx}(\cos 3x) + \cos 3x \times \dfrac{d}{dx}(x)$ product rule

$\qquad = x \times (-3\sin 3x) + \cos 3x \times (1)$

$\qquad = \cos 3x - 3x\sin 3x$

c $\dfrac{d}{dx}\left[\dfrac{x^2}{\sin\left(2x + \dfrac{\pi}{4}\right)}\right] = \dfrac{\sin\left(2x + \dfrac{\pi}{4}\right) \times \dfrac{d}{dx}(x^2) - x^2 \times \dfrac{d}{dx}\left[\sin\left(2x + \dfrac{\pi}{4}\right)\right]}{\left[\sin\left(2x + \dfrac{\pi}{4}\right)\right]^2}$ quotient rule

$\qquad = \dfrac{\sin\left(2x + \dfrac{\pi}{4}\right) \times (2x) - x^2 \times \left[2\cos\left(2x + \dfrac{\pi}{4}\right)\right]}{\sin^2\left(2x + \dfrac{\pi}{4}\right)}$

$\qquad = \dfrac{2x\sin\left(2x + \dfrac{\pi}{4}\right) - 2x^2\cos\left(2x + \dfrac{\pi}{4}\right)}{\sin^2\left(2x + \dfrac{\pi}{4}\right)}$

d $\dfrac{d}{dx}\left[(1 + 3\tan 2x)^5\right] = 5(1 + 3\tan 2x)^4 \times 6\sec^2 2x$ chain rule

$\qquad = 30\sec^2 2x(1 + 3\tan 2x)^4$

Exercise 15.3

1 Differentiate with respect to x.

     a $2 + \sin x$ **b** $2\sin x + 3\cos x$ **c** $2\cos x - \tan x$

     d $3\sin 2x$ **e** $4\tan 5x$ **f** $2\cos 3x - \sin 2x$

     g $\tan(3x + 2)$ **h** $\sin\left(2x + \dfrac{\pi}{3}\right)$ **i** $2\cos\left(3x - \dfrac{\pi}{6}\right)$

2 Differentiate with respect to x.

a $\sin^3 x$
b $5\cos^2(3x)$
c $\sin^2 x - 2\cos x$
d $(3-\cos x)^4$
e $2\sin^3\left(2x+\dfrac{\pi}{6}\right)$
f $3\cos^4 x + 2\tan^2\left(2x-\dfrac{\pi}{4}\right)$

3 Differentiate with respect to x.

a $x \sin x$
b $2\sin 2x \cos 3x$
c $x^2 \tan x$
d $x\tan^3\left(\dfrac{x}{2}\right)$
e $\dfrac{5}{\cos 3x}$
f $\dfrac{x}{\cos x}$
g $\dfrac{\tan x}{x}$
h $\dfrac{\sin x}{2+\cos x}$
i $\dfrac{\sin x}{3x-1}$
j $\dfrac{1}{\sin^3 2x}$
k $\dfrac{3x}{\sin 2x}$
l $\dfrac{\sin x + \cos x}{\sin x - \cos x}$

4 Differentiate with respect to x.

a $e^{\cos x}$
b $e^{\cos 5x}$
c $e^{\tan x}$
d $e^{(\sin x + \cos x)}$
e $e^x \sin x$
f $e^x \cos \dfrac{1}{2} x$
g $e^x (\cos x + \sin x)$
h $x^2 e^{\cos x}$
i $\ln(\sin x)$
j $x^2 \ln(\cos x)$
k $\dfrac{\sin 3x}{e^{2x-1}}$
l $\dfrac{x \sin x}{e^x}$

5 Find the gradient of the tangent to

a $y = 2x\cos 3x$ when $x = \dfrac{\pi}{3}$
b $y = \dfrac{2-\cos x}{3\tan x}$ when $x = \dfrac{\pi}{4}$.

6 a By writing $\sec x$ as $\dfrac{1}{\cos x}$, find $\dfrac{d}{dx}(\sec x)$.

b By writing $\operatorname{cosec} x$ as $\dfrac{1}{\sin x}$, find $\dfrac{d}{dx}(\operatorname{cosec} x)$.

c By writing $\cot x$ as $\dfrac{\cos x}{\sin x}$, find $\dfrac{d}{dx}(\cot x)$.

7 Find $\dfrac{dy}{dx}$ for each of the following.

a $e^y = \sin 3x$
b $e^y = 3\cos 2x$

Hint:
Take the natural logarithm of both sides of the equation before differentiating.

CHALLENGE Q

8 A curve has equation $y = A\sin x + B\sin 2x$.

The curve passes through the point $P\left(\dfrac{\pi}{2}, 3\right)$ and has a gradient of $\dfrac{3\sqrt{2}}{2}$ when $x = \dfrac{\pi}{4}$.

Find the value of A and the value of B.

CHALLENGE Q

9 A curve has equation $y = A\sin x + B\cos 2x$.

   The curve has a gradient of $5\sqrt{3}$ when $x = \dfrac{\pi}{6}$ and has a gradient of $6 + 2\sqrt{2}$ when $x = \dfrac{\pi}{4}$.

   Find the value of A and the value of B.

15.4 Further applications of differentiation

You need to be able to answer questions that involve the differentiation of exponential, logarithmic and trigonometric functions.

WORKED EXAMPLE 9

A curve has equation $A\sin x + B\cos 2x$.

The curve passes through the point $P\left(\dfrac{\pi}{2}, a\right)$.

a Find the value of a.
b Find the equation of the normal to the curve at P.

Answers

a When $x = \dfrac{\pi}{2}$, $y = 3 \times \dfrac{\pi}{2} \times \sin\left(\dfrac{\pi}{2}\right) + \dfrac{\pi}{6}$

$$y = \dfrac{3\pi}{2} + \dfrac{\pi}{6} = \dfrac{5\pi}{3}$$

Hence, $a = \dfrac{5\pi}{3}$.

b $y = 3x \sin x + \dfrac{\pi}{6}$

$\dfrac{dy}{dx} = 3x \cos x + 3 \sin x$

When $x = \dfrac{\pi}{2}$, $\dfrac{dy}{dx} = 3\left(\dfrac{\pi}{2}\right)\cos\left(\dfrac{\pi}{2}\right) + 3\sin\left(\dfrac{\pi}{2}\right) = 3$

Normal: passes through the point $\left(\dfrac{\pi}{2}, \dfrac{5\pi}{3}\right)$ and gradient $= -\dfrac{1}{3}$

$$y - \dfrac{5\pi}{3} = -\dfrac{1}{3}\left(x - \dfrac{\pi}{2}\right)$$

$$y - \dfrac{5\pi}{3} = -\dfrac{1}{3}x + \dfrac{\pi}{6}$$

$$y = -\dfrac{1}{3}x + \dfrac{11\pi}{6}$$

WORKED EXAMPLE 10

A curve has equation $y = x^2 \ln x$.

Find the approximate increase in y as x increases from e to e + p, where p is small.

Answers

$y = x^2 \ln x$

$\dfrac{dy}{dx} = x^2 \times \dfrac{1}{x} + \ln x \times 2x$ product rule

$= x + 2x \ln x$

When $x = e$, $\dfrac{dy}{dx} = e + 2e \ln e$

$= 3e$

Using $\dfrac{\delta y}{\delta x} \approx \dfrac{dy}{dx}$

$\dfrac{\delta y}{p} \approx 3e$

$\delta y \approx 3ep$

WORKED EXAMPLE 11

Variables x and y are connected by the equation $y = \dfrac{\ln x}{2x + 5}$.

Given that y increases at a rate of 0.1 units per second, find the rate of change of x when $x = 2$.

Answers

$y = \dfrac{\ln x}{2x + 5}$ and $\dfrac{dy}{dt} = 0.1$

$\dfrac{dy}{dx} = \dfrac{(2x + 5)\dfrac{1}{x} - 2 \ln x}{(2x + 5)^2}$ quotient rule

$= \dfrac{(2x + 5) - 2x \ln x}{x(2x + 5)^2}$

When $x = 2$, $\dfrac{dy}{dx} = \dfrac{(4 + 5) - 4 \ln 2}{2(4 + 5)^2}$

$= \dfrac{9 - 4 \ln 2}{162}$

Using the chain rule, $\dfrac{dx}{dt} = \dfrac{dx}{dy} \times \dfrac{dy}{dt}$

$= \dfrac{162}{9 - 4 \ln 2} \times 0.1$

$= 2.6014\ldots$

Rate of change of x is 2.60 units per second correct to 3 sf.

Chapter 15: Differentiation 2

WORKED EXAMPLE 12

A curve has equation $y = e^{-x}(2\sin 2x - 3\cos 2x)$ for $0 < x < \dfrac{\pi}{2}$ radians.

Find the *x*-coordinate of the stationary point on the curve and determine the nature of this point.

Answers

$y = e^{-x}(2\sin 2x - 3\cos 2x)$

$\dfrac{dy}{dx} = e^{-x}(4\cos 2x + 6\sin 2x) - e^{-x}(2\sin 2x - 3\cos 2x)$ product rule

$\phantom{\dfrac{dy}{dx}} = e^{-x}(7\cos 2x + 4\sin 2x)$

Stationary points occur when $\dfrac{dy}{dx} = 0$.

$e^{-x}(7\cos 2x + 4\sin 2x) = 0$

$7\cos 2x + 4\sin 2x = 0$ or $e^{-x} = 0$

$\tan 2x = -\dfrac{7}{4}$ no solution

$2x = 2.0899$ There are other values of *x* for which

$x = 1.045$ $\tan 2x = -\dfrac{7}{4}$ but they are outside the

range $0 < x < \dfrac{\pi}{2}$.

$\dfrac{d^2y}{dx^2} = e^{-x}(-14\sin 2x + 8\cos 2x) - e^{-x}(7\cos 2x + 4\sin 2x)$

$\phantom{\dfrac{d^2y}{dx^2}} = e^{-x}(\cos 2x - 18\sin 2x)$

When $x = 1.045$, $\dfrac{d^2y}{dx^2} < 0$.

Hence the stationary point is a maximum point.

WORKED EXAMPLE 13

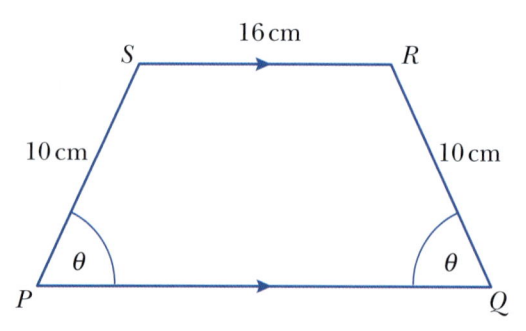

The diagram shows an isosceles trapezium $PQRS$ with area $A\,\text{cm}^2$.
Angle SPQ = angle $PQR = \theta$ radians.
$PS = QR = 10\,\text{cm}$ and $SR = 16\,\text{cm}$.

a Show that $A = 160\sin\theta + 100\sin\theta\cos\theta$.
b Find the value of θ for which A has a stationary value.
c Determine the nature of this stationary value.

Answers

a $A = \dfrac{1}{2}(a+b)h$ \hspace{2em} use $h = 10\sin\theta$

$= \dfrac{1}{2}(PQ + SR) \times 10\sin\theta$ \hspace{2em} use $PQ = 10\cos\theta + 16 + 10\cos\theta = 16 + 20\cos\theta$

$= \dfrac{1}{2}[(16 + 20\cos\theta) + 16] \times 10\sin\theta$

$= 5\sin\theta(32 + 20\cos\theta)$

$= 160\sin\theta + 100\sin\theta\cos\theta$

b $\dfrac{dA}{dx} = 160\cos\theta + [100\sin\theta(-\sin\theta) + 100\cos^2\theta]$ \hspace{1em} use the product rule on $100\sin\theta\cos\theta$

$= 160\cos\theta - 100\sin^2\theta + 100\cos^2\theta$ \hspace{2em} use $\sin^2\theta = 1 - \cos^2\theta$

$= 160\cos\theta - 100(1 - \cos^2\theta) + 100\cos^2\theta$

$= 200\cos^2\theta + 160\cos\theta - 100$

Stationary values occur when $\dfrac{dA}{dx} = 0$.

$200\cos^2\theta + 160\cos\theta - 100 = 0$

$10\cos^2\theta + 8\cos\theta - 5 = 0$ \hspace{2em} use the quadratic formula

$\cos\theta = 0.412$ \hspace{2em} or \hspace{1em} $\cos\theta = -1.212$

$\theta = 1.146$ radians \hspace{4em} no solution

c $\dfrac{d^2A}{dx^2} = -400\cos\theta\sin\theta - 160\sin\theta$

When $\theta = 1.146$, $\dfrac{d^2A}{dx^2} < 0$.

Hence the stationary value is a maximum value.

Exercise 15.4

1. A curve has equation $y = 3\sin\left(2x + \dfrac{\pi}{2}\right)$.

   Find the equation of the normal to the curve at the point on the curve where $x = \dfrac{\pi}{4}$.

2. A curve has equation $y = x \sin 2x$ for $0 \leqslant x \leqslant \pi$ radians.
   a. Find the equation of the normal to the curve at the point $P\left(\dfrac{\pi}{4}, \dfrac{\pi}{4}\right)$.
   b. The normal at P intersects the x-axis at Q and the y-axis at R.
      Find the coordinates of Q and R.
   c. Find the area of triangle OQR where O is the origin.

3. A curve has equation $y = e^{\frac{1}{2}x} + 1$.

   The curve crosses the y-axis at P.

   The normal to the curve at P meets the x-axis at Q.

   Find the coordinates of Q.

4. A curve has equation $y = 5 - e^{2x}$.

   The curve crosses the x-axis at A and the y-axis at B.
   a. Find the coordinates of A and B.
   b. The normal to the curve at B meets the x-axis at the point C.
      Find the coordinates of C.

5. A curve has equation $y = xe^x$.

   The tangent to the curve at the point $P(1, e)$ meets the y-axis at the point A.

   The normal to the curve at P meets the x-axis at the point B.

   Find the area of triangle OAB, where O is the origin.

6. Variables x and y are connected by the equation $y = \sin 2x$.

   Find the approximate increase in y as x increases from $\dfrac{\pi}{8}$ to $\dfrac{\pi}{8} + p$, where p is small.

7. Variables x and y are connected by the equation $y = 3 + \ln(2x - 5)$

   Find the approximate change in y as x increases from 4 to $4 + p$, where p is small.

8. Variables x and y are connected by the equation $y = \dfrac{\ln x}{x^2 + 3}$.

   Find the approximate change in y as x increases from 1 to $1 + p$, where p is small.

9. Variables x and y are connected by the equation $y = 3 + 2x - 5e^{-x}$.

   Find the approximate change in y as x increases from $\ln 2$ to $\ln 2 + p$, where p is small.

10. A curve has equation $y = \dfrac{\ln(x^2 - 2)}{x^2 - 2}$.

    Find the approximate change in y as x increases from $\sqrt{3}$ to $\sqrt{3} + p$, where p is small.

11 Find the coordinates of the stationary points on these curves and determine their nature.
  a $y = xe^{\frac{x}{2}}$
  b $y = x^2 e^{2x}$
  c $y = e^x - 7x + 2$
  d $y = 5e^{2x} - 10x - 1$
  e $y = (x^2 - 8)e^{-x}$
  f $y = x^2 \ln x$
  g $y = \dfrac{\ln x}{x^2}$
  h $y = \dfrac{\ln(x^2 + 1)}{x^2 + 1}$

12 Find the coordinates of the stationary points on these curves and determine their nature.
  a $y = 4\sin x + 3\cos x$ for $0 \leqslant x \leqslant \dfrac{\pi}{2}$
  b $y = 6\cos\dfrac{x}{2} + 8\sin\dfrac{x}{2}$ for $0 \leqslant x \leqslant 2\pi$
  c $y = 5\sin\left(2x + \dfrac{\pi}{2}\right)$ for $-\dfrac{\pi}{6} \leqslant x \leqslant \dfrac{5\pi}{6}$
  d $y = \dfrac{e^x}{\sin x}$ for $0 < x < \pi$
  e $y = 2\sin x \cos x + 2\cos x$ for $0 \leqslant x \leqslant \pi$

13 A curve has equation $y = Ae^{2x} + Be^{-2x}$.
   The gradient of the tangent at the point (0, 10) is −12.
   a Find the value of A and the value of B.
   b Find the coordinates of the turning point on the curve and determine its nature.

14 A curve has equation $y = x \ln x$.
   The curve crosses the x-axis at the point A and has a minimum point at B.
   Find the coordinates of A and the coordinates of B.

15 A curve has equation $y = x^2 e^x$.
   The curve has a minimum point at P and a maximum point at Q.
   a Find the coordinates of P and the coordinates of Q.
   b The tangent to the curve at the point $A(1, e)$ meets the y-axis at the point B.
      The normal to the curve at the point $A(1, e)$ meets the y-axis at the point C.
      Find the coordinates of B and the coordinates of C.
   c Find the area of triangle ABC.

Chapter 15: Differentiation 2

16 The diagram shows a semi-circle with diameter *EF* of length 12 cm.

Angle $GEF = \theta$ radians and the shaded region has an area of $A\,\text{cm}^2$.

  a Show that $A = 36\theta + 18\sin 2\theta$.

  b Given that θ is increasing at a rate of 0.05 radians per second, find the rate of change of A when $\theta = \dfrac{\pi}{6}$ radians.

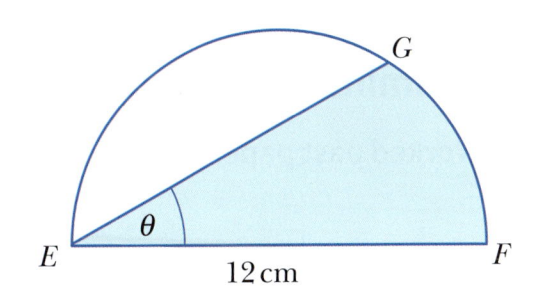

CHALLENGE Q

17 The diagram shows an isosceles triangle *PQR* inscribed in a circle, centre *O*, radius r cm.

$PR = QR$ and angle $ORP = \theta$ radians.

Triangle *PQR* has an area of $A\,\text{cm}^2$.

  a Show that $A = r^2 \sin 2\theta + r^2 \sin 2\theta \cos 2\theta$.

  b Find the value of θ for which A has a stationary value and determine the nature of this stationary value.

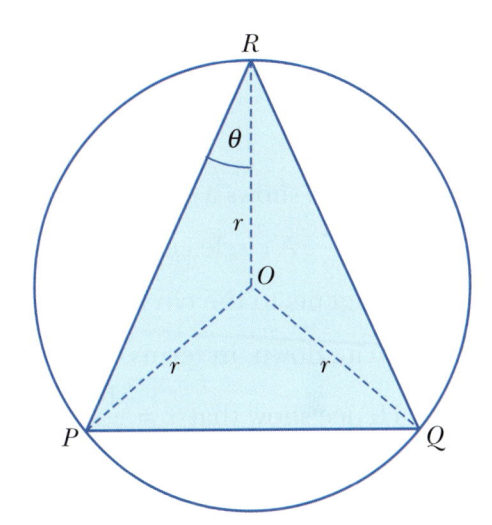

Summary

Exponential functions

$\dfrac{d}{dx}(e^x) = e^x$ $\qquad$ $\dfrac{d}{dx}\left[e^{ax+b}\right] = ae^{ax+b}$ $\qquad$ $\dfrac{d}{dx}\left[e^{f(x)}\right] = f'(x) \times e^{f(x)}$

Logarithmic functions

$\dfrac{d}{dx}(\ln x) = \dfrac{1}{x}$ $\qquad$ $\dfrac{d}{dx}\left[\ln(ax+b)\right] = \dfrac{a}{ax+b}$ $\qquad$ $\dfrac{d}{dx}\left[\ln(f(x))\right] = \dfrac{f'(x)}{f(x)}$

Trigonometric functions

$\dfrac{d}{dx}(\sin x) = \cos x$ $\qquad$ $\dfrac{d}{dx}\left[\sin(ax+b)\right] = a\cos(ax+b)$

$\dfrac{d}{dx}(\cos x) = -\sin x$ $\qquad$ $\dfrac{d}{dx}\left[\cos(ax+b)\right] = -a\sin(ax+b)$

$\dfrac{d}{dx}(\tan x) = \sec^2 x$ $\qquad$ $\dfrac{d}{dx}\left[\tan(ax+b)\right] = a\sec^2(ax+b)$

Examination questions

Worked past paper example

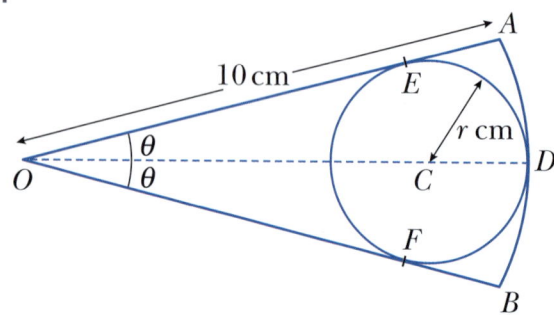

The figure shows a sector OAB of a circle, centre O, radius 10 cm. Angle $AOB = 2\theta$ radians where $0 < \theta < \dfrac{\pi}{2}$. A circle centre C, radius r cm, touches the arc AB at the point D. The lines OA and OB are tangents to the circle at the points E and F respectively.

a Write down, in terms of r, the length of OC. [1]

b Hence show that $r = \dfrac{10\sin\theta}{1+\sin\theta}$. [2]

c Given that θ can vary, find $\dfrac{dr}{d\theta}$ when $r = \dfrac{10}{3}$. [6]

d Given that r is increasing at 2 cm s^{-1}, find the rate at which θ is increasing when $\theta = \dfrac{\pi}{6}$. [3]

Cambridge IGCSE Additional Mathematics 0606 Paper 11 Q10(part) Nov 2011

Answers

a $OC = OD - CD$

$OC = 10 - r$

b Using triangle OCE:

$\sin\theta = \dfrac{r}{OC}$ — use $OC = 10 - r$

$\sin\theta = \dfrac{r}{10-r}$ — multiply both sides by $(10 - r)$

$r = 10\sin\theta - r\sin\theta$ — collect terms involving r

$r + r\sin\theta = 10\sin\theta$ — factorise

$r(1 + \sin\theta) = 10\sin\theta$ — divide both sides by $(1 + \sin\theta)$

$r = \dfrac{10\sin\theta}{1+\sin\theta}$

c $r = \dfrac{10\sin\theta}{1+\sin\theta}$ use the quotient rule

$\dfrac{dr}{d\theta} = \dfrac{(1+\sin\theta)10\cos\theta - 10\sin\theta\cos\theta}{(1+\sin\theta)^2}$

$\dfrac{dr}{d\theta} = \dfrac{10\cos\theta}{(1+\sin\theta)^2}$ ----------------(1)

When $r = \dfrac{10}{3}$, $\dfrac{10}{3} = \dfrac{10\sin\theta}{1+\sin\theta}$

$30\sin\theta = 10 + 10\sin\theta$

$20\sin\theta = 10$

$\sin\theta = \dfrac{1}{2}$

If $\sin\theta = \dfrac{1}{2}$, then $\cos\theta = \dfrac{\sqrt{3}}{2}$.

Substituting in equation (1) gives: $\dfrac{dr}{d\theta} = \dfrac{10 \times \dfrac{\sqrt{3}}{2}}{\left(1+\dfrac{1}{2}\right)^2} = \dfrac{20\sqrt{3}}{9}$

d When $\theta = \dfrac{\pi}{6}$, $\sin\theta = \dfrac{1}{2}$, $\cos\theta = \dfrac{\sqrt{3}}{2}$ and $\dfrac{dr}{d\theta} = \dfrac{20\sqrt{3}}{9}$.

Using the chain rule: $\dfrac{d\theta}{dt} = \dfrac{d\theta}{dr} \times \dfrac{dr}{dt}$

$= \dfrac{9}{20\sqrt{3}} \times 2$

$= \dfrac{9}{10\sqrt{3}}$

$= \dfrac{3\sqrt{3}}{10}$

Exercise 15.5

Exam Exercise

1 a Find the equation of the tangent to the curve $y = x^3 - \ln x$ at the point on the curve where $x = 1$.   [4]

  b Show that the tangent bisects the line joining the points (−2, 16) and (12, 2).   [2]

Cambridge IGCSE Additional Mathematics 0606 Paper 11 Q5i,ii Nov 2014

2 Find $\dfrac{dy}{dx}$ when

  a $y = \cos 2x \sin\left(\dfrac{x}{3}\right)$,   [4]

  b $y = \dfrac{\tan x}{1+\ln x}$.   [4]

Cambridge IGCSE Additional Mathematics 0606 Paper 21 Q10i,11 Jun 2014

Cambridge IGCSE and O Level Additional Mathematics

3 Variables x and y are related by the equation $y = 10 - 4\sin^2 x$, where $0 \leqslant x \leqslant \dfrac{\pi}{2}$.

Given that x is increasing at a rate of 0.2 radians per second, find the corresponding rate of change of y when $y = 8$. [6]

Cambridge IGCSE Additional Mathematics 0606 Paper 21 Q3 Jun 2013

4 Given that $y = \dfrac{x^2}{\cos 4x}$, find

a $\dfrac{dy}{dx}$, [3]

b the approximate change in y when x increases from $\dfrac{\pi}{4}$ to $\dfrac{\pi}{4} + p$, where p is small. [2]

Cambridge IGCSE Additional Mathematics 0606 Paper 11 Q5i,ii Nov 2012

5 Variables x and y are such that $y = e^{2x} + e^{-2x}$.

a Find $\dfrac{dy}{dx}$. [2]

b By using the substitution $u = e^{2x}$, find the value of y when $\dfrac{dy}{dx} = 3$. [4]

c Given that x is decreasing at the rate of 0.5 units s^{-1}, find the corresponding rate of change of y when $x = 1$. [3]

Cambridge IGCSE Additional Mathematics 0606 Paper 11 Q10i,ii,iii Jun 2012

6

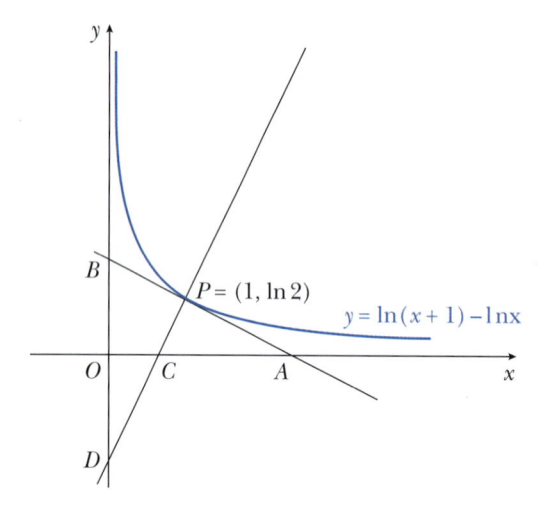

The diagram shows part of the curve $y = \ln(x + 1) - \ln x$. The tangent to the curve at the point $P(1, \ln 2)$ meets the x-axis at A and the y-axis at B. The normal to the curve at P meets the x-axis at C and the y-axis at D.

a Find, in terms of $\ln 2$, the coordinates of A, B, C and D. [8]

b Given that $\dfrac{\text{Area of triangle } BPD}{\text{Area of triangle } APC} = \dfrac{1}{k}$, express k in terms of $\ln 2$. [3]

Cambridge IGCSE Additional Mathematics 0606 Paper 21 Q12(part) Nov 2011

7 A curve has equation $y = 2x \sin x + \dfrac{\pi}{3}$. The curve passes through the point $P\left(\dfrac{\pi}{2}, a\right)$.

a Find, in terms of π, the value of a. [1]

b Using your value of a, find the equation of the normal to the curve at P. [5]

Cambridge IGCSE Additional Mathematics 0606 Paper 11 Q5i,ii Nov 2010

Chapter 16
Integration

This section will show you how to:

- use integration as the reverse process of differentiation
- integrate sums of terms in powers of x, excluding $\dfrac{1}{x}$
- integrate functions of the form $(ax+b)^n$, e^{ax+b}, $\sin(ax+b)$, $\cos(ax+b)$
- evaluate definite integrals and apply integration to the evaluation of plane areas.

Cambridge IGCSE and O Level Additional Mathematics

> **RECAP**
>
> In Chapter 12, you learnt about the process of obtaining $\dfrac{dy}{dx}$ when you know y. This process was called differentiation.
>
> You learnt the rule for differentiating power functions: If $y = x^n$, then $\dfrac{dy}{dx} = nx^{n-1}$.
>
> Applying this rule to functions of the form $y = x^2 + c$ you obtain:
>
> $$\left. \begin{array}{l} y = x^2 + 5.3 \\ y = x^2 + 2 \\ y = x^2 \\ y = x^2 - 3 \end{array} \right\} \dfrac{dy}{dx} = 2x$$
>
> In this chapter you will learn about the reverse process of obtaining y when you know $\dfrac{dy}{dx}$. This reverse process is called **integration**.
>
> **Note:** There are an infinite number of functions that when differentiated give $2x$.

16.1 Differentiation reversed

> **CLASS DISCUSSION**
>
> Find $\dfrac{dy}{dx}$ for each of the following functions.
>
> $y = \dfrac{1}{4}x^4 + 3$
>
> $y = \dfrac{1}{7}x^7 - 0.8$
>
> $y = \dfrac{1}{3}x^3 + 4$
>
> $y = \dfrac{1}{-2}x^{-2} + 1$
>
> $y = \dfrac{1}{\left(\dfrac{1}{2}\right)}x^{\frac{1}{2}} - 7$
>
> Discuss your results with your classmates and try to find a rule for obtaining y if $\dfrac{dy}{dx} = x^n$. Describe your rule in words.

From the class discussion you should have concluded that:

> If $\dfrac{dy}{dx} = x^n$ then $y = \dfrac{1}{n+1}x^{n+1} + c$, where c is an arbitrary constant and $n \neq -1$.

It is easier to remember this rule as:

'increase the power n by 1 to get the new power, then divide by the new power'.

Chapter 16: Integration

WORKED EXAMPLE 1

Find y in terms of x for each of the following.

a $\dfrac{dy}{dx} = x^4$ **b** $\dfrac{dy}{dx} = \sqrt{x}$ **c** $\dfrac{dy}{dx} = \dfrac{1}{x^3}$

Answers

a $\dfrac{dy}{dx} = x^4$

$y = \dfrac{1}{4+1} x^{4+1} + c$

$= \dfrac{1}{5} x^5 + c$

b $\dfrac{dy}{dx} = x^{\frac{1}{2}}$

$y = \dfrac{1}{\frac{1}{2}+1} x^{\frac{1}{2}+1} + c$

$= \dfrac{2}{3} x^{\frac{3}{2}} + c$

$= \dfrac{2}{3} \sqrt{x^3} + c$

c $\dfrac{dy}{dx} = x^{-3}$

$y = \dfrac{1}{-3+1} x^{-3+1} + c$

$= \dfrac{1}{-2} x^{-2} + c$

$= -\dfrac{1}{2x^2} + c$

WORKED EXAMPLE 2

Find y in terms of x for each of the following.

a $\dfrac{dy}{dx} = 6x^2 - \dfrac{5}{x^2} + 4x$ **b** $\dfrac{dy}{dx} = 8x^3 - \dfrac{4}{3x^5} - 2$ **c** $\dfrac{dy}{dx} = \dfrac{(x-2)(x+5)}{\sqrt{x}}$

Answers

a $\dfrac{dy}{dx} = 6x^2 - 5x^{-2} + 4x^1$ write in index form ready for integration

$y = \dfrac{6}{3} x^3 - \dfrac{5}{(-1)} x^{-1} + \dfrac{4}{2} x^2 + c$

$= 2x^3 + 5x^{-1} + 2x^2 + c$

$= 2x^3 + \dfrac{5}{x} + 2x^2 + c$

b $\dfrac{dy}{dx} = 8x^3 - \dfrac{4}{3} x^{-5} - 2x^0$ write in index form ready for integration

$y = \dfrac{8}{4} x^4 - \dfrac{4}{3(-4)} x^{-4} - \dfrac{2}{1} x^1 + c$

$= 2x^4 + \dfrac{1}{3} x^{-4} - 2x + c$

$= 2x^4 + \dfrac{1}{3x^4} - 2x + c$

c $\dfrac{dy}{dx} = \dfrac{x^2 + 3x - 10}{\sqrt{x}}$

$= x^{\frac{3}{2}} + 3x^{\frac{1}{2}} - 10x^{-\frac{1}{2}}$ write in index form ready for integration

$y = \dfrac{1}{\frac{5}{2}} x^{\frac{5}{2}} + \dfrac{3}{\frac{3}{2}} x^{\frac{3}{2}} - \dfrac{10}{\frac{1}{2}} x^{\frac{1}{2}} + c$

$= \dfrac{2}{5} x^{\frac{5}{2}} + 2x^{\frac{3}{2}} - 20x^{\frac{1}{2}} + c$

Cambridge IGCSE and O Level Additional Mathematics

> **WORKED EXAMPLE 3**
>
> A curve is such that $\dfrac{dy}{dx} = (1-x)(3x-2)$, and $(2, 8)$ is a point on the curve.
>
> Find the equation of the curve.
>
> **Answers**
>
> $\dfrac{dy}{dx} = (1-x)(3x-2)$ expand brackets
>
> $\quad = -3x^2 + 5x - 2$
>
> $\quad = -3x^2 + 5x^1 - 2x^0$ write in index form ready for integration
>
> $y = -x^3 + \dfrac{5}{2}x^2 - 2x + c$
>
> When $x = 2$, $y = 8$
>
> $8 = -(2)^3 + \dfrac{5}{2}(2)^2 - 2(2) + c$
>
> $8 = -8 + 10 - 4 + c$
>
> $c = 10$
>
> The equation of the curve is $y = -x^3 + \dfrac{5}{2}x^2 - 2x + 10$.

Exercise 16.1

1 Find y in terms of x for each of the following.

    a $\dfrac{dy}{dx} = 12x^4$ **b** $\dfrac{dy}{dx} = 5x^8$ **c** $\dfrac{dy}{dx} = 7x^3$

    d $\dfrac{dy}{dx} = \dfrac{4}{x^3}$ **e** $\dfrac{dy}{dx} = \dfrac{1}{2x^2}$ **f** $\dfrac{dy}{dx} = \dfrac{3}{\sqrt{x}}$

2 Find y in terms of x for each of the following.

    a $\dfrac{dy}{dx} = 7x^6 + 2x^4 + 3$ **b** $\dfrac{dy}{dx} = 2x^5 - 3x^3 + 5x$

    c $\dfrac{dy}{dx} = \dfrac{3}{x^4} - \dfrac{15}{x^2} + x$ **d** $\dfrac{dy}{dx} = \dfrac{18}{x^{10}} + \dfrac{6}{x^7} - 2$

3 Find y in terms of x for each of the following.

    a $\dfrac{dy}{dx} = 3x(x-2)$ **b** $\dfrac{dy}{dx} = x^2(4x^2 - 3)$

    c $\dfrac{dy}{dx} = (x + 2\sqrt{x})^2$ **d** $\dfrac{dy}{dx} = x(x-3)(x+4)$

    e $\dfrac{dy}{dx} = \dfrac{x^5 - 3x}{2x^3}$ **f** $\dfrac{dy}{dx} = \dfrac{(2x-3)(x-1)}{x^4}$

    g $\dfrac{dy}{dx} = \dfrac{x^5 - 4x^2 + 1}{2x^2}$ **h** $\dfrac{dy}{dx} = \dfrac{(3x+5)(x-2)}{\sqrt{x}}$

4 A curve is such that $\frac{dy}{dx} = 3x^2 - 4x + 1$.

Given that the curve passes through the point (0, 5) find the equation of the curve.

5 A curve is such that $\frac{dy}{dx} = 6x(x - 1)$.

Given that the curve passes through the point (1, −5) find the equation of the curve.

6 A curve is such that $\frac{dy}{dx} = \frac{2x^3 + 6}{x^2}$.

Given that the curve passes through the point (−1, 10), find the equation of the curve.

7 A curve is such that $\frac{dy}{dx} = \frac{(2 - \sqrt{x})^2}{\sqrt{x}}$.

Given that the curve passes through the point (9, 14), find the equation of the curve.

8 A curve is such that $\frac{dy}{dx} = kx^2 - 2x$ where k is a constant.

Given that the curve passes through the points (1, 6) and (−2, −15) find the equation of the curve.

9 A curve is such that $\frac{d^2y}{dx^2} = 12x - 12$.

The gradient of the curve at the point (2, 9) is 8.

a Express y in terms of x.

b Show that the gradient of the curve is never less than 2.

10 A curve is such that $\frac{dy}{dx} = kx - 5$ where k is a constant.

The gradient of the normal to the curve at the point (2, −1) is $-\frac{1}{3}$.

Find the equation of the curve.

16.2 Indefinite integrals

The special symbol $\int$ is used to denote integration.

When you need to integrate x^2, for example, you write

$$\int x^2 \, dx = \frac{1}{3}x^3 + c.$$

$\int x^2 \, dx$ is called the **indefinite integral** of x^2 with respect to x.

It is called 'indefinite' because it has infinitely many solutions.

Using this notation the rule for integrating powers of x can be written as:

$$\int x^n \, dx = \frac{1}{n+1}x^{n+1} + c, \text{ where } c \text{ is a constant and } n \neq -1$$

Cambridge IGCSE and O Level Additional Mathematics

This section provides you with practice at using this new notation together with the following rules:

$$\int k f(x)\, dx = k \int f(x)\, dx, \text{ where } k \text{ is a constant}$$

$$\int \left[f(x) \pm g(x) \right] dx = \int f(x)\, dx \pm \int g(x)\, dx$$

WORKED EXAMPLE 4

Find: **a** $\int x^2 (10x^2 - 8x + 3)\, dx$ **b** $\int \dfrac{x^4 - 2}{x\sqrt{x}}\, dx$

Answers

a $\int x^2 (10x^2 - 8x + 3)\, dx = \int (10x^4 - 8x^3 + 3x^2)\, dx$

$= \dfrac{10x^5}{5} - \dfrac{8x^4}{4} + \dfrac{3x^3}{3} + c$

$= 2x^5 - 2x^4 + x^3 + c$

b $\int \dfrac{x^4 - 2}{x\sqrt{x}}\, dx = \int \dfrac{x^4 - 2}{x^{\frac{3}{2}}}\, dx$

$= \int \left(x^{\frac{5}{2}} - 2x^{-\frac{3}{2}} \right) dx$

$= \dfrac{1}{\left(\frac{7}{2}\right)} x^{\frac{7}{2}} - \dfrac{2}{\left(-\frac{1}{2}\right)} x^{-\frac{1}{2}} + c$

$= \dfrac{2}{7} x^{\frac{7}{2}} + 4 x^{-\frac{1}{2}} + c$

$= \dfrac{2}{7} x^3 \sqrt{x} + \dfrac{4}{\sqrt{x}} + c$

Exercise 16.2

1 Find each of the following.

a $\int 4x^7\, dx$ **b** $\int 12x^5\, dx$ **c** $\int 2x^{-3}\, dx$

d $\int \dfrac{4}{x^2}\, dx$ **e** $\int \dfrac{3}{\sqrt{x}}\, dx$ **f** $\int \dfrac{6}{x^2 \sqrt{x}}\, dx$

2 Find each of the following.

a $\int (x+2)(x+5)\, dx$ **b** $\int (x-1)(2x+3)\, dx$ **c** $\int (x-5)^2\, dx$

d $\int (\sqrt{x}+3)^2\, dx$ **e** $\int x(x-1)^2\, dx$ **f** $\int \sqrt[3]{x}\,(x-4)\, dx$

3 Find each of the following.

a $\int \dfrac{x^2 - 5}{x^2}\,dx$ **b** $\int \dfrac{x^4 - 8}{2x^3}\,dx$ **c** $\int \dfrac{(x+1)^2}{3x^4}\,dx$

d $\int \dfrac{4x^2 - 3\sqrt{x}}{x}\,dx$ **e** $\int \dfrac{x^5 + 5}{x^3\sqrt{x}}\,dx$ **f** $\int \left(\sqrt{x} + \dfrac{3}{x^2\sqrt{x}}\right)^2 dx$

16.3 Integration of functions of the form $(ax+b)^n$

In Chapter 12 you learnt that:

$$\dfrac{d}{dx}\left[\dfrac{1}{2 \times 8}(2x+5)^8\right] = (2x+5)^7$$

Hence $\int (2x+5)^7\,dx = \dfrac{1}{2 \times 8}(2x+5)^8 + c.$

This leads to the general rule:

$$\int (ax+b)^n\,dx = \dfrac{1}{a(n+1)}(ax+b)^{n+1} + c,\ n \neq -1 \text{ and } a \neq 0$$

WORKED EXAMPLE 5

Find

a $\int (3x-8)^5\,dx$ **b** $\int \dfrac{8}{(4x+1)^3}\,dx$ **c** $\int \dfrac{12}{\sqrt{2x-7}}\,dx.$

Answers

a $\int (3x-8)^5\,dx = \dfrac{1}{3(5+1)}(3x-8)^{5+1} + c$

$= \dfrac{1}{18}(3x-8)^6 + c$

b $\int \dfrac{8}{(4x+1)^3}\,dx = 8\int (4x+1)^{-3}\,dx$

$= \dfrac{8}{4(-3+1)}(4x+1)^{-3+1} + c$

$= -(4x+1)^{-2} + c$

$= -\dfrac{1}{(4x+1)^2} + c$

c $\int \dfrac{12}{\sqrt{2x-7}}\,dx = 12\int (2x-7)^{-\frac{1}{2}}\,dx$

$= \dfrac{12}{2\left(-\dfrac{1}{2}+1\right)}(2x-7)^{-\frac{1}{2}+1} + c$

$= 12\sqrt{2x-7} + c$

Exercise 16.3

1 Find:

   a $\displaystyle\int (x+2)^9 \, dx$
   b $\displaystyle\int (2x-5)^6 \, dx$
   c $\displaystyle\int 2(3x+2)^9 \, dx$

   d $\displaystyle\int 3(2-3x)^4 \, dx$
   e $\displaystyle\int (7x+2)^{\frac{1}{3}} \, dx$
   f $\displaystyle\int \sqrt{(3x-1)^3} \, dx$

   g $\displaystyle\int \frac{6}{\sqrt{x+1}} \, dx$
   h $\displaystyle\int \left(\frac{2}{5x+3}\right)^3 \, dx$
   i $\displaystyle\int \frac{3}{2(3-2x)^4} \, dx$

2 A curve is such that $\dfrac{dy}{dx} = (4x+1)^4$.

   Given that the curve passes through the point $(0, -1.95)$ find the equation of the curve.

3 A curve is such that $\dfrac{dy}{dx} = \sqrt{2x+1}$.

   Given that the curve passes through the point $(4, 11)$ find the equation of the curve.

4 A curve is such that $\dfrac{dy}{dx} = \dfrac{1}{\sqrt{10-x}}$.

   Given that the curve passes through the point $(6, 1)$, find the equation of the curve.

5 A curve is such that $\dfrac{dy}{dx} = k(2x-3)^3$ where k is a constant.

   The gradient of the normal to the curve at the point $(2, 2)$ is $-\dfrac{1}{8}$.

   Find the equation of the curve.

6 A curve is such that $\dfrac{dy}{dx} = 2(kx-1)^5$ where k is a constant.

   Given that the curve passes through the points $(0, 1)$ and $(1, 8)$ find the equation of the curve.

16.4 Integration of exponential functions

In Chapter 15, you learnt the following rules for differentiating exponential functions:

$$\frac{d}{dx}(e^x) = e^x \qquad\qquad \frac{d}{dx}(e^{ax+b}) = ae^{ax+b}$$

Since integration is the reverse process of differentiation, the rules for integrating exponential functions are:

$$\int e^x \, dx = e^x + c \qquad\qquad \int e^{ax+b} \, dx = \frac{1}{a} e^{ax+b} + c$$

Chapter 16: Integration

> **WORKED EXAMPLE 6**
>
> Find
> **a** $\displaystyle\int e^{2x}\,dx$ **b** $\displaystyle\int e^{-7x}\,dx$ **c** $\displaystyle\int e^{6x-5}\,dx$.
>
> **Answers**
>
> **a** $\displaystyle\int e^{2x}\,dx = \frac{1}{2}e^{2x} + c$
>
> **b** $\displaystyle\int e^{-7x}\,dx = \frac{1}{-7}e^{-7x} + c$
>
> $= -\dfrac{1}{7}e^{-7x} + c$
>
> **c** $\displaystyle\int e^{6x-5}\,dx = \dfrac{1}{6}e^{6x-5} + c$

Exercise 16.4

1 Find:

  a $\displaystyle\int e^{5x}\,dx$ **b** $\displaystyle\int e^{9x}\,dx$ **c** $\displaystyle\int e^{\frac{1}{2}x}\,dx$

  d $\displaystyle\int e^{-2x}\,dx$ **e** $\displaystyle\int 4e^{x}\,dx$ **f** $\displaystyle\int 2e^{4x}\,dx$

  g $\displaystyle\int e^{7x+4}\,dx$ **h** $\displaystyle\int e^{5-2x}\,dx$ **i** $\displaystyle\int \frac{1}{3}e^{6x-1}\,dx$

2 Find:

  a $\displaystyle\int e^{x}(5 - e^{2x})\,dx$ **b** $\displaystyle\int (e^{2x} + 1)^2\,dx$ **c** $\displaystyle\int (3e^{x} + e^{-x})^2\,dx$

  d $\displaystyle\int \frac{e^{2x} + 4}{e^{x}}\,dx$ **e** $\displaystyle\int \frac{5e^{3x} - e^{2x}}{2e^{x}}\,dx$ **f** $\displaystyle\int \frac{(e^{4x} - 2e^{x})^2}{e^{3x}}\,dx$

3 Find:

  a $\displaystyle\int \left(2e^{x} + \frac{1}{\sqrt{x}}\right)dx$ **b** $\displaystyle\int (x^2 - 3e^{2x+1})\,dx$ **c** $\displaystyle\int \frac{3x^2 e^{2x} - 4e^{x}}{12x^2 e^{x}}\,dx$

4 A curve is such that $\dfrac{dy}{dx} = 2e^{2x} + e^{-x}$.

Given that the curve passes through the point $(0, 4)$, find the equation of the curve.

5 A curve is such that $\dfrac{dy}{dx} = ke^{2-x} + 4x$, where k is a constant.

At the point $(2, 10)$ the gradient of the curve is 1.

  a Find the value of k.

  b Find the equation of the curve.

6 A curve is such that $\dfrac{d^2 y}{dx^2} = 8e^{-2x}$.

Given that $\dfrac{dy}{dx} = 2$ when $x = 0$ and that the curve passes through the point $\left(1, \dfrac{2}{e^2}\right)$, find the equation of the curve.

7 The point $P\left(\dfrac{3}{2}, 5\right)$ lies on the curve for which $\dfrac{dy}{dx} = 2e^{3-2x}$.

The point $Q(1, k)$ also lies on the curve.

a Find the value of k.

The normals to the curve at the points P and Q intersect at the point R.

b Find the coordinates of R.

16.5 Integration of sine and cosine functions

In Chapter 15, you learnt how to differentiate sine and cosine functions:

$\dfrac{d}{dx}(\sin x) = \cos x$ $\qquad$ $\dfrac{d}{dx}[\sin(ax+b)] = a\cos(ax+b)$

$\dfrac{d}{dx}(\cos x) = -\sin x$ $\qquad$ $\dfrac{d}{dx}[\cos(ax+b)] = -a\sin(ax+b)$

Since integration is the reverse process of differentiation, the rules for integrating sine and cosine functions are:

$$\int \cos x \, dx = \sin x + c \qquad \int [\cos(ax+b)] \, dx = \dfrac{1}{a}\sin(ax+b) + c$$

$$\int \sin x \, dx = -\cos x + c \qquad \int [\sin(ax+b)] \, dx = -\dfrac{1}{a}\cos(ax+b) + c$$

Note:
It is important to remember that that the formulae for differentiating and integrating these trigonometric functions only apply when x is measured in radians.

WORKED EXAMPLE 7

Find:

a $\displaystyle\int \sin 2x \, dx$ $\quad$ **b** $\displaystyle\int \cos 5x \, dx$ $\quad$ **c** $\displaystyle\int 3\sin\dfrac{x}{2} \, dx$

Answers

a $\displaystyle\int \sin 2x \, dx = -\dfrac{1}{2}\cos 2x + c$

b $\displaystyle\int \cos 5x \, dx = \dfrac{1}{5}\sin 5x + c$

c $\displaystyle\int 3\sin\dfrac{x}{2} \, dx = 3\int \sin\dfrac{x}{2} \, dx$

$\qquad\qquad\qquad = 3 \times \left(-2\cos\dfrac{x}{2}\right) + c$

$\qquad\qquad\qquad = -6\cos\dfrac{x}{2} + c$

WORKED EXAMPLE 8

Find:

a $\int (3\cos 2x + 5\sin 3x)\,dx$ **b** $\int [x^2 + 2\cos(5x-1)]\,dx$

Answers

a $\int (3\cos 2x + 5\sin 3x)\,dx = 3\int \cos 2x\,dx + 5\int \sin 3x\,dx$

$= 3 \times \left(\dfrac{1}{2}\sin 2x\right) + 5 \times \left(-\dfrac{1}{3}\cos 3x\right)$

$= \dfrac{3}{2}\sin 2x - \dfrac{5}{3}\cos 3x + c$

b $\int [x^2 + 2\cos(5x-1)]\,dx = \int x^2\,dx + 2\int \cos(5x-1)\,dx$

$= \dfrac{1}{3}x^3 + 2 \times \left[\dfrac{1}{5}\sin(5x-1)\right] + c$

$= \dfrac{1}{3}x^3 + \dfrac{2}{5}\sin(5x-1) + c$

Exercise 16.5

1 Find:

a $\int \sin 4x\,dx$ **b** $\int \cos 2x\,dx$ **c** $\int \sin \dfrac{x}{3}\,dx$

d $\int 2\cos 2x\,dx$ **e** $\int 6\sin 3x\,dx$ **f** $\int 3\cos(2x+1)\,dx$

g $\int 5\sin(2-3x)\,dx$ **h** $\int 2\cos(2x-7)\,dx$ **i** $\int 4\sin(1-5x)\,dx$

2 Find:

a $\int (1 - \sin x)\,dx$ **b** $\int \left(\sqrt{x} - 2\cos 3x\right)\,dx$

c $\int \left(3\cos 2x - \pi \sin \dfrac{5x}{2}\right)\,dx$ **d** $\int \left(\dfrac{1}{x^2} - \cos \dfrac{3x}{2}\right)\,dx$

e $\int (e^{2x} - 5\sin 2x)\,dx$ **f** $\int \left(\dfrac{2}{\sqrt{x}} + \sin \dfrac{x}{2}\right)\,dx$

3 A curve is such that $\dfrac{dy}{dx} = \cos x - \sin x$.

Given that the curve passes through the point $\left(\dfrac{\pi}{2}, 3\right)$, find the equation of the curve.

4 A curve is such that $\dfrac{dy}{dx} = 1 - 4\cos 2x$.

Given that the curve passes through the point $\left(\dfrac{\pi}{4}, 1\right)$, find the equation of the curve.

5 A curve is such that $\dfrac{dy}{dx} = 4x - 6\sin 2x$.

Given that the curve passes through the point $(0, -2)$, find the equation of the curve.

6 A curve is such that $\dfrac{d^2y}{dx^2} = 45\cos 3x + 2\sin x$.

Given that $\dfrac{dy}{dx} = -2$ when $x = 0$ and that the curve passes through the point $(\pi, -1)$, find the equation of the curve.

7 A curve is such that $\dfrac{dy}{dx} = k\cos 3x - 4$, where k is a constant.

At the point $(\pi, 2)$ the gradient of the curve is -10.

a Find the value of k.

b Find the equation of the curve.

8 The point $\left(\dfrac{\pi}{2}, 5\right)$ lies on the curve for which $\dfrac{dy}{dx} = 4\sin\left(2x - \dfrac{\pi}{2}\right)$.

a Find the equation of the curve.

b Find the equation of the normal to the curve at the point where $x = \dfrac{\pi}{3}$.

9 The point $P\left(\dfrac{\pi}{3}, 3\right)$ lies on the curve for which $\dfrac{dy}{dx} = 3\cos\left(3x - \dfrac{\pi}{2}\right)$.

The point $Q\left(\dfrac{\pi}{2}, k\right)$ also lies on the curve.

a Find the value of k.

The tangents to the curve at the points P and Q intersect at the point R.

b Find the coordinates of R.

16.6 Further indefinite integration

This section uses the concept that integration is the reverse process of differentiation to help integrate complicated expressions.

If $\dfrac{d}{dx}[F(x)] = f(x)$, then $\int f(x)\,dx = F(x) + c$

WORKED EXAMPLE 9

Show that $\dfrac{d}{dx}\left(\dfrac{x^2+1}{\sqrt{4x-3}}\right) = \dfrac{2(3x^2-3x-1)}{\sqrt{(4x-3)^3}}$.

Hence find $\displaystyle\int \dfrac{3x^2-3x-1}{\sqrt{(4x-3)^3}}\,dx$.

Answers

Let $y = \dfrac{x^2+1}{\sqrt{4x-3}}$

$\dfrac{dy}{dx} = \dfrac{(\sqrt{4x-3})2x - (x^2+1)\left[\dfrac{1}{2}(4x-3)^{-\frac{1}{2}}(4)\right]}{4x-3}$ quotient rule

$= \dfrac{2x\sqrt{4x-3} - \dfrac{2(x^2+1)}{\sqrt{4x-3}}}{4x-3}$ multiply numerator and denominator by $\sqrt{4x-3}$

$= \dfrac{2x(4x-3) - 2(x^2+1)}{(4x-3)\sqrt{4x-3}}$

$= \dfrac{2(4x^2-3x-x^2-1)}{\sqrt{(4x-3)^3}}$

$= \dfrac{2(3x^2-3x-1)}{\sqrt{(4x-3)^3}}$

$\displaystyle\int \dfrac{3x^2-3x-1}{\sqrt{(4x-3)^3}}\,dx = \dfrac{1}{2}\int \dfrac{2(3x^2-3x-1)}{\sqrt{(4x-3)^3}}\,dx$

$= \dfrac{x^2+1}{2\sqrt{4x-3}} + c$

WORKED EXAMPLE 10

Differentiate $x \sin x$ with respect to x.

Hence find $\displaystyle\int x \cos x\, dx$.

Answers

Let $y = x \sin x$

$\dfrac{dy}{dx} = (x)(\cos x) + (\sin x)(1)$ product rule

$= x\cos x + \sin x$

Hence $\displaystyle\int (x\cos x + \sin x)\,dx = x\sin x$

$\displaystyle\int x\cos x\,dx + \int \sin x\,dx = x\sin x$

$\displaystyle\int x\cos x\,dx = x\sin x - \int \sin x\,dx$

$\displaystyle\int x\cos x\,dx = x\sin x + \cos x + c$

WORKED EXAMPLE 11

Differentiate $x^3\sqrt{2x-1}$ with respect to x.

Hence find $\displaystyle\int \dfrac{7x^3 - 3x^2 + 5}{\sqrt{2x-1}}\, dx$.

Answers

Let $y = x^3\sqrt{2x-1}$

$\dfrac{dy}{dx} = (x^3)\left[\dfrac{1}{2} \times 2 \times (2x-1)^{-\frac{1}{2}}\right] + \sqrt{2x-1} \times (3x^2)$ product rule

$= \dfrac{x^3}{\sqrt{2x-1}} + 3x^2\sqrt{2x-1}$

$= \dfrac{x^3 + 3x^2(2x-1)}{\sqrt{2x-1}}$

$= \dfrac{7x^3 - 3x^2}{\sqrt{2x-1}}$

$\displaystyle\int \dfrac{7x^3 - 3x^2 + 5}{\sqrt{2x-1}}\, dx = \int \dfrac{7x^3 - 3x^2}{\sqrt{2x-1}}\, dx + \int \dfrac{5}{\sqrt{2x-1}}\, dx$

$\displaystyle\qquad = \int \dfrac{7x^3 - 3x^2}{\sqrt{2x-1}}\, dx + 5\int (2x-1)^{-\frac{1}{2}}\, dx$

$\displaystyle\qquad = x^3\sqrt{2x-1} + \dfrac{5}{2 \times \dfrac{1}{2}}(2x-1)^{\frac{1}{2}} + c$

$\displaystyle\qquad = x^3\sqrt{2x-1} + 5\sqrt{2x-1} + c$

$\displaystyle\qquad = (x^3 + 5)\sqrt{2x-1} + c$

Exercise 16.6

1. **a** Given that $y = \dfrac{x+5}{\sqrt{2x-1}}$, show that $\dfrac{dy}{dx} = \dfrac{x-6}{\sqrt{(2x-1)^3}}$.

   b Hence find $\displaystyle\int \dfrac{x-6}{\sqrt{(2x-1)^3}}\, dx$.

2. **a** Differentiate $(3x^2 - 1)^5$ with respect to x.

   b Hence find $\displaystyle\int x(3x^2 - 1)^4\, dx$.

3. **a** Differentiate $x \ln x$ with respect to x.

   b Hence find $\displaystyle\int \ln x\, dx$.

4. **a** Show that $\dfrac{d}{dx}\left(\dfrac{\ln x}{x}\right) = \dfrac{1 - \ln x}{x^2}$.

   b Hence find $\displaystyle\int \left(\dfrac{\ln x}{x^3}\right) dx$.

5 a Given that $y = x\sqrt{x^2 - 4}$, find $\dfrac{dy}{dx}$.

 b Hence find $\displaystyle\int \dfrac{x^2 - 2}{\sqrt{x^2 - 4}} \, dx$.

6 a Given that $y = 3(x+1)\sqrt{x-5}$, show that $\dfrac{dy}{dx} = \dfrac{9(x-3)}{2\sqrt{x-5}}$.

 b Hence find $\displaystyle\int \dfrac{(x-3)}{\sqrt{x-5}} \, dx$.

7 a Find $\dfrac{d}{dx}\left(xe^{2x} - \dfrac{e^{2x}}{2}\right)$.

 b Hence find $\displaystyle\int xe^{2x} \, dx$.

8 a Show that $\dfrac{d}{dx}\left(\dfrac{\sin x}{1 - \cos x}\right)$ can be written in the form $\dfrac{k}{\cos x - 1}$, and state the value of k.

 b Hence find $\displaystyle\int \dfrac{5}{\cos x - 1} \, dx$.

9 a Given that $y = (x+8)\sqrt{x-4}$, show that $\dfrac{dy}{dx} = \dfrac{kx}{\sqrt{x-4}}$, and state the value of k.

 b Hence find $\displaystyle\int \dfrac{x}{\sqrt{x-4}} \, dx$.

10 a Given that $y = \dfrac{1}{x^2 - 7}$, show that $\dfrac{dy}{dx} = \dfrac{kx}{(x^2 - 7)^2}$, and state the value of k.

 b Hence find $\displaystyle\int \dfrac{4x}{(x^2 - 7)^2} \, dx$.

11 a Find $\dfrac{d}{dx}(2x^3 \ln x)$.

 b Hence find $\displaystyle\int x^2 \ln x \, dx$.

12 a Differentiate $x \cos x$ with respect to x.

 b Hence find $\displaystyle\int x \sin x \, dx$.

13 a Given that $y = e^{2x}(\sin 2x + \cos 2x)$, show that $\dfrac{dy}{dx} = 4e^{2x} \cos 2x$.

 b Hence find $\displaystyle\int e^{2x} \cos 2x \, dx$.

CHALLENGE Q

14 a Find $\dfrac{d}{dx}\left(x^2 \sqrt{2x - 7}\right)$.

 b Hence find $\displaystyle\int \dfrac{5x^2 - 14x + 3}{\sqrt{2x - 7}} \, dx$.

16.7 Definite integration

You have learnt about indefinite integrals such as

$$\int x^2 \, dx = \frac{1}{3}x^3 + c$$

where c is an arbitrary constant.

$\int x^2 \, dx$ is called the **indefinite integral** of x^2 with respect to x.

It is called 'indefinite' because it has infinitely many solutions.

You can integrate a function between two defined limits.

The integral of the function x^2 with respect to x between the limits $x = 1$ and $x = 4$ is written as: $\int_1^4 x^2 \, dx$

The method for evaluating this integral is

$$\int_1^4 x^2 \, dx = \left[\frac{1}{3}x^3 + c\right]_1^4$$

$$= \left(\frac{1}{3} \times 4^3 + c\right) - \left(\frac{1}{3} \times 1^3 + c\right)$$

$$= 21$$

Note that the c's cancel out, so the process can be simplified to:

$$\int_1^4 x^2 \, dx = \left[\frac{1}{3}x^3\right]_1^4$$

$$= \left(\frac{1}{3} \times 4^3\right) - \left(\frac{1}{3} \times 1^3\right)$$

$$= 21$$

$\int_1^4 x^2 \, dx$ is called the **definite integral** of x^2 with respect to x.

It is called 'definite' because there is only one solution.

Hence, the evaluation of a definite integral can be written as:

$$\int_a^b f(x) \, dx = \left[F(x)\right]_a^b = F(b) - F(a)$$

The following rules for definite integrals may also be used.

$$\int_a^b k f(x) \, dx = k \int_a^b f(x) \, dx, \text{where } k \text{ is a constant}$$

$$\int_a^b [f(x) \pm g(x)] \, dx = \int_a^b f(x) \, dx \pm \int_a^b g(x) \, dx$$

WORKED EXAMPLE 12

Evaluate: **a** $\int_1^2 \dfrac{x^5+3}{x^2}\, dx$ **b** $\int_0^5 \sqrt{3x+1}\, dx$ **c** $\int_{-1}^1 \dfrac{10}{(3-2x)^2}\, dx$

Answers

a $\int_1^2 \dfrac{x^5+3}{x^2}\, dx = \int_1^2 (x^3 + 3x^{-2})\, dx$

$= \left[\dfrac{1}{4}x^4 + \dfrac{3}{-1}x^{-1}\right]_1^2$

$= \left(\dfrac{1}{4}(2)^4 - 3(2)^{-1}\right) - \left(\dfrac{1}{4}(1)^4 - 3(1)^{-1}\right)$

$= \left(4 - \dfrac{3}{2}\right) - \left(\dfrac{1}{4} - 3\right)$

$= 5\dfrac{1}{4}$

b $\int_0^5 \sqrt{3x+1}\, dx = \int_0^5 (3x+1)^{\frac{1}{2}}\, dx$

$= \left[\dfrac{1}{(3)\left(\dfrac{3}{2}\right)}(3x+1)^{\frac{3}{2}}\right]_0^5$

$= \left[\dfrac{2}{9}(3x+1)^{\frac{3}{2}}\right]_0^5$

$= \left(\dfrac{2}{9} \times 16^{\frac{3}{2}}\right) - \left(\dfrac{2}{9} \times 1^{\frac{3}{2}}\right)$

$= \left(\dfrac{128}{9}\right) - \left(\dfrac{2}{9}\right)$

$= 14$

c $\int_{-1}^1 \dfrac{10}{(3-2x)^2}\, dx = \int_{-1}^1 10(3-2x)^{-2}\, dx$

$= \left[\dfrac{10}{(-2)(-1)}(3-2x)^{-1}\right]_{-1}^1$

$= \left[\dfrac{5}{3-2x}\right]_{-1}^1$

$= \left(\dfrac{5}{1}\right) - \left(\dfrac{5}{5}\right)$

$= 4$

Cambridge IGCSE and O Level Additional Mathematics

WORKED EXAMPLE 13

Evaluate:

a $\displaystyle\int_1^2 4e^{2x-3}\,dx$ **b** $\displaystyle\int_0^{\frac{\pi}{4}} (3\cos 2x + 5)\,dx$

Answers

a $\displaystyle\int_1^2 4e^{2x-3}\,dx = \left[\frac{4}{2}e^{2x-3}\right]_1^2$

$= (2e^1) - (2e^{-1})$

$= 2e - \dfrac{2}{e}$

$= \dfrac{2e^2 - 2}{e}$

b $\displaystyle\int_0^{\frac{\pi}{4}} (5 + 3\cos 2x)\,dx = \left[5x + \frac{3}{2}\sin 2x\right]_0^{\frac{\pi}{4}}$

$= \left(\dfrac{5\pi}{4} + \dfrac{3}{2}\sin\dfrac{\pi}{2}\right) - \left(0 + \dfrac{3}{2}\sin 0\right)$

$= \left(\dfrac{5\pi}{4} + \dfrac{3}{2}\right) - (0 + 0)$

$= \dfrac{5\pi + 6}{4}$

Exercise 16.7

1 Evaluate:

a $\displaystyle\int_1^2 7x^6\,dx$ **b** $\displaystyle\int_1^2 \frac{4}{x^3}\,dx$ **c** $\displaystyle\int_1^3 (5x+2)\,dx$

d $\displaystyle\int_0^3 (x^2+2)\,dx$ **e** $\displaystyle\int_{-1}^2 (5x^2-3x)\,dx$ **f** $\displaystyle\int_1^4 \left(2+\frac{2}{x^2}\right)\,dx$

g $\displaystyle\int_2^4 \left(x^2-3-\frac{1}{x^2}\right)\,dx$ **h** $\displaystyle\int_1^3 \left(\frac{2x^2-1}{x^5}\right)\,dx$ **i** $\displaystyle\int_{-3}^{-2} (2x-1)(3x-5)\,dx$

j $\displaystyle\int_1^4 \sqrt{x}(x+3)\,dx$ **k** $\displaystyle\int_1^2 \frac{(5-x)(2+x)}{x^4}\,dx$ **l** $\displaystyle\int_1^4 \left(2\sqrt{x}-\frac{2}{\sqrt{x}}\right)\,dx$

2 Evaluate:

a $\displaystyle\int_1^2 (2x+1)^3\,dx$ **b** $\displaystyle\int_0^6 \sqrt{2x+4}\,dx$ **c** $\displaystyle\int_0^3 \sqrt{(x+1)^3}\,dx$

d $\displaystyle\int_{-1}^2 \frac{12}{(x+4)^3}\,dx$ **e** $\displaystyle\int_{-1}^1 \frac{2}{(3x+5)^2}\,dx$ **f** $\displaystyle\int_{-4}^0 \frac{6}{\sqrt{4-3x}}\,dx$

3 Evaluate:

a $\displaystyle\int_0^1 e^{2x}\,dx$ **b** $\displaystyle\int_0^{\frac{1}{4}} e^{4x}\,dx$ **c** $\displaystyle\int_0^2 5e^{-2x}\,dx$

d $\int_0^{\frac{1}{3}} e^{1-3x}\,dx$ **e** $\int_0^1 \dfrac{5}{e^{2x-1}}\,dx$ **f** $\int_0^1 (e^x + 1)^2\,dx$

g $\int_0^1 (e^x + e^{2x})^2\,dx$ **h** $\int_0^1 \left(3e^x - \dfrac{2}{e^x}\right)^2 dx$ **i** $\int_0^2 \dfrac{3 + 8e^{2x}}{2e^x}\,dx$

4 Evaluate:

a $\int_0^\pi \sin x\,dx$ **b** $\int_0^{\frac{\pi}{2}} (3 + \cos 2x)\,dx$

c $\int_0^{\frac{\pi}{3}} \sin\left(2x - \dfrac{\pi}{6}\right) dx$ **d** $\int_{\frac{\pi}{6}}^{\frac{\pi}{3}} (2\cos x - \sin 2x)\,dx$

e $\int_0^{\frac{\pi}{4}} (2x - \sin 2x)\,dx$ **f** $\int_{\frac{\pi}{4}}^{\frac{\pi}{2}} (\sin 3x - \cos 2x)\,dx$

16.8 Further definite integration

This section uses the concept that integration is the reverse process of differentiation to help evaluate complicated definite integrals.

> **WORKED EXAMPLE 14**
>
> Given that $y = \dfrac{3x}{\sqrt{x^2 + 5}}$, find $\dfrac{dy}{dx}$.
>
> Hence evaluate $\int_0^2 \dfrac{3}{\sqrt{(x^2+5)^3}}\,dx$.
>
> **Answers**
>
> $y = \dfrac{3x}{\sqrt{x^2+5}}$
>
> $\dfrac{dy}{dx} = \dfrac{\left(\sqrt{x^2+5}\right)(3) - (3x)\left[\frac{1}{2}(x^2+5)^{-\frac{1}{2}}(2x)\right]}{x^2+5}$ quotient rule
>
> $= \dfrac{3\sqrt{x^2+5} - \dfrac{3x^2}{\sqrt{x^2+5}}}{x^2+5}$ multiply numerator and denominator by $\sqrt{x^2+5}$
>
> $= \dfrac{3(x^2+5) - 3x^2}{(x^2+5)\sqrt{x^2+5}}$
>
> $= \dfrac{15}{\sqrt{(x^2+5)^3}}$
>
> $\int_0^2 \dfrac{3}{\sqrt{(x^2+5)^3}}\,dx = \dfrac{1}{5}\int_0^2 \dfrac{15}{\sqrt{(x^2+5)^3}}\,dx$
>
> $= \dfrac{1}{5}\left[\dfrac{3x}{\sqrt{x^2+5}}\right]_0^2$
>
> $= \dfrac{1}{5}\left[\left(\dfrac{6}{\sqrt{4+5}}\right) - \left(\dfrac{0}{\sqrt{0+5}}\right)\right]$
>
> $= \dfrac{2}{5}$

Cambridge IGCSE and O Level Additional Mathematics

WORKED EXAMPLE 15

Given that $y = x\cos 2x$, find $\dfrac{dy}{dx}$.

Hence evaluate $\displaystyle\int_0^{\frac{\pi}{6}} 2x \sin 2x \, dx$.

Answers

Let $y = x\cos 2x$

$\dfrac{dy}{dx} = (x) \times (-2\sin 2x) + (\cos 2x) \times (1)$ product rule

$\qquad = \cos 2x - 2x\sin 2x$

$\displaystyle\int_0^{\frac{\pi}{6}} (\cos 2x - 2x\sin 2x) \, dx = [x\cos 2x]_0^{\frac{\pi}{6}}$

$\displaystyle\int_0^{\frac{\pi}{6}} \cos 2x \, dx - \int_0^{\frac{\pi}{6}} 2x\sin 2x \, dx = \left(\dfrac{\pi}{6} \times \cos \dfrac{\pi}{3}\right) - (0 \times \cos 0)$

$\left[\dfrac{1}{2}\sin 2x\right]_0^{\frac{\pi}{6}} - \displaystyle\int_0^{\frac{\pi}{6}} 2x\sin 2x \, dx = \dfrac{\pi}{12}$

$\displaystyle\int_0^{\frac{\pi}{6}} 2x\sin 2x \, dx = \left[\dfrac{1}{2}\sin 2x\right]_0^{\frac{\pi}{6}} - \dfrac{\pi}{12}$

$\qquad\qquad\qquad\qquad = \left(\dfrac{1}{2}\sin\dfrac{\pi}{3}\right) - \left(\dfrac{1}{2}\sin 0\right) - \dfrac{\pi}{12}$

$\qquad\qquad\qquad\qquad = \dfrac{\sqrt{3}}{4} - \dfrac{\pi}{12}$

$\qquad\qquad\qquad\qquad = \dfrac{3\sqrt{3} - \pi}{12}$

Exercise 16.8

1. **a** Given that $y = (x+1)\sqrt{2x-1}$, find $\dfrac{dy}{dx}$.

   b Hence evaluate $\displaystyle\int_1^5 \dfrac{x}{\sqrt{2x-1}} \, dx$.

2. **a** Given that $y = x\sqrt{3x^2 + 4}$, find $\dfrac{dy}{dx}$.

   b Hence evaluate $\displaystyle\int_0^2 \dfrac{3x^2 + 2}{\sqrt{3x^2 + 4}} \, dx$.

3. **a** Given that $y = \dfrac{1}{x^2 + 5}$, find $\dfrac{dy}{dx}$.

   b Hence evaluate $\displaystyle\int_1^2 \dfrac{4x}{(x^2 + 5)^2} \, dx$.

4 a Given that $y = \dfrac{x+2}{\sqrt{3x+4}}$, find $\dfrac{dy}{dx}$.

b Hence evaluate $\displaystyle\int_0^4 \dfrac{6x+4}{\sqrt{(3x+4)^3}}\, dx$.

5 a Show that $\dfrac{d}{dx}\left(\dfrac{x}{\cos x}\right) = \dfrac{\cos x + x\sin x}{\cos^2 x}$.

b Hence evaluate $\displaystyle\int_0^{\frac{\pi}{4}} \dfrac{\cos x + x\sin x}{5\cos^2 x}\, dx$.

CHALLENGE Q

6 a Find $\dfrac{d}{dx}(x\sin x)$.   **b** Hence evaluate $\displaystyle\int_0^{\frac{\pi}{2}} x\cos x\, dx$.

CHALLENGE Q

7 a Find $\dfrac{d}{dx}(x^2 \ln x)$.   **b** Hence evaluate $\displaystyle\int_1^e 4x\ln x\, dx$.

CHALLENGE Q

8 a Given that $y = x\sin 3x$, find $\dfrac{dy}{dx}$.   **b** Hence evaluate $\displaystyle\int_0^{\frac{\pi}{6}} x\cos 3x\, dx$.

16.9 Area under a curve

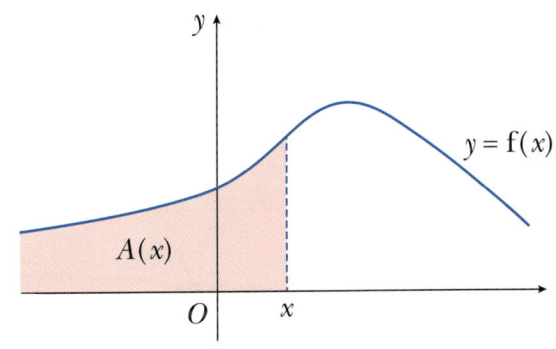

If you define the area under the curve $y = f(x)$ to the left of x as $A(x)$, then as x increases then $A(x)$ also increases.

Now consider a small increase in x, say δx, which results in a small increase, δA, in area.

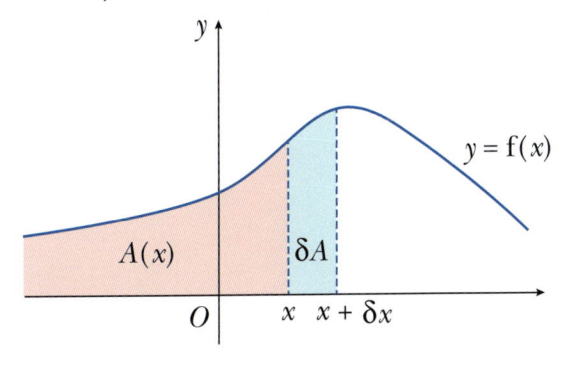

δA = area to the left of $(x + \delta x)$ − area to the left of x

$\delta A = A(x + \delta x) - A(x)$

Now consider the area δA which is approximately a rectangle.

$\delta A \approx y \delta x$

so $\dfrac{\delta A}{\delta x} \approx y$

As $\delta x \to 0$, then $\dfrac{\delta A}{\delta x} \to \dfrac{dA}{dx}$, hence $\dfrac{dA}{dx} = y$.

If $\dfrac{dA}{dx} = y$, then $A = \int y \, dx$.

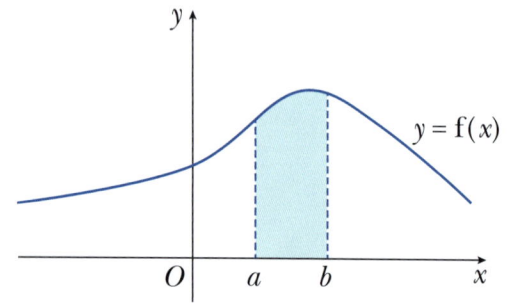

Hence the area of the region bounded by the curve $y = f(x)$, the lines $x = a$ and $x = b$ and the x-axis is given by the definite integral.

$$\text{Area} = \int_a^b f(x) \, dx, \text{ where } f(x) \geq 0$$

WORKED EXAMPLE 16

Find the area of the shaded region.

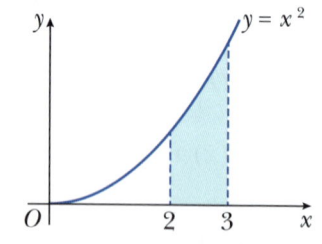

Answers

$\text{Area} = \displaystyle\int_2^3 x^2 \, dx$

$= \left[\dfrac{1}{3} x^3 \right]_2^3$

$= \left(\dfrac{27}{3} \right) - \left(\dfrac{8}{3} \right)$

$= 6 \dfrac{1}{3}$ units^2

WORKED EXAMPLE 17

Find the area of the shaded region.

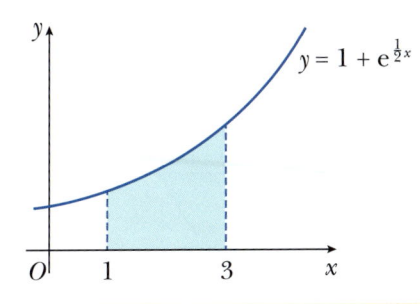

[Graph showing curve $y = 1 + e^{\frac{1}{2}x}$ with shaded region between $x=1$ and $x=3$]

Answers

$$\text{Area} = \int_1^3 \left(1 + e^{\frac{1}{2}x}\right) dx$$

$$= \left[x + \frac{1}{\frac{1}{2}} e^{\frac{1}{2}x} \right]_1^3$$

$$= \left[x + 2e^{\frac{1}{2}x} \right]_1^3$$

$$= \left(3 + 2e^{\frac{3}{2}}\right) - \left(1 + 2e^{\frac{1}{2}}\right)$$

$$= 2 + 2e^{\frac{3}{2}} - 2e^{\frac{1}{2}}$$

$$= 2\left[1 + \sqrt{e}\,(e - 1)\right]$$

$$\approx 7.67 \text{ units}^2$$

In the examples so far, the required area has been above the x-axis.

If the required area between $y = f(x)$ and the x-axis lies below the x-axis, then $\int_a^b f(x)\,dx$ will be a negative value.

Hence, for a region that lies below the x-axis, the area is given as $\left| \int_a^b f(x)\,dx \right|$.

Cambridge IGCSE and O Level Additional Mathematics

WORKED EXAMPLE 18

Find the area of the shaded region.

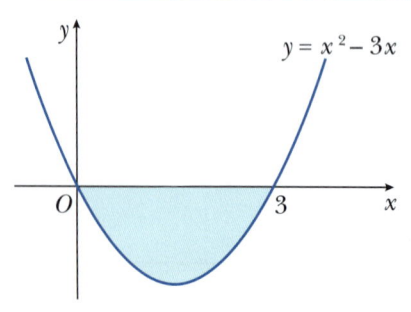

Answers

$$\int_0^3 (x^2 - 3x)\,dx = \left[\frac{1}{3}x^3 - \frac{3}{2}x^2\right]_0^3$$

$$= \left(9 - \frac{27}{2}\right) - (0 - 0)$$

$$= -4.5$$

Area is 4.5 units².

The required region could consist of a section above the x-axis and a section below the x-axis.

If this happens you must evaluate each area separately.

This is illustrated in the following example.

WORKED EXAMPLE 19

Find the total area of the shaded regions.

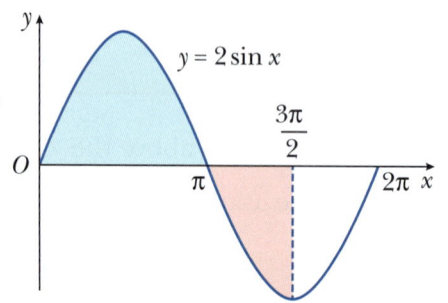

Answers

$$\int_0^\pi 2\sin x\,dx = [-2\cos x]_0^\pi$$

$$= (-2\cos \pi) - (-2\cos 0)$$

$$= (2) - (-2)$$

$$= 4$$

$$\int_\pi^{\frac{3\pi}{2}} 2\sin x\,dx = [-2\cos x]_\pi^{\frac{3\pi}{2}}$$

$$= \left(-2\cos\frac{3\pi}{2}\right) - (-2\cos \pi)$$

$$= (0) - (2)$$

$$= -2$$

Hence, the total area of the shaded regions = 4 + 2 = 6 units².

Exercise 16.9

1 Find the area of each shaded region.

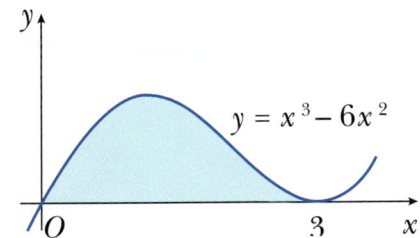

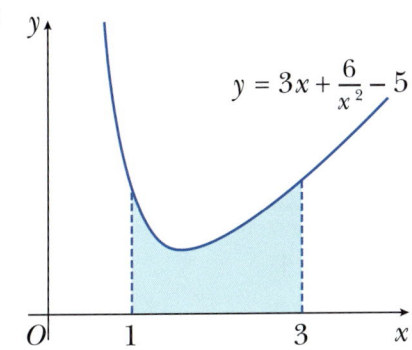

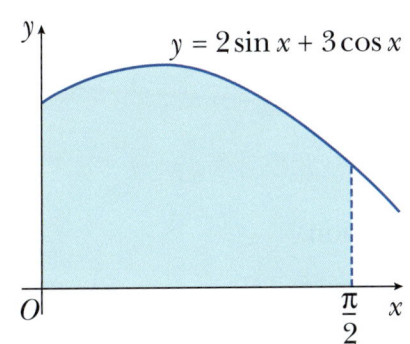

a $y = x^3 - 6x^2$, region from 0 to 3

b $y = 3\sqrt{x} - x$, region from 0 to 9

c $y = 3x + \dfrac{6}{x^2} - 5$, region from 1 to 3

d $y = e^x + 2e^{-x}$, region from 0 to 1

e $y = 2\sin x + 3\cos x$, region from 0 to $\dfrac{\pi}{2}$

f $y = 1 + \sin 2x$, region from $\dfrac{\pi}{4}$ to $\dfrac{\pi}{2}$

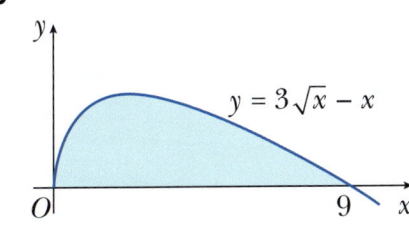

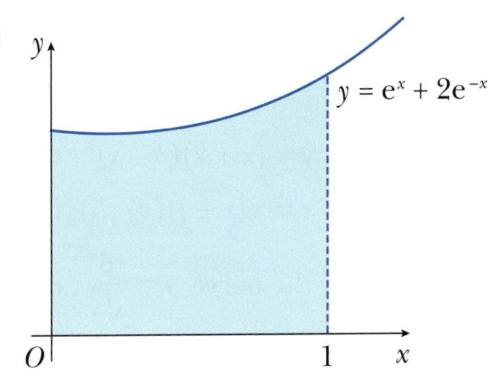

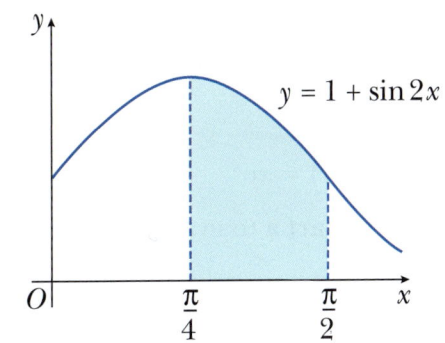

2 Find the area of each shaded region.

a $y = x(x-2)$, region from 0 to 2

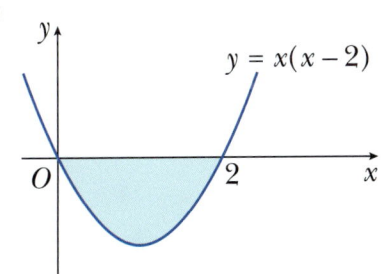

b $y = x - 5\cos\dfrac{x}{2}$, region from $\dfrac{\pi}{3}$ to $\dfrac{\pi}{2}$

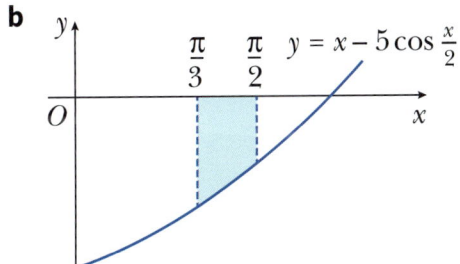

3

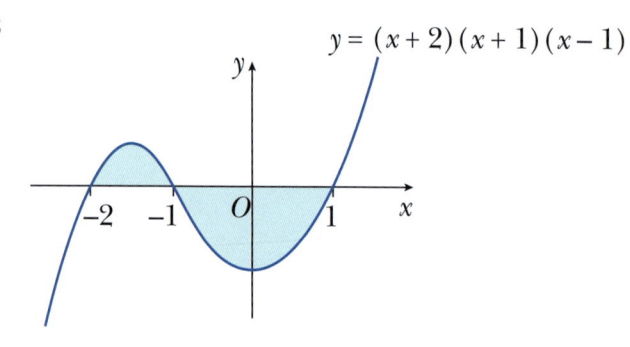

$y = (x+2)(x+1)(x-1)$

Find the total shaded region.

4 Sketch the following curves and find the area of the finite region or regions bounded by the curves and the x-axis.

   a $y = x(x+1)$ **b** $y = (x+2)(3-x)$ **c** $y = x(x^2 - 4)$

   d $y = x(x-2)(x+4)$ **e** $y = x(x-1)(x-5)$ **f** $y = x^2(4-x)$

5 Find the area enclosed by the curve $y = \dfrac{6}{\sqrt{x}}$, the x-axis and the lines $x = 4$ and $x = 9$.

6 **a** Find the area of the region enclosed by the curve $y = \dfrac{12}{x^2}$, the x-axis and the lines $x = 1$ and $x = 4$.

   b The line $x = p$ divides the region in **part a** into two equal parts. Find the value of p.

7 **a** Show that $\dfrac{d}{dx}(xe^x - e^x) = xe^x$.

   b Use your result from **part a** to evaluate the area of the shaded region.

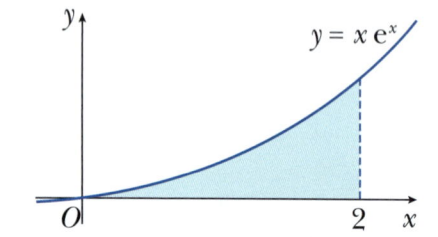

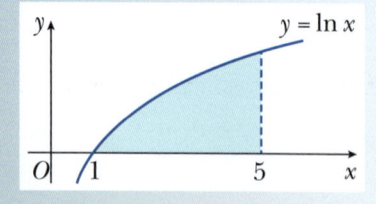

$y = xe^x$

CHALLENGE Q

8 **a** Show that $\dfrac{d}{dx}(x \ln x) = 1 + \ln x$.

   b Use your result from **part a** to evaluate the area of the shaded region.

$y = \ln x$

CHALLENGE Q

9 a Show that $\dfrac{d}{dx}(x\cos x) = \cos x - x\sin x$.

b Use your result from **part a** to evaluate the area of the shaded region.

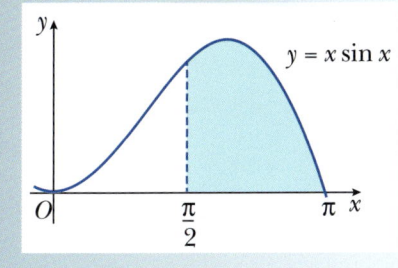

16.10 Area of regions bounded by a line and a curve

The following example shows a possible method for finding the area enclosed by a curve and a straight line.

WORKED EXAMPLE 20

The curve $y = 2\sqrt{x}$ intersects the line $y = x$ at the point $(4, 4)$. Find the area of the shaded region bounded by the curve and the line.

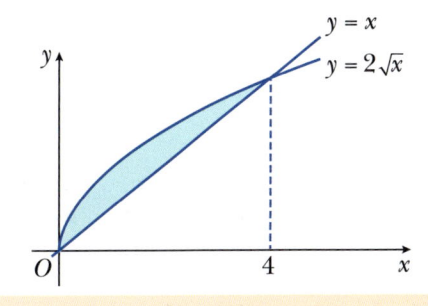

Answers

Area = area under curve − area of triangle

$= \displaystyle\int_0^4 2\sqrt{x}\,dx - \dfrac{1}{2} \times 4 \times 4$

$= \displaystyle\int_0^4 2x^{\frac{1}{2}}\,dx - 8$

$= \left[\dfrac{2}{\frac{3}{2}} x^{\frac{3}{2}}\right]_0^4 - 8$

$= \left(\dfrac{4}{3} \times 4^{\frac{3}{2}}\right) - \left(\dfrac{4}{3} \times 0^{\frac{3}{2}}\right) - 8$

$= 2\dfrac{2}{3}$ units^2

There is an alternative method for finding the shaded area in the previous example.

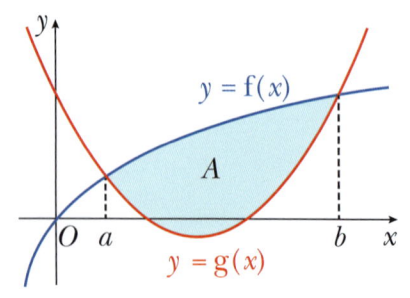

If two functions f(x) and g(x) intersect at $x = a$ and $x = b$, then the area, A, enclosed between the two curves is given by:

$$A = \int_a^b f(x)\,dx - \int_a^b g(x)\,dx$$

So for the area enclosed by $y = 2\sqrt{x}$ and $y = x$:

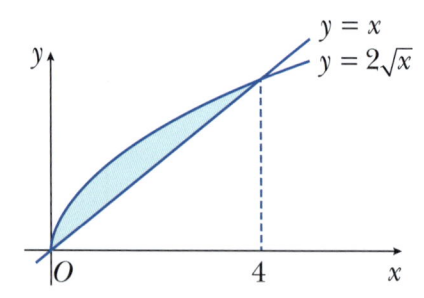

using $f(x) = 2\sqrt{x}$ and $g(x) = x$

$$\begin{aligned}
\text{area} &= \int_0^4 f(x)\,dx - \int_0^4 g(x)\,dx \\
&= \int_0^4 2\sqrt{x}\,dx - \int_0^4 x\,dx \\
&= \int_0^4 \left(2\sqrt{x} - x\right)dx \\
&= \left[\frac{2}{\frac{3}{2}}x^{\frac{3}{2}} - \frac{1}{2}x^2\right]_0^4 \\
&= \left(\frac{4}{3} \times 4^{\frac{3}{2}} - \frac{1}{2} \times 4^2\right) - \left(\frac{4}{3} \times 0^{\frac{3}{2}} - \frac{1}{2} \times 0^2\right) \\
&= 2\frac{2}{3}\ \text{units}^2
\end{aligned}$$

This alternative method is the easiest method to use in this next example.

WORKED EXAMPLE 21

The curve $y = x^2 - 4$ intersects the x-axis at the points A and B and intersects the line $y = x - 2$ at the points B and C.

a Find the coordinates of A, B and C.
b Find the area of the shaded region bounded by the curve and the line.

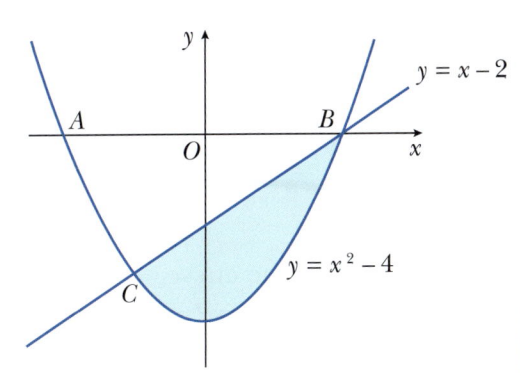

Answers

a When $y = 0$, $x^2 - 4 = 0$
$$x = \pm 2$$
A is the point $(-2, 0)$ and B is the point $(2, 0)$
For intersection of curve and line:
$$x^2 - 4 = x - 2$$
$$x^2 - x - 2 = 0$$
$$(x + 1)(x - 2) = 0$$
$$x = -1 \text{ or } x = 2$$
When $x = -1$, $y = -3$
C is the point $(-1, -3)$

b Area $= \int_{-1}^{2} (x - 2) \, dx - \int_{-1}^{2} (x^2 - 4) \, dx$

$= \int_{-1}^{2} (x - 2 - x^2 + 4) \, dx = \int_{-1}^{2} (x + 2 - x^2) \, dx$

$= \left[\dfrac{1}{2}x^2 + 2x - \dfrac{1}{3}x^3 \right]_{-1}^{2}$

$= \left(2 + 4 - \dfrac{8}{3} \right) - \left(\dfrac{1}{2} - 2 + \dfrac{1}{3} \right)$

$= 4.5$ units^2

CLASS DISCUSSION

Discuss with your classmates how you could find the shaded area, A, enclosed by the curve $y = x(8 - x)$ the line $y = 3x$ and the x-axis.

Can you find more than one method?

Calculate the area using each of your different methods.

Discuss with your classmates which method you preferred.

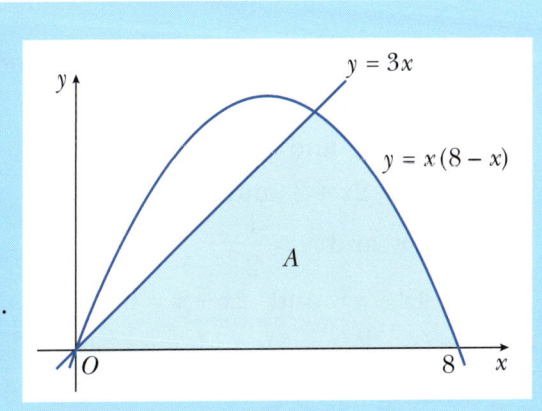

Cambridge IGCSE and O Level Additional Mathematics

Exercise 16.10

1. Find the area of the region enclosed by the curve $y = 1 + \cos x$ and the line $y = 1$.

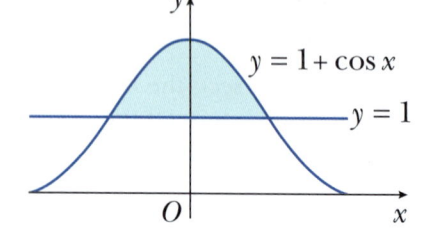

2. Find the area of the region bounded by the curve $y = 2 + 3x - x^2$, the line $x = 2$ and the line $y = 2$.

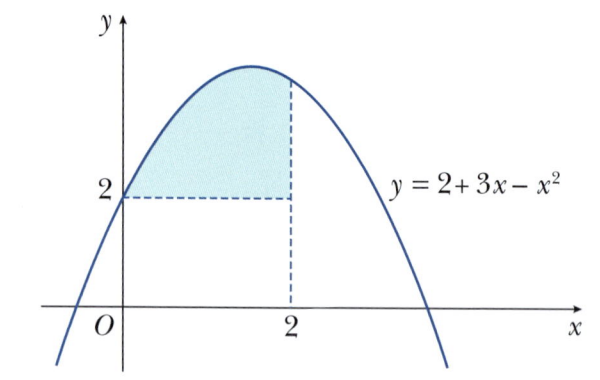

3. Find the area of the region bounded by the curve $y = 3x^2 + 2$, the line $y = 14$ and the y-axis.

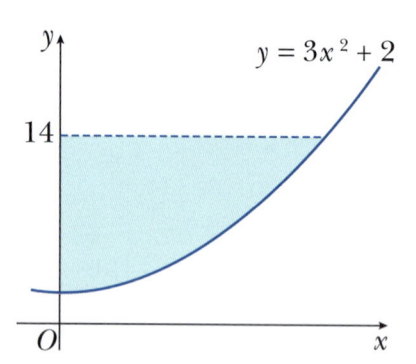

4. Find the area of the shaded region.

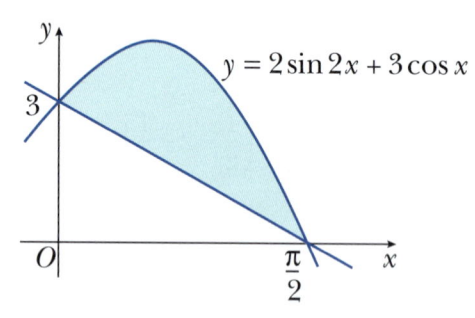

5. Sketch the following curves and lines and find the area enclosed between their graphs.
   a $y = x^2 + 1$ and $y = 5$
   b $y = x^2 - 2x + 3$ and $x + y = 9$
   c $y = \sqrt{x}$ and $y = \dfrac{1}{2}x$
   d $y = 4x - x^2$ and $2x + y = 0$
   e $y = (x-1)(x-5)$ and $y = x - 1$

6 Sketch the following pairs of curves and find the area enclosed between their graphs for $x \geqslant 0$.

a $y = x^2$ and $y = x(2-x)$

b $y = x^3$ and $y = 4x - 3x^2$

7 Find the shaded area enclosed by the curve $y = 3\sqrt{x}$ the line $y = 10 - x$ and the x-axis.

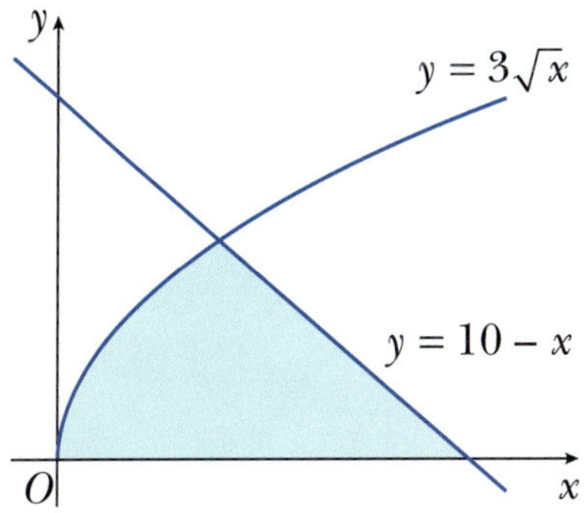

8 The tangent to the curve $y = 6x - x^2$ at the point $(2, 8)$ cuts the x-axis at the point P.

a Find the coordinates of P.

b Find the area of the shaded region.

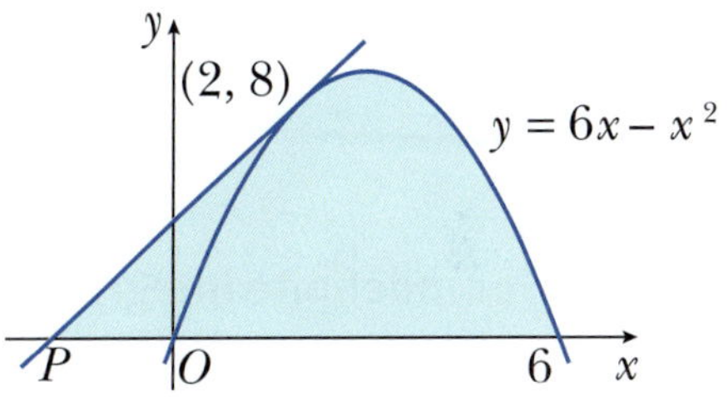

9 The curve $y = \sqrt{2x+1}$ meets the y-axis at the point P.

The tangent at the point $Q(12, 5)$ to this curve meets the y-axis at the point R.

Find the area of the shaded region PQR.

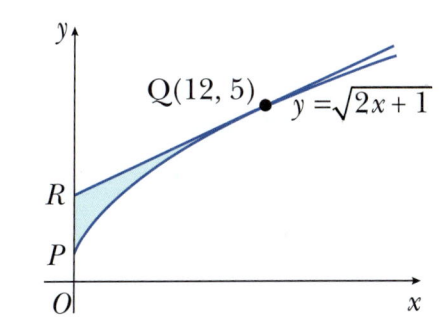

10 The diagram shows the graphs of $y = 2 + \cos 2x$ and $y = 1 + 2\cos 2x$ for $0 \leqslant x \leqslant \pi$.

Find the area of the shaded region.

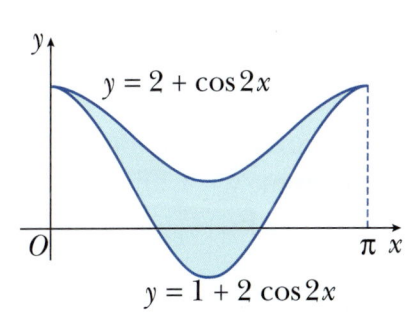

Summary

Integration as the reverse of differentiation

If $\dfrac{d}{dx}[F(x)] = f(x)$, then $\int f(x)\,dx = F(x) + c$.

Integration formulae

$\int x^n\,dx = \dfrac{1}{n+1}x^{n+1} + c$, where c is a constant and $n \neq -1$

$\int (ax+b)^n\,dx = \dfrac{1}{a(n+1)}(ax+b)^{n+1} + c$, $n \neq -1$ and $a \neq 0$

$\int e^x\,dx = e^x + c$ $\qquad \int e^{ax+b}\,dx = \dfrac{1}{a}e^{ax+b} + c$

$\int \cos x\,dx = \sin x + c$ $\qquad \int [\cos(ax+b)]\,dx = \dfrac{1}{a}\sin(ax+b) + c$

$\int \sin x\,dx = -\cos x + c$ $\qquad \int [\sin(ax+b)]\,dx = -\dfrac{1}{a}\cos(ax+b) + c$

Rules for indefinite integration

$\int k f(x)\,dx = k \int f(x)\,dx$, where k is a constant

$\int [f(x) \pm g(x)]\,dx = \int f(x)\,dx \pm \int g(x)\,dx$

Rules for definite integration

If $\int f(x)\,dx = F(x) + c$, then $\int_a^b f(x)\,dx = [F(x)]_a^b = F(b) - F(a)$.

$\int_a^b k f(x)\,dx = k \int_a^b f(x)\,dx$, where k is a constant

$\int_a^b [f(x) \pm g(x)]\,dx = \int_a^b f(x)\,dx \pm \int_a^b g(x)\,dx$

Area under a curve

The area, A, bounded by the curve $y = f(x)$, the x-axis and the lines $x = a$ and $x = b$ is given by the formula

$A = \int_a^b f(x)\,dx$ if $f(x) \geq 0$.

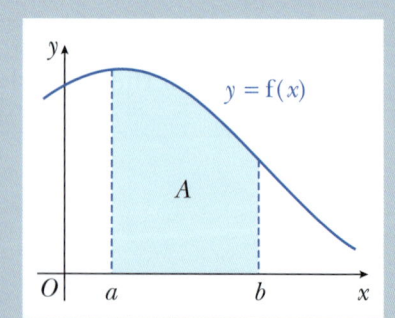

Area bounded by the graphs of two functions

If two functions $f(x)$ and $g(x)$ intersect at $x = a$ and $x = b$, then the area, A, enclosed between the two curves is given by the formula:

$A = \int_a^b f(x)\,dx - \int_a^b g(x)\,dx$.

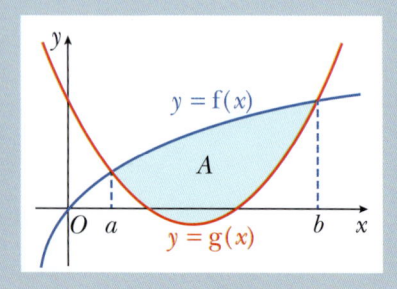

Examination questions

Worked past paper example

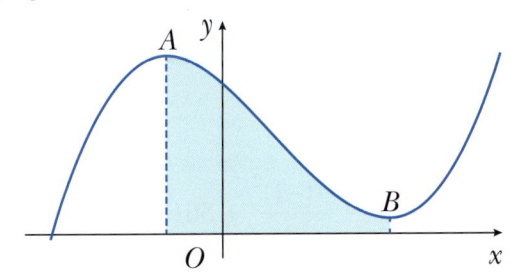

The diagram shows part of a curve such that $\frac{dy}{dx} = 3x^2 - 6x - 9$.

Points A and B are stationary points of the curve and lines from A and B are drawn perpendicular to the x-axis. Given that the curve passes through the point $(0, 30)$, find

a the equation of the curve, [4]

b the x-coordinates of A and B, [3]

c the area of the shaded region. [4]

Cambridge IGCSE Additional Mathematics 0606 Paper 11 Q12(part) Nov 2012

Answers

a $\frac{dy}{dx} = 3x^2 - 6x - 9$

$y = x^3 - 3x^2 - 9x + c$

Using $x = 0$, $y = 30$ gives $c = 30$.

The equation of the curve is $y = x^3 - 3x^2 - 9x + 30$.

b Stationary points occur when $\frac{dy}{dx} = 0$

$3x^2 - 6x - 9 = 0$

$x^2 - 2x - 3 = 0$

$(x + 1)(x - 3) = 0$

$x = -1$ or $x = 3$

The x-coordinate of A is -1 and the x-coordinate of B is 3.

c Area $= \int_{-1}^{3} y \, dx$

$= \int_{-1}^{3} (x^3 - 3x^2 - 9x + 30) \, dx$

$= \left[\dfrac{x^4}{4} - x^3 - \dfrac{9x^2}{2} + 30x \right]_{-1}^{3}$

$= \left(\dfrac{(3)^4}{4} - (3)^3 - \dfrac{9(3)^2}{2} + 30(3) \right) - \left(\dfrac{(-1)^4}{4} - (-1)^3 - \dfrac{9(-1)^2}{2} + 30(-1) \right)$

$= 76$

Area of shaded region is 76 units^2.

Exercise 16.11
Exam Exercise

1 a Given that $y = e^{x^2}$, find $\dfrac{dy}{dx}$. [2]

  b Use your answer to part **a** to find $\int x e^{x^2} \, dx$. [2]

  c Hence evaluate $\int_{0}^{2} x e^{x^2} \, dx$. [2]

  Cambridge IGCSE Additional Mathematics 0606 Paper 11 Q5i,ii,iii Jun 2014

2 A curve is such that $\dfrac{dy}{dx} = 4x + \dfrac{1}{(x+1)^2}$ for $x > 0$. The curve passes through the point $\left(\dfrac{1}{2}, \dfrac{5}{6} \right)$.

  a Find the equation of the curve. [4]

  b Find the equation of the normal to the curve at the point where $x = 1$. [4]

  Cambridge IGCSE Additional Mathematics 0606 Paper 11 Q7i,ii Jun 2014

3 a Find $\int \left(1 - \dfrac{6}{x^2} \right) dx$. [2]

  b Hence find the value of the positive constant k for which $\int_{k}^{3k} \left(1 - \dfrac{6}{x^2} \right) dx = 2$. [4]

  Cambridge IGCSE Additional Mathematics 0606 Paper 11 Q5i,ii Jun 2013

4 The diagram shows part of the curve of $y = 9x^2 - x^3$, which meets the x-axis at the origin O and at the point A. The line $y - 2x + 18 = 0$ passes through A and meets the y-axis at the point B.

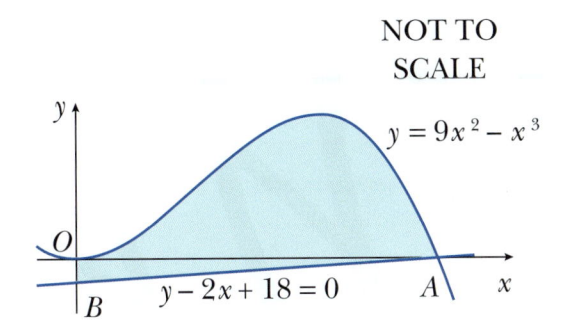

NOT TO SCALE

a Show that, for $x \geqslant 0$, $9x^2 - x^3 \leqslant 108$. [4]

b Find the area of the shaded region bounded by the curve, the line AB and the y-axis. [6]

Cambridge IGCSE Additional Mathematics 0606 Paper 11 Q11(part) Jun 2012

5 The diagram shows part of the curve $y = 2 \sin 3x$. The normal to the curve $y = 2 \sin 3x$ at the point where $x = \dfrac{\pi}{9}$ meets the y-axis at the point P.

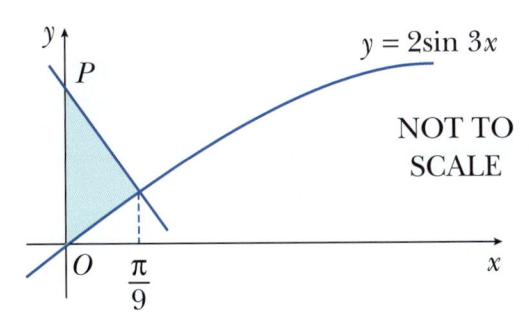

NOT TO SCALE

a Find the coordinates of P. [5]

b Find the area of the shaded region bounded by the curve, the normal and the y-axis. [5]

Cambridge IGCSE Additional Mathematics 0606 Paper 11 Q11(part) Jun 2012

Chapter 17
Kinematics

This section will show you how to:

- apply differentiation to kinematics problems that involve displacement, velocity and acceleration of a particle moving in a straight line with variable or constant acceleration.

Chapter 17: Kinematics

RECAP

You should already know about distance-time graphs and speed–time graphs.

Distance-time graphs can be used to find out how the distance changes with time.

- The gradient of a distance-time graph represents the speed.

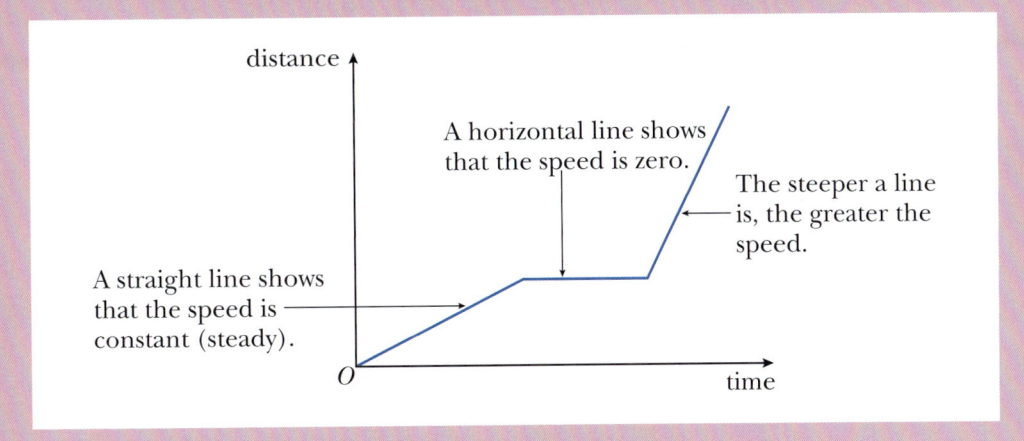

A straight line shows that the speed is constant (steady).

A horizontal line shows that the speed is zero.

The steeper a line is, the greater the speed.

Speed-time graphs can be used to find out how the speed changes with time.

- The gradient of a speed-time graph represents the acceleration.
- The area under a speed-time graph represents the distance travelled.

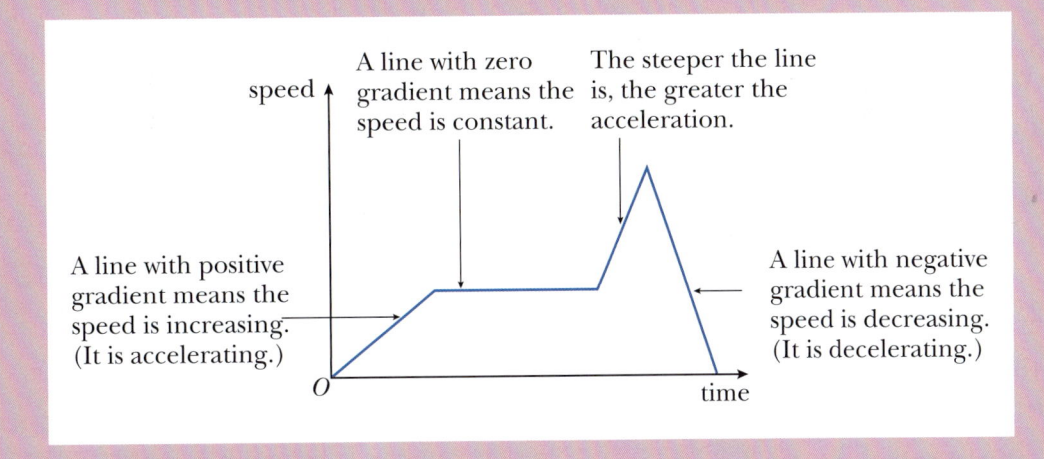

A line with positive gradient means the speed is increasing. (It is accelerating.)

A line with zero gradient means the speed is constant.

The steeper the line is, the greater the acceleration.

A line with negative gradient means the speed is decreasing. (It is decelerating.)

Distance and speed are examples of **scalar** quantities.
(Scalar quantities have magnitude but no direction.)

In this chapter you will learn about displacement, velocity and acceleration.

Displacement, velocity and acceleration are examples of **vector** quantities.
(Vector quantities have magnitude and direction.)

17.1 Applications of differentiation in kinematics

Displacement

Consider a particle, P, travelling along a straight line such that its displacement, s metres, from a fixed point O, t seconds after passing through O, is given by $s = 4t - t^2$.

The graph of s against t for $0 \leq t \leq 5$ is:

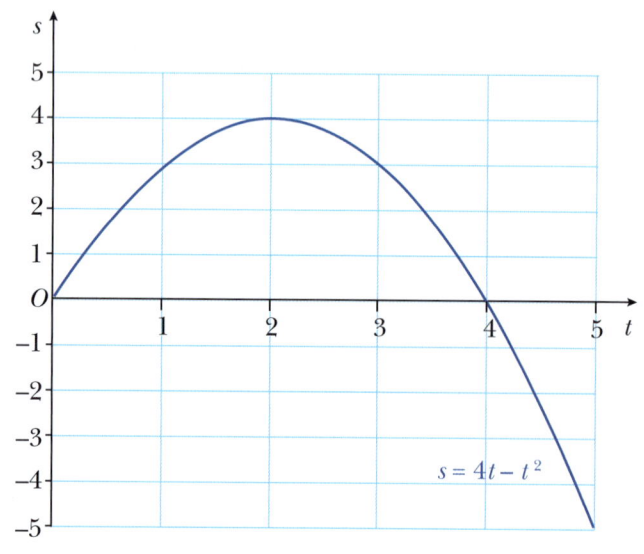

This can be represented on a motion diagram as:

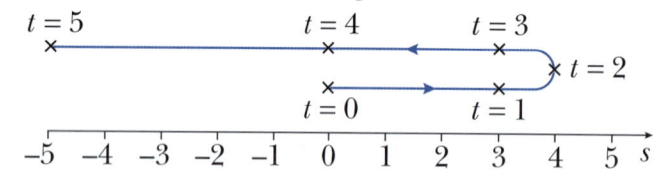

At time $t = 2$, the displacement of the particle from O is 4 m.

When $t = 2$ the particle stops instantaneously and reverses its direction of motion.

At time $t = 3$, the **displacement** is 3 m and the total distance travelled is $4 + (4 - 3) = 5$ m.

At time $t = 4$, the displacement is 0 m and the total distance travelled is $4 + 4 = 8$ m.

At time $t = 5$, the displacement is -5 m and the total distance travelled is $4 + 9 = 13$ m.

Velocity and acceleration

If a particle moves in a straight line, with displacement function $s(t)$, then the rate of change of displacement with respect to time, $\dfrac{ds}{dt}$, is the **velocity**, v, of the particle at time t.

$$v = \dfrac{ds}{dt}$$

If the velocity function is $v(t)$, then the rate of change of velocity with respect to time, $\frac{dv}{dt}$, is the **acceleration**, a, of the particle at time t.

$$a = \frac{dv}{dt} = \frac{d^2s}{dt^2}$$

CLASS DISCUSSION

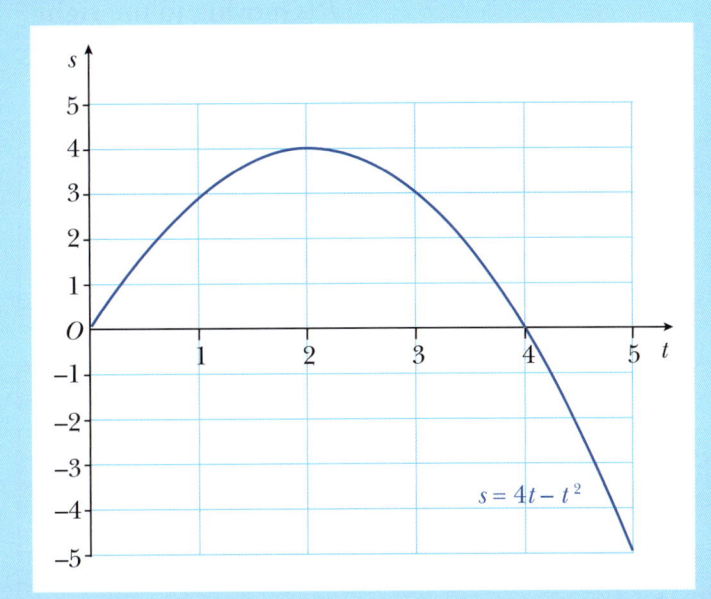

Earlier in this chapter you considered this displacement-time graph for the first 5 seconds of the motion of a particle P. The displacement of the particle, s metres, from a fixed point O, t seconds after passing through O, was given by $s = 4t - t^2$.

Working in small groups, complete the following tasks.

1. Find an expression, in terms of t, for the velocity, $v\,\text{m s}^{-1}$, of this particle.
2. Draw the graph of v against t for $0 \leqslant t \leqslant 5$.
3. State the values of t for which v is
   - **a** positive   **b** zero   **c** negative.
4. What can you say about the direction of motion of the particle when v is
   - **a** positive   **b** zero   **c** negative?
5. Find the acceleration, $a\,\text{m s}^{-2}$, of this particle and interpret your answer.

Now, discuss your conclusions with the whole class.

It is important that you are able to interpret the signs for displacements, velocities and accelerations.

These interpretations for a particle P relative to a fixed point O are summarised in the following tables.

Signs for displacement s

$s < 0$	$s = 0$	$s > 0$
P is to the left of O	P is at O	P is to the right of O

Signs for velocity v

$v < 0$	$v = 0$	$v > 0$
P is moving to the left	P is instantaneously at rest	P is moving to the right

Signs for acceleration a

$a < 0$	$a = 0$	$a > 0$
velocity is decreasing	velocity could be maximum or minimum or constant	velocity is increasing

WORKED EXAMPLE 1

A particle moves in a straight line so that, t seconds after passing a fixed point O, its displacement, s metres, from O is given by $s = t^3 - 12t^2 + 45t$.

a Find the velocity when $t = 2$.
b Find the acceleration when $t = 4$.
c Find the values of t when the particle is instantaneously at rest.
d Find the distance of the particle from O when $t = 7$.
e Find the total distance travelled by the particle during the first 7 seconds.

Answers

a $s = t^3 - 12t^2 + 45t$

$v = \dfrac{ds}{dt} = 3t^2 - 24t + 45$

when $t = 2$, $v = 3(2)^2 - 24(2) + 45 = 9$

The velocity is $9\,\text{m s}^{-1}$ when $t = 2$.

b $v = 3t^2 - 24t + 45$

$a = \dfrac{dv}{dt} = 6t - 24$

when $t = 4$, $a = 6(4) - 24 = 0$

The acceleration is $0\,\text{m s}^{-2}$ when $t = 4$.

c The particle is at instantaneous rest when $v = 0$.

$$3t^2 - 24t + 45 = 0$$
$$t^2 - 8t + 15 = 0$$
$$(t-3)(t-5) = 0$$
$$t = 3 \text{ or } t = 5$$

The particle is at instantaneous rest when $t = 3$ and $t = 5$.

d When $t = 7$, $s = (7)^3 - 12(7)^2 + 45(7) = 70$.

The particle is 70 m from O when $t = 7$.

e When $t = 0$, $s = 0$.

Critical values are when $t = 3$ and $t = 5$.

When $t = 3$, $s = (3)^3 - 12(3)^2 + 45(3) = 54$.

When $t = 5$, $s = (5)^3 - 12(5)^2 + 45(5) = 50$.

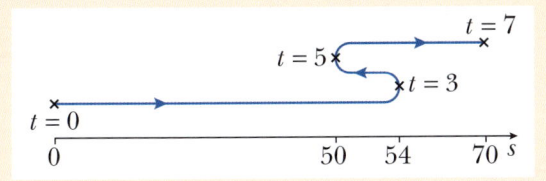

Total distance travelled $= 54 + (54 - 50) + (70 - 50) = 78$ m.

WORKED EXAMPLE 2

A particle moves in a straight line so that the displacement, s metres, from a fixed point O, is given by $s = \ln(2t + 5)$, where t is the time in seconds after passing a point X on the line.

a Find OX.
b Find the velocity when $t = 10$.
c Find the distance travelled during the third second.
d Find the acceleration of the particle when $t = 2.5$.

Answers

a When $t = 0$, $s = \ln[2(0) + 5] = \ln 5$ — the particle is at X at time $t = 0$

$OX = \ln 5 \approx 1.61$ m

b $s = \ln(2t + 5)$

$v = \dfrac{ds}{dt} = \dfrac{2}{2t + 5}$

When $t = 10$, $v = \dfrac{2}{2(10) + 5} = 0.08$

The velocity is 0.08 m s^{-1}.

c Since $v > 0$ for all values of t, there is no change in the direction of motion of the particle.

The third second is from $t = 2$ to $t = 3$.

When $t = 2$, $s = \ln[2(2) + 5] = \ln 9$.

When $t = 3$, $s = \ln[2(3) + 5] = \ln 11$.

Distance travelled during the third second $= \ln 11 - \ln 9 = \ln \dfrac{11}{9} \approx 0.201 \text{ m}$.

d $v = \dfrac{2}{2t + 5} = 2(2t + 5)^{-1}$

$a = \dfrac{dv}{dt} = -2(2t + 5)^{-2} \times 2 = -\dfrac{4}{(2t + 5)^2}$

When $t = 2.5$, $a = -\dfrac{4}{[2(2.5) + 5]^2} = -0.04$

The acceleration is -0.04 m s^{-2}.

WORKED EXAMPLE 3

A particle moves in a straight line such that its displacement, s metres, from a fixed point O on the line at time t seconds is given by $s = 20[e^{-2t} - e^{-3t}]$.

a Find value of t when the particle is instantaneously at rest.
b Find the displacement of the particle from O when $t = 1$.
c Find the total distance travelled during the first second of its motion.

Answers

a $s = 20[e^{-2t} - e^{-3t}]$

$v = \dfrac{ds}{dt} = 20[-2e^{-2t} + 3e^{-3t}]$

$v = 0$ when $-2e^{-2t} + 3e^{-3t} = 0$

$2e^{-2t} = 3e^{-3t}$

$e^t = \dfrac{3}{2}$

$t = \ln \dfrac{3}{2}$

It is instantaneously at rest when $t = \ln \dfrac{3}{2} = 0.405 \text{ s}$.

b When $t = 1$, $s = 20[e^{-2(1)} - e^{-3(1)}] \approx 1.711$.

Displacement from O is 1.71 m.

c When $t = 0$, $s = 0$.

Critical value is when $t = \ln\dfrac{3}{2}$.

When $t = \ln\dfrac{3}{2}$, $s = 20\left[e^{-2\left(\ln\frac{3}{2}\right)} - e^{-3\left(\ln\frac{3}{2}\right)}\right] \approx 2.963$.

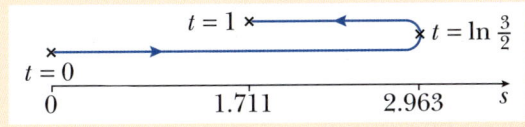

Total distance travelled = $2.963 + (2.963 - 1.711) \approx 4.21$ m.

WORKED EXAMPLE 4

A particle travels in a straight line so that, t seconds after passing through a fixed point O, its velocity v m s^{-1}, is given by $v = 5\cos\left(\dfrac{t}{2}\right)$.

a Find the value of t when the particle first comes to instantaneous rest.

b Find the acceleration of the particle when $t = \dfrac{\pi}{3}$.

Answers

a The particle is at rest when $v = 0$.

$$5\cos\left(\dfrac{t}{2}\right) = 0$$

$$\cos\left(\dfrac{t}{2}\right) = 0$$

$$\dfrac{t}{2} = \dfrac{\pi}{2}$$

$$t = \pi$$

It is at instantaneous rest when $t = \pi$.

b $v = 5\cos\left(\dfrac{t}{2}\right)$

$a = \dfrac{dv}{dt} = -\dfrac{5}{2}\sin\left(\dfrac{t}{2}\right)$

When $t = \dfrac{\pi}{3}$, $a = -\dfrac{5}{2}\sin\left(\dfrac{\pi}{6}\right) = -1.25$

When $t = \dfrac{\pi}{3}$ the acceleration is -1.25 m s^{-2}.

Exercise 17.1

1. A particle, moving in a straight line, passes through a fixed point O.
   Its velocity $v\,\mathrm{m\,s^{-1}}$, t seconds after passing through O, is given by $v = \dfrac{50}{(3t+2)^2}$.
   a Find the velocity of the particle as it passes through O.
   b Find the value of t when the velocity is $0.125\,\mathrm{m\,s^{-1}}$.
   c Find the acceleration of the particle when $t = 1$.

2. A particle, moving in a straight line, passes through a fixed point O.
   Its velocity $v\,\mathrm{m\,s^{-1}}$, t seconds after passing through O, is given by $v = 6e^{2t} - 2t$.
   a Find the initial velocity of the particle.
   b Find the initial acceleration of the particle.

3. A particle starts from rest and moves in a straight line so that t seconds after passing through a fixed point O, its velocity $v\,\mathrm{m\,s^{-1}}$, is given by $v = 5(1 - e^{-t})$.
   a Find the velocity of the particle when $t = \ln 100$.
   b State the value which v approaches as t becomes very large.
   c Find the acceleration of the particle when $v = 4$.
   d Sketch the velocity-time graph for the motion of the particle.

4. A particle moves in a straight line such that its displacement, s metres, from a fixed point O on the line at time t seconds is given by $s = 9[\ln(3t+2)]$.
   a Find the value of t when the displacement of the particle from O is $36\,\mathrm{m}$.
   b Find the velocity of the particle when $t = 1$.
   c Show that the particle is decelerating for all values of t.

5. A particle moves in a straight line so that, t seconds after passing through a fixed point O, its displacement, s metres, from O is given by $s = \ln(1 + 2t)$.
   a Find the value of t when the velocity of the particle is $0.4\,\mathrm{m\,s^{-1}}$.
   b Find the distance travelled by the particle during the third second.
   c Find the acceleration of the particle when $t = 1.5$.

6. A particle travels in a straight line so that, t seconds after passing through a fixed point O, its velocity $v\,\mathrm{m\,s^{-1}}$, is given by $v = 8\cos\left(\dfrac{t}{4}\right)$.
   a Find the value of t when the velocity of the particle first equals $4\,\mathrm{m\,s^{-1}}$.
   b Find the acceleration of the particle when $t = 5$.

7. A particle, moving in a straight line, passes through a fixed point O.
   Its velocity $v\,\mathrm{m\,s^{-1}}$, t seconds after passing through O, is given by
   $v = \cos 3t + \sin 3t$.
   a Find the value of t when the particle is first instantaneously at rest.
   b Find the acceleration of the particle when $t = \pi$.

8 A particle starts from rest and moves in a straight line so that, t seconds after leaving a fixed point O, its displacement, s metres, is given by $s = 2 - 2\cos 2t$.
   a Find an expression for the velocity and the acceleration of the particle in terms of t.
   b Find the time when the particle first comes to rest and its distance from O at this instant.

9 A particle moves in a straight line such that its displacement, s metres, from a fixed point O on the line at time t seconds is given by $s = 50\left[e^{-2t} - e^{-4t}\right]$.
   a Find the time when the particle is instantaneously at rest.
   b Find the displacement of the particle from O when $t = 2$.
   c Find the total distance travelled during the first 2 seconds of its motion.

10 A particle moves in a straight line so that its displacement from a fixed point O, is given by $s = 2t + 2\cos 2t$, where t is the time in seconds after the motion begins.
   a Find the initial position of the particle.
   b Find an expression for the velocity and the acceleration of the particle in terms of t.
   c Find the time when the particle first comes to rest and its distance from O at this instant.
   d Find the time when the acceleration of the particle is zero for the first time and its distance from O at this instant.

11 A particle, moving in a straight line, passes through a fixed point O. Its velocity $v\,\text{m s}^{-1}$, t seconds after passing through O, is given by $v = k\cos 4t$, where k is a positive constant.
   a Find the value of t when the particle is first instantaneously at rest.
   b Find an expression for the acceleration, a, of the particle t seconds after passing through O.
   c Given that the acceleration of the particle is $10\,\text{m s}^{-2}$ when $t = \dfrac{7\pi}{24}$, find the value of k.

CHALLENGE Q

12 A particle moves in a straight line such that its displacement, s metres, from a fixed point O at a time t seconds, is given by

$s = 2t$ for $0 \leqslant t \leqslant 4$,

$s = 8 + 2\ln(t-3)$ for $t > 4$.

a Find the initial velocity of the particle.

b Find the velocity of the particle when   **i** $t = 2$ **ii** $t = 6$.

c Find the acceleration of the particle when   **i** $t = 2$ **ii** $t = 6$.

d Sketch the displacement-time graph for the motion of the particle.

e Find the distance travelled by the particle in the 8th second.

CHALLENGE Q

13 A particle moves in a straight line so that the displacement, s metres, from a fixed point O, is given by $s = 2t^3 - 17t^2 + 40t - 2$, where t is the time in seconds after passing a point X on the line.

a Find the distance OX.

b Find the value of t when the particle is first at rest.

c Find the values of t for which the velocity is positive.

d Find the values of t for which the velocity is negative.

17.2 Applications of integration in kinematics

In the last section you learnt that when a particle moves in a straight line where the displacement from a fixed point O on the line is s, then:

$$v = \frac{ds}{dt}$$

and

$$a = \frac{dv}{dt} = \frac{d^2s}{dt^2}$$

Conversely, if a particle moves in a straight line where the acceleration of the particle is a, then:

$$v = \int a \, dt \quad \text{and} \quad s = \int v \, dt$$

In this section you will solve problems that involve both differentiation and integration.

The following diagram should help you remember when to differentiate and when to integrate.

$$v = \frac{ds}{dt} \qquad \text{displacement } (s) \qquad s = \int v \, dt$$

$$\text{velocity } (v)$$

$$a = \frac{dv}{dt} = \frac{d^2s}{dt^2} \qquad \text{acceleration } (a) \qquad v = \int a \, dt$$

WORKED EXAMPLE 5

A particle moving in a straight line passes a fixed point O with velocity $8 \, \text{m s}^{-1}$. Its acceleration $a \, \text{m s}^{-2}$, t seconds after passing through O is given by $a = 2t + 1$.

a Find the velocity when $t = 3$.

b Find the displacement from O when $t = 3$.

Answers

a $a = 2t + 1$

$$v = \int a \, dt$$

$$= \int (2t + 1) \, dt$$

$$= t^2 + t + c$$

Using $v = 8$ when $t = 0$, gives $c = 8$

$$v = t^2 + t + 8$$

When $t = 3$, $v = (3)^2 + (3) + 8 = 20$

The particle's velocity when $t = 3$ is $20 \, \text{m s}^{-1}$.

b $v = t^2 + t + 8$

$$s = \int v \, dt$$

$$= \int (t^2 + t + 8) \, dt$$

$$= \frac{1}{3}t^3 + \frac{1}{2}t^2 + 8t + c$$

Using $s = 0$ when $t = 0$, gives $c = 0$

$$s = \frac{1}{3}t^3 + \frac{1}{2}t^2 + 8t$$

When $t = 3$, $s = \frac{1}{3}(3)^3 + \frac{1}{2}(3)^2 + 8(3) = 37.5$

Its displacement when $t = 3$ is $37.5 \, \text{m}$.

WORKED EXAMPLE 6

A particle, moving in a straight line, passes through a fixed point O.
Its velocity v m s^{-1}, t seconds after passing through O, is given by $v = 6e^{3t} + 2t$.
a   Find the acceleration of the particle when $t = 1$.
b   Find an expression for the displacement of the particle from O.
c   Find the total distance travelled by the particle in the first 2 seconds of its motion.

Answers

a $v = 6e^{3t} + 2t$

$a = \dfrac{dv}{dt} = 18e^{3t} + 2$

When $t = 1$, $a = 18e^{3(1)} + 2 \approx 364$

Its acceleration when $t = 1$ is 364 m s^{-2}.

b $v = 6e^{3t} + 2t$

$s = \int v \, dt$

$= \int \left(6e^{3t} + 2t\right) dt$

$= 2e^{3t} + t^2 + c$

Using $s = 0$ when $t = 0$, gives $c = -2$
The displacement, s metres, is given by $s = 2e^{3t} + t^2 - 2$.

c   Since $v > 0$ for all values of t, there is no change in the direction of motion of the particle.
When $t = 0$, $s = 0$
When $t = 2$, $s = 2e^{3(2)} + (2)^2 - 2 = 2e^6 + 2$
Distance travelled during the first 2 seconds $= 2e^6 + 2 \approx 809$ m.

Alternative method

Since there is no change in direction of motion:

$s = \int v \, dt$

$= \int_0^2 \left(6e^{3t} + 2t\right) dt$

$= \left[2e^{3t} + t^2\right]_0^2$

$= \left(2e^6 + 4\right) - \left(2e^0 + 0\right)$

$= 2e^6 + 2$

≈ 809 m

IMPORTANT
This alternative method can only be used when there has been no change in direction of motion during the relevant time interval.

WORKED EXAMPLE 7

A particle starts from rest and moves in a straight line so that, t seconds after leaving a fixed point O, its velocity, v m s^{-1}, is given by $v = 4 + 8\cos 2t$.

a Find the range of values of the velocity.
b Find the range of values of the acceleration.
c Find the value of t when the particle first comes to instantaneous rest.
d Find the distance travelled during the time interval $0 \leqslant t \leqslant \dfrac{\pi}{2}$.

Answers

a $v = 4 + 8\cos 2t$ and $-1 \leqslant \cos 2t \leqslant 1$
$v_{min} = 4 + 8(-1) = -4$ and $v_{max} = 4 + 8(1) = 12$
Hence, $-4 \leqslant v \leqslant 12$.

b $v = 4 + 8\cos 2t$
$a = \dfrac{dv}{dt} = -16\sin 2t$ and $-1 \leqslant \sin 2t \leqslant 1$
$a_{min} = -16(1) = -16$ and $a_{max} = -16(-1) = 16$
Hence, $-16 \leqslant a \leqslant 16$.

c When $v = 0$, $4 + 8\cos 2t = 0$
$$\cos 2t = -\dfrac{1}{2}$$
$$2t = \dfrac{2\pi}{3}$$
$$t = \dfrac{\pi}{3}$$
The particle first comes to rest when $t = \dfrac{\pi}{3}$.

d $s = \int v \, dt$
$= \int (4 + 8\cos 2t) \, dt$
$= 4t + 4\sin 2t + c$
Using $s = 0$ when $t = 0$, gives $c = 0$
$s = 4t + 4\sin 2t$
Particle changes direction when $t = \dfrac{\pi}{3}$.

When $t = \dfrac{\pi}{3}$, $s = 4\left(\dfrac{\pi}{3}\right) + 4\sin\left(\dfrac{2\pi}{3}\right) \approx 7.6529$

When $t = \dfrac{\pi}{2}$, $s = 4\left(\dfrac{\pi}{2}\right) + 4\sin(\pi) = 2\pi \approx 6.2832$

Total distance travelled = $7.653 + (7.653 - 6.283) \approx 9.02$ m.

Exercise 17.2

1 A particle, moving in a straight line, passes through a fixed point O.

Its velocity v m s^{-1}, t seconds after passing through O, is given by $v = 10t - t^2$.

  a Find the velocity of the particle when the acceleration is 6 m s^{-2}.

  b Find the time taken before the particle returns to O.

  c Find the distance travelled by the particle in the 2nd second.

  d Find the distance travelled by the particle before it comes to instantaneous rest.

  e Find the distance travelled by the particle in the first 12 seconds.

2 A particle, moving in a straight line, passes through a fixed point O.

Its velocity v m s^{-1}, t seconds after passing through O, is given by $v = \dfrac{32}{(t+2)^2}$.

  a Find the acceleration of the particle when $t = 2$.

  b Find an expression for the displacement of the particle from O.

  c Find the distance travelled by the particle in the 3rd second.

3 A particle, moving in a straight line, passes through a fixed point O.

Its velocity v m s^{-1}, t seconds after passing through O, is given by $v = 4e^{2t} + 2t$.

  a Find the acceleration of the particle when $t = 1$.

  b Find an expression for the displacement of the particle from O.

  c Find the total distance travelled by the particle in the first 2 seconds of its motion. Give your answer correct to the nearest metre.

4 A particle, moving in a straight line, passes through a fixed point O.

Its velocity v m s^{-1}, t seconds after passing through O, is given by

$v = t + 2\cos\left(\dfrac{t}{3}\right)$.

Find the displacement of the particle from O when $t = \dfrac{3\pi}{2}$ and its acceleration at this instant.

5 A particle, moving in a straight line, passes through a fixed point O.

Its velocity v m s^{-1}, t seconds after passing through O, is given by $v = 4e^{2t} + 6e^{-3t}$.

  a Show that the velocity is never zero.

  b Find the acceleration when $t = \ln 2$.

  c Find, to the nearest metre, the displacement of the particle from O when $t = 2$.

6 A particle moves in a straight line, so that, t seconds after leaving a fixed point O, its velocity, $v\,\text{m s}^{-1}$, is given by $v = pt^2 + qt - 12$, where p and q are constants.

When $t = 2$ the acceleration of the particle is $18\,\text{m s}^{-2}$.

When $t = 4$ the displacement of the particle from O is $32\,\text{m}$.

Find the value of p and the value of q.

7 A particle moving in a straight line passes a fixed point O with velocity $10\,\text{m s}^{-1}$.

Its acceleration $a\,\text{m s}^{-2}$, t seconds after passing through O is given by $a = 3 - 2t$.

  a Find the value of t when the particle is instantaneously at rest.

  b Sketch the velocity-time graph for the motion of the particle.

  c Find the total distance travelled in the first 7 seconds of its motion. Give your answer correct to 3 sf.

8 A particle moving in a straight line passes a fixed point O with velocity $18\,\text{m s}^{-1}$.

Its acceleration $a\,\text{m s}^{-2}$, t seconds after passing through O is given by $a = 3t - 12$.

  a Find the values of t when the particle is instantaneously at rest.

  b Find the distance the particle travels in the 4th second.

  c Find the total distance travelled in the first 10 seconds of its motion.

9 A particle starts from rest and moves in a straight line so that, t seconds after leaving a fixed point O, its velocity, $v\,\text{m s}^{-1}$, is given by $v = 3 + 6\cos 2t$.

  a Find the range of values for the acceleration.

  b Find the distance travelled by the particle before it first comes to instantaneous rest. Give your answer correct to 3 sf.

10 A particle starts from rest at a fixed point O and moves in a straight line towards a point A. The velocity, $v\,\text{m s}^{-1}$, of the particle, t seconds after leaving O, is given by $v = 8 - 8e^{-2t}$.

  a Find the acceleration of the particle when $t = \ln 5$.

  b Given that the particle reaches A when $t = 2$ find the distance OA. Give your answer correct to 3 sf.

11 A particle travels in a straight line so that, t seconds after passing through a fixed point O, its speed, $v\,\text{m s}^{-1}$, is given by $v = 2\cos\left(\dfrac{t}{2}\right) - 1$.

  a Find the value of t when the particle first comes to instantaneous rest at the point P.

  b Find the total distance travelled from $t = 0$ to $t = 2\pi$.

CHALLENGE Q

12 A particle moves in a straight line so that t seconds after passing through a fixed point O, its acceleration, $a\,\text{m s}^{-2}$, is given by $a = pt + q$, where p and q are constants.

The particle passes through O with velocity $3\,\text{m s}^{-1}$ and acceleration $-2\,\text{m s}^{-2}$.

The particle first comes to instantaneous rest when $t = 2$.

a Find the value of p and the value of q.

b Find an expression, in terms of t, for the displacement of the particle.

c Find the second value of t for which the particle is at instantaneous rest.

d Find the distance travelled during the 4th second.

Summary

The relationships between displacement, velocity and acceleration are:

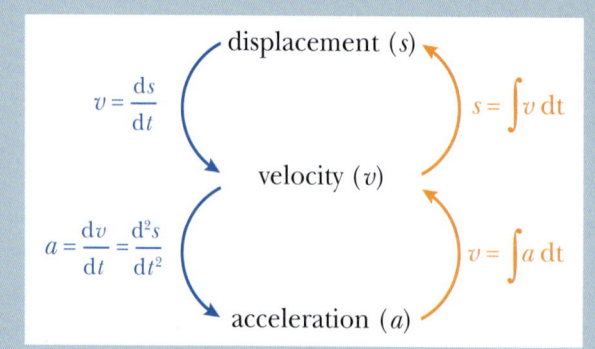

$$v = \frac{ds}{dt}$$

$$a = \frac{dv}{dt} = \frac{d^2s}{dt^2}$$

$$s = \int v\, dt$$

$$v = \int a\, dt$$

displacement (s) → velocity (v) → acceleration (a)

A particle is at instantaneous rest when $v = 0$.

Chapter 17: Kinematics

Examination questions

Worked past paper example

A particle travels in a straight line so that, t s after passing through a fixed point O, its velocity, $v\,\text{cm s}^{-1}$, is given by $v = 4e^{2t} - 24t$.

a Find the velocity of the particle as it passes through O. [1]

b Find the distance travelled by the particle in the third second. [4]

c Find an expression for the acceleration of the particle and hence find the stationary value of the velocity. [5]

Cambridge IGCSE Additional Mathematics 0606 Paper 21 Q11(part) Nov 2012

Answer

a When $t = 0$, $v = 4e^{(2 \times 0)} - 24(0) = 4$.

The velocity of the particle as it passes through O is $4\,\text{cm s}^{-1}$.

b The third second is from $t = 2$ to $t = 3$.

$v \geq 0$ for $2 \leq t \leq 3$, hence there is no change in direction of motion in this time interval.

$$\text{Distance travelled} = \int_2^3 v\,dt$$

$$= \int_2^3 \left(4e^{2t} - 24t\right) dt$$

$$= \left[2e^{2t} - 12t^2\right]_2^3$$

$$= \left(2e^6 - 108\right) - \left(2e^4 - 48\right)$$

$$= 2e^6 - 2e^4 - 60$$

Distance travelled in third second $\approx 638\,\text{m}$.

c $\text{Acceleration} = \dfrac{d}{dt}(v)$

$$= \dfrac{d}{dt}\left(4e^{2t} - 24t\right)$$

$$= 8e^{2t} - 24$$

Acceleration is $(8e^{2t} - 24)\,\text{cm s}^{-2}$.

Stationary values of v occur when $\dfrac{dv}{dt} = 0$.

$$8e^{2t} - 24 = 0$$

$$e^{2t} = 3$$

$$2t = \ln 3$$

$$t = \dfrac{1}{2}\ln 3$$

When $t = \dfrac{1}{2}\ln 3$, $v = 4e^{\ln 3} - 12\ln 3 = 12 - 12\ln 3$.

Stationary value of velocity is $12(1 - \ln 3)\,\text{cm s}^{-1}$.

Exercise 17.3
Exam Exercise

1

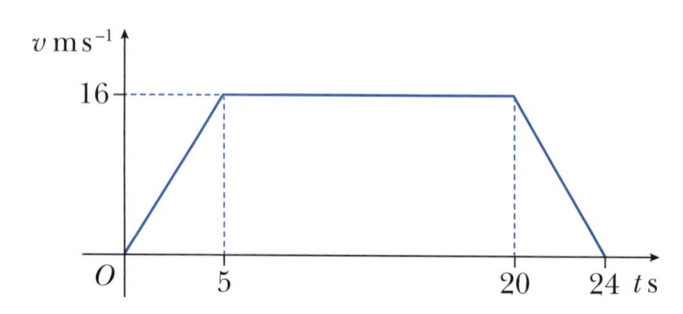

The velocity-time graph represents the motion of a particle moving in a straight line.
- **a** Find the acceleration during the first 5 seconds. [1]
- **b** Find the length of time for which the particle is travelling with constant velocity. [1]
- **c** Find the total distance travelled by the particle. [3]

Cambridge IGCSE Additional Mathematics 0606 Paper 21 Q2i,ii,iii Jun 2013

2 A particle moves in a straight line so that, t s after passing through a fixed point O, its velocity, v m s^{-1}, is given by $v = 2t - 11 + \dfrac{6}{t+1}$. Find the acceleration of the particle when it is at instantaneous rest. [7]

Cambridge IGCSE Additional Mathematics 0606 Paper 21 Q9 Jun 2012

3 A particle moves in a straight line such that its displacement, x m, from a fixed point O at time t s, is given by $x = 3 + \sin 2t$, where $t \geq 0$.
- **a** Find the velocity of the particle when $t = 0$. [2]
- **b** Find the value of t when the particle is first at rest. [2]
- **c** Find the distance travelled by the particle before it first comes to rest. [2]
- **d** Find the acceleration of the particle when $t = \dfrac{3\pi}{4}$. [2]

Cambridge IGCSE Additional Mathematics 0606 Paper 11 Q5i-iv Nov 2011

4 A body moves in a straight line so that, t s after passing through a fixed point O, its displacement from O is s m. The velocity v m s^{-1} is such that $v = 5\cos 4t$.
- **a** Write down the velocity of the body as it passes through O. [1]
- **b** Find the value of t when the acceleration of the body is first equal to 10 m s^{-2}. [4]
- **c** Find the value of s when $t = 5$. [4]

Cambridge IGCSE Additional Mathematics 0606 Paper 11 Q9i,ii,iii Jun 2011

Answers

Chapter 1
Exercise 1.1

1 {6, 7, 8, 9, 13, 14, 15}

2 a {7, 8}
   b {1, 2, 3, 4, 5, 6, 9, 10, 11, 12}
   c {1, 2, 4}

3 a 1, 5   b 1, 2, 3, 4
   c 1   d 6, 7, 8, 9

4 a $\{x : 1 \leq x \leq 3 \cup 8 < x \leq 10\}$
   b $\{x : 1 \leq x \leq 5 \cup 9 \leq x \leq 10\}$
   c $\{x : 5 < x \leq 8\}$
   d $\{x : 3 < x < 9\}$

5 a $n(\mathcal{E}) = 52$
   b $n(R) = 35$
   c $n(R \cap C) = 21$
   d $R \subset W$

6 a members who like music or rock-climbing (or both)
   b members who like music and sailing
   c members who do not like rock-climbing
   d no members like rock-climbing and sailing

7 a i $P \subset M$
      ii $A \cap P = \emptyset$
   b i students who study art and maths but not physics
      ii students who study maths or physics (or both) but not art

8 a $17 \in P$ b $30 \notin C$
   c $n(C) = 3$ d $n(P') = 35$
   e $S \cap P = \emptyset$

9 a $C \subset G$
   b $F \subset G'$
   c $A \cap C = \emptyset$
   d $n(A \cap F) = 3$

10 a straight line, gradient 1, y-intercept 2
   b straight line, gradient -1, y-intercept 3
   c straight line, gradient 2, y-intercept -1
   d straight line, gradient -1, y-intercept 2, region above line shaded

11 a i (0, 3)   ii (1, 5)
   b i 1   ii 0

12 a i 1   ii 2
      iii 1   iv 0
   b i {−2, 0, 5, 7}   ii {−2}
   c $C \cap D = \emptyset$

Exercise 1.2

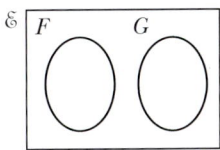

1 a, b, 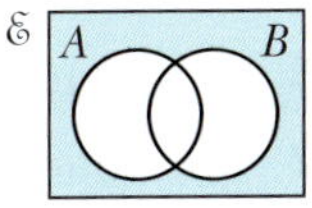 c, 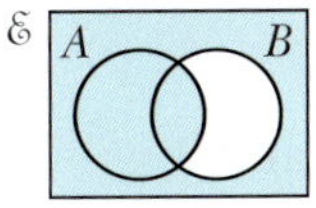 d — Venn diagrams

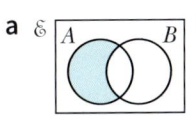

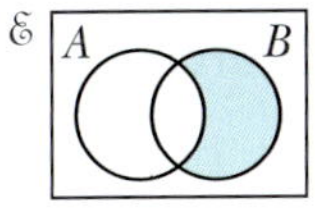

2 Venn diagram with F, G

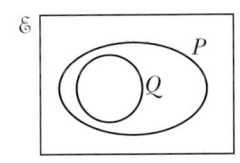

3 Venn diagram with P, Q

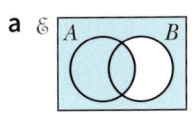

4 a Venn diagram with A, B
   b $(A' \cap B)'$

5 a False   b False

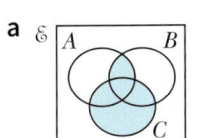

6 a, b — Venn diagrams with A, B, C

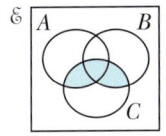

c, 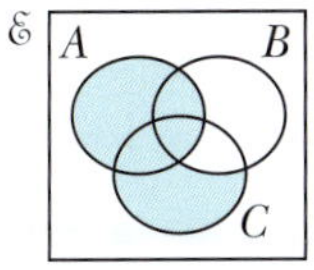 d, 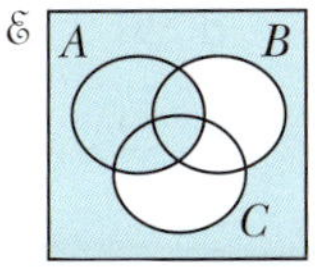 e, 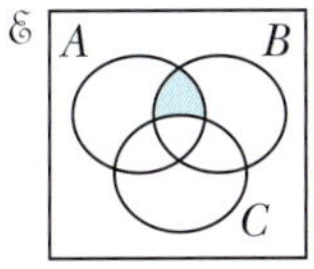 f, 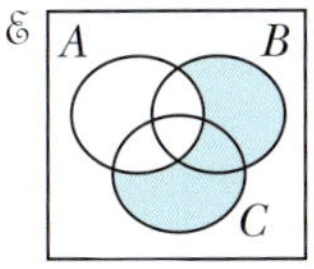 g, 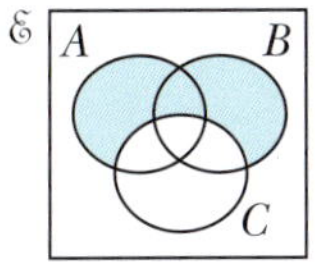 h — Venn diagrams with A, B, C

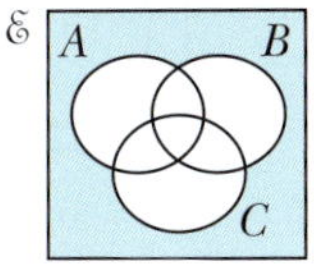

7 a True   b True

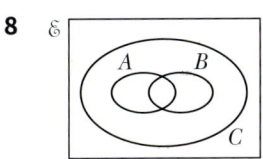

8 Venn diagram with A, B, C

9 Venn diagram with A, B, C

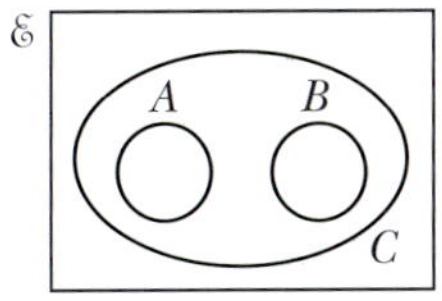

10 True

11 Venn diagram with A, B, C

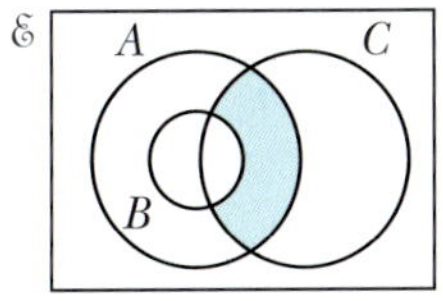

12 a, 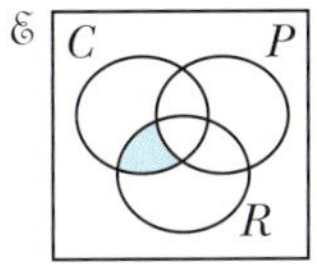 b — Venn diagrams with C, P, R

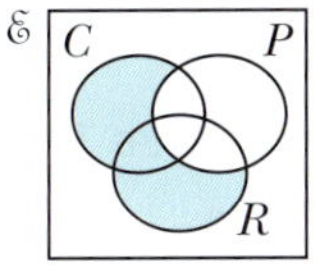

Exercise 1.3

1 a $(A \cup B)'$ b $A' \cup B$
   c $(A \cap B)'$

2 a $(A \cup C)' \cap B$
   b $A' \cap B \cap C$
   c $(A \cup C) \cap B'$
   d $A \cap (B \cup C)$
   e $(A \cap B) \cup (A \cap C) \cup (B \cap C)$
   f $(A \cap B' \cap C') \cup (A' \cap B' \cap C)$

3 $(A \cup C) \cap B'$

Exercise 1.4
1. a 16 b 18 c 4
   d 26 e 24 f 8
   g 22 h 12 i 18
2. 23   3. 6   4. 22
5. 5
6. [Venn diagram: A and B with 15, 11, 10]
7. 16
8. a 11, 0   b 29, 18
9. 21   10. 26   11. 44
12. a, b [Venn diagram: ℰ, O, M, P with 7, 5, 20, 12]
    c i 4   ii 8

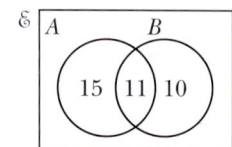

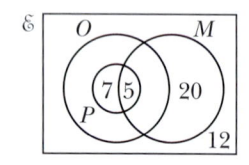

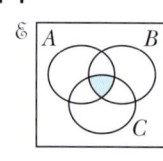

Exercise 1.5
1. 5   2. 7   3. 5
4. a 7   b 14
5. a 16   b 27   c 8   d 26
6. a 5   b 4   c 15   d 7

Exercise 1.6
1. a [Two Venn diagrams with A, B, C]
   b 14
2. a i [Venn diagram] ii [Venn diagram]
   iii [Venn diagram]

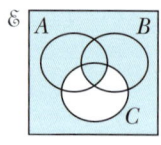

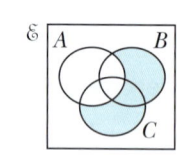

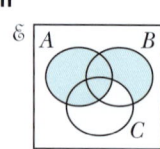

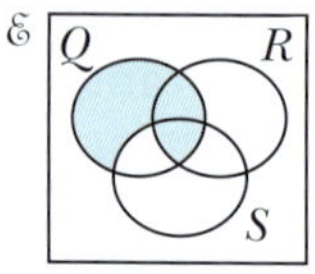

b i 2   ii 0
3. a i $n(P) = 11$
      ii $18 \notin F$ iii $T \subset F$
   b i [Venn diagram A, B]   ii [Venn diagram Q, R, S]
4. a [Venn diagram A, B, C] [Venn diagram A, B, C]
   [Venn diagram A, B, C]

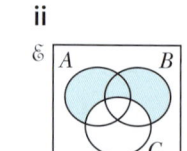

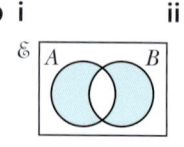

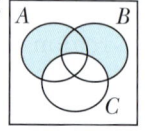

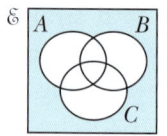

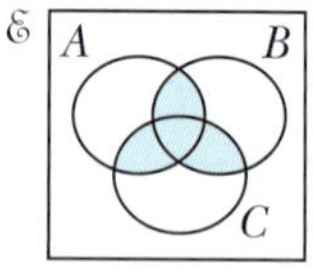

Chapter 2
Exercise 2.1
1. one-one   2. many-one
3. one-one   4. one-one
5. one-one   6. one-one
7. one-one   8. one-many

Exercise 2.2
1. 1, 2, 3, 4, 5, 6 and 7
2. a $-7 \leqslant f(x) \leqslant 2$
   b $2 \leqslant f(x) \leqslant 17$
   c $-1 \leqslant f(x) \leqslant 9$
   d $0 \leqslant f(x) \leqslant 9$
   e $\frac{1}{8} \leqslant f(x) \leqslant 8$
   f $\frac{1}{5} \leqslant f(x) \leqslant 1$
3. $g(x) \geqslant 2$ 4. $f(x) \geqslant -4$
5. $f(x) \geqslant 5$ 6. $f(x) \geqslant -5$
7. $f(x) \leqslant 10$ 8. $f(x) \geqslant 3$

Exercise 2.3
1. 9   2. 51   3. 675   4. 1
5. 67
6. a hk   b kh

7. $x = -\frac{1}{3}$
8. $x = -\frac{2}{3}$ or $x = 4$
9. $x = \pm\frac{3}{4}$
10. $x = 2.5$
11. $x = 5$
12. $x = 3$ or $x = 4$
13. a fg   b gf   c g^2 d f^2

Exercise 2.4
1. a $-2\frac{2}{3}, 4$ b $-2, -7$
   c $0.8, 1.6$ d $-23, 25$
   e $-5, -2$ f $-0.5, 7.5$
   g $16, 24$ h $-5, 3\frac{8}{9}$
   i $1\frac{2}{3}, 5$
2. a $-4\frac{5}{6}, -1.9$ b $-0.8, 0$
   c $-5.6, 4$ d $0.75, 3.5$
   e 6.5 f $x = 3\frac{1}{3}$
3. a $-2, 2$ b $-3, 3$
   c $-3, -1, 2$ d $0, 4, 6$
   e $-2, 1, 3$ f $-2, -1, 0, 3$
   g $0.5, 1$ h $-1, 2$
   i $0, 2, 6$
4. a $(-4, 0), (3, 7), (5, 9)$
   b $(0, 0), (1, 1), (2, 2)$
   c $(1, 3), (2.5, 7.5)$

Exercise 2.5
1. a ∨ shape, vertex at $(-1, 0)$, y-intercept 1
   b ∨ shape, vertex at $(1.5, 0)$, y-intercept 3
   c ∨ shape, vertex at $(5, 0)$, y-intercept 5
   d ∨ shape, vertex at $(-6, 0)$, y-intercept 3

e ∨ shape, vertex at (5, 0), y-intercept 10

f ∨ shape, vertex at (18, 0), y-intercept 6

2 a
x	-2	-1	0	1	2	3	4
y	7	6	5	4	3	4	5

b

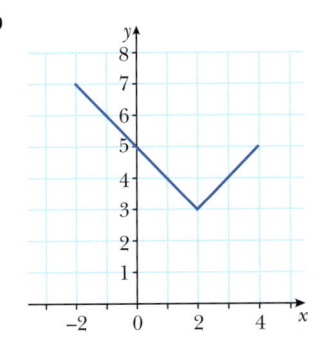

3 a ∨ shape, vertex at (0, 1)
  b ∨ shape, vertex at (0, −3)
  c ∧ shape, vertex at (0, 2)
  d ∨ shape, vertex at (3, 1), y-intercept 4
  e ∨ shape, vertex at (−3, −3), y-intercept 3

4 a $-3 \leq f(x) \leq 11$
  b $0 \leq g(x) \leq 11$
  c $-3 \leq h(x) \leq 5$

5 $-5 \leq f(x) \leq 5, 0 \leq g(x) \leq 5,$
   $-5 \leq h(x) \leq 3$

6 a ∨ shape, vertex at (−2, 0), y-intercept 4
  b straight line through (−5, 0), (0, 5)
  c −3, 1

7 a ∨ shape, vertex at (3, −3), y-intercept 3
  b $-3 \leq f(x) \leq 7$
  c 0.5, 5.5

8 a ∨ shape, vertex at $\left(\frac{4}{3}, 0\right)$, y-intercept 4

b straight line through (−2, −4), (5, 10)

c 0.8, 4

9 a

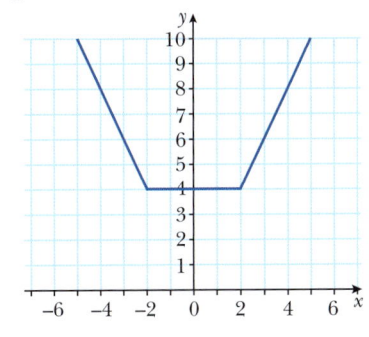

b −3, 3

Exercise 2.6

1 $f^{-1}(x) = \sqrt{x+7} - 5$

2 $f^{-1}(x) = \dfrac{6 - 2x}{x}$

3 $f^{-1}(x) = \dfrac{3 + \sqrt{x-1}}{2}$

4 $f^{-1}(x) = (8-x)^2 + 3$

5 $f^{-1}(x) = \dfrac{x+3}{5}$, $g^{-1}(x) = \dfrac{2x-7}{x}$

6 a $f^{-1}(x) = \sqrt{x+5} - 2$ b 20

7 a $f^{-1}(x) = 4 + \sqrt{x-5}$ b 294

8 a $g^{-1}(x) = \dfrac{x+3}{x-2}$ b 3.25

9 a $f^{-1}(x) = 2(x-2)$
  b no solution

10 0   11 −2, 3.5

12 $f^{-1}(x) \geq 0$ 13 $f^{-1}g^{-1}$

14 f, h

15 a $x \geq 2$ b $g(x) \geq 0$

16 a $f^{-1}(x) = \dfrac{x+k}{3}$, $g^{-1}(x) = \dfrac{x+14}{5-x}$
   b 13   c x

17 a $f^{-1}g$ b $g^{-1}f$
   c gf^{-1} d $f^{-1}g^{-1}$

Exercise 2.7

1

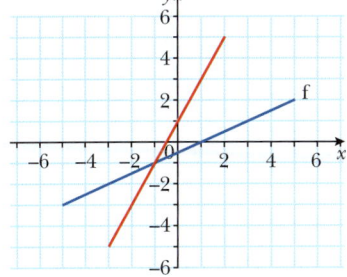

2

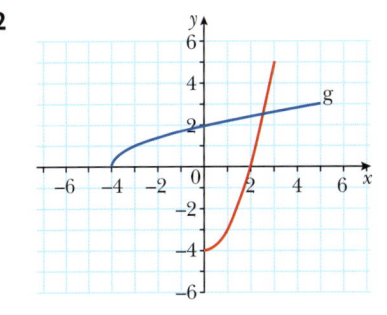

3

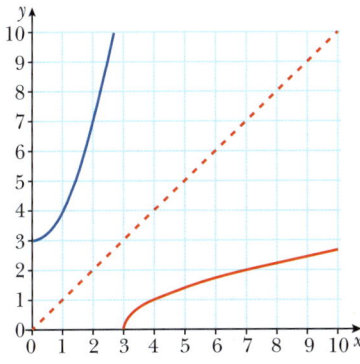

4

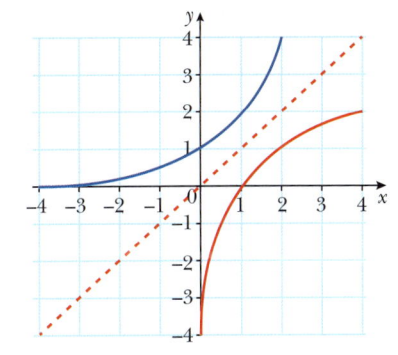

5

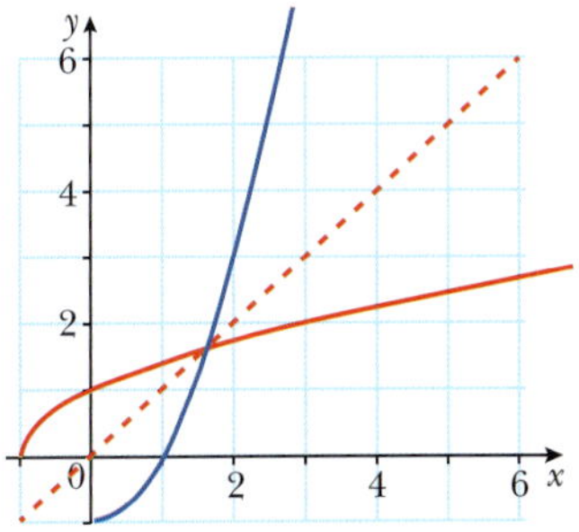

6 [graph]

7 a f is a one-one function
  b $f^{-1}(x) = \sqrt{3-x} - 1$
  c [graph]

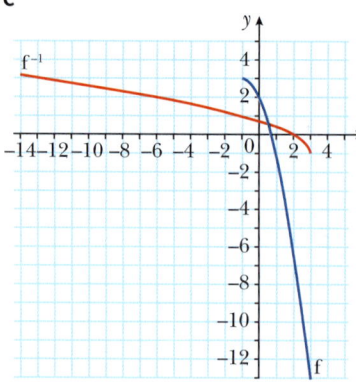

8 a $f^{-1}(x) = \dfrac{2x+7}{x-2}$
  b The curve is symmetrical about the line $y = x$

Exercise 2.8

1 6.5, −4
2 a V shape, vertex at (−0.6, 0), y-intercept 3
  b −0.2, −1
3 a V shape, vertex at (2.5, 0), y-intercept 5
  b 1, 4
4 a $-1 \leq f(x) \leq 299$ **b** $x \geq 0$
5 a $\dfrac{1}{3}$
  b $f^{-1}(x) = (x+3)^2 + 1$
  c $g^{-1}(x) = \dfrac{3x-2}{2x-1}$
6 a $0.2 \leq g(x) \leq 1$
  b $g^{-1}(x) = \dfrac{1+x}{2x}$
  c $0.2 \leq x \leq 1$
  d 1.25

7 a 33
  b i kh **ii** h^2
    iii $h^{-1}k^{-1}$ or $(kh)^{-1}$
8 a i $2(x-2)^2 - 3$ **ii** $x \geq 2$
  b i $g(x) \geq 4$, $h^{-1}(x) \geq 0$
    ii [graph]
    iii 8.5

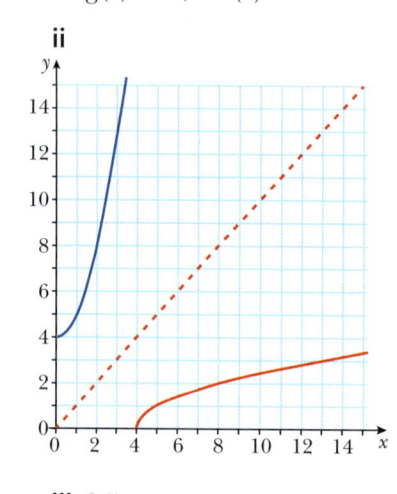

Chapter 3

Exercise 3.1

1 $x = 3, y = 9$ and $x = -2, y = 4$
2 $x = -1, y = -7$ and $x = 4, y = -2$
3 $x = -3, y = -4$ and $x = 4, y = 3$
4 $x = 1, y = 4$ and $x = -2, y = -2$
5 $x = 0.5, y = 0.5$ and $x = 0, y = 1$
6 $x = -1, y = -3$ and $x = 2, y = 1$
7 $x = 1.5, y = 4$ and $x = 2, y = 3$
8 $x = 3, y = 1$ and $x = 9, y = 7$
9 $x = 1.8, y = 2.6$ and $x = 1, y = 3$
10 $x = -1, y = -2$ and $x = 1, y = 2$
11 $x = 1, y = 2$ and $x = 2, y = 1$
12 $x = 1, y = 2$ and $x = 4, y = -4$
13 $x = 1, y = -\dfrac{1}{3}$ and $x = -\dfrac{1}{2}, y = \dfrac{1}{6}$
14 $x = 3, y = 1$ and $x = 1, y = 3$
15 $x = -1, y = -3$ and $x = 1, y = 3$
16 $x = 0, y = -0.5$ and $x = -1, y = -1$
17 $x = -1, y = 2$ and $x = 7\dfrac{1}{2}, y = -1.4$
18 $x = -1.5, y = -8$ and $x = 4, y = 3$
19 (−0.2, 1.4) and (1, −1)
20 a $x + y = 11$, $xy = 21.25$
  b $x = 2.5, y = 8.5$ and $x = 8.5, y = 2.5$
21 17 cm and 23 cm
22 $6\sqrt{5}$ or 13.4 to 3 sf
23 (0.5, 0)
24 $5\sqrt{2}$ or 7.07 to 3 sf
25 (2, 2)
26 $y = -2x - 1$

Exercise 3.2

1 a min (2.5, −12.25), axis crossing points (−1, 0), (6, 0), (0, −6)
  b min (0.5, −20.25), axis crossing points (−4, 0), (5, 0), (0, −20)
  c min (−2, −25), axis crossing points (−7, 0), (3, 0), (0, −21)
  d min (−1.5, −30.25), axis crossing points (−7, 0), (4, 0), (0, −28)
  e min (−2, −3), axis crossing points $(-2-\sqrt{3}, 0)$, $(-2+\sqrt{3}, 0)$, (0, 1)
  f max (1, 16), axis crossing points (−3, 0), (5, 0), (0, 15)
2 a $(x-4)^2 - 16$
  b $(x-5)^2 - 25$
  c $(x-2.5)^2 - 6.25$
  d $(x-1.5)^2 - 2.25$
  e $(x+2)^2 - 4$
  f $(x+3.5)^2 - 12.25$
  g $(x+4.5)^2 - 20.25$
  h $(x+1.5)^2 - 2.25$
3 a $(x-4)^2 - 1$
  b $(x-5)^2 - 30$

Answers

c $(x-3)^2 - 7$
d $(x-1.5)^2 + 1.75$
e $(x+3)^2 - 4$
f $(x+3)^2 + 0$
g $(x+2)^2 - 21$
h $(x+2.5)^2 - 0.25$

4 a $2(x-2)^2 - 5$
b $2(x-3)^2 - 17$
c $3(x-2)^2 - 7$
d $2(x-0.75)^2 + 0.875$
e $2(x+1)^2 - 1$
f $2(x+1.75)^2 - 9.125$
g $2(x-0.75)^2 + 3.875$
h $3\left(x-\dfrac{1}{6}\right)^2 + 5\dfrac{11}{12}$

5 a $9-(x-3)^2$
b $25-(x-5)^2$
c $2.25-(x-1.5)^2$
d $16-(x-4)^2$

6 a $6-(x+1)^2$
b $12-(x+2)^2$
c $16.25-(x+2.5)^2$
d $9.25-(x+1.5)^2$

7 a $13.5-2(x+1.5)^2$
b $3-2(x+1)^2$
c $15-2(x-2)^2$
d $4\dfrac{1}{12} - 3\left(x-\dfrac{5}{6}\right)^2$

8 a $4\left(x+\dfrac{1}{4}\right)^2 + 4.75$
b No, since $4.75 > 0$

9 a $2(x-2)^2 - 7$ b $(2,-7)$
10 a $-5.25, 0.5$ b $x \geq 0.5$
11 a $11\dfrac{1}{8} - 2\left(x+1\dfrac{3}{4}\right)^2$
b $x \leq 11\dfrac{1}{8}$

12 a $18.5 - 2(x-1.5)^2$
b $(1.5, 18.5)$
c ∩ shaped curve, vertex $= (1.5, 18.5)$

13 a $13.25 - (x-2.5)^2$
b $(2.5, 13.25)$, maximum
c $-7 \leq f(x) \leq 13.25$
d No, it is not a one-one function.

14 a $2(x-2)^2 - 5$ b $x \geq 2$
15 -0.75
16 a $5-(x-2)^2$
b $(2, 5)$ maximum
c One-one function, $f^{-1}(x) = 2 + \sqrt{5-x}$

Exercise 3.3

1 a

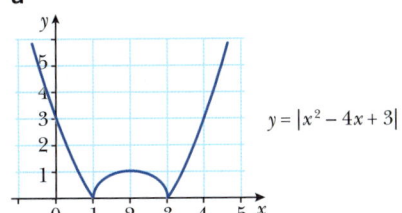

$y = |x^2 - 4x + 3|$

b

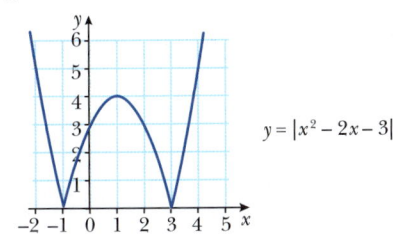

$y = |x^2 - 2x - 3|$

c

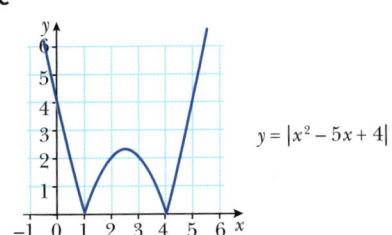

$y = |x^2 - 5x + 4|$

d

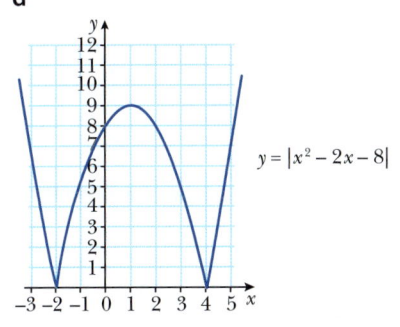

$y = |x^2 - 2x - 8|$

e

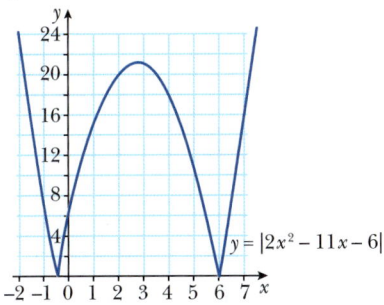

$y = |2x^2 - 11x - 6|$

f

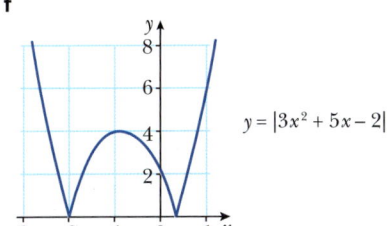

$y = |3x^2 + 5x - 2|$

2 a $5-(x+2)^2$
b ∩ shaped curve, vertex $= (-2, 5)$
c

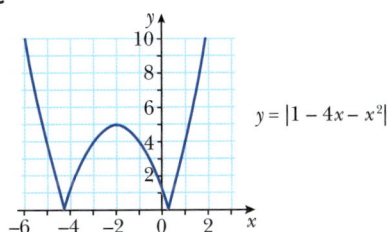

$y = |1 - 4x - x^2|$

3 a $2(x+0.25)^2 - 3.125$
b

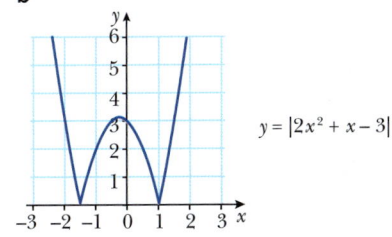

$y = |2x^2 + x - 3|$

423

4 a (3, 16)

b

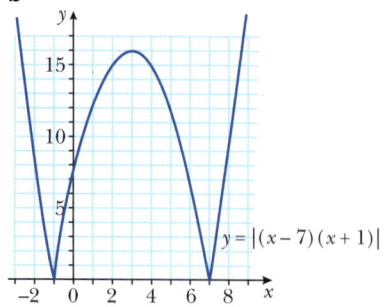

[Graph of $y = |(x-7)(x+1)|$]

c $0 < k < 16$

5 a (−3, 4)   **b** $k > 4$

6 a (5.5, 6.25)   **b** 6.25

7 a −4, 4   **b** −2, 0, 2
   c −1, 2, 3, 6   **d** −6, 4
   e $\dfrac{5 - \sqrt{33}}{2}$, 1, 4, $\dfrac{5 + \sqrt{33}}{2}$
   f −4, −2, −1, 1
   g $-1 - \sqrt{10}$, −1, $-1 + \sqrt{10}$
   h $\dfrac{1 + \sqrt{7}}{2}$, $\dfrac{-1 + \sqrt{7}}{2}$
   i −1, 3

8 a (−1, 0), (2, 3), (4, 5)
   b (−2, 1), (−1, 1.5), (2, 3), (5, 4.5)
   c (1, 2), (2, 4)

Exercise 3.4

1 a $x < -3$, $x > 4$
   b $1 < x < 5$
   c $x \leqslant -7$, $x \geqslant 3$
   d $0 < x < 5$
   e $-0.5 < x < 4$
   f $-1 \leqslant x \leqslant 3$
   g $-1.5 < x < 5$
   h $-\infty < x < \infty$
   i $x = 3$

2 a $-7 < x < 2$
   b $x \leqslant -3$, $x \geqslant 2$
   c $4 \leqslant x \leqslant 5$

   d $x < -8$, $x > 6$
   e $-2.5 \leqslant x \leqslant 3$
   f $x < -1$, $x > -0.8$

3 a $-6 < x < 3$
   b $x < 5$, $x > 7$
   c $x \leqslant 0.5$, $x \geqslant 1$
   d $-3 < x < 2$
   e $x < -4$, $x > 1$
   f $-0.5 < x < 0.6$

4 a $3 < x < 5$
   b $1 < x \leqslant 6$
   c $0.5 < x < 1$
   d $3 < x < 5$
   e $x < -2$, $x \geqslant 3$

5 a $-5 < x < 3$
   b $0 < x < 2$, $6 < x < 8$
   c $0 < x < 2$, $4 < x < 6$

6 $-1\dfrac{1}{3} < x < 2$

Exercise 3.5

1 a two equal roots
   b two distinct roots
   c two distinct roots
   d no roots
   e two distinct roots
   f two equal roots
   g no roots
   h two distinct roots

2 $k = \pm 6$

3 $k < 0.5$

4 $k > \dfrac{1}{3}$

5 $0, -\dfrac{8}{9}$

6 $k > -1.5$

7 $k > 3\dfrac{2}{3}$

8 $k = -10$, $k = 14$

9 $k = 1$, $k = 4$

Exercise 3.6

1 $k = -3$, $k = 5$

2 $k = -7$, $k = -3$

3 $c = \pm 4$

4 $k < 1$, $k > 5$

5 a $k = \pm 10$
   b (−2, 6), (2, −6)

6 $k > -5$

7 $k \geqslant 0.75$

8 $-11 < m < 1$

9 $m = -2$, $m = -6$

Exercise 3.7

1 $3 < k < 4$

2 $-1 < x < 0$

3 a $2\left(x - \dfrac{1}{4}\right)^2 + \dfrac{47}{8}$
   b $\dfrac{47}{8}$ when $x = \dfrac{1}{4}$

4 $k < -\dfrac{5}{2}$

5 $-6 < x < 1$

6 −2, −18

7 a $a = 20$, $b = -4$, (4, 20)
   b ∩ shaped curve, vertex = (4, 20), y-intercept = (0, 4)

8 $k = c + 9$

9 $k < -6$, $k > 10$

10 a $a = -12$, $b = -4$ **b** −4

11 $m < 2$, $m > 14$

12 a

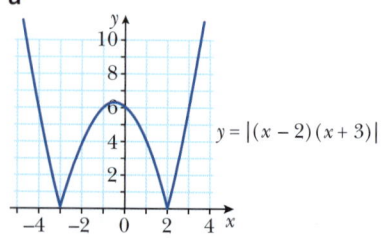

[Graph of $y = |(x-2)(x+3)|$]

   b $\left(-\dfrac{1}{2}, \dfrac{25}{4}\right)$

   c $k > \dfrac{25}{4}$

Answers

Chapter 4

Exercise 4.1

1. a x^{15} b x^{16} c x^{-3}
   d x^5 e x^{-2} f x^{-15}
   g x^2 h x^2 i $15x^6y^4$
   j $5x^3y^{-2}$ k $16x^{12}y^6$ l $6x^6y^{-3}$

2. a x^4 b x^5 c x^4
   d $\frac{9}{4}x^{-4}y^{-1}$

3. a $a=1, b=3, c=5$

4. a $a=-\frac{7}{2}, b=1$

5. $x=\frac{3}{5}, y=-1$

6. $x=5, y=8$

7. $x(1+x)^{\frac{1}{2}}$

Exercise 4.2

1. a $\frac{1}{5}$ b 3
   c -3 or 2 d $-\frac{1}{2}$ or 5

2. a 4 b 2 c 5
   d 1 e -1 f -3
   g -4 h ± 4

3. a 6 b -1 c -7
   d -10 e $-4\frac{2}{3}$ f $-\frac{4}{5}$
   g -3 h $4\frac{1}{3}$ i $\frac{5}{16}$
   j 1 or 3 k -1 or 4
   l -0.5 or 2

4. a 0.8 b 1.5 c $-\frac{5}{3}$
   d 8

5. a 0 b 3 c 0.4
   d $\frac{1}{7}$

6. a -1 b 3 c -1.5

7. a $x=\frac{11}{6}, y=-\frac{1}{3}$
   b $x=\frac{3}{4}, y=\frac{1}{4}$
   c $x=\frac{7}{6}, y=\frac{3}{2}$

8. a $-\frac{1}{2}$ or 4 b 2

9. a $-\frac{5}{4}$ or 3 b 1

10. a $-\frac{1}{3}$ or 3 b 9

Exercise 4.3

1. a $10\sqrt{5}$ b $5\sqrt{10}$
   c $9\sqrt{11}$ d $5\sqrt{3}$

2. a $5\sqrt{5}+4\sqrt{3}$
   b $4\sqrt{5}+5\sqrt{3}$
   c $12\sqrt{5}+5\sqrt{3}$
   d $20\sqrt{5}+27\sqrt{3}$

3. a $2+13\sqrt{7}$
   b $10+35\sqrt{7}$
   c $2+(2n-1)\sqrt{7}$

4. a $\sqrt{33}$ b $11+\sqrt{33}$

5. $x=5-3\sqrt{2}, y=8+4\sqrt{2}$,
   $z=12-7\sqrt{2}$.

Exercise 4.4

1. a 6 b 12 c $\sqrt{30}$
   d 2 e 13 f $5\sqrt{5}$
   g $15\sqrt{6}$ h $14\sqrt{35}$

2. a 2 b $\sqrt{2}$ c 2
   d $\frac{1}{2}$ e $\frac{1}{3}$ f $\sqrt{5}$
   g 3 h $\frac{2}{5}$ i $\frac{\sqrt{5}}{9}$
   j $\sqrt{2}$ k 6 l $\sqrt{5}$

3. a $2\sqrt{2}$ b $2\sqrt{3}$ c $2\sqrt{5}$
   d $2\sqrt{7}$ e $5\sqrt{2}$ f $6\sqrt{2}$
   g $3\sqrt{2}$ h $4\sqrt{2}$ i $4\sqrt{5}$
   j $3\sqrt{10}$ k $3\sqrt{7}$ l $3\sqrt{11}$
   m $2\sqrt{11}$ n $5\sqrt{5}$ o $3\sqrt{13}$
   p $10\sqrt{2}$ q $5\sqrt{3}$ r $10\sqrt{30}$
   s $\sqrt{5}$ t $\sqrt{3}$ u $2\sqrt{5}$
   v $10\sqrt{2}$ w $2\sqrt{10}$ x $4\sqrt{3}$
   y 35

4. a $9\sqrt{3}$ b $3\sqrt{3}$ c $5\sqrt{5}$
   d $7\sqrt{3}$ e 0 f $9\sqrt{5}$
   g $2\sqrt{5}$ h $-3\sqrt{5}$ i $6\sqrt{7}$
   j $8\sqrt{2}$ k $10\sqrt{2}$ l 0
   m $20\sqrt{5}$ n $8\sqrt{3}$ o $6\sqrt{2}$

5. a $2+3\sqrt{2}$ b 12
   c $-4+5\sqrt{2}$ d $9+5\sqrt{3}$
   e $3-\sqrt{3}$ f 20
   g 1 h $-2+4\sqrt{3}$
   i $12+5\sqrt{5}$ j 7
   k 13 l -4
   m 4 n $17+3\sqrt{35}$
   o $23+16\sqrt{2}$

6. a $9+4\sqrt{5}$ b $28-10\sqrt{3}$
   c $91+40\sqrt{3}$ d $5+2\sqrt{6}$

7. $(10+12\sqrt{2})$ cm^2

8. a 293 b $a=9, b=10$
   c $p=45, q=2$

9. $(11+7\sqrt{2})$ cm^3

10. $\sqrt{2}$

Exercise 4.5

1. a $\frac{\sqrt{5}}{5}$ b $\frac{3\sqrt{2}}{2}$ c $3\sqrt{3}$
   d $\frac{\sqrt{3}}{3}$ e $\frac{4\sqrt{5}}{5}$ f $4\sqrt{3}$
   g $\frac{2\sqrt{3}}{3}$ h $\frac{5\sqrt{2}}{2}$ i $\frac{3\sqrt{2}}{4}$
   j $\frac{1}{4}$ k $\frac{\sqrt{5}}{5}$ l $\frac{\sqrt{13}}{13}$
   m $\frac{5\sqrt{2}}{4}$ n $\frac{7\sqrt{3}}{6}$ o $\frac{5+\sqrt{5}}{5}$
   p $\frac{3-\sqrt{3}}{3}$ q $\frac{-2+3\sqrt{2}}{2}$
   r $-1+2\sqrt{7}$

2. a $-1+\sqrt{2}$ b $\frac{3-\sqrt{5}}{4}$

c $\dfrac{3-\sqrt{7}}{2}$ d $3+\sqrt{5}$

e $-10+5\sqrt{5}$ f $\dfrac{-7-2\sqrt{7}}{3}$

g $4+2\sqrt{3}$ h $\dfrac{15+10\sqrt{3}}{3}$

i $\dfrac{2\sqrt{3}+\sqrt{2}}{10}$ j $4\sqrt{7}+4\sqrt{5}$

3 a $7-4\sqrt{3}$ b $\dfrac{5+4\sqrt{2}}{7}$

c $\dfrac{5+3\sqrt{2}}{7}$ d $\dfrac{9-2\sqrt{14}}{5}$

e $2+\sqrt{5}$ f $\dfrac{14-\sqrt{187}}{3}$

g $\dfrac{-5+\sqrt{21}}{2}$ h $\dfrac{30+\sqrt{851}}{7}$

4 a $\sqrt{3}$ b $\dfrac{3\sqrt{7}-\sqrt{2}}{5}$

c $\dfrac{12+\sqrt{3}}{13}$

5 $(2\sqrt{5}-\sqrt{2})$ cm

6 $(4-\sqrt{5})$ cm

7 $7-2\sqrt{3}$ cm

8 a $\dfrac{1+5\sqrt{2}}{7}$ b $\dfrac{15+14\sqrt{2}}{2}$

9 $\dfrac{23-4\sqrt{7}}{30}$

10 $6-4\sqrt{2}$

Exercise 4.6

1 a $\dfrac{6+\sqrt{15}}{7}$ b $\dfrac{\sqrt{10}+2\sqrt{5}}{5}$

c $\dfrac{\sqrt{85}+2\sqrt{15}}{5}$

2 a $1+\sqrt{2}, 3-2\sqrt{2}$

b $2+\sqrt{6}, 3-\sqrt{6}$

c $2+\sqrt{5}, -3\sqrt{5}$

d $3+\sqrt{7}, 5-2\sqrt{7}$

e $3-\sqrt{2}, 5+\sqrt{2}$

3 a $\dfrac{100}{9}$ b $\dfrac{1}{9}$

c no solution   d 5

e 19.5   f 2

g 15   h $2\sqrt{2}$

i 20

4 a 1   b 3   c 3

d -3 e 1   f 5

g 4   h no solution

i 4   j 0 or 1   j 0 or 2

5 a -3 or 1   b 9   c 0 or 4

d 0   e 3   f -4.5

6 $\dfrac{7+2\sqrt{6}}{5}$

7 $\dfrac{2+\sqrt{2}}{2}$

Exercise 4.7

1 2 or 3

2 $x=3, y=-0.5$

3 -4.5

4 $a=-3, 2$ $b=-18, 12$

5 $6-3\sqrt{3}$

6 $17\sqrt{5}+1$

7 a i $45-12\sqrt{10}+8$
$=53-12\sqrt{10}$

ii $-3\sqrt{5}+2\sqrt{2}$

b $-1+\sqrt{6}$

8 $7+3\sqrt{5}$

Chapter 5

Exercise 5.1

1 a $3x^4+2x^3+3x^2$

b $9x^4+2x^3+7x^2-2$

c $3x^4-4x^3-3$

d $6x^7+3x^6+4x^5+5x^4-2x^3+x^2-1$

2 a $8x^4-4x^3+2x^2+3x-2$

b $3x^4+8x^3+4x^2-3x-2$

c $3x^5+5x^4-3x^3+7x^2+8x-20$

d $3x^5+12x^4+13x^3+3x^2-4$

e $x^4-10x^3+29x^2-20x+4$

f $27x^3-27x^2+9x-1$

3 a $3x^2+x-7$

b $2x^3+17x^2+21x-4$

c $2x^5+5x^4-8x^3-x^2-19x$

4 a x^3+7x^2+x-4

b $4x^4-4x^3-15x^2+8x+16$

c $8x^4-8x^3-32x^2+17x+32$

d $4x^4-4x^3-5x^2+3x-2$

Exercise 5.2

1 a $x^2+2x-48$

b x^2+x-1

c $x^2-15x+25$

d x^2+2x+1

e x^2+4x-5

f x^2-9

2 a $3x^2+2x-1$

b $2x^2+3x-2$

c $3x^2-5x-10$

d $3x^2+4$

3 a $3x^2-4$

b $2x^2-x+5$

c $x-4$

d $x+3$

4 a x^3-x^2+x-1

b x^2+2x+4

Exercise 5.3

2 a 29

b 546

c 12

3 $b=-2-2a$

4 a $a=0, b=-19$

b $a=2, b=38$

c $a=-12, b=-7$

Answers

5 −66, 18

6 $a = 13.5, b = 5.5$

7 a $p = 1, q = 9$

8 b 0, 1, 3

Exercise 5.4

1 b $(2x − 1)(x + 1)(x − 1)$

2 a $(x − 2)(x^2 + 4x + 5)$
   b $(x + 4)(x + 2)(x − 2)$
   c $x(2x + 3)(x − 6)$
   d $(x − 7)(x + 1)(x − 2)$
   e $(2x + 1)(x − 3)(x − 4)$
   f $(x − 2)(x + 3)(3x − 1)$
   g $(2x − 1)(2x + 1)(x − 2)$
   h $(2x − 1)(x − 3)(x + 5)$

3 a −5, 1, 7   **b** 1, 2, 3
   c $-4, -2, \frac{1}{3}$ **d** −4, 1, 1.5
   e −2, 0.5, 3   **f** $-4, -\frac{1}{2}, 1$
   g −2, −1.5, 0.5   **h** −4, 2.5, 3

4 a $1, -3 \pm \sqrt{7}$
   b $-3, -\frac{5}{2} \pm \frac{1}{2}\sqrt{37}$
   c $2, -2 \pm \sqrt{3}$
   d 1.5, 1, 4

5 $-0.5, -2 \pm \sqrt{13}$

6 −5.54, −3, 0.54

7 b 2

8 a $x^3 − 4x^2 − 7x + 10$
   b $x^3 + 3x^2 − 18x − 40$
   c $x^3 + x^2 − 6x$

9 a $2x^3 − 11x^2 + 10x + 8$
   b $2x^3 − 7x^2 + 7x − 2$
   c $2x^3 − 9x^2 − 8x + 15$

10 $x^3 + x^2 − 7x − 3$

11 $2x^3 − 9x^2 + 6x − 1$

12 b $2, \frac{1 \pm \sqrt{33}}{8}$

Exercise 5.5

1 a 5   **b** −1
   c 76   **d** 2

2 a 5   **b** 57
   c 11

3 $a = 4, b = 0$

4 $a = −6, b = −6$

5 a $a = −8, b = 15$
   b $3, \frac{-1 + \sqrt{21}}{2}, \frac{-1 - \sqrt{21}}{2}$

6 a $a = −9, b = 2$
   b 5

7 $b = 2$

8 $a = 6, b = −3$

9 a $b = 12 − 2a$
   b $a = 5, b = 2$

10 a 5   **b** −72

11 a $a = −8, b = −5$
   b −30

12 32

13 b $3, \frac{-7 + \sqrt{13}}{6}, \frac{-7 - \sqrt{13}}{6}$

14 a 3   **b** −5

15 b −3, 6

Exercise 5.6

1 b $(x − 2)(x − 4)(3x + 4)$

2 $a = −2, b = 2.5$

3 b $b^2 − 4ac = −11$

4 a −17   **b** 71

5 $(x + 1)(x − 7)(2x + 1)$

6 $a = 7, b = −6$

Chapter 6

Exercise 6.1

1 a $\lg 1000 = 3$
   b $\lg 100 = 2$
   c $\lg 1\,000\,000 = 6$
   d $x = \lg 2$
   e $x = \lg 15$
   f $x = \lg 0.06$

2 a 1.88   **b** 2.48
   c 2.86   **d** 1.19
   e −1.70   **f** −2.30

3 a $10^5 = 10\,000$
   b $10^1 = 1$ **c** $10^{-3} = \frac{1}{1000}$
   d $x = 10^{7.5}$ **e** $x = 10^{1.7}$
   f $x = 10^{-0.8}$

4 a 126 000   **b** 1450
   c 145   **d** 0.501
   e 0.0316   **f** 0.00145

5 a 4   **b** −2
   c 0.5   **d** $\frac{1}{3}$
   e 1.5   **f** 2.5

Exercise 6.2

1 a $\log_4 64 = 3$
   b $\log_2 32 = 5$
   c $\log_5 125 = 3$
   d $\log_6 36 = 2$
   e $\log_2 \frac{1}{32} = -5$
   f $\log_3 \frac{1}{81} = -4$
   g $\log_a b = 2$
   h $\log_x 4 = y$
   i $\log_a c = b$

2 a $2^2 = 4$ **b** $2^6 = 64$
   c $5^0 = 1$ **d** $3^2 = 9$
   e $36^{\frac{1}{2}} = 6$ **f** $8^{\frac{1}{3}} = 2$
   g $x^0 = 1$ **h** $x^y = 8$
   i $a^c = b$

3 a 16   **b** 9
   c 625   **d** $\sqrt{3}$

427

e 12   f 3   g 17
  h 4   i −41
4 a 2   b 4   c 3
  d −2   e 5   f 3.5
  g 2.5   h −1.5   i 0.5
  j −0.5   k $\dfrac{1}{3}$ l −0.5
5 a 2   b $\dfrac{1}{3}$ c 1.5
  d −2   e −6   f 3.5
  g $\dfrac{2}{3}$ h $\dfrac{7}{6}$
6 a 8   b 625

Exercise 6.3
1 a $\log_2 15$ b $\log_3 6$
  c $\log_5 64$ d $\log_7 2$
  e $\log_3 20$ f $\log_7\left(\dfrac{1}{2}\right)$
  g $\log_4 12$ h $\lg\dfrac{1}{20}$
  i $\log_4 6.4$
2 a 3   b 2   c 1
  d 1   e 1.5   f −2
3 a $\log_5 36$ b $\log_2 \dfrac{4}{3}$
4 a $2^4, 2^{-2}$ b −2
5 a 2   b 3   c −3
  d −1
6 a 5^u b $u − 2$
  c $1 + \dfrac{1}{2}u$ d $\dfrac{3}{2}u − 3$
7 a $1 + x$ b $2 − x$
  c $x + 2y$ d 4^{x+y}
8 a −8   b −5.5
  c 13   d 34
9 a 8   b 20
  c 14   d 0

Exercise 6.4
1 a 5   b 7.5   c 25
  d 77
2 a 12   b 8   c 10
  d 3   e 0.7   f 7.5
3 a 2, 8   b 5   c 6
  d 4   e 3   f $\dfrac{1}{4}, \dfrac{3}{2}$
  g 5   h 20
4 a 16   b 4   c $\dfrac{2}{3}$
  d $\sqrt{3}$
5 a 5, 25   b $\dfrac{1}{125}, 3125$
  c $\dfrac{1}{125}, 15625$ d $\dfrac{1}{512}, 16$
6 a $x = 4, y = 16$
  b $x = 20, y = 10$
  c $x = 4, y = 12$
  d $x = 40, y = 16$
  e $a = 6.25, b = 2.5$
  f $x = 1.25, y = 2.5$
7 b $\lg x = 8, \lg y = 2$

Exercise 6.5
1 a 6.13   b 2.73   c 0.861
  d 2.41   e 2.65   f 1.66
  g 6.90   h 5.19   i 1.15
  j −13.4   k 0.641   l 0.262
2 b 10   c 3.32
3 a 0.415   b 2.42   c 2.46
  d 1.63   e 1.03
4 −0.751, 1.38
5 a 0, 1.46
  b 1.40   c 2.32   d 0.683
6 0.683, 1.21
7 a 1.58
  b 0.257, 0.829
  c 0.631, 1.26

  d 0.792, 0.161
8 a 2.32   b 1.16
  c 0.631, 1.26
  d 0.431, 1.43
9 a 0.6   b −0.189

Exercise 6.6
1 a 3.32   b 3.18
  c 1.29   d −3.08
2 a $\dfrac{1}{u}$ b $\dfrac{2}{u}$
  c $\dfrac{1}{2u}$ d $\dfrac{3}{2u}$
3 a $\dfrac{1}{x}$ b $1 + x$
  c $2x$ d $4 + 2x$
4 a 4   b 0.4
5 $\dfrac{1}{3}$
6 a 23   b 23
7 a $\dfrac{1}{2}\log_2 x$
  b 256
8 a 16   b 9
  c 1.59   d 1.87
9 a $\dfrac{1}{\log_3 x}$ b 3, 9
10 a $\dfrac{1}{27}, 27$ b 5
  c $\dfrac{1}{256}, 4$ d 16, 64
  e $\dfrac{1}{2}, 512$ f 25
11 a $\dfrac{1}{2}\log_2 x$ b $\dfrac{1}{3}\log_2 y$
  c $x = 32, y = 2$
12 $x = 6.75, y = 13.5$

Exercise 6.7
1 a 7.39   b 4.48   c 1.22
  d 0.0498

2   a 1.39   b 0.742   c −0.357
    d −0.942
3   a 5   b 8   c 6
    d −2
4   a 7   b 2.5   c 6
    d 0.05
5   a 4.25   b 1.67   c 1.77
    d 1.30
6   a $\ln 7$ b $\ln 3$
    c $\frac{1}{2}(5+\ln 3)$ d $\frac{1}{3}(1+3\ln 2)$
7   a 20.1   b 0.135   c 1100
    d 12.5
8   a 3.49   b −2.15   c 0.262
9   a $3+e^2$ b $\frac{1}{2}(1+\ln 7)$
    c $2\ln 2$ d $\frac{1}{2}\ln 2$
    e $2\ln 2, \ln 5$ f $\ln 2, \ln 3$
10 a 1.79   b 0, 1.39
    c −3.69, 4.38
11 a $x = \frac{1}{e^2}, y = \frac{1}{e}$
    b $x = \ln 0.6, y = \ln 0.12$

Exercise 6.8
1   a 409 600   b 16.61
2   a 43 000   b 2091
3   a 0.0462   b 724
4   a 500   b 82.6
    c 2.31
5   a $250 000   b 0.112
    c 6.18
6   a $\frac{4}{3}$
    b $\frac{81}{80}$, A_0 represents the area of the patch at the start of the measurements
    c 6.72

Exercise 6.10
1   a asymptote: $y = -4$,
       y-intercept: (0, −2)
       x-intercept: (ln 2, 0)
    b asymptote: $y = 6$,
       y-intercept: (0, 9)
    c asymptote: $y = 2$,
       y-intercept: (0, 7)
    d asymptote: $y = 6$,
       y-intercept: (0, 8)
    e asymptote: $y = -1$,
       y-intercept: (0, 2)
       x-intercept: (ln 3, 0)
    f asymptote: $y = 4$,
       y-intercept: (0, 2)
       x-intercept: (−ln 2, 0)
    g asymptote: $y = 1$,
       y-intercept: (0, 5)
    h asymptote: $y = 8$,
       y-intercept: (0, 10)
    i asymptote: $y = 2$,
       y-intercept: (0, 1)
       x-intercept: $\left(\frac{1}{4}\ln 2, 0\right)$
2   a asymptote: $x = -2$,
       x-intercept: (−1.5, 0)
       y-intercept: (0, ln 4)
    b asymptote: $x = 2$,
       x-intercept: $\left(2\frac{1}{3}, 0\right)$
    c asymptote: $x = 4$,
       x-intercept: (3.5, 0)
       y-intercept: (0, ln 8)
    d asymptote: $x = -1$,
       x-intercept: (−0.5, 0)
       y-intercept: (0, 2 ln 2)
    e asymptote: $x = 2$,
       x-intercept: (2.5, 0)
    f asymptote: $x = 1.5$,
       x-intercept: $\left(1\frac{2}{3}, 0\right)$

Exercise 6.11
1   a $f^{-1}(x) = \ln(x-4)$, $x > 4$
    b $f^{-1}(x) = \ln(x+2)$, $x > -2$
    c $f^{-1}(x) = \ln\left(\frac{x+1}{5}\right)$, $x > -1$
    d $f^{-1}(x) = \frac{1}{2}\ln\left(\frac{x-1}{3}\right)$, $x > 1$
    e $f^{-1}(x) = \frac{1}{2}\ln\left(\frac{x-3}{5}\right)$, $x > 3$
    f $f^{-1}(x) = -\frac{1}{3}\ln\left(\frac{x-5}{4}\right)$, $x > 5$
    g $f^{-1}(x) = \ln(2-x)$, $x < 2$
    h $f^{-1}(x) = -\frac{1}{2}\ln\left(\frac{5-x}{2}\right)$, $x < 5$
2   a $f^{-1}(x) = e^x - 1$
    b $f^{-1}(x) = e^x + 3$
    c $f^{-1}(x) = e^{0.5x} - 2$
    d $f^{-1}(x) = \frac{1}{2}\left(e^{0.5x} - 1\right)$
    e $f^{-1}(x) = \frac{1}{2}\left(e^{\frac{1}{3}x} + 5\right)$
    f $f^{-1}(x) = \frac{1}{3}\left(e^{-0.2x} + 1\right)$
3   a $f(x) > 1$
    b $f^{-1}(x) = \frac{1}{2}\ln(x-1)$
    c $x > 1$ d x
4   a i $5x$ ii $x + \ln 5$
    b $\sqrt{5}$
5   a i x^3 ii $3x$
    b $\frac{1}{2}\ln 2$
6   a $(2x+1)^2$
    b $x = \ln 2$

Exercise 6.12
1   a $5y^2 - 7y + 2 = 0$
    b 0, −0.569
2   $x = 5.8, y = 2.2$
3   a $g^{-1}(x) = \ln\left(\frac{x+2}{4}\right)$
    b $x = 1$
4   a 10   b −5   c $\frac{1}{7}$
5   a 2   b 4, 6

6 3.14

7 $\lg \dfrac{ab^3}{1000}$

8 −0.569

9 a 70   b 39.7   c 17.0

Chapter 7
Exercise 7.1

1 a 3   b 4   c 10
   d 13   e 5   f 25
   g $\sqrt{74}$ h $\sqrt{13}$ i $12\sqrt{2}$

2 a $2\sqrt{5}$, $3\sqrt{5}$, $\sqrt{65}$; right-angled
   b $2\sqrt{13}$, 10, $4\sqrt{10}$; not right-angled
   c $4\sqrt{5}$, $3\sqrt{5}$, $5\sqrt{5}$; right-angled

4 5 and −5

5 1 and 3

6 a (6, 4)   b (6.5, 7)
   c (3, 8)   d (0.5, 1.5)
   e (−4.5, −2.5)
   f (3a, b)

7 $a = 18, b = -8$

8 a (0, 4.5)   b (1, 1)

9 1

10 $A(-5, 2), B(9, 4), C(-3, 6)$

Exercise 7.2

1 a −2   b −3   c 0
   d $3\dfrac{1}{3}$ e $\dfrac{1}{3}$ f $-\dfrac{3}{4}$

2 a $-\dfrac{1}{3}$ b 2   c $-\dfrac{5}{2}$
   d $-\dfrac{4}{5}$ d $\dfrac{2}{5}$

3 a $\dfrac{2}{3}$ b $-\dfrac{3}{2}$

4 (−3, −1)

6 a $-\dfrac{3}{5}, -\dfrac{1}{2}$
   b not collinear

7 5

8 1, 2

9 (11, 0)

Exercise 7.3

1 a $y = 3x - 13$
   b $y = -4x + 7$
   c $y = -\dfrac{1}{2}x + 1$

2 a $2y = 5x - 11$
   b $3x + 2y = 9$
   c $x + 2y = 1$

3 a $y = 2x - 10$
   b $x + 2y = -8$
   c $2y = 3x - 15$
   d $x + 4y = 0$

4 a $4x - 5y = -17$
   b (0, 3.4)
   c 3.4 units^2

5 a $y = -2x$
   b $3x + 4y = 2$
   c $5x + 7y = -26$

6 a $P\left(1\dfrac{1}{2}, 0\right), Q\left(0, 2\dfrac{1}{4}\right)$
   b $\dfrac{3\sqrt{13}}{4}$
   c 1.6875 units^2

7 a (3, 2)
   b $3y = 2x + 5$

8 a (5, 6)   b $k = 8$

9 a $y = -2x + 13$
   b (6, 1)
   c $6\sqrt{5}, 3\sqrt{5}$
   d 45 units^2

10 a i $2x + 3y = 14$,
       ii $y = \dfrac{1}{2}x$
    b (4, 2)

Exercise 7.4

1 a 27.5 units^2
   b 22 units^2

2 a 54.5 units^2
   b 76 units^2

3 a $k = -9$
   b 50 units^2

4 a (−1, 1.5), (2, −4.5)
   c 22.5 units^2

5 a (4, 5), (0, −3)
   b 20 units^2

6 a (0, −7)
   b 60 units^2

7 a (7.5, 9)
   b 38.25 units^2

8 a (2, 2), (4, −2), (0, 6)
   b 40 units^2

9 a (5.5, 1)
   b (6, 7)
   c 116 units^2

Exercise 7.5

1 a $y = ax^2 + b$, $Y = y$, $X = x^2$, $m = a, c = b$
   b $yx = ax^2 + b$, $Y = xy$, $X = x^2$, $m = a, c = b$
   c $\dfrac{y}{x} = ax - b$, $Y = \dfrac{y}{x}$, $X = x$, $m = a, c = -b$
   d $x = -b\dfrac{x}{y} + a$, $Y = x, X = \dfrac{x}{y}$, $m = -b, c = a$
   e $y\sqrt{x} = ax + b$, $Y = y\sqrt{x}$, $X = x, m = a, c = b$

Answers

   f $x^2y = bx^2 + a$, $Y = x^2y$,
$X = x^2$, $m = b$, $c = a$

   g $\dfrac{x}{y} = ax + b$, $Y = \dfrac{x}{y}$,
$X = x$, $m = a$, $c = b$

   h $\dfrac{\sqrt{x}}{y} = ax - b$, $Y = \dfrac{\sqrt{x}}{y}$,
$X = x$, $m = a$, $c = -b$

2 a $\lg y = ax + b$, $Y = \lg y$, $X = x$,
$m = a$, $c = b$

   b $\ln y = ax - b$, $Y = \ln y$, $X = x$,
$m = a$, $c = -b$

   c $\lg y = b \lg x + \lg a$, $Y = \lg y$,
$X = \lg x$, $m = b$, $c = \lg a$

   d $\lg y = x \lg b + \lg a$, $Y = \lg y$,
$X = x$, $m = \lg b$, $c = \lg a$

   e $\ln y = -\dfrac{a}{b}\ln x + \dfrac{2}{b}$, $Y = \ln y$,
$X = \ln x$, $m = -\dfrac{a}{b}$, $c = \dfrac{2}{b}$

   f $\lg x = -y \lg a + \lg b$, $Y = \lg x$,
$X = y$, $m = -\lg a$, $c = \lg b$

   g $x^2 = -by + \ln a$, $Y = x^2$,
$X = y$, $m = -b$, $c = \ln a$

   h $\ln y = bx + \ln a$, $Y = \ln y$,
$X = x$, $m = b$, $c = \ln a$

Exercise 7.6

1 a $y = 2x$

   b $y = \dfrac{1}{5}x^3 + 3$

   c $y = \sqrt{x} + 1$

   d $y = -\dfrac{1}{2}x^4 + \dfrac{11}{2}$

   e $y = -2 \times 2^x + 7$

   f $y = -\dfrac{5}{4}\ln x + \dfrac{27}{4}$

2 a ii $y = \dfrac{1}{x^2 - 1}$ **ii** $\dfrac{1}{3}$

   b ii $y = 2x^2 + 3x$ **ii** 14

   c ii $y = \dfrac{8}{x} - 1$ **ii** 3

   d ii $y = (13 - 2x^2)^2$ **ii** 25

   e ii $y = \dfrac{5}{4}x^2 - x - \dfrac{9}{2}$ **ii** $-\dfrac{3}{2}$

   f ii $y = x^{0.5} - x^{-0.5}$

   ii $\dfrac{3\sqrt{2}}{2}$

3 $y = -2x^5 + 16x^2$

4 a $y^2 = 3(2^x) + 25$ **b** 5

5 a $y = -2x^2 + 8x$

   b $x = 2.5$, $y = 7.5$

6 a $e^y = x^2 + 1$

   b $y = \ln(x^2 + 1)$

7 a $\lg y = \dfrac{3}{2}x - 7$

   b $y = 10^{-7} \times 10^{\frac{3}{2}x}$.

8 a $y = 100x^{\frac{3}{2}}$

   b 0.64

9 a $\ln y = 3\ln x - 1$

   b $y = \dfrac{x^3}{e}$

10 a 12.7

   b $a = e^{12.7}$, $b = -2$

Exercise 7.7

1 a

x	0.5	1.0	1.5	2.0	2.5
xy	0.5	3	5.51	8	10.5

   c $y = 5 - \dfrac{2}{x}$

   d $x = 0.8$, $y = 2.5$

2 a

$\dfrac{1}{x}$	10	5	3.33	2.5	2
$\dfrac{1}{y}$	9.01	6.49	5.68	5.29	5

   c $y = \dfrac{2x}{1 + 8x}$ **d** 0.22

3 b $y = 0.8x + \dfrac{12}{x}$

   c $x = 0.6$, $y = 20.48$

4 b $m_0 = 50$, $k = 0.02$

   c 29.1

5 b $k = 3$, $k = 0.7$

6 b $a = 5$, $b = 1.6$

7 b $a = 1.8$, $n = 0.5$

8 b $a = 0.2$, $b = 3$ **c** 4.56

9 b $a = -1.5$, $b = 1.8$ **c** 8.61

10 b $a = 3.6$, $b = -0.1$

   c gradient = 3.6, intercept = 0.1

11 b $y = e^3 \times x^{-0.8}$

   c gradient = −0.8, intercept = 3

Exercise 7.8

1 a $y = 7$ **b** $3x + 4y = 31$

   c 12.5

2 b allow -1.4 to -1.6

   c allow 13 to 16

3 a $2\sqrt{5}$ **b** $y = -2x + 6$

   c $(3, 0)$, $(-1, 8)$

4 $A = e^2$, $b = e$

5 55

6 a

$x\sqrt{x}$	1	2.83	5.20	8	11.18
$y\sqrt{x}$	3.40	4.13	5.07	6.20	7.47

   c $a = 3$, $b = 0.4$

   d 3.05

7 12.5

8 a 6.8

   b $A = 898$, $b = -0.5$

Chapter 8

Exercise 8.1

1 a $\dfrac{\pi}{18}$ **b** $\dfrac{\pi}{9}$ **c** $\dfrac{2\pi}{9}$

   d $\dfrac{5\pi}{18}$ **e** $\dfrac{\pi}{12}$ **f** $\dfrac{2\pi}{3}$

   g $\dfrac{3\pi}{4}$ **h** $\dfrac{5\pi}{4}$ **i** 2π

j 4π k $\dfrac{4\pi}{9}$ l $\dfrac{5\pi}{3}$

m $\dfrac{\pi}{20}$ n $\dfrac{5\pi}{12}$ o $\dfrac{7\pi}{6}$

2 a 90° b 30° c 15°
   d 20° e 120° f 144°
   g 126° h 75° i 27°
   j 162° k 216° l 540°
   m 315° n 480° o 810°

3 a 0.559 b 0.960 c 1.47
   d 2.15 e 4.31

4 a 74.5° b 143.2° c 59°
   d 104.9° e 33.2°

5 a

Degrees	0	45	90	135	180
Radians	0	$\dfrac{\pi}{4}$	$\dfrac{\pi}{2}$	$\dfrac{3\pi}{4}$	π

Degrees	225	270	315	360
Radians	$\dfrac{5\pi}{4}$	$\dfrac{3\pi}{2}$	$\dfrac{7\pi}{4}$	2π

b

Degrees	0	30	60	90	120
Radians	0	$\dfrac{\pi}{6}$	$\dfrac{\pi}{3}$	$\dfrac{\pi}{2}$	$\dfrac{2\pi}{3}$

Degrees	150	180	210	240	270
Radians	$\dfrac{5\pi}{6}$	π	$\dfrac{7\pi}{6}$	$\dfrac{4\pi}{3}$	$\dfrac{3\pi}{2}$

Degrees	300	330	360
Radians	$\dfrac{5\pi}{3}$	$\dfrac{11\pi}{6}$	2π

6 a 0.964 b 1.03 c 0.932
   d 1 e 0.5 f 1

Exercise 8.2

1 a $\dfrac{3\pi}{2}$ cm b 2π cm
   c $\dfrac{15\pi}{4}$ cm d 15π cm

2 a 9.6 cm b 2 cm
3 a 1.25 rad b 1.5 rad
4 a 12.4 cm b 32 cm
   c 31 cm
5 a 10 cm b 1.85 rad
   c 38.5 cm
6 a 23 cm b 18.3 cm
   c 41.3 cm
7 a 13.6 cm b 21.1 cm
   c 34.7 cm

Exercise 8.3

1 a 6π cm² b $\dfrac{135}{2}\pi$ cm²
   c 35π cm² d $\dfrac{135}{4}\pi$ cm²
2 a 10.4 cm² b 4.332 cm²
3 a 1.11 rad b 1.22 rad
4 a 0.8 rad b 40 cm²
5 $r(75 - r)$
6 a $9\sqrt{2}$ cm
   b $\dfrac{\pi}{2}$
   c $\dfrac{81}{2}\pi$ cm²
7 a 1.24 rad b 89.3 cm²
   c 121 cm²
8 a 1 rad b 49.8 cm²
   c 17.8 cm²
9 a 24.3 cm² b 37.7 cm²
   c 13.4 cm²
10 b $54\pi - 36\sqrt{2}$
11 a $\dfrac{3}{7}$ rad b 18 cm²
12 a 4.39 cm b 2.40 cm
   c 15.5 cm d 15.0 cm²
13 34.4 cm
14 a 45.5 cm² b 57.1 cm²
   c 80.8 cm² d 21.7 cm²

Exercise 8.4

1 a $0.4x^2$ b 19.8 or 19.9
   c 24.95 to 25
2 a 74.1 b 422 or 423
3 b 54.6 or 54.5 or 54.55
   c 115.25 or 115.3 or 115
4 a 54.3 c 187

Chapter 9

Exercise 9.1

1 a $\dfrac{2\sqrt{13}}{13}$ b $\dfrac{3\sqrt{13}}{13}$
   c $\dfrac{4}{13}$ d 1
   e $\dfrac{7+\sqrt{13}}{9}$
2 a $\dfrac{\sqrt{23}}{5}$ b $\dfrac{\sqrt{46}}{23}$
   c $\dfrac{23}{25}$ d $\dfrac{\sqrt{2}+\sqrt{23}}{5}$
   e $\dfrac{23\sqrt{2}-2\sqrt{23}}{10}$
3 a $\dfrac{4\sqrt{3}}{7}$ b $4\sqrt{3}$
   c $\dfrac{4\sqrt{3}}{7}$ d 1
   e $\dfrac{7-196\sqrt{3}}{48}$
4 a $\dfrac{1}{2}$ b 3
   c $\dfrac{2}{3}$ d $\dfrac{\sqrt{3}+\sqrt{2}}{2}$
   e $\dfrac{2}{7}$
5 a $\dfrac{\sqrt{2}}{4}$ b $\dfrac{1}{2}$
   c $\dfrac{\sqrt{6}}{3}$ d $\dfrac{-6+10\sqrt{3}}{3}$
   e $2-\sqrt{2}$ f $2\sqrt{3}-\sqrt{6}$

Answers

Exercise 9.2

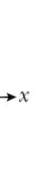

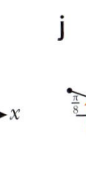

1 a, b, 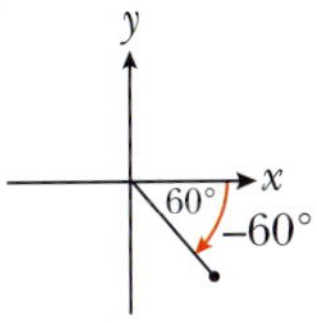 c, 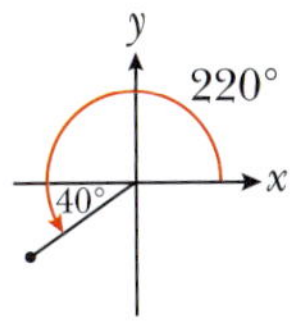 d, 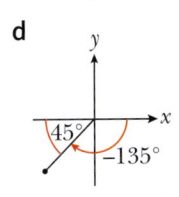 e, 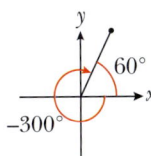 f, 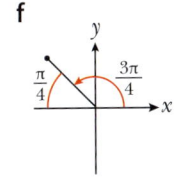 g, 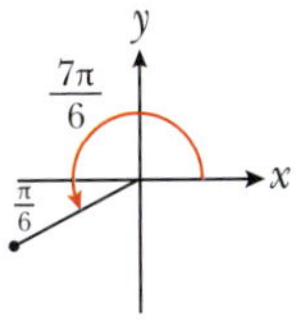 h, 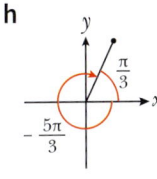 i, 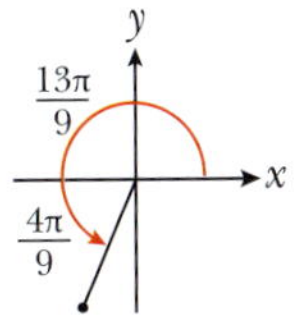 j (diagrams showing angles: 70°/110°, -60°/60°, 40°/220°, 45°/-135°, -300°/60°, π/4, 3π/4, 7π/6, π/6, π/3, -5π/3, 13π/9, 4π/9, π/8, -5π/8)

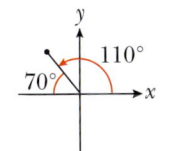

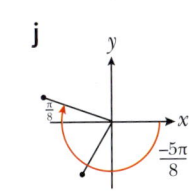

2 a second b fourth c third
   d third e third f first
   g fourth h third i first
   j first

Exercise 9.3

1 a $-\sin 40°$ b $\cos 35°$
   c $-\tan 40°$ d $\cos 25°$
   e $\tan 60°$ f $\sin \frac{\pi}{5}$
   g $-\tan \frac{\pi}{4}$ h $\cos \frac{\pi}{6}$
   i $-\tan \frac{\pi}{3}$ j $\sin \frac{\pi}{4}$

2 a $-\frac{\sqrt{21}}{2}$ b $-\frac{\sqrt{21}}{5}$

3 a $\frac{\sqrt{3}}{2}$ b $-\frac{1}{2}$

4 a $-\frac{12}{13}$ b $-\frac{5}{12}$

5 a $-\frac{2\sqrt{13}}{13}$ b $-\frac{3\sqrt{13}}{13}$

6 a $-\frac{4}{5}$ b $-\frac{3}{5}$
   c $-\frac{\sqrt{6}}{3}$ d $\sqrt{2}$

7 a $\frac{5}{13}$ b $-\frac{12}{5}$
   c $-\frac{4}{5}$ d $-\frac{4}{3}$

Exercise 9.4

1 a i amplitude = 7, period = 360°, (0, 7), (180, −7), (360, 7)
   ii amplitude = 2, period = 180°, (45, 2), (135, −2), (225, 2), (315, −2)
   iii amplitude = 2, period = 120°, (0, 2), (60, −2), (120, 2), (180, −2), (240, 2), (300, −2), (360, 2)
   iv amplitude = 3, period = 720°, (180, 3)
   v amplitude = 4, period = 360°, (0, 5), (180, −3), (360, 5)
   vi amplitude = 5, period = 180°, (45, 3), (135, −7), (225, 3), (315, −7)

2 a i amplitude = 4, period = 2π, $\left(\frac{\pi}{2}, 4\right), \left(\frac{3\pi}{2}, -4\right)$
   ii amplitude = 1, period = $\frac{2\pi}{3}$, $(0, 1), \left(\frac{\pi}{3}, -1\right), \left(\frac{2\pi}{3}, 1\right), (\pi, -1), \left(\frac{4\pi}{3}, 1\right), \left(\frac{5\pi}{3}, -1\right), (2\pi, 1)$
   iii amplitude = 2, period = $\frac{2\pi}{3}$, $\left(\frac{\pi}{6}, 2\right), \left(\frac{\pi}{2}, -2\right), \left(\frac{5\pi}{6}, 2\right), \left(\frac{7\pi}{6}, -2\right), \left(\frac{3\pi}{2}, 2\right), \left(\frac{11\pi}{6}, -2\right)$
   iv amplitude = 3, period = 4π, $(0, 3), (2\pi, -3)$
   v amplitude = 1, period = π, $\left(\frac{\pi}{4}, 4\right), \left(\frac{3\pi}{4}, 2\right), \left(\frac{5\pi}{4}, 4\right), \left(\frac{7\pi}{4}, 2\right)$
   vi amplitude = 4, period = π, $(0, 3), \left(\frac{\pi}{2}, -5\right), (\pi, 3), \left(\frac{3\pi}{2}, -5\right), (2\pi, 3)$

3 $a = 2, b = 4, c = 1$

4 $a = 3, b = 2, c = 4$

5 $a = 3, b = 2, c = 3$

6 a i period = 90°, $x = 45°, x = 135°, x = 225°, x = 315°$
   ii period = 360°, $x = 180°$
   iii period = 60°, $x = 30°, x = 90°, x = 150°, x = 210°, x = 270°, x = 330°$

7 a i period = $\frac{\pi}{4}$, $x = \frac{\pi}{8}, x = \frac{3\pi}{8}, x = \frac{5\pi}{8}, x = \frac{7\pi}{8}, x = \frac{9\pi}{8}, x = \frac{11\pi}{8}, x = \frac{13\pi}{8}, x = \frac{15\pi}{8}$
   ii period = $\frac{\pi}{3}$, $x = \frac{\pi}{6}, x = \frac{\pi}{2}, x = \frac{5\pi}{6}, x = \frac{7\pi}{6}, x = \frac{3\pi}{2}, x = \frac{11\pi}{6}$
   iii period = $\frac{\pi}{2}$, $x = \frac{\pi}{4}, x = \frac{3\pi}{4}, x = \frac{5\pi}{4}, x = \frac{7\pi}{4}$

8 $a = 2, b = 1, c = 3$

9 $a = 9, b = 4, c = 6$

10 a $A = 2, B = 5$

b 3

c

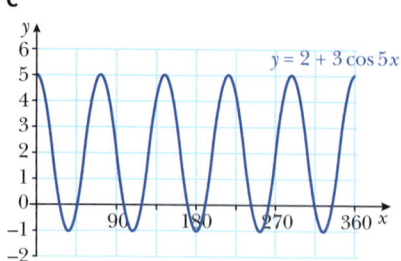

$y = 2 + 3\cos 5x$

11 a $A = 1, B = 3, C = 4$

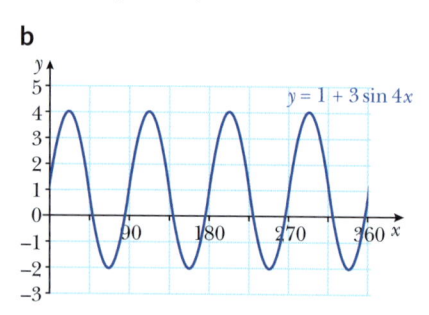

b

$y = 1 + 3\sin 4x$

12 b 2

13 b 2

14 b 4

Exercise 9.5

1 a $f(x) \geq 0$

b $0 \leq f(x) \leq 1$

c $0 \leq f(x) \leq 3$

d $0 \leq f(x) \leq 1$

e $0 \leq f(x) \leq 2$

f $0 \leq f(x) \leq 2$

g $1 \leq f(x) \leq 3$

h $0 \leq f(x) \leq 6$

i $0 \leq f(x) \leq 7$

2 c 4   3 c 2

4 c 3   5 b 2

6 b 5   7 b 2

8 b 4

9 $1 < k < 5$

10 $a = 1, b = 4, c = 2$

Exercise 9.6

1 a 17.5°, 162.5°

b 41.4°, 318.6°

c 63.4°, 243.4°

d 216.9°, 323.1°

e 125.5°, 305.5°

f 233.1°, 306.9°

g 48.6°, 131.4°

h 120°, 240°

2 a $\dfrac{\pi}{3}, \dfrac{5\pi}{3}$

b 0.197, 3.34

c no solutions

d 1.89, 5.03

e 3.99, 5.44

f 2.15, 4.13

g 0.253, 2.89

h 3.55, 5.87

3 a 26.6°, 63.4°

b 63.4°, 116.6°

c 31.7°, 121.7°

d 108.4°, 161.6°

e 18.4°, 161.6°

f 98.3°, 171.7°

g 80.8°, 170.8°

h 20.9°, 69.1°

4 a 150°, 270°

b 95.7°, 129.3°

c 225°, 315°

d $\dfrac{\pi}{2}, \dfrac{7\pi}{6}$

e 1.82, 2.75

f $\dfrac{\pi}{6}, \dfrac{7\pi}{6}$

5 a 14.0°, 194.0°

b 126.9°, 306.9°

c 31.0°, 211.0°

d 25.7°, 115.7°, 205.7°, 295.7°

6 0.648, 2.22

7 a 0°, 30°, 180°, 210°, 360°

b 0°, 38.7°, 180°, 218.7°, 360°

c 70.5°, 90°, 270°, 289.5°

d 0°, 135°, 180°, 315°, 360°

e 11.5°, 90°, 168.5°, 270°

f 0°, 45°, 180°, 225°, 360°

8 a 30°, 150°, 210°, 330°

b 31.0°, 149.0°, 211.0°, 329.0°

9 a 45°, 108.4°, 225°, 288.4°

b 30°, 150°, 270°

c 0°, 109.5°, 250.5°, 360°

d 60°, 180°, 300°

e 0°, 180°, 199.5°, 340.5°, 360°

f 19.5°, 160.5°, 210°, 330°

g 19.5°, 160.5°, 270°

h 30°, 150°, 270°

i 19.5°, 160.5°

10 0.848

Exercise 9.8

1 a 73.3°, 253.3°

b 75.5°, 284.5°

c 210°, 330°

d 53.1°, 306.9°

2 a 0.201, 2.94

b 0.896, 4.04

c 1.82, 4.46

d 2.55, 5.70

3 a 25.7°, 154.3°

b 5.8°, 84.2°

c 67.5°, 157.5°

d 112.8°, 157.2°

4 a 100.5°, 319.5°

b 73.3°, 151.7°

Answers

    d 2.56, 5.70
    e 1.28, 2.00
5   a 60°, 120°, 240°, 300°
    b 56.3°, 123.7°, 263.3°, 303.7°
    c 106.3°, 253.7°
6   a 41.4°, 180°, 318.6°
    b 113.6°, 246.4°,
    c 71.6°, 153.4°, 251.6°, 333.4°
    d 19.5°, 160.5°
    e 48.2°, 311.8°
    f 18.4°, 30°, 150°, 198.4°
    g 60°, 300°
    h 23.6°, 30°, 150°, 156.4°

Exercise 9.10
1   b i 4
       ii 60°
2   a 10°, 50°
    b $\frac{\pi}{6}, \frac{5\pi}{6}$
3   b 54.7°, 125.3°, 234.7°, 305.3°
5   a 164.1°, 344.1°
    b 0.898, 1.67, 4.04, 4.81
6   c 3
8   b 0.902, 2.24
9   a $a = 3, b = 8, c = 7$
    b i 120°
       ii 5

Chapter 10
Exercise 10.1
1   a 5040   b 12   c 840
    d 336   d 6   e 60
    f 20   g 4200
2   a 2!   b 6!   c $\frac{5!}{2!}$
    d $\frac{17!}{13!}$ e $\frac{10!}{7!3!}$ f $\frac{12!}{7!4!}$

3   a $\frac{n!}{(n-4)!}$ b $\frac{n!}{(n-6)!}$
    c $\frac{n!}{(n-3)!5!}$ d $\frac{n!}{(n-5)!3!}$

Exercise 10.2
1   a 24   b 5040
2   a 120   b 40320
    c 3628800
3   a 24
    b i 6   ii 6
4   a 5040   b 144
5   a 120   b 72   c 72
    d 42
6   a 12   b 36   c 24
7   a 720   b 120   c 48
8   a 600   b 312
9   288

Exercise 10.3
1   a 6720   b 360
    c 6652800   d 5040
2   360
3   15120
4   336
5   480
6   18
7   a 1680   b 840   c 630
    d 330
8   a 60   b 300
9   720

Exercise 10.4
1   a 5   b 20   c 1
    d 70   e 1   f 35
2   $\frac{8!}{3!5!} = \frac{8!}{5!3!}$
3   a 120   b 21   c 364
4   10
5   56

6   700
7   a 210   b 84
8   a 30045015   b 142506
9   67200
10 a 56   b 30   c 6
11 a 1287   b 756
12 1709
13 a 462   b 350
14 a 45   b 45
15 a 252   b 126   c 42
16 2000

Exercise 10.5
1   a 28
    b i 420   ii 240
2   a i 3628800   ii 17280
    b i 150   ii 110
3   a i 15120   ii 210
    b i 15504   ii 3696
       iii 56
4   a 720   b 240   c 480
    d 168
5   a i 40320   ii 2880
    b 350
6   a 840   b 240   c 80

Chapter 11
Exercise 11.1
1   1, 6, 15, 20, 15, 6, 1
    1, 7, 21, 35, 35, 21, 7, 1
2   a $1 + 3x + 3x^2 + x^3$
    b $1 - 4x + 6x^2 - 4x^3 + x^4$
    c $p^4 + 4p^3q + 6p^2q^2 + 4pq^3 + q^4$
    d $8 + 12x + 6x^2 + x^3$
    e $x^5 + 5x^4y + 10x^3y^2 + 10x^2y^3$
       $+ 5xy^4 + y^5$
    f $y^3 + 12y^2 + 48y + 64$

435

g $a^3 - 3a^2b + 3ab^2 - b^3$
h $16x^4 + 32x^3y + 24x^2y^2 + 8xy^3 + y^4$
i $x^3 - 6x^2y + 12xy^2 - 8y^3$
j $81x^4 - 432x^3 + 864x^2 - 768x + 256$
k $x^3 + 6x + \dfrac{12}{x} + \dfrac{8}{x^3}$
l $x^6 - \dfrac{3}{2}x + \dfrac{3}{4}x^{-4} - \dfrac{1}{8}x^{-9}$

3 a 16   b 10   c −12
   d 8   e 40   f 160
   g 5760 h $-\dfrac{3}{2}$

4 $A = 2048$, $B = 1280$, $C = 40$
5 $1 + 14x + 74x^2 + 216x^3 + 297x^4 + 162x^5$
6 $a = 8$
7 a $81 + 108x + 54x^2 + 12x^3 + x^4$
   b $376 + 168\sqrt{5}$
8 a $1 + 5x + 10x^2 + 10x^3 + 5x^4 + x^5$
   b i $76 + 44\sqrt{3}$
      ii $76 - 44\sqrt{3}$
   c 152
9 a $16 - 32x^2 + 24x^4 - 8x^6 + x^8$
   b 64
10 90
11 $\dfrac{3}{4}$
12 a $32 + 80y + 80y^2$
   b 400
13 $\dfrac{1}{5}$

Exercise 11.2
1 a $^3C_0\ ^3C_1\ ^3C_2\ ^3C_3$
   b $^4C_0\ ^4C_1\ ^4C_2\ ^4C_3\ ^4C_4$
   c $^5C_0\ ^5C_1\ ^5C_2\ ^5C_3\ ^5C_4\ ^5C_5$
2 a $1 + 4x + 6x^2 + 4x^3 + x^4$
   b $1 - 5x + 10x^2 - 10x^3 + 5x^4 - x^5$

c $1 + 8x + 24x^2 + 32x^3 + 16x^4$
d $27 + 27x + 9x^2 + x^3$
e $x^4 + 4x^3y + 6x^2y^2 + 4xy^3 + y^4$
f $32 - 80x + 80x^2 - 40x^3 + 10x^4 - x^5$
g $a^4 - 8a^3b + 24a^2b^2 - 32ab^3 + 16b^4$
h $16x^4 + 96x^3y + 216x^2y^2 + 216xy^3 + 81y^4$
i $\dfrac{1}{16}x^4 - \dfrac{3}{2}x^3 + \dfrac{27}{2}x^2 - 54x + 81$
j $1 - \dfrac{x}{2} + \dfrac{x^2}{10} - \dfrac{x^3}{100} + \dfrac{x^4}{2000} - \dfrac{x^5}{100\,000}$
k $x^5 - 15x^3 + 90x - \dfrac{270}{x} + \dfrac{405}{x^3} - \dfrac{243}{x^5}$
l $x^{12} + 3x^8 + \dfrac{15}{4}x^4 + \dfrac{5}{2} + \dfrac{15}{16x^4} + \dfrac{3}{16x^8} + \dfrac{1}{64x^{12}}$

3 a $40x^3$ b $175\,000x^3$
   c $160x^3$ d $720x^3$
   e $-20x^3$ f $-5376x^3$
   g $-9\,450\,000x^3$
   h $-954\,204\,160\,000x^3$
4 a $1 + 10x + 45x^2$
   b $1 + 16x + 112x^2$
   c $1 - 21x + 189x^2$
   d $729 + 2916x + 4860x^2$
   e $19683 - 59049x + 78732x^2$
   f $256 + 512x + 448x^2$
   g $1953125 - 3515625x^2 + 2812500x^4$
   h $1048576x^{10} - 13107200x^9y + 73728000x^8y^2$

5 a $1 + 12x + 60x^2 + 160x^3$
   b 140
6 a $1 + \dfrac{13}{2}x + \dfrac{39}{2}x^2 + \dfrac{143}{4}x^3$
   b $\dfrac{377}{4}$
7 a $1 - 30x + 405x^2 - 3240x^3$
   b −4860
8 a $1 + 14x + 84x^2$
   b 47
9 a $1 + 7x + 21x^2 + 35x^3$
   b 7
10 −945
11 $\dfrac{21}{2}$
12 $a = \dfrac{3}{n-2}$

Exercise 11.3
1 a $64 + 192x + 240x^2 + 160x^3$
   b 64
2 a $x^6 + 12x^3 + 60$ b 72
3 a $n = 6$ b −5
4 a −27.5   b 38.5
5 a $64 - 960x + 6000x^2$ b −640

Chapter 12
Exercise 12.1
1 a $4x^3$ b $9x^8$ c $-3x^{-4}$
   d $-6x^{-7}$ e $-x^{-2}$ f $-5x^{-6}$
   g $\dfrac{1}{2}x^{-\frac{1}{2}}$ h $\dfrac{5}{2}x^{\frac{3}{2}}$ i $-\dfrac{1}{5}x^{-\frac{6}{5}}$
   j $\dfrac{1}{3}x^{-\frac{2}{3}}$ k $\dfrac{2}{3}x^{-\frac{1}{3}}$ l $-\dfrac{1}{2}x^{-\frac{3}{2}}$
   m 1   n $\dfrac{3}{2}x^{\frac{1}{2}}$ o $\dfrac{5}{3}x^{\frac{2}{3}}$
   p $6x^5$ q $3x^2$ r $2x$
   s $\dfrac{1}{2}x^{-\frac{1}{2}}$ t $-\dfrac{3}{2}x^{-\frac{5}{2}}$

Answers

2
- a $6x^2 - 5$
- b $40x^4 - 6x$
- c $-6x^2 + 4$
- d $6x - 2x^{-2} + 2x^{-3}$
- e $2 + x^{-2} + \frac{1}{2}x^{-\frac{3}{2}}$
- f $\frac{1}{2}x^{-\frac{1}{2}} - \frac{5}{2}x^{-\frac{3}{2}}$
- g $1 + 3x^{-2}$
- h $5 + \frac{1}{2}x^{-\frac{3}{2}}$
- i $\frac{3}{2}x^{\frac{1}{2}} - \frac{1}{2}x^{-\frac{1}{2}} + \frac{1}{2}x^{-\frac{3}{2}}$
- j $15x^2 + 10x$ k $-2x^{-2} + 10x^{-3}$
- l $1 + 2x^{-2}$ m $18x + 6$
- n $-6x^2 + 6x^5$ o $12x + 5$

3
- a 6 b 4 c -2
- d 0 e -0.2 f $\frac{2}{9}$

4 $(2, 5)$

5 0.25

6 5

7 $-11, 11$

8 $a = 3, b = -4$

9 $a = -2, b = 5$

10 $\left(1, 2\frac{5}{6}\right), \left(4, 4\frac{1}{3}\right)$

11
- a $(-3, 2), (0, 5), (9, 14)$
- b $13, -8, 37$

12
- a $12x^2 + 6x - 6$
- b $x \leq -1$ and $x \geq 0.5$

13
- a $3x^2 + 2x - 16$
- b $-\frac{8}{3} \leq x \leq 2$

Exercise 12.2

1
- a $9(x + 2)^8$
- b $21(3x - 1)^6$
- c $-30(1 - 5x)^5$
- d $2\left(\frac{1}{2}x - 7\right)^3$
- e $4(2x + 1)^5$
- f $12(x - 4)^5$
- g $-30(5 - x)^4$
- h $8(2x + 5)^7$
- i $8x(x^2 + 2)^3$
- j $-28x(1 - 2x^2)^6$
- k $5(2x - 3)(x^2 - 3x)^4$
- l $8\left(x - \frac{1}{x^2}\right)\left(x^2 + \frac{2}{x}\right)^3$

2
- a $-\dfrac{1}{(x + 4)^2}$
- b $-\dfrac{6}{(2x - 1)^2}$
- c $\dfrac{15}{(2 - 3x)^2}$
- d $-\dfrac{64x}{(2x^2 - 5)^2}$
- e $-\dfrac{8(x - 1)}{(x^2 - 2x)^2}$
- f $\dfrac{5}{(x - 1)^6}$
- g $-\dfrac{30}{(5x + 1)^4}$
- h $-\dfrac{6}{(3x - 2)^5}$

3
- a $\dfrac{1}{2\sqrt{x + 2}}$
- b $\dfrac{5}{2\sqrt{5x - 1}}$
- c $\dfrac{2x}{\sqrt{2x^2 - 3}}$
- d $-\dfrac{3x^2 + 2}{2\sqrt{x^3 + 2x}}$
- e $-\dfrac{2}{3(3 - 2x)^{\frac{2}{3}}}$
- f $\dfrac{4}{\sqrt{2x - 1}}$
- g $-\dfrac{3}{2(3x - 1)^{\frac{3}{2}}}$
- h $\dfrac{5}{(2 - 5x)^{\frac{4}{3}}}$

4 8

5 2

6 0.75, -3

7 $(3, 2)$

8 $a = 8, b = 3$

Exercise 12.3

1
- a $2x + 4$
- b $12x + 10$
- c $(x + 2)^2(4x + 2)$
- d $x(x - 1)^2(5x - 2)$
- e $\dfrac{3x - 10}{2\sqrt{x - 5}}$
- f $\dfrac{3x + 2}{2\sqrt{x}}$
- g $\dfrac{5x^2 + 12x}{2\sqrt{x + 3}}$
- h $\dfrac{(3 - x^2)^2(13x^2 - 3)}{2\sqrt{x}}$
- i $2(3x^2 + x + 5)$
- j $(4x + 9)(x - 3)^2$
- k $2(x - 1)(x + 2)(2x + 1)$
- l $14(x - 1)(x - 3)^3(2x + 1)^2$

2 9 **3** 85

4 49, 0 **5** $-2, 0, 1.5$

6 $1\dfrac{2}{3}$

Exercise 12.4

1
- a $\dfrac{11}{(5 - x)^2}$
- b $\dfrac{10}{(x + 4)^2}$
- c $\dfrac{7}{(3x + 4)^2}$
- d $-\dfrac{1}{(3 - 8x)^2}$
- e $\dfrac{x(5x - 4)}{(5x - 2)^2}$
- f $-\dfrac{x^2 + 1}{(x^2 - 1)^2}$
- g $-\dfrac{15}{(3x - 1)^2}$
- h $-\dfrac{x^2 + 8x + 2}{(x^2 - 2)^2}$

2   −4

3   (0, 0), (1, 1)

4   $\dfrac{25}{9}$

5   a $\dfrac{1-2x}{2\sqrt{x}(2x+1)^2}$

    b $\dfrac{1-x}{(1-2x)^{\frac{3}{2}}}$

    c $\dfrac{x(x^2+4)}{(x^2+2)^{\frac{3}{2}}}$

    d $\dfrac{-5(x-3)}{2\sqrt{x}(x+3)^2}$

6   4

7   (3, −2)

8   a   (−2, −2.4), (0.4, 0), (2, 1.6)

    b $-\dfrac{23}{25}, \dfrac{125}{29}, -\dfrac{7}{25}$

Exercise 12.5

1   a $y = 4x - 6$
    b $y = -x - 2$
    c $y = 16x - 10$
    d $y = -\dfrac{1}{2}x + 3$
    e $y = -3x - 3$
    f $y = \dfrac{1}{4}x + 2\dfrac{1}{4}$

2   a $y = -\dfrac{1}{3}x - 4\dfrac{1}{3}$
    b $y = -\dfrac{1}{8}x + 5\dfrac{1}{4}$
    c $y = \dfrac{1}{4}x - 3\dfrac{3}{4}$
    d $y = 2x + 7.5$
    e $y = -0.1x - 3.8$
    f $y = 4x - 22$

3   $y = 8x - 6$, $y = -\dfrac{1}{8}x + \dfrac{17}{8}$

4   (0, 5.2)

5   $y = \dfrac{9}{16}x - \dfrac{1}{2}$, $y = -\dfrac{16}{9}x - \dfrac{1}{2}$

6   (2, −3)

7   $y = 2x - 20$

8   a $y = x + 8$
    b   (1, 6)
    c $y = -\dfrac{1}{2}x + \dfrac{13}{2}$

9   (1, 5.25)

10 a   (7, 4)
    b   12 units²

11 b $y = -0.4x - 0.6$

12 216 units²

13 22.5 units²

Exercise 12.6

1   0.21   2   0.68
3   −0.8p   4   2p
5   25p   6 $\dfrac{11}{3}p$
7   $\dfrac{\pi}{20}$
8   a $y = \dfrac{180}{x^2}$
    c   −254p, decrease

Exercise 12.7

1   0.15 units per second
2   0.125 units per second
3   −4 units per second
4   −0.25 units per second
5   0.5 units per second
6   $\dfrac{1}{150}$ units per second
7   −0.08 units per second
8   0.025 cm s⁻¹
9   $\dfrac{1}{96}$ cm s⁻¹
10 324 cm³ s⁻¹
11 $\dfrac{1}{480}$ cm s⁻¹
12 12π cm³ s⁻¹
13 a $\dfrac{4}{5\pi}$ cm s⁻¹   b $\dfrac{1}{5\pi}$ cm s⁻¹
14 a $\dfrac{1}{7}$ cm s⁻¹   b $\dfrac{1}{12}$ cm s⁻¹

Exercise 12.8

1   a   10   b $12x + 6$
    c $-\dfrac{18}{x^4}$ d $320(4x+1)^3$
    e $-\dfrac{1}{(2x+1)^{\frac{3}{2}}}$ f $\dfrac{3}{(x+3)^{\frac{5}{2}}}$

2   a $12(x-4)(x-2)$
    b $\dfrac{8x-6}{x^4}$
    c $\dfrac{8}{(x-3)^3}$
    d $\dfrac{2(x^3+6x^2+3x+2)}{(x^2-1)^3}$
    e $y = \dfrac{50}{(x-5)^3}$
    f $y = \dfrac{102}{(3x-1)^3}$

3   a   −3   b   −9   c   −8

4   b   −18, 18

5
x	0	1	2	3	4	5
$\dfrac{dy}{dx}$	+	0	−	−	0	+
$\dfrac{d^2y}{dx^2}$	−	−	−	+	+	+

Exercise 12.9

1   a   (6, −28)   minimum
    b   (−2, 9)   maximum
    c   (−2, 18) maximum,
        (2, −14) minimum
    d $\left(-2\dfrac{2}{3}, 14\dfrac{22}{27}\right)$ maximum,
        (2, −36) minimum
    e   (−3, −18) minimum, $\left(\dfrac{1}{3}, \dfrac{14}{27}\right)$ maximum

Answers

   f $\left(\dfrac{2}{3}, \dfrac{14}{27}\right)$ maximum, $(4, -18)$ minimum

2 a $(4, 4)$ minimum

   b $(-1, 3)$ minimum

   c $(4, 3)$ minimum

   d $\left(-3, -\dfrac{1}{3}\right)$ minimum,

      $\left(3, \dfrac{1}{3}\right)$ maximum

   e $(-2, -4)$ maximum, $(0, 0)$ minimum

   f $(-4, -13)$ maximum, $(2, -1)$ minimum

3 $\dfrac{dy}{dx} = -\dfrac{3}{(x+1)^2}$, numerator of $\dfrac{dy}{dx}$ is never zero

4 $a = 3$

5 a $a = -3, b = 5$

   b minimum

   c $(-1, 7)$, maximum

6 a $a = 2, b = -4$

   b minimum

7 a $a = 8, b = -4$

   b maximum

Exercise 12.10

1 a $y = 8 - x$

   b i $P = 8x - x^2$

      ii 16

   c i $S = x^2 + (8 - x)^2$

      ii 32

2 b $A = 1250, x = 50$

3 a $y = \dfrac{288}{x^2}$

   c $A = 432$, 12 cm by 6 cm by 8 cm

4 a $h = \dfrac{V}{4x^2}$

   c $\dfrac{5\sqrt{6}}{3}$

5 a $\theta = \dfrac{60}{r} - 2$

   c $30 - 2r, -2$

   d 15

   e 225, maximum

6 a $h = 3 - \dfrac{1}{2}r(\pi + 2)$

   c $6 - 4r - \pi r, -4 - \pi$

   d $\dfrac{6}{4 + \pi}$

   e $\dfrac{18}{4 + \pi}$, maximum

7 a $BC = 4 - p^2$

   c $\dfrac{2\sqrt{3}}{3}$

   d $\dfrac{32\sqrt{3}}{9}$, maximum

8 a $h = \dfrac{250}{r^2}$

   c $4\pi r - \dfrac{500\pi}{r^2}$, $4\pi + \dfrac{1000\pi}{r^3}$

   d 5

   e 150π, minimum

9 a $h = \dfrac{144}{r} - \dfrac{3}{2}r$

   c $\dfrac{12\sqrt{10}}{5}$

10 a $r = \dfrac{25 - 2x}{\pi}$

    c $A = 87.5, x = 7.00$

11 a $r = \sqrt{25 - h^2}$

    c $\dfrac{5\sqrt{3}}{3}$

    d maximum

12 a $h = 24 - 2r$

    c 512π

13 a $r = \sqrt{20h - h^2}$

    c $13\dfrac{1}{3}$

    d $\dfrac{32000}{81}\pi$, maximum

Exercise 12.11

1 $(2, 12)$

2 $k = 4$

3 a $-\dfrac{1}{x^2} + \dfrac{1}{\sqrt{x}}$

   b $\dfrac{2}{x^3} - \dfrac{1}{2x^{\frac{3}{2}}}$

   c $(1, 3)$, minimum

4 b 56.25 cm^2

5 a $2\left(\dfrac{1}{4}x - 5\right)^7$

   b $-256p$

6 $y = \dfrac{1}{2}x + 10$

7 a $y = -3x + 4$

   b $(-2, 10)$

9 $x = 9$

10 b $x = 10$

Chapter 13

Exercise 13.1

1 a $\mathbf{i} - 3\mathbf{j}$ b $3\mathbf{i} - 2\mathbf{j}$ c $4\mathbf{i} - \mathbf{j}$

   d $2\mathbf{i}$ e $\mathbf{i} + 3\mathbf{j}$ f $-2\mathbf{i} + \mathbf{j}$

   g $-2\mathbf{i}$ h $-3\mathbf{i} - 2\mathbf{j}$ i $-\mathbf{i} - \mathbf{j}$

2 a 2   b 5   c 13

   d 10   e 25   f 17

   g $4\sqrt{2}$ h $5\sqrt{5}$

3 $16\mathbf{i} + 12\mathbf{j}$

4 $36\mathbf{i} - 15\mathbf{j}$

5 a $\dfrac{1}{5}(3\mathbf{i} + 4\mathbf{j})$

   b $\dfrac{1}{13}(5\mathbf{i} + 12\mathbf{j})$

   c $-\dfrac{1}{5}(4\mathbf{i} + 3\mathbf{j})$

   d $\dfrac{1}{17}(8\mathbf{i} - 15\mathbf{j})$

   e $\dfrac{\sqrt{2}}{2}(\mathbf{i} + \mathbf{j})$

6 a $4\mathbf{i}$ b $14\mathbf{i} - 9\mathbf{j}$

439

c $-26\mathbf{i} - 3\mathbf{j}$ d $-\mathbf{i} + 3\mathbf{j}$

7 a 15 **b** $\sqrt{461}$

8 $\mu = -3, \lambda = 5$

9 $\mu = 3, \lambda = -2$

Exercise 13.2

1 a $-\mathbf{i} - 3\mathbf{j}$ **b** $2\mathbf{i} - 10\mathbf{j}$
  c $3\mathbf{i} + \mathbf{j}$ **d** $-12\mathbf{i} + 3\mathbf{j}$
  e $\mathbf{i} + 7\mathbf{j}$ **f** $-6\mathbf{i} - \mathbf{j}$

2 a $\begin{pmatrix} 4 \\ 10 \end{pmatrix}$ **b** $\begin{pmatrix} -5 \\ 11 \end{pmatrix}$
  c $\begin{pmatrix} 1 \\ 3 \end{pmatrix}$

3 a $-15\mathbf{i} + 20\mathbf{j}$ **b** $24\mathbf{i} + 10\mathbf{j}$
  c $15\mathbf{i} + \mathbf{j}$ **d** $\sqrt{226}$

4 a $16\mathbf{i} + 12\mathbf{j}$ **b** $\frac{1}{5}(4\mathbf{i} + 3\mathbf{j})$
  c $5\mathbf{i} + 2\mathbf{j}$

5 a $10\mathbf{i} + 24\mathbf{j}$ **b** 26
  c $\frac{1}{13}(5\mathbf{i} + 12\mathbf{j})$ **d** $3\mathbf{i} + 8\mathbf{j}$

6 7

7 a $\begin{pmatrix} 20 \\ -21 \end{pmatrix}$ **b** $\begin{pmatrix} 30 \\ -32 \end{pmatrix}$

8 a i 29
  ii 30
  iii 38.1
  b $\begin{pmatrix} 22.5 \\ -1 \end{pmatrix}$

9 a $12\mathbf{i} + 9\mathbf{j}$ **b** $7\mathbf{i} + \mathbf{j}$

10 a $6\mathbf{i} - 8\mathbf{j}$ **b** $7.5\mathbf{i} + 4\mathbf{j}$

11 $\begin{pmatrix} 9 \\ 7 \end{pmatrix}$

12 3

13 a 22 or -8 **b** -9
  c 1

14 $6\mathbf{j}$

15 $\frac{20}{7}\mathbf{i}$

16 a i $2\sqrt{10}$
  ii $\sqrt{130}$
  iii $3\sqrt{10}$
  c $\lambda = \frac{7}{3}, \mu = \frac{2}{3}$

Exercise 13.3

1 a $(1 - \lambda)\mathbf{a} + \lambda\mathbf{b}$
  b $\left(\frac{1}{2} - \frac{1}{2}\mu\right)\mathbf{a} + 3\mu\mathbf{b}$
  c $\lambda = \frac{3}{5}, \mu = \frac{1}{5}$

2 a i $2\mathbf{a} - \mathbf{b}$
  ii $3\mathbf{a} + \mathbf{b}$
  b i $\lambda(5\mathbf{a} - \mathbf{b})$
  ii $\mu(3\mathbf{a} + \mathbf{b})$
  c $\lambda = \frac{5}{8}, \mu = \frac{3}{8}$

3 a $\lambda(\mathbf{a} + 2\mathbf{b})$
  b $\mu\mathbf{a} + (3 - 3\mu)\mathbf{b}$
  c $\lambda = \frac{3}{5}, \mu = \frac{3}{5}$

4 a $(1 - \lambda)\mathbf{a} + 2\lambda\mathbf{b}$
  b $\frac{5}{3}\mu\mathbf{a} + (1 - \mu)\mathbf{b}$
  c $\lambda = \frac{2}{7}, \mu = \frac{3}{7}$

5 a i $-\mathbf{a} + \mathbf{b}$
  ii $\frac{1}{2}\mathbf{a} + \frac{1}{2}\mathbf{b}$
  b $\frac{1}{2}\lambda\mathbf{a} + \frac{1}{2}\lambda\mathbf{b}$
  c $\frac{3}{4}\mu\mathbf{a} + (1 - \mu)\mathbf{b}$
  d $\lambda = \frac{6}{7}, \mu = \frac{4}{7}$

6 a $\frac{3}{5}\lambda\mathbf{a} + \frac{2}{5}\lambda\mathbf{b}$
  b $\frac{5}{7}\mu\mathbf{a} + (1 - \mu)\mathbf{b}$
  c $\lambda = \frac{25}{31}, \mu = \frac{21}{31}$

7 a i $\lambda\mathbf{a} - \mathbf{b}$
  ii $-\mathbf{a} + \mu\mathbf{b}$
  b i $\frac{2}{5}\lambda\mathbf{a} + \frac{3}{5}\lambda\mathbf{b}$
  ii $\frac{1}{4}\mathbf{a} + \frac{3}{4}\mu\mathbf{b}$
  iii $\lambda = \frac{5}{8}, \mu = \frac{4}{5}$

8 a i $-9\mathbf{a} + 18\mathbf{b}$
  ii $-5\mathbf{a} + 10\mathbf{b}$
  b $\overrightarrow{AC} = \frac{9}{5}\overrightarrow{AB}$, so AB and AC are parallel and A lies on both lines

9 a i $4\mathbf{a}$
  ii $2\mathbf{b}$
  iii $-2\mathbf{a} + 3\mathbf{b}$
  b i $6\mathbf{a} - 3\mathbf{b}$
  ii $2\mathbf{a} - \mathbf{b}$
  iii $4\mathbf{a} - 2\mathbf{b}$
  b $\overrightarrow{CE} = 3\overrightarrow{CD}$, so CE and CD are parallel and C lies on both lines
  d $1 : 2$

Exercise 13.4

1 a $(3.5\mathbf{i} + 9\mathbf{j})$ m s^{-1}
  b $(30\mathbf{i} - 36\mathbf{j})$ m
  c 12.5 hours

2 $(-22\mathbf{i} + 11.6\mathbf{j})$ km h^{-1}

3 $125\mathbf{i}$ km

4 a $(18\mathbf{i} + 18\mathbf{j})$ km h^{-1}
  b $(10\mathbf{i} + 10\sqrt{3}\mathbf{j})$ km h^{-1}
  c $(-50\sqrt{3}\mathbf{i} - 50\mathbf{j})$ m s^{-1}

5 a 20 m s^{-1}
  b i $(-68\mathbf{i} + 44\mathbf{j})$ m
  ii $(-56\mathbf{i} + 28\mathbf{j})$ m
  iii $(-44\mathbf{i} + 12\mathbf{j})$ m
  c $\mathbf{r} = \begin{pmatrix} -80 \\ 60 \end{pmatrix} + t\begin{pmatrix} 12 \\ -16 \end{pmatrix}$

Answers

6 a $10\,\text{km}\,\text{h}^{-1}$

    b $(28\mathbf{i} + 14\mathbf{j})\,\text{km}$

    c $\mathbf{r} = \begin{pmatrix} 10 \\ 38 \end{pmatrix} + t\begin{pmatrix} 6 \\ -8 \end{pmatrix}$

    d 2030

7 a $(12\mathbf{i} - 12\mathbf{j})\,\text{km}\,\text{h}^{-1}$

    b i $(29\mathbf{i} - 12\mathbf{j})\,\text{km}$

       ii $(14\mathbf{i} + 3\mathbf{j})\,\text{km}$

    c $\mathbf{r} = \begin{pmatrix} 5 \\ 12 \end{pmatrix} + t\begin{pmatrix} 12 \\ -12 \end{pmatrix}$

8 a $(10\mathbf{i} + 6\mathbf{j})\,\text{km}$

    b $(5\mathbf{i} + 12\mathbf{j})\,\text{km}\,\text{h}^{-1}$

    c $13\,\text{km}\,\text{h}^{-1}$

    d 52

9 a $(15\mathbf{i} + 20\mathbf{j})\,\text{km}$

    b $(8\mathbf{i} + 6\mathbf{j})\,\text{km}\,\text{h}^{-1}$

    c $(111\mathbf{i} + 92\mathbf{j})\,\text{km}$

10 a $(50\mathbf{i} + 70\mathbf{j})\,\text{km}$,
       $(40\mathbf{i} + 100\mathbf{j})\,\text{km}$

     b 31.6 km

11 a $(6\mathbf{i} + 8\mathbf{j})\,\text{km}$, $21\mathbf{j}\,\text{km}$

     b 14.3 km

Exercise 13.5

1 a $(11\mathbf{i} + 8\mathbf{j})\,\text{m}$ at 1400 hours

    b Do not meet

    c Do not meet

    d $(19\mathbf{i} + 7\mathbf{j})\,\text{m}$ at 1600 hours

    e $(30\mathbf{i} + 42\mathbf{j})\,\text{km}$ at 1130 hours

2 -2

3 a $57.6\,\text{km}\,\text{h}^{-1}$ b $047.9°$

Exercise 13.6

1 $19.2\,\text{km}\,\text{h}^{-1}$

2 $7.71\,\text{km}\,\text{h}^{-1}$

3 $81.9\,\text{km}\,\text{h}^{-1}$

4 a $5\,\text{m}\,\text{s}^{-1}$

    b $36.9°$ to the riverbank

5 a $9.64\,\text{m}\,\text{s}^{-1}$

    b $21.1°$ to the riverbank

6 a $3.66\,\text{m}\,\text{s}^{-1}$ b $65.8°$

7 a $60°$ b 13.5 seconds

8 a $5.23\,\text{m}\,\text{s}^{-1}$

    b $64.0°$ to the riverbank

9 a $68.0°$ to the riverbank

    b 21.6 seconds

10 a $4.79\,\text{m}\,\text{s}^{-1}$

     b $44.2°$ to the riverbank

11 37.7 seconds

12 Bearing of $028.6°$

13 a $500\,\text{km}\,\text{h}^{-1}$

     b Bearing of $347°$

14 $219\,\text{km}\,\text{h}^{-1}$, bearing of $046.8°$

15 2 hours 56 minutes

16 $56.0\,\text{km}\,\text{h}^{-1}$, bearing of $103°$

17 $133\,\text{km}\,\text{h}^{-1}$, bearing of $200°$

Exercise 13.7

1 a $5\mathbf{i}\,\text{m}\,\text{s}^{-1}$, $5\,\text{m}\,\text{s}^{-1}$

    b $26\mathbf{i}\,\text{m}\,\text{s}^{-1}$, $26\,\text{m}\,\text{s}^{-1}$

    c $(11\mathbf{i} + 2\mathbf{j})\,\text{m}\,\text{s}^{-1}$, $5\sqrt{5}\,\text{m}\,\text{s}^{-1}$

    d $(-2\mathbf{i} - 13\mathbf{j})\,\text{m}\,\text{s}^{-1}$, $\sqrt{173}\,\text{m}\,\text{s}^{-1}$

    e $(-11\mathbf{i} + 7\mathbf{j})\,\text{km}\,\text{h}^{-1}$,
       $\sqrt{170}\,\text{km}\,\text{h}^{-1}$

2 $(5\mathbf{i} + 5\mathbf{j})\,\text{km}\,\text{h}^{-1}$

3 $(3\mathbf{i} + 3\mathbf{j})\,\text{m}\,\text{s}^{-1}$

4 a $(16\mathbf{i} + 16\mathbf{j})\,\text{km}\,\text{h}^{-1}$

    b $(-4\mathbf{i} + \mathbf{j})\,\text{km}\,\text{h}^{-1}$

5 a $(240\mathbf{i} + 120\mathbf{j})\,\text{km}\,\text{h}^{-1}$

    b $063.4°$

6 a $109°$

    b 51.3 minutes

7 a $(60\mathbf{i} - 60\mathbf{j})\,\text{km}\,\text{h}^{-1}$

    b $60\sqrt{2}\,\text{km}\,\text{h}^{-1}$

    c $135°$

Exercise 13.8

1 $5.23\,\text{m}\,\text{s}^{-1}$, $39.6°$

2 a $9\mathbf{i} + 45\mathbf{j}$

    b 13

    c $\dfrac{4}{3}\mathbf{i} - 2\mathbf{j}$

3 a $\mu\left(\dfrac{3}{5}\mathbf{a} + \dfrac{2}{5}\mathbf{b}\right)$

    b $\mu = \dfrac{5}{3}$, $\lambda = \dfrac{2}{3}$

4 $(5\mathbf{i} + 12\mathbf{j})\,\text{km}$, 13 km

5 107 minutes

Chapter 14

Exercise 14.1

1 a 2×2 b 2×1

    c 3×3 d 1×5

2 a $\begin{pmatrix} 6 & 8 \\ 2 & 10 \end{pmatrix}$ b $\begin{pmatrix} -10 & 0 \\ 5 & 10 \end{pmatrix}$

    c $\begin{pmatrix} 1 & 4 \\ 2 & 7 \end{pmatrix}$ d $\begin{pmatrix} 5 & 4 \\ 0 & 3 \end{pmatrix}$

    e $\begin{pmatrix} -4 & 8 \\ 7 & 20 \end{pmatrix}$ f $\begin{pmatrix} 3 & 12 \\ 6 & 21 \end{pmatrix}$

    g $\begin{pmatrix} 4 & 4 \\ 0.5 & 4 \end{pmatrix}$ h $\begin{pmatrix} 5 & 8 \\ 2.5 & 11 \end{pmatrix}$

3 $x = 7$, $y = 3$

4 a $\begin{pmatrix} 11 & -1 \\ 2 & 5 \end{pmatrix}$ b $\begin{pmatrix} 11 & -1 \\ 2 & 5 \end{pmatrix}$

    c $\begin{pmatrix} 3 & -3 \\ 4 & 5 \end{pmatrix}$ d $\begin{pmatrix} -3 & 3 \\ -4 & -5 \end{pmatrix}$

    e $\begin{pmatrix} 16 & -1 \\ 5 & 3 \end{pmatrix}$ f $\begin{pmatrix} 16 & -1 \\ 5 & 3 \end{pmatrix}$

    $\mathbf{A} + \mathbf{B} = \mathbf{B} + \mathbf{A}$, $\mathbf{A} - \mathbf{B} \neq \mathbf{B} - \mathbf{A}$,
    $\mathbf{A} + (\mathbf{B} + \mathbf{C}) = (\mathbf{A} + \mathbf{B}) + \mathbf{C}$

5 a $\begin{pmatrix} 20 \\ 15 \end{pmatrix} + \begin{pmatrix} 15 \\ 20 \end{pmatrix} + \begin{pmatrix} 18 \\ 14 \end{pmatrix}$

    b $\begin{pmatrix} 53 \\ 49 \end{pmatrix}$

441

Exercise 14.2

1. **a** not possible

    b $\begin{pmatrix} 6 & 6 \\ 0 & -4 \\ 8 & 16 \end{pmatrix}$ **c** $\begin{pmatrix} 0 & 0 \\ 0 & 0 \\ 0 & 0 \end{pmatrix}$

    d $\begin{pmatrix} 3 \\ -7 \\ 18 \end{pmatrix}$ **e** $\begin{pmatrix} 3 & 0 \\ 1 & -2 \\ 2 & 4 \end{pmatrix}$

    f $\begin{pmatrix} 1 \\ 4 \end{pmatrix}$ **g** $\begin{pmatrix} 30 \\ -16 \\ 72 \end{pmatrix}$

    h $\begin{pmatrix} 0 \\ 0 \end{pmatrix}$

2. AB, AC, BA, BAC

3. $\begin{pmatrix} 7 & -18 \\ -3 & -19 \end{pmatrix}$

4. $(-7 \ -20)$

5. **a** $\begin{pmatrix} 5 & 2 & 8 \\ 8 & -13 & 2 \end{pmatrix}$

    b $\begin{pmatrix} -6 \\ 3 \end{pmatrix}$

6. $\begin{pmatrix} 28 & -4 \\ 6 & 1 \end{pmatrix}$

7. **a** $\begin{pmatrix} 8 & -10 \\ 9 & -6 \end{pmatrix}$

    b $\begin{pmatrix} -1 & -3 \\ 15 & 3 \end{pmatrix}$

    c $\begin{pmatrix} -8 \\ 6 \end{pmatrix}$

8. **a** $\begin{pmatrix} 5 & -15 & 35 \\ -5 & 10 & 30 \end{pmatrix}$

    b $\begin{pmatrix} 15 & 6 \\ -6 & 3 \end{pmatrix}$

    c $\begin{pmatrix} 3 & -10 & 34 \\ -3 & 7 & 5 \end{pmatrix}$

9. $p = -1, q = 2$

Exercise 14.3

1. **a** $(60 \ 30 \ 100)\begin{pmatrix} 2 \\ 5 \\ 1 \end{pmatrix}$

    b (370)

2. **a** $(5 \ 9 \ 14)\begin{pmatrix} 5 \\ 3 \\ 1 \end{pmatrix}$

    b (66)

3. **a** $\begin{pmatrix} 5 & 3 & 2 \\ 4 & 3 & 3 \\ 3 & 4 & 3 \\ 2 & 4 & 4 \end{pmatrix}\begin{pmatrix} 3 \\ 1 \\ 0 \end{pmatrix}$

    b $\begin{pmatrix} 18 \\ 15 \\ 13 \\ 10 \end{pmatrix}$

4. **a** $\begin{pmatrix} 19 & 20 & 15 \\ 18 & 18 & 16 \end{pmatrix}\begin{pmatrix} 50 \\ 60 \\ 80 \end{pmatrix}$

    b $\begin{pmatrix} 3350 \\ 3260 \end{pmatrix}$

5. **a** $\begin{pmatrix} 14 & 4 & 2 \\ 13 & 2 & 5 \end{pmatrix}\begin{pmatrix} 2 \\ -1 \\ 0 \end{pmatrix}$

    b $\begin{pmatrix} 24 \\ 24 \end{pmatrix}$

6. **a i** $(20 \ 12 \ 6)\begin{pmatrix} 500 \\ 100 \\ 50 \end{pmatrix}$

    ii (11500)

    b i $(15 \ 10 \ 5)\begin{pmatrix} 600 \\ 150 \\ 50 \end{pmatrix}$

    ii (10750)

    c $\$22\,250$

7. **a** $(0.4 \ 0.15 \ 0.15)$

    $\begin{pmatrix} 70 & 60 & 80 \\ 15 & 15 & 20 \\ 12 & 10 & 15 \end{pmatrix}\begin{pmatrix} 60 \\ 40 \\ 50 \end{pmatrix}$

    b (4895.5)

8. **a** $(800 \ 600)$

    $\begin{pmatrix} 0.25 & 0.35 & 0.4 \\ 0.2 & 0.3 & 0.5 \end{pmatrix}\begin{pmatrix} 2.3 \\ 1.5 \\ 1.2 \end{pmatrix}$

    b (2170)

9. **a** $(0.4 \ 0.6 \ 0.3)$

    $\begin{pmatrix} 10 & 12 & 15 & 12 \\ 50 & 160 & 180 & 100 \\ 2 & 4 & 4 & 3 \end{pmatrix}\begin{pmatrix} 100 \\ 200 \\ 200 \\ 150 \end{pmatrix}$

    b (56755)

10. **a** $(0.6 \ 0.4)$

    $\begin{pmatrix} 4 & 4 & 2 \\ 5 & 2 & 3 \end{pmatrix}\begin{pmatrix} 5 \\ -1 \\ 0 \end{pmatrix}$

    b (18.8)

Exercise 14.4

1. **a** $\begin{pmatrix} 3 & -4 \\ -2 & 3 \end{pmatrix}$

    b $\dfrac{1}{2}\begin{pmatrix} 2 & 4 \\ 3 & 7 \end{pmatrix}$

    c $\dfrac{1}{3}\begin{pmatrix} 2 & 1 \\ -1 & 1 \end{pmatrix}$

    d $\dfrac{1}{3}\begin{pmatrix} 3 & -2 \\ -6 & 5 \end{pmatrix}$

    e $\begin{pmatrix} 1 & -3 \\ -2 & 7 \end{pmatrix}$

    f $\dfrac{1}{4}\begin{pmatrix} 1 & -2 \\ 1 & 2 \end{pmatrix}$

    g $\dfrac{1}{3}\begin{pmatrix} -1 & 2 \\ -5 & 7 \end{pmatrix}$

    h $\dfrac{1}{8}\begin{pmatrix} 1 & -1 \\ -2 & -6 \end{pmatrix}$

2. $-3\dfrac{1}{3}$

3. $\dfrac{1}{4}\begin{pmatrix} 1 & 0 \\ -3 & 4 \end{pmatrix}$

4. $\begin{pmatrix} -8 & -3.5 \\ 6 & 2 \end{pmatrix}$

5. **a** $\dfrac{1}{5}\begin{pmatrix} 3 & -4 \\ 2 & -1 \end{pmatrix}$ **b** $\begin{pmatrix} -4 & 2.2 \\ -1 & 0.8 \end{pmatrix}$

Answers

6 $\begin{pmatrix} 9 & 4 \\ 20 & 11 \end{pmatrix}$

7 $\begin{pmatrix} 1 & -3 \\ 2 & -1 \end{pmatrix}$

8 a $\dfrac{1}{5}\begin{pmatrix} 6 & -7 \\ -1 & 2 \end{pmatrix}$ b $\begin{pmatrix} 3 & -5 \\ -1 & 0 \end{pmatrix}$

9 a $\dfrac{1}{11}\begin{pmatrix} 4 & -1 \\ 3 & 2 \end{pmatrix}$ b $\begin{pmatrix} 5 & 1 \\ 0 & 2 \end{pmatrix}$

10 $\begin{pmatrix} -3 & 1 \\ 2 & 1 \end{pmatrix}$

11 a $\dfrac{1}{10}\begin{pmatrix} 2 & 2 \\ -1 & 4 \end{pmatrix}$ b $\begin{pmatrix} 1.4 \\ 1.3 \end{pmatrix}$

12 a $\dfrac{1}{4}\begin{pmatrix} -4 & 2 \\ -2 & 2 \end{pmatrix}$

   b $\begin{pmatrix} -6 & 3.5 \\ -0.5 & 1 \end{pmatrix}$

Exercise 14.5

1 a $\begin{pmatrix} 1 & 3 \\ 5 & -2 \end{pmatrix}\begin{pmatrix} x \\ y \end{pmatrix} = \begin{pmatrix} 21 \\ 10 \end{pmatrix}$

   b $\begin{pmatrix} 3 & 7 \\ 5 & -2 \end{pmatrix}\begin{pmatrix} x \\ y \end{pmatrix} = \begin{pmatrix} 22 \\ 2 \end{pmatrix}$

   c $\begin{pmatrix} 2 & -3 \\ 1 & 5 \end{pmatrix}\begin{pmatrix} x \\ y \end{pmatrix} = \begin{pmatrix} 1 \\ 0 \end{pmatrix}$

   d $\begin{pmatrix} 2 & -5 \\ 7 & 8 \end{pmatrix}\begin{pmatrix} x \\ y \end{pmatrix} = \begin{pmatrix} 1 \\ 4 \end{pmatrix}$

2 a $x = 3, y = 5$
   b $x = 1.625, y = 7.75$
   c $x = 3, y = -2.5$
   d $x = -2, y = 1$
   e $x = -10, y = 9$
   f $x = 8, y = -2$
   g $x = 2, y = 4$
   h $x = 4, y = 1$

3 a $\dfrac{1}{13}\begin{pmatrix} 3 & 2 \\ -5 & 1 \end{pmatrix}$
   b $x = 1, y = -3$

4 a $\dfrac{1}{5}\begin{pmatrix} -3 & 2 \\ -4 & 1 \end{pmatrix}$

   b $x = 5, y = -4$

   c $\begin{pmatrix} -4.6 & 4.4 \\ 5.8 & -2.2 \end{pmatrix}$

5 a $\begin{pmatrix} k & 4 \\ 9 & k \end{pmatrix}\begin{pmatrix} x \\ y \end{pmatrix} = \begin{pmatrix} 7 \\ 4 \end{pmatrix}$

   b ± 6

Exercise 14.6

1 a $\begin{pmatrix} 10 & 19 \\ 32 & 37 \\ 14 & 14 \end{pmatrix}$

   b $\dfrac{1}{7}\begin{pmatrix} 5 & -1 \\ -3 & 2 \end{pmatrix}$

   c $x = 0.5, y = -2.5$

2 a $\begin{pmatrix} 4 & 3 \\ 4 & 3 \end{pmatrix}$

   b $\begin{pmatrix} 16 & 9 \\ 12 & 13 \end{pmatrix}$

   c $\dfrac{1}{100}\begin{pmatrix} 13 & -9 \\ -12 & 16 \end{pmatrix}$

3 a $\dfrac{1}{13}\begin{pmatrix} 5 & 1 \\ -3 & 2 \end{pmatrix}$
   b $a = 4, b = 2, c = 1, d = 1$

4 a $\dfrac{1}{26}\begin{pmatrix} 5 & 3 \\ -2 & 4 \end{pmatrix}$
   b $x = 0.5, y = 4$

5 a $\begin{pmatrix} 5 & 0 \\ 4 & -13 \end{pmatrix}$

   b $\begin{pmatrix} 7 & -18 \\ -3 & -19 \end{pmatrix}$

   c $\dfrac{1}{17}\begin{pmatrix} 5 & 2 \\ 1 & -3 \end{pmatrix}$

   d $x = 9, y = -2$

6 a AB, AC
   b $x = 4, y = 12$

7 $(5\ \ 1\ \ -2)\begin{pmatrix} 7 & 6 & 5 \\ 1 & 3 & 5 \\ 2 & 1 & 0 \end{pmatrix}\begin{pmatrix} 0.2 \\ 0.3 \\ 0.5 \end{pmatrix}$, 30.7

Chapter 15
Exercise 15.1

1 a $7e^{7x}$ b $3e^{3x}$
   c $15e^{5x}$ d $-8e^{-4x}$
   e $-3e^{-\frac{x}{2}}$ f $3e^{3x+1}$
   g $2xe^{x^2+1}$ h $5 - \dfrac{3e^{\sqrt{x}}}{2\sqrt{x}}$
   i $-3e^{-3x}$ j $-4e^{2x}$
   k $\dfrac{e^x - e^{-x}}{2}$ l $10x(1 + e^{x^2})$

2 a $xe^x + e^x$
   b $2x^2e^{2x} + 2xe^{2x}$
   c $-3xe^{-x} + 3e^{-x}$
   d $\sqrt{x}\,e^x + \dfrac{e^x}{2\sqrt{x}}$
   e $\dfrac{xe^x - e^x}{x^2}$
   f $\dfrac{e^{2x}(4x - 1)}{2x^{\frac{3}{2}}}$
   g $-\dfrac{2e^x}{(e^x - 1)^2}$
   h $2xe^{2x}$
   i $\dfrac{e^x(x^2 + 2xe^x + 2x + 5)}{(e^x + 1)^2}$

3 a $5x + 8y = 10$
   b $5x - 6y + 15\ln 5 = 0$
   c $y = 3ex + 2x - 2e - 1$

4 $A\left(-\dfrac{1}{3}, 0\right)$

Exercise 15.2

1 a $\dfrac{1}{x}$ b $\dfrac{1}{x}$
   c $\dfrac{2}{2x + 3}$ d $\dfrac{2x}{x^2 - 1}$
   e $\dfrac{6}{3x + 1}$ f $\dfrac{1}{2x + 4}$

443

g $\dfrac{20}{5x-2}$ h $2-\dfrac{1}{x}$

i $\dfrac{3}{3x-2}$ j $\dfrac{1}{x\ln x}$

k $\dfrac{1}{(\sqrt{x}+1)\sqrt{x}}$ l $\dfrac{2x^2+1}{x(x^2+\ln x)}$

2 a $1+\ln x$ b $2x+4x\ln x$

c $1-\dfrac{1}{x}+\ln x$ d $10+5\ln x^2$

e $\dfrac{x}{\ln x}+2x\ln(\ln x)$

f $\dfrac{1-\ln 2x}{x^2}$ g $-\dfrac{4}{x(\ln x)^2}$

h $\dfrac{2}{x^2(2x+1)}-\dfrac{2\ln(2x+1)}{x^3}$

i $\dfrac{3x^2(2x+3)-2(x^3-1)\ln(x^3-1)}{(2x+3)^2(x^3-1)}$

3 $2+4\ln 6,\ 3+2\ln 6$

4 a $\dfrac{3}{6x+2}$

b $\dfrac{2}{5-2x}$

c $\dfrac{5(x-1)}{x(x-5)}$

d $\dfrac{-3}{(2x+1)(x-1)}$

e $\dfrac{x-4}{x(2-x)}$

f $\dfrac{x^2+4x+2}{x(x+1)(x+2)}$

g $\dfrac{2-6x-2x^2}{(x-5)(x+1)(2x+3)}$

h $\dfrac{-3x-1}{(x+3)(x-1)}$

i $\dfrac{-x^2+6x-3}{x(x-1)(x+1)(2x-3)}$

5 a $\dfrac{1}{x\ln 3}$

b $\dfrac{2}{x\ln 2}$

c $\dfrac{5}{(5x-1)\ln 4}$

6 a $\dfrac{8x}{4x^2-1}$

b $\dfrac{15x^2-2}{5x^3-2x}$

c $\dfrac{2x-1}{(x+3)(x-4)}$

7 0.2

Exercise 15.3

1 a $\cos x$

b $2\cos x-3\sin x$

c $-2\sin x-\sec^2 x$

d $6\cos 2x$

e $20\sec^2 5x$

f $-6\sin 3x-2\cos 2x$

g $3\sec^2(3x+2)$

h $2\cos\left(2x+\dfrac{\pi}{3}\right)$

i $-6\sin\left(3x-\dfrac{\pi}{6}\right)$

2 a $3\sin^2 x\cos x$

b $-30\cos 3x\sin 3x$

c $2\sin x\cos x+2\sin x$

d $4(3-\cos x)^3\sin x$

e $12\sin^2\left(2x+\dfrac{\pi}{6}\right)\cos\left(2x+\dfrac{\pi}{6}\right)$

f $-12\sin x\cos^3 x$
$+8\tan\left(2x-\dfrac{\pi}{4}\right)\sec^2\left(2x-\dfrac{\pi}{4}\right)$

3 a $x\cos x+\sin x$

b $-6\sin 2x\sin 3x$
$+4\cos 2x\cos 3x$

c $x^2\sec^2 x+2x\tan x$

d $\dfrac{3}{2}x\tan^2\left(\dfrac{x}{2}\right)\sec^2\left(\dfrac{x}{2}\right)$
$+\tan^3\left(\dfrac{x}{2}\right)$

e $15\tan 3x\sec 3x$

f $\sec x+x\tan x\sec x$

g $\dfrac{x\sec^2 x-\tan x}{x^2}$

h $\dfrac{1+2\cos x}{(2+\cos x)^2}$

i $\dfrac{(3x-1)\cos x-3\sin x}{(3x-1)^2}$

j $-6\cot 2x\,\text{cosec}^3 2x$

k $\dfrac{3\,\text{cosec}\,2x-6x\cot 2x}{\text{cosec}\,2x}$

l $\dfrac{-2}{(\sin x-\cos x)^2}$

4 a $-\sin x\,e^{\cos x}$

b $-5\sin 5x\,e^{\cos 5x}$

c $\sec^2 x\,e^{\tan x}$

d $(\cos x-\sin x)e^{(\sin x+\cos x)}$

e $e^x(\sin x+\cos x)$

f $\dfrac{1}{2}e^x\left(2\cos\dfrac{1}{2}x-\sin\dfrac{1}{2}x\right)$

g $2e^x\cos x$

h $xe^{\cos x}(2-x\sin x)$

i $\cot x$

j $x[2\ln(\cos x)-x\tan x]$

k $\dfrac{3\cos 3x-2\sin 3x}{e^{2x-1}}$

l $\dfrac{x\cos x+\sin x-x\sin x}{e^x}$

5 a -2

b $\dfrac{3\sqrt{2}-8}{6}$

6 a $\tan x\sec x$

b $-\cot x\,\text{cosec}\,x$

c $-\text{cosec}^2 x$

7 a $3\cot 3x$

b $-2\tan 2x$

8 $A=3,\ B=-5$

9 $A=4,\ B=-3$

Exercise 15.4

1 $4x-24y=\pi$

2 a $2x+2y=\pi$

… Answers

b $Q\left(\frac{\pi}{2}, 0\right)$, $R\left(0, \frac{\pi}{2}\right)$

c $\frac{\pi^2}{8}$ units^2

3 $Q(1, 0)$

4 a $A\left(\frac{1}{2}\ln 5, 0\right)$, $B(0, 4)$

  b $C(-8, 0)$

5 $\frac{1}{2}e(2e^2 + 1)$

6 $\sqrt{2}\,p$ 7 $\frac{2}{3}p$

8 $\frac{1}{4}p$ 9 $\frac{9}{2}p$

10 $2\sqrt{3}\,p$

11 a $(-2, -2e^{-1})$ minimum

   b $(-1, e^{-2})$ maximum, $(0, 0)$ minimum

   c $(\ln 7, 9 - 7\ln 7)$ minimum

   d $(0, 4)$ minimum

   e $(-2, -4e^2)$ minimum, $(4, 8e^{-4})$ maximum

   f $\left(e^{-\frac{1}{2}}, -\frac{1}{2}e^{-1}\right)$ minimum

   g $\left(\sqrt{e}, \frac{1}{2}e^{-1}\right)$ maximum

   h $(-\sqrt{e-1}, e^{-1})$ maximum, $(0, 0)$ minimum, $(\sqrt{e-1}, e^{-1})$ maximum

12 a $(0.927, 5)$ maximum

   b $(1.85, 10)$ maximum

   c $(0, 5)$ maximum, $\left(\frac{\pi}{2}, -5\right)$ minimum

   d $\left(\frac{\pi}{4}, 3.10\right)$ minimum

   e $\left(\frac{5\pi}{6}, -\frac{3\sqrt{3}}{2}\right)$ minimum

13 a $A = 2$, $B = 8$

   b $\left(\frac{1}{4}\ln 4, 8\right)$ minimum

14 $A(1, 0)$, $B(e^{-1}, -e^{-1})$

15 a $P(0, 0)$, $Q(-2, 4e^{-2})$

   b $B(0, -2e)$, $C\left(0, e + \frac{1}{3e}\right)$

   c $\frac{1}{2}\left(3e + \frac{1}{3e}\right)$

16 b 2.7 cm^2 per second

17 $\frac{\pi}{6}$ maximum

Exercise 15.5

1 a $y = 2x - 1$

2 a $\frac{1}{3}\cos 2x \cos\left(\frac{x}{3}\right) - 2\sin 2x \sin\left(\frac{x}{3}\right)$

   b $\dfrac{(\sec^2 x)(1 + \ln x) - \frac{1}{x}(\tan x)}{(1 + \ln x)^2}$

3 -0.8

4 a $\dfrac{2x \cos 4x + 4x^2 \sin 4x}{\cos^2 4x}$

   b $-\frac{\pi}{2}p$

5 a $2e^{2x} - 2e^{-2x}$

   b 2.5

   c -7.25

6 a $A(1 + 2\ln 2, 0)$, $B\left(0, \frac{1}{2} + \ln 2\right)$, $C\left(1 - \frac{1}{2}\ln 2, 0\right)$, $D(0, -2 + \ln 2)$

   b $k = (\ln 2)^2$

7 a $a = \frac{4\pi}{3}$

   b $2y = \frac{19\pi}{6} - x$

Chapter 16

Exercise 16.1

1 a $y = \frac{12}{5}x^5 + c$

  b $y = \frac{5}{9}x^9 + c$

  c $y = \frac{7}{4}x^4 + c$

  d $y = -\frac{2}{x^2} + c$

  e $y = -\frac{1}{2x} + c$

  f $y = 6\sqrt{x} + c$

2 a $y = x^7 + \frac{2x^5}{5} + 3x + c$

  b $y = \frac{x^6}{3} - \frac{3x^4}{4} + \frac{5x^2}{2} + c$

  c $y = -\frac{1}{x^3} + \frac{15}{x} + \frac{x^2}{2} + c$

  d $y = -\frac{2}{x^9} - \frac{1}{x^6} - 2x + c$

3 a $y = x^3 - 3x^2 + c$

  b $y = \frac{4}{5}x^5 - x^3 + c$

  c $y = \frac{8}{5}x^{\frac{5}{2}} + \frac{x^3}{3} + 2x^2 + c$

  d $y = \frac{x^4}{4} + \frac{x^3}{3} - 6x^2 + c$

  e $y = \frac{x^3}{6} + \frac{3}{2x} + c$

  f $y = -\frac{2}{x} + \frac{5}{2x^2} - \frac{1}{x^3} + c$

  g $y = \frac{x^4}{8} - 2x - \frac{1}{2x} + c$

  h $y = \frac{6}{5}x^{\frac{5}{2}} - \frac{2x^{\frac{3}{2}}}{3} - 20\sqrt{x} + c$

4 $y = x^3 - 2x^2 + x + 5$

5 $y = 2x^3 - 3x^2 - 4$

6 $y = x^2 - \frac{6}{x} + 3$

7 $y = 8\sqrt{x} - 4x + \frac{2}{3}x^{\frac{3}{2}} + 8$

445

8   $y = 2x^3 - x^2 + 5$

9   a $y = 2x^3 - 6x^2 + 8x + 1$

10   $y = 2x^2 - 5x + 1$

Exercise 16.2

1   a $\dfrac{x^2}{8} + c$ b $2x^6 + c$

   c $-\dfrac{1}{x^2} + c$ d $-\dfrac{4}{x} + c$

   e $6\sqrt{x} + c$ f $-\dfrac{4}{x\sqrt{x}} + c$

2   a $\dfrac{x^3}{3} + \dfrac{7x^2}{2} + 10x + c$

   b $\dfrac{2x^3}{3} + \dfrac{x^2}{2} - 3x + c$

   c $\dfrac{x^3}{3} - 5x^2 + 25x + c$

   d $4x^{\frac{3}{2}} + \dfrac{x^2}{2} + 9x + c$

   e $\dfrac{x^4}{4} - \dfrac{2x^3}{3} + \dfrac{x^2}{2} + c$

   f $\dfrac{3x^{\frac{7}{3}}}{7} - 3x^{\frac{4}{3}} + c$

3   a $x + \dfrac{5}{x} + c$

   b $\dfrac{x^2}{4} + \dfrac{2}{x^2} + c$

   c $-\dfrac{1}{3x} - \dfrac{1}{3x^2} - \dfrac{1}{9x^3} + c$

   d $2x^2 - 6\sqrt{x} + c$

   e $\dfrac{2x^{\frac{5}{2}}}{5} - \dfrac{2}{x^{\frac{5}{2}}} + c$

   f $\dfrac{x^2}{2} - \dfrac{6}{x} - \dfrac{9}{4x^4} + c$

Exercise 16.3

1   a $\dfrac{1}{10}(x+2)^{10} + c$

   b $\dfrac{1}{14}(2x-5)^7 + c$

   c $\dfrac{1}{15}(3x+2)^{10} + c$

   d $-\dfrac{1}{5}(2-3x)^5 + c$

   e $\dfrac{3}{28}(7x+2)^{\frac{4}{3}} + c$

   f $\dfrac{2}{15}(3x-1)^{\frac{5}{2}} + c$

   g $12\sqrt{x+1} + c$

   h $-\dfrac{4}{5(5x+3)^2} + c$

   i $\dfrac{1}{4(3-2x)^3} + c$

2   $y = \dfrac{(4x+1)^5}{20} - 2$

3   $y = \dfrac{\sqrt{(2x+1)^3}}{3} + 2$

4   $y = 5 - 2\sqrt{10-x}$

5   $y = (2x-3)^4 + 1$

6   $y = \dfrac{(3x-1)^6 + 8}{9}$

Exercise 16.4

1   a $\dfrac{e^{5x}}{5} + c$ b $\dfrac{e^{9x}}{9} + c$

   c $2e^{\frac{1}{2}x} + c$ d $-\dfrac{e^{-2x}}{2} + c$

   e $4e^x + c$ f $\dfrac{e^{4x}}{2} + c$

   g $\dfrac{e^{7x+4}}{7} + c$ h $-\dfrac{e^{5-2x}}{2} + c$

   i $\dfrac{e^{6x-1}}{18} + c$

2   a $5e^x - \dfrac{e^{3x}}{3} + c$

   b $\dfrac{e^{4x}}{4} + e^{2x} + x + c$

   c $\dfrac{9e^{2x}}{2} - \dfrac{e^{-2x}}{2} + 6x + c$

   d $e^x - 4e^{-x} + c$

   e $\dfrac{5e^{2x}}{4} - \dfrac{e^x}{2} + c$

   f $\dfrac{e^{5x}}{5} - 2e^{2x} - 4e^{-x} + c$

3   a $2e^x + 2\sqrt{x} + c$

   b $\dfrac{1}{3}x^3 - \dfrac{3e^{2x+1}}{2} + c$

   c $\dfrac{e^x}{4} + \dfrac{1}{3x} + c$

4   $y = e^{2x} - e^{-x} + 4$

5   a $k = -7$

   b $y = 7e^{2-x} + 2x^2 - 5$

6   $y = 2e^{-2x} + 6x - 6$

7   a $6 - e$

   b $\left(\dfrac{4e^2 - e - 2}{2e - 2}, \dfrac{24e - 4e^2 - 21}{4e - 4} \right)$

Exercise 16.5

1   a $-\dfrac{1}{4}\cos 4x + c$

   b $\dfrac{1}{2}\sin 2x + c$

   c $-3\cos\dfrac{x}{3} + c$

   d $\sin 2x + c$

   e $-2\cos 3x + c$

   f $\dfrac{3}{2}\sin(2x+1) + c$

   g $\dfrac{5}{3}\cos(2-3x) + c$

   h $\sin(2x-7) + c$

   i $\dfrac{4}{5}\cos(1-5x) + c$

2   a $x + \cos x + c$

   b $\dfrac{2}{3}\left(x^{\frac{3}{2}} - \sin 3x\right) + c$

   c $\dfrac{3}{2}\sin 2x + \dfrac{2}{5}\pi\cos\dfrac{5x}{2} + c$

   d $-\dfrac{1}{x} - \dfrac{2}{3}\sin\dfrac{3x}{2} + c$

   e $\dfrac{1}{2}\left(e^{2x} + 5\cos 2x\right) + c$

   f $4\sqrt{x} - 2\cos\dfrac{x}{2} + c$

3   $y = \sin x + \cos x + 2$

4   $y = x - 2\sin 2x + 3 - \dfrac{\pi}{4}$

5   $y = 2x^2 + 3\cos 2x - 5$

6   $y = 5\cos 3x - 2\sin x + 4$

7   a $k = 6$
   b $y = 2\sin 3x - 4x + 2 + 4\pi$

8   a $y = 5 - 2\cos\left(2x - \dfrac{\pi}{2}\right)$
   b $y = -\dfrac{1}{2}x + \dfrac{\pi}{6} + 5 - \sqrt{3}$

9   a $k = 2$
   b $\left(\dfrac{3\pi - 2}{6}, 3\right)$

Exercise 16.6

1 b $\dfrac{x+5}{\sqrt{2x-1}} + c$

2 a $30x(3x^2 - 1)^4$
   b $\dfrac{1}{30}(3x^2 - 1)^5 + c$

3 a $\ln x + 1$
   b $x\ln x - x + c$

4 b $-\dfrac{1}{x} - \dfrac{\ln x}{x} + c$

5 a $\dfrac{2(x^2 - 2)}{\sqrt{x^2 - 4}}$
   b $\dfrac{1}{2}x\sqrt{x^2 - 4} + c$

6 b $\dfrac{2}{3}(x+1)\sqrt{x-5} + c$

7 a $2xe^{2x}$
   b $\dfrac{1}{2}xe^{2x} - \dfrac{1}{4}e^{2x} + c$

8 a $k = 1$
   b $\dfrac{5\sin x}{1 - \cos x} + c$

9 a $k = \dfrac{3}{2}$
   b $\dfrac{2}{3}(x+8)\sqrt{x-4} + c$

10 a $k = -2$
   b $-\dfrac{2}{x^2 - 7} + c$

11 a $2x^2 + 6x^2 \ln x$
   b $\dfrac{1}{3}x^3 \ln x - \dfrac{1}{9}x^3 + c$

12 a $\cos x - x\sin x$
   b $\sin x - x\cos x + c$

13 b $\dfrac{1}{4}e^{2x}(\sin 2x + \cos 2x) + c$

14 a $\dfrac{5x^2 - 14x}{\sqrt{2x - 7}}$
   b $(x^2 + 3)\sqrt{2x - 7}$

Exercise 16.7

1 a 127   b 1.5   c 24
   d 15   e 10.5   f 7.5
   g $12\dfrac{5}{12}$ h $\dfrac{52}{81}$ i 75.5
   j 26.4   k $3\dfrac{13}{24}$ l $5\dfrac{1}{3}$

2 a 68   b $18\dfrac{2}{3}$ c 12.4
   d 0.5   e 0.25   f 8

3 a $\dfrac{1}{2}(e^2 - 1)$ b $\dfrac{1}{4}(e - 1)$
   c $\dfrac{5(e^4 - 1)}{2e^4}$ d $\dfrac{1}{3}(e - 1)$
   e $\dfrac{5(e^2 - 1)}{2e}$
   f $\dfrac{1}{2}(e^2 + 4e - 3)$
   g $\dfrac{1}{12}(3e^4 + 8e^3 + 6e^2 - 17)$
   h $\dfrac{9}{2}e^2 - \dfrac{2}{e^2} - \dfrac{29}{2}$
   i $4e^2 - \dfrac{3}{2e^2} - \dfrac{5}{2}$

4 a 2   b $\dfrac{3\pi}{2}$
   c $\dfrac{\sqrt{3}}{4}$ d $\sqrt{3} - \dfrac{3}{2}$
   e $\dfrac{\pi^2 - 8}{16}$ f $\dfrac{1}{6}(3 - \sqrt{2})$

Exercise 16.8

1 a $\dfrac{3x}{\sqrt{2x - 1}}$ b $5\dfrac{1}{3}$

2 a $\dfrac{6x^2 + 4}{\sqrt{3x^2 + 4}}$ b 4

3 a $-\dfrac{2x}{(x^2 + 5)^2}$ b $\dfrac{1}{9}$

4 a $\dfrac{3x + 2}{2\sqrt{(3x + 4)^3}}$ b 2

5 b $\dfrac{\pi\sqrt{2}}{20}$

6 a $\sin x + x\cos x + c$
   b $\dfrac{1}{2}(\pi - 2)$

7 a $x + 2x\ln x + c$
   b $1 + e^2$

8 a $\sin 3x + 3x\cos 3x$
   b $\dfrac{1}{18}(\pi - 2)$

Exercise 16.9

1 a $6\dfrac{3}{4}$ b $13\dfrac{1}{2}$
   c 6   d $1 + e - \dfrac{2}{e}$
   e 5   f $\dfrac{2 + \pi}{4}$

2 a $1\dfrac{1}{3}$
   b $5\sqrt{2} - 5 - \dfrac{5\pi^2}{72}$

3 $3\dfrac{1}{12}$

4 a $\dfrac{1}{6}$ b $20\dfrac{5}{6}$
   c 8   d $49\dfrac{1}{3}$
   e $32\dfrac{3}{4}$ f $21\dfrac{1}{3}$

5 12

6 a 9   b 1.6

7 b $1 + e^2$

8 b $5\ln 5 - 4$

9 b $\pi - 1$

Exercise 16.10

1 2

2 $3\dfrac{1}{3}$

3 16

4 $5 - \dfrac{3\pi}{4}$

5 a $10\dfrac{2}{3}$ b $20\dfrac{5}{6}$ c $1\dfrac{1}{3}$
   d 36 e $20\dfrac{5}{6}$

6 a $\dfrac{1}{3}$ b $\dfrac{3}{4}$

7 34

8 a $(-2, 0)$ b $42\dfrac{2}{3}$

9 $4\dfrac{4}{15}$

10 π

Exercise 16.11

1 a $2xe^{x^2}$ b $\dfrac{1}{2}e^{x^2}$ c 26.8

2 a $y = 2x^2 - \dfrac{1}{x+1} + 1$
   b $8x + 34y = 93$

3 a $x + \dfrac{6}{x} + c$ b $k = 2$

4 b 628 units^2

5 a $(0, 1.85)$ b 0.292 units^2

Chapter 17
Exercise 17.1

1 a $12.5\,\text{m}\,\text{s}^{-1}$ b 6
   c $-2.4\,\text{m}\,\text{s}^{-2}$

2 a $6\,\text{m}\,\text{s}^{-1}$ b $10\,\text{m}\,\text{s}^{-2}$

3 a $4.95\,\text{m}\,\text{s}^{-1}$ b 5
   c $1\,\text{m}\,\text{s}^{-2}$
   d

4 a $\dfrac{1}{3}(e^4 - 2)$ b $5.4\,\text{m}\,\text{s}^{-1}$

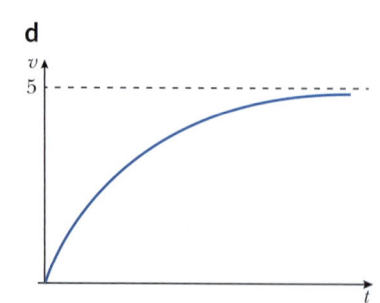

5 a 2 b $\ln\left(\dfrac{7}{5}\right)$ m
   c $-0.25\,\text{m}\,\text{s}^{-2}$

6 a $\dfrac{4\pi}{3}$ b $-1.90\,\text{m}\,\text{s}^{-2}$

7 a $t = \dfrac{\pi}{4}$ b $-3\,\text{m}\,\text{s}^{-2}$

8 a $v = 4\sin 2t$, $a = 8\cos 2t$
   b $t = \dfrac{\pi}{2}$, $s = 4$

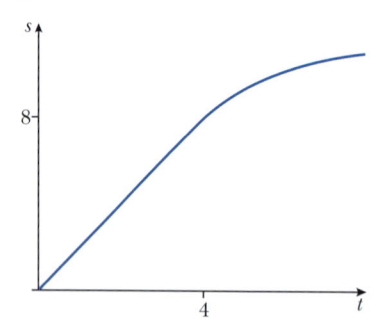

9 a $t = \dfrac{1}{2}\ln 2$ b 0.899 m
   c 24.1 m

10 a 2 m away from O
   b $v = 2 - 4\sin 2t$, $a = -8\cos 2t$
   c $t = \dfrac{\pi}{12}$, $s = \dfrac{\pi}{6} + \sqrt{3}$
   d $t = \dfrac{\pi}{4}$, $s = \dfrac{\pi}{2}$

11 a $t = \dfrac{\pi}{8}$
   b $a = -4k\sin 4t$
   c $k = 5$

12 a $2\,\text{m}\,\text{s}^{-1}$
   b i $2\,\text{m}\,\text{s}^{-1}$
     ii $\dfrac{2}{3}\,\text{m}\,\text{s}^{-1}$
   c i $0\,\text{m}\,\text{s}^{-2}$
     ii $-\dfrac{2}{9}\,\text{m}\,\text{s}^{-2}$
   d
   e $2\ln\dfrac{5}{4}$ m

13 a 2 m
   b $t = \dfrac{5}{3}$
   c $0 \leq t < \dfrac{5}{3}$ and $t > 4$
   d $\dfrac{5}{3} < t < 4$

Exercise 17.2

1 a $16\,\text{m}\,\text{s}^{-1}$ b 15 seconds
   c $12\dfrac{2}{3}$ m d $166\dfrac{2}{3}$ m

   e $189\dfrac{1}{3}$ m

2 a $-1\,\text{m}\,\text{s}^{-2}$ b $s = \dfrac{16t}{t+2}$
   c 1.6 m

3 a $2(4e^2 + 1)$ m
   b $s = 2e^{2t} + t^2 - 2$
   c 111 m

4 $\left(\dfrac{9\pi^2}{8} + 6\right)$ m, $\dfrac{1}{3}\,\text{m}\,\text{s}^{-2}$

5 b $29.75\,\text{m}\,\text{s}^{-2}$ c 109 m

6 $p = 6$, $q = -6$

7 a $t = 5$
   b
   c 62.5 m

8 a $t = 2$, $t = 6$ b 5.5 m
   c 112 m

9 a $-12 \leq a \leq 12$ b 5.74 m

10 a $0.64\,\text{m}\,\text{s}^{-2}$ b 12.1 m

11 a $t = \dfrac{2\pi}{3}$
   b $\left(4\sqrt{3} + \dfrac{2\pi}{3}\right)$ m

12 a $p = \dfrac{1}{2}$, $q = -2$
   b $s = \dfrac{1}{12}t^3 - t^2 + 3t$
   c $t = 6$ d $\dfrac{11}{12}$ m

Exercise 17.3

1 a 3.2 b 15 c 312

2 $\dfrac{11}{6}$

3 a 2 b $\dfrac{\pi}{4}$ c 1
   d 4

4 a 5 b $\dfrac{7\pi}{24}$ c 1.14

Index

absolute value *see* modulus
acceleration 403, 410–11, 416
  signs for 403–4
addition
  of matrices 320–1, 336
  of polynomials 89–90
  of vectors 289
addition/subtraction rule, for differentiation 250, 283
amplitude 190, 192–3
angles
  between 0° and 90° 181–4
  general definition 184–5
  negative 184, 214
  positive 184, 214
approximations 264–6, 283
arcs 170
  length 170–2
areas
  bounded by graphs of two functions 392, 396
  rectilinear figures 144–7
  regions bounded by line and curve 391–5
  sector 173–6
  under curves 385–91, 396
arrangements 220–3
  rule for 220

base 68
  change of 120–2
binomial 237
binomial expansions 236–45
binomial theorem 242–4
boxing in method 145, 146

Cartesian plane 184
chain rule 253–5, 283
change of base rule 120–2
chords 170
  gradients of 264
circular measure 166–76
collinear points 289
combinations 226–31
  order and 226–7
  rule for finding 227
completing the square method 43, 47–8
composite functions 23–5
conjugate surds 78

cosecant function (cosec) 210–11
cosine function (cos) 181, 186
  amplitude 190, 193
  derivative of 350–5
  graphs of 189–90, 193–4, 196
  integration of 374–6
  period 190, 193
  sign of 186–7, 214
cotangent function (cot) 210–11
cubic equations 96–100
cubic polynomials 89, 96–100
curve
  area of region bounded by line 391–5
  area under 385–91, 396
  intersection of line and 60–2

definite integrals 380–5, 396
degree, of polynomial 89
degrees 167
  converting from radians to 168
  converting to radians from 168
denominator, rationalising 78–81
derivatives 249
  of cos $(ax + b)$ 352
  of $e^{f(x)}$ 343
  of exponential functions 342–6, 355–61
  first 271
  of ln f(x) 346–7
  of logarithmic functions 346–50, 355–61
  second 271–2
    and stationary points 275–6
  of sin $(ax + b)$ 352
  of tan $(ax + b)$ 352
  of trigonometric functions 350–61
  see also differentiation
determinants, of matrices 330, 337
differentiation 247–84, 341–61
  addition/subtraction rule 250, 283
  applications in kinematics of 402–10
  approximations 264–6, 283
  chain rule 253–5, 283
  first derivative 271
  from first principles 249
  notation 249
  power rule 249–53, 283
  product rule 255–7, 283
  quotient rule 258–60

rates of change 267–71
  connected 268
  reversed, integration as 366–9, 376, 396
  scalar multiple rule 250, 283
  second derivatives 271–2
    and stationary points 275–6
  see also derivatives; stationary points
discriminant 57–8
displacement 289, 402, 410–11, 416
  signs for 403–4
distance 401
distance–time graphs 401
dividend 91
division
  of polynomials 91–3
  of surds 76
division law 114
divisor 91
domain 21, 30

e 122, 343
elimination method 42
empty set 2
equations
  cubic 96–100
  involving indices *see* exponential equations
  involving surds 81–4
  logarithmic 116–17
  quadratic *see* quadratic equations roots 57
exponential equations
  practical applications 124–5
  solving 69–72, 118–19
exponential functions 107–31
  derivatives of 342–6, 355–61
  graphs of 125–8
  integration of 372–4
  inverse of 129–30
exponents *see* indices

factor theorem 93–6, 104
factorial notation 219
factorisation method 43
factors, of polynomials 93–104
Ferris wheel 189
fractions, rationalising denominator 78–81
frames of reference 307
functions 19–36
  composite 23–5
  definition 21
  domain 21, 30

exponential *see* exponential functions
gradient 248–53
inverse 30–3
  of exponential functions 129–30
  graphs of 33–6
  of logarithmic functions 129–30
logarithmic *see* logarithmic functions
modulus 25–7
periodic 190
range 21, 30
trigonometric *see* trigonometric functions

geometry, of vectors 296–300
gradient
  curve 248
  line 135, 248
  parallel lines 135, 139–41
  perpendicular lines 135, 139–41
gradient function 248–53
graphs
  of exponential functions 125–8
  of functions and inverses 33–6
  of logarithmic functions 125–8
  straight-lines *see* straight-line graphs
  of trigonometric functions/ratios 189–99
  of $y = a \cos bx + c$ 190, 193
  of $y = a \sin bx + c$ 190, 193
  of $y = a \sin x$ 191
  of $y = a \tan bx + c$ 190, 193
  of $y = \cos x$ 189–90
  of $y = e^x$ 125
  of $y = k e^{nx} + a$ 126–8
  of $y = k \ln ax = b$ 126–8
  of $y = \sin bx$ 191–2
  of $y = \sin x$ 189–90
  of $y = \sin x + c$ 192
  of $y = \tan x$ 190
  of $y = |f(x)|$
    where f(x) is linear 28–30
    where f(x) is quadratic 52–5
    where f(x) is trigonometric function 199–201

identity matrix 323, 337
image set *see* range
indefinite integrals 369–71, 376–9, 380, 396
indices 67–72
  rules of 68, 85
  simplifying expressions involving 68–9
  solving equations involving 69–72, 118–19

Index

inequalities
   linear 55
   quadratic 55–7
inflexion, points of 274–5
instantaneous rest 404, 416
integers 3
integration 365–96
   applications in kinematics of 410–16
   area of regions bounded by line and curve 391–5
   area under curve 385–91, 396
   areas bounded by graphs of two functions 392, 396
      of cosine functions 374–6
   definite 380–5, 396
      as differentiation reversed 366–9, 376, 396
      of exponential functions 372–4
   formulae for 396
      of functions of form $(ax+b)^n$ 371–2
   indefinite 369–71, 376–9, 380, 396
      of powers of x 369
      of sine functions 374–6
   symbol for 369
interception problems 304–7
intersection of sets 2
inverse functions 30–3
   of exponential functions 129–30
   graphs of 33–6
   of logarithmic functions 129–30
inverse matrices 330–4, 337
   solving simultaneous equations with 334–6

kinematics 400–16
   applications of differentiation in 402–10
   applications of integration in 410–16

laws of logarithms 114–15, 130
length
   arc 170–2
   line 135
      problems involving 136–9
linear inequalities 55
linear polynomials 89
line(s)
   coincident 335
   equations of straight 135, 141–4
   gradient 135, 248
   intersecting 335
   intersection of curve and 60–2
   length 135
   mid-point 135
   parallel 135, 139–41, 335
   perpendicular 135, 139–41
   problems involving length and mid-point 136–9
   see also straight-line graphs
logarithmic equations, solving 116–17
logarithmic functions 107–31
   change of base of 120–2
   derivatives of 346–50, 355–61
   graphs of 125–8
   inverse of 129–30
   laws/rules of logarithms 114–15, 130
   natural logarithms 122–3, 131
   product rule for 131
   to base 10 108–11
   to base a 111–13

many-one mappings 20
mappings 20
   many-one 20
   one-many 20
   one-one 20
matrices 319–37
   addition 320–1, 336
   determinants of 330, 337
   identity 323, 337
   inverse 330–4, 337
      solving simultaneous equations with 334–6
   multiplication by scalar 320–1, 336
   multiplication of *see* matrix products
   non-singular 330, 337
   order 320, 336
   singular 330, 337
   subtraction 320–1, 336
   zero 323, 337
matrix products 322–4, 337
   practical applications 325–30
maximum points 46–51, 273
   first derivative test for 273, 284
   practical problems 278–83
   second derivative test for 275, 284
mid-point of line 135
   problems involving 136–9
minimum points 46–51, 273
   first derivative test for 273, 284
   practical problems 278–83
   second derivative test for 276, 284
modulus
   of number 25–7
   of vector 289

motion diagrams 402
multiplication
    of matrices *see* matrix products
    of matrix by scalar 320–1, 336
    of polynomials 89–90
    of surds 75–6
    of vector by scalar 289
multiplication law 114

natural logarithms 122–3, 131
natural numbers 3
non-linear equations
    converting from linear form to 151–4
    converting to linear form 147–50
    finding relationships from data 155–60
non-singular matrices 330, 337
normals 260–4
    equations of 261, 283

one-many mappings 20
one-one mappings 20
order
    and combinations 226–7
    of matrix 320, 336
    and permutations 223–4

parabola 46
    intersection of line and 60–2
Pascal's triangle 237–41
period 190, 193
periodic functions 190
permutations 223–6
    notation 223
    order and 223–4
    rule for finding 223
points of inflexion 274–5
polynomials 88–104
    addition 89–90
    definition 89
    degree 89
    division 91–3
    factor theorem 93–6, 104
    factors of 93–104
    multiplication 89–90
    remainder theorem 100–4
    subtraction 89–90
position vectors 292–6, 315
power law 114
power rule 249–53, 283
powers *see* indices

product rule
    for differentiation 255–7, 283
    for logarithms 131

quadrants 184–5
quadratic equations 43, 46–55, 57–9
    completing the square method 43, 47–8
    condition for real roots 60, 63
    and corresponding curves 63
    factorisation method 43
    graphs of $y = |f(x)|$ where $f(x)$ is quadratic 52–5
    maximum values 46–51
    minimum values 46–51
    quadratic formula method 43
    roots of 57–9
quadratic formula 57
quadratic formula method 43
quadratic inequalities 55–7
quadratic polynomials 89
quartic polynomials 89
quotient 91
quotient rule 258–60

radians 167
    converting from degrees to 168
    converting to degrees from 168
range 21, 30
rates of change 267–71
    connected 268
rational numbers 3
real numbers 3
rectilinear figures, areas 144–7
relative velocity 307–13, 315
    using **i**, **j** notation 314–15
remainder theorem 100–4
rest, instantaneous 404, 416
roots
    of equations 57
    of quadratic equations 57–9

scalar multiple rule, for differentiation 250, 283
scalars 289, 401
secant function (sec) 210–11
sectors 170
    area 173–6
segments 170
sets 1–15
    complement 2
    disjoint 2
    elements 2

Index

empty 2
intersection 2
language of 2–6
notation 3
symbols 2
union 2
universal 2
shoestring/shoelace method 145
simultaneous equations 41–2, 43–5
   elimination method 42
   one linear and one non-linear 43–5
   solving with inverse matrices 334–6
   substitution method 42
sine function (sin) 181, 186
   amplitude 190, 192–3
   derivative of 350–5
   equivalent trigonometric expressions for 209
   graphs of 189–93, 195–6
   integration of 374–6
   period 190, 193
   sign of 186–7, 214
singular matrices 330, 337
small increments 264–6
speed 401
   constant 300
   see also velocity
speed–time graphs 401
stationary points (turning points) 46, 273–7, 283
   of inflexion 274–5
   second derivatives and 275–6
   see also maximum points; minimum points
stepping stone game 241
straight-line graphs 134–61
   areas of rectilinear figures 144–7
   converting from linear form to non-linear equation 151–4
   converting from non-linear equation to linear form 147–50
   equations of straight lines 135, 141–4
   finding relationships from data 155–60
   see also line(s)
subsets 2
substitution method 42
subtraction
   of matrices 320–1, 336
   of polynomials 89–90
   of vectors 289
surds 73–85
   conjugate 78
   division 76
   multiplication 75–6
   rationalising denominator of fraction 78–81
   rules of 85
   simplification 75–8
   solving equations involving 81–4

tangent function (tan) 181, 186
   derivative of 351–5
   graphs of 190, 193
   period 190, 193
   sign of 186–7, 214
tangents 63, 260–4
   equations of 261, 283
translation 192–3
trigonometric equations 202–7, 210–11
trigonometric functions/ratios 181
   derivatives of 350–61
   of general angles 186–8
   graphs of 189–99
   graphs of $y = |f(x)|$ where $f(x)$ is trigonometric function 199–201
   signs of 186–7, 214
   sketching 194–6
   see also cosecant function; cosine function; cotangent function; secant function; sine function; tangent function
trigonometric identities 208–9, 212–13, 214
trigonometry 180–214
   equivalent trigonometric expressions 209
   see also angles; trigonometric equations; trigonometric functions/ratios; trigonometric identities
turning points *see* stationary points

union of sets 2
universal set 2

vector triangles 309–11
vectors 288–315
   addition 289
   component form 290
   constant velocity problems 300–3
   definition 289, 401
   equal 289
   geometry 296–300
   i, j notation 290
   interception problems 304–7

magnitude 289
modulus 289
multiplication by scalar 289
notation 289, 290–2
position 292–6, 315
relative velocity 307–13, 315
   using **i**, **j** notation 314–15
subtraction 289
unit 290
velocity 300, 315, 402–3, 410–11, 416
   constant, problems 300–3
   relative 307–13, 315
      using **i**, **j** notation 314–15
   signs for 403–4
   splitting into components 301–2
Venn diagrams
   describing sets on 9–10
   number of elements in regions on 10–14
   shading sets on 6–8

zero matrix 323, 337